THE AMERICAN BUSINESS CREED

THE
AMERICAN
BUSINESS CREED

FRANCIS X. SUTTON

SEYMOUR E. HARRIS

CARL KAYSEN

JAMES TOBIN

SCHOCKEN BOOKS · NEW YORK

First SCHOCKEN PAPERBACK *edition 1962*

This edition is published by arrangement with
Harvard University Press

Library of Congress Catalog Card Number: 56–8553

Printed in the United States of America

TO THE LATE OLIVIA THORNDIKE CHEEVER,
WHO CONTRIBUTED SO MUCH TO
THIS VOLUME

PREFACE

This study is an examination of the ideology of American business, as it is revealed in the public statements of business leaders, the institutional advertisements of large corporations, the literature of such business associations as the United States Chamber of Commerce, the Committee for Economic Development, and the National Association of Manufacturers. The material is ubiquitous in our daily life; from magazine ad to Congressional testimony it constitutes a substantial part of the vast stream of public communication, oral and written, in which our society swims. Its importance is commensurate with its prevalence: in a complex, literate, open, and democratic society ideological statement and argument are the core of the processes of public life, and in our society the business creed forms one of the major contributions to the total flow of public discussion.

Our aim in this study is to answer the questions: Why does the business ideology say what it does? On what theory can the themes, symbols, arguments, which form the business ideology be explained? To answer these questions we must, of course, first give an exposition of the content of the business ideology. To this task we devote Part I, after introducing the problem in Chapter I. Part II presents our analysis of the form and substance of the business creed. To reach the answer to our ultimate question, we first seek to define the general role of ideologies in social life. We find our answer, broadly speaking, in the strains and conflicts inherent in every institutional position in a complex society, whether the position be that of businessman, or university professor, or labor leader. These conflicts are of several kinds: conflicts between the demands of the particular position and the broader values of society; gaps between the demands of social positions and the capabilities of the human beings who hold them to fulfill these demands; inherently conflicting demands built into the social definition of certain positions. This general proposition is applied to an investigation of the particular strains inherent in the business role in the United States, and the major themes of business ideology are shown as verbal and symbolic resolutions of these conflicts. This is our central proposition. We also recognize and examine other forces which shape the business ideology: the general cultural inheritance of our society with which any acceptable ideology must be in consonance, and the particular means of producing and disseminating business ideology in the institutional setting of our society.

The purpose of this study is to analyze, not to debunk. We wish to explain the business creed as a social phenomenon, not to evaluate it in terms of "right" and "wrong." To be sure, every analytical study of social institutions tends to carry with it some nuance of criticism, if only by pointing out that things might possibly be otherwise than they are. We shall point to contradictions, ambiguities, exaggerations, and omissions in the business creed's account of the workings of our society; these are hallmarks of every ideology. To the extent that we do so, our account of the creed is "critical"; yet we wish to emphasize that the criticism appears in service of our analysis, not as an end in itself. We have our ideological commitments (which vary among ourselves), as do most people in the United States. But in this study we have aimed at a neutral scientific viewpoint and a scholarly description and analysis of the business creed from that viewpoint. We have tried to avoid the presentation of evaluative arguments from the standpoint of one or another anti- or pro-business ideology. Our success in this is, of course, for others to judge.

The material on which this study is based was drawn from the output of recent years, much of it from the period 1948-49. It includes business advertisements in newspapers and magazines, books, pamphlets, and speeches by individual business leaders, business testimony before Congressional committees, the publications of trade associations and other business associations, and the like. We have studied a great volume of this material, and are confident of the representative character of what we here set forth.

Our definition of ideology limits it to public statements; others have used the word in other ways. In particular, it has been used to refer to underlying "private" beliefs, and sometimes to the ideas believed to be implicit in the actions of particular persons or groups. In terms of our own analysis, neither of these concepts of ideology appears satisfactory. But it is appropriate to remark that such evidence as we have been able to gather strongly suggests a high degree of consonance between public statements and "private beliefs" on ideological matters, giving that rather slippery concept what appears to be a useful interpretation for operational purposes.

The book is in every sense a joint work, the product of all four authors. Our method of collaboration involved the joint discussion of the content of each chapter on the basis of an outline prepared by some one of us, the preparation of a draft, again discussed by all, and the revision and re-revision of the draft, frequently by another than its first author. Though we all are jointly responsible for the book, we have not all contributed in the same way. The study is basically a sociological analysis, though the propositions which it examines refer largely to the economic functioning of our society. The three economists among us therefore went to school to the

one sociologist, Francis Sutton, in the course of the work. The basic theoretical framework of our analysis is one that he had worked out in an earlier
study entitled *The Radical Marxist*.[1] In this sense his contribution was
fundamental and the order of listing of authors' names is used to indicate
this fact; the rest of us appear alphabetically.

Collaboration is a slow process, the more so when relatively new ideas
are being worked out. The pace of our efforts was slowed by the geographic
dispersion of the authors which occurred between the time we first undertook this study and its completion almost seven years later, as well as by
other enterprises in which we were severally engaged. The intervening
period saw many changes in the immediate external scene: Fair Dealism was
replaced by Progressive Conservatism, and a government "sympathetic" to
business came to power for the first time since the beginning of the Great
Depression. These changes and the corresponding reactions of business and
business propaganda reinforced our views on the importance of deep-lying
motivational forces in explaining business ideology, and the relatively
superficial influence of current political debate on the substance of the creed.
These views were further confirmed by a broad survey of stability and
change in the business creed during the first half of this century which we
undertook and which we report in the final chapter of this book. We thus
believe that we have analyzed a social and cultural phenomenon that has a
persisting form and character through the welter of current public arguments about current public issues.

Since completing this study we have found no reason to alter our views.
In our various capacities and from our different vantage points, we continue
to hear the same familiar themes and are persuaded that the creed as we
have described it is still living social reality. Some changes in balance and
emphasis have occurred as skirmishes develop along the New Frontier and
Senator Goldwater's forces rally around old ones. A new survey of the out-
pourings of the early sixties would doubtless have to give more place to
questions of foreign trade and the relevance of the free enterprise system to
the development of foreign lands than we have given. But such changes
still appear to us as at most variations and developments on the basic
themes we have analyzed. In focusing on these persisting themes, we do not
mean to minimize the interest of studies that might concentrate on the
changes that occur in business ideology from decade to decade. There is
fascinating historical study to be done here, and we hope that others will
undertake what we have not tried to do.

In the course of this long work we benefited from the help of more
people than we can individually recall here. We had able and devoted research assistants, one of whom we recall in the dedication of the volume;

[1] F. X. Sutton, "The Radical Marxist," unpublished doctoral dissertation deposited
in Harvard College Library.

we had patient typists to produce our various drafts and generous colleagues who gave their time to read and criticize them.

Two research grants from Harvard University made the initiation and completion of this study possible. The Society of Fellows gave the funds which enabled us to gather and order our basic material. A grant from the Joseph H. Clark Bequest paid for typing and editorial assistance. The Society of Fellows did much more than provide funds. Sutton, Kaysen, and Tobin were all Junior Fellows at Harvard when this work was begun; the Society gave them the leisure in which to think about it, and organize their early ideas. And, true to Mr. Lowell's vision of the Society, it provided the meeting ground for sociologist and economist without which this study would not have been undertaken.

Our wives struggled with the burdens of collaboration actively as well as passively. All served as guinea pigs, on whom successive drafts were tried out. Jacqueline Y. Sutton prepared a bibliography, without which our footnotes could not have been checked, and Annette N. Kaysen typed a large part of the first draft.

For all this assistance, we are thankful. For what we have written, we ourselves are, of course, alone responsible.

FXS

SEH

CK

JT

New York, Cambridge, Washington
December 1961.

CONTENTS

THE AMERICAN BUSINESS CREED

1

INTRODUCTION: THE AMERICAN BUSINESS CREED AS IDEOLOGY

SURE AMERICA'S GOING AHEAD IF WE ALL PULL TOGETHER. American teamwork is management that pays reasonable wages and takes a fair profit.[1]

WE CAN'T LEGISLATE HAPPINESS. We run the risk in this country of substituting law for conscience; of feeling that passing a law makes something so. Laws are easy, work is hard. But only work, hard work, ever got anybody anything worth having.[2]

TODAY, AS IN 1935, American industry is being hampered by ignorant political interference.[3]

WHY YOU CANNOT GET AHEAD AS YOUR FATHER DID. The United States is being forced towards socialism by a tax revolution of far-reaching consequences.[4]

THE SPIRIT OF 1776. One hundred and seventy-two years ago, the ringing of the Liberty Bell announced to mankind the birth of a nation founded upon freedom and justice . . . We must face the fact that there are forces at work striving to deprive us of those fundamental rights . . . The origin of those forces lies in foreign lands where people live in poverty, misery and fear . . . Let us compare our American way of life and its system of competitive free enterprise with that of people who live under other forms of government.[5]

These statements were made in advertisements by business firms. The attitudes, opinions, arguments, values, and slogans of the American busi-

[1] Advertisement approved by the Public Policy Committee of the Advertising Council and contributed "as a public service" by the *Woman's Home Companion,* November 1948.

[2] Warner & Swasey advertisement, *Business Week,* April 9, 1948.

[3] Hearst Newspaper advertisement, *New York Times,* July 6, 1948.

[4] McGraw-Hill advertisement, *New York Herald Tribune,* March 8, 1948.

[5] Firestone Tire and Rubber advertisement, *New York Times,* July 4, 1948.

ness community are a familiar part of the landscape of most Americans. In recent years, the business point of view has found abundant expression in every kind of medium: placards in buses on the economics of the "miracle of America"; newspaper and magazine advertisements on the perils of excessive taxation; speeches of business executives on the responsibilities and rights of management; editorials deploring the size of the national debt; textbooks, sponsored by business associations, explaining the workings of a free enterprise economy; pamphlets exposing the dangers of unwise political interventions in business affairs; testimony by business spokesmen before Congressional committees on a host of specific issues of public policy. These public expressions of the views of American businessmen constitute the "American Business Creed," the subject of this book.

This is a book, then, about what American businessmen and their spokesmen say or write in public in the hope of influencing the actions and attitudes of other businessmen and of the rest of the community. Our interest is in the question: Why do businessmen and their spokesmen say and write the things they do? What determines the content of the American Business Creed? In Part II we apply a theory of ideology to this problem, and we argue that our theory provides a more satisfactory explanation of American business ideology than alternative hypotheses. The nature of our explanation is briefly set forth later in this introductory chapter. Before offering an explanation of the content of the business creed, we must be clear what that content is. Part I is a systematic examination of what business ideology says.

IDEOLOGY AND DEMOCRACY

When we refer to the American Business Creed as "ideology," we are not, of course, using that word in the derogatory sense the term often carries in popular and polemical discussion. For us the term is neutral and describes any system of beliefs publicly expressed with the manifest purpose of influencing the sentiments and actions of others.[6] In this sense

[6] The theoretical discussion of ideologies in social science has been closely associated with the name of Karl Mannheim. See his *Ideology and Utopia* (New York, n.d.) and *Essays in the Sociology of Knowledge,* ed. by P. Kecskemeti (London, 1952) where, however, a number of points of view are maintained which are at variance with those developed in this work. A recent systematic discussion of the place of ideologies in social systems is contained in Talcott Parsons, *The Social System* (Glencoe, Ill., 1951), ch. VIII. On the psychological side, see the major effort of T. W. Adorno, *et al., The Authoritarian Personality* (New York, 1950). The theory of ideology has a long tradition, in which the names of Marx and Weber occupy the most prominent place.

The term "ideology" now has a wide usage outside the familiar meaning of popular discussion as, for example, in describing accounts which African peoples give of their own kinship systems; compare A. Southall, *Lineage Formation Among the Luo* (New York, 1952).

ideology is an essential element of all social life. One has no more cause to feel dismayed or aggrieved by having his own views described as "ideology" than had Molière's famous character by the discovery that all his life he had been talking prose. Ideology may be true as well as false. According to one's personal values, any particular ideology may be good or bad. Ideology is no monopoly of totalitarians, of the Left or of the Right; there is democratic ideology too. In fact, ideologies proliferate under democracies. Democracy provides both the motivation and the opportunity for individuals and organized groups to try to influence the actions and attitudes of others — the votes of plain citizens and Senators, the decisions of bureaucrats and the President, the economic demands of workers, businessmen, and farmers, and the loyalties and values of housewives and children.

CHARACTERISTICS OF IDEOLOGY

Ideologies, whatever their content and whoever their adherents, possess certain common features. They are selective in subject matter and in use of empirical evidence and logical argument. They are simple and clear-cut even when their subject matter is complicated. They are expressed in language that engages the emotions, as well as the understanding, of their readers and listeners. At the same time, their content is limited to what is publicly acceptable. In the course of Part I, our examination of the business creed, we shall show how business ideology exemplifies these common characteristics.

These characteristics of ideology stand out when ideology is compared with science. Science, like ideology, is public; but, unlike ideology, its objective is not to influence social action but to enlarge understanding. Democratic institutions, we have argued above, tend by their very nature to nurture ideologies. At the same time the institutions of Western culture have developed the quite different kind of public communication that we know as science. This distinction between science and ideology is fundamental to the approach of this book. We shall introduce it by examining the common features of ideologies listed in the preceding paragraph.

Selectivity. First of all, an ideology is generally selective. It is selective in the subjects that it chooses to discuss. For example, the publications of trade unions and the pronouncements of union leaders are not promising sources of information concerning jurisdictional strikes, secondary boycotts, and the problems of democratic control of union leadership. These are subjects which union ideology is likely to omit from its picture of the world of labor. Ideology is selective in citing empirical evidence. The reader who has followed any recent American political campaign has heard both parties cite figures, in themselves accurate enough, "proving" contradictory conclusions about such matters as changes in the average citizen's standard of living. Ideology is selective also in its use of logical argument. Labor ideology frequently argues that increases in wages relative to profits are essential to ward off recession or to recover from depression. The logic of this argument implies that, when the danger is inflation rather than deflation, the indicated change in wages is downward. But from this implication the ideology shrinks; and arguments quite different from a logical standpoint are brought forth to justify wage increases in inflation too.

To appreciate the incompleteness of the picture of the world presented by the ideologist, we must compare it with the picture drawn by the scientist. The question "Is the average American better off?" has a simple Democratic answer and a simple Republican answer. The economist who tried to answer it would find both the question and the answer much more complicated than an ideologist of either party. Similarly, the student of labor relations would not fail, in any comprehensive survey of the American labor scene, to discuss subjects — jurisdictional strikes, etc. — that command scant attention in labor ideology. Nor would the economist shrink from following a logical argument concerning the effects of increasing wages to whatever conclusions it led.

Science is, of course, selective. The very notion of understanding or explaining reality implies abstraction, classification, and simplification, in which attention is focused on some aspects of reality while others are ignored. From the vantage point of the twentieth century, we can appreciate the incompleteness and selectivity of science in the past, with full confidence that the science of our own day will appear similarly limited to future observers. And in the social sciences especially, we must give some credit to ideologies for widening scientific horizons in special directions. But, imprisoned by the confines of our present knowledge, we can judge the selectivity of a current ideology only by comparing it with the scope of current science.

Why is ideology selective in comparison with science? A key to the answer is in the difference between the objectives of ideology and of science. The institutionally defined objective of science is to seek understanding. If a question is complicated, if there is much conflicting evidence, if there are empirical uncertainties, if there are logical arguments leading in divers directions, the discipline of the scientist demands that he recognize these facts. The ideologist seeks to influence action and attitude. His objective leads him to overlook complications of logic and of evidence which would dilute his argument and weaken his influence. His selectivity is not necessarily deliberate deception, although at times it may be. More often the possibilities he overlooks simply never occur to him.

Oversimplicity. For the same reason, ideology tends to be simple and clear-cut, even where its simplicity and clarity do less than justice to the subject under discussion. The ideological picture uses sharp lines and contrasting blacks and whites. The ideologist exaggerates and caricatures in the fashion of the cartoonist. In contrast, a scientific description of social phenomena is likely to be fuzzy and indistinct. In recent labor ideology the Taft-Hartley Act has been a "slave labor act." By no dispassionate examination does the Act merit this label. Any detached assessment of the Act would have to consider its many provisions individually. On any set of values, even those of trade unions themselves, such an assessment would yield a mixed verdict. But mixed verdicts are not the stuff of ideology. They are too complicated, too fuzzy. Ideology must categorize the Act as a whole with a symbol to rally workers, voters, and legislators to action. Or, to take an example from another sphere, "truth" is always a good in the ideology of academicians. No attention is given in this ideology to the possibility that the discovery and dissemination of particular truths may cause social harm rather than social benefit.

Language. The use of expressive symbols is another important characteristic of ideology which differentiates it from science. An expressive symbol is a word or set of words which excites in the reader feelings of like or dislike or other emotional reactions. A symbol of this kind not only conveys some meaning; it arouses some emotion. The scientist *qua* scientist does not use words in this way; in scientific discussion "Taft-Hartley Act" is just a shorthand reference to a particular piece of legislation enacted by the Eightieth Congress. In ideological discussion "Taft-Hartley Act" is a symbol, and reference to it is intended to mobilize emotional approval or disapproval. Ideology is oriented to influence action and sentiment. To influence action, it is necessary to do more than merely inform. It is necessary to engage the likes and dislikes, and the moral feelings, of the audience.

Public acceptability. The orientation of ideology subjects it, to a greater measure than science, to control by its audience. Thus, labor ideology cannot and does not attack "free enterprise." To the vast majority of Americans, workers included, "free enterprise" is a positive symbol; the words connote something they like and approve. The cognitive content of the words may be low — few people can say just what "free enterprise" means — but the affective content is high — they feel that "free enterprise" is something good. Whatever restrictions by unions or governments on the discretion of business management the unions may advocate, they must propose in the name of "free enterprise." To cite another example, "racial discrimination" is a strongly established negative symbol in America. Whatever specific policies one may advocate or practice with respect to Negroes or Jews, it is virtually impossible, at least outside the South, to describe them publicly as "racial discrimination." To do so would be to throw away all prospect of public acceptance. The emotions associated with many words thus limit the way in which ideology can be expressed in public. A scientist, on the other hand, does not solicit diffuse public acceptance for his statements and does not use words in contexts where their symbolic associations matter to any comparable degree. A scientific statement is consequently much less affected by the values and sentiments of its audience; it is limited only by logical consistency with the existing body of scientific knowledge. A nutritionist in Wisconsin, "America's Dairyland," could say, and would be expected to say what no politician would dare to say — that margarine can be just as nutritive as butter.

IDEOLOGY AND SOCIAL SCIENCE

Science stands in contrast to ideology because its fundamental objective is not to influence action or opinion but to enlarge understanding. In practice the distinction between the two is not always as sharp as this statement implies. Ideological and scientific objectives are often intertwined. Ideology has often advanced science by raising problems and suggesting methods of analysis which the science of the day would have ignored without the impetus of ideological discussion. At the same time, much that has passed for neutral scientific inquiry has certainly had ideological objectives and presuppositions. Nevertheless, a tradition of scientific inquiry, the pursuit of knowledge for its own sake, has become firmly established in the institutions of Western societies. Neutral and objective investigation gains its strength from this tradition and from these social institutions.

Fortunately, science does not depend on the personal motivations of scientists but rests on a more secure foundation. Whatever the personal motivations of the scientist, the social institutions of science impose a discipline that tends to force his research to conform to the scientific objective and to discard it from the corpus of science if it does not. His results and his methods will be scrutinized by other scientists. Weaknesses, errors, inaccuracies, and biases are liable to be exposed. Both the weight accorded to his conclusions and his professional prestige and advancement depend on the outcome of this process of scrutiny and criticism. This is the process by which scientific content is extracted from ideologies, and by which the ideological motivations of individual scientists are kept in the long run from influencing the cumulative body of accepted scientific conclusions. The impact of scientific discipline on the individual investigator is sometimes too weak to overcome his personal motivations; and the process of criticism and correction of his results is often slow. Indeed, in some cases the time consumed by the process may be very long because whole generations of scientists share the same ideology and are unaware of its influence on their work. Despite these difficulties the institutions that support scientific neutrality are sufficiently strong in the Western world to give meaning to our distinction between science and ideology.[7]

Many persons will readily accept this distinction in the sphere of natural phenomena, but not in that of social phenomena. The claim of the social sciences to be sciences is not fully respected. There are evidently two reasons for this reluctance, and it may clarify matters if we examine both of them briefly.

The first reason is, from the standpoint of our distinction between ideology and science, largely irrelevant. It is, in effect, that the social sciences are not very successful sciences; some would add that they never can be successful because of the impossibility of controlled experiments in social science. But success is not the criterion of scientific orientation. Much work of natural scientists is proved by later investigators to be wrong; it does not thereby lose its status as scientific effort or become ideology. Meteorology is a recognized science whose success, measured by accuracy of prediction, has not been conspicuous. The claim of the social sciences to be sciences cannot rest on any pretensions to success and precision comparable to the achievements of the older natural sciences. It must rest rather on the claim that social scientists approach their subject matter with the same objective and the same orientation as natural scientists bring to the study of their phenomena.

This brings us to the second reason for denying to social science the status of science. It is that a neutral attitude toward social phenomena and adherence to the objective of scientific curiosity are impossible, because the investigator cannot escape the prejudices and values engendered by his own social experience.[8]

It cannot be denied that it is far more difficult to sustain scientific objectivity in the study of human societies than in the investigation of bacteria or atoms or stars, and this is particularly true when the investigator studies his own society. The outcome will depend largely on (1) the success of social scientists in developing a compelling tradition that demands of the members of the profession that, when they go to their studies or their laboratories, they make every effort to leave their personal values and emotions at home; (2) the development of the arts and techniques of self-knowledge that will enable them to succeed in this endeavor;

[7] For an excellent statement of the relations between science and ideology, with illuminating examples from the history of economics, the reader is referred to the Presidential address of Joseph A. Schumpeter before the American Economic Association, "Science and Ideology," *American Economic Rev.* XXXIX: 345–359 (March 1949).

[8] A classic exposition of this position may be found in the methodological section, Gunnar Myrdal, *American Dilemma* (New York, 1946), Appendix II, where it is argued that social "scientists" must therefore attempt to state explicitly their own ideological predispositions. The effectiveness of this precept is limited, however, when predilections are too deeply ingrained to be revealed by even the most conscientious self-examination.

and (3) the development of objective techniques for assaying the validity of conclusions and methods so that scientific discipline is enforceable. The strength of a professional tradition fortified by such techniques should not be underestimated. The examples of the natural sciences and of other professions testify that there is nothing psychologically impossible in control of personal attitude by professional role. The nuclear physicist does not let his views on atomic bombing distort the results of his research. The physician does not let his fondness or dislike for the patient influence his diagnosis or prescription. The lawyer defends in court a criminal he may despise.

In the social sciences, the tradition of scientific neutrality is one of growing strength, and the techniques necessary to implement it and to enforce it are steadily becoming more effective. It is in the spirit of this growing tradition that we have tried to write this book. To the extent that we here fail to act as neutral observers and analysts we shall have failed in our scientific purpose. We are, of course, citizens who vote and who have opinions — opinions often differing among ourselves — on the controversial issues discussed in the business creed. We have tried not to let our personal politics, values, and opinions distort our report and analysis of business ideology. We do not wish to persuade the reader of anything beyond the reasonableness of our analytical explanation of the content of the business creed. How well we succeed in our purpose the reader will, of course, judge for himself.

An attempt to be neutral and dispassionate on live social issues, which arouse strong emotions throughout the society, confronts still another obstacle. This attitude is almost bound to appear annoyingly and presumptuously Olympian, as if the authors place themselves outside and above their own society. We are all too keenly aware that much in this volume will give such an impression. For example, on the subject of corporate profits taxation we shall find some truth and some exaggeration both in business ideology and in labor union ideology. We shall point out that the areas of ignorance and doubt on the subject are much too great to justify the certainty with which ideological positions are asserted on both sides. But this is an issue, like many others, which in practice must be continually resolved, regardless of the judicious uncertainties of social scientists. In its resolution many persons feel deep personal involvement; they cannot afford the luxury of leisurely study and balanced or suspended judgment. If we seem aloof in discussing such matters, it is not because we are unaware that issues of policy must be decided or that people rightly feel strongly about how they are decided. The moral is that science alone cannot run a society. Ideology is required too — otherwise social decisions would never be reached, or once reached, carried out.

THE CONTENT OF THE BUSINESS CREED

In Part I we shall expound the content of the American Business Creed. In the process of reporting the articles of the creed, we shall wish to point out their ideological characteristics. We shall show how the business creed possesses the features of ideology which have been reviewed above and illustrated with examples from other ideologies. Since these ideological features stand out only in contrast to science, we shall compare the business creed's treatment of many subjects with the treatment of the same subjects in the social sciences. Usually this does not lead to any categorical conclusion that the ideology is true or false, right or wrong. Many ideological statements are evaluative, and social science provides no basis for classing them as right or wrong; for non-evaluative statements, social science is often not definite enough to support categorical conclusions on the truth or falsity of business ideology. We shall point out, instead, that ideology exaggerates and oversimplifies, that it is dogmatically certain where social science is uncertain, that it tells only parts of many stories. We shall also be interested in the symbols of the business creed and in the part which symbols widely diffused in American culture play in business ideology. And we shall note the restraining influence of public admissibility on the content of the business creed.

We speak of *the* American business creed, but we do not mean to give the impression that business ideology is monolithic. Businessmen disagree among themselves on many matters, and these disagreements find public expression. Indeed, there is a pervasive divergence between adherents of what we call the *classical* and the *managerial* strands in the creed, and we examine their differences at length in Part I. The diversity of business ideology, in comparison with certain other ideological movements, is easy to understand. Business ideology has no official sacred text, such as the works of Marx provide for the movement he founded. There is no priesthood or hierarchy to establish an official "line." Business ideology is not a set of ready-made beliefs which potential adherents must take or leave. Rather, it is created and revised by its own adherents.

The time reference of the book is the period since the Second World War. We shall refer occasionally to earlier business ideology and to changes that have occurred in ideological viewpoints. But we are writing an analysis of contemporary American business ideology, not a history of American business ideology. The report in Part I of the content of the business creed relies almost entirely on publications since the Second World War and uses illustrations of earlier date where the points of view expressed are representative of contemporary business opinion or shed light on the current creed.

Our report is based upon an extensive survey of: (a) advertisements of business firms and of associations of business firms in periodicals of general circulation and of business circulation, (b) articles, speeches, public letters, and books by business authors, (c) articles and editorials in business periodicals or in the business and financial sections of other publications, (d) pamphlets, leaflets, and books distributed by business firms, associations of business firms, or organizations supported by businessmen and devoted to the propagation of the business point of view, (e) statements of businessmen or their representatives before Congressional hearings.

We have surveyed the output of literature from the major relevant organizations: the National Association of Manufacturers, the Committee for Economic Development, the Chamber of Commerce of the United States, the Foundation for Economic Education, and others.[9] We have examined business testimony in major Congressional hearings during the period.[10] We have systematically clipped every issue of fifteen representative periodicals of popular and business circulation over a period of a year (July 1, 1948 to June 30, 1949).[11] Beyond these systematic efforts, we have been, of course, sensitive to many other published expressions of the business creed.

However, we cannot in the nature of the case claim to have based our report of the content of the business creed on a statistical sample. The universe of business ideology is too vaguely defined for the application of formal sampling concepts. The material that we have examined discloses such homogeneity in its major themes that we have no fears that our report suffers from an unrepresentative selection of sources.[12] The

[9] Organizations from which literature has been received and studied are listed in Appendix.

[10] The hearings which have been studied are listed in the Appendix.

[11] The list of periodicals clipped is given in the Appendix.

[12] There are some questions, on which we wished to obtain a business viewpoint, which the creed seldom considers. In these cases we have had to rely on a small number of sources, sometimes even on a single source. On such questions our report obviously runs a great risk of being unrepresentative. But generally we attach more significance to the relative silence of the creed on these matters than to the substance of the few opinions which are expressed.

There is also the related question of "crackpot" expressions of opinion by individual businessmen which cannot be taken as "representative" of the creed. No hard and fast rule can be laid down for distinguishing "crackpot" from "representative" material; the boundaries of the expressions which constitute the business creed are simply too vague, at the margins, to permit of hard and fast distinctions. In general, the authors considered such criteria as the frequency with which particular points were repeated in various sources, the position of the writer in the business community, the nature and standing of the agency which disseminates a particular document, and so forth. The problem of the range of opinion expressed in the creed and the relation of extreme views to the central core of the creed receives further treatment in Chapter 18 below.

A similar problem exists in deciding when writings or statements made or cir-

same themes, arguments, facts, and symbols recur again and again. We are confident that the reader who cares to survey the literature will find that the chapters which follow report faithfully the substance of the creed.

OUR THEORY: ROLES, STRAINS AND BUSINESS IDEOLOGY

The central purpose of the book, to which Part II is devoted, is to provide an explanation of the content of the creed, as reported in Part I. The comparisons between ideology and social science in Part I provide material for our answer in Part II to the question, "What determines the content of business ideology?" For the discrepancies between ideology and science — the contexts of exaggerations, omissions, special emphases, dogmatic certainties, and symbolic appeals — are clues to the motivations that lie behind the ideological beliefs.

Briefly, our thesis is that the content of the business ideology can best be explained in terms of the *strains* to which men in the business role are almost inevitably subject. Businessmen adhere to their particular kind of ideology because of the emotional conflicts, the anxieties, and the doubts engendered by the actions which their roles as businessmen compel them to take, and by the conflicting demands of other social roles which they must play in family and community. Within the resources of the cultural tradition and within the limits of what is publicly acceptable, the content of the ideology is shaped so as to resolve these conflicts, alleviate these anxieties, overcome these doubts. For the individual businessman, the function of the ideology is to help him maintain his psychological ability to meet the demands of his occupation. It follows that the ideology has functional importance also for those on whom the actions of businessmen impinge and for the whole society.

We do not imply, of course, that the business role is the only one in our society which is subject to strains. All roles involve strains in varying degree, and many are undoubtedly harder to play than that of business-men. Nor do we imply that business ideology is the only set of beliefs which is related to the strains of some role. Indeed we expect that workers, professors, and bureaucrats — to name some outstanding examples — also have ideologies connected with the strains of their respective social roles. In this book, however, we will make the business ideology a test case of our theory.[13]

---

culated by businessmen are to be considered as science rather than ideology. Again discretion was the rule, and such writings as, for example, those of Chester Barnard on organization, or Oswald Knauth on the character of the business corporation are here treated as scientific rather than ideological. Beardsley Ruml, *Tomorrow's Business* (New York, 1945), exemplifies a mixture of scientific and ideological material which could be discussed as either.

[13] One of us, Mr. Sutton, has examined the role strains that motivate certain workers, intellectuals, and others to adhere to Marxist ideology. See F. X. Sutton, "The Radical Marxist," unpublished doctoral dissertation, Harvard, 1950.

We recognize that businessmen vary in the extent to which they find the requirements of the role a source of strain. Some indeed may be nearly perfectly adapted to the role. Yet the typical child of American culture who undertakes a business career is bound to find some of the demands of the role uncongenial. Moreover, one can reasonably infer, on the basis of psychological assumptions, that businessmen feel certain common or *patterned strains* as a result of the institutional features of business and certain pervasive characteristics of American society.

Some readers may expect us to rely on psychoanalytic study of individual businessmen in our search for the sources of ideology. Even if we were able to do so, we would not consider such an approach necessary or sufficient. Our inferences are primarily derived from the institutional structure of society, not from the structure of individual personalities. We expect them to hold on the average for large numbers, not for specific individuals. Just as we cannot expect every businessman to be equally subject to the patterned strains of the role, so we cannot expect every businessman to react to these strains in the same manner. There can be as great a variety of individual reactions as there are varieties of individual histories and personalities. The difficulties of the business office may be reflected in family troubles, in hobbies and avocations, in religion, in alcoholism, in hypochondria, or in a host of other ways. Ideological belief and expression provide for businessmen a reaction which is socially acceptable, available to all, and mutually reinforcing. Whatever forms their personal reactions to the strains of the role may take, it seems likely that ideology will be a reaction common to a great many businessmen.

THE INTEREST THEORY REJECTED

We have rejected the "interest" theory, that ideologies simply reflect the economic self-interest, narrowly conceived, of their adherents.[14] Ideology, in this view, is merely an attempt to manipulate symbols and marshal arguments which will persuade others to take actions from which the ideologist stands to profit financially. The ideologist may or may not believe the things he says. If he does happen to believe them, it is maintained, it is only because he has succeeded by wishful thinking in convincing himself that truth and self-interest coincide.

The "interest theory" contains important elements of truth. It is easy to understand why the ideology of the domestic watch industry, both management and labor, features support of tariff protection and includes all the venerable arguments and symbols which might persuade the Tariff

[14] Nowadays many people rightly reject the notion that economic self-interest is the sole motivation of men in their economic behavior. Yet it continues to be fashionable and sophisticated to accept the thesis that economic self-interest is virtually the sole motivation of men in the field of social and political ideas and words.

Commission, the Congress, and the public of the protectionist case. Were this the model for all ideology, there would indeed be little problem of explanation and little need for our book. Actually the relationship between specific ideologies and economic interest is seldom so clear. A more typical example is provided by the passionate support a businessman gives to the principle of a balanced federal budget. We surely cannot conclude that he has reached this position by sober calculation of his profit prospects under balanced and unbalanced budgets. Assessing the ultimate effects of alternative budgetary policies on the profits of a specific business firm is a formidable econometric problem. Yet businessmen speak on the subject with such confidence, emotion, and unanimity that, in the "interest theory" of ideology, we would be forced to conclude that they have no trouble knowing on which side of the issue their economic interests lie, and that varying effects on different groups of businessmen are never to be anticipated.

It is true that with sufficient ingenuity one can construct a chain which reconciles practically any ideological position to the economic interest of its holder. Or one can make the task easier by attributing to the ideologist a mistaken or unduly certain conception of his own interest. One can make the task still easier by widening the notion of self-interest to encompass psychological satisfactions other than economic returns. But these expedients are really the end of the theory they are designed to salvage. They reduce it to a tautology: "Men act in their own interests" becomes "Men act as they are motivated to act." [15]

THE EXPLICIT AND PUBLIC NATURE OF IDEOLOGY

In discussing ideology in this introductory chapter, we have identified ideology only with *explicit public statements*. On this point we must make ourselves unmistakably clear. Often the term "ideology" has been used with much wider connotation. For example, sometimes ideology is interpreted to include not just what is explicitly said but also what is, or seems to the observer, implicit in actions and institutions. [16] On this interpretation, it is possible to deduce the ideology of a group not from what they say but from what they do. What must they believe in order to act as they do? What is the outlook on the world implicit in their institutions? This seems to involve a hazardous kind of speculation and raises the very difficult question of the relation between beliefs and actions. Actions are not simply consequences of *beliefs;* and where the interest is in expressed beliefs, it seems desirable not to complicate matters by trying from the very first to treat action as evidence of beliefs.

[15] The interest theory and other theories of ideology are discussed further in Chapter 14 below.

[16] See Thurman Arnold, *The Folklore of Capitalism* (New York, 1941); *Ideological Differences and World Order* edited by F. S. C. Northrop (New Haven, 1949). Also see discussion in Chapter 14 below.

Often the definition of ideology is widened to include private beliefs as well as public statements. We have focused attention on public statements largely, of course, because the content is much more accessible, and partly because we believe the determination of the content of public statements is an interesting problem in itself. There may seem to be a risk that in paying attention to public statements we are examining a relatively superficial phenomenon, that we are not finding out what businessmen "really believe," but only what they are forced to say if they hope for a sympathetic response in a particular situation. It is often assumed that people are only able to say what they "really think" in sympathetic, private conversations and that what they say in public is more or less "window dressing." Since we shall argue later that many of the business creed's statements are linked to deep-seated feelings of businessmen (and in this sense are "really believed"), it is important for us to analyze the possible discrepancies between beliefs expressed in public and in private.

As a general principle, it may be assumed that any social action (including the verbal expression of a belief) is subject to two determining influences: (1) the subjective orientations of the persons initiating the action, and (2) external situational conditions, including the expectations of those persons to whom the action is oriented.[17] It follows that the beliefs which a person expresses in any social situation are to some extent determined by the expectations of others in that situation. The common feeling that we "really" express ourselves in those intimate, familiar contexts we call "private," rests not on the fact that there are *no* constraints on what we say in these contexts, but on a difference in degree of constraint.

It is true, as we have remarked above, that some views are possible as unexpressed beliefs or as opinions shared by a small group which are not admissible as more public expressions. For example, one may advocate in private a property qualification for voting; but one is compelled to be for universal suffrage in public. The extent and significance of divergencies of this kind can easily be exaggerated. There is a strong tendency for the social constraints which make some statements inadmissible in public to be *internalized* in individuals. That is, the controlling norms become part of the individual's own structure of attitudes and beliefs; and the inhibitions become personal and automatic rather than controlled by the social situation.[18] Insofar as this happens, we may say that a man "believes" what he

[17] See *Toward a General Theory of Action,* edited by T. Parsons and E. Shils (Cambridge, 1951), part 2, ch. 1, pp. 53 ff.

[18] In a society like the United States where "sincerity" is strongly valued, there are perhaps especial pressures toward internalizing the values which control public statements and thus toward making expressed beliefs invariant from one context to another. The situation might be somewhat different in Japanese or French society. In Japanese society, for example, there is an accepted distinction between

says in public and that this will not differ significantly from at least some of the things he says in private. Thus, our private advocate of a restricted suffrage is not likely to be thoroughly consistent in always rejecting universal suffrage in his private discussions, nor is he necessarily purely expedient in his public acceptance of it.

If the relations between public and private expressions of belief are thus somewhat more complicated than the relations between "real belief" and "window dressing," they still merit close inspection. We shall return to this question in Chapter 15 below, when we have made clear how we propose to analyze the public statements we take as the business ideology. There we shall compare the ideology with what is known (chiefly from polls) about what businessmen say in more private contexts. The divergences prove to be on the whole small.

"front-door" and "back-door" talk. It is fully recognized that one puts on different codes of behavior in different situations without there being cynical derogation of "front-door" talk as "insincere." The American pressure to be "natural" or "sincere" at all times is lacking. We are indebted to Professor J. Pelzel for illuminating discussions of this point.

PART I

THE CONTENT OF THE CREED

The general task of Part I is to expound the content of the contemporary American Business Creed. The place of this exposition in our argument and the spirit in which it is undertaken have already been set forth in the Preface and in Chapter 1. Here it is necessary only to explain the structure of the eleven chapters that make up Part I.

The notion of a coherent, unique, and consciously designed American economic "system" is the central concept of the business creed. The ideology finds in this system the decisive explanation of the remarkable achievements of the American nation since the eighteenth century. The concept of the system, and the claims made on its behalf are the subjects of Chapter 2.

The key institutional unit in the system is the business enterprise, and the next five chapters are devoted to the creed's description of the enterprise and of its relationships with individuals. Chapter 3 is concerned with over-all views of the enterprise, both classical and managerial. Chapters 4, 5, and 6 set forth the details of these views regarding relationships to, successively, owners, managers, employees, and customers.

Beginning with Chapter 8, we turn from ideology concerning the individual business enterprise to ideology concerning the operation of the system as a whole. Chapter 8 itself examines the ideology's description of the mechanism by which competition among businesses and individuals leads to optimal over-all results, including the claimed benefits of Chapter 2. The creed's picture of government as outside the system and as a menace to the mechanism is discussed in Chapter 9. Chapters 10 and 11, still on this macroscopic level, set forth the doctrines found in the business creed concerning the causes and cures of depressions and inflations. In these four chapters, classical views receive the most attention because the managerial creed has not yet worked out a theory of the economy-wide consequences of the interactions of managerial business corporations. But we find managerial views less emphatic regarding the benefits of free competition and less hostile to government interventions than the dominant classical strand.

Finally, the business creed contains a definite and consistent set of judgments on what constitutes the good individual and the good society. The ethics and social values of the creed, which provide a framework for the discussion of all kinds of specific subjects, are the subjects of Chapter 12, which thus serves as a kind of summary of Part I and transition to Part II.

2

THE AMERICAN SYSTEM
AND ITS ACHIEVEMENTS

PRAISE FOR THE ACHIEVEMENTS of American capitalism is one of the dominant themes in the literature of the Business Creed. Material achievements — especially the high and rising standard of living — take first place; discussion of non-material achievements is subordinate in frequency of repetition throughout the body of ideology and in prominence of place in systematic expositions of it. Both the material and the non-material achievements are explained by a rigid cause-and-effect link with the System: the achievements flow from and validate the System, and the two are inseparably bound together. The lesson for the future is clear.

MATERIAL ACHIEVEMENTS OF AMERICAN CAPITALISM

The central achievement of the system has been the great rise in standard of living to its present level, high in comparison with the past and in comparison with other countries today. All elements of this rise are praised: the great increase in total output, the introduction of new goods, the conversion of the luxuries of yesterday's rich to the necessities of today's masses, and the great reduction of working time. But the first three are praised more frequently than the last. A typical expression of the claims of progress is provided by the Advertising Council's pamphlet, *The Miracle of America:*

Today the American way of life provides the highest standard of living ever enjoyed by any people in the world.

This is no mere boast. It is a statement of thrilling fact — that men can raise their level of living by greater productivity if they are free to do it.

Electricity, running water, central heating, one house or apartment per family, are quite general in America. To the Russian or Chinese worker, whose whole family is often crowded in one room, with no private kitchen or bath and no central heating, our homes would represent dreams of luxury.

With only one-fifteenth of the world's population and about the same proportion of the world's area and natural resources, the United States — has more than half the world's telephone, telegraph and radio networks — more than three-quarters of the world's automobiles — almost half the world's radios — and consumes more than half the world's copper and rubber, two-thirds of the silk, a quarter of the coal and nearly two-thirds of the crude oil.[1]

An hour's work in 1914 and 1948 would buy the following:[2]

	1914	1948
Men's Work Shoes	9 hours	3 hours
Baby Carriage	21 hours	15½ hours
Electric Light Bulbs	102 minutes	12 minutes
Electric Fan	49 hours	4 hours

Another example, emphasizing the comparison between the United States and the U.S.S.R., which is now common in the context of the world political struggle, appears in an advertisement of the Columbia Steel and Shafting Company:

It may seem a small thing to you that an average worker in the U.S. earns more than enough in two 8-hour shifts, even at this year's prices, to put a Thanksgiving dinner fit for a king on the family table — plump-breasted gobbler and all the other fixin's, down to pumpkin pie and whipped cream and a cherry on top.

But it isn't a small thing at all. It's one more instance of the direct results of a productive system that has brought more health and happiness to more people, more things and better things at less cost, than any other system ever has or ever will.

The average Russian worker, now — he'd have to work four full 40-hour weeks, plus a couple of hours of over-time to set the same dinner in front of his wife and kids. It's lucky for him that Russia doesn't have a Thanksgiving Day. Very appropriate, too. After all, under the Communistic system of slave labor, with no freedom of action, speech, religion or anything else, what would he be thankful for?[3]

Benson Ford, of the Ford Motor Company, in a speech before the Los Angeles Chamber of Commerce emphasizes the great rate of material progress:

In the year 1900, there was one automobile for every 9,500 people in this country. Today there is one automobile for every 4½ to 5 people in the United States.

In the year 1925, 2,700,000 families had radios. Today 37,000,000 families — or 95 per cent of all American families — have radios.

In 1935, 16 per cent of families or spending units in this country had an

---

[1] *The Miracle of America, as discovered by one American family,* Advertising Council, Inc. (New York, n.d.), pp. 11–12.
[2] *Ibid.,* p. 12.
[3] Columbia Steel & Shafting Company advertisement, *Business Week,* Nov. 20, 1948.

income of over $2000. Last year 64 per cent had incomes over $2000 a year,
. . . Progress is always an unfinished business in America.[4]

Both time and space comparisons which portray the success of the
American System are often put into dramatic form. Thus McGraw-Hill
shows how much of the world's production the United States accounts for,
despite its relatively small size:

The United States contains only about 6 per cent of the world's population. But our national income, before the war, amounted to almost 25 per cent
of the world's income. Our industrial output as a whole approximates 45 per
cent of world totals. We are now producing a like percentage of the world's
railroad mileage; 25 per cent of merchant fleet tonnage; 50 per cent of the
world's telephones; 45 per cent of steel production; 40 per cent of aluminum
production; 33 per cent of coal output. We are refining (though part of the
production comes from imports) 55 per cent of the world's copper, and 70 per
cent of its petroleum. We are now producing 50 per cent of the world's rubber
(though post-war resumption of natural rubber production will sharply reduce
this balance). Our shares of agricultural production are, of course, much smaller,
but just before the war we accounted for 35 per cent of world cotton production, 15 per cent of wheat, and 10 per cent of wool.[5]

Paul Hoffman makes a similar point:

. . . Ours may not be a perfect system but under it 7 per cent of the
people of the world do produce nearly 50 per cent of the world's manufactured
goods . . .[6]

And the Advertising Council tells us:

*Compared to the record of all civilization, this free world of yours is ten
minutes old.*
Yet in ten short minutes it's done more *good for more people* than anything that ever happened on earth.[7]

The last examples serve to illustrate another important aspect of
progress which is emphasized in the creed — sheer productivity and
efficiency in itself. There is, of course, a logical connection between a rise

[4] Benson Ford (Vice President of Ford Motor Company), *Five Jobs for Young
Men,* address before the Los Angeles Chamber of Commerce, Los Angeles, Calif.,
Feb. 28, 1949, p. 7.
[5] "What Does America Want?," McGraw-Hill advertisement, *Washington Post,*
December 1944.
[6] Address by the Honorable Paul G. Hoffman before the National Board of
Fire Underwriters, May 25, 1950, p. 8.
[7] "A Tremendous Thing Has Happened in the Last 10 Minutes," an advertisement approved by the Public Policy Committee of the Advertising Council. This is
a favorite metaphor; see for example, S. Wells Utley, *The American System, Shall
We Destroy It?* (Detroit, 1936), p. 74, where United States history is compressed
into the last twenty-five seconds of twelve hours of human history.

in the standard of living and an increase in productivity. But frequently, increases in efficiency are celebrated as achievements in themselves without reference to their fruits in terms of increased living standards. A General Electric Company advertisement tells how G.E. products have become increasingly efficient.

> Fluorescent lamps, introduced by General Electric Scientists, give about 2½ times as much light as filament lamps of the same voltage . . . often last from three to six times longer . . . G.E. research and engineering have improved the household refrigerator so that today's model runs on less than half the current used 20 years ago . . .[8]

The Advertising Council, in the *Miracle of America,* tells us:

> . . . the average worker can produce about five times as much per hour as in 1850 without expending any more energy than he did then. That's why net output of goods and services increased 29 times from 1850 to 1944, though working hours were much shorter and the population only six times greater. *If we were still producing at the 1850 rate per hour, we would need over 300 million workers, each putting in 43 hours a week to produce as much as we did in 1944!* [9]

This same pamphlet illustrates another, and somewhat curious, form of the emphasis on production for its own sake; in summarizing the progress of the American system, it cites the rise in the proportion of the population gainfully employed from 320 per thousand in 1850 to 420 per thousand today.

The business creed is not exaggerating when it emphasizes the high standard of living in the United States compared with the rest of the world, the great speed with which output and consumption have grown in the last 100 years, and the introduction of countless new goods; any historian would see these facts in much the same perspective. In the material sense, industrialization has changed the world with unbelievable rapidity and has done so more rapidly in the United States than elsewhere.

NONMATERIAL ACHIEVEMENTS

Among the nonmaterial achievements of the system, three are given particular importance in the business creed: the creation by and in business of the spirit of service; the opportunity for personal achievement and social recognition which the business world presents to all who have the talents to use it; and, broadest of all, the achievement of Freedom — political, religious, and personal — which the system and the system alone makes possible.

According to the creed, business creates a spirit of service and its

[8] General Electric advertisement, *Boston Globe,* June 13, 1948.
[9] *Miracle of America,* p. 13.

objectives go far beyond meeting the needs of the cash customers, or even creating new needs for new cash customers. Thus the authors of *USA, The Permanent Revolution,* picture the heavy social responsibilities of a business executive and their importance to society at large:

"There are times, as I sit behind a desk piled high with the day's unread correspondence, when I stare darkly out of the window," Walter H. Wheeler, Jr., President of Pitney-Bowes, Inc., of Stamford, Connecticut, was speaking on the *Social Responsibility of Business.* "Trying to see me are three conscientious executives, who would like to remind me, if they dared, that we're in business to make a profit and that I must spend *some* time on the problem of sales, manufacturing, and development. There is a Community Chest meeting in five minutes, and a directors' meeting tomorrow morning, neither of which I am prepared for . . . It seems to me that none of us can look forward with hope over the years unless all of us can find solutions to problems bigger than our immediate material progress."

Every American man-of-affairs will recognize Mr. Wheeler's complaint . . . The truth is that Americans are just about as busy with their non-official, unremunerated, voluntary activities as they are with their official duties; and these unpaid, unofficial, off-duty activities have a deeper and more lasting effect upon American life, and even American policies, than do the official ones.[10]

Another variation on the service theme is provided by the picture of Henry Ford drawn in a life insurance company advertisement:

Young Henry Ford saw something quite different in the shadows of the shop that night.

He saw his little automobile speeding a doctor to a remote farmhouse to save a life.

He saw a million miles of roads opening up for all Americans the glories of their big country . . . making the man from Maine a neighbor of the man from California.

He saw people riding to work, to market, to school, to church freed at last from the old tyranny of distance.

And he saw new jobs, better incomes, more free time for everybody . . .

Such was the vision of young Henry Ford in the little shop on Bagley Avenue . . . Like every enterprise we look upon as basic . . . the auto industry has earned its success by contributing something deep and lasting to the welfare of all Americans.[11]

The emphasis on disinterested and nonmaterialistic motivations in this quotation provides a counterpoint to the more usual materialistic themes; it might be called a spiritualization of material progress.

The picture of business as the provider of the sinews of war and na-

---

[10] *USA, The Permanent Revolution,* by the Editors of *Fortune* with the collaboration of Russell Davenport (New York, 1951), pp. 128–129.

[11] John Hancock Life Insurance Company advertisement, *Newsweek,* Jan. 24, 1949.

tional defense is also part of the service theme. This picture, with its appeal to patriotic sentiments and national solidarities, first became important in the Second World War, and for a time became the staple ingredient of advertising. The theme is frequently repeated today in the context of the cold war, often in terms of "first in war, first in peace." But the implied obligation, that business should be first in the hearts of its countrymen, is not always honored as business feels it should be. Thus the President of the United States Steel Company pictures the achievements of business in winning the war in a somewhat plaintively defensive context:

It was only a few years ago — in the war years — that the government gloried in the size of its industrial giants and honored them for doing successfully the giant tasks — the almost impossible production tasks — that our national security demanded. It called upon United States Steel to outproduce, single handed, all the Axis nations put together. We did it. It called upon our great research laboratories and our skilled technicians to design and to create such storybook miracles as a "portable" landing field for aircraft. We did so. It called upon our management to use all of its experience, ingenuity, efficiency and know-how, to build, to man and to operate vast new steel-making plants for the government. We did so. And the government sang our praises.

. . . After World War I those who had produced the weapons that defeated our enemies were denounced as "merchants of death." Today, after World War II, they are branded as "oligopolists." [12]

A second nonmaterial benefit claimed in the creed is that the business system creates equality of opportunity and rewards those who take advantage of it. The Bell Telephone advertisement which tells us:

Year by year the next half century will be increasingly theirs [those starting out]. New leaders will appear from among them. Step by step, rung by rung, they will mount the ladder to the top. For telephone management is employee management and comes up from the ranks.

There will be more good jobs in the telephone business in 1958 and 1998 than now. It just can't help being this way . . .[13]

is typical. Similarly, the paper of the Eastern Railroad Presidents' Conference has a column entitled "Career Open to Merit," which tells us, for example, that the new Chairman of the Board of the Pennsylvania Railroad started as a rodman on a track engineering corps in 1901 and that the new President of the Erie Railroad began as a yard clerk in 1908.[14]

Opportunity is often linked with freedom and together they are por-

[12] B. J. Fairless, *Business — Big and Small — Built America*, U.S. Steel Corporation, 1950, pp. 5–6. Statement in *Study of Monopoly Powers, Hearings* before the Subcommittee of the House Committee of the Judiciary (Celler Subcommittee), Eighty-first Congress, 2nd session, February–July 1950.

[13] Bell Telephone System advertisement, *Harper's*, March 1948.

[14] *Railroad Data*, June 1949, September 1949.

trayed as the crowning achievement of the system. Freedom as an achievement is usually given a place of honor in comparisons with the slavery and low living standards of the Communist world. Thus a Warner and Swasey advertisement states:

If every Communist knew what every sane person in a capitalist country knows — the high standard of living which capitalism makes possible, the pride of individual accomplishment, the satisfaction of knowing you can go as far as your own abilities and ambition will take you, the security of justice, the joy of knowing your son can go even farther than you have gone . . . if every Communist knew the facts about capitalism, there wouldn't be any Communists.[15]

Freedom also appears in contrast with government control in a broad sense, rather than specifically with the lack of freedom in a totalitarian Communist state. This is especially the case in discussions of the proper role of government; the Chamber of Commerce argues that without the freedoms embodied in the right "to keep his living where he can find it, and to venture his means where profit seems likely, it is pure delusion to imagine that political freedom, even if it exists, can long endure." [16] And, in a somewhat different context, the then Chairman of the Board of the United States Steel Corporation celebrated another aspect of Freedom:

. . . No other nation possesses so many private universities as we do; and no nation, I suppose, enjoys the same full measure of individual liberty that we have known. That can hardly be a coincidence.
. . . But I am suggesting that Freedom of Education and Freedom of Enterprise are part and parcel of the same thing — and they are inseparable — and that neither can survive without the other.[17]

These nonmaterial benefits claimed in the creed cannot be measured as can output, consumption per head, or productivity.[18] One cannot define precisely, far less quantify, how much freedom there is in one society compared with another; much the same thing is true of opportunity, although the problems here are not quite so great. Yet it can fairly be said that the creed is rather selective in claiming nonmaterial achievements for the System. This is not to say that its claims are false; the major claims of freedom and free opportunity are certainly justified on any fair view

---

[15] Warner & Swasey advertisement, *Newsweek,* Aug. 9, 1948.
[16] *Measuring Monopoly: A New Approach,* A statement of the U.S. Chamber of Commerce (Washington, 1949), p. 23.
[17] I. S. Olds, *Our Mutual Ends,* address at a dinner celebrating the 250th Anniversary of Yale University (19 October 1951), published by the U.S. Steel Corporation, pp. 1, 8.
[18] Of course, a sufficiently sophisticated economist will reject the notion that any of these magnitudes can be measured with any precision for the purposes of intertemporal or international comparisons, but such refinement is hardly in order in the context of this discussion.

of American society. But they are one-sided. No rounded account of the matter would push so far the claims of the uniqueness of American freedom, and of its necessary association with a particular set of economic arrangements. With respect to equality of opportunity, there is an even clearer process of selection at work. Individual success stories abound, but no attempt is made to examine the overall statistical situation. Such an examination might well lead to more tempered conclusions about American freedom of opportunity.[19]

EXPLAINING THE ACHIEVEMENTS — THE AMERICAN SYSTEM

These great achievements are, according to the business creed, mainly due to the American System of free enterprise and limited government. James B. Walker, "an active participant in the business system," [20] concludes his history of business on this continent with a careful consideration of the factors responsible for the spectacular success of America. He gives credit to the environment: climate, geography, natural resources. The people, he finds, had spiritual as well as physical strength. But the climactic position in his list goes to the Constitution, "a Bill of Rights for a free enterprise economy," which fostered inventiveness, business acumen, and thrift.[21] Similarly, the authors of the National Association of Manufacturers' two-volume study give credit to a variety of factors but place of honor to the system:

No one factor has been responsible for this progress. The character of our people, our abundant supply of natural resources, our form of government, the type of business system we have developed, the international environment in which we have operated — all these and many other factors have played their part.

Nevertheless, two of these things have been of outstanding and dominating importance in our development: our system of representative democracy and our system of individual enterprise.

. . . inevitably and irrevocably the two go hand in hand.[22]

[19] See, for example, the studies of William Miller in the social origins of American business leaders: "American Historians and the Business Elite," *Journal of Economic History,* November 1949; "The Recruitment of the Business Elite," *Quarterly Journal of Economics,* May 1950; and "American Lawyers in Business and Politics," *Yale Law Journal,* January 1951; F. W. Taussig and C. Jocelyn, *American Business Leaders;* and Upsell and Bendix, in the *American Journal of Sociology,* January and March, 1952.

[20] James B. Walker, *The Epic of American Industry* (New York, 1949), p. xi.

[21] *Ibid.,* pp. 476–479.

[22] National Association of Manufacturers, Economic Principles Commission, *The American Individual Enterprise System, Its Nature and Future,* 2 vols., New York: McGraw-Hill, 1946, p. 873. This treatise will be cited NAM, I or II. This book is the single most important systematic exposition of the business creed in the current literature.

Other ideologists are even more emphatic. They see nothing distinctive in America's endowment of natural resources or in the quality of the population. The System is the unique element, and to it must be credited the unique achievements.

It is true that our land is richly endowed with fertile fields and raw materials, but this can be said with equal truth of Mexico, Central America, and South America. Our people have been thrifty, diligent, and intelligent, but there is no sound basis for the assumption that they overstep the rest of the world in these qualities by any such margin as is shown by their material progress.[23]

> *To say that it's because of our natural resources is hardly the answer.* The same rich resources were here back when the mound builders held forth. Americans have had no monopoly on iron, coal, copper, aluminum, zinc, lead, or other materials. Such things have always been available to human beings. China, India, Russia, Africa, all have great natural resources.
> *Is it because we work harder?*
> Again the answer is "NO" because in most countries the people work much harder on the average than we do.
> *Can it be that we are a people of inherent superiority?*
> . . . Down through the centuries our ancestors, including the Anglo-Saxons, have starved right along with everyone else.[24]

Both of these authors, after rejecting other explanations, find the answer in the discovery, in this country in the late eighteenth century, of the way to release human energy.

There is no mystery as to the causes . . . The reasons . . . are clear and definite forces which have been exerted in the lives of human beings, forces as eternal in their action as the laws of physics or gravitation. We, as a people, can continue to be guided by them and keep on to still greater heights, or we can cast them aside and return to the same stagnation which enveloped the race in former times.

During the last quarter of the eighteenth century, man evolved a new basis for human relationships.[25]

The System would not be a logically adequate explanation of American achievements if it had been tried elsewhere and failed to produce similar results. It is important, therefore, for the creed to distinguish the American system from other versions of capitalism and limited government, and the American Revolution from other revolutions. A characteristic example of the manner of drawing the distinction is provided by the following

[23] Utley, *The American System*, p. 79.
[24] Henry Grady Weaver, *Mainspring, the Story of Human Progress and How NOT to Prevent It*, Irvington-on-Hudson, N.Y., 1947, p. 4 (italics as in original).
[25] Utley, *The American System*, p. 79.

colloquy between Mr. Tyre Taylor, General Counsel of the Southern States Industrial Council and Senator Willis Robertson (D., Va.). Mr. Taylor was testifying before the Senate Committee on Banking and Currency, then holding hearings on the Economic Power of Labor Organizations. Senator Robertson described the discussion as "lay(ing) a foundation for what you are going into."

SENATOR ROBERTSON. . . . Isn't it true that both at Jamestown and at Plymouth the first settlers tried communism, found it to be a failure and abandoned it?

MR. TAYLOR. They did try communism both at Jamestown and at Plymouth, as I recall.

SENATOR ROBERTSON. Isn't it true that after they abandoned it, both in Virginia and Massachusetts, and later in all of the Thirteen Original Colonies, they definitely went to a system of private enterprise?

MR. TAYLOR. That is correct, sir; individual initiative.

SENATOR ROBERTSON. Isn't it true that that was the first bona fide experiment in a system of private enterprise that the world had ever known? Do you know of any other nation that ever gave the same free rein to private enterprise that we enjoy in this country?

MR. TAYLOR. I can't think of any at the moment, Senator.

SENATOR ROBERTSON. I have studied the problem quite at length and I do not know of any other nation. Isn't it true that under a system such as that we have grown to be the most prosperous nation in the world with the highest standard of living in the world?

MR. TAYLOR. Not only the highest standard, but the highest actual effective scale of living in the world at any time.

SENATOR ROBERTSON. So that we are now being called upon to render great financial aid to what we may call the mother country, Great Britain, and to European democracies on the Continent of Europe, and we are receiving demands from Asia and other parts of the globe for financial assistance; we the youngest of those nations are being called upon to repair the ravages of war and get them back on their feet; isn't that true?

MR. TAYLOR. Not only repair the ravages of war, Senator, but to shore up the inefficiencies of socialism. We have the strange situation where the present American free enterprise, competitive capitalistic system, is being called upon and is actually subsidizing socialism in all parts of the world.

SENATOR ROBERTSON. Isn't it true that when at Philadelphia Thomas Jefferson framed the immortal Declaration of Independence, he by necessary inference, supported a system of private enterprise when he said that among others the inalienable rights of mankind were life, liberty and the pursuit of happiness?

MR. TAYLOR. Certainly, Senator, the concept of individual liberty is inseparable from a private, free-enterprise system.

SENATOR ROBERTSON. Well, Thomas Jefferson was not a frivolous man. He was an austere man. He was a disciplined man, and he certainly didn't have in mind when he referred to the pursuit of happiness that we had inalienable rights to go to picture shows, horse races, boxing matches, baseball games, and things of that kind; he was thinking of those fundamental happinesses which were the freedom to work, the freedom to control your own business, the freedom to achieve something for yourself in the world; isn't that true?

MR. TAYLOR. That is. As I see it, one of the most important things it involves is the right to own and control property.

SENATOR ROBERTSON. You can't be happy if you are the economic slave of somebody, can you?

MR. TAYLOR. I don't think so, and I think there has been a great deal of very loose thinking which finds expression in what you hear a lot of people say, talking about human rights as distinguished from property rights. They are indistinguishable; they are inseparable.

SENATOR ROBERTSON. After adopting that Declaration of Independence, we went to war, fought for seven years, and won our freedom from the tyranny of George III, and a group assembled again in Philadelphia to frame a constitution under which a new government could be established.
Isn't it true that what we now call the American System, not only of constitutional liberty, but of private enterprise, was definitely written into that Constitution?

MR. TAYLOR. I think of course the law and the Constitution is what the Supreme Court says it is. We have had a lot of change of thinking within the Supreme Court on those issues in recent years, but my own opinion is that the very concept of private, free enterprise, and the ownership and enjoyment of property is imbedded in the Constitution of the United States.[26]

The substance of this colloquy is widely repeated in the American Business Creed. The United States is conceived as a nation uniquely blessed by a remarkable economic system, which is the central part of the larger American System. Like any ideology, the creed is chiefly concerned with the immediate historical situation in which it arises; it may reach out to view Socialist Britain, or the lessons of the fall of Rome, but most of the writings and speeches by which it is conveyed deal with concrete problems in contemporary America. Through the material of the creed there runs a persistent effort to define the essential features of the United States as a whole. The result is the definition and characterization of an

[26] In *Economic Power of Labor Organizations, Hearings* before the Committee on Banking and Currency of the U.S. Senate (Robertson Committee), Eighty-first Congress, 1st session, July–August 1949, part I, pp. 184–185.

American System, grounded in a particular economic organization, which, as Senator Robertson argued, was inherent in the System from its start.

THE NATURE OF THE SYSTEM — ECONOMY AND SOCIETY

As seen in the business creed, the economy is the central core of the American System, around which the rest of the society is built. Like Marxism, the creed views modern society as a single, consistent, highly integrated pattern. Both ideologies see the economic engine as the prime mover of the social vehicle, though Marxism is much more explicit in this respect than the business creed. In any broad comparative perspective, this is remarkable; rarely has the economic structure of a society been given so central a place in the society's total view of itself as in the modern West. In most societies, fairly stable patterns of economic activity become so traditionalized, so interwoven with kinship, community, and political systems that the economy and its workings occupy a relatively minor place in prevailing ideology.[27]

The idea of the tight interdependence of economy and society is central to the business ideology. The comprehensive statement of the creed prepared by the National Association of Manufacturers opens with this expansive treatment of the "economic system":

The term "economic system" means not merely business as this word is commonly used. It includes all those activities and relations which have an influence upon, or affect, our making a living. It is concerned just as much with the organization of government as with the organization of business, with social problems as with production problems, and with training workers. All these elements are a part of the whole which is the "American way of life" . . . and anything that affects one part will alter the whole.[28]

A little later, the authors in an even more embracing statement appear to make the "economic and political system" coextensive with the whole of American society:

Our political and economic system is simply you and I and the millions like us. It is you as you argue with your neighbors over politics, religion, working conditions, foreign policy, and the weather. It is you as you work at your jobs alongside a lathe, behind a plow, or in front of a kitchen stove. It is you as you sit at night and help your boys and girls with their lessons, and as you fret and worry and plan for their future. It is you as you sit and read the evening paper, or listen to the radio, or go for a ride in the country, or gossip over the back fence. It is you as you say "the blessing" when you sit down to eat and as you go to worship.

---

[27] See the account of the Kula in B. Malinowski, *Argonauts of the Western Pacific* (London, 1932), for a striking case in which social and ritualistic aspects have obscured the functioning of the economy.

[28] NAM, I:1.

These — the thousand and one things which make "our day, our daily bread" — are the American political and economic system.[29]

The tendency of the ideology to intertwine "economy" and other aspects of society reflects, in part, the realistic problems of making distinctions of this sort in a complex society; in part it reflects a more general ideological tendency to emphasize the integrated wholeness of society.

In contexts where the lines between economic and other institutions are more clearly drawn, the business creed again parallels that of its Marxist critics: the one finds American society good, and the source of its virtues lies in its "economic system"; the other finds America wicked, and the same "economic system" is the source of its vices. A favorite linkage between the economic system and the rest of society in the business creed is the edifice of American freedoms. Thus a former president of the NAM told that society on its fiftieth anniversary:

. . . [more Americans must be made to] realize that competitive enterprise, civil and religious freedom, and political freedom are inseparably bound up together and that when one of the three is undermined, all the liberty they now so smugly enjoy will soon be devoured in the maw of dictatorship.[30]

The indivisibility of freedom demands that the economic system be both "free" and free from competition from another system in the same society. No departures from the creed's model of a competitive economy are admitted; the business creed denies the viability of a "mixed" economy in which government economic activity plays a significant and legitimate role. If the economy now shows features which do not accord with the unitary model of the creed, the portentous nature of this situation is sharply urged:

. . . The road we are traveling is sufficiently clear. We cannot delude ourselves with the expectation that we may go a little way further and then stop in the belief that we can combine socialism and capitalism and preserve the best features of each. The very first hard and cold fact that we must face is that *these two systems cannot live together in the same society* . . .[31]

Other authors are scarcely less emphatic on the immiscibility of "systems":

[29] NAM, I:17–18.
[30] H. W. Prentis, Jr., President of Armstrong Cork Co., *Competitive Enterprise versus Planned Economy,* address, issued as a pamphlet by the NAM, August 1945, p. 9.
[31] John T. Flynn, *The Road Ahead* (New York, 1949), p. 151.
On the distribution of this volume by businessmen and business-financed organizations, see Chapter 14 below, p. 294. A condensation of the book by the *Reader's Digest* has been privately distributed by H. R. Cullen of Houston, Texas, a wealthy oilman, with the inscription, "This reprint is presented to you in the belief that its shocking challenge cannot be ignored by any citizen who wishes to preserve America's heritage of freedom."

It is doubtful that we can stop with a mixed economy, part government and part private enterprise. Our country a century ago found that it could not continue to exist half free, half slave.[32]

Or again:

From past experience, a middle-of-the-road course in respect to planned economy is out of the question.[33]

The emphasis in the creed on the proposition that a society is indeed an organized structure, the parts of which are significantly interconnected, and not merely a random congeries of institutions, is one which a neutral social science description of society would share. Indeed, the very nature of the process of apprehending "a society" at all involves seeing it as a system on some level of abstraction. But where the social scientist would point out that "integration is more a tendency than a fact," [34] the ideologist plunges on to define his tightly integrated, consistent system as the reality. The ideologist simplifies complexity and unifies diversity, neglecting the inevitable incongruities of any historically developing social order.

Moreover, the interconnections among various institutions in a society operate in more than one direction. The creed emphasizes the dependence of noneconomic on economic institutions, but ignores interconnections running the other way. No mention of the dependence of a competitive economy and a mobile labor force on the particular type of family and kinship structure and status system based largely on occupational achievement which exist in our society is recognized in the literature of the creed.[35]

Both the emphasis on the integrated character of the social order and the central role of the economy are reflected in the frequent ideological discussion of the "proper" name for the system. Past captains of industry and present-day social scientists have been satisfied with the classic label "capitalism." But other terms now seem to sound better.[36]

The dominant tendency in the ideology is to use the word "capitalism"

[32] NAM, II:1–21. Some economists, it should be noted (for example, F. A. von Hayek) give support to this view, though rarely is the future left so fully open to rational choice, so little to the pressures of events.

[33] Prentis, *Competitive Enterprise*, p. 12.

[34] Clyde Kluckhohn, in *Toward a General Theory of Action*, p. 416.

[35] See Max Weber, *Theory of Social and Economic Organization* (New York, trans. 1947) for a pioneer work in this field.

[36] One reason for concern with the name is indicated by the remarks of A. J. Hayes, president of the International Association of Machinists, to a group of businessmen and others, in which he spoke of "the economic system which grew along with industry, which we and the textbooks used to call capitalism, and which we now sheepishly refer to as free enterprise." See *Creating an Industrial Civilization*, edited by E. Staley, p. 20. This volume (New York, 1952), is a report on a conference sponsored by the Corning Glass Works, and held May 17–19, 1951 at Corning, New York.

only with the modifier, "American," or to substitute other terms. This stems from the intense nationalism of the creed in part and in part it reflects the avoidance of the unfavorable overtones that critics have attached to the term "capitalism" in the past century. The authors of the NAM treatise, after a careful review of several alternatives, fixed on the title *The American Individual Enterprise System* as "the term which most closely approximates accuracy." [37] Individual businessmen have followed suit. Edgar Queeny, of the Monsanto Chemical Company, after "pondering carefully" an argument for the use of the name "capitalism" [38] rejected it in favor of the "free enterprise system . . . an American mutant of age-old capitalism." [39] A more recent writer speaks of an earlier age:

. . . before the word capitalism became perverted by left-wing propaganda to mean exploitation of workers, and (when) there was a general understanding that every drayman with a horse, or every urchin with a shoe shine kit, was a capitalist, i.e., owner of tools of production.[40]

Occasionally in hard-boiled, no-nonsense accounts of the working of the system, "capitalism" remains the designation. Thus the President of the Chamber of Commerce of the United States in 1943, Mr. Eric Johnston, argued:

We fear that word capitalism is unpopular. So we take refuge in a nebulous phrase and talk about the "Free Enterprise System." And we even run to cover in the folds of the flag and talk about the "American Way of Life."

Such language dangerously obscures the main issue. You cannot take a whiff of "free enterprise" or a stretch of a "way of life" and start a factory with it. To start a factory . . . you have to have capital.

People will never understand this point unless we say capitalism.[41]

CLASSICAL AND MANAGERIAL VIEWS OF THE SYSTEM

So far we have spoken of the ideological description of the System as if it were unitary. In fact, we must distinguish between two strands of thinking in the creed, which differ substantially on certain points in their treatment of the American System as well as throughout the creed in general. We shall call these two strands of thought the "classical" and "managerial" versions of the creed. The classical strand centers around the model of a decentralized, private, competitive capitalism, in which the forces of supply and demand, operating through the price mechanism, regulate the economy in detail and in aggregate. The managerial strand

---

[37] *Ibid.*, pp. 2–4.
[38] See quotation from Eric Johnston, below.
[39] Edgar M. Queeny, *The Spirit of Enterprise*, 1943, pp. 244–246.
[40] Ernest L. Klein, *How to Stay Rich* (New York, 1950), p. 189. The book carries the subtitle, *The Story of Democratic American Capitalism.*
[41] Eric Johnston, "Your Stake in Capitalism," *Reader's Digest,* February 1943.

differs chiefly in the emphasis it places on the role of professional managers in the large business firm who consciously direct economic forces for the common good. Examined abstractly, the two strands of thought are quite different in fundamental conception, and, indeed, are hardly entirely consistent. In the literature of the creed, they frequently make their appearance in different contexts, and sometimes as parallel explanations of the same phenomenon; but usually neither is pressed to the logical goal of excluding the other. Macroscopic discussions of the system as a whole are cast in classical terms; the managerial strand is most prominent in discussions of the organization and operation of the business firm.[42] The most coherent exposition of the classical view is that of the authors of the NAM treatise; managerial themes are most completely articulated in *USA, The Permanent Revolution*. The two views will be unfolded as we proceed; it is worth noting at the outset, however, that the classical strand is basic in the business ideology; managerial views represent a variant diverging widely on many specific points, but not sufficiently different nor sufficiently complete to stand as a separate creed.

With respect to their view of the American System, classical and managerial strands are alike in their nationalistic emphasis on the "American" quality of the system, and in their assignment to the economy of the central position in the whole society. It is U.S.A. which is the scene of the permanent revolution; it is the "American proposition" which is the principle of that revolution.[43] And, as we have already seen, the authors of the NAM text, after a careful examination of alternatives, find that it is the American system of individual enterprise whose principles they are expounding.

The editors of *Fortune,* like the NAM authors and others cited in the preceding section above, see the economy as crucial in the whole system. In writing about the "Transformation of American Capitalism," [44] they say:

. . . The revolution was not and is not a mere exercise in political theory . . . It involved the transformation of all aspects of human society — not only political but cultural and economic . . .

[42] Thus in Chapters 3–12 below, in which the business ideology is presented, the classical strand is dominant in the material treated in Chapter 8, on the working of the economic system as a whole, and in Chapter 9, on the role of government; managerial themes are most important in the material presented in Chapter 3, on the business firm, and in Chapter 5, on the role of management. The materials presented in Chapter 4, on business ownership, Chapter 6, on labor, Chapter 7, on consumers, Chapter 10, on money, and Chapter 11, on business fluctuations show mixtures of both classical and managerial views. In Chapter 12, which explores the value system of the creed, no distinction between classical and managerial themes can be made.

[43] *Permanent Revolution,* ch. II. Similarly, ch. III is entitled "The American System."

[44] *Ibid.,* ch. IV.

After protesting their inability to discuss the cultural aspects of the revolu-tion, they propose to focus on "the economy," not only because of their superior competence in this field but because:

. . . it has been the major domestic battleground of our time. Probably the fundamental problem of freedom is cultural, but for the last quarter-century the struggle for freedom has manifested itself chiefly in questions of political economy all over the world. This area, therefore, we believe, is the strategic one to choose in showing how the permanent revolution is being carried out by Americans in the modern world.[45]

The major difference between classical and managerial discussions of the System lies in their varying treatments of history. In the typical classical expression, the American System has been homogeneous in time and space. The system which the Founding Fathers established is the system under which we live today;[46] it is the same system which embraces the whole economy and the whole society, multi-billion dollar utility enter-prise and corner grocery store.[47]

By contrast, the managerial strand emphasizes the fundamental trans-formation of the past fifty years, and sees in the present economic system a radical break with the past. The editors of *Fortune* find that the American economy "bears little resemblance" to that of a century ago.[48] The General Cable Corporation states this theme with rhapsodic simplicity in a full page ad:

I am Industry — 1952

. . . .

---

[45] *Ibid.*, pp. 65–66.
The very fact of making what the authors call "a somewhat arbitrary decision" to exclude the cultural field from discussion is indicative of its ideological unim-portance in their scheme.

[46] Or at least the system under which we lived until 1932; see below.

[47] For example, John M. Hancock, a prominent investment banker, in a state-ment entitled "The Freedom to Compete" made to the Senate Committee on Inter-state and Foreign Commerce, Nov. 9, 1948 (later reprinted as a pamphlet), in connection with hearings on a bill to legalize basing-point pricing said:

"The idea of free competition is part of the American soil. Since the very beginnings of American trade in the days of the Colonies — from the time that Conestoga wagons crossed the Alleghanies carrying goods from seaboard to the new interior — since the time that flat boats first floated goods up and down the Ohio and the Mississippi — in the opening of the West by wagon train and railroad — the abhorrence of monopoly and the refusal to permit conspiracies in restraint of trade have been articles of political faith of, the American people."

Or more explicitly, we find the U.S. Chamber of Commerce attacking the Welfare State by reference to the real intentions of the Founding Fathers and the real significance of the phrase "to promote the general welfare" in the Preamble to the Constitution. See *The Welfare State and the State of Human Welfare*, Chamber of Commerce of the United States (Washington, n.d.), pp. 12–13.

[48] *Permanent Revolution*, p. 189.

People were hurt when I first stirred in life;
Then I grew and learned;
. . . .
I am the people!

With maturity, I have grown, too, in social responsibility
To the people,
    To America!
    And even to those beyond our shores.
My efforts are not in selfish interest;
Rather all my brains and brawn strain for the good of the many;
I am the American way! [49]

Indeed, managerial writers see the break with the past as so sharp that the whole system is moving toward a new kind of homogeneity — of large professionally managed, socially oriented corporations.[50]

Both these sweeping viewpoints are ideologically emphatic and selective. There are important elements of continuity in American economic history; but to identify today's world with the "economic system" of 1776, when nineteen out of twenty Americans lived on the farm, traveled by horse, and manufactured by hand, is as little realistic as to see every American business in the mold of the few largest publicly owned corporations, and to identify the activities of business with the public statements of some businessmen.

ATTRIBUTES OF THE SYSTEM

The American System is characterized in the literature of business ideology by four attributes; they are grouped in the form of two somewhat contradictory pairs of statements. The system is unique (as we have already seen) and, especially in the classical versions, the result of a special act of creation. Yet, at the same time, it is in some sense natural, based on universal laws of human nature. The system is inherently stable, and, unless attacked from without, it functions smoothly and beneficially. This is in sharp contrast to the way the system is viewed in Marxist ideology, which sees it as full of contradictions, and creating within itself forces which will ultimately destroy it. But much emphasis is also placed on the fact that the system is voluntarily "chosen" by its participants, with the implication that they could choose an inferior competing system. Indeed, correct choice and continued adherence become moral duties.

---

[49] General Cable Corp. advertisement, *New York Times,* April 8, 1952.

[50] "What counts, however, is that certain business leaders *are* setting the pace, and *are* being followed. What counts is that the old concept that the owner has a right to use his property just the way he pleases has evolved into the belief that ownership carries social obligations, and that a manager is trustee not only for the owner but for society as a whole. Such is the Transformation of American Capitalism." *Permanent Revolution,* p. 88. See also ch. IV.

Unique. The ideology is unanimous on the proposition that our American system is unique, unlike anything anywhere else in the world. Ernest Klein begins a chapter on "Democracy, the U.S.A. and Capitalism" with:

It is no historical accident that Democracy, the United States of America and Capitalism all were born during the latter half of the eighteenth century. The hour for them had struck. Together they developed and today, welded into the great entity of Democratic American Capitalism, they dominate the world. Still so welded they should mold the future.[51]

And then goes on to say:

At the middle of the eighteenth century, democracy, as we know it, existed only in a few books, principally those of Locke, Voltaire and Rousseau. Capitalism did not exist even on paper, although in England foreshadowings of it might have been discerned . . . Within a magic fifty years, the entire face and future of Western European and American civilization had been changed by the birth of the three tremendous historical factors with which we have to deal in this chapter.[52]

Weaver, in writing about the American Revolution and the founding of the United States, says:

That is what makes the American concept of constitutionalism different from that of the British or anything else that had ever gone before. The difference is the very essence — the very foundation of the Revolution. Ours is the only basic innovation in political structure since the beginning of recorded history.[53]

A two-page spread in *Business Week* puts the theme of uniqueness in appealing terms. A picture of a ten- or twelve-year-old boy, stretched out on the bank of a stream, a can of worms at one side and a fishing pole on the other is headed, "Thank your lucky Stars (and Stripes), Son!" The text reads:

UNDER NO OTHER FLAG IN THE WORLD could this youngster dream his dreams with the same hope of achieving them — with as many great opportunities of realizing them — as under Old Glory! Doesn't that say just about everything for the American system of free enterprise — for the American teamwork of men and machines that makes possible this Good Living? [54]

USA, The Permanent Revolution also emphasizes the uniqueness of the American system, although with the difference that it is the recent managerial system which it pictures:

. . . U.S. capitalism has been in the process of a transformation, with the result that it now bears little resemblance to the classical brand (against which,

---

[51] Klein, *How to Stay Rich,* p. 35.
[52] *Ibid.,* pp. 35, 36.
[53] Weaver, *Mainspring,* p. 168.
[54] Allis-Chalmers advertisement, *Business Week,* Jan. 1, 1949.

for example, Karl Marx launched his attack more than a hundred years ago)
. . . When Europeans talk about capitalism they are referring to something
that no longer exists in America.[55]

The contrast between the American system and European economies
has been especially frequent in recent years, in the context of large American foreign aid programs. Klein, discussing "British socialism" remarks:

. . . the British system which preceded socialism was capitalism in name
only. Competition was stifled by cartel arrangements to restrict production,
fix prices, and allocate markets, all for the protection of the least efficient.[56]

The same ideas can be found earlier. In the early forties, Queeny asserted
that "only in the United States have all the conditions of free and private
enterprise been common to all manufacture and trade and service." [57]

In the classical strand, assertions about the uniqueness of the American
system often take the form of a nationalistic creation myth in which the
System is viewed as coeval with the nation, fashioned completely and
consciously by the Founding Fathers, and embodied (implicitly) in the
texts of the Declaration of Independence and the Constitution. We have
seen some examples of this idea above. The myth is often implicit in the
use of symbolism which associates the free-enterprise system of today
with the events of 1776 and 1787. An Atchison, Topeka and Santa Fe
Railway ad headed "A July Fourth Scoreboard of Freedom" compares the
reader's rights as a U.S. citizen with those he might have under a dictatorship. Under the caption, "YOUR RIGHTS, Here are some of the basic
ones. There are many more," sixteen rights are listed: ten correspond to
sections of the Constitutional Bill of Rights and one to the Thirteenth
Amendment to the Constitution; two are the common law presumption
of innocence of an accused and the right of the secret ballot; the other
three are:

Freedom of the individual to own property of his own selection in communities of his own choosing.
Freedom of each person to work in callings and localities of his own
choice.
Freedom of anyone to have his own business, to start and manage any
enterprise and profit thereby, to contract about his affairs, to invest in a profit
and loss system, to buy and sell in a free market.[58]

A similar technique of symbolic identification is shown in a short film,
entitled "Letter to a Rebel," released by RKO Pathe.[59] The film was

[55] *Permanent Revolution,* p. 189.
[56] Klein, *How to Stay Rich,* p. 111.
[57] Queeny, *Spirit of Enterprise,* p. 245.
[58] Atchison, Topeka and Santa Fe Railway advertisement, *Look,* July 6, 1948.
[59] Quotations are from the cutting continuity of the film, which was kindly made
available to us by the Company.

produced on behalf of the Motion Picture Association, and is introduced by the statement:

The American story of freedom, abundance and opportunity is the great drama in the world today. It is a story that should never be taken for granted. That is why the Motion Picture Association commends this picture to you.

The film tells and shows the comments and thoughts of a small-town newspaper editor as he answers a letter from his son. The letter encloses an editorial from the college newspaper which the son has written. The boy's editorial talks about the "vicious capitalistic system," and it is to the errors in this view that his father addresses his reply. The answer begins:

You'll be pleased to know that you come from a long line of outspoken "liberals" . . . but you'll probably be shocked to discover that they were practically all "capitalists." You know that old flintlock rifle we keep over the mantlepiece? The one I showed you how to handle for the High School history pageant last summer? Well, that rifle belonged to an ancestor of yours . . . a "big businessman" if you will, from Cambridge, Mass. He carried it up Bunker Hill and finally dropped it, in his own blood, along the Brandywine. He was a "liberal," if you want one — a revolutionist, a rebel, like you. But he wasn't fighting against the profit system. He was fighting for his *share* in it . . . and his family's and his country's. And there was your great-grandfather. He was considered a barn-burning radical, back in the 1850's. . . . That was before he came to Monroe and started the Gazette. He put out Abolitionist newspapers in Copperhead communities. His papers, naturally, were never popular, and he was run out of town after town because he was against slave labor, and believed in human rights and the dignity of man. I guess that would make him a "liberal" by any definition. You know, of course, son that I am a capitalist. Oh, I don't wear a plug hat or have dollar signs all over my vest. But I own the paper and employ the help. . . . "slaves" you'd call them . . . who labor for the wages they use to buy the things that are advertised in the paper they put out.[60]

Later in the letter we have:

. . . Your mother and I went strolling over by the old grist mill last Sunday. That mill ground corn, free of charge, for Washington's army. But the farmers paid a fair price and, from the increase of his capital, the miller could build a home and rear his family and bequeath some money to help build the church. He's buried there now, along with generations of townsmen, rich and poor, who shared a common faith in God and the American way.[61]

[60] Continuity, pp. 3, 4. The dots are in the original, and do not indicate omissions. This passage is a treasure of ideological symbols of all sorts; the pictures, of course, add immensely to the effect.
[61] *Ibid.*, p. 10.

Natural. Although our system is a unique creation, it corresponds to fundamental and eternal laws of human nature, presumably valid for all societies. The author of *Mainspring,* like Mr. Utley quoted above,[62] argues that the great American invention rested on the recognition of "a principle as inexorable as any law of physics." [63] The inevitable failings of other systems are rooted in the fact that they are not in accord with these inexorable laws of human nature. Mr. Weaver concedes, "in all fairness" that "communism recognizes the *human equality* and *brotherhood* of man — but it fails to recognize the *real nature of man.*" The root of communist authoritarianism is "an ancient, infantile assumption, a pagan superstition" about human nature.[64] Frequently, the authoritarianism which the creed sees as inevitable in socialist systems arises from a crude effort to make them function, though they are fundamentally unsound. Thus Mr. Flynn:

> Socialism is impossible under any conditions, but if it can be made to work at all it must be under an all-powerful State with the vast powers necessary to enforce its decrees governing every sector of our lives.[65]

The authors of the NAM volumes see the future hopefully, in the face of the growth of "statism"; the "inherent inefficiencies of their economic systems" will force other nations to reverse their course. "They will . . . surely return, either gradually or suddenly, toward the principles of free enterprise." [66]

Competition, as well as freedom, is fundamental to human nature. The creed warns against "intellectual theorists" who offer the delusive "dream of an inanimate heaven," a non-competitive system. Such systems are fantasies; "The only time when the competitive spirit of a human being is stilled is when the human heart ceases to beat." [67]

Serious logical problems confront any effort to combine these two themes: (a) the correspondence of the American system to fundamental laws of human nature, and (b) the historical uniqueness of the American system. But these logical problems are nowhere recognized in the business creed.

Stable. From a system which is "natural" to one which is inherently stable is an easy step; the creed makes it, and views the System as essentially permanent, unless upset by "outside" forces. The possibility that the forces of growth within the System will lead to fundamental changes in it is denied, or ignored.[68] Thus the NAM authors find that there is nothing in

---

[62] Above, p. 27.
[63] Weaver, *Mainspring,* p. 203.
[64] *Ibid.,* p. 36 (emphasis in original).
[65] Flynn, *The Road Ahead,* p. 150.
[66] NAM, II: 1027. This prospect holds for the totalitarian communist nations too.
[67] Donald Richberg, in the NAM monthly, *U.S.A.,* July 1952, p. 120.
[68] The contrast with the Marxist view of capitalist society has already been mentioned. But there is just as great a contrast with views of fundamentally conservative

"the innate character of technological development, the maturity of the economy, or the superiority of mind of government planners over the minds of businessmen" which will lead, by "economic necessity," to the demise of private enterprise.[69] Ideologies critical of the System often raise the problem of its economic stability, and doubt that *laissez faire* can maintain full employment. In some contexts, the creed accepts the inevitability of depressions — especially in the classical version;[70] but not in the context of a discussion of the potential permanence of the System. In the NAM treatise, the "challenge of 'full employment' " is "formulated and voiced by persons known more for their wishful thinking than for their economic or industrial competence, and not too much attention is paid to the economic possibilities of meeting this challenge." [71]

Insistence on the permanence of the System is much stronger in the classical than in the managerial strand of the creed. This is in keeping with the classical picture of a system which has persisted fundamentally unchanged in time, governed by internally consistent economic laws working toward harmony. Managerial writings, having already recognized a "great transformation" of business and society in the recent past, do not present the same unchanging picture. In terms of its view of the future, however, even the managerial strand embodies faith in the permanence of the System. The revolution which the *Fortune* editors celebrate is, after all, a permanent one, which will continue to operate to meet the new problems of the future. And all the time, past and future, the American Proposition remains constant and continues to be at the heart of successful change.[72]

Although the System is potentially permanent, the ideology sees its existence as continuously endangered by forces "outside" the System. Today, of course, Soviet Communism and the Communist bloc of nations are the "outside" threats most obvious. Advertisements and other popular literature of the creed are filled with comparisons of Soviet and American productivity, Soviet and American freedoms, and so on. But many phenomena within American society are also viewed as threats to the System, and the creed is heavy with warnings of one sort or another. These phenomena appear as the result of malevolent and essentially foreign propaganda, or else as "errors," and in either case, outside the System, not the

---

orientation; for instance, those of Joseph A. Schumpeter in *Capitalism, Socialism, and Democracy* (New York, 1942).

[69] NAM, II: 1022.

[70] See Chapter 10 below.

[71] NAM, II: 1021.

[72] *Permanent Revolution,* ch. VIII, esp. pp. 163–167, 174–179. What is seen as constant here is much broader and vaguer than what the classical strand views as the fixed elements of the system, and also less particular to the business creed, as such, as distinguished from the broader stream of American ideology of which it is a part. Compare below, Chapter 13.

products of its normal operation. The NAM authors, in cataloguing the dangers we face speak of a "misguided security hankering," the attachment of people to destructive policies despite their "manifest failure," the adverse indoctrination of the young, the propaganda of intellectuals, and the pressures of the world growth of socialism.[73] A writer for business readers described the driving force behind the full Employment Act of 1946 — a piece of legislation frequently attacked as inconsistent with the System — as follows:

. . . This American version of the thoroughly un-American British Beveridge Plan was supplied by a heterogeneous group comprised largely of economic planners, inflation-minded Congressmen, representatives of labor, and "spokesmen for the small but vociferous group of farmers who may be classified broadly as 'union-minded.' " [74]

This remark not only makes the characteristic identification of "hostile" and "foreign," but also exemplifies the broad tendency in the classical strand of the creed to consider trade unionism, and especially its political manifestations, as "outside" the system. This is less true of managerial versions of the creed, and at least some managerial writings tend to recognize Big Labor and Big Government as products of the same forces that produced the Great Transformation.[75]

Chosen. The existence of a variety of threats to continued operation of the System, despite its conformity to natural law and its incredible beneficence, poses a problem for the creed. Since these threats are viewed as "external," meeting them is seen as a matter of choice: adhering to the true free enterprise system, or going over to its enemies. This "choice" is never the result of a social process; it is a moral choice which each individual citizen must make. A good deal of the writing we have already reviewed is exhortation; much of it expresses the manifest purpose of the author to show his readers the right choice. The authors of the NAM treatise tell us that "the very writing of this book was occasioned by deep apprehension lest the American people unwittingly allow their precious birthright to slip from their possession or be traded for a 'mess of pottage.' " [76] Ernest Klein announces that now is the time to stand up and be counted for democratic American capitalism, and provides a solemn creed for those who will.[77] *Barron's,* the financial weekly, warns that "the

---

[73] NAM, II: 1021–1023.

[74] Edward H. Collins, *N.Y. Times* financial page, Aug. 25, 1952.

[75] *Permanent Revolution* exemplifies this line. But a discussion of "Businessmen's Responsibilities to Employees," in a consistently managerialist symposium, can fail to mention the word "union" even once. See Richard Deupree, President of Procter and Gamble Company, in *Responsibilities of Business Leadership,* edited by H. F. Merrill (Cambridge, Mass., 1948).

[76] NAM, II: 1017.

[77] Klein, *How to Stay Rich,* ch. X.

mania for central planning threatens everything you own" and invites readers of its ad to "stand up for private property and a return to the free market." [78]

Voluntary choice among various systems appears in broader contexts than the discussion of current ideological attacks and counterattacks. The creation myth itself embodies the notion that the Founding Fathers deliberately chose the System from among a wide field of possible systems. A pamphlet explaining the free enterprise system says:

> That you live in America is circumstance; but that America lives as she does is not. For a century and a half Americans have *planned it that way*.
> The American system of free enterprise, on its record indisputably is the most progressive and completely democratic form of capitalism yet devised by man.[79]

The managerial version of the creation myth — the Great Transformation — also embodies the idea of voluntary moral choice. The transition from irresponsible tycoon to principled manager is the product of a moral effort by businessmen, made in response to a perceived need, not the result of a complex social evolution.[80]

Just as the choice of the free enterprise system was deliberate, and deliberate continued adherence is required to maintain it, adherents of rival systems consciously plan to substitute them — *in toto* — for free enterprise. John T. Flynn, contemplating the fate of Great Britain, concludes, "that once great country — the home of modern capitalism and modern free government — was led stealthily . . . to her present state." What the Fabians did to England, a sinister coalition is now planning in the United States:

> We must see this English experiment clearly because the plan by which England was sneaked into socialism is now being promoted in this country by a coalition of politicians and revolutionary crusaders who are the counterpart of the British Fabian Socialists. It is being carried out with startling fidelity and promptness with the aid of the ignorance of the American businessman and politician.[81]

Viewed broadly, the most striking aspect of the way the creed characterizes the System is the complete absence of any recognition of historical processes. Complex societies change slowly; different parts of them change in different degrees, and a society at any one time includes institutions of diverse temporal origins — survivals of the past, foreshadowings of the

[78] Advertisement, *New York Times,* financial section, April 20, 1952.
[79] *The Free Enterprise System,* Phelps Adams, Chief of the Washington Bureau, *The New York Sun*, originally an article in *The Sun*, Jan. 5, 1948, reprinted and distributed by NAM, pp. 4, 5 (emphasis added).
[80] *Permanent Revolution,* p. 68.
[81] Flynn, *The Road Ahead,* p. 11.

future. At any particular time, "voluntary choice" of institutions takes place, if at all, in a situation which constrains the choice sharply; such choice as there is is limited to particular institutions; history shows to the historian no grand choices among alternative systems. Almost as striking is the difficulty of dealing with counter-ideologies within the logical framework of the creed. On the one hand, the creed emphasizes the tight integration of the whole System; on the other, it consigns such major products of recent American development as the New Deal and the trade union movement to the role of "outside" forces, in no way the result of the System's operation.

SYSTEM AND REALITY

When the ideology is expounded, its exponents typically identify the System with the concrete reality of the United States. Thus, Phelps Adams' account of "what (free enterprise) is, how it works, and what it has done" begins by congratulating the reader on his luck in living in the United States, and continues in a way in which the U.S. and the Free Enterprise System are completely equated.[82] In general, in any positive context, this identification is made. In polemical contexts, however, the existence of the System in the United States is seen as threatened, or impaired, and in extreme cases, the identification is broken: the United States no longer enjoys the Free Enterprise System.

Characteristically, ideological discussion of specific issues of policy involve appeals to the integrity of the whole System; changes, however small, are viewed as "first steps" to the abandonment of the System. For example, John M. Hancock, an investment banker testifying before a Senate Committee on "the legality of delivered price systems and competitive freight absorption" — a matter which might well be considered narrow and technical — begins his statement:

Because I believe that the future of the democratic way of life — where it still exists — is inevitably bound up with the maintenance of American free enterprise — and never was this so clearly true as now — I have accepted your gracious invitation to appear here today to discuss with members of the Sub-Committee your responsibilities under Senate Resolution 241 . . . The areas you must explore and the questions you will have to probe are not only complicated and delicate — they reach ultimately to the bedrock of the principles and premises on which the American way of life is founded.[83]

Such appeals are not in any way peculiar to the business creed; "entering wedge" arguments, and appeals to basic principles are characteristic of all ideological discussion of actions which, on any neutral view, are obscure in their outcomes and quite limited in their scope.

---

[82] Adams, *Free Enterprise*.
[83] John M. Hancock, *The Freedom to Compete* (Washington, 1948), p. 1.

The NAM authors weave a ragged course on the present state of the Free Enterprise System. Broadly, of course, the history of America is the history of the Free Enterprise System; but it is not clear whether we are still living under it or not. Thus, in dealing with the problems America now faces, the authors lament that youth "had had little if any experience under real private enterprise"; a few pages later we learn that "if the question of the *restoration* of the private enterprise system were submitted to the voting electorate of our country, there seems to be no question that it would be *restored* forthwith" and that "millions have not really changed at heart, they are still believers in the traditional American Way of Life and *long for its return*." [84]

Private enterprise weathered the depression, although it had a narrow escape. But then it went under a "long and comprehensive subjection to the state";[85] yet it was the private enterprise system which won the war, and thus it must have been in existence in 1941, even though our young people do not remember it. But in spite of these ambiguities, the NAM authors are confident of the future:

. . . unfavorable as present conditions are, the outlook need not be entirely black. The system can take an enormous amount of pounding and of restriction and still remain in existence; and even in this bruised and bound state it can confer greater benefits upon mankind than has any other economic organization yet devised.[86]

The extreme proponents of the classical view are much less temperate and confident. Mr. Flynn sees "our system wilting away before our very eyes." [87] And there are some who frankly pronounce it gone. To F. A. Harper we have already adopted socialist-communist measures, ostensibly for the purpose of defense against Russia; he asks if these are necessary, "Why fight them? Why not join them in the first place and save all the bloodshed? . . . There is no sense in conjuring up in our minds a violent hatred against people who are the victims of communism in some foreign nation, when the same government shackles are making us servile to illiberal forces at home." [88] Garet Garrett, in a pamphlet entitled *Ex America,* is more explicit and gloomier:

And when this end has come to pass not only will we be through with the fiction of free prices, free markets, free contracts, and free enterprise; we shall probably be through also with inflation . . .

---

[84] NAM, II: 1023, 1025 (emphasis added).
[85] *Ibid.,* p. 1023.
[86] *Ibid.,* pp. 1026, 1027.
[87] Flynn, *The Road Ahead,* p. 157.
[88] F. A. Harper, *In Search of Peace,* Irvington-on-Hudson: Foundation for Economic Education, 1951, pp. 36, 37. Mr. Harper is a member of the Foundation staff.

The consuming delusion is that because of what Americans were this may not or cannot happen.[89]

Such views are those of a minority, however; the more typical position sees the system as seriously threatened, and currently suffering from violation of its rules, but ultimately maintaining its integrity.

THE SYSTEM AND ITS ACHIEVEMENTS — SOME SPECIFIC SYMBOLS

While the business creed puts major burden of explanation of the achievements of our society on the System, viewed *in toto,* certain symbols of the System receive special mention. One of these is teamwork. For example:

How have we achieved all this? Through the American kind of teamwork! And what is teamwork?

American teamwork is management that pays reasonable wages and takes fair profits — that provides the best machines, tools, materials and working conditions it possibly can — that sees new methods, new markets, new ideas; that bargains freely and fairly with its employees.

Our teamwork is labor that produces as efficiently and as much as it can — that realizes its standard of living ultimately depends upon how much America produces — that expects better wages as it helps increase that production.

Teamwork is simply working together to turn out more goods in fewer man-hours — making things at lower costs and paying higher wages to the people who make them and selling them at lower prices to the people who use them.

. . . .

It will continue to take teamwork, but if we work together, there's no limit on what we can all share together of even greater things.[90]

Competition is another aspect of the system frequently mentioned in the creed's explanations of American progress.

. . . In my end of the business, we're breaking records every day. That's what happens when you have thousands of different companies trying to out-do each other in producing more oil more efficiently.

That's the kind of competition that makes America go — and it goes on in every other branch of our business — research, refining, marketing, transportation . . .[91]

[89] Garet Garrett, *Ex America* (Boise, Idaho, 1951), p. 42. This pamphlet is one of a series of Caxton Books for Libertarians. The author, now retired, was chief editorial writer for the *Saturday Evening Post,* and then for *American Affairs,* the monthly publication of the National Industrial Conference Board.

[90] Advertisement approved by the Public Policy Committee of the Advertising Council and contributed by *Woman's Home Companion,* November 1948.

[91] "Oil Builds for America's Future," Oil Industry Information Bureau advertisement, *Newsweek,* May 16, 1949.

G. L. Wood, of S. H. Kress Company:

. . . our economic system has, and still does, depend on incentive and competition for its greatest degree of success, which has resulted in the highest standard of living ever known on earth. Profit is the incentive for savers, competition guarantees that profits will not be too high, competition is the first enforcement agency available . . .[92]

And, from a Chamber of Commerce publication:

Under the free market, aided by effective anti-trust legislation, the march of science and technology inevitably expresses itself in a higher and richer standard of living for all groups of people. For example, wholesale prices in 1930 were at almost the same level that they were in 1840, 90 years earlier; but, meantime, average wages had increased by 700 per cent. The competition of job-seekers for the services of workers pulled wages up, while the competition in goods market helped to keep prices down . . .[93]

The growth of capital, made possible by individual and corporate saving, is also frequently cited in connection with the achievements of American capitalism.

. . . And surely, there is something worth pondering in the fact that strong nations are those having the biggest stock of tools, that tools come from savings and the pledging of anticipated savings, and that savings taxed away mean fewer tools for productive enterprise and the easier satisfaction of men's needs.[94]

One hundred years ago it took only $557 worth of capital to provide the tools, machines and plant facilities used by a single American factory worker. He labored seventy hours a week for a bare existence.

Today it takes eleven times as much capital to provide tools for this worker. He puts in forty hours a week. His hourly earnings, in terms of dollars, are about sixteen times as high as they were 100 years ago. In terms of purchasing power they are about five and one-half times as great.

Over the century, the gross value of this worker's product has increased in almost exact proportion to the amount of capital invested in his job . . .[95]

Science and industrial research also figure as explanatory factors. The association between technological progress, increased standards of living, and industrial research is pointed out increasingly in advertisements and similar media. This association borrows for business some of the mystique which our society attaches to the laboratory and the man in the

[92] *Senate Banking and Currency Hearings on Defense Production Act of 1951*, part 3, p. 2211.

[93] Chamber of Commerce of the United States, *The Welfare State and the State of Human Welfare*, p. 10.

[94] J. A. Stephens, *Mature Collective Bargaining — Prospects and Problems*, U.S. Steel Corporation (New York, n.d.) p. 18.

[95] Phelps Adams, *The Free Enterprise System*, p. 11.

white coat. Industrial research is emphasized but the relation of applied research to fundamental science is not stressed in the same way. Typical of this sort of advertising is the following:

> Millions of machines turned out canned goods, cars, textiles, radios — better and better each year. There's no stopping Science and Industry now . . . no limit to good things to come! [96]
>
> United States Steel plants have been breaking production records to help fill these and many other needs. In United States Steel research laboratories, scientists have developed better steels for today's exacting demands. Nothing else can do what steel can do.[97]

> . . . G. E. research and engineering have improved the household refrigerator so that today's model runs on less than half the current used 20 years ago.[98]

> The Richest Frontier of All.
>
> In the mind and the will! Here lies the unbounded frontier of today. On that frontier, the nation's research laboratories are prospecting for new wealth in which everyone shares . . . through improved processes, new materials.
>
> Millions of dollars backed the patient determination to conquer just one of these frontiers in the glass industry . . . After years of searching, Fiberglas materials — glass in fiber form — had become practical. Born in November, 1938 . . . ten years ago this month . . . the new company was formed to develop that frontier, to carry on further research, to explore additional uses, and to adapt Fiberglas to uses for which their inherent properties qualify them. Then hundreds of other minds, attuned to industrial exploration, wove Fiberglas materials, braided them, matted and impregnated them, built them into a host of superior products.
>
> . . . .
>
> Every day, new ideas take form from the opportunities which Fiberglas has opened. As a result, small businesses have been launched, markets expanded, jobs created . . .[99]

Teamwork, competition, capital accumulation and thrift, invention and research — these and other features of the System are invoked to explain how and why it has led to so much progress in America. But they are only intermediate explanations, logically subordinate to the central thesis. The basic explanation is the System of freedom itself, from which all other factors are derivative. For example, the author of *Mainspring* remarks in regard to technological progress: "Free minds are inventive minds." [100]

[96] Allis-Chalmers advertisement, *Newsweek,* April 11, 1949.

[97] U.S. Steel Company advertisement, *Business Week,* April 23, 1949.

[98] General Electric advertisement, *Boston Sunday Globe,* June 13, 1948.

[99] Owens-Corning Fiberglas advertisement, *New York Times,* Mar. 30, 1949.

[100] Weaver, *Mainspring,* p. 202. This is quoted with approval by Walker, *American Industry,* p. 479.

SELECTIVITY OF THE CREED

In both its discussion of what constitute the achievements of American capitalism, and its explanation of these achievements, the business ideology is highly selective, in comparison with a broader, more neutral social science discussion of these problems.

The creed, as we have seen, concentrates on the material and the practical in its enumeration of achievements. Claims that the business system has yielded significant cultural or esthetic gains are almost completely absent. Spiritual and moral achievements are limited largely to Freedom.

It is hardly surprising that the creed rarely makes any claim on the esthetic quality of modern life, the superiority of the moral standards of our present society over those of earlier societies or of other countries,[101] or the piety of life under the System. To concentrate on such matters would be foreign to the fundamental American value system within which the values of the business creed are framed. Nowhere in the creed is there any suggestion that conflict exists between religion and capitalism, humanitarianism and money seeking, although discussion of such conflicts is frequent in European writing.

Little space is given to other noneconomic achievements of the society which are more compatible with our value system and might well be credited to the System. The great improvement in health over the last century and the resultant increase in the average length of life are little discussed, although they are clearly achievements of industrial capitalism. True, they are listed among the achievements of the System in the NAM treatise,[102] but they rarely appear in the more popular conveyors of the creed — advertisements, pamphlets, and speeches. The same can be said of equal opportunity in education.[103]

---

[101] Both these claims appear occasionally. See, for example, Ernest Elmo Calkins, *Business the Civilizer* (Boston, 1928), p. 22, where the first of these claims is made. Although the emphasis on "service" smacks of a claim of moral superiority, it is not usually made explicit. While the superiority of American moral standards over those of other nations is not part of the business creed, it certainly is a part of popular American ideology, and forms an important sentimental base for isolationism in international politics.

[102] NAM, II: 891–892.

[103] Again, the NAM volumes devote some space to the spread of schooling in the United States, pp. 892–94. The chapter on "Achievements under the Enterprise System," ch. XVII, in which these pages and those cited above on health appear, is the most systematic exposition of the "achievements" which our ideological material shows. As such, the distribution of space among various topics furnishes an interesting indication of their relative importance. The whole chapter is thirty-eight pages long: two of these are devoted to an introduction which links achievements with the System; the seventeen pages which follow are occupied by an account of

The growth of industrialism in the United States has been accompanied by striking changes in family structure.[104] The small nuclear family comprising parents and minor children rather than the extended family including several generations, the free choice of marriage partners based on romantic love, democracy within the family, and the independence of women are all recent developments and to some extent they are peculiar to American society. They are in the individualistic tradition which the business creed shares with the broader American value system. Yet they are rarely celebrated as achievements of the System in the literature of the creed.[105]

A further element of selectivity in the creed lies in its neglect of the possibility of adverse effects of the System's working to set off against the achievements which it praises. The type of progress of which the business creed boasts carries with it certain problems. Innovation and growth in a decentralized, private-property economy create instability; change has its costs. Recognition of these costs and discussion of who bears them and who should bear them is an old but lively topic in economic literature.[106] One of the greatest costs of change and instability is unemployment, cyclical and structural. These problems have received little attention in the business creed, except for indirect and polemical treatment in the

---

the material achievements of the system — the increase in output and productivity, the accumulation of capital, the rise in real incomes and real wages, the growth in the use of automobiles, vacuum cleaners, refrigerators, and other luxuries-become-necessities; in addition four more pages are occupied with a discussion of the growth of national income and of savings and life insurance in the hands of households, likewise aspects of the material progress of the system, and the two concluding pages repeat chiefly the figures on material growth. Thus only ten of the thirty-eight pages are devoted to claims of a nonmaterial sort, described as "social gains": of these five are devoted to a discussion of the social security system which here is claimed as an achievement of the System without any indication of the extent to which advocates of welfare-statism and even socialism used the power of the government to create it against the bitter opposition of the business community; two to the benefactions of private philanthropy; two to education; and less than a page each to health and the decline in child labor.

[104] See R. M. Williams, Jr., *American Society, a Sociological Interpretation* (New York, 1951), ch. 4, "Kinship and Family in the United States."

[105] An omission of this sort can hardly be adequately explained by an "interest theory" of ideology. Such a theory would lead to the expectation that every positive claim which has any appeal would be used in defense of the *status quo* by the interests. The motivational analysis developed in Part II below seeks the factors which guide the selection of material included in the business creed, and thus seeks to explain omissions of this sort.

[106] See, for example, J. A. Schumpeter, *Theory of Economic Development* (Cambridge. Mass. 1934; first German ed., 1911); D. H. Robertson, *A Study of Industrial Fluctuations* (London, 1915); A. G. B. Fisher, *The Clash of Progress and Security* (London, 1935); J. R. Hicks, *The Trade Cycle* (London, 1950); D. M. Wright, *Capitalism* (New York, 1951); A. H. Hansen, *Business Cycles and National Income* (New York, 1952).

form of attacks on the welfare state or on the dangers of workers' demands for security.

The explanation of America's achievements offered by the creed is even more selective than its catalogue of them.

The identification of "achievements" with the "System" in an integral fashion — the major explanatory hypothesis of the creed — is hardly objective. Undoubtedly there is considerable connection between the peculiar social, political, and economic structure of American society and the pace and character of American industrial development. But the character of this connection is complicated and involves many more variables and many more complex interrelations than the creed suggests. Any neutral discussion of the subject could hardly lead to dogmatic certainty on the basis of present knowledge.

One aspect of the explanation is especially striking — its nationalism. The System which accounts for the achievements is an American system. It is American Free Enterprise, not capitalism in general, which leads to the celebrated results. It is, very often, American ingenuity, rather than international science, which creates the new goods and the new factories. One need scarcely point out the extreme one-sidedness of these notions. America has borrowed from the foreigner at least as much as she has given him. The tremendous importance of the nineteenth-century imports of capital and techniques from Europe in our industrial growth, the intellectual imports from the Enlightenment on which our political philosophy was based, the imports of pure science and scientists from Europe on which, until very recently, American technology rested — all these have helped to make the American System what it is.

The specific features of the System which appear as factors accounting for its achievements all possess some relevance. The teamwork explanation is relevant to American achievement if it is applied to labor-management relations, which have been more peaceful and less shot through with class conflict than those in many other countries. Saving and capital accumulation are undoubtedly linked with economic development and the growth of output and consumption. The link between capital formation and "free enterprise," however, is less clear, as is the identification of saving with voluntary private saving and the reinvestment of corporate earnings. Other methods of financing capital formation — for example: inflation, taxation, government savings — have been known to function effectively in other economies and even in American economic history. Soviet Russia, hardly a stronghold of free enterprise, also has a very high rate of investment and a very rapid growth of industrial output. Again, industrial research certainly plays an important part in the production of new products and new techniques of production; but this is true only of the recent past. The role played by such research can easily be overrated as an explanation of past industrial growth.

The explanations used by the creed neglect factors which are at least as important as those they emphasize. One of these is the fortunate geographical position of America, which gave it security from external aggression and for a long time made a large military establishment unnecessary. Another is America's newness as a society and the historical circumstances which, far more than conscious design, freed it from all the archaic hangovers of feudalism. Third, there is the size of the American free trade area, which permits low-cost large-scale production of many more products than would be possible in a smaller country. Fourth, there is the great stream of immigration in the nineteenth century, which provided a huge labor force, much of which was already trained abroad. Our borrowings from European science and technology, and the time sequence of our industrial growth which made these borrowings possible are also important. And while the business ideology never tires of dwelling on government obstruction of its processes, it makes no mention of the important constructive role of government in stimulating and financing economic development, especially in the road, canal, and railroad building periods. In short, the business version of the "Miracle of America" is not a rounded objective history of our economic development.

3

THE AMERICAN BUSINESS ENTERPRISE

THE BUSINESS ENTERPRISE AS A SOCIAL INSTITUTION

THE HEART OF THE SYSTEM is the business enterprise. According to the creed, it is this institution more than any other that is responsible for the distinctive character of American society. Leaving the ideology aside for the moment, what is a business enterprise, and what distinguishes it from other social institutions? The term "business enterprise" covers millions of institutions vastly different in size, organization structure, age, and activity. It covers General Motors and the corner drugstore, the Pennsylvania Railroad and the street vendor calling his wares, the Chase-Manhattan Bank and the local undertaker. At the same time, other institutions which have many points of similarity with these are clearly not business enterprises. Consider, as examples, the Post Office, the New York subways, a hospital, Harvard University, a medical practitioner, a subsistence farm, and a baby-sitter. Still other institutions are on the border line: a producers' or consumers' cooperative, a commercial farm, a law partnership.

A business enterprise has certain distinguishing features, recognized both in the business creed and in society at large. These are at least five in number:

(1) A business enterprise presupposes a market outside itself in which it sells goods or services. Hence subsistence farming is not considered a business.

(2) A business enterprise requires property, distinguishable in kind or amount from the personal property that individuals use for their own satisfactions as consumers. This capital investment may be the pushcart and vegetable inventory of a street vendor or the furnaces, mills, ore boats, and mines of U.S. Steel. The absence of such capital investment is the principal reason for excluding persons who merely sell their own labor services, whether hired workers, domestic servants, or baby-sitters, from the category of businessmen.

(3) This property is owned directly or indirectly by one or more

private individuals; government-owned activities are, by common consent, not business enterprises.

Legally a business is its ownership, and its operations are simply the exercise of the right of the owner of private property to dispose of his property as he sees fit and to make contracts with others. When ownership is plural, complications arise over the rights of the owners with respect to each other in controlling the common property, and over the obligations of the owners to fulfill the contracts of the joint enterprise. Incorporation solves these difficulties by creating a fictitious legal individual of indefinite life, independent of its temporary owners, and by limiting both the control and the liability of the individual owners. But the central legal importance of ownership in the enterprise is retained. In an important sense the stockholders are the corporation, and each stockholder is the corporation in proportion to his equity. Hired management, other employees, creditors, customers, suppliers — all are merely outsiders with whom the stockholders, like the owner of an individual proprietorship, make contracts. Obviously the real position of stockholders is usually much less central than their position in this legal model. But formal congruence with the legal model is nonetheless important as a distinguishing characteristic of a business enterprise.

(4) However, private ownership is not enough; the exclusion of privately owned "non-profit" institutions, such as hospitals and universities, suggests that a business enterprise must be run primarily for the profit of its owners. Where orientation to profit is not socially acceptable, an organization is not considered a business enterprise in the true sense of the term. Legally, an independent professional practice is as clear an example of an individual proprietorship as an independent grocery store. Nevertheless between "business" and "the professions" both society at large and the groups themselves make a careful distinction. The code of behavior which society expects of a professional practitioner restricts his pursuit of private gain more than the code imposed on other individual proprietors. The relationship of a doctor to his patients and to the public is governed by quite a different set of legal and "ethical" rules than the relationship of a shopkeeper to his customers. A proper business enterprise is free to act in its pecuniary self-interest subject only to very general legal and customary restraints which apply to the whole society. Within these limits, a businessman, unlike a professional practitioner, is not considered under any obligation to engage in transactions from which he does not anticipate gain or to refrain from actions from which he does anticipate gain. One must be able to say without malice of a business enterprise, "After all, they're not in business for their health." [1]

---

[1] On the distinction between business and the professions, see Talcott Parsons, "The Professions and the Social Structure," *Essays in Sociological Theory, Pure and Applied* (Glencoe, Ill., 1949).

However, the importance of the profit orientation of business is often exaggerated; it can best be kept in perspective by bearing three points in mind. First, the "profit motive" is characteristic of the enterprise as an institution, rather than of the personalities of managers and owners. To recognize that making profits is the main purpose of a business enterprise is not to imply that businessmen are more selfish or more strongly motivated by pecuniary gain than individuals in other roles. It is simply that an altruistic businessman will display his benevolence in the disposition of profits once they are earned rather than in unbusinesslike conduct of his business. In contrast, a professional man cannot seize every opportunity for making a profit even if he wants to. He is prevented by his professional code and by social sanctions at the disposal of his profession and of society at large.[2]

Second, despite this contrast there are also limits on the extent that a business enterprise can be run for profit. They are far wider, but social pressure is slowly enforcing a stricter standard than that required by law or custom.

Third, the legal model of the business enterprise exaggerates the central position of the owners. Legally, a business is a voluntary employment of the private property of its owners; if its affairs are managed rationally and economically, with an eye on the balance sheet, the owners are the automatic beneficiaries. Socially a business is much more than its ownership. The "outsiders," whose formal bonds to the enterprise are only contractual, have often much more permanent, vivid, and complete identification with the organization than the owners. They develop expectations and demands that go beyond their contractual status and challenge any exclusive orientation of the enterprise to the owners. The management and employees of a corporation constitute a social system that inherently involves authority and hierarchy. For many purposes it is more meaningful to identify the corporation with this social system, in which the owners scarcely participate, than to identify it with scattered and passive stockholders.

(5) One other feature of the business enterprise is the fairly sharp separation of business from personal and family life — in location, time, property, financial accounting, and interpersonal relationships. It would be "unbusinesslike" for even the sole proprietor of a business not to distinguish between purchases for personal consumption and those for occupational supplies. The institution of business enterprise enforces a division between business accounting and family accounting; the owner of a business sees himself as earning from his business not his ultimate satisfactions but a money income which he can dispose of as he and his family see fit. This way of looking at things has important consequences. Personal

---

[2] The social norms which conflict with a complete orientation to profit will be considered at length in Chapters 16 and 17.

and business expenditures are subject to different kinds of scrutiny and discipline. In disposing of personal income, only the subjective judgment of the household decides whether the benefits are worth the cost. In business accounting, all benefits and costs are reduced to money figures and recorded on the balance sheet; rationality and "economy" are required.

Commercial farming meets all the criteria of the business enterprise except this sharp separation of business and personal life. It is the most frequent and important example of that legal form of business organization known as the individual proprietorship. Although this is universally recognized in discussions of legal forms of business organization, there is nevertheless an irresistible impulse, evident both in the business creed and elsewhere, to view "agriculture" and "business" as distinct and frequently divergent interests. No doubt this failure to count farmers as business entrepreneurs is due in part to the special political problems connected with agriculture. But it also seems to reflect a feeling that the family farm is not a true business enterprise, because it mixes inseparably the two spheres of business activity and family life. There is no reluctance to include as business an agricultural operation, like California fruit-growing, which is conducted not on family farms but mainly on absentee-owned land with hired labor.

This separation is as important for interpersonal relationships as it is for financial accounting. A business enterprise is expected to deal with individuals, inside or outside the organization, on coldly rational and universalistic criteria. Status in a business enterprise at any level, except as it arises from property ownership in the business, is not supposed to be inherited as a right of birth; nor are the jobs, purchases, and sales of an enterprise "spoils" of which successful candidates for business leadership can dispose as favors to their personal friends or as payments of personal debts. Jobs and status are supposed to go to the most able individuals available; purchases and sales decisions are to be made on the basis of the objective terms of the contracts offered to the firm, with no regard for the personalities and identities of the individuals involved. It is true that universalism — treating all individuals, regardless of who they are, according to a common standard — is a pervasive feature of American culture; it is not peculiar to business. For example, universities and governments, as well as business firms, are supposed to treat individuals on their merits. But the discipline of the balance sheet to which the business enterprise is subject gives a special support to rationality and universalism absent in other institutions. Decisions made on extraneous personal grounds will result in less profit. Of course everyone knows that nepotism, favoritism, and "politics" occur in business. The point is that they are considered not only unjust but also "unbusinesslike."

Business ideology provides two basic descriptions of the institutional nature of the business enterprise. These two views are related to the two main descriptions of the System as a whole: the classical and managerial themes of business ideology.

The classical view of the business enterprise starts from the legal model of the institution. The enterprise is viewed as an exercise of the owners' rights to dispose of their property as they see fit. It is expected, and it is deemed entirely proper, that the owners of business property will see fit to employ it to their own maximum profit. Employees, customers, suppliers, and the general public are outsiders, and, in dealings with them, the firm has no responsibilities other than to seek lawful contracts and bargains most advantageous to the owners. The role of management is simply to obtain maximum long-run profits for the owners.

By itself, this description of the individual enterprise is not promising ideological material. Its appeal depends on the symbol of the rights of private property, either in its eighteenth-century form or in its modern version, freedom of enterprise. But the classical creed has a much stronger string to its bow. Its main emphasis is on the System as a whole rather than on its elementary units. From classical economics it draws a theory which transmutes individual selfishness into maximum social welfare, a theory which relies heavily on the mechanism of free competition, and in which the business enterprise is capable of exercising very little power in the markets in which it deals. In short, classical ideology emphasizes that business firms are generally small and that the powers of business firms, even of the few which are big, are narrowly circumscribed by competition.

The managerial theme does not rely on esoteric economic theory to reconcile private business decisions and the social welfare. In this view the actions of individual enterprises are and should be dominated by considerations of the public interest; profit-seeking takes a lesser place. If enterprises act directly in the public interest, there is much less need to rely on the competitive mechanism to demonstrate that individual actions which appear to be self-seeking are socially beneficial in the System as a whole. Where the principal focus of the classical view is on the System, that of the managerial view is on the individual business enterprise. Accordingly, the enterprise is not conceived in the narrow terms of its legal model. Instead emphasis is placed on the enterprise as a social system. Employees, customers, and suppliers are not regarded as outsiders but as integral parts of the organization; their relations to management are not purely, or even mainly, contractual and economic.

Owners, particularly corporation stockholders, are deposed from their central position. Whereas in the classical view they *are* the enterprise, in the managerial view they are on a par with other groups who have stakes in, and just claims on, the organization. Managers are assigned a more important and more autonomous role than that of agents for the owners. Theirs is the statesman's function of mediating among the groups dependent on the enterprise, satisfying their just claims, and preserving the continuity of the organization — while always remembering that "private office is a public trust" and keeping the interest of the general public paramount. The classical theme is taken from classical economics; the managerial approach has common origins with studies of "human relations" and of industrial management within the social sciences.

By implication, the managerial view assigns much more power to the individual enterprise and claims that this power is used fairly and wisely. The classical view pictures the firm as helpless before the inexorable forces of supply and demand in the competitive market. The newer approach emphasizes the role of justice and wisdom in the determination of prices, wages, and profits and so attaches more importance to managerial decisions. Thus managers as a group must deliberately create the balance which, in the classical view, results automatically from a proper functioning of the System.[3]

Naturally, most ideological expressions that bear directly on the nature of business enterprise and the function of the businessman follow the managerial approach. Business firms are not likely to advertise themselves as profit-seeking, and management is not likely to disavow all responsibility except to owners. Since the main proponents of managerial themes are the managements of large corporations, the contention that American business is small business is less important in managerial than in classical ideology. But the symbol of "small business" is not abandoned.

THE CREED'S DESCRIPTION OF THE BUSINESS ENTERPRISE

The Size of the American Business Enterprise. The question of the size of American businesses and the concentration of wealth and economic power is a very sensitive one. Consequently, it calls forth extreme statements and selective use of fact and logic by both business and opposing ideologies.

The typical American business enterprise is small, and there are many

---

[3] The managerial exposition of the creed really lacks an explanation of how proper balance in the individual firm leads to proper balance in the economy as a whole. Such an explanation, in terms of the competitive price system, is the core of the classical exposition of the creed. See Chapter 8 below for a detailed discussion of this contrast; its implications for the relative roles of classical and managerial themes in the creed are discussed in Chapters 17 and 18.

throughout the nation. This is the repeated claim of the business creed, both in its popular appeals and its learned texts. The word "business" should make one think, not of a giant, impersonal corporation with offices in lower Manhattan, but of the machine shop an enterprising friend has started in his backyard. When thinking of businessmen, one should think, not of the big executives of that remote corporation, but of the fellows who sit down to the weekly Rotary luncheon in Middletown. Statistics are mobilized to show: 70 per cent of all manufacturing establishments have fewer than twenty employees;[4] the number of business firms is growing faster than the population;[5] there are 34,000 companies in the oil industry;[6] the National Association of Manufacturers is predominantly composed of small firms.[7]

Large business corporations do exist, of course. Indeed, they are the firms which disseminate the creed via national advertising; concerns with fewer than twenty employees are unlikely to buy space to proclaim how small and how typical they are. Large corporations reconcile their existence with the doctrine that business is decentralized in several ways.

First, the large enterprise takes pride in the number of independent small businesses which it fosters. These are its suppliers — the makers of automobile parts — or its customers — the fabricators of Alcoa aluminum — or simply its neighbors. The large business pictures itself as a kindly big brother offering encouragement, cooperation, and technical assistance to firms within its orbit and to newcomers who wish to enter the field (especially to veterans after World War II).[8]

Second, the large enterprise emphasizes its humble beginnings. Once it was the backyard machine shop in your neighborhood. To aspire to grow is as natural and as acceptable a feature of the model business enterprise as to be small. Thus a witness before a Congressional committee said: ". . . that is the kind of thing that made American business move along; John Jones starting up in the woodshed in a small way and getting in a little money, putting in a little money of his own and his father-in-law putting in $500 and so on, with the expectation of the thing

---

[4] NAM, I: 30–31.

[5] *Ibid.*

[6] Oil Industry Information Committee advertisement, *Look,* April 6, 1948.

[7] NAM Advertisement, *Atlantic Monthly,* July 1948.

[8] Many examples of this theme could be cited. An American Iron and Steel Institute advertisement, *Saturday Evening Post,* May 7, 1947, features a small town plumber as typical of the businesses related to steel. W. J. Cameron broadcast on Feb. 23, 1938 that the growth of Ford has doubled and tripled the opportunities for small business. An Aluminum Company of America advertisement stresses small businesses based on aluminum and the Company's relations with them. In *Profits, Hearings* before the Subcommittee of the Joint Committee on the Economic Report (Flanders Subcommittee), Eightieth Congress, 2nd session, December 1949, both Mr. Coyle of General Motors (p. 522) and Mr. Wilson of General Electric (p. 501) stressed the importance of their contributions to related small businesses.

rolling into a big business some day." [9] The history of today's large enterprise helps to assimilate it to the typical firm of the creed.[10]

Third, the large enterprise claims that its scattered plants are good neighbors and good citizens just as if they were independent local businesses.[11]

The business creed's picture of economic decentralization is the counterpart of the picture of extreme and growing concentration painted by Marxism and other hostile ideologies. In both cases ideological purposes are served by selective emphasis both in citing facts and in using logical argument. The same statistical data are used to show the numerical preponderance of small firms and the economic preponderance of large firms, measured by the shares in total employment, production, or capital assets accounted for by the few largest firms. The question whether the degree of concentration in the United States is increasing or decreasing over time is an extremely tough one, both conceptually and statistically. There are many possible measures, leading to different results; serious students of the subject agree only that it is a field where dogmatism is unjustified.[12] Flat statements that the degree of concentration is increasing or that it is decreasing[13] must acquire their confidence from ideological, not scientific, conviction.

Although the main emphasis of the ideology is on the smallness of the typical American business and on the decentralized aspects of the untypical large corporation, the creed also expounds the social benefits of Bigness. The creed reflects American ambivalence on the question of size. In the first place, Growth is a much more acceptable symbol than Bigness. And both Growth and Bigness are more acceptable if what is Growing and Big is technological rather than financial. Where scientific and engineering marvels are concerned, large enterprises are proud to proclaim their own size and growth.[14] In the second place, the proposition that Big Business is required in a Big Country has recently achieved cur-

[9] William A. Paton, *Hearings on Profits* (Flanders), p. 56.
[10] Alcoa advertisement, *Atlantic Monthly*, April 1948.
[11] See the Bell Telephone System advertisement, *Atlantic*, September 1948, and the descriptions of U.S. Steel subsidiaries in *The Radio Story of the Industrial Family that Serves the Nation*, especially the activities of Tennessee Coal & Iron Railroad Company in aid of Southern agriculture.
[12] See Adelman, *Review of Economics and Statistics*, November 1951, p. 269.
[13] The NAM volumes' evidence, that the number of concerns has grown faster than the population, is not very relevant. Such growth would not be inconsistent with a growth of concentration in the sense that a few large firms acquire greater shares of many markets.
[14] See, for example, the testimony of C. E. Wilson, President, and C. G. Suits, Director of Research, of General Electric, Pt. 2B, pp. 1158–1166, 1208–1238. Parts of this were later reprinted as a pamphlet, *Big Business and Big Progress Go Together*, and distributed by the Corporation.

rency. Thus Mr. Fairless, President of the United States Steel Corporation, says: "United States Steel is large because it has had to be, in order to do the big jobs that a big nation has demanded of it in war and in peace — and to do them well. It has grown as America has grown; and it has contributed at every step of the way toward the growth, prosperity and security of America." [15] Finally, challenges to Bigness are part of the stock in trade of hostile ideologies. The spokesmen of business reply by pointing to the economies of large-scale production, organization, and research; at the same time they claim that the largest enterprise is never free from the sobering discipline of actual or potential competition. Faced with government action to force business into its own ideological mold, the cult of Smallness tends to evaporate into the position that Bigness is not in itself sinful, that there are "good" and "bad" businesses of all sizes.[16]

The Dispersion of Business Ownership. The stigma of big business is also counteracted by emphasis on the fact that its ownership is widely dispersed. The large corporation proclaims that it is owned by thousands of ordinary people; its stockholders are workers, farmers, housewives, widows, retired farmers, all over the country. They live, not just in big cities, but in farms, villages, small towns. The ownership is a "cross-section of America." [17] The creditors of the corporation include anyone who owns an insurance policy or a savings account. If a corporation is big, it is only because thousands of little people have seen fit to entrust their savings to it, just as the local shopkeeper has put his savings into his business. "A business owned by the people," as American Telephone & Telegraph Company styles itself,[18] turns a socialist promise of industrial democracy into a description of the actual state of one of America's largest private corporations. In the same vein, S. Wells Utley finds in the dispersion of stock ownership the fulfillment of the socialists' dream of public ownership.[19] And the Chairman of the Board of General Foods calls his and thousands of other American companies "publicly owned" and "ventures in economic democracy." [20] Granting that the plain people who own the corporation may have little power over its policies, the Santa Fe

[15] Celler Committee (Subcommittee on Study of Monopoly Power of the Committee of the Judiciary, House of Representatives, Eighty-first Congress, 2nd session), *Hearings*, Pt. 4A, p. 465 (26 April 1950).

Similar views are expressed in the testimony of Crawford Greenewalt, President of E. I. duPont de Nemours, in his testimony before the Committee, *Hearings*, Pt. 2A, pp. 543–592.

[16] See testimony of Greenewalt, *Ibid.;* also testimony of Earl Bunting, President of NAM, immediately following, pp. 592–620.

[17] U.S. Steel, *The Radio Story*, p. 34 (broadcast Dec. 16, 1945).

[18] *Atlantic*, May 1948. See also the Bell Telephone System advertisement, *Harper's*, September 1948 (200,000 employees buying stock), and the publicity given the millionth A. T. & T. stockholder in 1951.

[19] Utley, *The American System*, p. 117.

[20] *Hearings on Profits* (Flanders), p. 209.

Railroad carries the analogy with democracy farther. The nice old lady from a small town whom the corporation introduces as a representative stockholder[21] cannot alone control its policies, but neither can she alone choose a President of the United States.

Obviously, the ideology is highly selective here. The fact that a few persons may hold most of the shares is played down, just as it is played up in opposing ideologies. The analogy of the corporation to political democracy is inexact. Even if the shareholders control the corporation, control resides in a majority of shares rather than in a majority of shareholders. As sympathetic an observer as *Fortune* has found this theme of business ideology objectionable and has suggested that corporations would do better to tell frankly not just the number of their shareholders but also the numbers who hold various given amounts of stock.

The Business Enterprise as a Family or a Team. In the managerial view, the business enterprise consists of an association of individuals who are voluntarily cooperating for their own mutual benefit as well as for that of the general public.

The concept of a business enterprise as a family softens the hard edges of economic relationships and the conflicts between employer and employee, buyer and seller, manager and owner. It implies that interpersonal relationships in the firm are like those within the family, of which it is impossible to disapprove. In the "family" workers, managers, owners, and even customers and suppliers are united in a common interest. "How's our railroad doing, young man?" says the nice old lady in the Sante Fe ad to the smiling young brakeman on the steps of the caboose.[22] United States Steel is "the industrial family that serves the nation." [23] A colored picture of the Avondale family, with representatives of all American races, sexes, ages, and classes features an advertisement of that particular textile firm.[24]

Long association with the firm is emphasized in this context. The workman who is proudly introduced in advertising is a veteran of years of faithful service to his firm; better yet, he followed in his father's footsteps and his sons have joined the family too. In a kinship family the junior members of yesterday are the seniors of today, in authority no less than in age. When an executive is honored by publicity, he is one who boasts many years of membership and gradual promotion in the same organization. He has, however, earned his high status by merit and experience and not by mere seniority. The war, of course, provided an excellent opportunity for business to display its familial instincts. During

---

[21] *Business Week,* Dec. 9, 1948.
[22] Santa Fe advertisement, *Business Week,* Oct. 9, 1948.
[23] See *The Radio Story,* especially p. 109 (broadcast Dec. 8, 1946).
[24] Avondale advertisement, *New York Times,* May 16, 1948.

the war "our boys" in service were proudly counted and listed. Afterward, their reemployment was proudly proclaimed.[25]

If a business enterprise does not style itself a family, it is likely to be a team, another irreproachable American institution. From childhood we are taught the virtue and success of athletic teamwork, and we learn the nature of a team. It is a group of individuals bound by a common goal which will best be achieved by intelligent and practiced cooperation. Every member is indispensable, and success requires competent and devoted performance by everyone. The code of the team requires subordination of individual objectives and idiosyncrasies and, above all, unswerving loyalty to team and teammates.

Both the family analogy and the team analogy emphasize the role of close cooperation between all the individuals associated with an enterprise. Conflicts of interest among them are not part of the picture. Like the family analogy, the team symbol imputes to association with the firm content and meaning beyond the implications of economic relationship. Loyalty and continuity of membership are no part of a wage-earner's bargain with a corporation, but they are implied by membership in a team.[26] A further implication is that, just as in a proper football team, each member must respect and not encroach upon the function assigned to a teammate. Management is the quarterback, and for the good of the whole team, labor should not try to call the signals.[27]

These interpretations are even more prevalent than the actual use of the two symbols "family" and "team." Management is increasingly adopting the view that it is and should be satisfying to participate in the work of a corporation, quite apart from the earnings involved. Corporations take public pride in providing economic security for their employees, in providing all kinds of group recreational facilities, in health and safety programs, in pointing out any evidence of management-labor camaraderie, etc. This new conception of the corporation is part of the "transformation of American capitalism" discovered by that wing of business opinion which is anxious to disassociate modern business from the "socially irresponsible" business of fifty years ago.[28]

It is as characteristic of orthodox ideologies to emphasize the integrative features of existing social institutions as it is characteristic of radical

[25] In U.S. Steel, *The Radio Story,* one of the themes of this paragraph was the subject of at least one of the two messages in twenty-one broadcasts of a total of ninety-three. Similar emphasis on continuity of personnel is found in advertising of the Standard Oil Company of New Jersey (Esso): see *New York Times* and *Boston Herald,* May 20, 1949.

[26] Typical use of "team" and "teamwork" can be seen in a NAM folder on the bequest of Lt. Ben Toland, and in SKF advertisements, *Business Week,* April 16, 1949 and May 14, 1949.

[27] *Business Week* (editorial) Sept. 25, 1948.

[28] See *Permanent Revolution,* pp. 78 ff.

ideologies to see nothing but their divisive features. Marx, in a famous metaphor, likened the factory of capitalism to a military barracks. The managerial creed stresses the voluntary, cooperative, and egalitarian features of the enterprise and pays little attention to problems of discipline, authority, and differential status. The managerial conception is nearer the mark than its Marxist opponent or classical twin. The network of contractual relationships and lines of authority based on property rights, which constitutes the classical picture of the enterprise, could not function in real life. The enterprise is a social system, and its members must be motivated by some identification with the organization so that it can function and continue to exist.

In addition, the business unit can use family and team analogies with more justification than could other hierarchical organizations such as the military services and, perhaps, governmental bureaucracies. For example, a military unit is expected to operate as if its personnel were interchangeable parts.[29] As a rule this does not hold true for business, at least where executives are concerned. But the "family" and "team" analogies undoubtedly overstate the case. Compared with families and athletic teams, the business organization has a serious problem of integration. A family does not require any external purpose to give it unity; it is an end in itself. A team has a very obvious purpose of unambiguous appeal to its members. The case is very different for the business enterprise. As a consequence, divisive forces and problems of hierarchical discipline are much more important than managerial ideology implies.

The Responsibilities and Rights of Business Management. In public statements, corporation managers generally claim that they have four broad responsibilities: to consumers, to employees, to stockholders, and to the general public;[30] sometimes a fifth is added: to suppliers and other business contracts, or responsibilities to the immediate and ultimate customers of a firm may be stressed separately. In any case, each group is on an equal footing; the function of management is to secure justice for all and unconditional maxima for none.[31] Stockholders have no

[29] Chester Barnard, *Organization and Management* (Cambridge, Mass., 1948), pp. 200–202.

[30] "It is our aim and our purpose to so conduct our business that our customers will be better served at lower prices, that our employees will have more and better jobs at high wages, and that we can continue to contribute to and meet the needs of an expanding economy through the products and services we offer. It is our belief that in order to fulfill this objective, we must seek to make more profits for our stockholders." C. E. Wilson of General Electric, *Hearings on Profits* (Flanders), p. 475.

[31] "We in our business feel most keenly the need for balance in administering out three-way responsibility to the American consumer, to our associates in this business, and to the 68,000 men and women whose faith has been shown by their investment in General Foods. We . . . would serve (the company's) interests badly by shifting the fruits of the enterprise too heavily toward any one of these groups." Francis of General Foods, *Hearings on Profits* (Flanders), p. 212.

special priority; they are entitled to a fair return on their investment, but profits above a "fair" level are an economic sin. The multiple responsibilities of corporate management are so inclusive that its objective can be summarized as "administration of the business in the best long range interest of the public at large." Some exponents of the social gospel go so far as to commend a Kantian criterion to individual managements for every decision: to consider what would be the consequences for society if every management acted thus.[32]

The classical interpretation of the business enterprise is rarely applied to an individual firm. No management would publicly announce that its sole objective is maximum profits. But the interpretation is found in abstract analyses — the NAM textbook,[33] for example. And it is frequently used in defensive arguments when the prerogatives of management and ownership are threatened by government encroachment. These arguments generally invoke fundamental rights of private property which should be applied equally to the great corporation and the small proprietorship.[34] Proposals to limit profits or to compel management decisions to reflect the very nonprofit considerations and interests which, according to the managerial interpretation, are already voluntarily respected, lead naturally to the rebuttal that pursuit of profit is not only a right implied by private ownership of property but is, thanks to the competitive mechanism, in the public interest.

Allied with property rights in this defense are "rights of management." Property rights protect ownership, and they protect management when it acts on the owners' behalf. The newer and separate concept of rights of management reflects the institutional split between management and ownership; it is designed to defend for management a sphere of unhampered discretion and authority which is not merely derivative from the property rights of owners. Management's rights are the inherent counterpart of its responsibilities, whether these are conceived in the broad terms of the managerial interpretation or the narrow terms of the classical view.

[32] For an extreme statement, from which the quotation is taken, see T. R. Jones (President of ATF), "Obligations of Leadership in an Evolving Society," *Dun's Review,* March 1949, p. 11. The theme of "serving all four" is featured in advertising of the Shell Oil Co., *New York Times,* April 10, 1949. It was also the theme of a conference on "The Area of Business Leadership" concluding a series of University of Rochester Management Clinics, as reported in *Trends in Industry — Education Cooperation* (an NAM publication), September 1949, p. 15. The formula appears again in the Presidential address of Lawrence A. Appley to the American Management Association, reported in *New York Times,* Jan. 9, 1949.

[33] Chapters 2 and 3.

[34] A typical instance of the defensive use of the classical model of the firm is provided by the testimony of President Dunlop of the Sun Oil Company in *Hearings on Profits* (Flanders), p. 266. Mr. Dunlop described the plowing back of profits in these terms: the owners of the oil industry, the stockholders, to whom the profits rightfully belong, have permitted their companies to reinvest a major portion of their profit money.

As the "quarterback" parallel noted above indicates, even those who espouse the managerial view of the enterprise draw some lines beyond which familial cooperation and teamwork cannot go. The literature is vague about the content of management's rights; in the past management has had to retreat from positions from which retreat had previously been said to be unthinkable.

Business Institutions and Other Institutions. The features which differentiate business enterprises from other social institutions are seldom mentioned in the business creed. Indeed, the distinction is often blurred by applying terms such as family or team to the business enterprise. However, in some contexts the institutional differences are given ideological significance. Discussion of political institutions generally evokes both unfavorable comparison with business and the suggestion that government badly needs the application of sound business principles. The argument is that political institutions lack the characteristics which lead to efficiency in business: orientation to private profit; the discipline of the balance sheet; rationality, impersonality, and universalism in human relations — and are therefore naturally prone to waste, corruption, and favoritism. More generally, the creed expresses the feeling that non-business organizations fail to call individuals to account for their use of funds and economic resources and for their decisions. This feeling makes for one line of argument in defense of profits. It is also involved in business' distrust of government and in the claim that businessmen are peculiarly fitted to be the natural leaders of society outside the business firm as well as within it. These themes are both openly expressed in the business creed.

4

THE FUNCTIONS AND REWARDS
OF OWNERSHIP

THIS CHAPTER CONCERNS the business creed's explanation of the functions, motivations, and rewards of the owners of business enterprises. The prominence of discussion about profits — their basic legitimacy, their place as incentives, their size — is one of the most striking features of contemporary business ideology. The roles of owner and executive frequently overlap in practice; but, for the sake of convenience, this chapter will confine itself to the ideology's treatment of the owner *qua* owner, and Chapter 5 with its treatment of the managerial role.

PROFITS AS AN IDEOLOGICAL ISSUE

> When Adam delved and Eve span
> Who was then the gentleman?

The fact that incomes in our society may be based simply on the facts of ownership and not necessarily on services rendered through "work" obviously offers a target for criticism. John Ball's ancient ditty reminds us of the long history of resentments among those who delve and spin against those who live idly on a return from property. As long as business ideology could emphasize individual proprietorship as the dominant type of business organization, it could ignore the problem of idle, absentee ownership of business. Interest and rent might need defense, but profits were solidly based in the labors of the proprietor. Even in a proprietorship, it is possible to distinguish logically between the functions of executive control and ownership; but such distinction requires an academic fussiness not convenient for ideological symbols. The "capitalist" as owner-manager has, of course, been an ideological symbol charged with negative feelings through the Western world, but he has not typically been depicted as idle and inattentive to business. He has been, in Sir John Maynard's phrase, a "fat gentleman with a gift for arithmetic," and if his girth suggested physical sluggishness, his business garb and cigars suggested a continuous, occupational attention to his arithmetic. Saint-Simon's anger at *les oisifs* has a quaint air now, viewed across a century and a half of anger at more industrious exploiters of property rights.

The appearance of the corporation, a conspicuous feature of the modern world, has provided a very tangible separation of ownership and management and occasioned a number of problems for ideology. The functions of ownership and executive control are less readily confused, and the legitimacy of property incomes is potentially a sharper issue. Confusion between the two may indeed be maintained, as we shall see below in the NAM's discussion of the "enterpriser." It may also be used to deny the existence of a large army of drones living on their dividends. Thus S. Wells Utley argued that very few capitalists (whom he defines as any persons who spend less than they earn), except widows and orphans, are idle people; since, in his claim, most security holders also hold jobs, the capitalist should not be conceived as an idle rich man.[1]

Nevertheless, the accrual of income to the "impersonal" corporation conspicuously divorces income from any specific personal occupational activity. Corporate profits become a target for resentments against property incomes and for anti-business ideology; and the vast amount of attention to profits in the business creed may be viewed as a defense. Even so, this focus of ideological discussion upon profits is extraordinary in the perspective of a broad survey of questions about incomes which might become ideological issues.

Income inequality is doubtless one of the issues involved in controversy over profits, but it does not appear to be the main issue. The *nature* of incomes receives more attention than the *size* of individual incomes. The functional distribution of the national income (the percentage shares of profits, wages, etc.) is scrutinized more closely than the size distribution (percentage of families with income over a specified amount). Substantial inequality among individuals in wage and salary earnings provokes relatively little comment. It is not necessary to defend the fabulous earnings of Hollywood stars and baseball players; even the high salaries of business executives themselves receive relatively little discussion, as we shall see in the next chapter.

The distinction between "earned" and "unearned" incomes is loaded with more ethical content in our culture than the contrast between high and low incomes, but the distinction is highly conventional. Thus, the wages or salaries of any employee, however large, are considered "earned," and this honor is extended to the incomes of the self-employed from their own work, for example, the incomes of professionals in independent practice. On the other hand, incomes requiring no current personal effort but rewarding the ownership of some kind of property are likely to be considered "unearned" and therefore present an ideological problem. Thus

[1] Utley, *The American System*, p. 89.

the distinction between "earned" and "unearned" incomes tends to become in practice one between "work" and "property" incomes.

Moreover, the "work-property" distinction is itself inconsistently applied, and classification of incomes according to these two categories is greatly influenced by conventional labels. "Wages and salaries" and "earnings of self-employed," on the one hand, and "profits," on the other, certainly do not correspond to the distinction between the rewards of current personal effort and the rewards of past accumulations. Several examples will make this clear. The income of a doctor from his practice would not be called profit, nor would its size be questioned so long as the doctor was thought to have earned it in a proper professional manner. But it generally includes a return on an investment: not just the doctor's investment in professional equipment but, what is more important, the money invested by the doctor or his parents in his professional training. Men of wealth understand that an alternative to bequeathing their fortunes to their children as property is to pass it on in the form of education (it is, incidentally, an alternative which saves taxes). A farmer or an individual business proprietor receives in addition to "wages" for his work a return on his investment in his enterprise, and this is an income for owning property in the same sense as the dividends of a corporation shareholder. But it is not called "profits," and its legitimacy as "earned" income is little questioned. In contrast, corporate profits are clearly labeled, and, by definition, since the wages of management are "costs" deducted in reckoning profits, cannot be confused with the rewards of current personal effort. Again, the label is in many cases arbitrary. For many reasons, including the tax laws, an entrepreneur may incorporate his business and convert into "profits" what was formerly merely the income of an individual proprietor. The same considerations may lead such a corporation to pay its owner-manager only a nominal salary; by taking his gains in the form of corporate profits which increase the value of his stock or pay dividends, he causes a different label to be placed upon what is essentially the same income as if he had received it as an individual proprietor or a salaried corporation executive.

It is more difficult to understand why, among various kinds of property incomes, corporate profits are singled out for attention. There is very little discussion nowadays of the justification for interest income. Interest has been an important ideological issue in the past. The Populist movement made extensive use of the money-man as a negative symbol; and later, especially after the stock market crash of 1929, "Wall Street finance," contrasted with "productive enterprise," was under attack. Today it is not a hot issue, even when it takes the form of receiving income for holding the perfectly safe and highly liquid obligations of the federal government. In this respect our society diverges sharply from many other cultures, where usury is abhorred but uncertain and variable returns on property are unquestioned.[2] What is perhaps more surprising in an Anglo-Saxon tradition which includes Ricardo and Henry George, rental incomes — when they accrue directly to individuals rather than to corporations — attract little attention, outside such specific contexts as rent control.

The literature of the business creed reveals remarkably little resistance to defining the issues in these curious terms. The creed is, by and large, prepared to do battle on the nature of incomes called profits, taking for granted that they are quite distinct from other kinds of income and that the legitimacy of incomes of other names is beyond question.

It is true that some attempt is made to escape the burden of the label "profits" by arguing that profit, under other names but no different in essence, pervades the whole economy. General Motors heads a comparison of a 1929 Buick and a 1948 Chevrolet, "Profits for the Customer."[3] A Warner & Swasey advertisement resurrects the Iron Law of Wages in arguing that the concept of "excess profits" is no less appropriate to wages above minimum subsistence standards than to corporate profits.[4] It is claimed that every exchange, whether between employer and employee, or consumer and retailer or any other buyer and seller, yields "profit" to both parties, in the sense that they receive more value than they give up.[5]

In the main, however, the ideology accepts the conventional, narrower concept of profits and makes their legitimacy a central article of the creed. The System is a profit system; to question profits is to attack the System, according to *Business Week*.[6] Warner and Swasey says, "Such attacks are beginning to show their foreign accent,"[7] and attributes them to "furtive people."[8] The Standard Steel Spring Company blames them on "questionable influences."[9] Alternatively, attacks on profits are "either political claptrap, or evidence of economic illiteracy."[10] The very existence of a

---

[2] See Raymond Firth, *The Elements of Social Organization,* pp. 147–153.

[3] *Hearings on Profits* (Flanders), p. 523.

[4] "Every workman is a miniature corporation," Warner & Swasey advertisement, *Business Week,* July 16, 1949.

[5] "Under our competitive system, no business can last, much less produce a profit for its owners for any prolonged period, unless it is able to provide for its customers the ever better values which in a very real sense represent a profit for them." M. E. Coyle (General Motors), *Hearings on Profits* (Flanders), p. 523.

[6] "Profits Are Easy to Criticize — and Defend" (Editorial), *Business Week,* Oct. 1, 1949.

[7] Warner & Swasey advertisement, *Newsweek,* May 16, 1948.

[8] Warner & Swasey advertisement, *Business Week,* Feb. 26, 1949.

[9] Standard Steel Spring Company advertisement, *New York Times,* April 26, 1949.

[10] "Wanted, a Better Understanding of Profits," United Business Service release, Sept. 7, 1948.

Congressional inquiry into corporate profits so outraged Ernest R. Klein that he wrote *How to Stay Rich* to set straight the illiterate and ward off the malevolent.

PROFITS AND PROFITABILITY

The business creed contains two distinct lines of defense for the profit system; these are closely related to an important ambiguity in the meaning of "profit":

On the one hand, profits are incomes accruing first to enterprises and, through their mediacy, to individuals. Here the main defense lies in an attempt to prove that profits are "earned" just as truly as wages and salaries are "earned." Anxiety on this score is illustrated by the NAM text's exclusion from profits of "so-called windfall or fortuitous gains . . . Such gains are the result of luck or good fortune which has no relation to any risk taken, or any effort made by the recipient . . . (and) . . . are no more 'profit' than they are wages, or interest or rent." [11] There are two ways of showing that profits are earned. One is to show that each recipient, individual or firm, has performed a service for society that merits the return it gets. The other is to show that, taken as a whole, profits fulfill a social function which would not otherwise be performed so well or so cheaply. In the business creed, explanations of both kinds are intertwined and are not kept logically separate.

On the other hand, "profits" may be defended, not as incomes, but as a symbol of accountability and rational economic calculation. There is some advantage, in many contexts, in speaking of profits as if no one receives them, and this manner of discussion is facilitated by the impersonality of the corporation. According to the business creed, the discipline of the balance sheet is an important reason for the unique efficiency and practicality of businessmen. In defending "the profit system" or, as it is often styled, the "profit and loss system," businessmen are defending a principle of objective accountability for the performance of individuals and enterprises. This principle, in the business view, is all that holds the dike against a host of sometimes well-intentioned but impractical proposals by labor leaders, politicians, reformers, bureaucrats, social workers, et al. Such people represent inattention to the balancing of costs against values and the replacement of objective measures of value by sloppy, subjective judgments. Although the main message of the ideology is that the profit system is uniquely American, concern with profit in the accounting sense leads to another theme. This is the theme that profit — or profitability, as Peter Drucker[12] calls it in this meaning — is inherent in economic

---

[11] NAM, I: 495–560.
[12] Peter Drucker, "The Function of Profits," *Fortune*, March 1949.

law and must exist in some form in any system which attempts to allocate economic resources rationally.

Thus, the ambiguity in the meaning of "profit system" apparently leads business ideology to defend two quite different aspects of business enterprise at the same time. The second of these aspects, the principle of objective accountability, would seem to be intrinsically easy to defend. But in practice its defense is jeopardized by its association with the first aspect, private property incomes, which is intrinsically much more vulnerable.[13]

COMPETITIVE PROFITS OF THE ENTERPRISE

The primary justification of the profits of the enterprise is that they are earned in free competition under the exacting sovereignty of consumers. In neo-classical economic theory the ultimate source of value is the freely expressed choice of consumers in a competitive market. If consumers are willing to pay the price for something, it must be "worth it," and if that price includes some profit, consumers have automatically given that profit their stamp of approval. Their approval not only legitimizes the profit as income, but sanctions the stewardship of the enterprise for the economic resources entrusted to its use. Thus the "competitive profits" argument is in part a defense of a system of accountability and rational economic calculation.

Certainly there is nothing antisocial in profit. I think the truth of the matter is that — given access to all as buyers and sellers — the profit earned by the wise businessman is a measure of the service he has rendered to his market, in terms of a value placed on those services by the buyers, individually and collectively.[14]

Certainly profits cannot be arithmetically too high if they are made competitively in fair dealings in a competitive economy.[15]

Competition is recognized as an essential condition, in this argument, for profits to derive legitimacy from consumers' votes. Under competitive conditions "large profits are an indication that the company earning them is playing a useful role." [16]

. . . any larger or smaller profit we could make, as compared with any of our competitors, would be due to the relative ingenuity, experience, and energy we put into supplying the customer with what we have found he wants.[17]

[13] A point of interest for the analysis of the ideology which will come later is involved here. This fact is evidence against the simple view that business ideology is only cleverly contrived propaganda consciously tailored to obtain the most favorable popular reception.

[14] C. E. Wilson (General Electric), *Hearings on Profits* (Flanders), p. 475.

[15] Clarence Francis (General Foods), *Hearings on Profits* (Flanders), p. 210.

[16] United Business Service, "Wanted, a Better Understanding."

[17] Wilson, *Hearings on Profits* (Flanders), p. 473.

. . . the free play of competition, plus the long-range interests of the producer, as he seeks the consumer market, will assure that the profits which are earned are not excessive.[18]

. . . the margin of profit serves as a recorder or yardstick of the efficiency of the managers of the enterprise, unless the latter enjoys some kind of monopoly position.[19]

The ethical status of actual corporate profits depends, therefore, on identifying actual markets with the competitive model.[20] The large corporations which justified their profits before the Flanders Subcommittee had no worries on this score. They denied having significant control over their selling prices.[21] They emphasized that profits are an unplanned "residual" rather than an item added to costs in setting prices. When Senator Flanders referred to a union charge that General Electric enjoyed "monopoly profits," Mr. Wilson replied with a jokingly regretful denial. Later, anxious lest his denial be considered too equivocal and frivolous, he wrote: "The General Electric Company is not engaged and does not wish to be engaged in any enterprise resulting in monopolistic profits . . . it is our policy to observe both the letter and the spirit of the anti-trust laws in every respect." [22]

Just as competition gives profits the ethical standing of having been "earned" by their recipients, it provides the institution of profits with an important macroscopic social function. Profits "are the gauges in our general office control rooms which signal the economic temperatures and pressures of the times. For example, profits, when they become large, signal the need for expansion in those lines of production in which demand is increasing. Contrariwise, a lack of profits indicates the necessity of contraction in those industries which have been overexpanded or whose products are in diminishing demand." [23] Thus profits are a key part of the mechanism, to be examined in Chapter 8, by which productive resources are optimally allocated among alternative uses. According to the logic of this argument, however, the profits and losses which are the governors of the competitive machine are essentially transient. In the process of performing their function of inducing expansion in one line and contraction

---

[18] *Ibid.*, pp. 475–476.

[19] Robert G. Dunlop (Sun Oil Co.), *Hearings on Profits* (Flanders), p. 262.

[20] NAM, I: 460–464.

[21] "We have got another boss who finally reviews the price policy and approves or disapproves it. That boss is your wife and mine, buying in a highly competitive market where pennies count." Francis, *Hearings on Profits* (Flanders), p. 207.

[22] *Ibid.*, pp. 488, 505.

This unquestioning identification of the economy with the competitive model is characteristic of the business creed, and will be examined in Chapter 8, where some of the difficulties it involves are pointed out.

[23] Dunlop, *Hearings on Profits* (Flanders), p. 262.

74   THE AMERICAN BUSINESS CREED

in another, they disappear. Competition does not legitimize permanent profits.

THE MAGNITUDE OF POSTWAR CORPORATE PROFITS

In the years following World War II, the subject of corporate profits became particularly lively. Business leaders blamed "wage-rounds" for the inflation, and labor leaders blamed the high profits disclosed in corporation reports. Corporations, in Labor's view, could afford both to raise wages *and* to lower prices.

In this setting the standard explanations of profits were supplemented by special arguments appropriate to the times. Some of these were specific applications of the standard explanations. For example, inflation was held to accentuate the need for high profits as an incentive for capital expansion, for two reasons. Inflation reveals the urgency of the community's desire for more production, which can only be obtained with the aid of more tools. Since tools cost more at inflated prices and wages, it naturally takes much higher money profits to provide the incentive to invest in them.[24] The history of the oil industry in the postwar period was cited as a case study in the function of high profits in eliminating scarcity.[25] Other arguments were *ad hoc*. Practically every business spokesman before the Flanders Subcommittee referred to the legitimacy and necessity of making high profits in good times to protect business against an adverse turn of the cycle in the future. ". . . surely it is the business of management to make as much money as possible when the making is good . . . to protect the properties under its control against possible economic recession." [26] But the most frequent of the *ad hoc* arguments was that profits are not really as large as people, including the tax collectors, think. Two facets of this discussion are worth examining in some detail; both illustrate that the use of numbers for ideological purposes may be highly selective and artful.

(1) Corporate profits appear to be exact in corporation income statements, but their computation is actually the result of many rather crude guesses and arbitrary conventions. The numerical approximation to this concept depends on conventional rules of accounting. In the postwar inflation, business came to the conclusion that these rules were systematically

---

[24] An example of this line of argument is the following statement of Wilson in *Hearings on Profits* (Flanders), p. 482: ". . . the true test of the adequacy of profits . . . (is) . . . whether a corporation's profits are bringing about as fast an expansion of industrial capacity as the community desires . . . the replacement cost of our plant at today's prices is estimated to be more than $300,000,000 in excess of the actual cost." For a professional statement of this point of view, on which business spokesmen leaned heavily, see the testimony of Sumner Slichter before the same committee, 3–26.

[25] See testimony of Joseph E. Pogue (Vice-President, Chase National Bank), *Hearings on Profits* (Flanders), pp. 159–198.

[26] TGM's column, *Boston Globe,* Mar. 8, 1949.

exaggerating corporate net income. This argument was espoused by both business executives and by some professional economists and accountants in the Flanders Subcommittee hearings and elsewhere.[27] The conservatism of the accounting profession has prevented widespread correction of corporate accounts for the alleged exaggeration, but corporate reports commonly warn readers that accounting profits are larger than true profits and many firms, for example, U.S. Steel, actually make numerical corrections.

A corporation holds stocks of goods: "inventories" of raw materials, goods in process, and finished commodities; it also has "fixed" plant and equipment. Its operations during a year use up part of the stocks with which the corporation began the year. The reduction in stocks is clearly one of the costs which the firm must deduct from its sales receipts in reckoning its net income, or profits, for the year. Provision must be made for the restoration of stocks to their initial level. The appropriate size of this allowance is very difficult to estimate, and in practice the uncertainties are overcome only by the use of arbitrary accounting conventions. In the first place, the physical amount of consumption of stocks is not easy to ascertain. In the case of inventories, it is quite definite — so many tons of coal or yards of wool — but in the case of durable installations of machinery and plant it is vague. How much less is there of a blast furnace after it has been used for a year? The accountant must use a formula based on some estimate of the life of the furnace and of its "depreciation" at various ages. For example, he may simply assume that one-twentieth of the furnace is "used up" for each of twenty years. The second problem, which is our present interest, is to translate the estimate of the physical consumption of stocks into dollar costs. Some price must be attached to each kind of good used up. In periods of changing prices, there are a number of prices which might be used in making the calculation; the corporation's income statement will look different depending on which price is selected. Accounting convention has been to use those prices which the corporation paid originally for the goods used up at a later date; in the case of inventories of identical goods acquired at various times and prices the usual convention is to assume that goods are used up in the sequence in which they were bought — "first in, first out." In periods of rising prices these conventions automatically choose the lowest possible price. If a blast furnace was built in 1939, one-twentieth of its total 1939 cost is charged against operations in 1948. If at the beginning of 1948 the coal inventory includes (from an accounting point of view) some coal purchased in 1947 at 1946 prices, the dollar cost of "using up" coal in 1948 partially reflects the lower 1946 price of coal. This is the basis for the contention commonly made by businessmen that conventional accounting exaggerates profits dur-

---

[27] The subtlety of the argument did not prevent its occurrence in popular media. See, for example, Union Oil Co. advertisement, *New York Times*, April 20, 1952.

ing inflation. They claim that current rather than historical prices should be used; otherwise, costs of restoring stocks of goods to their levels at the beginning of the year are understated. If one-twentieth of a blast furnace is used up during 1948, the true cost to the corporation is one-twentieth of what it would cost in 1948 to replace that blast furnace. The cost of depleting the coal inventory in 1948 is what it would actually cost the corporation to purchase that coal at the end of 1948. In a situation of continuous inflation, the appropriate replacement cost figure would be the cost as of the actual time of replacement. Thus, in the previous example, the cost of using up one-twentieth of a blast furnace in 1948 should be figured as one-twentieth of the (assumed higher) replacement costs of 1959, when a new blast furnace will be needed. Original costs are irrelevant; their use in inflationary times conceals the true costs of doing business, exaggerates the profit base for taxation, and invites excessive wage demands.[28]

This is true, but it is not the whole story; it is, of course, characteristic of ideology that the rest of the story is not always told. If a corporation is to revalue its stocks of goods at current prices in reckoning its costs, it should also revalue them at current prices in reckoning its assets. If a 1939 blast furnace is depreciated at one-twentieth of its 1948 replacement cost, the undepreciated ten-twentieths of the furnace should be carried as an asset on the corporation's books at one-half the 1948 replacement cost rather than at one-half the original 1939 cost. If coal consumption is to be charged as a cost at current high prices, then the whole inventory of coal should be valued at these prices too, regardless of the prices at which the coal was bought.

As a holder of goods over a period of rising prices, a corporation is in the same position as anyone else who was fortunate or foresighted enough to buy when prices were low. During inflation, holders of money or of bonds suffer a decline in the purchasing power of their capital. But holders of goods enjoy an appreciation of the money value of their holdings, so that the purchasing power of their investment is maintained. (Of course, they may gain or lose in purchasing power depending on whether the goods they hold advance in price more or less rapidly than the general

---

[28] Mr. Voorhees, chairman of the finance committee of U.S. Steel, warns against the "hidden erosion of the American tools of production that is resulting from a lack of understanding of costs," as if accounting procedures could cause blast furnaces to waste away. *Hearings on Profits* (Flanders), p. 591. The Socony-Vacuum Oil Company makes a typical statement: "It is our sincere conviction that unless the oil industry is permitted to deduct from its taxable profits amounts which will enable it to replace equipment and crude oil, it will gradually lose its purchasing power as well as its productivity." *Hearings on Profits* (Flanders), p. 585. It should be noted that this argument is quite a distinct one from the argument, examined on p. 74, that high profits are needed as an incentive to investment in high-cost facilities; the present argument denies that those profits exist.

price level.) Still more fortunate in inflationary times are those who hold goods and owe money; the money value of their goods increases while their debts remain the same. It is better to have owned a house over the past decade than to have owned savings bonds. It is still better to have mortgaged the house. Corporations are generally debtors. Just as inflation benefits the titular owner of a home at the expense of the holder of the mortgage, it favors the stockholders of a corporation at the expense of the creditors.

Inflation, then, increases the money value of the corporation's stock of goods. Conventional accounting practice notices these monetary capital gains when, and only when, they are realized. That is, conventional accounting practice includes in profits the monetary gains on the goods used up or depreciated during the year. Thus the appreciation in money value of the one-twentieth of the blast furnace assumed to have been used up in 1948 is included in "profits" for 1948. The business creed rightly points out that this appreciation in dollars reflects no gain in terms of purchasing power. Counting it in profits gives a misleading impression of the profitability of the enterprise; if inflation stopped, the corporation would in time realize all such monetary gains and from then on would make only the net income indicated by replacement cost accounting.[29]

But if conventional accounting overstates the current profits and profitability of the corporation during inflation, it also understates the equity of the shareholders and fails to show their gains in purchasing power at the expense of their creditors.[30] The ideology frequently emphasizes the one defect of conventional accounting but not the other.

In a somewhat different context, business spokesmen recognize the increase in the value of the stockholders' equity in the corporation. One of the many measures of profits is as a percentage of "net worth," indicating the rate of return which stockholders are earning, though not necessarily receiving, on their equity in the corporation. If a firm now values its physical assets at their prewar costs of acquisition, it understates this equity or net worth and consequently overstates the rate of return. Therefore, business finds two counts on which profits, by this measure, are overstated in conventional accounting. One is that the dollar amount of profits is exaggerated; the second is that the base for computing the rate of

[29] There is some justice to the view that monetary capital gains that reflect no gain in purchasing power should not be taxed as if they were real gains. Congress has recognized this view in exempting from tax homeowners who realize a capital gain in selling a home to the extent that they use the proceeds of sale to buy a new home. Otherwise, our tax laws are based on dollars as units rather than units of constant purchasing power, and their wholesale revision to avoid the injustice of taxing illusory monetary gains has scarcely been considered either within the business creed or elsewhere.

[30] Conversely, during deflation conventional accounting understates the current profits of a business and overstates the stockholders' equity.

return is underestimated. Businessmen contend that the only relevant measure for determining the attractiveness of a corporation (particularly if prices become stabilized) is the rate of return which results from replacement cost accounting. But it follows that the increase in net worth is also relevant in a context to which businessmen do not apply it: the question of how stockholders fare, relative to other groups, during inflation.

(2) A measure of profits which lends itself to skillful ideological use is that of profits as a percentage of sales. Profits which look large by other standards may look small when they are expressed in this way. The campaign to make profits seem small by expressing them as a percentage of sales is, unlike the accounting arguments just reviewed, one of the cases in which the content of the ideology seems to have been shaped by a conscious exploitation by advertising experts of the most effective techniques of manipulating mass opinion.

Why does this measure of profits make them seem small? In the first place, it does not relate them to the owners' investment in the enterprise. It is possible to take a very small chunk of each sales dollar and nevertheless achieve a handsome rate of return on investment. Every shopkeeper, whose investment is largely in stocks on the shelves, knows the secret — rapid turnover. If he need hold inventory equal to only two weeks' sales, he can make, from a 1 per cent return on sales, a return of 26 per cent per year on his inventory investment. In the second place, it is entirely possible for each firm to take only a small percentage of its sales as profit while profits in the aggregate amount to a large share of the national incomes. This is simply because many firms handle the same material on its way from unfinished to finished state. Suppose, for example, that each firm took exactly a quarter as much profit as it paid out in wages and other kinds of income. Suppose that twenty firms worked on a given article at various stages of fabrication, and that each made a dollar of profit. In its final sale, the article would sell for $100 and the firm making the sale could truthfully say that *its* profit was only 1 per cent of sales. But a fact of much more significance is that $20 of that $100 was somebody's profit.

With this background let us examine a concerted campaign waged by the NAM in a long series of full-page advertisements to correct with "straightforward facts" the "fantastic idea" of "the average American" "about how big the profits of business are."

. . . surveys show that most Americans think industry's peacetime profits range from 18% to 25% a year. Paradoxically, the same people estimate that 10 to 15 cents out of each sales dollar would be a fair profit for business to make. Actually, industry averages less than half that much profit." There follows a table on "Profit Margins on Sales, All Manufacturing Corporations," 1938–1947, in which the highest entry is 6.2% for 1941 and 1947.[31]

This point was dramatized in a series of advertisements featuring average Americans who, shrewd as they may be about most things, are mistaken about the size of profits. "Joe Vaughn 'knows his onions'!" " 'But,' says Joe, 'I wonder if a lot of business firms today aren't making too much profit.' " [32] "Ed Taintor isn't fooled often. But, about business Ed says, 'Could be that profits are too high these days.' " [33] The NAM sets Joe and Ed, and others straight:

> Smart as he is, Ed's missing the nail on that one. For, as it happens, Government figures show that industry actually averages *less than half* what Ed — and perhaps you too — believe would be a *fair* profit.

The NAM chooses to believe that the respondents to the survey answered in terms of the profit-sales ratio of individual firms or groups of firms rather than the profit-sales ratio for all industry with inter-firm sales transactions eliminated. If a consumer is asked how much profit there is or there should be in an article for which he pays $100, will he think only of the profit of the retailer, or only of the profit of the final manufacturer? Or will he think of all the profit made by everyone connected with the production and sale of the article? In terms of our example above, will he think of a number corresponding to the 1 per cent or a number corresponding to the 20 per cent? Shrewd as he is, Ed Taintor probably isn't aware of the subtleties of the problem, although the NAM should be. But the context in which he, and Joe Vaughn, and Bob Johnston — a "plenty hep" high school sophomore[34] — worry about profits may well be their size relative to wages, salaries, and other incomes. If so, their answers would show that they do not have an exaggerated notion of the size of profits and that their idea of a fair profit is not larger than what industry actually makes.

Consider the ratio of profits to all income — profits, wages, salaries, interest, rent — originating in manufacturing corporations, the subject of the NAM advertisements. In 1947 this figure was 21 per cent for profits before taxes and 13 per cent for profits after taxes. The NAM assumes without question that the survey respondents were thinking of profits *after* taxes; otherwise its 6 per cent on sales for 1947 would have to be 10 per cent.[35] But this is by no means certain. In estimating "fair" profits and

[31] NAM advertisement, *Harper's*, June 1948.
[32] NAM advertisement, *Saturday Evening Post*, Sept. 11, 1948.
[33] NAM advertisement, *Saturday Evening Post*, Oct. 9, 1948.
[34] NAM advertisement, *Trends* in Education-Industry Cooperation, Sept. 1948.
[35] NAM pamphlet, *Who Profits from Profits?*, which shows the breakdown of the manufacturer's sales dollar ending with 6¢ for profits, 9¢ is deducted early in the game for taxes, without explanation that 4 of those 9 cents are taxes on profits.

actual profits, Joe and Ed and Bob may not have been uninfluenced by knowledge that corporations have to pay taxes. If the share of profits after taxes is to be compared with other income shares, those incomes also should be calculated net of taxes. This would lead to a figure somewhere in between the 13 per cent and 21 per cent cited above.

The NAM is not alone among business ideologists in exploiting the survey of public opinion on profits and the subtleties of profits-sales statistics. National Dairy Products Corporation concluded each of a long series of advertisements with the following:

An impartial national survey shows that most Americans consider 10%– 15% on sales a fair profit for business. Compared to this, the average profit in the food industry is less than 5%. And National Dairy's profit in its milk divisions in 1947 was less than 2%.[36]

Fractions of a cent are even more trifling than small percentages.

. . . in many cases, if profits to the producer were eliminated entirely, *there would be no difference at all in price to the consumer* . . . On a loaf of bread, the profit, after taxes, of the 4 largest bakers in America is less than ⅗ of a cent.

This is repeated for a quart of milk (½¢), a pound of sugar (⅙¢), a pound of meat (½¢), a can of food (⅔¢). No recognition is given to the fact that, for example, the sugar refiner's profit is not the sole profit in the price of a pound of sugar. And, of course, had the writer chosen as his unit a pint of milk instead of a quart, or an ounce of sugar instead of a pound, he could have made the fractions even smaller.[37]

JUSTIFICATION OF THE STOCKHOLDERS' RETURNS

When the creed turns from profits earned by the corporation to those passed on to individual stockholders, business is faced with two conflicting problems: how to justify such profits in the eyes of the general public; and how to convince the stockholders that the corporation adequately represents their interests.

In some contexts a tenuous relation of the absentee stockholder to the productive process in industry is implicitly recognized. Thus, SKF Industries tell the public how a pound of steel is changed into a pound of gold (as ball bearings). The needed ingredients are skilled labor, efficient machines, and the know-how of management, with no word for the functions of ownership.[38] In other contexts investment becomes the decisive agent in the whole economic process by the characteristic ideological

[36] For example, *Newsweek*, Dec. 20, 1948.
[37] N. W. Ayer & Son, Inc. advertisement, *Saturday Evening Post*, May 14, 1949.
[38] SKF Industries advertisement, *Business Week*, May 14, 1949.

device of taking one indispensable factor and arguing that the employment of all others is (asymmetrically) dependent on this one. In an argument reminiscent of Marx's labor theory of value, Mr. Utley tells us that the capitalist "is actually the man who provides us our jobs and our luxuries . . . He is the most vital factor in making our progress possible." [39] The claim is supported by the argument that no business can start unless someone is willing to risk his capital, and temporal priority is readily construed as implying priority in importance. [40]

It is now common to stress the manifold blessings which flow from the tools of production provided by stockholders' investment. A great deal of business ideology in popular media merely describes these blessings, and asserts without explanation that "adequate" profits are an indispensable prerequisite. Profits encourage capital accumulation and thus they raise employment, real wages, productivity, and the standard of living. The ideology implies that society should be willing to pay almost anything to achieve these benefits and is most ungrateful if it begrudges the trifling amounts which it actually has to pay.

Thus N. W. Ayer and Son, Inc., asks: [41]

"How secure is your job? As secure as the profits of the firm you work for."

A statement attributed to Samuel Gompers: "The worst crime against working people is the corporation which fails to operate at a profit" is probably the most quoted and approved saying of any labor leader which appears in the business ideology. It is in the Ayer advertisement cited above, and also in two Warner & Swasey advertisements. [42] Another Warner & Swasey advertisement compares a man with a pick, who can produce only enough to earn $7 per day, with a man with a power shovel, who can earn $20.

What makes him worth $13 more per day? The *machine*. Then shouldn't the *machine* earn something, too? What would you say would be fair — the amount it *added* to the man's income — $13? Actually the machine will get only a trifle. [43]

The same company puts the following words in the mouth of a worker whose grandfather earned $1 a day:

. . . with that $11,000 machine working for me, I get $12 a day. I'm $11 a day better off because of that machine. So I figure the man who saved up and

[39] Utley, *The American System*, p. 94.

[40] *Ibid.*, pp. 92–93.

[41] N. W. Ayer and Son advertisement, *Saturday Evening Post*, June 11, 1949.

[42] Warner & Swasey advertisement, 1949, *Business Week*, Feb. 26, and June 18, 1949.

[43] Warner & Swasey advertisement, *Newsweek*, May 16, 1948.

bought it for me to use is entitled to a little something too. I understand they call that "profit on investment." I just call it fair play.[44]

The calculations of the amount of investment it takes to provide a job are numerous. The prize for exactitude goes to the Association of American Railroads: "It takes $20,265 to keep a man working on the railroad." [45] The prize for magnitude goes to the Humble Oil Company, which puts the figure at $92,500 and tells its employees, "It takes a lot of money to keep us in jobs." [46] Of the investment plans of business for 1950–53, J. H. McGraw writes:

> The program of capital expenditures planned by American industry is one of the greatest bargains ever offered the American people.[47]

The ideology's explanation of why profits must be paid to obtain these benefits proceeds along two main lines. First, profits are the indispensable incentive for individuals to save and to invest their savings in productive equipment. Second, profits are the major source, and almost the only possible source today, of investment funds.

The first line of thought explains that the incentive function of profit is a very simple matter.

> Every schoolboy knows that the *incentive* back of every business is *profit* . . . every one of the 18 million shareholders, the *real owners of business* bought those shares under the self-same incentive — *to receive a profit.*[48]

Why is this incentive needed, and how much profit is required to provide it? Warner & Swasey say that the machine-provider "denied himself, and saved up";[49] in another advertisement they liken profits to the interest on savings accounts and dividends on insurance policies enjoyed by "70,000,-000 Americans." [50] The necessity of a rate of return to induce savings would not explain the need for a rate higher than that on government bonds, and the usual explanation of the business creed goes farther.

The central argument stresses the responsibility for the risks of business, and the stress may be a solemn one as in the NAM volumes.

> . . . it is (the investor's) function to bear the non-insurable risks of business . . . This ultimate financial responsibility, this liability for losses . . . cannot be delegated . . . No one who does not have such responsibility can

[44] Warner & Swasey advertisement, *Business Week*, May 7, 1948.

[45] Assn. of American Railroads advertisement, *New Yorker*, Sept. 11, 1948, p. 109.

[46] "The High Cost of Staying in Business" in the Humble house organ.

[47] McGraw-Hill advertisement, "Messages to American Industry," No. 72, *Business Week*, Feb. 26, 1949.

[48] Standard Steel Spring advertisement, *New York Times*, April 26, 1949.

[49] Warner & Swasey advertisement, *Business Week*, May 7, 1948.

[50] Warner & Swasey advertisement, *Business Week*, Jan. 15, 1949.

be an enterpriser; everyone who does have such responsibility is an enterpriser." [51]

It will be remembered that in the NAM treatise the "system" is an "enterprise system" and here we find owners — not managers — vested with the critical label, "enterpriser." [52] Other examples of this theme are abundant. "Profit must pay a sufficiently attractive return to the man who has saved his money to turn that money into risk capital." [53] Both Standard Oil of New Jersey and General Motors explain the high profits of their industries in terms of the high risks of failure;[54] they cite the disappearance of many enterprises from these fields as evidence of the risk involved. Utility companies — telephone, power, railway — repeatedly remind us that expansion of their services is contingent upon their earning enough to attract additional risk capital.[55]

This theme raises two questions: what is the contribution of the passive stockholder as risk-bearer and what return must be paid for risk? The NAM authors get into difficulties over the first. They argue that the contribution of the "enterpriser" is an increase in productivity and that the extent of this increase is somehow related to profits. The function of the "enterpriser" is universally essential to economic activity; it must be performed in the simplest economic system of an isolated family or in a communist, governmentally controlled economy.[56] However, in so arguing the authors are led to shift the meaning of the term "enterpriser"; he becomes concerned with "organization and direction" and as such he is closer to the executive than to the mere owner.[57] What is in effect argued is the indispensability of executive control rather than of risk-bearing. Thus the risk theory of profits shades into another theme, which could receive more explicit ideological emphasis than it does. This is that profits are the reward and incentive for innovation, foresight, and skillful management. The connection between profits and innovation is raised in the specific context of patents and copyrights,[58] but seldom noted elsewhere.

[51] NAM, I: 449.
[52] Compare the qualifying note, NAM, I: 447.
[53] Francis, *Hearings on Profits* (Flanders), p. 209.
[54] *Hearings on Profits* (Flanders), pp. 282, 508.
[55] Examples are numerous. A few are: "Between Ourselves," a public relations release of the New England Telephone and Telegraph Company mailed out with the bills, January 1949; *The Way to Better Rail Transportation,* a statement by R. V. Flc̈cher, President of the Association of American Railroads, published by the Association in Washintgon, March 1947; advertisements of Consolidated Edison Companies, *New York Times,* May 5 and 6, 1949, "Between Ourselves," April 1949; statements at rate hearings by executives of the New York Telephone Company, *New York Times* news story, May 10, 1948; and a Bell System advertisement in *Newsweek,* Nov. 15, 1948.
[56] NAM, I: 464.
[57] The shift in meaning starts early (see NAM, I: 454–455), when an argument is presented that the supply of competent enterprisers is limited.
[58] NAM, I: 593–594.

An evaluation of the theory that profits are the indispensable incentive for undertaking the risks of owning productive equipment raises a number of difficult problems; one can only make a subjective judgment as to whether any particular level of profits is adequate to perform this function. It is important not to draw conclusions for the whole economy from the experience of a particular firm or industry. Clearly, a single firm or industry cannot attract capital without offering a rate of return commensurate with the rewards obtainable elsewhere. This does not prove that society could not obtain the same amount of aggregate capital formation with a lower rate of profit all around. The claim that profit is necessary to reward risk-bearing rests on the assumption that most people do not like to take chances and must be paid for doing so.[59] This is not as self-evident as the business creed's exposition makes it appear; every day millions of people pay to take chances in various kinds of gambling.

The relation between risk and reward must be a loose one in any individual case. The example of General Motors' success serves as an "incentive" for prospective "enterprisers" in quite unrelated lines, and the example of the Tucker Corporation as a disincentive. The whole range of experience of business, from the big prizes to the total losses, influences the investor. Consequently, it may be true from a social point of view that the high profits of General Motors are a necessary incentive: without such examples no one would start a television business. But it is quite consistent with this that the high profits are in the nature of the "windfall or fortuitous gains" which the NAM text is so anxious to dissociate from true profit. Finally, the justification of profits is part of the defense of the System; consequently, it is relevant to ask how much of the risk for which society must pay profits is peculiar to our particular economic organization, that is, to the System itself, and how much is an inherent cost of economic activity under any set of institutions. Competition itself involves risks which might be eliminated in a less decentralized economic order.

The business creed takes a pessimistic view of the adequacy of postwar profits as an incentive for individual investors, ". . . the forgotten man of the present era is the common stockholder, the chap who provides risk capital." [60] A series of advertisements in the *New York Times* suggests that "no other important group in the community has been squeezed as much as has the investor" and that "the stock market, where industry traditionally has raised money from people willing to risk their savings, has been limping along, giving business no chance to get enough money

---

[59] The precise relation of a stockholder's risks to the risks of the enterprise in which he invests is not a simple one. Buying securities in the market, he is subject to risks only very mediately related to the earnings of the companies in which he invests. It may be that the risks of the market serve an ideological function in strengthening the presumption that the stockholder is performing a risk-bearing function for particular companies.

[60] W. A. Paton, *Hearings on Profits* (Flanders), p. 60.

on satisfactory terms." [61] Almost to a man, the business spokesmen who appeared before the Flanders Committee testified that it was impossible to raise equity capital. A *Saturday Evening Post* article, in discussing the financial needs of A.T. & T., compared investors with the kulaks liquidated in the Soviet Union.[62] The usual explanation is the double taxation of corporate profits: they are taxed once when earned by the corporation and again as individual income when they are paid out as dividends. But the government is also blamed in a more general sense. Uncertainty about government policy destroys confidence; McGraw-Hill castigated the President for saying nothing in his 1949 inaugural to resolve the "vital issues now freezing the capital markets." [63] Then there is a quite different explanation: "Selling capital stock is becoming more and more difficult and this condition will continue as long as most corporate earnings must be reinvested in the business instead of being paid out to stockholders as dividends." [64] This leads us to the second function of profits, that of providing a source of funds for tools of production.

The Johns-Manville Company puts it this way: "Profits provide dividends. Dividends help create savings. Savings and industry's profit dollars reinvested in plants and equipment produce new jobs as well as more goods." Adequate profits are "the cake of yeast necessary to make a capitalistic loaf of bread." Plowed-back earnings, "like good fertilizer on good soil, create enlarged crops of new jobs . . . more goods . . . more dividends." [65] But of the two methods by which profits generate investment funds, the retention of earnings receives far greater emphasis than savings from disbursed earnings.

"Plowing-back" is *the* American method of capital formation, according to the business creed. Like profits themselves, it is the essence of the System. The Standard Steel Spring Corporation defines "The American Business System — a System which permits management to assure progress for itself, its employees, and its stockholders by plowing earnings back into the business." [66] The NAM concludes a description of plowing-back, "that's the way the American system works." Plowing-back plays a key role in a primer of the System, "The American Triangle of Plenty." [67]

So enchanted is the business creed with the social beneficence of plowing-back that in some circumstances it is reluctant to count retained earnings as profits at all. "Most profits are never seen by the owners." [68] Part

[61] McGraw-Hill advertisement, *New York Times*, Nov. 19, 1948.

[62] *Saturday Evening Post*, March 19, 1949.

[63] McGraw-Hill advertisement, *Business Week*, Feb. 26, 1949.

[64] Seal (Socony-Vacuum), *Hearings on Profits* (Flanders), p. 586.

[65] Johns-Manville advertisement, *Business Week*, Feb. 26, 1949.

[66] Standard Steel Spring advertisement, *New York Times*, April 5, 1949.

[67] F. C. Crawford, *The American Triangle of Plenty*, distributed by NAM, 1943, p. 67.

[68] Warner & Swasey advertisement, *Business Week*, March 26, 1952.

of the NAM campaign to convince people that profits are not very large is to point out that "about half of what industry does make goes 'right back into the pot' to help pay for the development and expansion that bring more products, more jobs, and greater security for all." [69] Discussing demands for industrial expansion, Warner & Swasey deplores that "profits retained . . . were only large enough to meet 42% of these demands. In order to provide factories, machines, and materials to keep business and employment high, American corporations had to risk their futures by borrowing billions of dollars . . . The question is not whether American corporations made too much money. It is, did they make enough . . ." [70] The *New York Times* says that it is a confusion to identify the corporation with its stockholders and although undistributed profits increase stockholders' equity "They are, broadly speaking, in the nature of a social dividend in which the whole community shares through lower prices, improved quality of product, and greater employment." [71]

The reliance on retained earnings and the weakness of the equity capital market are interconnected, but which is cause and which is effect is not clear. Some hold that the market is weak because earnings are retained and not disbursed as dividends. But the dominant business opinion is that earnings have to be retained because it is impossible to obtain capital otherwise. ". . . if you give it all to the stockholders, by what rhyme or reason do we assume that they are going to save enough and have it ready for you when you want it? . . . we have to take calculated risks in business, but as an administrator I would not care to take that risk." [72] This is backed up by the argument that retaining earnings saves the company and the stockholder both the costs of marketing securities and the personal income tax on dividends.[73] Furthermore, many do not agree that failure to pay profits out in dividends depresses the stock market. They believe, with Mr. Batcheller, that investors are more interested in "the prospects of a continuing return and an increasing return, in the building up of an equity." [74]

There is some inconsistency between the doctrine that plowing-back is the American way of capital formation and the contention that profit is necessary as an incentive for individual investors. If investors are not to be called upon for capital anyway, why worry about the adequacy of their incentive to provide it? Utility companies ruefully note that, since they are regulated, they cannot meet their capital needs from their own

[69] NAM advertisement, *Saturday Evening Post,* July 17, 1948.

[70] Warner & Swasey advertisement, *Business Week,* Nov. 6, 1948.

[71] Editorial, Dec. 18, 1948, quoted in *Businessman's Book of Quotations,* edited by R. L. Woods (New York, 1951).

[72] Francis, *Hearings on Profits* (Flanders), p. 211. See also Coyle (General Motors), *ibid.,* pp. 524–525.

[73] See Francis, *Hearings on Profits* (Flanders), p. 211, and Batcheller (Allegheny-Ludlum Steel Co.), *ibid.,* p. 317.

[74] *Ibid.*

earnings as the rest of industry does, and so they must attract outside funds.[75] Plowing-back means that management, rather than individual stockholders, makes the judgment whether investment in capital facilities promises enough profits to justify the risk. This divorces the stockholder from the direct operation of the profit incentive to undertake capital investment. But management considers itself as a trustee for the stockholder and therefore requires the same incentive. General Motors, according to its spokesman before the Flanders Subcommittee, seeks "expansion of volume on a sustained basis to the maximum extent consistent with stockholder interests . . . employment of the additional capital required for expanding volume may be subject to added hazards and risks and has to be justified by a reasonable prospect for a satisfactory average rate of return over the long term on such additional capital." [76]

The acceptance of plowing-back as a normal and natural method of capital formation is appropriate enough in the managerial version of the business creed. In this strand of the creed, the separation of management from ownership in the large publicly owned corporation is explicitly recognized.[77] The apportionment of profits between dividends to stockholders and retained earnings for reinvestment is only one aspect of the general function of balancing competing economic interests which devolve on corporate management.

But this acceptance is a remarkable departure from the individualism which otherwise pervades the classical version of the creed. The individual stockholder does not have free choice over the disposition of the earnings on his investment. This is decided for him; to say that he participates in such decisions in proportion to his equity flies in the face of reality.[78] The NAM authors remark that plowing-back is most "conservative" and note its great importance as a source of capital; but they make no comment on the relations between plowing-back and the position of the stockholder-entrepreneurs.[79]

---

[75] Bell System advertisement, *Newsweek,* Nov. 15, 1948. "This money cannot come out of the rates you pay for service. It must come from investors . . ." "Between Ourselves," June 1948, a New England Telephone and Telegraph Company publicity document, points out that utilities have "scant profit to plow in."

[76] *Hearings on Profits* (Flanders), p. 511.

[77] *Permanent Revolution,* pp. 77–88. Also, see Peter Drucker, *The Concept of the Corporation* (New York, 1946); W. B. Given, Jr., Chairman of the Board of the American Brake Shoe Corporation in *The Social Responsibilities of Management,* a symposium published by New York University, School of Commerce, Accounts and Finance (1940); J. F. Bell, Chairman of the Board, General Mills, "The Shadow of Dead Men's Reasoning," *The Management Review,* 36: 620–622 (1947).

[78] The statement of Mr. Dunlop that the "owners of the oil industry, the stockholders, to whom the profits rightfully belong, have permitted their companies to reinvest a major portion of their profit money" (*Hearings on Profits* (Flanders), p. 266) is not distinguished by its realism.

[79] NAM, I: 383. The whole discussion occupies one paragraph of a fifty-six-page chapter on "Savings and Capital Formation." Three pages are given to a discussion of the functions of investment bankers.

In neo-classical economic theory (upon which the classical version of the business creed is largely modeled), established enterprises with plans for expansion must compete with new ventures in the market for investment funds and both must compete for funds with consumption. Theoretically, this competition ensures that the amount of resources drawn away from consumption for investment purposes accords with the preferences of the owners of investible resources. It should also ensure that the investment projects actually undertaken are those which, in the eyes of the individual investors, promise the best rate of return, and consequently the best use of the community's resources.[80] Plowing-back insulates the expansion projects of existing firms from the test of the market, and further, gives them an important advantage over projected new firms in securing funds.

A solution to these difficulties is sometimes found in the freedom of the dissatisfied stockholder to sell his stock, a freedom which the NAM text invokes as the general protection of the individual stockholder.[81] Assuming that the retention of earnings adds to the market value of the stock, the individual stockholder can reap what is denied him in dividends by realizing some capital gains. These he can then invest — or consume — according to his own preferences. In this case one can assume that the market has approved the management's use of the retained earnings; but presumably the market would also have taken up a new issue of stock for the same purpose. But if the market appraises unfavorably the prospects of further investment in the company, the stockholders will not be able to capture their earnings by selling stock. Under these circumstances, the management would also have had difficulty selling new stock. But plowing-back enables the management to go ahead with its investment projects anyway, even if the appraisal of the market is that the funds could be better used elsewhere. Any satisfactory reconciliation of plowing-back with the interests and free choices of individual stockholders is bound to undermine both the business creed's claim that retained earnings should not be counted in reckoning the size of profits and its contention that profits are inadequate to attract new equity capital in the market.

SEPARATION OF OWNERSHIP AND CONTROL

The difficulties of reconciling extensive plowing-back with the classical version of the creed is only one example of the ideological problems posed by the separation of ownership from management in the large corporation

---

[80] Dunlop, *Hearings on Profits* (Flanders), p. 262, reflects this view in listing as one of the functions of profits that "they act as a guide and a regulator of the flow of capital funds."

[81] NAM, I: 452.

today.[82] The dispersion of corporate ownership, even though it makes conspicuous the rewarding of mere passive ownership, can be favorably exploited by the ideology on another front. We have heard in Chapter 3 the boasts of corporations about the great armies of everyday Americans who are their stockholders. But it leads to embarrassment, evident in abundant ideological discussion, on another score — justifying the divorce of the property-owner from control over his property. In general, the classical strand in the creed emphasizes the various controls stockholders have over management, without attempting a rounded assessment of their relations. Thus, Mr. Queeny can point to the power of minority stockholders to sue the directors if they are unfairly treated, and can argue that in general the Board of Directors controls only so long as it commands the confidence of the shareholders. Where directors have held long tenure, as in A.T. & T., it is because of the "general wisdom and excellence of their stewardship." [83]

The NAM treatise puts its chief emphasis on the power of the dissatisfied stockholder to express his disapproval by selling his holdings, although it also mentions the power of a dissatisfied majority to change the management.[84] While discussing the propriety of calling stockholders "enterprisers" although they are divorced from active participation in the management of the company, the NAM authors admit that many stockholders cannot identify the board of directors or executive officials of the companies in which they invest.[85] Yet the man who buys stock from a dissatisfied holder "necessarily is satisfied with the management and the outlook for the company, or else he would not buy the stock." [86] A decline in the market price of a company's stock is thus an appraisal of the management by the combined judgment of the sellers; thus the market is a control on management. While it suffers from the limitations of indirection, it has the virtues of diffusing ownership and permitting those of small means to participate as enterprisers in large corporations. The dubious character of this argument does not need to be labored.

[82] First discussed by A. A. Berle, Jr. and G. C. Means in *The Modern Corporation and Private Property* (New York, 1932). For a recent discussion, see R. A. Gordon, *Business Leadership in the Large Corporation* (Washington, 1945).

[83] Queeny, *Spirit of Enterprise*, p. 98. The discussion is in the context of an attack on the TNEC findings on centralization of control in corporations. There is no discussion, other than the mention of the right to sue, of the machinery by which directors and managers are removed when they cease to command the confidence of the shareholders.

[84] NAM, I: 452–453.

[85] NAM, I: 450–451.

[86] NAM, I: 452.

5

THE BUSINESS EXECUTIVE

THE LABOR OF MANAGEMENT

HOW IS THE MANAGER OF THE ENTERPRISE, as distinguished from the owner, described in business ideology? Although open accusations that the manager is an idle parasite are by no means as common in America as elsewhere, business executives feel that their functions and problems are not widely understood. A correspondent of *Dun's Review* offers a formidable picture of executives' problems to counter the alleged belief of employees that "an executive has nothing to do." [1] *Business Week,* editorializing on the length of a work week, impresses on its readers how hard managers work.[2] The Fortune Executive Forecast's effort to survey executives' working hours was surely motivated by more than simple curiosity.[3]

THE MANAGERIAL TALENT

It is more difficult to define just what the executive does during his long hours, and to explain why the executive role is so important.

In groping for a central element in the activities of management a recent spokesman suggested, "Primarily, we make decisions." [4] The importance of decision-making is, not surprisingly, widely stressed.[5] Mr. Ruml sees the business system as one which concentrates decision-making in the managers and provides an escape from decision-making for most employees.[6] The businessman is also distinguished by the manner in which

[1] Letter of Walter E. Johnson, Industrial and Management Engineer, Chicago, *Dun's Review,* July 1951, p. 8.

[2] *Business Week,* Jan. 22, 1949.

[3] *Fortune,* October 1946, p. 5. Reproduced in detail in *Management Review,* 36: 66–67 (1947).

[4] T. R. Jones, "Obligations of Leadership in an Evolving Society," *Dun's Review,* March 1949, pp. 11 ff.

[5] Calumet & Hecla Consolidated Copper Company, Inc. advertisement, "The Man of Decisions . . . the Plant Manager," *Fortune,* February 1951, p. 136.

[6] "Business does not eliminate from life the necessity for decision, but it does change the position of those who exercise decision by removing the power and responsibility from those for whom it is a burden." Ruml, *Tomorrow's Business,* p. 42.

he makes decisions; emphasis is put on his "hard-boiled" rationality, realism, and "practicality." Examples of such claims are most abundant where businessmen are scolding the executives of other organizations for deficiencies in these qualities. Mr. Boulware, a vice president of General Electric, writes that unions apparently ignore the "hard rule" learned early in business that "we can make good decisions only on the basis of full information" and goes on to claim that "we accordingly withhold making decisions until after we are sure we have all the important facts." [7]

Business executives "do not think on emotional grounds. Reason dominates their thinking." Here Mr. Queeny contrasts the sober rationality of business executives with the vagaries of "New Dealers," those "underpaid and underworked professors (who) have theory as their forte (and) no commercial experience." [8] He takes the allegation that Thorstein Veblen was weak at mathematics as an occasion to link business and the queen of the sciences.

Mathematics is the key to business accounts . . . Business' books must mathematically balance . . . Workers in fields founded on mathematics have confidence in facts and reason. They usually have vision and faith, and seek adventure.[9]

Presumably as a consequence of this careful resort to facts and ratiocination, a peculiarly sober realism is claimed for business executives. They are sharply aware that "it is impractical to obtain something for nothing and on general principles they do not try." [10] They are sensible about the difficulties of commercial success and know it is a "slow and painful process." [11] In short, compared with everyone else the business manager "is, or should be, the smartest; is, with the agriculturalist, the most practical; knows how to get things done." [12]

Any evaluation of these ideological claims requires some examination of executive roles in general, and of the business executive's role in particular. Mr. Queeny's linking of business and mathematics provides a convenient starting point. The comparison is curious. In contrast to the proverbial certainty of mathematical demonstrations, it is precisely the uncertainty involved in executive decisions which distinguishes the executive role from many others. Compare, for example, the role of a technical specialist, which is free of uncertainty, and involves little "decision-making." The need for genuine decisions, in contrast to routine application of

[7] L. R. Boulware, *What About a Fourth Round of Wage Increases?* May 16, 1949, p. 4.

[8] Queeny, *Spirit of Enterprise,* pp. 40–41.

[9] *Ibid.,* pp. 64–65.

[10] G. Carpenter, *Dollars and Sense* (New York, 1928), p. 7.

[11] Queeny, *Spirit of Enterprise,* pp. 40–41.

[12] Jones, "Obligations of Leadership," p. 44.

rules, is born of uncertainty. Walter Bagehot, a nineteenth-century English businessman, came nearer to the truth than Mr. Queeny when he said that businessmen "have lived all their lives in an atmosphere of probabilities and of doubt, where nothing is very clear." [13] This is the essence of executive roles in institutions other than businesses, too. Whether businessmen themselves are peculiarly rational and clearheaded compared with, say, labor leaders or civil servants, is a difficult judgment.

Hostile remarks about "experts" suggest that business executives are sometimes uncomfortably aware of the differences between their own and specialized technical roles. *Business Week* once interviewed a crusty North Carolinian businessman, who proclaimed, "I don't like that damned word 'experts'" and berated the ignorance of various aspirants to the label.[14] Mr. Batcheller, of Allegheny-Ludlum Steel, brought forth a time-honored condemnation when he contradicted "various experts who do not have to meet a payroll." [15] Executive roles are intrinsically vulnerable in this sort of comparison with "experts." The executive's functions of coordination and supervision imply that he cannot become too closely engaged with details, and it is easy to draw the conclusion that he knows "nothing in particular." Mr. Johnson, writing in *Dun's Review,* gets over this hurdle by asserting aggressively that the higher level executive has to watch patiently while his subordinates fumble through tasks which he could do more efficiently himself. Yet even this leaves open the difficult question of assigning a clear domain of knowledge and capacity to the executive; he is a "specialist in generality."

In this context it is frequently pointed out that business ability is not a widely distributed talent. There is real content to the job of business management, and not everybody can run a business. The Chamber of Commerce of the United States reports with satisfaction the failure of a trade union attempt to run a grocery store; it invites unions to make further adventures into business in order to give their members some appreciation of the skills which businessmen possess.[16] Similarly, *Business Week* reports that the success of a group of Cleveland businessmen in restoring solvency to a hospital is a lesson to the doctors involved and to the general public in the unique skills of business.[17] The ideology further

[13] *English Constitution* (Oxford World Classics edition), p. 127.

[14] *Business Week,* May 7, 1949, pp. 58 ff. A Moore and White Co., advertisement (*Fortune,* February 1951, p. 205), proclaims, "The Long Hair Approach is Out. We don't do it a certain way just because the book says so. Our engineers are strictly grass-roots operators . . . practical men . . . (with) experience, and the desire to serve."

[15] *Hearings on Profits* (Flanders), p. 299. The fact that probably the great majority of present-day corporate executives have never "met a payroll" (in the sense of personal financial responsibility) has not caused the phrase to disappear.

[16] U.S. Chamber of Commerce, *Economic Intelligence,* July 1949.

[17] *Business Week,* Feb. 19, 1949, pp. 30–34.

claims that business skills are trained skills, not simply unusual native apti-
tudes. This implies some common fund of knowledge which businessmen
acquire and others do not. Increasing stress has been placed in recent years
on the specialized knowledge and skills required of business executives.
This attempt to establish management as a profession is prominent in the
managerial theme in business ideology. Each year, in awarding the degree
of Master of Business Administration to the graduating class of the Business School, the President of Harvard refers to business as "the oldest of
the arts and the youngest of the professions." "The mid-century business
man has had to go to school — in labor, in politics, and in social welfare,"
according to *Fortune*. Evidently he doesn't necessarily have to go to a
formal school of business; but if he doesn't, he has to acquire the same
schooling on the job and by independent study.

"Today's business man," continues *Fortune,* "brings a new professional
responsibility to his day-to-day problems." [18] The standards of this professional responsibility are also a concern of the ideology. They are defined
in the "serving all four" formulas discussed in Chapter 3 above and more
elaborately and formally, in suggested codes of business conduct.[19]

Despite these efforts, it is clear that society does not yet recognize
business as a profession or accord to it the same prestige which the leading professions command.[20] It is interesting to note that pharmacists and
undertakers seek professional status by differentiating themselves from
the run of businessmen.[21] One obvious objective difference between business and the established professions may be superficial in itself but nonetheless important in shaping attitudes. There is no established legal requirement for admission to the occupation of business. No examination
must be passed or educational degree obtained, and no certificate or
license is granted the individual entering the occupation.

Despite these efforts to establish management as a profession, the
theme that unsystematic "practicality" is the key attribute of the business
executive still takes first place in the ideology. Its prominence is related
to a central institutional feature of the business executive's role. It is commonly accepted in our society that the success or failure of an enterprise
depends almost entirely on the efficiency or inefficiency of its management.
This belief survives in the face of obvious evidence to the contrary; the
general state of the economy is clearly beyond the individual's control;

[18] *Fortune* advertisement in New York *Herald Tribune,* Sept. 4, 1951.

[19] See the Hippocratic oath for businessmen suggested by Clarence Francis in
Responsibilities of Business Leadership, p. 10.

[20] See, for example, polls reported in *Public Opinion 1935–1946,* edited by
H. Cantril (Princeton, 1951), p. 529. For further discussion of this matter, see Chapter 16.

[21] See *Casket and Sunnyside,* the undertakers' journal; a student paper, "The
Retail Druggist," by Charles A. Sletten of Harvard has reviewed for us the efforts of
pharmacists to obtain professional status.

and many important contingencies may be so difficult to predict that any correct prediction can only be a lucky one. Yet if a small business firm is unable to meet its financial obligations, the owner-manager must "fail." His work is not evaluated, say, by some impartial board which might come out with the conclusion that he has been an admirable businessman even though his business is bankrupt. The basic definition is that he has "failed." [22] In the same way the Lynds in *Middletown in Transition* reported the extraordinary assumptions of personal responsibility among unemployed workers during the depression; even though they were aware that great numbers like themselves were out of work and that "conditions were bad," they assumed that if they really had had the intelligence and initiative they would have been able to find a job.[23] Within this tradition individuals have had to assume heavy responsibilities for failures but they are also free to claim credit for successes. Managing a successful business has been treated as a legitimate claim to high regard, on the assumption that executive competence is crucial in the success attained.

The ideological reactions to this situation are of the greatest interest; as we shall see, the creed makes little attempt to alter the definitions to make them easier on the businessman or more clearly suited to his effective powers.

An NAM vice-president has used the well-known high rates of establishment and failure of small businesses as a pretext for quoting Emerson's remark that "a successful business is but the lengthening shadow of a man." [24] This spokesman argued that there is essentially no profit in the American System because investors in business never get their money back; businesses grow through the genius of some individual and then recede and fail when he passes on. Insofar as the small firm becomes the ideological model for the total economy, there is in this theme an obvious way in which the decisions of a single individual, the owner-manager, can be raised to crucial importance.

The growth of large, impersonal, and enduring managerial enterprises has not, however, muted the claims of the importance of business executives. Indeed, Beardsley Ruml has argued that the corporation has made differential executive abilities even more important. "Modern science and technology has multiplied the differential productivity of talent manyfold." [25] If General Motors is big and able to stay big relative to its competitors, the reason is said to lie in the ability of the people operating the business. "So long as GM can attract and retain capable people that will

[22] Compare the boards which investigate the responsibility of military officers for accidents and reverses.

[23] R. S. and H. M. Lynd, *Middletown in Transition*, New York 1937, pp. 127, 447.

[24] Utley, *The American System*, p. 137.

[25] Ruml, *Tomorrow's Business*, p. 110.

do a better competitive job than the other fellow, we can't help but be larger than the other fellow." [26]

High executive talent is assumed to be scarce and at least one author has analyzed the reasons for this scarcity in terms of the distribution of complex abilities.[27] This assumption, combined with that of the manager's responsibility for the success or failure of an organization, leads to statements like those of Gerald W. Loeb:

> No price was too high to have paid Walter P. Chrysler to go to work for the obscure and failing Maxwell-Chalmers Corp. and build it up into one of the big three motormakers. No low figure, paid the managements of the small independents that at the same time fell by the wayside, could possibly have been a bargain.[28]

Ruml shares this judgment of the importance of executive competence and thinks it unlikely that a small company which pays for high talent will be a small company for long.[29] The problem of recognizing executive talent in advance, spotting a Chrysler *before* he has succeeded, is not faced. But unless there is some definition of talent other than achieved success and achieved high salary, there is little meaning to the argument that it is necessary to pay high for talent.

This emphasis of the business ideology makes a striking comparison with Marxism, in which no value was originally attached to executive competence. For example, Lenin thought that a socialist society could be effectively run with no specially qualified executives.[30] Such views have been relatively inconspicuous in America, although they appeared in the thought of Veblen and the technocrats.

There can be no doubt that Lenin grossly underestimated the importance of executive talent. Business ideologists are much nearer the mark;[31] but they exaggerate the critical importance of the executive for

[26] Mr. Coyle before the *Hearing on Profits* (Flanders), p. 573.

[27] Carl Synder, *Capitalism the Creator* (New York, 1940), chs. XIV, XV.

[28] From the *Investor,* quoted in *Time,* April 10, 1950, p. 84. Mr. Loeb is a partner in the Wall Street firm of E. F. Hutton & Company.

The writer continues with remarks about the "mistakes of corporate officers hired purely on a low-price basis." Is it presumed that there is a clear relation between the "supply-price" of executives and their susceptibility to error? Compare the following moral tale: "We once knew a chap who with a total capital of $15,000 started in competition with his former employer and spent $5,000 the first year advertising that the reason he could undersell his former employer was because he had no expense for high-salaried executives. Naturally he went broke." Carpenter, *Dollars and Sense,* p. 169.

[29] Ruml, *Tomorrow's Business,* p. 113.

[30] B. Moore, Jr., *Soviet Politics* (Cambridge, Mass., 1950), reviews the ideology and Soviet experience in this matter.

[31] Businessmen stress the crucial importance of executive talent in contexts which are definitely non-ideological. See Oswald Knauth, *Managerial Enterprise* (New York, 1948), pp. 58–79, 186–187; Powell in *Individual Initiative in Business,* edited by G. H. Allen (Cambridge, Mass., 1950), pp. 158–162, where presumed executive

the success or failure of the enterprise. As noted above, business ideology makes the manager fully responsible for results while he lacks full control over the factors which produce them. This exaggeration may be a convenient source of proud boasts, but when things go badly, it may involve acceptance of unjustified blame. The ideology takes a sporting stand. If it accords high honors for achievement, it does not readily admit excuses for failures. Altogether, it is far from obvious why the ideology should follow these institutionalized definitions of the managerial role and reinforce such extremes of responsibility.[32]

MANAGERIAL RESPONSIBILITIES

The ideology does not ignore uncomfortable implications of this stand. On the contrary, the special responsibilities of business executives are given great emphasis. "Business" is often contrasted favorably with "government" or "bureaucracy" on this score. Mr. Queeny declares that business is much freer from "buck-passing" than government. In business, "every manufacturer is responsible for the quality of his finished product." Not only in the top levels of management but all down the line in business, responsibility is assigned in ways not characteristic of bureaucracies, which "trust no one." If the abhorred "planned state" should come "businessmen would no longer have a near monopoly on gastric ulcers and bad hearts"; the ex-businessmen would probably have lower salaries but much lighter responsibilities.[33]

This particular business executive puts "competition" as the determining factor behind the exceptional responsibilities imposed on businessmen. It is not simply that businessmen are "naturally" morally superior to governmental bureaucrats: they are forced to be more responsible themselves and to exact responsibility from subordinates if their businesses are not to be eliminated by competition (p. 125). But there are many statements elsewhere which have a simple categorical moral stress to them. In discussing the difficult markets of the thirties, W. J. Cameron once put the issue in uncompromising terms:

(The businessman's) job is to *sell;* if he thinks he does that when he merely urges others to buy, he is mistaken. He is asking them to do their part and his part too. Anything that encourages a businessman to rely on anyone's doing what he is responsible for, is . . . harmful to him . . .[34]

competence appears as the crucial concern of an organization seeking small business investments. Thus the evidence is strong that businessmen "really believe" what the ideology proclaims on this point.

[32] This is a problem that will be considered below.

[33] Queeny, *Spirit of Enterprise,* pp. 125–131, 159–160.

[34] Ford Hour, Nov. 13, 1938.

See also Boulware, "Fourth Round," pp. 14–15, and the responsibility for activity and optimism noted in Chapter 12 below.

Mr. Cameron was not explicit on what more businessmen could do to increase sales than to "urge others to buy," and it seems perfectly clear that he was not offering them concrete advice. He was rather urging an extreme assumption of "responsibility" under which *no* appeal to difficult conditions could be an admissible excuse for inadequate sales; the only accounting that Mr. Cameron will hear is that the businessman with insufficient sales has not done his part. He would subject the businessman to a harsh and categorical moral precept.

The difficulties imposed by "responsibility" are often welcomed cheerfully in the ideology, not regarded as an unfortunate burden of the business executive. Mr. Boulware of General Electric hailed the return of a buyer's market after the easier markets of the war years. Businessmen may find it hard "really to go to work again" but it is only in a buyer's market that they exercise ingenuity and courage, and so make "real progress!" [35] Mr. Boulware would also remind us that we have a profit *and loss* system, an emphasis which is commonly directed at businessmen themselves. Thus S. Wells Utley proclaims that if businessmen are to have the right to run their own businesses and share in profits, they "must take responsibility for accepting losses." [36]

It is hardly surprising that the business ideology treats success in business as evidence of the possession of fine personal qualities. Whereas in a hostile tradition, like the Marxian, those who triumph in the competitive struggle may be looked on simply as more rapacious or scheming than others, the presumption in the business creed is that successful executives have been "smart," "practical," and "sound." Proven capacity to "meet a payroll" may indeed be deemed a qualification for a great variety of tasks.[37]

MANAGERIAL AUTHORITY

Compared to its abundant treatment of the responsibilities of the business executive, the business creed makes little mention of his authority over other individuals. This is perhaps because executive authority has not been seriously challenged in America. There have been no extreme claims for "industrial democracy" of the sort which were made after World War

[35] Boulware, "Fourth Round," pp. 11–12.
[36] Utley, *The American System*, p. 215.
[37] The charges that F. D. R. was not a fit president of the United States because of his business history may be recalled. Business success may be a qualification for general discourse on the economy. Some two decades ago an American businessman chose to answer Stuart Chase and F. R. Schlink, *Your Money's Worth* (New York, 1937), in a book we have cited. He prefaced his reply with a statement of his own and his opponents' qualifications to discuss the questions in hand. Chase and Schlink, he found, had "never met a payroll" whereas "under our management our company has paid every obligation promptly when due with one hundred cents on the dollar." (Carpenter, *Dollars and Sense*, pp. x, xi.)

I in Germany or in the Soviet Union, with broad demands for "control from below" in industrial organizations. Subsidiary to general arguments for socialism, there have been assaults on the right of ownership to ultimate control. But the authoritarian structure of the enterprise has *in itself* hardly been a focus of much discussion. It is usually accepted that the executives of a business enterprise should be determined by the owner, and not "democratically" by the "workers" or some other interested body. The actual operation of business has been to a striking degree "monarchical," that is, with a single head directing normal operations. The powers of executives to determine the formal organization and to select personnel have been very extensive; they have been jealously defended where felt to be subject to "encroachment." Explicit definition of their own authority by business executives has largely tended to be *ad hoc,* as our consideration of labor relations in Chapter 6 below will show.

The creed resists in various ways any image of the business executive as an authoritarian figure of high status. The businessman is depicted as one who either has built up his own business from small beginnings or has risen through a long organizational hierarchy. N. W. Ayer and Sons urge: "When you think of the head of a big business, think of a young man who once drew an envelope at the end of the week with $13.40 in it." [38] Individual corporations[39] like to report the modest beginnings of their own top executives.

The "human relations" movement with its emphasis on "teamwork" and "telling people what's going on" has generally tended to minimize explicit stress on authority as such. A recent survey by *Dun's Review* reported answers by prominent executives to the question "What Should a President Do?" [40] Stress on teamwork and analogies to baseball were so prominent in the replies that the editors evoked the memory of Tinker-to-Evers-to-Chance and provided a cut of the first baseman of this legendary combination. Benjamin Fairless of United States Steel considered himself a playing manager, while A. S. Igleheart of General Foods Corporation prefered to manage from the dugout. The analogy, as pointed out in Chapter 3, stresses the need for common effort toward a common goal rather than discipline over subordinates interested only in their pay.

The emphasis of the creed on wide diffusion of information about management's activities suggests anxiety on the part of the business managers that they might be suspected of possessing "hidden power." In the *Dun's Review* symposium, Mr. Specht, President of Armour and Company, urges that full information be given to all employees. The management of Standard Oil of New Jersey stresses that they have tried

[38] See note 67.
[39] Bell System, railroads, etc.
[40] *Dun's Review,* July 1951, pp. 13 ff.

sincerely to keep stockholders and the general public informed on their activities.[41] Whereas Marxist ideology emphasizes that economic relationships are power relationships, business ideology tends to view private economic relationships as purely voluntaristic. The business creed treats market relationships as voluntary contracts between equals; similarly, it views the firm as a network of voluntary cooperative relationships, either contractual bonds in the classical creed or quasi-familial bonds in the managerial creed. In this fashion the business creed tends to eliminate power problems from the discussion of the business firm and to confine them to discussions of the coercive authority of government. Some writers express distaste for the whole question of the locus and distribution of power,[42] but there are others who take pains to examine the question in detail.[43] Chapter 4 has already examined the creed's treatment of the division of power between owners and managers. In subsequent chapters the ideology's discussion of business power toward other groups in the society will be discussed.

THE MOTIVATIONS AND REWARDS OF THE BUSINESS EXECUTIVE

The motivations of an individual in any role are characteristically manifold and complex. Motivations may include intrinsic satisfaction in the tasks expected, instrumental advantages of varied sorts (money income is one type), the "self-satisfaction" of behaving "decently," and many other factors. A balanced and systematic picture of the motivational forces characteristic in a role is by no means easy. This is one of the core problems of social science, and at present there are certainly no more than rough beginnings of a satisfactory systematic approach. In view of the difficulty of the problem, it is not surprising that the business creed fails to provide a systematic treatment of the motivations of the business executive, although it contains considerable reference to the importance of incentives, of the profit motive, of feelings of responsibility.

An examination of the creed's discussion of the motivations of the businessman can conveniently begin with the classical strand of business ideology, although its analysis is not very conspicuous in the present-day creed. The "classical" strand of business ideology is historically rooted in the broad philosophical tradition known as utilitarianism, to which the dominant Anglo-American tradition in economics is closely related. It shares with more academic economic thought a central concern with certain special empirical features of our Western society. These are the data of market transactions and pecuniary calculations. Commodity

---

[41] *Report of the Annual Meeting,* 1949, p. 16.

[42] Chester Barnard, in a talk reported in *Change and the Entrepreneur* (Cambridge, Mass., 1949).

[43] Ruml, *Tomorrow's Business,* ch. IV, *passim.*

prices, wage rates, interest, and profits are analyzed with an eye to understanding their quantitative variation; and this analysis requires some theoretical assumptions relating to motivation. The assumptions suggested by the term "economic man" have been a fruitful source of analytical results. In professional economics this apparatus has been subjected to the restraints of parsimony and elegance and kept to certain minimal assumptions about preference schedules. But the tradition leads, especially in ideology, to stronger presumptions about motivations.

Concerning the occupational role of an individual, economics has asked only, "What price must be paid to secure the participation of the individual?" It follows that the economist need analyze motivations only insofar as they have a direct bearing on the wage, salary, or profit that must be paid to secure the individual's participation. Within this narrow context, the economist is justified in treating people as if their only positive interest in their jobs were in the rewards. Other motivations are excluded from economic analysis because they are irrelevant, not because their existence or their importance is denied.

The restricted interest of the economist is not logically bound up with any particular set of views on occupational motivations. In fact, it has become so through the common tendency to assume that an abstract idea mirrors a concrete situation; in this process certain elements of the original idea are given more specific and elaborate meaning than they possessed originally. Ideologies in particular are peculiarly susceptible to this "misplaced concreteness" and the business ideology is no exception.[44] Here the abstract assumption of the economist is extended to an empirical proposition as to which motivations are most important. In the classical view, the motivation of workers is intimately and exclusively related to wages; "work" is conceived to be a deprivation or burden with the wage reward as pecuniary compensation for the "disutility" of work. (The classical view is undoubtedly influenced by a tradition of rather sharp distinction between "work" and "leisure"; with the presumption that one "enjoys" leisure but "works" only to provide means for other enjoyments.) The motivations of the independent entrepreneur and of the business executive have been less clearly interpreted along these lines. But there has certainly been a tendency to treat performance in these roles as involving only "disutility," with the pecuniary return in profits or salaries as compensation for the tedium, worry, and effort endured. It is obvious that such views are at best abstract or one-sided. Intuitively, and hence unsystematically, those acquainted with our society know better than to regard the view as comprehensive of all strategic factors.

In the sphere of the business executive, the classical tradition in both economics and business ideology has spoken in terms of a "profit

---

[44] See, for example, Utley, *The American System,* p. 143.

motive." As Professor Parsons has shown in a well-known essay,[45] to speak of a "profit motive" is misleading, since the term "motive" suggests a part of the given, natural equipment of individuals, regardless of their participation in particular social institutions. It is certainly evident that the businessman's motivation to make a profit is not a simple acquisitiveness in this sense; profits are made only in the contexts of business enterprises, in other words in a particular kind of social organization and the "profit motive" thus must refer to motivations understandable only within an institutional context. All of this becomes very clear and explicit in the managerial strands of the business ideology, as we shall see, but it has often been obscured in the classical tradition. Where the institutional framework of business is not explicitly noted, the fact that motivations are dependent on that framework can hardly receive proper recognition. Thus, the motivation of the businessman to make a profit very readily appears as simple "selfishness" or "lust for money." Here again the conceptual scheme used for dealing with economic problems focuses attention on certain abstract categories; these are then confused with concrete reality and are given an exclusive or at least a prominent position.

In the classical view, then, a businessman is interested in the financial state of his business primarily because it determines his income. Any source of satisfaction in the role other than money income is ignored. Our NAM vice-president once admitted that there are some people who work because they somehow enjoy it, but in good classical fashion he regarded this as more or less accidental and atypical.[46] In an interesting argument, Klein interprets the "profit motive" in terms of the uses of the personal income so attained:

Search history as we may, and we can find but two motives which ever have stimulated man to economic activity beyond the most meager requirements of subsistence. Those two motives are (1) the desire for personal advancement and (2) fear . . . The desire for self-aggrandizement may be evidenced by the purchase of the finest yacht afloat. It may also be expressed in the much less obtrusive personal satisfaction which comes from doing well for one's family and appearing well before one's neighbors. Fear is fear . . .
. . . Personal advancement is whatever raises the individual in his own estimation. Such increased self-esteem may come with clothes and jewelry. It may come from the ability to contribute largely to charities. It need not be, and usually is not, unworthy. The personal desires most Americans strive to satisfy are decent and honorable.[47]

This discussion is specifically tied to a justification of profits. The motivations to profit-making are the two listed; once "fear" is allayed "personal

[45] Parsons, "The Motivation of Economic Activities," *Sociological Theory*.
[46] Utley, *The American System*, pp. 143–145.
[47] Klein, *How to Stay Rich*, pp. 99, 100.

advancement" becomes important and here, curiously, the only specified modes are in the form of expenditures. Such things as the prestige of running a large organization are neglected.

Views like Klein's, which interpret profits and the money compensation of businessmen primarily from the point of view of consumption behavior, are not widespread. The notion that businessmen go into business primarily to make money in order to increase their personal consumption has been widely resisted in this country. American businessmen express surprise at their European colleagues who seem indeed to go into business in the hope of accumulating sufficient means to get out of it as soon as possible.[48] To W. J. Cameron, those who retire when they have "made enough" are "deserters."[49] Mr. Queeny criticizes high salaries in good Puritan fashion; they may encourage extravagant living at the expense of devotion to work and duty.[50] Such statements confirm a general impression that American businessmen do not really work for money alone; for an adult male American, having a job is so much the expected pattern that there is little place for the wealthier man of leisure. The feeling that a man should go on working even though his wealth would permit him to retire at an early age is certainly not restricted to a few unreconstructed Puritans in our society but is very widely accepted.[51]

The strong intrinsic motivations of business roles are so manifest on the American scene that it is not surprising that they gain some expression in business ideology. Discussions of executives' salaries and their relation to corporate profits bring these motivations to the fore. The conspicuous fact that most of the executives in large enterprises are compensated by salaries and bonuses set at the discretion of others (usually the Board of Directors) makes apparent a gap between profits and rewards. Yet in the classical view the profits are supposedly the outcome of and incentive for executives' efforts. The common solution is to treat profits as "markers" or indices of achievement and thus as symbols.[52] Queeny has suggested that other symbols such as "scrambled eggs on visors" might be used. But he argues that, for top management at least, profits are a "natural marker, since they are directly related to the expressions of approval or disapproval of the ultimate judges — the consumers."[53]

[48] Jesse Rainsford Sprague, *High Pressure: What it is doing to my town and to my neighbors* (New York, 1938).

[49] Ford Hour, March 16, 1941.

[50] Queeny, *Spirit of Enterprise*, p. 41.

[51] The widespread fear of retirement is evidence in point. This tends to be expressed in pecuniary terms as a fear of loss of income, "economic security," and the like, but American men are so strongly motivated to regard their status and activities as contingent on an occupation that they tend to be "lost without a job."

[52] See, for example, *Hearings on Profits* (Flanders), p. 262.

[53] Queeny, *The Spirit of Enterprise*, p. 41.

How is the spectacularly high remuneration of some executives treated in the ideology? In most societies one finds a reasonably good correspondence between income and prestige, but in America there are extraordinary exceptions to the rule. For instance, eight executives in General Motors each receive compensation more than three times that of the President of the United States.[54] A Justice of the Supreme Court, whose job has been shown in repeated surveys to possess higher prestige than any other in the country,[55] receives $25,000 a year. Yet in 1950, both E. I. duPont de Nemours and General Motors were paying eight not-so-old men salaries and bonuses to the tune of $300,000 each. Top-ranking executives generally receive far more than top-ranking professionals, although the professions tend to outrank business executive roles in prestige. However, there is reason to believe that within the business world itself the correlation between income and prestige holds good.[56]

The theme most commonly found in the ideology is that high compensations are necessary to induce the best talent, which is assumed to be scarce,[57] to take on the responsibilities of high executive positions. Thomas McElroy, president of Procter and Gamble, sees in the present income tax structure a serious barrier to offering the requisite inducements.[58] An identification of "responsibility" and "disutility" seems to be assumed; there is no suggestion that the prestige and nonpecuniary advantages of a high position might compensate for additional "worry" even if the salary were actually less. The well-known pressures on people in business hierarchies to be ambitious[59] and to accept the challenge of new responsibilities are also neglected in this view. A man who dislikes heavy responsibility is unlikely to say so when he refuses a promotion; he will rationalize his decision in terms of income and say, for instance, that he cannot afford to move.

Beardsley Ruml has devoted himself with characteristic independence

[54] SEC figures reported in the *New York Times,* June 10, 1951, p. 60.

[55] The leading study is that of Cecil North and Paul Hatt. Compare W. Kolb & L. Wilson, *Sociological Analysis* (New York, 1950); or R. Bendix & S. M. Lipsett, *Class, Status, and Power* (Glencoe, Ill., 1954).

[56] It is true that some professional men, notably the famous corporation lawyers, have made very large incomes. This is even true of some physicians. But there is a very poor relation within the professions between income and prestige. Certainly Charles Evans Hughes's status in the legal profession was much more enhanced by being Chief Justice than by his reputedly huge income as a corporation lawyer.

[57] Sometimes the issue of the abundance of the requisite talent may be neglected, and it is simply assumed that people who handle large sums of money ought to be well paid. "If commerce is cursed with anything it is the habit of buying cheap talent. We have known of purchasing agents who have been responsible for the purchase of five million dollars of commodities per year who have been paid a clerk's salary." Carpenter, *Dollars and Sense,* p. 189.

[58] Allen, *Individual Initiative in Business,* pp. 14–15.

[59] Stressed by Chester Barnard and others; compare E. P. Learned, D. N. Ulrich, and D. R. Booz, *Executive Action* (Cambridge, Mass., 1951), p. 40.

and originality to these problems. He refuses to argue that very high incomes are wholesome for those able to get them, or that they are wholesome for the community or nation.[60] That they occur he takes to be a consequence of competitive bidding for scarce talents. The assumed motivation only appears when he traces out the consequences of a law limiting compensation. The consequence would be "to deprive the generation of a substantial and irreplaceable portion of the productiveness of its highest genius," since "high talent can work part time, and that is exactly what would happen if the rate of pay per month, per year, or per lifetime were to be limited by law." Thus, while he asserts that high executives should never get high incomes merely for "applied time," he seems to conclude that capable executives will adjust their working time to pecuniary compensation.[61] Here we have a striking classical remnant put forward by a sophisticated exponent of managerial views.

Ruml remarks further that high compensation should never be a mere "reward for honor earned," and there is very little attention anywhere in the ideology to the correlation between prestige and income. It is difficult to rationalize this correlation in an egalitarian tradition, thus it is not surprising that the ideology does not give realistic weight to high income as evidence that a man and his organization are important and successful. However, the belief that practicality is the key attribute of the business executive and his role one in which "results count" introduces a helpful ambiguity. The president of Procter and Gamble speaks of executives' salaries as a "compensation for achievement" and, incidentally, offers the remarkably teleological argument that money is the "acceptable" form of compensation since it is the only form giving individuals freedom to choose those material things of greatest importance to them.[62] High compensation for executives is thus suggested to be not merely a non-rational symbolic recognition of their high status but a reward for high accomplishment.

Concerning the nonpecuniary motivations of business executives a heterogeneous array of factors are discussed in the business ideology. The classical view focuses attention on pecuniary rewards and provides a narrow but clear analysis of motivations. Once the classical view is abandoned, a variety of possibilities opens up. The managerial view, as was noted in Chapter 3, stresses the various responsibilities of business. These discussions hover between description and exhortation; but the

---

[60] Ruml, *Tomorrow's Business*, p. 111.

[61] *Ibid.*, pp. 112–114.

[62] Ruml presents a number of arguments in support of high salaries mostly from the viewpoint of the firm. He notes: (1) the range of choice is increased; (2) more recruits are attracted by the existence of large prizes; (3) high-paid executives can more readily be discharged, since the firm which does so can be free from qualms about depriving them of material security. *Ibid.*, pp. 113–116.

picture which emerges is of a corporation manager motivated by these feelings of responsibility, rather than a manager who is responsible merely because this is the most profitable way to behave. Thus, in the managerial strand of the ideology, the modern entrepreneur tends to stand in contrast to the classical entrepreneur for whom moral responsibilities are treated simply as conditions restricting and defining the range of means he may use in his rational pursuit of profit.

This extreme, moralistic view of the motivations of businessmen has long been represented in the unsystematic effusions of the service ideology. It is alleged to have increasing application as business has matured and large, stable enterprises have emerged. The old wickedness of ruthless self-aggrandizement is said to be declining. Motivational analyses involve a different sort of intrinsic concern with the day-to-day management of a business enterprise than the instrumental analysis of the classical view. The appeal of the risks and competitive struggle of business are an important part of Queeny's argument about the place of profits in motivation. He compares business gains to poker winnings and argues that the game, not only the wins and losses, has intrinsic importance in both.[63] The comparison of business with a game — not mere "gambling" but a game with "elements of luck, skill, risk and calculation of chances" as he says — is a common metaphor in American usage and may indeed point to a peculiarity of American Society.[64]

It should be noted that the model for this comparison is certainly that of the independent entrepreneur or the top levels in corporate hierarchies. The picture of the "intrinsic" motivations and rewards of executives whose positions are far removed from that of the classical entrepreneur is much less developed in the ideology. The fact that top executives have climbed long to reach their present eminence may be cited to show that "management has served its apprenticeship," [65] but the obvious conclusion that hopes and expectations are intimately bound to promotions is not drawn. In government, preferment through the favor of others is recognized and labeled as "politics"; but the fact that a junior executive in business is completely dependent on the good will of a few of his superiors for promotion is not recognized in the ideology. The model of the modern corporation with an elaborated executive hierarchy presents a number of awkward problems for ideology, and these deserve a little attention.

The relation of participation in an organization to the total pattern of an individual's motivations is always a complex matter. In our society

[63] Queeny, *Spirit of Enterprise,* pp. 39–40.

[64] Compare Adam G. de Gurowski, "The Practical Genius of the Americans," in *America in Perspective,* edited by H. S. Commager (New York, 1947), p. 169.

[65] N. W. Ayers advertisement with much data, cited in *The Management Review,* 36: 58 (1947).

individuals are admitted a considerable latitude of self-interest in their own careers, while at the same time there are demands for loyalty to the various organizations in which they work. This is, of course, true not only in the business world but also in politics, the universities, and probably even the churches. But the business executive is faced with a special problem. The implications of the stress on teamwork and organizational loyalty which we have encountered are, in this context, limitations on the admissible range of self-concern for executives. Extreme self-abnegation, say, as in a religious order or the Communist Party, is not demanded; Ruml speaks of subjection to business organization as tolerable for executives only if they have the ability to get jobs elsewhere and the courage to do so.[66] Still, the pressures on the executive are considerable as compared to, say, the loyalty demanded by a university from one of its professors. Executives, particularly at the higher levels, do shift from organization to organization; but in the nature of their functions they lack the core of independence which specialized technical competence, and external evidence thereof, gives to the career of a professor. While attached to a particular organization they cannot continue their "own work" in anything like the same sense. Executives are expected to be ambitious and independent (and, in this sense, self-interested), while at the same time they are subjected to a rather severe organizational discipline.

Complexities of this sort do not readily make for clear ideological symbols; if the businessman is pictured as "loving adventure," the independent entrepreneur makes a much more convenient image. The motivations of the corporate executive get scant treatment in ideology; when they are discussed, individual self-interest is played down and merged with the interests of the organization. The possibility of conflict between self-interest and loyalty is thus ignored. An executive is ambitious for the organization in which he works.

The boasts of business firms about their successes feed the vicarious ambitions of their executives. In its house organ The Houghton Company tells how it has "again led the industry," and "intends to stay in the front ranks." [67] Mr. Queeny has given a strong statement of the importance of power and position as a goal of businessmen. The ambition of a typical successful businessman is never satisfied. "If he is producing six things and employs 1,000 people, his ambition is to exceed a competitor twice his size . . . Every businessman has an ideal; he wants a large and successful business, bigger and more profitable than that of his competitors." This picture is fairly close to that of the independent entrepreneur, but there is a protective distinction between the businessman and his organization. It is not simply personal aggrandizement which is at issue, but the growth

[66] Ruml, *Tomorrow's Business*, p. 67.
[67] *The Houghton Line, Not a Yes-Magazine*, 17: 4: 5, 7 (June 1949).

of an organization. Within this organization Queeny's businessman is little motivated by the enjoyment of power. He wants a loyal, harmonious, hard-working organization with contented employees in a well-designed and efficient plant. This organization is not simply a "lengthened shadow" of himself which will fade at his death but a continuing organism, "well balanced . . . with young talent coming along." [68]

In this sort of emphasis on the organizational context it is, then, possible to give some expression to the satisfactions of power and control. Among the rewards of high executive position such satisfactions are certainly always represented; but their ideological expression is not easy, particularly in the democratic atmosphere of American society. The ideology offers little in the way of analysis of the relation of the "greatness" of a firm to the personal satisfactions of a particular executive. This is another thorny problem. That executives derive satisfaction from being a part of a great firm can hardly be doubted, but the delicate problems involved in judging the strength of such satisfaction and the contexts of its importance hardly suit the straightforward simplicities of ideology.

One final point deserves brief notice. Chester Barnard has given emphasis to a fact which seems to be widely attested by experience not only in large businesses but in very small ones as well. [69] It is the fact that the fear of failure seems to be a far stronger spur than the hope of profit. The realistic importance of this side of a business executive's motivation can hardly be doubted, but it is completely neglected in the ideology. It is in a sense the "maintenance" aspect of role performance; not failing may be tremendously important but in itself it "doesn't get you anywhere." As such, it makes poor material for ideology.

[68] Queeny, *Spirit of Enterprise*, pp. 38, 40.
[69] In a talk reported in *Change and the Entrepreneur*.

6

BUSINESS AND LABOR

THE NATURE OF THE RELATIONSHIP between employer and employee is exceedingly complex and lends itself to description and interpretation from a number of different points of view. An appreciation of this complexity is essential for understanding the selective emphasis of any ideological description of the relationship. Analytically, the relationship can be viewed from various angles.

1. Legally, it is *a voluntary contract* between equal individuals. Neither the employer nor the employee is under any legal compulsion to enter this contract. Their agreement is an exercise of their fundamental freedom of contract. It is the responsibility of the state to respect and to protect this freedom and to enforce valid contracts. Like other private contracts, employment contracts are subject to governmental regulation, which is supposed to be general and uniform in its incidence, that is, common to all employment agreements. An employment contract can be terminated virtually at will by the employee — a feature designed to prevent involuntary servitude. The employer cannot compel the employee to work for him, but his obligations under the contract are, of course, contingent on the performance of work by the employee. Under the "wage system," in its pure form, the relationship can be terminated virtually at will by the employer. These rights exist no matter how long one may have worked for the other in a given post, no matter what their kinship relationship, no matter what employment relationship may have existed between their fathers. There is no slavery, and there are no prescriptive rights or acquired property rights in jobs.

The legal situation described here was considerably modified by the federal labor legislation of the 1930's. That legislation is still controversial, and one important criticism is that it is inconsistent with our *fundamental* legal institutions. Consequently, the traditional legal interpretation of the employment relationship continues to be of great ideological importance.

2. In economic theory it is *a market transaction* between buyer and

seller; labor service is the commodity exchanged, while the wage or salary is the price. It is assumed that each party rationally pursues his own self-interest. The employer enters a particular transaction only after he has considered such questions as: how much labor is it worth while for him to buy from whatever source; how much he would have to pay to get other employees; and so on. In particular, he will have made sure that the value of the employee's services to him are no less than their cost. Similarly the employee enters the transaction only after he has considered any other employment opportunities open to him, weighed the advantages of leisure against those of work, and made sure that the compensation is no less than his own valuation of his labor. This conception of the employment relationship is quite incomplete. But that the classical economists could picture the relationship in these terms is significant; among human societies past and present, modern Western society is unique in the weakness of institutional barriers to mobility and to the pursuit of self-interest.

3. In both the legal and economic conceptions employer and employee enter the relationship on a perfectly equal footing. But, from another viewpoint, the employer's ownership of productive property makes the relationship *one-sided*. The asymmetry arises out of a combination of modern technology and the institution of private ownership. It is no longer possible for the average worker to own the tools he uses; he usually works on premises and with tools which are owned by the employer or by persons for whom the employer is an agent. He works in the company of other employees. There are necessarily fewer employers than employees, and in the absence of trade unions the initiative belongs to the employers or buyers of labor. They set the wages and see what supply is forthcoming. In this matter of the location of price-setting initiative, the labor market differs from consumers' goods markets and most others. Moreover, many workers acquire specialized skills with the use of tools and equipment which are not their own. This effectively reduces the range of alternative employment open to them.

4. The employment relationship typically involves both parties in participation in *an authoritarian and hierarchical organization*. The employee sells a major portion of his time to one employer over a long period — perhaps weeks, perhaps years. As a result he becomes a member of a group to which his employer also belongs. For both, this social group is distinct from other social affiliations, such as family and neighborhood. This distinction we take for granted, though it is by no means inevitable — even in our society the employment group may coincide with the family group, as on a farm. The nature of this social group and the places of employer and employee within it are therefore important aspects of the employer-employee relationship.

The complexity and formality of the hierarchy vary tremendously with the size of the enterprise. The hierarchy of a small firm may have only two levels: the owner-manager, and a few employees equal in status. At the other extreme, imagine the table of organization of General Motors. In a small firm the entire hierarchy is within the range of personal acquaintance and familiarity, and the exercise of authority can be informal and flexible. But well over half of the nonagricultural employed labor force are employed in enterprises of which this is not true.

In accepting employment an employee subjects himself to a definite discipline. He is obliged to abide by certain rules and to obey orders. Yet, in the absence of trade unions, he has no part in the formation of these rules or orders; they are communicated to him and enforced upon him by a well articulated chain of command. He knows exactly where he stands in the hierarchy, who is above him and who is below him. It is true that the employer has only private sanctions with which to enforce this discipline; his ultimate sanction is dismissal.[1] But being fired may well be a calamity, particularly since other employers generally inquire into an applicant's previous work record. Of course, at the end of the working day the employee escapes from the formal control of his employer, and the hierarchical rankings of the firm do not automatically apply outside it. He does not have to defer to his foreman in the movie queue, and he may have higher status and even authority over his work-time superiors in, say, church or athletic groups.

Some of the underlying causes for labor-management conflict arise from difficulties of integration of the business enterprise as a social system. There is nothing inherent in the business enterprise to ensure that its members, down to the lowest echelons, will identify themselves with the whole organization and count its successes as their successes. There are three broad reasons why this should be so.

In the first place, the social mobility of the worker is an obstacle to his identification with the enterprise. The worker's attachment to the enterprise is a matter of voluntary choice on both sides. The worker has no permanent right to his employment, acquired by birth, family connections, residence or other nonoccupational characteristics. Similarly, the employer has no permanent claim to the service of the employee. If the worker leaves for a better paying job, neither the laws nor the moral sentiments of the community condemn his action. Both employer and employee are expected to evaluate the wisdom of continuing their relationship on universalistic rather than particularistic criteria: the employer to choose his work force on the basis of their specific abilities rather than

---

[1] The punitive powers of the state are behind the employer in case of crime; but disobedience of company rules or management orders is not a crime and only private sanctions can be applied.

on the basis of their individual total personalities; the employee to choose his employer on the basis of the terms of employment offered without regard to who the employer is. The mobility of the worker is double-edged. On the one hand, it gives him a measure of independence and freedom unparalleled in societies where employment is a matter of ascribed status. On the other hand, it deprives him of the sense of psychological security provided by a social system within which he is always sure of having a place. Not only the discretion of the employer, but the discretion of the worker himself, contributes to his feeling of insecurity. He must always wonder whether he is doing the right thing in sticking to his present job. He must wonder because society not only defines his job as voluntary and impermanent but also imposes on him the goal of occupational success. He will be judged by himself, his family, and others on his achievement in the general society's ladder of social status; this assessment will not confine itself to his performance in a given job or even his place in the hierarchy of a single employer but will take the whole of society as its field of comparative reference. And society does not accord high status to the hired worker. These features of Western social structure clearly militate against any strong identification of the worker with the enterprise which employs him. In contrast, consider the nature of his membership in his family or in the nation. These are permanent and inescapable ties, on which the individual can rely; their ability to command loyalty stems in large part from this fact.

In the second place, any social system has difficulty in supplying unifying emotional symbols to enlist the loyalties of its members in all ranks. The business enterprise encounters especially serious difficulty in creating organization-wide *esprit de corps*. There is no definition of the achievement of the total organization which would lead employees to identify themselves with it. The aims which the legal and economic nature of the enterprise impose upon its management are certainly not promising symbols of integration: profits, sales, share in the market. The volume of production is more promising, but its appeal to employer and employee alike is limited to wartime. Only then is it possible for the enterprise to define its goal as the maximization of production. At other times this objective must be subject to various financial constraints — a fact which is bound to be apparent to employees from variations in the rate at which capacity is utilized. Moreover, these variations inspire in workers the suspicion that maximum production today may simply mean less production and fewer jobs tomorrow. The notion of "making the work last" has been found to be strongly ingrained in workers, whether organized or unorganized. In wartime it can be overcome because the needs of the government are well understood to be insatiable. But in peacetime it runs counter to the possible appeal to pride in joint productive achievement. In a large productive organization, if the individual employee is excited about output at all, it is more likely to be the output of his own shop or unit than the performance of the whole organization. The division of labor so submerges the contribution of any one individual or small group to the finished product that it is difficult for the worker to feel any pride of accomplishment or craftsmanship in the quality or quantity of the final product.

Lacking any strong integrating symbol, a hierarchical organization might preserve loyalty to the top by the lure of the hope of advancement up through the hierarchy. But this has great limitations in business organizations as well as in other hierarchies. Pyramids are necessarily narrower higher up, and only those fairly near the top already can be expected to identify themselves with the top leadership because of expectation or hope of becoming that leadership. There is a sharp cleavage between those ranks where one automatically casts his lot with the official organization and entrusts his career to competing up its ladder and lower ranks where personal goals are customarily more modestly defined. An ensign fresh from Annapolis may have visions of becoming an admiral; a new apprentice seaman doesn't set his sights above Chief Petty Officer. A junior executive fresh from the Harvard Business School may see in himself a prospective vice-president; few newly employed workers picture themselves as more than foremen.[2]

The business organization must therefore rely heavily on discipline; but here the third set of difficulties arises. This discipline does not always inspire unquestioning compliance or keep competition for approval and promotion among employees. After all, employees are free of both hierarchy and discipline off the job, and they naturally bring to their working-hours society some of the standards of their other personal relationships. They do not uncritically accept orders and decisions from above, but apply their own standards of reasonableness, justice, and equity. The employee's fear of arbitrary authority, combined with the real limitations on his freedom to move from job to job, make him anxiously concerned about his security. This is reflected in the standards he applies to the actions of management. There is great concern over "precedents," and management is considered committed to established procedures and unwritten customs. Employees' standards of reasonableness and consistency conflict with the natural business objectives of the employer over, for example, work loads, order of promotions, layoffs, and rehirings. From the employer's point of view, these standards are unwarranted restrictions on his freedom of action in adapting his firm to an ever-changing external environment; from the employees' point of view any departure from them

[2] For evidence on the infrequency of executive or managerial aspirations among workers, see Richard Centers, "Motivational Aspects of Occupational Stratification," *Journal of Social Psychology*, 28: 187–217 (1948) esp. table 9, p. 200.

is simply unfair. In this situation, loyalty to a small group replaces loyalty to the whole organization; and the attitude toward the official chain of command, enforced by the social climate of opinion, is not conducive to acquiescence in the official system of incentives and disincentives. An individual who responds to this system wholeheartedly, whether from innocence or from hope of gain, finds himself the victim of the ridicule or hostility of his fellow workers.

Many of these difficulties are present in other forms of social organization; here they are aggravated because the economic element in the employer-employee relationship is divisive. Buyers want to pay as little as possible, and sellers to obtain as much as possible; this is as true of transactions involving labor as of other exchanges.

For the same reasons the business enterprise has failed to enlist the loyalty of employees, the trade union has succeeded. We have already noted the sense of insecurity generated by the impermanence and universalism characteristic of employment relationships in our society, and we have seen that this is intensified by the low status which society accords to hired labor. The labor union alleviates this insecurity. It gives to the worker as a worker the same sense of belonging to a group which his family affiliation gives him as a son or husband or father and which his nation gives him as a citizen. The union treats him, and endeavors to make his employer treat him, more as a particular individual to whom specific obligations are due. It is no accident that much union activity is geared to the ascription of status to individuals: in respect to hiring, firing, and promotion, on the basis of criteria, principally seniority, which are foreign to the universalistic criteria of management. The union also succeeds in providing an integrating symbol, namely opposition to the employer. We have noted before that there is some point in the hierarchy above which individuals identify themselves with the enterprise and below which they do not. Union affiliation by those below the dividing line makes the split more concrete, and increases the difficulties of integration which beset the social system of a business enterprise.

The conclusion from this brief analysis is not that the business enterprise is not a viable organization: obviously, these organizations do function, work is done. It is that the positions of the employer and the employee within their common social system are so different that they cannot fail to view the relationship between them in radically different terms. This leads inevitably to conflict and controversy over the nature of the relationship and the governing of the organization. Unlike other buyers and sellers, whose relationships are transient and involve no differentiation of status, employers and employees are thrown together in a continuing stratified social system; and all kinds of "political" problems intrude upon their economic transactions. It is symptomatic of the intensity of feeling generated by these problems that, on both sides, the ideology of the subject is studded with the uncompromising political language of "rights" — each "right" asserted is countered by an opposing "right" — to an extent unparalleled in discussion of other economic relationships.

INDIVIDUAL AND COLLECTIVE BARGAINING

Selectivity and special emphasis are, we have seen before, characteristics of ideological treatment of any subject. Of the four aspects of the employer-employee relationship noted above, Marxism concentrates on the third — the separation of workers from ownership of the means of production — and draws an exaggerated picture of the economic weakness of the employee. The classical theme of the business creed emphasizes the first two of the four aspects, interpreting the relationship as a symmetrical contract and a market transaction.[3] The "managerial" theme of the business creed is preoccupied with the fourth aspect, the business enterprise as a human society.

The context in which the classical view of the labor market is usually set forth in the business creed is opposition to labor unions. The classical model is individualistic. It contemplates bargaining between employer and individual employee, and collective action by employees spoils the picture. The key slogan of the ideology is "the Right to Work." [4] This is the right of the *individual* worker to make such employment agreement as he sees fit with an employer, without interference from other workers or from the government. The state is held to be remiss in its duty to maintain individuals' freedom of contract when it does not preserve the individual's access to employment from the coercion of labor unions. The "Right to Work" is the symbol of opposition to the closed shop and other union security arrangements and to effective strikes. It is the counterright which limits the "right to bargain collectively," which unions have claimed so successfully that it cannot be explicitly denied.

The classical creed does not question the workers' right to form and join unions:

Any group of people has the right to organize for any purpose that the members wish to carry through and that does not injure others; and no other group in the community is entitled to try to suppress such organizations as long as they do not take illegal and coercive steps . . .[5]

The NAM text mentions with approval the functions of unions in providing centers of social activity, standards of experience and craftsmanship,

---

[3] See exposition of "the wage system" in NAM, I: 98–100.

[4] This is to be distinguished, of course, from a different kind of "right to work": the right of every worker to a job opportunity, which is espoused in labor ideology in connection with the issue of government guarantee of full employment. On this, see p. 121 below.

[5] NAM, I: 89.

death and sickness benefits, and Americanization of immigrants.[6] More important, the business creed now generally concedes that the "right to join" a union should be protected from coercion by employers, even from economic coercion. The demise of the "yellow-dog contract" is not mourned, and the stipulation of the Wagner Act that employees should not be fired just for union membership or activity is accepted. These concessions lay the groundwork for appeal for symmetrical protection of the "right not to join."

However, there are exceptions to the "right to join." These stem from the "rights of management," the necessity of maintaining an unambiguous chain of authority and of assuring the undivided loyalty of personnel above a certain point in the hierarchy. The issue has centered on the status of foremen. The NAM text says:

Actually, of course, the foreman is a management representative, and as such he cannot consistently be a member of the same union as the workers under his supervision, or of any union affiliated with such a union.[7]

One of the essentials of national labor legislation, according to *Business Week* at a time when this publication was — unnecessarily as it turned out — reconciled to considerable modification of the Taft-Hartley Act, is that foremen be on the management team.[8] Actually, the Taft-Hartley Act, in response to sentiment of this kind, does deny foremen the status of "employee"; this means that they are not protected from discrimination because of union affiliation by the employer in hiring and firing. Professional employees, and plant guards and watchmen are also treated as special cases.

The confidence with which the creed makes these distinctions is scarcely justified by the existence of clear lines dividing the hierarchy of business organization between "management representatives" and others. In a sense, anyone who gives orders is a management representative and anyone who receives them is a worker. Almost everyone in the hierarachy, except the very bottom and top rungs, does both.

Although the classical version of the creed concedes in general the "right to join," it does not admit that many employees would of their own free choice avail themselves of that right. The first of the NAM text's three answers to "Why do workers join unions?" is "coercion." They have to in order to get a job. (The other two are "psychological pressure" and "desire for betterment.")[9] The authors complain that, in occupations where strong unions protected by union security agreements exist, the individual worker can gain and hold employment only at the pleasure of the union

⁶ NAM, I: 188.
⁷ NAM, I: 229.
⁸ *Business Week,* Feb. 19, 1949.
⁹ NAM, I: 188–189.

leadership. He is compelled to join the union, even if he does not wish to. He is compelled to support the leadership after he becomes a member, for fear of losing his membership and so being disqualified from his job.

The closed shop is one of the principal targets of business attack; against it are summoned the "right to work" and the "right not to join." These rights are asserted in Constitutional language: "Every man regardless of race, color, creed, or union affiliation has a right to apply to an employer for a job." [10] The NAM authors claim that the closed shop (a term which they use to cover all union security agreements including union shops, maintenance-of-membership provisions, etc.) menaces "equality of opportunity, freedom of contract, and individual liberty" and destroys "the liberty of Americans to make contracts and to work, to decide for themselves whether they want to join any organization." Not only is the "closed shop" politically sinful; it is economically inefficient:

> In the interest of productive efficiency there should be no arbitrary discrimination in the hiring, retention, or promotion of employees based upon membership or nonmembership in any lawful labor organization. Employers should be free to select, retain, and promote employees on the basis of competency . . .[11]

Individual workers are to be protected equally against discrimination by employers because of their membership and discrimination by unions because of their nonmembership. In this respect, as in others, the Taft-Hartley Act is described as rectifying the one-sided Wagner Act. This balanced objective is expressed by other business spokesmen who are more cautious in their approach to the closed shop.

> Unless the government regulates the closed shop, the individual human rights of wage earners may be disposed of as the union sees fit. Our laws must provide that free American citizenship is not violated by either employees or unions.[12]

Whatever the abstract merits of the various rights involved in the discussion of union security arrangements, there is little evidence that workers are anxious to be liberated. Besides outlawing the closed shop, the Taft-Hartley Act permitted the union shop only in bargaining units where a majority of the employees had voted for it in a special election.

Admittedly this was one point where the Act did not work as expected. The basic philosophy behind the Act was a belief that individual employees needed protection from the union, and given an opportunity would in many if not most cases vote against compulsory union membership requirements. Experience was quite to the contrary. Overwhelmingly large proportions of em-

[10] J. M. Swigert on Taft-Hartley Act in *Saturday Evening Post,* Oct. 30, 1948.
[11] NAM, I: 194.
[12] Editorial in *Business Week,* Feb. 19, 1949.

ployees voted — and voted for the union shop. No support was given to the theory that employees themselves who wanted union representation were to any large degree opposed to union security.[13]

Ultimately, this provision of the Act was abandoned by Congress, with the approval of Senator Taft himself, as entailing unnecessary expense to the government. The issue of the individual or minority versus the closed-shop union has frequently arisen, but in a form quite different from its presentation in the business creed. The issue generally arises, not over workers who object to any union affiliation, but over workers who wish to form or join a different union. The punishment for dual unionism is generally expulsion from the recognized union. The National Labor Relations Board has wrestled for years with the problem of how to protect workers from losing their jobs because of such expulsion.[14] In practice the "right not to join" in which workers are usually interested is the "right to join" another union, to persuade a majority of their fellows to switch affiliation, and to obtain for the new union the bargaining privileges and union security protection of the old. But these realities receive no recognition in the creed's discussion of the closed shop.

The "right to bargain collectively," like the existence of unions, is now beyond direct attack.[15] According to the NAM text it is "not an issue," and collective bargaining is to be judged pragmatically by its results in particular cases, rather than in the abstract.[16] This descent from abstract classical principles covers a significant retreat. The individualistic model of the labor market could, without too much logical strain, admit the legitimacy of groups of workers joining together to negotiate their contracts with an employer, so long as the employer is free to bargain separately with other groups and with unaffiliated individuals. Indeed,

[13] H. A. Millis and E. C. Brown, *From the Wagner Act to Taft-Hartley* (Chicago, 1950), p. 436.

[14] *Ibid.*, pp. 210–216.

[15] However, this has not been the situation very long, and there are in the ranks of business both individuals and minorities in business associations who are uncompromisingly opposed to collective bargaining. John W. Scoville, economist for Chrysler Corporation, in 1944 denounced collective bargaining and called for repeal, not amendment, of all federal labor legislation (address before Detroit Kiwanis Club, Aug. 8, 1944). In 1946, this policy was advocated by influential groups within both the Chamber of Commerce of the U.S. and the NAM, but was rejected in favor of the policy of accepting collective bargaining but seeking amendment of the Wagner Act. (Millis and Brown, *Wagner to Taft-Hartley*, p. 287.) Acceptance of the principle of collective bargaining of the Wagner Act has been a difficult process for the NAM, which opposed the Act in the beginning, claimed it was unconstitutional until the Supreme Court decided otherwise, and has advocated first its repeal and later its drastic amendment. In 1935, its position on collective bargaining was uncompromisingly "classical": that "employer and employees be free to bargain collectively or individually in such forms as are mutually satisfactory to them without coercion from any source." (Quoted in Millis and Brown, *Wagner to Taft-Hartley*, p. 285 n.)

[16] NAM, I: 189–190.

Senator Taft stated his objective in just such terms: "assuring complete freedom of choice to employees who do not wish to be represented collectively as well as those who do." [17] But both the NAM and Senator Taft's legislation have retreated farther from the classical model. The appropriateness of a *single* collective bargaining agency for a given body of employees chosen by majority vote is not questioned, although there is still debate on the proper size of a bargaining unit. Moreover, it is accepted that the wages and terms of employment determined by collective bargaining with this single group should apply to all employees of the unit, whether or not they are members of the bargaining group. The classical symbols of individual rights could be invoked against these practices, but they are not.[18]

Of the many rights asserted by both sides, the "right to strike" is one of the most solidly entrenched in general public opinion. To oppose it is to risk the appearance of advocating slavery, a fact which Senator Taft was quick to exploit when President Truman proposed drafting railroad employees into the Army to keep the trains running. The business creed recognizes the "right to strike" but seeks to limit it by other "rights." The classical model clearly grants to the individual the "right to quit work" whenever he pleases. (Although even this, Henry Hazlitt points out, is not absolute — an engineer cannot abandon his train in the middle of the desert.)[19] There can be no objection on broad classical grounds to a simultaneous and even collusive[20] decision by a group of individuals to quit work. Were all railroad workers to decide independently to leave their jobs on the same day in favor of other occupations or leisure, society has no protection which is consistent with the concept of employment as a voluntary agreement. The trains could run again only as the railroads attracted and trained new recruits. This is a chance which the exponents of the classical view are willing to take, and it is in this sense that they accept the "right to strike." What they object to is the extension of the "right to strike" to include "the spurious right to prevent others from working by force." Those who voluntarily quit work abandon all claims on the jobs they have vacated; the classical view resists any attempt to place jobs in the sphere of property rights. They have no right to "prevent others from taking the jobs they have vacated." ". . . The right to work is as

[17] U.S. Senate, Committee on Labor and Public Welfare, *Federal Labor Relations Act of 1947*, Report No. 105, 80–81, p. 3.

[18] This is an example of the way in which ideological argument shifts its specific targets and omits all discussion in one context of what was a hot issue in another context. See Chapter 18 where some shifts over time in the focus of ideological discussion of these problems are noted.

[19] Henry Hazlitt, "The Right to Strike," *Newsweek*, May 16, 1949.

[20] The objection to collusion on the basis of the old common-law doctrine against conspiracy in restraint of trade has long since been abandoned when the ends to which a combination is directed are legitimate.

sacred as the right to quit work and no less in need of protection." [21]
This application of pure individualism to labor disputes forms one criticism
of the Wagner Act, under which strikers were legally "employees" and
thus entitled to collective bargaining rights and protection against dis-
criminatory "dismissal" by the employer. The NAM authors proposed
legislation to "modify or eliminate the act's treatment of 'strikers' as
'employees.'" [22] The Taft-Hartley Act did modify these provisions of the
Wagner Act, by narrowing considerably the eligibility of strikers for
reinstatement and for participation in representation elections. Demands
like Mr. Hazlitt's for the protection of nonstrikers and replacement
workers from violence, threats, mass picketing, etc. on the part of strikers
have been widespread among businessmen. The Taft-Hartley Act included
these practices under "unfair labor practices," for which the responsible
unions are subject to various penalties.

Again, whatever the merits of the various "rights" involved, the realities of the large strike are generally quite different from the impression
given in business ideology. Nowadays there is little need for "coercion"
in order to make a strike effective. No one imagines that enforcing the
"right to work" during strikes in the coal, steel, railroad, or automobile
industries would enable the employers to obtain the work forces they need
to resume normal operations. In such cases picketing is more a propaganda
device than a method of excluding willing workers from struck plants.
However, it is true that in less well-organized industries and areas, strike-
breaking by means of what organized labor calls "scabs" is still possible;
and there are certainly cases where employees are forced to stop work
involuntarily — although this is perhaps more frequently because their
operations are meshed with those of strikers than because they are forcibly
denied access to their work. But the business creed's stereotype of the
coerced strike, in which reluctant strikers are pulled off the job by union
leaders and eager new workers are denied access to the jobs, is atypical.

There are two dominant and interrelated themes in the ideology's treatment of individual versus collective bargaining.

1. Individual workers need to be saved from the oppression of union
leaders. Union members, as well as other workers, are considered to be
unwilling or, at worst, deluded captives of their leaders. Henry Hazlitt
and the 1948 Republican National Committee contended that the only real
opposition to the Taft-Hartley Act was the personally selfish resistance of
"union bosses." [23] The Act was represented, by these and others, as a
measure to liberate the rank and file of workers from the despotism of

[21] Hazlitt, "The Right to Strike."
[22] NAM, I: 218.
[23] Henry Hazlitt, "A Pro-Labor Law," *Newsweek,* Aug. 11, 1947. Republican
National Committee 1948 campaign pamphlet, *Before and After the Labor-Management Relations Act of 1947.*

their leaders. A McGraw-Hill advertisement[24] is dramatically headed "Taft-Hartley Act frees 'Slave' Labor" (incidentally, another example of ideological turnabout in the use of symbols).

But experience shows that the ideological position that, given the opportunity, the rank and file of union members would repudiate their leadership is far from accurate. "When governmental intervention in a labor dispute takes the form of asking workers publicly to support or repudiate their leadership, they tend strongly to do the former." [25] This remark was prompted by experience during the war when union leaders had no difficulty winning strike votes which Congress had required in the expectation that they would act as a brake on the striking proclivities of the leaders. The experience of union security elections under Taft-Hartley has already been cited. There are many examples where leaders restrain impetuous actions by the rank and file, and where national leaders exert a sobering influence on local unions. These are omitted from business ideology.

2. Individual rights must not be restricted by majority rule. This raises an ancient problem in political theory in a relatively new setting, the employee society instead of society at large. That problem is the reconciliation of majority rule and individual rights: the delineation of the sphere in which individual differences can be permitted from the sphere in which they cannot and in which individual right must be limited to equal participation in deciding on a common action. On a national level in the United States, for example, it is clear that foreign policy belongs to the second sphere — we can have only one foreign policy, and the rights of individuals are limited to equal participation in choosing a President. Expressions of opinion about foreign policy, on the other hand, belong to the first sphere; there is free play of individual differences and majority rule is not imposed. For a society of employees, business ideology assigns to the second sphere only the right of collective bargaining, everything else to the first. Indeed, the classical model, as we have seen, does not even conceive of employees as a social system and therefore does not accept this definition of the issue. Union ideology, in contrast, is inclined to assign everything to the sphere of majority rule; the conception of protecting the rights of individual workers embodied in the Wagner Act was principally to safeguard their voting rights so that elections would reflect genuine majority decision.

One thing is clear: the issues are much too complex to be resolved by the straightforward application of a few basic "rights." What appears to business as clear infringement of individual freedom of choice is to labor an indispensable safeguard of collective freedom of choice. The latter

---

[24] *New York Times* and other newspapers, week of Oct. 20, 1947, #62 of series.
[25] Millis and Brown, *Wagner to Taft-Hartley*, p. 299.

interpretation is as neglected in the ideology of business as the former in the ideology of organized labor. The difficulties of pursuing a consistent and balanced course through the variety of actual situations are illustrated by the experience of the National Labor Relations Board under both its successive legislative mandates.

RIGHTS OF MANAGEMENT

So far the argument has been cast almost entirely in terms of the rights of employees, not in terms of the rights, obligations, and interests of employers. This corresponds to the emphasis of the ideology in its campaigns regarding federal labor legislation. Representative Hartley called his bill "the workingman's bill of rights." Even the theme of "equalizing" the positions of unions and management under the law played a subsidiary role in the campaign for amendment of the Wagner Act. However, the creed also contains a discussion of the rights and duties of employers in respect to their employees.

The "classical" theme of the ideology seeks to limit the obligations of the employer to the employee to those implied in the legal interpretation of the contract between them. Any attempt to extend the notion of property rights to the interests of workers in their jobs encounters determined ideological resistance;[26] it conjures up terrible memories of the sit-down and stay-in strikes of the 1930's in which the traditional rights of private property of the employers were dramatically threatened.[27] The response to the milder challenge presented by labor's slogan "Right to a Job" is also negative. The classical view recognizes no obligation on the part of the employer to give a particular worker employment at any time when he is not worth his wage to the employer — no matter how great the worker's need or how long he has been employed.

> From the standpoint of economics and productive efficiency it may be stated that it is not the business or proper function of the employer to determine whether any work applicant, or present employee . . . does or does not need a job.[28]

This opposition to any job rights which imply employment obligations on the part of employers extends to opposition to any over-all guarantee of full employment.[29] Business opposition to "full employment" plans shows anxiety lest the right to a job in general be interpreted at the level of

[26] See Hazlitt, "The Right to Strike."

[27] Even the editors of *Fortune,* who are fairly sympathetic to the labor movement, are horrified. See *Permanent Revolution,* pp. 99–100.

[28] NAM, I: 228.

[29] See, for example, statement of the Machinery and Allied Products Institute on the Full Employment Bill of 1945 before the House Committee on Expenditures in the Executive Departments, Oct. 23, 1945.

specific firms. It is stressed that neither the economy as a whole nor any individual employer has any obligation to employ a worker unless he can "earn" his wage by his contribution to the value of output.

Although employment contracts for long periods — for example, for a year as contemplated in "guaranteed annual wage" proposals — are no less consistent with freedom of contract than contracts for a week, the business creed is wedded to the short-term agreement at present institutionalized in the "wage system." A longer contract, it is feared, would result in the employer's paying for useless work or for work not performed if sales fell off during the year. It would impair management's "right to dismiss." [30]

Union demands for "fair" methods of promotion, dismissal, and hiring on bases such as seniority invade a province which, in the classical view of the business enterprise, belongs excusively to management discretion. Seniority, the NAM text insists, is a legitimate criterion in personnel decisions only where the normal criteria of an unfettered management are indecisive:

> From the standpoint of efficient production, promotion of employees should be solely on the basis of demonstrated ability and indicated aptitude for the job ahead. If two employees are equal in these respects, then the promotion may be given, and because of its effect on individual and plant morale should be given, to the one with the greater seniority or period of past service . . .
>
> In the case of layoffs, consideration should be given ability and productivity, to increase over-all efficiency in the plant; and if two employees are equal in this respect, the one retained should, again from the psychological standpoint, be the one with the longer service." [31]

Actually organized labor has succeeded through its collective bargaining agreements over a large sector of American industry in establishing complicated systems of individual priorities and claims on jobs. Whether these interferences with management's selection of personnel do or do not impair efficiency is not a simple question; it involves balancing the loss due to a non-optimal matching of individuals and jobs against the gain due to the general improvement in employee morale from satisfying some of the desires for security and fairness.

The "rights of management" are a general defense against widening the agenda of employer-union negotiations. Hazlitt takes the extreme position that the government's requirement — retained by the Taft-

---

[30] Irving S. Olds (Chairman of the Board of U.S. Steel), "Some Aspects of the Proposed Guaranteed Wage," address before the Economic Club of Detroit, May 14, 1945. The creed will now have to adjust to the principles of supplementary unemployment compensation embodied in labor contracts in the automobile industry in 1955.

[31] NAM, I: 196.

Hartley Act — that management "bargain collectively" itself "abridges management's freedom to manage." [32] The NAM text attempts to draw a line between "matters directly affecting employment conditions," in which labor participation is legitimate, and "management as management," in which it is not.[33] The rights of management are defined more precisely when specific union demands are being resisted. For example, during a Ford strike about alleged "speed-up" the company asserted its right "to establish work standards which will assure efficient operation without impairing in any way the health and safety of our employees." The *Times* commented editorially, "Perpetuation of a vigorous free enterprise system will depend to a very large degree on how jealously management resists efforts to take over in part or whole its particular sphere of activity and responsibility." [34] That the boundaries of this sphere are vague was indicated by a story in the same paper the following day, in which the president of the Hickey-Freeman Company stated that 100 per cent cooperation with the union was the salvation of the clothing industry.

UNIONS AS MONOPOLIES

In attacking unions as "labor monopolies," business ideology leans heavily on the classical economics of the labor market. For theoretical reasons, to be examined in Chapter 8, monopoly is the snake in the laissez-faire Garden of Eden. For historical reasons, monopoly is a strong negative symbol in America. To tag labor unions successfully with this label would be a major victory for business in the war of ideologies.

The "monopoly" label turns against labor the charge which has long been leveled against business itself. Terms reminiscent of concentration and abuse of business power are applied to national labor unions: "huge combinations of 'holding companies' in the field of labor." [35] A common diagnosis is disarmingly impartial: once, it is admitted, the evil was Big Business, which the public rightly cut down to size; now the evil is Big Labor. Whether or not past business sins are confessed, it is agreed that at present labor monopoly is by far the greater peril.

In our Nation during the last half century, successful monopolization of business by combinations not licensed or sponsored by government has been rare, largely because . . . of the Sherman Act, and illegal agreements entered into surreptitiously are very hard to enforce . . . By contrast, monopolization generated by combination of employees is an exceedingly common phenomenon, for such monopolization has been encouraged and promoted by government . . .[36]

[32] Henry Hazlitt, "Legally Certified Monopolists," *Newsweek,* May 2, 1949.
[33] NAM, II: 235, 111.
[34] *New York Times,* May 11, 1949.
[35] NAM, I: 218.
[36] W. I. King, of the Committee for Constitutional Government, *Hearings on Labor Organizations* (Robertson), p. 644.

The charge of monopoly is closely related to the charge of coercion already considered. The creed contends that unions' monopoly power is based in the first place on coercion of workers and is used to coerce workers, employers, government, and the general public.

> Far too common . . . is the case of the labor monopoly which by intimidation or the actual use of violence, prevents nonmonopolized workers from taking jobs in a unionized plan or industry.[37]

In keeping with the business creed's careful distinction between union leadership and the workers, the monopolist is identified as the union boss rather than the collectivity of members.

> Most labor unions are now treating the worker's services as a commodity or property which they can dispose of on terms and in such manner as the union leaders consider best.[38]

The last quotation gains added significance because revulsion against the treatment of human labor as a commodity has long been an obstacle to public acceptance of the classical economic analysis of the labor market. This is more than a verbal quibble; the Clayton Act embodies the finding of Congress that labor is not a commodity or article of commerce either in fact or, what is more important, for the purpose of antitrust legislation. One of the remedies sought by the opponents of labor monopoly is the removal of this exemption and the exposure of labor organizations to the same peril of antitrust prosecution as business. Business spokesmen now adopt the line that it is the leaders of the labor movement itself who have chosen to regard labor as a commodity, by "monopolizing" it, setting its price, and laying down its terms of sale.[39]

Industry-wide bargaining is a special target of the antimonopoly crusade, especially since no legislation on this subject emerged in the final version of the Taft-Hartley Act. Opinions differ on whether its prohibition should be accomplished by specific legislation or left to antitrust action following the removal of labor's immunity. Experience in the railroad and coal industries in this country and in many industries abroad is cited to demonstrate the antisocial consequences of industry-wide bargaining. The specter of economy-wide bargaining, to which the present practice is but a first step, is raised. Not only is industry-wide bargaining an instrument of labor monopoly; it also encourages business monopoly, as employers are compelled to join together in order to deal with the union. It protects both the employers and employees in organized firms from the competition of unorganized rivals. For this very reason, the business creed has not

[37] *Ibid.*
[38] NAM, I: 240.
[39] See, for example, testimony of George Christensen, *Hearings on Labor Organizations* (Robertson), pp. 250–257.

really jelled on this issue; many employers welcomed industry-wide bargaining as a means of escape from the competitive disadvantage of a strong local. In 1946, the NAM text opposed the practice but only after giving a balanced list of advantages and disadvantages.[40] In 1949, the NAM statement to the Robertson committee unequivocally denounced industry-wide bargaining and called for legislative remedy.[41]

PRODUCTIVITY AND WAGES

The business creed hammers home again and again the lesson that real wages are inseparably connected with the productivity of labor. This lesson is repeated in many different contexts, at various levels of sophistication, with numerous ideological overtones.

1. Throughout the ideology runs the doctrine that higher productivity is the sole and sovereign remedy for all economic ills. This and this alone can relieve unemployment, stop inflation, and raise real wages.

2. The productivity theory of wages, like the "more production" doctrine of which it is one application, is generally given a puritanical and ascetic flavor. It is a hard, inescapable fact of life. Those who face it squarely don a Churchillian mantle. *They* do not delude the people. There is no easy road; there is no panacea; there is no short cut. There is only hard work. You cannot get something for nothing.

> . . . the path to higher wages is along the route of greater production — increased output per worker and per machine — and . . . there are no safe shortcuts.[42]

A Warner & Swasey advertisement entitled "Let's look at the record" begins:

> That's the American way of doing things — dealing in honest facts, with all the cards above the table. Well here are the facts: *The workman decides his real wage by his production.*

[40] NAM, I: 231–234.

[41] *Hearings on Labor Organizations* (Robertson), pp. 959–966. The solidification of opinion is described in Leo Wolman, *Industry-Wide Bargaining,* Foundation for Economic Education (1948), pp. 7–13, a good statement of the negative. Much of the testimony of the Robertson Committee hearings, which were inspired by a coal stoppage, is devoted to opposition to industry-wide bargaining. See also Clarence B. Randall, *A Creed for Free Enterprise* (Boston, 1952), pp. 34–35, where industry-wide bargaining is described "as this strangely un-American pattern type of existence in industry." These pages also point up the conflicts of interest on this issue between firms which are generally wage leaders, such as U.S. Steel, and firms which are not, like Mr. Randall's Inland Steel Corporation. The former generally favor formal industry-wide bargaining, since it protects them from the danger that "followers" will strike better bargains than they have achieved.

[42] Editorial, *Business Week,* Aug. 13, 1949.

This is supported by a chart plotting real hourly wage against output per manhour from 1914–1945 and followed by four other "facts." The advertisement concludes:

> There's nothing hopeless in these figures — but there is a warning. It is that we'd all better quit dealing in half-truths and get back quickly to hard facts — and hard work.[43]

> It's just that simple: if you want lower prices, a steady job, and more pay, you start with more efficient production. And there's *no other way*.[44]

> If we can set just one boy straight . . . If these messages can get even one confused American boy, with ears assaulted by the twisted ideologies of the world, to think through to the truth . . . if they can make him *know* he can be paid in this world only out of what he produces *for* the world . . .[45]

> One of the most deeply rooted fallacies in the mind of the working man is the idea that to produce less per hour will benefit him, because it will make his work last longer. This is a complete misconception of the fundamental truth that the source of all wealth lies in increased production. The worker fails to understand that the raises in wages, the better job, the continued employment he wants, and the high standard of living he enjoys, all depend upon increasing the rate of production.[46]

> Better productivity holds the promise of still better living. It is the way to make good on the things that people are talking about, and wanting, today: better wages, pensions . . . for all workers, better social services . . . But we can only have better living standards . . . if we increase our efficiency to produce more in each hour of work.[47]

3. One moral to be drawn from this sobering fact is that workers should work harder, unions should abandon rules and practices which restrict output, and employees should cooperate with management to increase efficiency. It is commonly complained that in fact labor does the opposite, at the same time as it demands higher wages.

A McGraw-Hill advertisement congratulates national labor leaders for their realization that "increased output per man-hour is the only road to increased 'real' wages," and says:

> If these expressions, *which still remain to be substantiated by practical performance*, come to be accepted by the rank and file of labor in each community, Labor Day, 1946, can usher in a period of great and perhaps unprece-

---

[43] Warner & Swasey advertisement, *Business Week*, Sept. 11, 1948.

[44] Warner & Swasey advertisement, *Business Week*, Aug. 28, 1948 (italics theirs).

[45] Warner & Swasey advertisement, *Newsweek*, Sept. 20, 1948 (italics and punctuation theirs).

[46] Fred C. Crawford, speech, August 1943, *Businessman's Book of Quotations*, p. 194.

[47] Editorial, *Business Week*, March 18, 1950.

dented improvement in the economic wellbeing of wage earners — as well as
the wellbeing of the country at large.

A survey of executives is cited:

> Worker effort has been below prewar. Since V-J day . . . labor, led on by
> a misguided government has had its sights on higher money wages instead of
> improving productivity which would have laid the foundation for increased
> "real" wages.[48]

> Despite three rounds of wage increases since the end of the war employees
> have failed to increase industrial productivity to any appreciable extent by
> putting forth greater effort, an economist and two industrial leaders declared
> yesterday.[49]

During the Ford strike, in which the issue was an alleged speed-up, the
Boston Herald was able to form its judgment on general principles:

> . . . the history of unionism since 1935 would make most objective stu-
> dents a bit doubtful as to the justification of the union speed-up charges against
> Ford. One would be inclined to think, short of knowing all of the facts, that a
> strong union like the UAW had seen to it that what they call "the standard
> production rate" was fixed at a pretty comfortable level for the workers.[50]

> Almost every response to the survey indicated company concern about a
> lack of employee interest in increased production . . . Several companies re-
> ported indifference by employees even to opportunities to earn higher pay on
> incentive plans rewarding greater than standard output.[51]

One of the reasons that the business creed favors paying by piecework
rates instead of by time rates is that it makes the basic connection between
productivity and wages crystal clear to the worker.

> Strikes for higher wages disappear when incentive wages are properly
> used.[52]

> If workmen were paid in the goods they produce (instead of in money),
> we would have industrial peace, greater production, lower prices.[53]

4. The second moral to be drawn is that workers should have more
tools to work with, because this is the major determinant of their pro-

---

[48] McGraw-Hill advertisement, *New York Herald Tribune* and other newspapers,
week of Aug. 26, 1946, #50 in series.

[49] *New York Times*, Sept. 24, 1948, reporting a conference of the American
Management Association on the "Relation of Wages to Productivity."

[50] Editorial, *Boston Herald*, May 11, 1949.

[51] *New York Times*, Nov. 4, 1948, reporting a survey of 1,000 companies by the
American Management Association.

[52] McGraw-Hill advertisement, widely distributed and published by various sponsors in World War II.

[53] Warner & Swasey advertisement, *Business Week*, Aug. 28, 1948.

ductivity. (This argument has already been encountered in the ideology's defense of profits.)

His tools, more than anything else, determine how much a worker can turn out; and what his paycheck will buy depends in large part on what he turns out — not on how long or how hard he works.[54]

Average output per man hour *does* increase largely because of arm-lengthening improvements in design, equipment, and method supplied by stockholders through management. Output per man hour can increase somewhat by added interest, care, skill, and effort by the non-supervisory worker, but unfortunately the tendency of the average worker has been in the opposite direction in recent years as a result of unwise union teachings and government encouragement.[55]

This moral is not entirely consistent with the exhortation to greater effort. But some reconciliation of the two morals along with a bow to management is achieved in the teamwork description of business operations. An advertisement headed "How to make a pork chop on a punch press in 9 minutes flat" concludes:

It's a job for advanced equipment, organization, techniques, and enterprise allied in cordial understanding with skill, care, cooperation, and drive. Productivity is a partnership achievement. It, and it alone, makes "real wages" real.[56]

In the postwar period, the contribution of tools to labor's well-being has been aggressively proclaimed. In the 1930's, the relation of machinery to labor was a subject on which business took a defensive attitude, against the charge of technological unemployment. Many of W. J. Cameron's Ford Hour broadcasts were devoted to proving that new machinery created many more jobs than it destroyed, increasing the standard of living in the process.[57] Nowadays the possibility that tools are substitutes for labor as well as complements receives recognition only in quite different context; for example, when a business writer predicts that John L. Lewis will destroy the jobs of his coal miners by inducing the industry to mechanize.[58]

5. The link between wages and productivity is not just a fact. It is an ethical principle. In discussing incentive wages, which are, it regrets to say, less prevalent in the U.S.A. than in the U.S.S.R., the NAM text says they rest

---

[54] McGraw-Hill advertisement, *New York Times,* #76 of series, May 23, 1949.
[55] Boulware, "What About a Fourth Round of Wage Increases?" May 16, 1949.
[56] SKF Industries Inc. advertisement, *Business Week,* April 16, 1949.
[57] For example, "Machinery Creates Employment," Feb. 13, 1938; "Nothing Good is Lost," Feb. 16, 1936; "Machines and Jobs," Dec. 1, 1935.
[58] Edward H. Collins, *New York Times,* July 12, 1948.

. . . on the premise that individuals differ in their ability and accomplishment, and that those who do most should receive most.[59]

6. Closely connected with the hard facts about productivity and wages are certain equally intractable accounting identities. Businessmen, because of their down-to-earth, practical bent are peculiarly aware of these truths. A business firm cannot, in the long run, disburse more than it collects from its customers, and a nation cannot receive more in income than it produces. In discussing the practicality of guaranteed annual wages, Olds devotes several pages to elaborating these points:

. . . the only continuing source of funds out of which the owner of a business can pay wages, or in fact meet any other cost, is the money received from the customers who buy his products.

. . . neither our concern, nor any other corporation, can endlessly generate funds to pay workers or stockholders beyond what is left out of the funds derived from sales of products after paying the costs of producing the things so sold. We are business men, not alchemists. Our budgets must balance, else before long we assemble in the bankruptcy courts.[60]

7. The productivity arguments so far discussed do not face the issue of the distribution of income, specifically the possibility of increasing wages at the expense of profits. The arguments ignore or pass lightly over it, giving the impression that there is no slack in the relation between productivity and wages or between industry's receipts and its wage disbursements.

The portion of the collections received from the consumers which is turned over to labor as a whole ranges from 65 to 85 per cent of the total national income. From the over-all viewpoint, it is therefore evident that wages as a whole cannot be greatly increased without changing the sums of the collections from the consumer.[61]

But business has to face an insistent challenge from labor on this score.[62] The creed's response is to minimize the level of profits and to defend their legitimacy and economic necessity; these arguments have been examined in Chapter 4. The creed is impatient with petty quibbling about the division of the economic pie and urges instead joint effort to increase the size of the pie. Its dramatic way of demonstrating the futility of this method of increasing wages is to divide total profits by the total number of employees, or by the whole population.

[59] NAM, I: 160.
[60] Olds, "Proposed Guaranteed Wage." See also, NAM, I: 124–125.
[61] NAM, I: 124–125.
[62] In the years following World War II, much debate on this issue was provoked by the "Nathan reports" for the CIO, which contended that business could and should grant substantial wage increases without raising prices.

. . . if the profits of 1936 were completely diverted to employees, the increase to each working-class family would be less than $3 per week.[63]

"Would *you* sell your country's future for $140.85?" asks the Standard Steel Spring Co., after dividing aggregate net profits for 1948 by the country's population.[64]

8. At the level of sophistication of the preceding arguments, the concept of productivity is left vague and undefined. But it appears that the productivity to which wages are rigidly related is what an economist would call "average physical productivity," that is, total output, measured in physical units, divided by total number of man-hours. Of course, real wages could not be equal to this quantity, or there would be nothing left for profits and other distributive shares; but problems like this are of little concern to crude productivity doctrines. In the more sophisticated versions it turns out that this is not the correct concept of productivity anyway. In the first place, "value productivity" has more significance than physical productivity. Converting the laborer's physical output into the dollars for which it sells provides a means of comparing the productivity of an auto worker and a coal miner. Moreover, it provides an opportunity for applying the general doctrine of consumers' sovereignty to the wage question; here again that doctrine minimizes the power, control, and responsibility of the businessman.

. . . most of the demand for labor is a derived demand which the enterpriser, a middleman, endeavors to satisfy . . . The price of the product received from the consumer must therefore be considered the ultimate source of the reward paid to labor . . . The employer, in general, is thus a channel for transferring the payments which the consumer makes for labor to the laborer . . .[65]

The second step in sophistication is to replace "average" with "marginal." The measure of the worth of a laborer to an employer is the amount of sales revenue the employer would lose if he had to operate without this one employee, every other condition of operation unchanged. This measure — "marginal productivity" — varies with the amount of labor hired by the employer; after a point, it declines as employment increases. Given the wage at which he can hire labor, the employer will fix the size of his work force at the level where its marginal productivity is equal to that wage. Any smaller amount of employment would mean foregoing an opportunity for profitable expansion; any larger amount would mean a scale of operations beyond the most profitable level. This sophistication solves the problem of the source of non-wage incomes, because the

[63] NAM, I: 125.
[64] Standard Steel Spring Co., advertisement, *New York Times,* April 5, 1949.
[65] NAM, I: 124.

marginal productivity of a given amount of labor, which determines its wage, is less than its average productivity.

Now this argument, which is nothing more than a logical deduction from the premise that a business firm maximizes its profits, plays an important role in a time-honored economic doctrine which is central to the "classical" strand of the business creed. That doctrine, to be discussed in some detail in Chapter 8, is that a competitive economy allocates productive resources among alternative uses in an optimum way: in other words, consumers could not be better satisfied by any other allocation. The relation of the marginal productivity theory to that doctrine is well understood by economists who contribute to ideological literature.

For the economics of minimum wage legislation, there is critical importance in our view of the relation between wage rate and worker (marginal) productivity. Do they actually tend to equalize?

Here it is important to see that this calls into question the validity of the whole body of basic principles with which (whether we always realize it or not) the whole case for competitive-market economy must stand or fall. The (marginal) productivity principle of wage determination is an indispensable, interlocking part of the fundamental reasoning by which we explain whatever orderliness, efficiency, and fairness we claim for that form of economic system.[1]

[1] [Footnote in original] For most trained economists, in fact, it is meaningful to say that the (marginal) productivity-wage principle is simply an inescapable derivative of the ultimate "economizing" principle, for any society in which wage differentials are principally relied upon for the mobilization and allocation of free labor in optimum consistency with free consumer-expenditure patterning of production.[66]

To play its role in this historic proposition, "marginal productivity" must be supplemented by two other arguments. First, it must be shown, as the above quotation indicates, that the labor market contains a mechanism which insures that the supply of labor seeking work will be employed at a wage equal to its marginal productivity. So far we have been told only that the wage will be no higher than that. Second, it must be shown that this determination of wages distributes labor among alternative uses in the pattern which best satisfies consumers. A necessary condition for these two conclusions is the existence of competition — in the special technical sense of "pure competition" in professional economics — throughout both the labor markets and the products markets. Competition among

[66] Chamber of Commerce of the United States, Committee on Economic Policy. *The Economics of Minimum Wage Legislation* (Washington, June 1947), p. 32. Our insertions of "marginal" are justified by the footnote, p. 33, which explains that this is what the authors mean, but they do not have space to explain the concept to laymen.

employers for the given supply of labor bids up its wage to equal marginal productivity and allocates to each use just enough labor to equate its marginal productivity in that use to the common competitive wage. Competition among employers in the sale of products insures that their demands for labor are true undistorted reflections of consumer preferences. In each use marginal productivity measures what consumers are willing to pay for expanding the employment of labor in that use; if these marginal productivities are everywhere equal, it is impossible to find a shift of labor from one use to another which consumers would ratify by valuing their gain of one kind of output more highly than their loss of another kind.

The question which the business creed slides over is whether the American economy in fact conforms to the rigorous competitive conditions necessary for the optimum-allocation argument. Professional economics recognizes the possibility, and indeed the prevalence, of market structures which depart from "pure competition." In its theory of wages, the creed stops short of some further sophistications of productivity theory. The addition to a firm's revenue due to adding more labor, which is the "marginal productivity" relevant to the firm's employment decisions, is in general not the same thing as the value to consumers of the additional physical output, but is smaller. This is the case in any firm which has any measure of control over its selling price; such a firm must count against the sales value of additional output the reduction in price, over its entire output, necessary to gain additional sales. This amendment weakens the connection between consumer valuations and wages; the connection is weakened even more by the recognition that in local labor markets competition among employers in buying labor may be far from "pure." [67]

9. The productivity theory of wages, at whatever level of sophistication, shows that union leaders are false prophets when they claim to raise the living standards of labor. In fact, by reducing labor's productivity and standing in the way of technological advance, unions keep living standards down. What happens when labor monopolies exert their power to try to force wages up? Inflation, unemployment, gains for some workers at the expense of others, distortions in the allocation of resources — these are the consequences of union, or government, interferences in the competitive labor market according to the business creed.

By its policy of slowing down the ambitious worker to the speed of the laggard, unionism has seriously retarded the increase in productivity. It has

[67] These complications are not mentioned in the exposition of wage theory in the NAM text, nor, except for the cursory dismissal of one possibility (Appendix D), in the Chamber of Commerce pamphlet cited above.

reduced, rather than increased, the annual real earnings of American labor, taken as a whole.

Labor monopolies have, of course, been very successful in pushing up the hourly pay of their members. However, higher wage rates inevitably mean higher-priced products, and the resulting increases in the "cost of living" penalize union members as well as the public in general. Furthermore, the higher prices cut sales, and many workers lose their jobs.[68]

Union wage practice, insisting on inflexible wage rates and refusing to make adjustments voluntarily, downward when necessary, in times of depression delays the period when unemployed labor can be reabsorbed into industry.

Use of monopolistic labor power for raising wages results in lower wages for excluded workers and higher prices for consumers.[69]

The general relationship of real wages to productivity, on which the business creed places so much emphasis, is undeniable. Over the broad sweep of history, or over the contemporary world, differences in productivity are the principal explanation of differences in labor's real income. They dwarf in importance differences in political and economic organization and differences in equality of income distribution. Marx predicted otherwise. He thought that capitalism would impoverish the worker at the same time that it made him more productive, and his prediction has been disproved. It is also undeniable that differences in capital per worker, along with associated differences in technology, are a major factor in differences in productivity. These are the important elements of truth in the business creed's theory of wages. On the other hand, the connection between the productivity of an individual worker and his wage is very loose. Moreover, the refinements which are necessary to make sense of the productivity theory of wages remove it a long way from any simple application of the appealing ethic that a worker should be paid what he produces. However useful productivity may be in explaining broad differences in wages, the theory does not provide, without further argument and the introduction of specific value judgments, any basis for evaluating one way or the other the existing distribution of income.

HUMAN RELATIONS AND THE INTEGRATION OF THE FIRM

Most of the discussions of labor problems in business ideology are in the classical vein and are bound up with the legal and economic aspects of employer-employee relations. But in recent years, business has paid increasing attention to the social nature of the business enterprise and to the problem of its integration. The keynote of this approach is that work-

[68] W. I. King, *What Raises Wages — Labor Unions or Better Tools?*, reprinted in *Hearings on Labor Organizations* (Robertson), p. 860.
[69] NAM, I: 148, 153.

ers "are human beings, not cogs in a machine." [70] This cliche gains significance beyond its apparent content for several reasons. First, the classical approach does treat labor in a mechanistic way and regards a contract and transaction involving labor little differently from any other contract and transaction. Second, the reminder that workers are human beings springs from a set of discoveries about the nature of human beings, especially in social groups. The burden of these discoveries is that wages have by no means the central importance in employee motivations which the classical approach assigns them. (See Chapter 5 for a discussion of the incompleteness of the classical view of occupational motivation.)

Because his daily job represents his "life center" it is of the greatest importance that management give full recognition to the personal hopes, fears, and pride of the individual.[71]

Management must apply itself with all the vigor it can command to the task of satisfying the complete wants of its personnel. Those wants are psychological as well as material.

The monotonous nature of much work in the modern mass production system puts it up to the employer to provide some recognition for his workers to give them real satisfaction in their jobs.[72]

The President of the American Management Association is concerned about "the satisfaction of individual desires for participating in constructive work in the factory and office." His wishes "to give employees at all levels a greater sense of dignity and recognition as individuals and respected members of the industrial community." [73] Third, the increasing ideological prominence of "human relations" has accompanied an institutional development in corporation management; personnel problems and policies have become a field for specialists and experts.

The spurt of interest in "human relations" is naturally associated with the "managerial" view of the business enterprise and of the responsibilities of management, discussed in Chapter 3. *Fortune* reports growing acceptance of the concept that the executive's No. 1 job is to keep his corporation in equilibrium, and lubricate it so "that it gives meaning and satisfaction to those within it." [74] But, of course, the new understanding of employee motivation does not necessarily compel any shift in the ultimate objective of business management; the art of human relations can be a new instrument in the quest for profits. The NAM pamphlet "Human Relations

[70] Harry A. Bullis, Chairman of Board of General Mills, Inc., in a speech before Congress of American Industry, reported in *New York Times,* Dec. 3, 1948.
[71] NAM, *Human Relations and Efficient Production,* p. 16.
[72] Bullis, see note 70, above.
[73] Speech of Lawrence A. Appley, reported in *New York Times,* Jan. 9, 1949.
[74] "Problem for the Front Office," *Fortune,* May 1951, pp. 5–51.

and Efficient Production" seems clearly to place "human relations" in the instrumental category:

Increased attention to employees as individuals brings about substantial improvement in productivity. Only as a man is able to secure satisfaction through his work, does he put forth his best efforts.

Many companies will testify that "going out for the good life" pays dividends.[75]

Fortune asks which is the objective, better morale or more profits, and answers that the businessman who denies any conflict "is simply following an old American custom, explaining away his decent instincts in terms of dollars and cents benefits." An executive is quoted:

We kid ourselves a lot. We talk about doing all this because it pays off in the annual report. We'd be scared to admit to ourselves anything else. But I think I know why we're doing it — it's because these people here have a right to express themselves.[76]

To some extent good personnel relations have the instrumental appeal of avoiding unions. Although the man who knows how to get along with unions may be the modern business hero, the man of whom it can be said, "His six thousand employees are nonunion in the very center of unionism," [77] certainly qualifies as a human relations expert.

The problem which "human relations" attempts to solve is nothing less than that of integrating the hierarchical society of employer and employees. It is the problem of motivating employees to act consistently with the objectives of the whole business organization. The classical solution, as we have seen, is a system of individual wage incentives and disincentives. It is based on the assumptions that the individual worker is immune to social influences, that his only concern in working is his take-home pay, that he really "lives" only after working hours. The human relations approach recognizes the inadequacy of this solution:

This view recognizes that incentives to action are not exclusively economic, and that management must, as well as it can, provide for the intellectual and spiritual values which all of us feel the need for.[78]

With some companies reporting the failure of financial incentives to interest workers in increasing production, there will be increased emphasis on nonfinancial incentives based on a common understanding of the cooperative effort necessary for a full production for American and world needs today.[79]

[75] NAM, "Human Relations," pp. 10, 18.
[76] "Problem for the Front Office," pp. 15, 156.
[77] Biographical note on one of the contributors to *Individual Initiative in Business,* p. 17.
[78] Ralph M. Hower, in *Individual Initiative in Business,* p. 111.
[79] Appley, speech in *New York Times.*

What are the non-financial incentives? They are commonly sought in the realm of communication, or understanding, or education. The sting of hierarchical authority and discipline can be removed, it is claimed, if the reasons for management's orders and actions are fully explained and employees are given a sense of participation in decisions. This was the main emphasis of a Harvard Business School Conference panel discussion on "Practical Human Relations in Management." During the discussion the issue was joined between profit-sharing, a classical if unconventional technique, and communication; which is the better method of enlisting employee cooperation?

It isn't so much the profit-sharing angle, but rather the failure to explain why the move was made. If that were done, you would sell the individual the *rightness* of the move. — J. S. Tomajan, President of The Washburn Company.

Make each employee a part of the organization, and explain at the beginning of each move the resulting good to everybody, thus taking out the impersonal and the machine slant on the whole thing. — J. S. Brown, Vice-President of Chemical Bank and Trust Company.[80]

This faith in communication applies not only to very specific matters but to the general orientation of the organization. Indeed, a large number of business spokesmen conceive the human relations problem as a public relations problem; employees need to be educated in the economics of free enterprise. This conception brings us full circle back to the classical business ideology; the only human relations problem is its successful propagation.

Wallace F. Bennett, President of the NAM, stated, "the most important problem facing American management today is the problem of human relationships" and went on to make clear his conception of this problem:

I feel that when each employee can understand the relation of his wages to the company's prices and to its costs, we can begin to hope for an intelligent approach to the problem of high prices.[81]

We are trying very hard to understand what it takes to make employee relations in an organization. An important part of that is the employee's understanding of what it takes to make a company work. I find an awful lot of effort wasted on employees simply because the employee doesn't understand the fundamentals of the business organization.

Now, I think we have got to go back home and start some work with the people we are talking about affecting here, so that they understand the man-

[80] Allen, in *Individual Initiative in Business,* pp. 99–128.
[81] Reported in *New York Times,* Dec. 30, 1948. See also Panel Discussion 5 of 1950 Harvard Business School conference, on "Education for Initiative and Enterprise within the Community," *Individual Initiative in Business,* pp. 209–229, which illustrates the importance attached to economic education.

agement problem and so that they understand the capital problem; so they understand what the management people are up against; that they have got to end up with a proper balance sheet or the employee will not continue to have a job there.[82]

The enthusiasts for "human relations" and "good communications" anticipate great achievements. Thomas G. Spates, Vice-President of General Foods Corp., believes the nation can be saved from socialism and communism if employers "start treating their workers like human beings." [83] He believes that the means of winning the "hot and cold running war against totalitarian communism" is to apply "the American code of personnel administration" which treats people "so that they will achieve and give the best that is in them, while getting the highest possible degree of individual satisfaction," eliminating "the disillusionments and frustrations, the emotional and mental illnesses from which are formed the subversive attitudes that influence the destinies of nations." [84] Even those who interpret "human relations" in the narrower terms of selling employees on the virtues of the free enterprise system believe "there is a growing hunger for economic education" which business can satisfy. "This is fortunate, for the salvation of our free system . . . depends on our being able to convey the basic economic facts of life." [85]

This optimism springs from a belief that the only threats to the "system" are external and artificial. In the light of the intrinsic difficulties of integration within the firm, examined at the beginning of this chapter, this optimism seems unjustified. Just as the classical approach selects for overemphasis the economic aspects of employer-employee relations, the "managerial" approach, in its reliance on "human relations," underestimates the economic aspects and underrates the difficulties of integrating the employer-employee social system. These difficulties are underrated even more, it appears, by those adherents of the classical creed whose conversion to the importance of human relations consists only in recognizing the need for disseminating the classical creed to employees.

[82] M. V. Cousins, Director of Personnel, United Gas Pipe Line Co., in panel discussion of "Practical Human Relations in Management," *Ibid.*, p. 127.

[83] Thomas G. Spates, speech reported in the *New York Times,* Apr. 2, 1949.

[84] Speech reported in the *New York Times,* June 29, 1948.

[85] L. R. Boulware, in *Individual Initiative in Business,* p. 210.

7

THE BUSINESSMAN
AND HIS CUSTOMERS

AN ENORMOUS BODY OF IDEOLOGY clusters about the relations of the businessman to his customers. Here, as elsewhere in our survey of the business creed, we emphasize that, from among the great variety of perspectives in which the phenomena under discussion might be viewed, the ideology selects only a few. For example, if a student of market phenomena were to allocate his attention according to dollar volume of transactions, he would focus primarily on interbusiness transactions and pay only secondary attention to retail markets for ultimate consumers. In so doing, he would be sharply reversing the relative emphases of the ideology.

The position of the businessman in American society and his special relation to markets and exchange are reflected in the ideology that accumulates about business-consumer relations. There are two views that we might expect. On the one hand, an ideology which stresses that the business system is uniquely American might logically be concerned with contrasting the American market with others. This is a fertile field. Even within the compass of the Western world, American markets have remarkable features, of which supermarkets and aggressive advertising are only among the more conspicuous examples. On the other hand, the cultural tradition embedded in economics textbooks and widely diffused in classical business ideology points in quite a different direction. Its concern is less with actual institutional arrangements than with the logical implications of markets where with freedom to enter into contracts buyer and seller may each rationally seek his own advantage.

The ideology actually exploits both these possibilities, in different and separate contexts. In over-all explanation of the whole economic system, business ideology usually follows the classical tradition. But in the great mass of popular ideology, the creed stresses quite different symbols and arguments. Indeed the symbol which has perhaps been most heavily used,

"Service," is one that suggests a direct contradiction of the classical view. It is true that the service theme involves no departure from classical views when it refers to the total business system as serving the needs of the whole society. But, as we shall see, the great bulk of service pronouncements refer to some disinterested orientation of individual firms to their particular customers. First we shall examine the classical theme of consumer sovereignty, and then the alternatives based on the service theme and on an emphasis on American institutional peculiarities.

CONSUMER SOVEREIGNTY

The doctrine that the ultimate consumer is a force of great power in the economy is one of the most prominent themes of business ideology. In a recent discussion of the position of management in American business, F. C. Crawford, President of the National Association of Manufacturers, depicted management in the middle of a "triangle of plenty." Labor and capital were at two corners of the triangle with ropes around the manager's legs. But:

> The top corner, the consumer corner, the market corner, is worse. It has a rope around management's neck, like a noose, yanking forever for bigger bargains.
> The people in this top corner are human beings and real mean. They want better goods and cheaper goods. They want bigger packages. The females, especially, have no hearts. They will do business with you on friendly affectionate terms for ten years and then switch their trade overnight to your sharpest competitor to save a nickel.[1]

This awesome description of power and exacting demands of customers is widely echoed. The President of Johnson and Johnson, George Frederick Smith, explained "our American economic system" to high school students of New Brunswick, New Jersey in these terms:

> The secret of a successful business . . . is a satisfied customer. The customer is the only person who finally determines whether a company stays in business or not. A business either meets the demands of its customers and succeeds . . . or does not meet the demands of its customers and fails.[2]

Queeny answers his own question "Who runs American enterprise?" with the simple claim, ". . . the ultimate consumers. You and I and 130 million other Americans." [3] The position of the businessman though seemingly powerful may only be that of an intermediary; thus we read, "It is the *customer,* not the employer, *who fills the pay envelope.*" [4] Even

---

[1] Crawford, *Triangle of Plenty,* p. 4.
[2] *Trends* in Educational-Industrial Cooperation, February 1949.
[3] Queeny, *Spirit of Enterprise,* p. 117.
[4] Utley, *The American System,* p. 91.

the "service which Americans enjoy in such abundance is directly the product of their own imagination, enterprise, and common sense." [5]

Examples of assertions of the power of consumers in the functioning of the total economy can easily be multiplied.[6] Individual firms like to remind their customers of their own importance. Standard Oil of New Jersey informs the public, "We either do a good job meeting your needs, or we just don't have any job . . . you're the real boss . . ." [7] The Gaylord Container Corporation has urged the business community that "the most important man in your business" is "Mr. Customer." [8]

The form in which the consumer exercises his great power is frequently described in an analogy to political elections. Thus the NAM volumes on *The American Individual Enterprise System* picture the customer in the market place as a "voter" confronted by a number of candidates vying for his purchasing power; in buying he "casts a vote" for the product of his choice.[9] Other writers speak of the "ballots cast for Henry Ford," [10] or the "daily referendum on competition." [11] A program fostered by the Advertising Council and the Advertising Federation of America seeks to explain the "American free-choice" system (and thus "to promote public understanding of advertising").[12]

It is not obvious that the consumer's freedom to choose among alternatives presented to him gives him the sovereign power the ideology attributes to him. To bridge this logical gap, certain arguments about the economic system in general, which will be considered in Chapter 8, are required. These arguments assume, among other things, two propositions about consumer behavior: first, that consumers' tastes are beyond the control or significant influence of business firms; and, second, that, when in the market place, consumers are able to act effectively in ac-

---

[5] Bell Telephone System, *Annual Report*, 1948, excerpted in advertisement.

[6] For example, "Economic forms will continue to exist or will be changed according to the effectiveness of their service . . . (and consumers determine this effectiveness). J. D. Houser, *What People Want from Business*, New York, 1938, p. 116. Utley, *The American System*, pp. 90–91. Queeny, *Spirit of Enterprise*, p. 114. A streetcar advertisement (Brand Names Foundation) widely seen in 1952 is a "Notice to All Passengers . . . You are the Boss in this Land of Brands." Also, NAM, I: 632–633.

[7] *New York Times*, 1948 (precise reference lost). The advertisement shows an employee, one Nason Clark, with the caption, "Sure he works for us . . . but he also works for you!"

[8] Gaylord Container Corporation advertisement, *Fortune*, February 1951, p. 51.

[9] NAM, I: 474–475.

[10] Utley, *Spirit of Enterprise*, pp. 90–91.

[11] Secretary of Commerce Sawyer in *Individual Initiative in Business*, p. 87. "The housewife votes every time she buys her groceries; she notices quality, price, and service as each seller competes for her favor."

[12] *New York Times*, April 8, 1949. A Brand Names Foundation streetcar advertisement in 1952 gives an eye-catching twist to these analogies: "The Lady Across the Way Was Proposed to Today."

cordance with these tastes. These two propositions can conveniently be made the focus of our survey of business ideology regarding consumer behavior, although the ideology's concentration on the problems they raise is probably a response less to logical exigencies than to outside criticisms. We shall consider first the problems raised by the second proposition, concerning the competence and power of the consumer, and then turn to the question raised by the first proposition, the autonomy of the consumer.

THE COMPETENCE AND POWERS OF THE CUSTOMER IN THE RETAIL MARKET

The doctrine of consumer sovereignty in logically elaborated form is characteristically embedded in the "classical" analysis of the functioning of the economy. As such it involves a high level of abstraction and neglects many empirical aspects of the market which give the opposite impression. If Beardsley Ruml argues that David Consumer has a potent weapon of free choice against Goliath Corporation, his very metaphor reflects an impression of great strength on the seller's side which threatens the plausibility of consumer sovereignty arguments.[13] Before examining the content of the ideology about the power and competence of the retail customer, we shall consider two broad aspects of retail markets, in order to provide a background for the impressions which ideology seeks to reinforce or combat. These are the concentration of initiative in the seller, and the uncertainties that inevitably beset the buyer.

1. Aggressive selling, in contrast to passive service, is the expected and accepted behavior of the business firm in our society. Modern business typically sells from prepared stocks to a shifting, anonymous market, and this means that the retail customer is much less obviously in the position of soliciting exchange than is the businessman. The situation is very different from that in which the seller produces only to order and may have to be urged to provide the desired goods. The typical asymmetry in the relationship between the modern businessman and his customer is considered a normal and legitimate part of most retail transactions.[14]

From any broad comparative perspective, the willingness of the customer in American retail markets to accept the offering price without any attempt to haggle is remarkable, but relatively little discussed in ideology. Ernest Elmo Calkins saw the elimination of haggling in retail purchases as one of the achievements of American business and derided the mysterious marks on merchandise in older times in favor of the clear, open statement of prices in more modern stores, and argued that under haggling "the odds were always in favor of the bank." [15] But such pride in the

[13] Ruml, *Tomorrow's Business*, p. 64.
[14] Knauth, *Managerial Enterprise*, p. 108.
[15] Calkins, *Business the Civilizer*, pp. 42–43.

use of fixed prices as an achievement of the system and a service to the customer is not common.

It might be argued that selling at fixed prices has helped to maintain the relatively high social status of retail business. Where haggling is accepted, there is an inevitable suggestion that the seller is trying to exploit his customer; reducing the original price suggests that the seller would have gotten more if he could have, that his dominant impulse was to maximize his pecuniary gain rather than give the customer the best "buy" he could afford to give him.[16] Resistance to haggling has developed to the point where it is assumed that under the fixed-price system the businessman is actually giving the best price he can afford.[17] Although business ideology shies away from terms such as "just" or "fair" prices, which would suggest that competition is not the proper determinant of prices, the conduct of ordinary retail business clearly involves the presumption that the price on the tab is in some sense a "fair" price and not "all the market will bear." The businessman nourishes this presumption with assertions of the "integrity" of the firm and the "value" of its products, but he rarely uses the opportunity to point to the fixed-price system as evidence of "deserved confidence."

There are obvious reasons why the system of fixed-pricing in retail trade does not make good ideology.[18] It thrusts the initiative of the seller and the question of his integrity into awkward prominence. By setting the selling price himself, he has an element of control which conflicts with the pervasive emphasis on consumer sovereignty found in the ideology.

There are certain limits to aggressiveness in soliciting custom that businessmen are expected not to overstep. Advertising, in the sense of broadcast appeals through mass media to an indefinite public, has had a more questionable status than other aspects of the seller's initiative. For instance, not long ago banks regarded advertising as illegitimate.[19] And there are

[16] The historical association of fixed-price selling with Protestant sects — notably the Quakers — was doubtless not a matter simply of their shrewdness in business. They were concerned to be engaged in a respectable calling, and an exploitative attitude toward customers is hardly conducive to such feelings.

[17] Persia Campbell, *The Consumer Interest* (New York, 1949), pp. 224–225, remarks: "It is coming to be looked upon as poor taste to question the integrity of the price tag, as it presents itself at any one time — this applied even during the war and was one of the problems encountered in price enforcement."

[18] Perhaps the absence of any significant "competition" from a system involving haggling is important. Where it has occurred in retail contexts in our society it has been associated with derogated groups and statuses. (Witness the curious locution, "to jew a man down.") Its prevalence outside the Western world has occasioned no troubles, since these societies were "backward" and no serious competitors to the "enterprise" system.

Also, the great importance of price negotiation in intra-business transactions might produce conflicts if haggling were generally deprecated.

[19] Carpenter, *Dollars and Sense,* p. 182.

still problems for special types of business, particularly those bordering on the professions or trying to claim professional status. Thus an insurance company recently protested that, while insurance is a profession, it is really different from law and medicine and "it is unethical for us *not* to solicit business." [20] The familiar prohibition of advertising in such professions as law and medicine occasions problems for the pharmacists and morticians, who accept advertising but try to keep it dignified.[21] However, these cases are exceptions: advertising is basically accepted in the business world.

The initiative of the businessman in the market place is not to be confused with authority. The customer is to be accommodated and pleased. The obsequiousness traditional among European tradesmen is out of place in the American egalitarian atmosphere, but an obliging manner is expected of retail sellers. Business ideology proudly contrasts the "unfailing courtesy" of the grocery clerk with the indifference of the "so-called public servant." [22] The slogan that the customer is always right has doubtless guided much business practice. Gimbels' recently advertised that they were continuing Adam Gimbel's 1846 policy of giving their customers "what they want, when they want it" even at the expense of maintaining dubious inventories — it was not Gimbel's function to scold people about trying to buy bathing suits late in the season when it is awkward for stores to stock them.[23]

These institutional features of the retail market do not offer easy support to the doctrine of the sovereign power of the consumer found in the business ideology. The deference to consumers' wishes readily fits with this doctrine, but aggressive advertising does not.

2. The second important feature of the retail market to which we would call attention in these preliminary remarks is the uncertainty which besets the ultimate consumer. As a rule he can judge the quality of any particular article only in a very limited sense. He cannot set up minute specifications or carry out careful tests as can the large-scale consumer of a few products. In the old days he could appeal to outside authorities for he had relatively fixed relationships with a number of small retailers. The old-fashioned grocer selling from bulk stores is often treated disparagingly by spokesmen of modern merchandising;[24] his methods may seem insanitary and unreliable today, but at least he could give his customers advice. He was, presumably, a reliable guide who could help the customer to make

---

[20] Travelers Insurance Company advertisement, *U.S. Investor,* Feb. 12, 1949, p. 8.
[21] See *Casket and Sunnyside,* the undertakers' trade journal.
[22] Utley, *The American System,* p. 153.
[23] Advertisement, "Will the boys at Harvard catch Gimbels' with its pants down?" *Times,* July 19, 1950, p. 13. Compare the very different relationship of a doctor to his patient. The patient is not merely to be "pleased," he is expected to do what the doctor tells him and may be scolded for not doing so. Also the patient is not to "shop around" without strong cause.
[24] Calkins, *Business the Civilizer,* p. 225.

a good buy. Today the ties between individual merchants and consumers have been weakened and are often non-existent, so that the consumer feels more uncertain of his choice. To some extent his anxieties have been relieved by brands and trade-marks; a familiar brand can always give some sense of what the psychologists call "a structured field." And a wide variety of merchandise is sold in packaged or other forms with some assurance of standard quality. Whether the present-day consumer is a better judge of quality than his predecessor or not is a moot point; the important thing is that he is not a completely independent judge — in the absence of personal advice he has to rely heavily on familiar brands.

Perhaps no area of modern American life has provided an easier mark for critics of the society than the advertising and selling practices of business. They have been a favored target of intellectuals and disillusioned members of the business community. Stuart Chase, William E. Woodward, Will Irwin, Sherwood Anderson, and Frederic Wakeman are among the better remembered of those who have given debunking or at least unflattering accounts of this feature of our society. In the business ideology, however, we find scant concession to these criticisms and a vigorous affirmation of the importance of salesmanship and advertising.

Although the role of salesman is accorded a very modest status in society, the NAM authors proclaim that "in our time, selling is an honored art," and explain how the price system becomes an "instrument of progress" through salesmanship and research.[25] The fact that top executive roles commonly involve some responsibility for the selling of products is used to give a glow to selling generally and to make the salesman a key to the "enterprise system":

The free enterpriser plans in order to foresee, to adapt himself and — at most — to modify the outside factors. His instrument of modification is the salesman.

The salesman can deepen a channel or construct a breakwater. He can modify by persuasion, but, by definition, he does not control. For many years the salesman, rather than the banker, the engineer, or the industrialist, has been the typical figure of American free enterprise.

Paul Hoffman is a salesman . . . And it is a salesman's planning, not a socialist's, that Paul Hoffman brings to Europe.[26]

Advertising in our economy is said to be as "staple as wheat or potatoes," [27] and to play an essential part in the economy. In a country "dedicated to a system of mass production," we must rely on advertising for the

[25] NAM, I: 638, 486–487
[26] *Time* advertisement, *Boston Herald,* April 7, 1949, p. 17.
[27] NAM, II: 640.

disposal of much of our production.[28] The planned state in doing away with advertising would present people with what bureaucrats not the people want, and quality of goods would deteriorate.[29] We are assured that "it has never been demonstrated that advertising is an economic waste" [30] and that it has played an essential role in building the American standard of living.

Advertising is not purely self-interested, it is asserted, but is a general service to the community. The growth of national advertising has made plausible the claim that most advertising does not directly benefit the individual advertiser. "What it does is to create a state of mind" which may benefit a competitor as well as the firm which pays for the advertisement.[31] The service theme is prominent not only in ideology but also in practical literature giving guidance with respect to effective advertising practice. Stressing "service" in advertising is advocated as an effective way of gaining sales but it may also be a way of removing the taint of aggressive self-interest. Thus we read that "The simple principle of offering service keeps advertisers from being beggars and peddlers . . ." [32]

Many of these claims in behalf of advertising have solid empirical grounding, and a strong case can be made that advertising is "vital to success of our economy." [33] Some other plausible claims are rarely encountered surprisingly enough. For example, the dependence of our great newspapers, magazines, and radio and television systems on advertising might well be turned to ideological use. The *New York Times* and the NBC Symphony might well be claimed as contributions of advertising to the national culture.

A central theme of the critics of advertising and aggressive selling has been that advertising misleads the customer so that he becomes a dupe rather than a sovereign judge. Nowadays this criticism is heard less than it was two decades ago when "Your Money's Worth" was a popular sensation and the consumers' movement was beginning. But occasional voices still denounce advertising as "a torrent of mendacity, imbecility and bilge." [34]

[28] Richard P. Deupree, President of Procter and Gamble, in *Individual Initiative in Business*, p. 14.

[29] Queeny, *Spirit of Enterprise*, pp. 170–172. Compare also a long fantasy in Calkins, *Business the Civilizer*, pp. 58–75.

[30] NAM, II: 461; see also Ruml, *Tomorrow's Business*, pp. 37–38, 97.

[31] Calkins, *Business the Civilizer*, p. 28. Calkins repeatedly stresses the "altruism" involved in national advertising; see p. 35.

[32] Mark O'Dea, *Preface to Advertising* (New York, 1937), p. 122. The assertion is in the context of a claim that "The best ads and the best commercials are created around the idea of satisfying selfish interests by offering service." See also H. Phelps Gates, "What is Successful Advertising," *U.S. Investor*, Oct. 1, 1949, pp. 19–22.

[33] Report of 31st Annual Meeting of the American Association of Advertising Agencies, *Time*, April 8, 1949.

[34] Bernard De Voto, "Why Professors are Suspicious of Business," *Fortune*, April 1951, pp. 114 ff.

In attempting to refute charges of dishonesty in advertising, a businessman once conceded that "there is only one way in which the buyer may swindle the seller and that is by not paying his bills, but there are a thousand and one ways in which the seller may impose on the buyer." [35] While modern business practices involving consumer's credit and return privileges broaden somewhat the customer's field for swindling, it is true that the greater initiative of the seller gives him more scope for behaving dishonestly. This asymmetry imposes special problems on the seller in securing the buyer's confidence. Popular suspicion of the sincerity of advertising and selling claims[36] makes natural some ideological discussion of the integrity of products and advertising.

Here the ideology's defense includes both assertions of fact and explanations of the facts. The alleged facts are that most advertising is basically honest. Bad, dishonest advertising is admitted, but it is small in volume and steadily being reduced. In 1926, the president of the International Advertising Association assured his readers that in twenty years his organization had succeeded in eliminating from our publications "that form of advertising which is untruthful in its essential details." [37] In 1949, this elimination was apparently still under way. At the 31st Annual Meeting of the American Association of Advertising Agencies, the members were assured that not only businessmen but "consumer leaders are of the opinion that advertising . . . is less misleading than it was some years ago." [38]

There are a number of ways in which this basic and improving honesty of advertising is accounted for, explicitly or implicitly. The competitive market provides one explanation. If advertising is to be profitable, it must be true.[39] Modern distribution is so expensive that without "repeat sales" there can be no profitable business; hence the seller cannot hope to profit by misleading the customer into buying an article with which he is not satisfied.[40] Honest mistakes as to the value of a product will bring economic death as surely as dishonest exaggeration.[41]

Advertising may indeed involve some exaggeration[42] while remaining

[35] Carpenter, *Dollars and Sense*, p. 184.

[36] There is, in general, a great suspicion of public utterances in our society — a suspicion which seems endemic and ineradicable. See Robert K. Merton, *Mass Persuasion* (New York, 1946).

[37] C. K. Woodbridge, in preface to Carpenter, *Dollars and Sense*, p. vi.

[38] *New York Times*, April 8, 1949.

[39] Carpenter, *Dollars and Sense*, p. 180.

[40] NAM, vol. II: 651 (Marketing chapter).

[41] Carpenter, *Dollars and Sense*, p. 175: "There are those who miscalculate the merits of their advertised commodities. Naturally they fail, and it is the cost of advertising which causes them to fail. In other words, advertising itself is the great scavenger of the commodity field, removing by its own power the inferior and perpetuating the superior."

[42] Carpenter blames the public for this. *Ibid.*, pp. 181–182.

basically honest; public boasting about products may in the long run assure that customers get not less than what is claimed but more. Advertising has taken the sand out of sugar, the beans out of coffee, the adulterations out of tea,[43] because modern producers make every effort to protect their brand names, and brand names are built up by advertising. Advertising not only improves the quality of products; it improves business practices both inside and outside the plant.[44]

The efforts of business to assure the quality of products and the honesty of advertising are given wide publicity. The attempts of Better Business Bureaus to control misleading advertising are regularly reported.[45] The Sears-Roebuck Company has had a display at the Museum of Science and Industry in Chicago showing how it makes scientific tests of the quality of various goods and the *New York Times* financial section comments: "Although the exhibit demonstrates the work of Sears' independent testing and development laboratories, it is typical of the efforts being made by most leading merchandisers to assure the quality of the goods they sell." [46] R. H. Macy's president verifies the *Times*' report that his company tries to test the products it sells.[47] In short, the business community claims that, whether because of simple good faith or because of the pressures of competition, it advertises honestly and provides goods which people want.

The ideology is affirmative as well as defensive in its assertion of the competence and power of the consumer in the market place. He is, according to the NAM authors, a perceptive judge of quality, and in the long run he buys what serves him best.[48] Women, despite their alleged non-rational susceptibilities, are really good judges of what they buy.[49] The 49th Annual Convention of the National Association of Retail Grocers saluted four Americans as "those who know their groceries best." The honored included Lady Mendl, the White House housekeeper, a Veterans' Hospital supply officer, and the secretary of the Independent Retail Food Distributors of Maryland.[50]

Jack I. Straus, President of R. H. Macy Co., recently used the housewife's competence as an argument for self-service in department stores. "She is today so much more enlightened in the quantity and quality of what she is buying that she has shown a real eagerness to go pick it out for herself." [51]

[43] *Ibid.*, p. 172; see also p. 169.
[44] Calkins, *Business the Civilizer*, p. 23.
[45] For example, *New York Times*, May 26, 1949, urging self-regulation on ammoniated dentifrice advertising.
[46] *New York Times*, Sunday, May 22, 1949.
[47] Merrill, *Responsibilities of Business Leadership*, pp. 41–51.
[48] NAM, II: 631.
[49] Roy M. Durstine, *This Advertising Business* (New York, 1929), p. 39.
[50] *New York Times*, June 21, 1948.
[51] Address at 32nd Annual convention of the Controllers Congress of the National

Advertising is given credit for the customer's alleged competence, because it supplies the necessary information.[52] In addition, there is a lively and aggressive campaign concerning the importance of branded merchandise. A "non-profit educational foundation," the Brand Names Foundation, acquires advertising space for this purpose. Under the caption, "By Appointment to the American People," we read:

Under our brand system, which is the very keystone in the structure of our free economy, people can separate the wheat from the chaff and make their purchases solely on the basis of merit and appeal to their personal tastes and preferences.

The brand names and trademarks which flourish in the American economy have "won esteem the hard way," they have developed broad markets and made possible cheap products, and they "spur manufacturers to greater efforts to please us." [53] In the NAM volumes, after a discussion of the indispensable place of advertising in the American economy, we read that "trade-marks have become the basis of advertising in America"; standards enforced by the government, such as grade labeling, are condemned as unworkable.[54] The customer is pictured buying a known brand with confidence because he is sure of its quality.

The advertisements of the Brand Names Foundation show that their authors are perceptive, if unsystematic, psychologists. An advertisement of the 1950–51 series asks readers to imagine how difficult life would be if "everybody had the same face." "What faces do for you on *people*

Retail Dry Goods Association, reported in *New York Times,* May 27, 1952. Mr. Straus's remarks indicate some anxiety lest "self-service" may mean less "service" from the retailer, "The housewife is meeting the new methods cheerfully more than half way. However, the job must be strictly professional, merchandise must be attractively displayed, readily accessible and visibly priced." But he warns that traditional methods "can sap the black ink out of the lifestream of net profit . . . (!)"

[52] Carpenter, *Dollars and Sense,* pp. 224–225.

[53] The Brand Names Foundation Inc. is sponsored by a large group of manufacturers, advertising agencies, and advertising media. A May 15, 1951 Roster of the Sponsors lists some 412 manufacturers of branded products. The Foundation supplies advertisements without charge to cooperating publishers who contribute the necessary space. A brochure of the Foundation displaying available advertisements has stated that between 1948 and 1951 there were some 730 advertising insertions of this sort by 222 publishers. The advertisements themselves are prepared by leading advertising agencies (such as Batten, Barton, Durstine, and Osborn, Inc. and Needham, Louis and Brorby, Inc.) for the Foundation without charge. Special series are prepared for consumers' journals and trade magazines, and for newspaper insertion. There is extensive use of radio, provision of study material for schools, a "complete program on the 'Economics of Today's Buying'" for women's clubs, a "Sam Brand" series to explain the brand system to plant employees, and help to local groups for "Brand Weeks" and other "civic promotions." Thanks are due to the Foundation for their cooperation in making their materials available to us.

[54] NAM, II: 633–634, 650. On the theme of brand competition as source and assurance of high quality: Queeny, *Spirit of Enterprise,* p. 172; Carpenter, *Dollars and Sense,* p. 205; Jenkins Valve advertisement, *Fortune,* February 1951, p. 52.

you meet . . . brand names do for you on *products* you buy." In the 1949–50 series, the plight of a family moving to a new community is depicted:

. . . so much would be strange — the schools, the church, their neighbors . . .

But not *everything* will be strange. The grocer and the druggist will have unfamiliar faces, but the *products* they carry will be old friends. The shelves of every store will be stacked with brand names the Johnsons recognize. Of course, it is a comfort to be able to shop by familiar brand name — the name the manufacturer gave his product so that people could tell it from any other.[55]

Many of these statements beg the question whether the customer's preferences are really satisfied or not, but they contain much solid realism. A customer's concern is often not so much to maximize the return for his money as to be assured of a reasonably satisfactory product at a standard price; a knowledge of trade-marks certainly increases his competence in this respect.[56]

The business creed, especially its classical strand, also attributes to consumers an alert and rational sensitivity to price differences in the market. At the beginning of our discussion of consumer sovereignty we heard Crawford's judgment on this matter,[57] and N. W. Ayer and Sons proclaim that "in the long run the public writes the price tag." [58] This view is difficult to reconcile with the uncertainties and ignorance that, we have argued, inevitably beset the modern consumer; and it ignores much irrationality in the customer's reactions to prices.[59] The prevalence of what may be called trivial decrement pricing ($9.95 instead of $10) is alone sufficient to suggest that sensitivity to prices does not always reflect a rational

[55] Another advertisement in this series is perhaps based on recognition of the great importance of gifts within and between households in some consumption items such as clothing in modern American life. A father buying stockings for his daughter is depicted as surmounting the uncertainties in meeting her special taste by using the guide of a brand name. A recent survey by the Bureau of Human Nutrition and Home Economics of the United States Department of Agriculture showed that consumers in the Minneapolis-St. Paul area got about 10 per cent of their clothing as gifts from people outside the family. (*New York Herald Tribune,* July 16, 1951, p. 22.) No doubt an appreciable further percentage of clothing used came in the form of intra-familial gifts, indicating a great importance of this type of purchase where there is a problem of the recipient's "being pleased" or "knowing what he's getting."

[56] Compare Calkins, *Business the Civilizer,* pp. 96–97, on the elimination of uncertainties provided by Yellow Cabs — a known, standardized service at a standardized price is assured.

[57] Crawford, *Triangle of Plenty.*

[58] N. W. Ayer and Sons advertisement, *Saturday Evening Post,* April 16, 1949, p. 127; and the same theme, *ibid.,* March 19, 1949, p. 73.

[59] Amusing instances in B. Kidd, *Women Never Go Broke* (Philadelphia and New York, 1948). See ch. VIII, "Cheap at $3.98: The Modern Mythology of Pricing," pp. 106–123.

calculation. The fact that consumers rely on price as a guide to quality instead of assessing quality independently has been offered by business critics as further evidence of consumer irrationality. In defense, business spokesmen argue that prices are in fact a reliable index of quality.[60]

THE AUTONOMY OF THE CONSUMER

We turn now to the other logical pillar of the theme of consumer sovereignty — the claim of the autonomy of consumer tastes, their ultimate independence of advertising and other efforts to mold them. The attacks on this claim have been strong, and the defense in the ideology has been hampered by the fact that businessmen would like to claim for advertising two conflicting functions: one that advertising is basically informative; the other that it molds and creates desires. The second function has considerable plausibility and there are contexts in which it is to the advantage of the ideology to stress it. The NAM authors note the possibility of "aggressive salesmanship" creating desires, and they assign an important historical place to salesmanship and advertising programs in increasing consumer demand.[61] Pride that advertising has stimulated demand and thus expanded the economy have been common; at one time advertising writers used to quote Calvin Coolidge and Winston Churchill on this point.[62] But this view is not easily consonant with autonomy of consumers' tastes. If toothpaste advertising has made us brush our teeth and thus given us the best teeth in the world (!)[63] or if soap advertising overcame our grandparents' fear of bathing thus ushering in "the prophylactic period in these United States," [64] the achievements may be admirable; but the sovereign power of the consumer to determine what the system will produce is logically brought into question.

Efforts to reconcile these conflicting claims are rare; those that occur are often very feeble. At one point the NAM authors assert rather lamely that "in the long run" the customer's discernment of what serves him best protects his autonomy.[65] In another place, they venture the more substantial argument that if advertising creates new desires it thereby has the effect of increasing the range of consumers' choices, hence of giving him "greater opportunity to develop along lines he selects for himself." [66] An older argument in the same vein is that a multiplicity of branded products bene-

[60] Carpenter, *Dollars and Sense*, p. 206.

[61] NAM, I: 485; NAM, II: 627, 632. Compare Durstine, *This Advertising Business*, p. 4.

[62] Durstine, *This Advertising Business*, p. 31 for Coolidge; Woodbridge in Carpenter, *Dollars and Sense*, p. 4 for Churchill.

[63] Queeny, *Spirit of Enterprise*, p. 172.

[64] O'Dea, *Preface to Advertising*, p. 85, "Advertising freed bathing from being dangerous."

[65] NAM, II: 632.

[66] NAM, I: 485.

fits the customers because of "the instinctive individuality of choice." "If there were only one brand of tooth paste in existence, it would be necessary to create another for the benefit of the tooth-paste customer . . . The interest of the consumer and the interest of the manufacturer are here identical." [67] The assertion of the Brand Names Foundation, that well-known brands have "won esteem the hard way" through competition for customers' favor and giving them *"exactly what they want,"* provides another link in a theory of the introduction of new products. It is admitted that, in the long run, tastes are molded by the advertising of new products. But, it is argued, advertising initially extends the range of the consumer's possible choices[68] and then wins his favor through superior gratification of his needs. The demand for a popular product is taken as evidence that this product has satisfied consumers better than its competitors.

This is a complex problem and, if the arguments of the business creed present difficulties, social science has not solved it satisfactorily either. It is by no means clear that advertising always increases the effective information available to consumers. In a market with an extensive array of advertised products, the choice problem is complicated and the consumer's information less likely to be adequate than if the range of choice were limited. In purchasing a particular product which he knows through advertising, the customer may be minimizing the anxiety of risk rather than maximizing the possible gratification of his individual taste. It is therefore not certain that an extended range of consumers' choice increases ultimate satisfactions or that a favored product has achieved its position by supplying greater satisfaction than its competitors.

The optimal gratification of consumers evidently depends on a delicate balance between the conflicting needs for standardization and variety. It is characteristic of ideology that the conflict of these needs is ignored; the business creed would have it both ways, extolling both the standardization of branded products and the variety of products which the "free enterprise" system makes possible. A serious, dispassionate study of this problem would have to compare the ways in which different institutional arrangements balance these needs. It might be true that a system of grade-labeling, vigorously enforced by the government, would deny variety to

[67] Calkins, *Business the Civilizer*, p. 10.

[68] An explicit admission that the molding of tastes occurs through substituting different goods primarily at the seller's initiative seems to be involved in some remarks of Jack Straus at a Harvard conference (Merrill, *Responsibilities of Business Leadership*, pp. 41–57).

The fact that tastes are molded not simply by extending information but by arousing feelings of emulation or anxiety does not gain an explicit place in systematic argument. (It is, on the other hand, not left entirely to discreet silence. Thus, "We've a better world with a bit of the proper kind of Fear in advertising — fear in women of being frumps, fear in men of being duds." O'Dea, *Preface to Advertising*, pp. 92–93.)

consumers to a point where optimal satisfaction is lower than it is under a free enterprise system. But this requires an argument which takes both the information and variety problems into consideration and no such arguments are to be found in the ideology.[69] The ideology steers clear of the problem of whether or not our present economy produces all the things which consumers want and could afford to buy. Richard Weil of Macy's in his response to Bernard DeVoto's polemic[70] really begs the question by assuming existing institutional arrangements.

The arguments found in the business ideology seem to follow orthodox economic thought in treating the tastes of the individual in isolation from those of other consumers. The satisfaction to be derived from consuming particular products is viewed as dependent on the intrinsic quality of the products in question. In taking this view, the ideology is reflecting not only the assumptions of economic theory but also those underlying much popular discussion. The critics of advertising, for example, have concentrated very heavily on the alleged misrepresentation of the intrinsic quality of goods and treated quality as the prime focus of consumer interest. The burden of Bernard DeVoto's criticism of business is suggested in his own maxim: "Build a worse mousetrap and the world will be forced to beat a pathway to your retail outlets." [71]

Common observation tells us that consumers are not concerned solely with quality and price. The consumer tends to purchase goods appropriate to his social status. Status considerations define for him the standards of a "decent" home, the "proper advantages" for his children, or "attractive" clothing for his wife. These considerations are rarely referred to overtly, but this is not because they are unimportant. It is rather because any discussion of whether or not a particular purchase is suited to one's social status would suggest the insecurity and exaggerated concerns of the parvenu, a danger which discussion of the intrinsic "quality" of goods does not raise. The American system of social stratification is one which places heavy emphasis on pragmatic achievements, particularly for men. An idle life involving sophisticated and "tasteful" consumption patterns is less highly regarded than in more aristocratic traditions, and there has been resistance to the possible competition of such bases for distinction with the norms of achievement in occupations. The emphasis on occupational achievement, combined with strong egalitarian values, has inhibited the cultivation, and even the recognition, of the importance of consumption patterns in symbolizing status. It is certainly no accident that the classic recognition of this point in American social science literature, Veblen's

[69] Compare the very fuzzy arguments in NAM, II: 633–634, or the rhetoric of Carpenter, *Dollars and Sense, passim,* against "standardization."
[70] DeVoto, *Fortune,* April 1951, p. 114. Weil, *Fortune,* June 1951, p. 19.
[71] *Ibid.,* p. 144. He asserts elsewhere: "the absolute question is the integrity of the end product."

Theory of the Leisure Class, was presented in an ironic, debunking guise.[72]

It follows that a great deal of popular discussion about the quality of goods, or the comforts and conveniences they offer, is probably rationalization. This is borne out by the observation of foreigners that the pressures to conform with conventional standards are peculiarly strong in America.[73] Observers from de Tocqueville to the present have found American consumers less distinguished as individualistic judges of quality than as anxious conformists to remarkably uniform and standardized patterns. There are good reasons why this should be so.[74] Since consumption patterns in any society symbolize social status, it seems probable that in a very mobile society such as America the patterns will differ from those in a less mobile one: for example, in a society based on ascribed status or one which has powerful local traditions. American consumption patterns would be expected to be more generalized throughout the society and more liable to change than, say, European patterns in which tradition plays a larger part in status differences and local variations are more prominent.

This makes it more difficult for the American consumer than for the European to know what standards are proper for him. What is the up-to-date pattern of consumption, in a culture where it is shifting all the time? What is the proper status for him to assume in his consumption pattern? This quest for standards is bound to cause anxiety to the American consumer.[75] Critics of American society sometimes exaggerate these anxieties, yet clearly they exist.

The business creed does not deny the obvious importance of standardized products in the American economy. Indeed, it often boasts of the benefits which have arisen from standardization. Beardsley Ruml claims that our writers no longer make fun of the fact that millions of Americans "eat the same cereals, drive the same cars, see the same movies, and wind the same watches," because we are beginning to understand the great values arising from standardization.[76] The chief benefit attributed to standardiza-

[72] Recently these matters have received a great deal of attention in the social science literature, in more sober and detached form. Compare David Riesman, Nathan Glazer, and Reuel Denney, *The Lonely Crowd* (New Haven, 1950), James S. Duesenberry, *Income, Saving, and the Theory of Consumer Behavior* (Cambridge, Mass., Harvard, 1949); Harvey Leibenstein, "Bandwagon, Snob, and Veblen Effects in the Theory of Consumers' Demand," *Quarterly Journal of Economics,* LXIV: 183–207 (1950).

[73] See, for example, the collection edited by Commager, *America in Perspective,* especially R. Mueller-Freienfels. See also André Siegfried, *America Comes of Age* (New York, 1927), p. 350; J. Hirsch, *Das Amerikanische Wirtschaftswunder* (Berlin, 1926), p. 219; H. Levy, *Volkscharakter und Wirtschaft* (Leipzig and Berlin, 1926), pp. 92–99.

[74] See Riesman, *Lonely Crowd,* chs. V–VII, where many of the relevant considerations are set forth.

[75] Note the amusing and perceptive article in *Life,* Sept. 3, 1951.

[76] Ruml, *Tomorrow's Business,* p. 38.

tion is that it enables higher productivity. Insofar as the implications of standardization for consumers' satisfactions are discussed, the main point stressed is that quality is assured and thus the picture of the individualistic consumer is preserved. The harassed conformist, so obvious to Europeans and to David Riesman, does not appear in this picture. Of course, consumers do choose among available goods on the basis of quality and price within the limitations imposed both by their financial resources and the standards imposed by their "reference groups." [77] But business ideology, in neglecting the role of socially determined standards, sketches only part of the picture and gives that part too large a share of the canvas.

In nonideological contexts, notably in advertisements of certain types of goods, businessmen show their intuitive awareness of the influence of status on consumption practices.[78] Thus we find a Cadillac advertisement discoursing like Thorstein Veblen or a modern sociologist:

It seems safe to say that there is no material possession which speaks more eloquently of the man who owns it than a Cadillac car.

Wherever it is driven, it offers authentic testimony as to its owner's good taste — his concern for the safety and comfort of his family and friends — and his general standing in the field of endeavor in which he has chosen to make his contribution to the world's affairs.

Indeed if a complete list were published of those who own and drive this distinguished car, it would be obvious that it has become a hall mark of achievement in almost every walk of life.[79]

Advertisements for those articles of personal use which present a wide scope for exercise of "personal taste" and concern for the sense of distinctiveness attaching to "good taste," exploit the consumers' need for "reference" models. Mrs. Orson Munn, Jr., "one of New York's most glamorous debutantes in 1947, and now one of the most charming hostesses in the younger set" has made the Camel 30-Day Mildness Test, we are told.[80] Mrs. Robert Bacon Whitney uses Pond's Vanishing Cream.[81] *Newsweek* appears "wherever people of importance and influence congregate." [82] This sort of advertising persists in the face of repeated criticism.[83]

[77] For this very useful concept, see R. K. Merton and A. S. Kitt, "Contributions to the Theory of Reference Group Behavior" in R. K. Merton and P. F. Lazarsfeld, *Studies in the Scope and Method of "The American Soldier"* (Glencoe, Ill., 1950).
[78] Calkins, *Business the Civilizer*, p. 159.
[79] *New York Times,* April 12, 1949. Note that "good taste" is really a solicitous concern for the "safety and comfort" of others.
[80] *Woman's Home Companion,* June 1949.
[81] *Woman's Home Companion,* April 1949, p. 80.
[82] *Newsweek* advertisement, *New Yorker,* May 22, 1948, pp. 60–61.
[83] It has been subject to criticism for a long time — particularly in its use of solicited individual testimonials from well-known figures. See Calkins, *Business the Civilizer,* and Durstine, *This Advertising Business,* O'Dea, *Preface to Advertising,* pp. 59–63. ". . . testimonials are as old as Eve, and so is their misuse" — p. 59.)

The dependence of American consumption patterns on social influences as well as on individual judgments of quality and price is recognized also in the obverse of snob appeal. The acceptability of relatively uniform, standardized products that "everybody likes" has been directly exploited by many advertisers. Thus, Old Golds flatter the competence of the general public, "You're the tobacco expert we seek to please." [84]

The relation between consumption patterns and social status in America is seldom considered — unless casually and unsystematically — in business writings. There are various reasons why this should be so. For one thing, recognition of "band-wagon effects" among consumers would imperil the claim that any product which beats out its competitors maximizes consumers' satisfactions. This claim is in danger of becoming a tautology if, among competing goods of similar qualities, the satisfaction of choosing the winner depends on the fact that it is the winner.[85] The autonomy of consumers' tastes and thus the whole framework of consumer sovereignty arguments become very dubious. If the doctrine of consumers' sovereignty is to be maintained in relatively clear form, one must cling to the classical picture of the consumer as an independent individual interested only in the quality and cost of his purchases.

THE "SERVICE" SYMBOL

Business ideology, then, has produced no clear alternative to the classical explanation of the relation between seller and consumer. In contrast to other subjects, where a well-developed managerial alternative has appeared, little systematic treatment of the consumer's place in "transformed" American capitalism has developed. Indeed, the peculiar institutional features of American markets and consumption patterns have been largely ignored, in favor of stressing the more abstract conceptions of markets borrowed from classical economics. If a somewhat different emphasis would endanger some of the claims that classical ideology bases upon consumer sovereignty, it would also have some compensating advantages. In any serious comparative study of the development of the American and other Western economies, the sociological determinants of demand should play an important role. The great achievements of the American economy have been dependent on a high receptivity of consumers to new and standardized products, and this receptivity can hardly be explained solely as a consequence of the initiative and aggressiveness of American entrepreneurs.

Some adumbrations of a different conception of the relation between

---

[84] Old Gold advertisement, *Saturday Evening Post*, April 2, 1949, p. 43.

[85] The "reference group" here may, of course, be limited. Thus the appeal of some products (like fancy cigarettes) may be precisely dependent on the fact that a select group, not everybody, is thought to use them.

seller and consumer have appeared in the ideology, particularly in the service theme, to which we now turn.

Some years ago, H. L. Mencken compiled a list of various occupations and professions which proclaimed themselves to be "in service." The list was a long one: ". . . bankers, druggists, grocers, superintendents of schools, proprietors of gents' furnishing stores, teachers, professors in third-rate universities, butchers, owners of Ford garages, proprietors of shoe stores, grain and feed dealers, vendors of stationery and school supplies, ice, coal and wood dealers, dentists, proprietors of soft-drink emporiums, agents for hygienic corsets, boarding-house keepers, insurance agents, proprietors of lunch rooms, advertising solicitors, station agents, secretaries to associations, promoters of daylight mausoleums, realtors, and postmasters." [86] In advertising and in ideology service is the major symbol used to describe the businessman's relationship to his customers. Evidently this was as true in 1925 as it is today. What does the ideology mean by service?

A sampling of uses of the "service" symbol reveals that it has a variety of meanings and ambiguities. In a 1949 advertisement, Revere Copper and Brass proclaims to its "colleagues in American business" the pride it takes in having brought copper flashing to homes. "This we regard as a valuable public service . . . It would be difficult for Revere to decide which provides the greater satisfaction; sales, or the knowledge that fine copper flashing has been brought to home owners . . . This is an excellent example of the way in which a search for expanded markets results in increased service to the people. It is thoroughly in the American tradition." [87] The advertising of the Bell Telephone System regularly stresses the devotion of the whole organization to providing "service." "All across the land, you will find teamwork and neighborliness among telephone people. They take satisfaction in providing a valuable service to the public." The system is actuated by the "traditional spirit of service to get the message through . . . we look forward to providing a service better and more valuable in the future than at any time in the past. We pledge our utmost efforts to that end." [88] The Association of American Railroads provides a "trackside report" entitled "You and Your Railroads," detailing how the railroads

[86] *American Mercury,* November 1925 (quoted in Siegfried, *America Comes of Age,* p. 178). Mencken's corresponding list of those not "in service" includes "cowboys, actors, bootleggers, opera singers, prize-fighters, lumbermen, head-waiters, pool champions, baseball players, stick-up men, writers, newspaper men, gangsters, sculptors, soldiers, prostitutes, acrobats, and doctors."

[87] Revere Copper and Brass advertisement, *New York Times,* April 10, 1949.

[88] Bell Telephone System. *1948 Annual Report,* excerpted in a widely appearing advertisement. Such matter is common in the widely distributed annual reports. See, for example, "Serving New England," pp. 18–19; *Annual Report, New England Tel. and Tel. Co.,* 1950.

"did their job of serving you last year." [89] The Oil Industry Information Committee reminds us: "Oil works round the clock for you . . . The efficient dependable service provided by your jobber symbolizes the progressiveness of the entire oil industry." [90] New investment in the oil industry is proudly connected with service; thus, Standard Oil of New Jersey — "We're spending One Thousand Million Dollars to meet your growing needs for oil." [91] Business sponsored research aims at better "service" or a "better life for all." [92]

Occasionally the obvious ambiguities of "service" become too great to be tolerated. Because "service is a misused word," Monroe Calculating Company takes a page to explain just exactly what "Monroe service" means.[93] But *Better Homes and Gardens,* in the same issue of *Time,* proudly describes itself as "America's First Service Magazine" and muddies the waters with an argument that fiction in a magazine is not "service" and that by eliminating fiction it sells "readers and advertisers exactly the same thing — 100% service." [94]

Although the ultimate consumer gets the lion's share of "service," the business world is not neglected. The motto of Monsanto Chemical Company is "Serving Industry — Which Serves Mankind," and a spokesman of a holding company can proclaim "(Electric) Bond and Share has always regarded itself as primarily a service institution." [95] Taking a global view, Cameron once rhapsodized:

> All life is a symphony, and industry is one of the choirs of the orchestra that produces it. A view of life is forming that will include the industrial world among the finer arts of human service.[96]

To other enthusiasts the course of business and indeed of human history has been determined by devotion to "service." If our own society has escaped the evil fate of Rome, we must look for explanation to our tradition of "service" whereby we plowed back profits which the selfish Roman capitalists used for themselves.[97] An older spokesman considers "service" the overriding aim and secret of success of American businesses.

[89] Assn. of American Railroads advertisement, *Saturday Evening Post,* Jan. 22, 1949.
[90] Oil Industry Information Committee advertisement, *Saturday Evening Post,* May 14, 1949, p. 69.
[91] Standard of New Jersey advertisement, *Harper's,* June 1949.
[92] Bell Telephone advertisement, *Look,* July 6, 1948, p. 7.
[93] Monroe Calculating Company advertisement, *Time,* Feb. 16, 1948, p. 115.
[94] Better Homes and Gardens advertisement, *Time,* Feb. 16, 1948, p. 83.
[95] G. G. Walker, President, in *Individual Initiative in Business,* p. 55.
[96] Ford Hour, Jan. 15, 1939.
[97] Hon. Hugh S. Butler, *How Profits Benefit the People.* Printed in the Appendix of the Congressional Record, July 6, 1950, at Butler's request and privately distributed separately.

Analyze the success of our great industrial corporations and you will find the secret of their success in service. Banks, insurance companies, department stores, public utilities, corporations and many others all feature service. The wonderful research facilities which have been described by our critics as conducted by the more prominent business concerns are all for the one purpose of service. And service is one of the great phases of modern economics. It is a modern blessing. Nothing contributes so much to the happiness of mankind as service.[98]

The American businessman's talk about "service" has long been a source of puzzled scepticism or scornful incredulity to domestic critics like Mr. Mencken and particularly to foreign observers.[99] These observers and critics have apparently been skeptical because they interpreted "service" as expressing benevolent concern. But it is not always clear that a benevolence toward the consumer is implied by the word "service." Its ambiguities should have been sufficiently exhibited in the examples we have given. They are, of course, rooted in common speech where we refer variously to "goods and services," the "service" provided by a durable good, or of "serving" an organization. American business literature may at times have deliberately exploited these ambiguities in making the inevitable economic references to "services" suggest benevolence, but certainly not all of the service proclamations have invited this interpretation. In some contexts "service" is clearly in the interests of good business, as in the Rotary Club motto — "He profits most who serves best." An NAM marketing spokesman argues, in an eloquent passage, that "The manufacturer can profit only as he serves." [100] Other examples range from this instrumental view of service toward pure benevolence. Sometimes the use of "service" implies that the businessman wants satisfied customers not merely because it "pays" but also because, like the Revere spokesman, the spectacle of satisfied customers is in itself gratifying, or like the Illinois Central, because he enjoys being a "good neighbor." [101] It is also easy to find more extravagant claims of disinterested concern for the customer or the general welfare. Cameron alleged that Henry Ford often said: "If I knew anything

[98] Carpenter, *Dollars and Sense,* p. 207. On p. 208, "service" is equated with "happiness."

[99] European observers have found it necessary to explain to their readers that the claims seem to be sincerely made. Siegfried, *America Comes of Age,* pp. 178–179, tried to account for it as a mixture of Protestantism, Benthamite materialism, and devotion to progress which the American might possibly believe, because the American deceives himself so easily. A German observer in the twenties — Hirsch, *Das Amerikanische Wirtschaftswunder,* pp. 227–229 — cautioned against regarding it as pure cant and tried to make of it an "unconscious American socialism."

[100] NAM, II: 666. The motto of Lincoln Electric Company, Cleveland, is almost identical with the Rotary motto: "He who serves best will profit most."

[101] *Fortune,* February 1951, p. 180.

better to do for the country than build motor cars, I would do it." [102] And General Foods' Chairman of the Board sees the next generation of business leadership measuring its success in terms of the greatest service to the greatest numbers of people.[103]

At least one common thread runs through all these various uses of the word "service": the relations of businessmen and customers are depicted in a way that minimizes the market transaction as such, and stresses the benefits to the customer. This view stands in contrast to the classical picture of a symmetrical relation between self-interested parties; here, the self-interest of the seller is replaced by concern that the customer be satisfied. The line between description of the advantages a customer gains from dealing with a businessman and the imputation that these advantages are the businessman's ruling and ultimate concern is apt to be a fuzzy one. It has commonly been ignored both by business and its critics, and "service" has easily meant benevolence.

In spite of the incredulity it arouses in some critics, the "service" theme surely contains a significant element of truth. The businessman is not entirely self-interested in relation to his customers; he is capable of disinterested behavior. On the other hand, it is not accurate to say that the businessman shows no sign of calculated self-interest. Profit-seeking behavior is an institutional requirement of the businessman's role, no matter how altruistic his character. The service ideology seems to overlook this institutional requirement completely, or at least to blur it beyond recognition. The classical strand in the ideology goes to the opposite extreme and gives exclusive attention to self-interest on both sides of the market.

The service symbol recognizes the continuing relationship between many a business firm and a body of customers. As in the case of labor relations, examined in Chapter 6, continuities of this kind provide an opportunity for stressing common interests and attachments in place of conflicting economic goals. For obvious reasons the public utilities have been among the first to stress the permanent link between customer and seller. New England Tel. and Tel. believes its annual report should be available not only to stockholders but also to customers who have "an equal stake in what goes on." [104] The Boston Consolidated Gas Company

---

[102] Ford Hour, Dec. 4, 1938. Mr. Ford made strong pronouncements on the subject of "service." In a published interview he once said, "(Service) is so often used just to cover cheap and easy gestures involving no thought or work, that it is necessary to point out that service, to be anything at all, must be the basic policy of a business and must carry through its every action." *A Basis for Stability*, p. 73, quoted by C. C. Chapman, *Development of American Business and Banking Thought, 1913–1936*, (London, New York, Toronto, 1936), p. 100.

[103] Merrill, *Responsibilities of Business Leadership*, p. 8.

[104] New England Telephone and Telegraph Company, leaflet, with the suggestive title *Between Ourselves*, regularly distributed with bills. March 1950.

explains a rate increase to its customers with regrets and an assurance that "We're All in This Together." [105] The use of these persisting ties to customers in any general theory of social organization, as Chester Barnard has attempted,[106] does not occur. Occasionally it may be claimed that "business" includes not only managers but employees and customers as well, but so far as customers are concerned, such claims hardly get beyond vague assertions of mutual dependence. The opportunities for describing relations to consumers in terms that stress the reassuring elements of the continuing responsibility of the business remain to be exploited in further development of managerial ideology.

[105] Leaflet, *Boston Gas News,* 1949, distributed with bills.
[106] Barnard, *Organization and Management,* ch. V. The spirit of this analysis seems definitely that of disinterested investigation rather than ideology.

8

THE FUNCTIONING OF A COMPETITIVE SYSTEM

GENERALIZED EXPLANATIONS of the over-all functioning of the economic system are naturally less frequent in the business creed than pronouncements on particular issues, such as the role of trade unions or the proper size of profits. While hostile ideologies attack the "system" in general terms, detailed discussion tends to focus on specific "vices" of the system, and the defense of the system by business ideology must be similarly specific. In the bulk of business ideology, therefore, the general laws of operation of the system are assumed to be known; they are referred to symbolically, not explained in detail. These laws, formal and abstract in character, make poor material for advertisements, speeches, Congressional testimony, and pamphlets. Their exposition is for the most part confined to a few books — some of them textbooks — which deal at length with the whole system or major parts of it.[1] While these treatises share with other ideological media the usual characteristics of ideology — selectivity and symbolic appeal — they are necessarily constrained more by the demands of logical coherence and consistency.

[1] Some of the more formal explanations of the System are found in:
National Association of Manufacturers (NAM), Economic Principles Commission, *The American Individual Enterprise System. Its Nature and Future* (1946)
Editors of Fortune, *USA: The Permanent Revolution* (1951)
E. M. Queeny, *The Spirit of Enterprise* (1943)
S. Wells Utley, *The American System, Shall We Destroy It?* (1936)
Henry Hazlitt, *Economics in One Lesson* (1946)
E. L. Klein, *How to Stay Rich: The Story of Democratic American Capitalism* (1950)
C. B. Randall, *A Creed for Free Enterprise* (1952)
W. A. Paton, *Shirtsleeve Economics* (1952)
H. G. Weaver, *Mainspring, The Story of Human Progress and How Not to Prevent It* (1947)
These books are not the only ones of this type written, and other representatives have been examined; but, as with the evidence in general, the high degree of identity of content in different sources makes the sampling problem relatively unimportant. Of these sources, the NAM volumes are by far the most ambitious attempt at systematization, thoroughness, and completeness.

The statement of general laws that govern the functioning of the whole economic system is, one might expect, a complicated task. Not so in the ideology: the economy is governed by natural, commonsense rules which anyone can understand — hence titles such as "Shirtsleeve Economics" and "Economics in One Lesson." The NAM authors draw a sharp distinction between the concepts of academic economists "so refined and so technical that (they) do not fit the realities of the business world" and their own simple analysis.[2] The emphasis on simplicity and practicality is partly dialectical — abstraction and complexity are attributed to New Deal Professors and theorists.[3] But it is also part of a basic anti-intellectual slant in the business ideology; "practical knowledge" gained in meeting payrolls is far more valuable than speculative abstract thought.

THE CLASSICAL EXPLANATION: "FUNCTIONAL" ARGUMENTS

The classical and managerial versions of how the economy functions are best exemplified in the NAM volumes and *USA: The Permanent Revolution* respectively. The classical explanation is like the model of a competitive, private enterprise economy found in economics textbooks. It combines two quite different streams of economic thought. The first is the "classical" economics of which the Physiocrats, Adam Smith and J. S. Mill were representative; the second is the "neo-classical" writings of Walras and Marshall. On what can be called the incentive level — the forces moving individuals in the market — the ideology borrows liberally from the laissez-faire views of the classical economists, and also from the view of the nature of human motivation held by early nineteenth-century utilitarians such as Jeremy Bentham. On what may be called the functional level of analysis — the prices, quantities, incomes, etc. generated by the system without much reference to the economic actors as individuals — the ideology selects from, and greatly dilutes, the neo-classical theory of perfectly competitive general equilibrium.[4] These two aspects of the analy-

---

[2] NAM, I: 589. This occurs in the context of a discussion of the meaning of competition and monopoly. The passage also contains the statement that "this vague concept of the general public is at least as valuable and as valid as the concept which has been developed by many recent writers on this subject."

[3] See, especially, Queeny, *Spirit of Enterprise.*

[4] It is striking that the ideology makes use of the general equilibrium model of perfect competition, one of the most remarkable achievements of abstract academic economics. First worked out in detail by Leon Walras in 1874, this model remained almost unknown to English economics, especially at the textbook level, until the last twenty-five years. The process of selection and redefinition by which this highly abstract model is adapted to the uses of the business ideology will be analyzed after the exposition of the ideology's content; but two broad features of the process are worth pointing out here. First, motivation is given an independent concrete existence, rather than viewed as a relationship between human actors and their social situation. Second, competition and other key concepts are used in a variety of meanings, not consistent with their meanings in the model from which the concepts were drawn.

sis are on somewhat different levels of abstraction. Analysis on the level of incentives is usually employed in the more popular explanations, such as Utley's or Queeny's, while the purely functional analysis is worked out in detail only in the relatively academic treatise of the NAM.[5]

In comparison with what is offered in the classical version of the creed, the managerial explanation of the over-all working of the competitive system is scanty. On the incentive level, the managerial version differs by placing emphasis on the responsible decisions of socially minded businessmen, absent in the classical version. On the functional level of analysis, the managerial creed simply lacks any fully defined explanation to supplant the competitive model of the classical creed. The managerial creed, in dealing with the individual enterprise, emphasizes the power of management decisions and the importance of responsible exercise of that power. However, when the creed deals with the whole economy, no similar single decision-making authority is envisaged, of course, yet there is no explanation — other than the competitive one of the classical creed — of just how the responsible decisions in each individual enterprise are coordinated for the whole economy. The result is a gap in the logical structure of the managerial version of the creed, which is usually filled with a general reference to the forces of competition, but which lacks the detailed working-out of the classical creed.

On the functional level, the two major characteristics of the classical explanation are freedom of consumer choice and a multitude of independent private enterprises striving to meet consumer demands under the stimuli and pressures of profits and losses. As long as there is free competition, each business serves the whole society, that is, the consumer, simply by striving to make a profit. Competition may take place in price, in quality, in salesmanship, in service, in credit, in courtesy, in packaging, or in any other way in which the businessmen can influence the consumers' choice of products. As long as the buyer has freedom to choose among sellers, all sellers strive to increase the degree to which they satisfy consumers. Just as there is competition among businessmen to satisfy consumers, there is competition among businessmen to hire workers, to use the flow of savings, the available raw materials, and the flow of new ideas. On the other side, there is competition among workers for jobs, among savers for investment outlets and among businessmen to seize opportunities for profit.

As long as competition flourishes, the NAM text states, the system will:

(1) tend to assure that goods and services will be produced and distributed at the lowest possible cost;

[5] See especially chs. 1, 3, 9, 10, 12, and 14. The exposition of the functional analysis which follows is drawn largely from the six chapters cited.

(2) tend to assure that profits will be held to the minimum, because prices have to be kept down;

(3) tend to assure that the energy and raw material and productive capacity of the nation will be used for providing those goods and services which the public wants and in proportion to the demands of the public as reflected in the market place;

(4) tend to assure that each factor in production will be paid, through wages, rent, interest, or profits, in harmony with the public's estimate of the contribution it makes;

(5) assure that a constant effort will be made to widen the choice of goods and services offered to the public;

(6) assure that a constant effort will be made to improve the attractiveness of goods offered for sale;

(7) assure freedom of opportunity, by making it possible for anyone at any time to enter any line of business he desires for which he has the necessary capital; and

(8) assure free and continuous progress and a gradually improving scale of living, through the production of more and more kinds of goods, of better and better quality, at prices which a large and larger proportion of the public can afford to pay.

"In a word," the statement continues, "from the point of view of the public welfare, competition serves as a regulator and reducer of prices, as an incentive to improved production efficiency, as a guarantee that we shall get what we want, and as a protector of the freedom of opportunity." [6]

According to the classical explanation, the competitive system functions through the mediation of the price mechanism; prices are the indicators which direct businessmen to those activities which are profitable. Since profit is the difference between the cost of providing a good or a service, and the price which consumers are willing to pay for it, the existence of profit in the provision of any good or service shows that it is worth more to consumers than it costs, and therefore that its production should be expanded. Similarly, the existence of loss shows that the good is worth less to consumers than it costs and that production should be contracted or abandoned altogether. Thus the bait of profits and the threats of losses are the guiding force which directs economic activity. Profits can change to losses, or losses to profits; as consumer tastes shift, new goods are introduced, new methods of production become available, old raw materials disappear. All these changes are reflected in the continual fluctuation of prices, which set in motion the appropriate responses of business. The free price mechanism regulates the market; it is the prerequisite of effective competition.

Under the competitive system there is a harmony of interests between producers and consumers and between labor and capital. A prime virtue

⁶ NAM, I: 58–59.

of the competitive market, as described in the ideology, is that it creates such harmony. Prices are determined at just that level where the interests of consumers and producers are balanced: prices lower than that level would at first deprive producers of profits to the benefit of consumers; this would ultimately lead to curtailment of supply, to the detriment of the consumers. Prices higher than that level would, in the first instance, take money from consumers to the advantage of producers; this would soon curtail demand so that producers would be forced to contract output or lower prices. Similarly, competition fixes the relative payments of labor and capital so that both are used to the best advantage. Wages and profits are not competing claims; both are paid out of production and both can be increased by increasing production.

In the classical version, over-all harmony flows automatically from the proper functioning of the system. This may be contrasted with the managerial version in which harmony is deliberately created within the enterprise by the managers.[7] The former is macroscopic, the latter microscopic. As we have already pointed out, the managerial version of business ideology really lacks an explanation of how the microscopic harmony the managers create within each enterprise results in macroscopic harmony in the system as a whole.

The classical explanation is full of warnings that the harmonious functioning of the system may be upset in various ways, principally by government intervention and monopoly; of these the former is the more important and indeed the latter often flows from it. "Most instances of monopoly power are either directly or indirectly government-made. Were it not for the policies of various governments, there would exist some local and regional monopolies, but only rare cases of national, and still less of international monopolies." [8] In castigating the New Deal, Queeny points to the monopolistic aspects of New Deal legislation on unions, of the NRA, and of the Guffey Act.[9] Sometimes, too, the government is called the greatest of all monopolies.[10] The more common complaint is that improper government intervention — which includes any attempt to fix prices or control outputs, as well as business activities on the part of the government — upsets the harmonious operation of the economic system, and results in waste and inefficiency.[11]

In dealing with the effects of monopoly, the classical creed broadly

[7] See Chapter 3 above.
[8] NAM, II: 621–622.
[9] Queeny, *Spirit of Enterprise,* p. 44.
[10] See, for example, First National Bank of Boston, *New England Letter,* 1949, quoting Senator B. H. Hill, "There is one corporation we may all dread. That corporation is the Federal Government." (1878.)
[11] See Chapter 9 below for a detailed discussion of the proper sphere of government activity as seen in business ideology.

follows neo-classical economic theory. The NAM authors find that, under conditions of monopoly, consumers will not get what they want produced most efficiently and sold at prices which correspond to costs, and monopolists will get excess profits.[12] Fortunately, the creed finds that monopoly is rare. Monopoly is the absence of competition — in price, in service, in quality, in salesmanship, in any of the other ways it may take place. The absence of competition arises only when businessmen agree not to compete, when they engage in a conspiracy in restraint of trade.[13] The creed suggests that such conspiracies are isolated incidents, in a class with embezzlement, fraud, and other occasional misdeeds of individual businessmen. That monopoly is something akin to a crime is emphasized by the extent to which "competing" is made a moral duty for businessmen.[14] This moral note is often sounded in contrasts between productive, efficient, competitive America and backward, slothful, cartelized Europe; the clear implication is that the difference is essentially one of American moral superiority.[15]

[12] NAM, II: 597–601.

An example of a more popular exposition of the virtues of competition and the vices of monopoly, still on the functional level of analysis, is a speech by President Robert Dunlop of the Sun Oil Company to the Petroleum Club of the Cleveland Chamber of Commerce on October 15, 1953, entitled "The Challenge of Free Markets." Its theme is the working of the free market to produce adequate supplies and lower prices; the retail gasoline market is held out as an example of "competition in action" which everybody can see for himself.

In the even more popular medium of a full-page newspaper advertisement, another oil company furnishes an example of the more compressed exposition of the same theme appropriate to the medium. The advertisement, entitled "American Incident," connects the discussion of "the age-old question whether rulers can plan the economic life of the people as well as the people themselves" with the then recent fears of oil shortage in the United States, and the way oil supply increased in response to price rises. "It was not a miracle, on the contrary, it was the natural American way of guiding production and consumption by the free operation of the price mechanism. The anticipated shortage caused competition to bid up the price of crude oil. This created greater incentive to discover and produce crude . . . Without the profit incentive, and the profits of earlier years, it would have been impossible for the oil industry to convert an economy of scarcity in 1948 to one of plenty today in 1949. Further, just as rising prices automatically stimulated production so today excess production swings the price pendulum downward. Economic law, unhampered, thus works day and night to bring back the balanced economy toward which it is always striving. It has never been done by executive order." Cities Service Oil Company advertisement, *New York Herald Tribune,* April 8, 1949.

[13] NAM, II: 593–594; Queeny, *Spirit of Enterprise,* 71–72.

[14] See Paton, *Shirtsleeve Economics,* pp. 178–185; Randall, *A Creed,* pp. 19–21.

[15] See Randall, p. 25; Paton, pp. 179–180. This is not to say that there are no real differences in the degree of competitiveness between the United States and the countries of Western Europe, and that those differences are unrelated to the large difference in productivity between the two areas. Rather, the specifically ideological elements involved in the passages referred to are their concentration on this factor to the exclusion of many other elements involved, and their implicit explanation of the difference as a matter of conscious choice by businessmen.

Harmful monopoly arises only from agreements in restraint of trade. Single suppliers of a particular product, say, under patent or copyright protection, or simply because no other seller has arisen to challenge them, are not monopolists in this sense; they do not interfere with the effective functioning of the system. The NAM writers, in making this point, speak of an author selling his book under copyright protection and a singer with unique talents as examples of such monopolies.

The author can refuse to sell his book for less than $50 a copy, and the singer can refuse to perform for less than $1,000 a song. Of course, no one may be willing to pay such prices, but that is beside the point. The important fact is that these sellers have complete ability to set the price at which the market will be supplied with their products, and that ability means that they have a monopoly. Now these, of course, are simple examples, and not of the type that we ordinarily have in mind when we think of monopolies. But just because of their simplicity they can be visualized free of all the ramifications of a complicated monopoly situation and hence serve perfectly to bring out what is perhaps the basic point of all in a sound appraisal of the problems of competition and monopoly. This point is that it is not the existence of monopoly itself (a single seller, in the sense of the discussion above) "which is contrary to the public interest." It is conspiracy in restraint of trade, including under the term "conspiracy" all contracts and combinations entered into for the purpose of restraining trade.[16]

The same point is made in another way by stressing "inter-industry" competition and competition for the consumer's dollar. Queeny sounds both these themes.

Though a company might have a monopoly of supply of a commodity such as aluminum, this monopoly loses much of its force because of competing commodities performing similar functions. Aluminum, for instance, competes with copper for power transmission lines, stainless steel in the production of railroad cars . . . (etc.) There is no aluminum use that cannot be satisfied by a competing article.

Each housewife has her budget. Naturally she allocates her expenditures to those goods or services from which she believes she gets the most enjoyment or utility. It may be a question of a trip or a new refrigerator; a chair or a new radio . . . (etc.) And the money goes where the best value is offered. Therefore, every businessman's enlightened self-interest demands that selling prices be kept to the lowest point compatible with reasonable profit.[17]

This theme parallels that of dollar voting by the consumer — a frequent element in advertisements and other unsystematic expressions of ideology.

Since restraint of trade arising from conspiracies is said to interfere with the effective functioning of the economy, the need for outlawing such

[16] NAM, II: 593–594.
[17] Queeny, *Spirit of Enterprise*, pp. 116, 117.

conspiracies is clearly recognized in the business creed. The Sherman Act performs this function, and performs it so effectively that such conspiracies are rare. The ideology frequently gives the impression that conspiracies were frequent in the nineteenth century but that the danger they presented was soon recognized by the public; in consequence, the Sherman Act outlawing such restraints (when they affected interstate commerce) was passed in 1890. The enforcement of this law soon led to the virtual disappearance of monopolies; and in the ideology monopoly is more an interesting historical curiosum than a current problem. Thus the NAM authors, in analyzing monopoly and the effects of the Sherman Act, choose the American Tobacco case of 1911 as an example for extended discussion; they also give a list of leading cases up to 1912, but nothing is said of Sherman Act prosecutions since that time.[18] Yet of the 1100-odd cases initiated by the United States Government under the Sherman Act from 1890 to the end of January 1952, more than 700 were brought since 1932.[19] In the same vein Queeny considers that the attempts of recent governments to enforce the Sherman Act have been misplaced; he referred to them as "Thurman Arnold's campaign against so-called monopolies, conspiracies in restraint of trade, alleged abuses of the patent system, and international cartels," but he approved of anti-trust activity directed against "new enterprise restricted, competition stifled, fellow citizens exploited," the true targets of anti-trust legislation.[20]

THE CLASSICAL EXPLANATION: INCENTIVE ARGUMENTS

Analyses in terms of incentives outweigh those on the functional level. Of the books listed at the beginning of this chapter, those by Utley, Weaver, and Queeny are entirely devoted to an analysis of the system from the point of view of incentives, and those by Randall and Klein, largely so. Even the NAM treatise and Paton's *Shirtsleeve Economics,* which offer the fullest exposition of the functional analysis, contain a large amount of material cast in terms of incentives. Advertisements and speeches frequently exhibit slogans drawn from the incentive level of analysis, which is suitable for such media; the demands for extended logical exposition implicit in the functional explanation of the system preclude its appearance in these forms.

The grand themes of this aspect of the ideology are freedom and the right of the individual to act in accordance with his own view of his own

[18] NAM, II: 604–614.

[19] Commerce Clearing House, *Blue Book of the Anti-Trust Laws* (New York, 1952 ed.). This listing includes some cases brought by the Department of Justice under other anti-trust legislation, including the Clayton Act, but does not include any cases initiated by the Federal Trade Commission.

[20] Queeny, *Spirit of Enterprise,* pp. 70, 89.

interests — Adam Smith's "obvious and simple system of natural liberty." [21] The essence of freedom is an organization which permits individuals to act in this way. The virtue of freedom is that individuals acting on their own initiative to further their own interests, act with efficiency, energy, determination, and spontaneity to a degree that is never present under any other social arrangement. The ideology gives to both individual freedom and individual interest a somewhat restricted interpretation: individual interest can always be measured in terms of income or wealth; individual freedom is essentially freedom to use and dispose of property and to sell or purchase goods and services in the market in accordance with one's wishes.

The NAM authors find that the four essential elements of our system of individual enterprise are: opportunities for earning profit in business activities as an incentive to business activity; the right to accumulate property and to transfer it by bequest as an incentive to the full use of productive ability; the legal sanctity of contract, as an encouragement to make future commitments; and competitive freedom in the choice of activities suitable to the abilities of each individual, to stimulate the full use of capacities and to keep the society fluid and progressive. While these principles have "at times, under misguided leadership . . . been seriously impaired," they have prevailed over our history as a whole, and should prevail in the future. [22]

The author of *Mainspring* begins by asking the question: "Why did men die of starvation (all over the world) for six thousand years? Why is it that we in America have never had a famine?" He finds the answer not in our superior endowment of natural resources, nor in harder work, nor in greater physical capacity for work but simply in one great invention: "our new and original concept of political structure based on a principle that is just as true, just as real, just as inexorable as any law of physics — the principle of individual liberty and freedom — the principle that each person controls his own life-energy and is responsible for his own acts and for his relationships with others." The central liberty is, of course, liberty to engage in economic activity without government regulation, direction, or control. This liberty is the cornerstone of all other liberties: "the misguided benevolence of complete social and economic power always leads to the ruthless suppression of religious freedom, personal freedom, freedom of expression — and even freedom of thought." The virtues of liberty and property arise simply from the fact that only through free institutions and private property can the energies of man be mobilized under "their own natural control"; any attempt at "authoritarian control" can only lead to

---

[21] Adam Smith, *Wealth of Nations, passim.*
[22] NAM, I: 6–8.

dissipation of human energies, and therefore to low productivity and no progress.[23]

Another student of human nature, Ernest Klein, asks: "Will an individual work harder for a slice of economic pie over which he has no control than he will for one which is seasoned to his taste and cut to his size? The answer appears to be, on the basis of totalitarian state examples to date, that he will not. Therefore the size of the national economic pie and the size of the individual slices all seemed to be doomed or impaired under controlled (as opposed to free) economies." [24]

Similarly, Utley announces that "in all human history there have been only two systems — the system of force and the system of freedom based on the hope of profit and the fear of loss. In present-day language, one is called the socialist philosophy, the other the capitalist system. We cannot have part of one and part of the other; they cannot be combined." [25] This last sentence makes an important and frequently repeated point: that freedom in the sense in which it is used in the ideology is absolute and indivisible, and any "encroachment" on it is a first step — if not more — to the destruction of the whole system. Lincoln's language, "We cannot exist half-slave and half-free" is frequently used in making this point; and advertisements embodying this theme in one form or another are often put out by industries subject to specific government regulation such as railroads and electric utilities.

The profit incentive is considered the motivation par excellence of the free society. While it is usually applied to seizing business opportunities in the market, it is not limited to this activity. All productive activity is attributed to a profit motive, and this motive is identified with the "human desire for betterment." Thus *Mainspring* finds that all human effort is motivated by Hope and Fear: the hope of reward and the fear of punishment. When Hope is dominant in the form of profit and Fear is at worst the fear of bankruptcy and personal insecurity, efforts are high. When Fear is dominant, as in all Authoritarian societies, efforts are low.[26]

The profit motive is said to be a fundamental natural law, rather than

[23] Weaver, *Mainspring*, p. 2.
[24] Klein, *How to Stay Rich*, p. 115.
[25] Utley, *The American System*, p. 21.
[26] Weaver, *Mainspring*, pp. 207–208.

A Warner & Swasey advertisement, *Business Week*, April 23, 1949, holds up the same hopes and fears. The caption warns, "The cake eaters are talking again." and the cake eaters are identified as those who want to "have government controls but keep your liberty . . . restrict corporations but keep individual opportunity for yourself and your children." The fallacy of these propositions is pointed out, and the reader is told that "more than anything else, what made this country great was — the chance for a man to go into business with hope of profit; the fear of loss, which drives him to work like ten men; the right to keep his profits in his business, to make it grow."

a socially conditioned institution. Thus Queeny tells us that incentives under capitalism correspond to fundamental human nature, while those on which socialism relies do not. Human nature is unchangeable, and socialist utopias ignore man's sinfulness.[27] And Utley speaks of Adam Smith and Thomas Jefferson as "discoverers, not makers, of laws" in the same sense as James Watt discovered rather than made the laws of gas pressure. In the same passage Utley says that Adam Smith outlines "the eternal laws of human conduct as applied to economic fields." [28]

THE SPHERES OF BUSINESS AND GOVERNMENT

Classical ideology, whether on the functional or on the incentive level of argument, finds a clear and natural demarcation between the sphere of business activity and that of government. The NAM volumes state that activities producing general public benefits which serve practically everybody, and whose benefits are not easily measured in money terms, are appropriate for government operation. Besides purely governmental functions — such as operating police departments or law courts — these activities include schools, highways, parks, fire protection, flood control, harbors, irrigation projects, water works, post offices. Any tendency to expand government operations beyond these limits would result in inefficiency and inject political pressures into situations in which decisions should be made on a businesslike basis. The Post Office provides an example of the best that can be expected when government is in business, and its operations are inefficient and uneconomical. This is shown by a comparison between the 50 per cent increase in the first-class mail rate with the 50 per cent decrease in the long distance phone rate in the past thirty years; as well as by the ability of private enterprises competing with it to make money on services on which the Post Office loses, for example, parcel post, or transfer of money.[29]

Government activity in those spheres properly reserved for business is inevitably harmful. On functional grounds, government-run enterprises are bad because they do not obey the rules. They do not operate at a profit; by their ability to run at a loss they drive out private competition and thus become monopolists, with all the evils of monopoly. Moreover, they do not obey the rules in terms of accounting, taxation, and the like, so that their costs are never honestly known. The objections on incentive grounds are even stronger and more fundamental. Governments are run by bureaucrats and bureaucrats are always irresponsible. They are motivated by political and not by businesslike aims; they are not judged by the conse-

[27] Queeny, *Spirit of Enterprise,* pp. 122, 160–167.
[28] Utley, *The American System,* pp. 55–56.
[29] NAM, II: 715–717.

quences of their actions; therefore they can never function as effectively as can the executives of businesses operating under the stimulus of the profit motive.[30]

It is noteworthy that the ideological division between the kinds of activities which are proper for government and those which form the natural sphere of business corresponds fairly well to the actual division of activities between the two spheres which prevailed about twenty-five years ago in the United States. In many of these areas some private activity exists, while in earlier periods in American history it was dominant. Private schools, parks, and water works now exist. Many industrial plants provide their own fire protection; there are some (but few) private highways. In earlier periods, private highways were important, private schools dominated our education system. Even postal systems have not always been public in Europe. Yet there is no ideological crusade to return those domains to private enterprise, although in terms of the arguments used to explain the "natural" dividing line this could easily be justified. For instance, many of the arguments which show the necessity of privately operated railroads could be turned in favor of privately operated toll roads.[31] While some advocacy of toll roads exists, it does not speak for private toll roads and could hardly be classified as business ideology, but rather as more or less disinterested academic study. This failure to carry the ideological argument to its logical conclusion may be explained on two grounds. The argument is usually advanced in a defensive context, as protest against some expansion of government activity. At the same time, arguments in favor of returning roads and schools to private hands would represent so extreme a deviation from accepted institutions as to lose the ideology the serious attention of its audience.

COMPETITION AND PROGRESS

According to the ideology, "progress" is built into the competitive system; it is the automatic result of the system's functioning. Conversely, "systems" other than Free Enterprise, such as British Socialism, Statism, the Welfare State, can never produce progress. Free Enterprise is the necessary and sufficient condition. This argument constitutes probably the most prevalent single theme in the current flow of ideology, especially on the more popular levels. A series of advertisements sponsored by Burlington Mills shows Howe working on the sewing machine, or the joining of the eastern and western halves of the first transcontinental railroad in Promontory, Utah, or similar American achievements, and asks the question, Why? The answer, of course, is Freedom of Enterprise, the same

[30] Klein, *How to Stay Rich,* ch. VIII.

[31] See Wilfred and Dearing, *A National Transportation Policy* (Washington, 1949).

force which explains Burlington Mills's own achievements in the field of rayon fabrics. And "if Burlington didn't do it, some other manufacturer would. And America would benefit, regardless of who profited. Freedom of Enterprise inevitably provides the greatest good for the greatest number. Better things for more people through the impetus of Free Enterprise." [32]

On the functional level of analysis, progress is said to be the result of competition: rival sellers striving to attract the consumer's dollar continually offer him more and better things. An Alcoa advertisement showing new developments in strong aluminum alloys says "A great and strongly competitive industry has sprung up in typically American fashion by making a better product to serve you more ways . . ." [33] The NAM authors speak of competition, especially competition in the advertisement, quality, styling and utility of products, in the provision of accessory services, delivery, and credit, and in price as "truly the life of trade and the breeding ground of progress." [34]

On the incentive level of analysis, freedom stimulates the activity of inventors and businessmen resulting in the production of new and better goods at lower costs. One example of this argument is provided by a Banker's Trust advertisement describing the wonders of an all-weather landing system, a product of industrial research "in this country, where companies are free to focus upon the future the unfettered ingenuity of man," with the result that its "industrial progress is unequalled anywhere on earth." [35] *Mainspring* devotes a chapter to Inventive Progress, the whole burden of which is the relation between Freedom and Invention.[36]

Sometimes the specific freedom of the saver to invest in hope of a return rather than freedom in general is held responsible for progress; savings become capital, and it is on capital accumulation that progress depends. Needless to say, this argument appears when profits are threatened, especially by higher wages or higher taxation. Then there is less emphasis on a vague and automatic connection between freedom and progress, and more emphasis on fostering the incentive of savers to invest in new and better "tools." A typical advertisement in an American Steel Spring series states, "Shackle profits and you INVITE NATIONAL DISASTER," and goes on to explain that profits are the major source from which business draws the means to progress; if profits are throttled, progress will disappear.[37]

[32] For example, those appearing in *Time*, Feb. 16, Mar. 29, Apr. 26, 1948.
[33] Alcoa advertisement, *Atlantic Monthly*, August 1948.
[34] NAM, I: 488.
[35] *Time*, Feb. 16, 1948. This is one of a series, all presenting similar ideas.
[36] Weaver, *Mainspring*, ch. 18.
[37] American Steel Spring Company advertisement, *New York Times*, April 26, 1949.

RETAINED CORPORATE EARNINGS

For classical ideology, a problem of consistency is raised by the fact that managerial discretion has displaced market competition in the matter of corporate dividends vs. retained earnings.[38] In fact, about half the profits of corporate business are usually retained and reinvested at the discretion of corporation managers, rather than being returned to the owners of the business — the stockholders — to reinvest or invest in other enterprises or spend on consumption as they see fit.[39] This fact is recognized without difficulty in the managerial version of the creed, which goes on to explain that retained earnings are "seed money" out of which future progress grows;[40] managements have a responsibility to the general public to use this seed money to improve their products and expand their businesses. The most systematic exposition of the managerial creed says no more than "any good manager can honestly argue that the growing importance of the hired management and its policy of self-capitalization have been of benefit to the stockholder," while at the same time pointing out that "management is no longer exclusively concerned with the stockholder." [41]

In the classical creed, as expounded by the NAM, retained earnings are acknowledged as an important source of business capital; but there is no mention of the implicit contradiction between this situation and the emphasis on individualism and the right of everyone to dispose of his own property which pervades the classical view. Thus, in its exposition of "Savings and Capital Formation" the NAM authors ask:

What are the sources open to you (a businessman with a successful new venture) for getting the needed capital for this expansion?

In general, there are only two sources available. The first and most "conservative" is to use your own profits; that is to reinvest your profits as you go along. This is commonly known as "plowing back earnings." It is a method of increasing capital which almost always is used to some extent by every company, and in small concerns just getting started it may be the only practical method available. The amount so reinvested in ordinary years aggregates hundreds of millions of dollars. It is one of the most significant sources of capital; that is, one of the most important methods of capital formation.

[38] See Chapter 4 above, where this point is developed at some length.
[39] In 1954, retained earnings were about 45 per cent of corporate profits after taxes; over the past ten years, retained earnings averaged 54 per cent of profits after taxes. See Report of the President's Council of Economic Advisors, January 1955, Table D-49. See also S. P. Dobrovolsky, *Corporate Income Retention, 1915–43,* National Bureau of Economic Research (New York, 1951).
The report of the stockholders' meeting of Standard Oil Company (N.J.) for 1950 shows that at least some stockholders differed from management in their views on retained earnings. See Report, pp. 34–35.
[40] See McGraw-Hill advertisement, *New York Herald Tribune,* July 27, 1943. This was one of a series.
[41] *Permanent Revolution,* pp. 80–81.

The argument then goes on to deal with "the savings of other people," and how they may be tapped through the capital market.[42]

Other classical writers show less facility in incorporating retention of a high proportion of corporate earnings for reinvestment as a normal feature of the system than do the authors of the NAM volumes. Klein argues the unfortunate necessity of plowing back earnings, and explains that it is due to the lack of equity capital which double taxation of corporate earnings has brought about.[43] Paton calls the plowing back of earnings a "controversial question." He says that it clearly means that corporations can dispose of the stockholders' money, but justifies it on two grounds: (1) this is the "easiest, most inexpensive method of financing growth," (2) the best evidence that 100 per cent distribution of earnings is not what stockholders want is their "apparent willingness to permit their hired men, in many cases, to retain a major part of earnings to finance corporate growth." [44]

THE BALANCE OF SAVINGS AND INVESTMENT

A second point at which managerial and classical views differ is the way in which decisions to invest and save are adjusted to each other over the whole economy. Managerial writers recognize that the undirected operation of the capital markets does not always channel all intended savings into investment; and that, therefore, various kinds of government direction and "planning" in this sphere may be required.[45] Here the classical ideologists follow — crudely — neo-classical economics; they deny that there is any problem of adjustment between the aggregate supply of savings and the aggregate demand for savings for investment purposes. The adjustment is made through normal market processes, just as free pricing balances supply and demand. Paton discusses the rewards — in the form of profits — needed to call forth capital for risky investments, makes a few minatory comments on the Keynesian attack on savings and then asks himself, "Do financial markets do a good job?" He answers, rather cautiously:

[42] NAM, I: 393.

The only other mention of retained earnings in the chapter consists of two pages in an appendix devoted to presenting some estimates of retained earnings in relation to total corporate uses of funds over the period 1925–40, in order to refute the theses presented in the TNEC Hearings that corporations are relying increasingly on internal funds to finance their capital formation. Thus, in a chapter of fifty-six pages plus an appendix of eight pages on "Savings and Capital Formation" only one paragraph in the text and two pages in the appendix are devoted to a discussion of retained earnings.

[43] Klein, *How to Stay Rich,* pp. 193 ff.

[44] Paton, *Shirtsleeve Economics,* p. 228.

[45] In particular, the managerialists think that the government should adopt some kind of fiscal policy designed to offset the trade cycle. See below, Chapter 10, where this subject is more fully discussed.

These financial institutions — the commercial and investment banking system, the insurance companies, the stock exchange, and so on — are among the most highly developed structures of the entire economic process. They permeate the economy, are provided with a great deal of information, and are sensitive to changing conditions. They are, moreover, closely scrutinized, and supervised in many respects by government agencies. The point may also be mentioned that the capital markets are subject to the attitudes and reactions of almost countless accumulators and users of funds. In view of these circumstances there are no outstanding reasons for assuming that our exchange economy falls down particularly in its appraisal of the efforts of capital-furnishers as compared with the job done in sizing up the contributions of those who furnish personal services.[46]

The NAM authors list four factors which control the volume of investment: the supply of available funds, the degree of confidence in the future, the possibilities of profit from prospective investments, and the prospects of keeping substantial parts of earnings from investment. All these factors have been and will continue to be subject to change; the proper relation between savings and investment fluctuate with them. "The proper relation is that which to the greatest possible degree satisfies, on the one hand, the demand of the public for goods, and on the other hand, the desire to save and attain an income from savings . . . If changes in public attitude are not too great and are gradual, the economic system can adjust itself to them without undue hardship." Drastic changes may cause trouble, but they are usually the consequence of wars, natural disasters, and bad government policies. NAM authors specifically deny that government spending or taxing can maintain equilibrium between savings and investment. "Government spending may create business activity, but not such as will counteract hoarding and unwillingness to invest." [47]

COMPETITION — MANAGERIAL AND CLASSICAL

A third point of difference between classical and managerial versions is the nature and significance of competition, although the difference is one of degree rather than substance. The managerialists carry to an extreme a tendency already present in the classical version — to broaden the meaning of "competition" without changing its function. Competition comes to mean any pressure from without the firm which impinges on management and influences management decisions, whether it arises from

---

[46] Paton, *Shirtsleeve Economics,* pp. 96–97.
[47] NAM, I: 362–363, 368–369, 370, marginal summary.

It is interesting that, in neither work quoted, does the rate of interest play the central role as equilibrator of savings and investment which is assigned to it in neo-classical economic theory. In general, little is said about interest in the ideology.

business firms in other markets, suppliers, customers, or the general public. Thus, *The Free Enterprise System*[48] describes American enterprise as providing gainful employment for 60 million persons who work only at the pleasure of their customers. These 60 million workers are the customers: as workers they constantly exact higher wages; as customers, they insistently demand lower prices. "Caught squarely in the middle, management is forced, under this tremendous competitive pressure, to operate more and more efficiently and to produce better goods at lower cost." *The American Triangle of Plenty,* says substantially the same thing.

The Permanent Revolution goes somewhat further in limiting the function of competition, as well as broadening its definition. "It is the modern manager's sense of responsibility to his customer and to the general public that gives him his best claim to being progressive. More goods at lower cost (and prices) is the basic principle of American industry . . . Many a chemical . . . has been sold at a progressively lower price without the spur of competition, simply to encourage the market." But, a little further, "Workable competition (which has been defined as the pragmatic concept which has succeeded the Darwinian notion of all-out competition) provides a good check on how a company is doing . . . and the soundest way to ensure survival." At another point, it is suggested that public opinion as well as managerial responsibility, serves the same function as competition. General Motors' program of "finding out what people like, doing more of it; finding out what people don't like, doing less of it" is offered as the approved example.[49]

Although they may imply that the modern manager's sense of responsibility can supplant competition, the managerialists never directly deny that competition is vital to the proper functioning of the system. They cite the Sherman Act as one of the key forces in the "Revolution," "Its success is among the chief reasons why American business today is so vastly different from European business." [50]

THE CREED AND NEUTRAL SOCIAL SCIENCE

How do the views of the over-all functioning of the economy found in business ideology differ from those found in current economics and sociology? The major differences can be classified under four heads:

(1) *The use of the symbol of "competition."* The model competitive economy found in neo-classical general equilibrium analysis gives much the same kind of results as the ideology attributes to the System, in particular the first four of the benefits listed above. But "competition" as used in that model has a very narrow and special sense: namely, that

[48] Adams, *Free Enterprise System.*
[49] *The Permanent Revolution,* pp. 84, 87.
[50] *Ibid.,* p. 72.

every product is offered for sale by a large number of sellers, each selling identically the same product and each so small as to have no influence on the market. Moreover, the competitive model makes certain unrealistic assumptions about the nature of consumers' preferences, particularly that consumers are independent of one another in their tastes, that they have perfect knowledge of the products on the market, and that they are not significantly influenced by advertising.[51]

It is true that the American economy has very broad features in common with the model of a competitive economy: consumers' choice is important in determining what is produced; production decisions are decentralized and are made by a large number of firms; these firms operate in their own interests under the restrictions of a price system which does coordinate the decisions of individual firms and households; entry into particular occupations or activities is not restricted by tradition or government regulation in any significant degree. In this broad sense, it is certainly appropriate to refer to the American economy as "competitive," particularly in contrast with a centrally planned economy such as the Soviet Union. But "competition" in this broad meaning does not necessarily have the same logical consequences as "competition" in the technical sense of the neo-classical economic model. And the use of competition as a symbol in the ideology covers at least as wide a ground as that marked out above.

The social scientist would describe our economy as a complex mixture of elements of competition and monopoly, the latter of varying degrees of strength and pervasiveness. In terms of the criteria previously referred to, the outcome of the functioning of a system of this character cannot be simply described as "optimal" in any well-defined sense. Taking the economy as a whole, it may well be true that consumers' wants tend to be satisfied at minimum costs; but it may not be true for large sections of the economy — depending on the degree of competition or monopoly present. At present, there is considerable disagreement among economists both on the economic implications of various mixtures of monopoly and competition and on empirical description of the particular mixture which actually exists.

Business ideologists and economists also part company on the identification of competition with *laissez faire*. In the ideology, intervention by government in economic activities outside its narrow "proper sphere" is always inimical to the proper functioning of the system. This view passes over several major problems. The most important is that of economic fluctuations; the whole trend of economic science for the last forty years has been to cut away every basis for the belief that a competitive

[51] These points are discussed in detail in Chapter 6.

system automatically reaches stable equilibrium and avoids violent fluctuations in aggregate output and employment. But even aside from this there are important difficulties in the identification of competition and *laissez faire*. Competition in the economists' sense may prove impossible to attain in many markets without government action which goes beyond prohibiting explicit agreements in restraint of trade (which the ideology approves) or even forbidding mergers (which the ideology does not approve) to more radical kinds of intervention in the form of subsidies, taxes, and even "direct controls," the most anathemized of all Government activities.[52]

The importance in our economy of "natural monopolies" such as electric utilities and transportation enterprises, which have traditionally been subject to government regulation in matters of price and output policy, is a specific example of the difficulty of identifying *laissez faire* and the benefits of competition. The detail of regulation which would be necessary if consumers of the outputs of these industries were to receive in full the "benefits of competition" as an economist would understand them would be very great, far exceeding the present degree of regulation which business ideologists find so intolerably burdensome.[53] Regulation of electric power rate structures and controls over the division of traffic between road and rail, for example, might have to go far beyond anything now practiced.[54] The problems created by the existence of natural monopolies in a competitive order are given scant recognition in the ideology. Discussion of these problems is sketchy and brief; what there is stresses heavily that such situations are exceptional and, while they do call for some regulation by the government as a substitute for control by the forces of competition, this regulation must be minimal. Indeed, far more of the discussion is devoted to the dangers of too much regulation than to an examination of why regulation is needed, and the range of the economy for which it is relevant.[55]

[52] See NAM, esp. II: 687–726, ch. on Government Regulation.

This is not to say that such intervention is always desirable, or that there are not market situations in which the lack of competition may be considered more desirable than the consequence of Government intervention; but merely to emphasize the illegitimacy of identifying competition and *laissez faire* as scientifically descriptive terms.

[53] See NAM, I: 489–490, 504, on electricity utilities; ch. XI on rail transportation, esp. pp. 560–575. Also Paton, *Shirtsleeve Economics,* pp. 268–269, 409–427.

[54] See W. Arthur Lewis, *Overhead Costs* (New York, 1949) chs. II, IV, for a penetrating discussion of these problems.

[55] In the NAM volumes there are only about two pages devoted to the need for and the nature of regulation of natural monopolies, pp. 489–90. The eleven other references to public utilities in the text, all brief, are concerned chiefly with mentioning difficulties created by regulation. There is one chapter, chapter XI, discussing transportation; most of it is narrative history; the discussion of regulation is in terms

It is really very difficult to draw a line between natural monopolies and "naturally competitive" sections of the economy; the problem of deciding what to regulate, and to what extent, is one of weighing attitudes toward the regulatory process itself as much as of determining where regulation is needed in order to achieve the benefits which competition cannot provide. Finally, government regulation does not consist of a few exceptional measures to cover a few exceptional circumstances; it ranges all the way from the prescription of quality standards as a protection against fraud to the imposition of fairly detailed controls over prices, outputs, and investment.

(2) *The link between competition and "automatic progress."* The fact of progress in the relevant sense — great increases in productivity and output, great increases in the standard of living of the average consumer — is strikingly clear,[56] and on any view is one of the most spectacular facts of recent history. But the connection between rising outputs, rising living standards, and competition is more obscure than the ideology would have us believe. On the functional level of analysis, the social scientist has found little evidence to support a close relationship between the main sources of progress — technical progress and capital investment — and competition in a technical sense. Indeed, the benefits of competition, in an ideal sense, are defined only in terms of a model which specifically excludes the change created by technological progress and capital investment. When such change is continuously present, as in modern industrial economies, the problems of stability of employment and income which always arise are not automatically and benevolently solved by a competitive price mechanism. This is true in terms either of the narrow technical sense of competition, or of its broader use in the ideology.[57]

---

of why there is too much of it, how transportation is a more competitive industry than has formerly been assumed, and why the present degree and kind of regulation is a threat to the whole system of private enterprise. Paton, *Shirstsleeve Economics,* has an eighteen-page chapter on public utility regulation (ch. XV). Again, the emphasis is on the exceptional character of situations in which regulation is called for. To Paton the public utility sector of the economy is a march which defends the main kingdom of private enterprise from the socialist hordes; holding the march, and preventing the barbarians from infiltrating it should be the great task of regulatory agencies.

[56] See Chapter 2 above for a detailed examination of the "progress" claims in the ideology.

[57] It is noteworthy that the writings of J. A. Shumpeter on economic progress are not more heavily drawn on by business ideologists. His work gives a central role to heroic creative activity by entrepreneurs in explaining progress under capitalism. *The Theory of Economic Development* and *Capitalism, Socialism and Democracy* are the chief sources for his views on this subject. Schumpeter relegates "competition" in the neo-classical sense to an unimportant position, and places prime emphasis on the "competition of the new" — innovation — as the central

On the ideology's incentive level of argument it is *laissez faire,* and the stimulus it provides to human effort, which is the guarantor of economic and thus general progress. This, too, is a drastic simplification. There is undoubtedly some historic connection between the growth of the scientific spirit, the growth of economic activities in towns outside the confines of feudal relations, the development of religious dissent, and the later application of invention to industry and the growth of *laissez faire.* Indeed, much of modern historical writing has been devoted to tracing and analyzing parts of these related streams of development. But the wide areas of space and time covered by these developments, their uneven pace from place to place and period to period, are alone enough to refute any simple one-way causal connection such as that found in the ideology. History shows *laissez faire* without progress, and progress without *laissez faire.*

(3) *Property rights and laissez faire.* Third, the business ideology implies, in its exposition of the relations between competition, freedom, and private property, that the particular set of property institutions in America today are precisely those which are best suited to convert private reward into public service through the mediation of competition and the price system. This is hardly a judgment which a neutral science examination of these institutions, bearing the marks of their diverse origins and their peculiar histories, would validate.

On the most obvious level, the inequalities of opportunity created by the inheritance of property make for great discrepancies between "rewards" and actual and potential "contributions" under *laissez faire.* Property inheritance creates great differences in access to capital and therefore in the ability to enter into business: business talent without capital may even fail to secure entry into the competitive race; sufficient

---

feature of capitalism. While Schumpeterian arguments identifying large firms with innovation and innovation with competition play some part in managerial statements, such as those of duPont, U.S. Steel, and General Electric executives cited in Chapter 2 above, the full range of his position is not relied on. Perhaps it is the fact that the Schumpeterian arguments justify monopoly, and indeed praise it, that limits their usefulness in ideological applications. This specific point, as well as the broader tone of his discussion, emphasizes rather than minimizes the power of businessmen. Such an emphasis is incompatible with the functional role that the theme of competition plays in the ideology. Schumpeter's writings also provide a convincing theory of profits as the reward for innovation and entrepreneurship; yet the creed has made scarcely any use of it. (See discussion Chapter 4 above.) This may be because the theory seems unsuited to justify the reward of absentee owners. Or it may be because the theory justifies too much: it embraces even monopoly profits which business ideology is more concerned to deny than to defend. Perhaps ignorance and time lag are also important, and the theory may be adapted to the uses of the creed: some examples of arguments similar to Schumpeter's have already been cited.

capital may enable men of little talent to remain in leading positions. More generally, access to occupations is limited by the inheritance not only of wealth but also of social status. The ability to earn a high income by making a highly valued contribution to the social product depends not only on talents and character, but frequently on expensive education and training. To a large extent, those born into families with high incomes, or with high social status even without high incomes, have preferential access to college and professional training, and the claims of ideology must be devalued accordingly. At a much simpler level, the ability of an ordinary worker to make a valued contribution and so receive a proportionately high income may be greater in a locality other than the one in which he lives. Yet he may be unable to finance the cost of moving himself and his family, even though that cost would be justified in terms of his prospective earnings. It is clear that problems of immobility and unequal access to education arising out of limited access to capital and out of the inheritance of social status, exist in every society. In fact, they may well be much smaller in contemporary America than they have been in most other societies, though this is a very difficult judgment to make. What is striking is not that such barriers exist, but that the ideology fails to mention them.

Inheritance is not the only problem which property institutions present in a laissez-faire economy. The very structure of property rights may make *laissez faire* unworkable. Thus the American landowner has title to all minerals which lie under his land, including oil. Yet a single oil pool generally underlies the land of many owners; and oil in the pool will flow underground from one parcel to another, depending on how wells are drilled. *Laissez faire* in the exploitation of property rights in oil lands has led literally to chaos — as in East Texas in the early thirties, when martial law was declared in order to prevent tremendous waste as well as to maintain the price of crude oil. It is now generally recognized that our property institutions are incompatible with *laissez faire* in crude oil production, and a complex — and inefficient — network of controls has been superimposed on the industry.[58]

This is one familiar example of many situations in which a given property owner may secure benefits without bearing costs, or incur costs, the benefits of which are redound to others. Yet the whole theory of the laissez-faire, private property, free-competition policy rests on the proposition that he who incurs the costs secures the associated returns, and he who benefits must bear the costs. Discussion of the problems created by departures from this norm — discrepancies between "social" and "private" costs — have been staple in economic literature since 1920, when the first

---

[58] See Northcutt Ely, "The Conservation of Oil," 51 *Harvard Law Review* 1209 (May 1938) for a discussion of the history of these measures.

edition of Pigou's *Economies of Welfare* appeared.[59] Yet this is a problem which the literature of the business creed does not recognize.

(4) *The Profit motive and human nature*. Finally, the creed, especially its classical strand, rests on the assumption that the stimulus of the profit motive and its exercise in the special and complex kind of "freedom" which characterizes our society are somehow expressions of fundamental unchangeable human nature. The ideological character of this assumption is so transparent as to need little comment. Sociology and cultural anthropology have for a half-century or more emphasized that human motivation and "human nature" are to a very great extent determined by society. Far from being biological constants that characterize the human species, whatever its social setting, human motivation and human nature vary with social institutions. The potential mutability of the way in which fundamental human drives are integrated into the institutions of different functioning human societies is one of the major conclusions which those disciplines have reached.

[59] See K. W. Kapp, *The Social Costs of Private Enterprise* (Cambridge, Mass., 1950), and W. J. Baumol, *Welfare Economics and the Theory of the State* (Cambridge, Mass., 1952) for recent discussions of this problem. Kapp attempts to estimate the dollar magnitude of some of the social costs not borne by private enterprise.

9

GOVERNMENT IN A
BUSINESS ECONOMY

INTRODUCTION

BUSINESS COMMENTS ON GOVERNMENT are rarely complimentary; that the government should have only limited powers and be restrained in their use is a fundamental and ever-recurring proposition in the business creed. The breach of these principles is viewed as a grave threat to the integrity of the economic system. Nevertheless, businessmen are ambivalent in their attitude to the government. According to the creed, free enterprise and free government were conceived and created together in this country in 1789, and both are uniquely American. This nationalism requires some abstract approval of Government as a symbol of the nation.

The requirement is met by the creed in several ways. First, the Constitution is admired as a symbol of wisdom, balance, and restraint in government. One can detect such admiration in the claim that the free enterprise system was consciously chosen by the Founding Fathers in 1776 and 1789,[1] and that the rights of free enterprise are parallel to, and an unspoken part of, the rights of civic and political freedom set forth in the first ten amendments to the Constitution. The separation of executive and legislative power is convenient for business' ambivalent feelings: one branch can be damned and another praised. Nearly always, at least in recent years, the executive is damned, and the legislative branch, at least by implication, praised.[2] Actions which are condemned in the business creed as unwarranted and dangerous extensions of government power into spheres which should be reserved for business enterprise are also condemned as unconstitutional intrusions by the executive into the domain of Congress. A Chamber of Commerce bulletin on "The Controlist Philos-

---

[1] See Chapter 2 above.
[2] It is conceivable, of course, that these roles might be exchanged in a radically different political situation.

ophy" [3] answers its question, "Who are the controlists," by pointing to officials of regulatory agencies of the government; it made no reference to the demands for price-and-wage control which were then being made in Congress. An advertisement giving one of James J. McGraw's messages to American industry told its readers that "The election of November 2, 1948 GAVE NO MANDATE FOR SOCIALISM," and went on to discuss the plans of the new Administration. All its warnings were addressed to the executive; no mention was made of the change in the party composition of Congress between the Eightieth and Eighty-First Congresses.[4]

Similarly, the judiciary, as the guardian of the Constitution, serves as a positive symbol in the business creed.[5] Finally the Armed Services are convenient symbols of the Nation for people who are hostile toward the "government" because of the relatively great separation of military and political activity traditional in the United States. Hence the frequent examples of partnership between business and the armed services found in the business creed.

So much for the positive side of business sentiment toward government. The rest of this chapter will be devoted to the creed's treatment of the nature of government, the proper functions of government, the inherent evils of government activity, the nature and dangers of the democratic process, and the threat of socialism which government action creates. On all these matters, the dominant tone of the creed is negative; government is at best a necessary evil; at worst, the evil far outweighs the necessity and, unchecked, can ruin society. While there are specific areas, especially in questions of fiscal policy, in which classical and managerial views of the role of government can be distinguished, in general there is

[3] *Economic Intelligence,* February 1949, no. 7, Economic Research Department, Chamber of Commerce of United States, Washington.

[4] "A Message to American Industry," 74th of a series by McGraw-Hill, *Business Week,* April 2, 1949, pp. 70–71. The figures were: 80th Congress, Senate, 45D: 51R, House, 188D: 244R; 81st Congress, Senate, 54D: 42R, House, 262D: 171R. See *Congressional Quarterly,* 1948 and 1949. In the Eightieth Congress, there were two vacancies and one third-party member in the House; in the Eighty-First, there was only one vacancy, and one third-party member.

[5] F. A. Harper, *Liberty, a Path to Its Recovery,* Foundation for Economic Education (Irvington-on-Hudson, N.Y., 1949), uses the fraction of consumer incomes taken as taxes as a measure of "loss of liberty." In an appendix on limitations of the measure, he points out that a very small part of this tax burden represents "allowable" governmental functions; his example: "Certain government functions are invaluable to liberty, but these are not highly expensive to operate; a Supreme Court, for instance, is not very costly . . ."

To be sure, individual decisions of the Court are vigorously attacked, and Justices pictured as lawless, but the institution is always referred to approvingly. An example of such an attack appears in *American Affairs* (published by the National Industrial Conference Board, quarterly), January 1948 in article entitled, "To Govern Without Law." This is a dissenting opinion, reprinted in its entirety, with an editorial headnote.

little difference between the two. In the main, the managerial line is a variant of the classical one.

NATURE OF GOVERNMENT

Government, as it is seen in the business creed, is inherently evil. It is always viewed negatively, as a restraint on the individual. While some restraints may be necessary, restraints in general are suspect because they are limitations of individual liberty. Thus government power is only tolerable at all when it is limited, no matter in whose behalf the power is exercised. The tyranny of the majority over the minority is as much — and even more — to be feared as the tyranny of the minority over the majority. In a pamphlet published by the Foundation for Economic Education, the case for limited government is stated in these terms:

> There is only one kind of freedom. And it is found only where the government is limited by a constitution. This protects the freedom of the individual against interference not only from other individuals but from government itself, even when government is doing the bidding of a majority . . . We have become great in this country because no power could prevent each individual from doing the things he wanted to do. Everybody may be against an individual and his ideas, all of his neighbors, all of his friends, all of the bankers, all of the state legislature, the governor, the Congress of the United States, and the President, yet this one man, believing in himself, can keep right on trying to create regardless of all the opposition of all the rest of the people in the United States. That is why in a few short years, there was ten times as much progress in the United States as was accomplished in all the balance of the world for a period of 6000 years.[6]

The same idea is stated more elegantly in *USA, The Permanent Revolution.*

> Constitutionalism, also sometimes called "pluralism" or "the principle of limitation" is a general name for a mechanical contraption of which almost every generation of Americans has brought forth a new model. Among these models have been checks and balances, states' rights, balance of power, concurrent majority, sectionalism, trust-busting, civil service, decentralization, "the TVA idea," what not. The unchanging purpose served by this changing machine is the negative one of keeping the power out of the hands of any one group of people whose common interest, whether economic or ideological, might prove too strong for the liberties of the rest. Constitutionalism expresses the conviction that all governments are a potential menace to liberty.[7]

That governmental power is inherently dangerous and that limited government is a great and unique American achievement are views the

---

[6] Sherman Rogers, *Why Kill the Goose,* Foundation for Economic Education, (Los Angeles, Calif., 1947), pp. 76–77.

[7] *Permanent Revolution,* pp. 41–42.

business creed shares with broader American ideology.[8] The special
quality of limited government in the United States arises from the
combination of two features of the political structure; the separation of
executive, legislative, and judicial powers (especially the separation of
the first two); and the system of federalism, with limited power in the
central government and residual power in the hands of the states and
the people. In much of the literature of the business creed limited government becomes identified with these particular devices of the American
Constitution; any attempts to alter them, or any recognition of actual
change in the relations among them, is occasion for alarm.

Hostility may be seen as a natural reaction to the actual intrusion of
government, particularly of the federal government, into economic affairs
today. Roughly 50 per cent of business income goes to the government
in taxes today; about 25 per cent of the total national product is represented by government activity. The extent and detail of federal regulation
of business is very great and covers many aspects of business, from the
Securities and Exchange Commission's controls on raising capital to the
National Labor Relations Board's controls on bargaining with workers.
Much of this regulatory power as well as the enormous growth in all
government economic activity is recent, the product of New and Fair
Deals. But business hostility toward government and mistrust of its powers
dates back at least fifty years before the presidency of F. D. Roosevelt.
Thus Frederick Lewis Allen, writing of J. P. Morgan, says:

> Naturally, Morgan had been opposed to the passage of the Interstate Com-
> merce Commission Act (1887). He had thought that the abuses in the railroad
> industry could best be cured by the sort of reform measures upon which he was
> engaged — substituting cooperation for competition and honest financing for
> buccaneering. He had a deep contempt for politicians, and thought that people
> like himself could handle things much better. He wanted to see the railroads
> of the country respectably run, at profits steady enough and large enough to
> maintain the value of their securities . . . The trouble with these ignoramuses
> in Washington, he felt, was that they seemed to make no distinction between
> the crying abuses of the industry and the perfectly sound action it must take
> to maintain values.[9]

Another banker of the time, Henry Lee Higginson, put the thought in his
own words:

> . . . All these new-fangled statesmen, including both Roosevelt and Bryan
> . . . are hell-bent on centralizing everything at Washington and wiping out
> state lines. These modern philosophers contend that the general government,
> because of the delegated power to regulate commerce among the states, can
> . . . say what this interstate carrier shall charge, what wages it shall pay, how

[8] See Chapter 12.
[9] F. L. Allen, *The Great Pierpont Morgan* (New York, 1949), p. 59.

and when it shall run its trains, and regulate every other detail of the railroad's operation. This is too much, and I do not believe the people will stand it. It is more than a question of law. It is a question of politics, of changing fundamentally our form of government, which is based on the idea of local self-government.[10]

And in 1927, at the height of the New Era, the President of the U.S. Chamber of Commerce warned:

As citizens we cannot permit the American government to be buried under a multiplicity of bureaus, and an avalanche of taxation. We serve neither our purpose nor those of our Government when we meekly submit to the growing idea that Government at will can step from its throne to enter the marts of trade to compete with the enterprise of its citizens.[11]

The last point which Higginson emphasized — the virtue of local and state as against federal government — is one which is still prominent in current ideology. State and local governments are less subject to the inherent evils of government power; they are closer to the people in some sense and this limits and guides their action. Local government tends to be in the hands of the real leaders of the community, the solid middle classes, and out of reach of demagogues who pander to special interests at the expense of the nation. Thus modern versions of States-rightism, especially in matters of taxation and expenditures, are strongly supported; for example, opposition to Federal aid for education or the (successful) advocacy of the de-federalization of the Employment Service.[12]

The true function of government is to take such action as is necessary to conserve and promote individual liberty. In the business creed, it is only the activities of individuals and "voluntary" associations which can be productive and creative, either in an economic or in a broader social sense. Government can act usefully, then, by promoting the activities of private persons and groups, and laying down such uniform rules for the conduct of these activities as will make for their smooth functioning with the minimum of mutual interference. Any government section not so directed is "coercive," and coercion, expressing the inherent evil in government power, is always sterile, incapable of producing any useful or desirable result.

This is, of course, the classic view of eighteenth- and nineteenth-century liberalism; it is the duty of government to hold the ring, within which the competitive struggle determines the activity of society. The holder

[10] Bliss Perry, *Life and Letters of Henry Lee Higginson* (Boston, 1921), p. 443.

[11] Lewis E. Pierson, President of the U.S. Chamber of Commerce, in an address at West Baden, Indiana, Oct. 18, 1927: quoted in Chapman, *The Development of American Business Thought*, 62–63.

[12] See NAM, II: 701–712, for a statement of "proper" divisions of responsibility which emphasizes the virtues of local government.

of the ring enforces the rules of fair competition, and in particular, sees that losers take their losses, and does not try to prevent winners from taking their gains. Thus the maintenance of the laws of property, and the enforcement of contracts become the most important aspects of "law and order" which it is the duty of the government to maintain.

The classic strand in the business creed repeats the Manchester philosophy with some enlargement. Thus the NAM study of the American System finds that the major legitimate functions of government are: the maintenance of law and order through the enforcement of the criminal law, the law of torts; the enforcement of contracts; the regulation of the health and safety of the population; the licensing of the professions; the conservation of natural resources; the provision of education and the relief of distress.[13] The conservation of natural resources and the provision of education would hardly have been recognized as government functions by the classic advocates of *laissez faire;* the rest of the list would have been familiar, though perhaps the regulation of health and safety and the relief of distress might have been given a different content in eighteenth-century England than the National Association of Manufacturers would give to them today. Principally, the government enforces the rules of the game; it does not make them, since they are the "natural" rules of the competitive system. Frequently, criticism of government activity in the business creed takes the form of attacks on attempts to change the rules; such attempts are thought to be necessarily harmful. But in addition to its major responsibility as an umpire, the government may legitimately perform certain kinds of positive functions. In the classic strand of the creed, these are narrowly circumscribed.[14] They include the provision of services of very general benefit which it is difficult to evaluate in money terms and thus impracticable for private business to provide through the market; the provision of services needed by everybody; and the operation of enterprises which must be public for police purposes.[15] The rather arbitrary nature of such classifications hardly needs comment. What is considered an obvious province for the police power in one country or at one time is thought to be just the opposite in another. Consider the difference in view between the citizens of Massachusetts and those of New Hampshire on whether the sale of alcoholic beverages through a state monopoly is or is not necessary for police purposes.

The managerialists take a broader view of proper governmental functions; indeed, this is one of the principal points at which the managerial is distinguished from the classical version in the discussion of the role of government. In particular, the managerialists approve government fiscal

[13] NAM, II: 714–717
[14] *Ibid.*
[15] See above Chapter 8.

policy designed to mitigate cyclical fluctuations even if this policy includes deficit spending, which is strongly condemned in the classic version of the creed. Thus, the editors of *Fortune* can say: "It is now almost universally accepted that . . . in the event of a serious depression government . . . undertake very large counter-cyclical spending programs." They then go on to discuss the possibility of "private planning" by individual business firms to diminish cyclical swings.[16] Of course, even here, the relative emphasis on the efficacy of private and government planning hardly corresponds to that of the economists: *Fortune*'s stress on individual private "planning" is clearly ideological, and serves to emphasize the small discrepancy between managerial and classical views in this area.[17]

Government activity which extends outside its proper limits is clearly bad; it upsets the regulatory mechanism of the price system.[18] This is the dominant, pragmatic theme in the ideology; hence the frequent use of the experience of rent control in France, and its deterrent effect on building there to show that rent control aggravates rather than ameliorates housing shortages.[19] But pragmatic arguments are not enough. Intervention is also bad in general and in principle, because it is "wrong" in a moral sense. It is an infringement by government of individual rights and liberties, and it is this character which makes it wrong whatever its pragmatic results. Enders Vorhees, Chairman of the Finance Committee of the United States Steel Corporation, says, in speaking of government price fixing:

Government, of course, can intervene. But its intervention, except to prevent fraud and coercion, only makes things worse. For if the government or labor unions — assuming to supreme economic insight — introduces rigidity into our affairs, we shall be unable to adjust the exchange relations of our products to the exchange relations of other products out of which comes automatically self-balanced progress. That is why we cannot have a mixed economy. A mixed economy must always be a messed economy. All government efforts to fix reasonable profits, or to determine price by profits or profits by prices are unalterably opposed to the American fundamental that producers must compete, while competing customers, the public, decide. All such government efforts are either open or disguised measures to protect the customer **from** himself. Actually the customer never needs protection — except in that ancient and continuing struggle to escape frustration and exploitation by government under the guise of protecting him.[20]

[16] *The Permanent Revolution*, pp. 203–204.
[17] The creed's views of business cycles, and differences between classic and managerial strands are treated more fully in Chapter 10 below.
[18] See Chapter 7.
[19] B. De Jouvenal, *No Vacancies* (Irvington-on-Hudson, N.Y., 1948), Foundation for Economic Education, pp. 1–15.
[20] E. M. Vorhees, "The State vs. Customers," an address before the 54th general meeting of the American Iron and Steel Institute, May 23, 1946.

Again there are managerial strands of the creed which are not so rigidly hostile to government action in principle. Paul Hoffman, first president of the CED, can say, "The people in this country want a good living, but they want security too . . . [To say that] because . . . social measures are sometimes necessary to give the people what they want, that means we are in a socialist state is nonsense." But such expressions are rare even in the managerial literature. The authors of *USA, The Permanent Revolution,* the most coherent exposition of the managerial viewpoint, find that government action generally indicates that private individuals have failed in their duties. They do not condemn government for filling the gap, but clearly prefer timely private action for its superior efficiency and harmony with the American Ideal.[21]

Comments on direct aid to individual producers via subsidies and tariffs are conspicuous by their absence in the business creed. Where such comments are made, they tend to minimize the general significance of the subsidies, find reasons for some of them, and paint the difficulties which might be created by withdrawing them. Thus the NAM authors recognize that "at no time in our national history has our economy been free of government subsidies of one kind or another." National defense is advanced as a reason for some subsidies; the possibility of retaliatory treatment in foreign markets, for others. It is proposed that the "systematic contraction of all non-military subsidies should be initiated at once, and the process carried to completion over a period of 20 years or so, with a view to giving each element of our population ample time for adjusting itself to the system of competitive prices . . ." [22] The emphases on particular justifications and on gradualism are a little out of line with the stern moral view taken of other kinds of government intervention.

Sometimes the treatment of subsidies is consistent. Thus, Clarence Randall says:

. . . We deny our heritage and jeopardize free enterprise when we ask special consideration for our own industry or our own company. If we seek to keep government out of business, we must not ourselves invite it in. Take all kinds of subsidy for example . . . Free enterprise means private capital, and the man who dares not risk is unworthy to share the rewards . . . Indirect subsidy is far more difficult to detect, but it can be found . . . Each time it happens a fraud is perpetuated on the public, the integrity of our economy is weakened, and the broad path to socialism made smoother.[23]

Particular justifications for specific subsidies are more familiar; the manufacturer who wants protection against cheap foreign labor so he can

---

[21] *The Permanent Revolution,* esp. chs. VIII, IX.

[22] NAM, II: 989–993. The first quotation appears on pp. 989–990; the second, on p. 992.

[23] Randall, *A Creed,* pp. 88–89.

provide jobs and maintain living standards at home; the publisher who wants low postal rates because his products serve an educational function; the airline and shipping operators whose activities contribute to national defense and therefore must be subsidized; the manufacturers and retailers who need resale price maintenance to protect their good will and prevent "unfair" competition. None of this justification is, in itself, a part of the business creed. But the creed tacitly accepts the legitimacy in these contexts of a kind of case-by-case justification which it strongly condemns elsewhere, as in discussions of price-control or profit limitation.

Government which stays within its proper sphere — the enforcement of the rules of competition and contract — nourishes confidence in the minds of businessmen. Any government action which goes outside the proper sphere destroys confidence, since its course is unpredictable and its consequences are bound to be detrimental. A wide variety of government actions are said to undermine business confidence: new taxes and government deficits, government controls of prices, profits, etc. Thus a McGraw-Hill advertisement in 1949, one of a series directed against the economic policy of the Democratic Administration, is entitled "YOUR ONLY CHANCE of Getting Ahead" and argues that only increased investment by business will increase output and productivity, but that Washington policy discourages such investment. Its concluding paragraph, in boldface type, is:

> The only sensibly safe national policy is to make it possible for American industry to do its job — not to terrorize private industry with proposals of ruinous taxation and paralyzing controls and threats of nationalization . . . American industry is the lifeblood of the American people and whatever makes industry do its work better contributes more to the common welfare than a bureaucratic government can ever hope to do.[24]

INHERENT EVILS OF GOVERNMENT ACTIVITY

Any government activity, according to the business creed, involves certain inherent evils. These evils are of two sorts: those connected with the kind of persons who man the government service, and those inherent in the very nature of the activities themselves, whoever performs them.

The creed classifies government servants into three groups: the politician, the routine bureaucrat, and the impractical academic bureaucrat. Viewed schematically, the activities of governments involve first the politician, who buys votes for the party in power; then the impractical theorist in the civil service — usually a professor in disguise — who conceives grandiose and unworkable plans; finally, these are executed and administered by the hidebound bureaucrat. The characteristic vices of

---

[24] McGraw-Hill advertisement, "A Message to American Industry," 76th of a series, *Business Week,* June 11, 1949.

these three species of homo politicus differ, but they share a common feature: the absence of those personal virtues possessed by businessmen. Their heads are neither clear, hard, nor level; none of them is really honest; all of them lack practical imagination and the desire to get things done.

The fat, back-slapping politico, who buys votes by handing out government jobs or government subsidies at the expense of the taxpayer is a familiar figure of the editorial page and the political cartoon.[25] The give-away politician is frequently the key figure in ideological attacks on the welfare state. It is his inability to say "No" to pressure groups that keeps the program in motion. The U.S. Chamber of Commerce describes this mechanism as follows:

The politician also needs, seeks and "discovers" everlastingly, new needs and issues. Pushing each program a little further, inventing new programs, discovering areas where more could be done, and "correcting" inequities caused by previous programs — this keeps the Welfare State in motion.[26]

The other two figures of the trinity of evil in government — the planning professor, and the civil servant, filling out useless forms in octuplicate — are familiar figures of scorn in the popular literature of the business creed. An amusing caricature of this view of government activity, which is effective in catching the tone of discussion because it is a caricature, appeared in the *Saturday Evening Post* of January 15, 1949, in the form of a "Washington Letter":

Chief problem facing the new Congress is what to do with the citizens. Leaders in both Houses have expressed the thought that citizens are of little value between elections, and add enormously to the cost of Government. Several plans are being studied, but the one most in favor would place large segments of the public in storage similar to the Navy's "mothball fleet" . . .

Labor Department statistics show clearly that there is great duplication of jobs among the public. In many sections of the country whole groups of people do the same work. Congress feels that many of these jobs could be eliminated, thus freeing thousands for Government work.

[25] The editorial page (pp. 10, 12) of the *Saturday Evening Post* for September 3, 1949, provides an example of both text and picture. The editorial is entitled: Jobocracy Cannot be Pruned Unless the People Holler; its theme is the political attractiveness of giving away jobs. The accompanying cartoon shows a fat, cigar-smoking figure labeled "political bureaucracy" sitting on a tiny, weary-looking taxpayer, reading a document labeled "Hoover Report" and saying "They can't do this to us servants of the people."

[26] *The Welfare State and the State of Human Welfare,* U.S. Chamber of Commerce (Washington, n.d.), p. 27.

On page 33, in a discussion of government agricultural programs we learn: "Furthermore, the politicians, against the wishes of most of the elected farm organization leaders, are trying vigorously to expand still further the programs, with higher parity targets and, inevitably, a comprehensive system of detailed regimentation of the farmer and all his activities.

Business Leaders pointed out that this type of economy is short-sighted, and would seriously curtail many of the services offered to Congress by the public. This type of thinking, according to Senate leaders, indicates a do-nothing attitude on the part of business, and a reluctance to face reality. As one leader stated, "How many of these businessmen ever had to meet a Government payroll?"

Even more serious objections to the "mothball" proposal were raised by the Department of Agriculture. This is due to a recent agreement with Great Britain in which we trade our wheat crop for their entire production of cricket bats. "We must create a demand for those bats," said one official. "How can we do it with people piled up in warehouses?"

The weaknesses of politicians and bureaucrats make good ammunition, especially in condemning the actions of past Fair and New Deal governments, but the business ideology has another string to its bow. Government activity as such is bad, even if administered by businessmen. Extravagance, inefficiency, and waste are inherent in government, because nothing which government does is forced to meet the text of the market. Further, government does not even meet the internal criteria of rationality which the balance sheet and the profit and loss statement impose on every individual business enterprise. The power of government to pay for itself through taxes and deficits, and to force on people things which they do not really want, deprives government activity of any semblance of restraint. These points are often made in reference to competition between government and private business. Thus "America's business-managed, tax-paying ELECTRIC LIGHT AND POWER COMPANIES" sponsor an advertisement — one of a series — showing a football umpire running with the ball, and straightening one of the players, with the caption: "What goes on here?" The text goes on to say:

You wouldn't stand for that sort of thing on a football field — but it happens every day in the electric light and power business. Government not only regulates the electric companies — but it is in competition with them at the same time.

The catch is that government sets up two different sets of rules. The government's electric agencies pay little or no interest on the money they borrow, and pay *no* Federal taxes — but electric companies do and expect to. When government-in-the-power-business can't make ends meet — it gets a handout of tax money from the U.S. Treasury. Who foots the bill? American taxpayers — of which you are one.

If government can get into the light and power business this way — it can get into every *other business* the same way.[27]

Or the president of a large casualty insurance company, speaking through a "public interest advertisement" says:

[27] Advertisement, *Newsweek*, Oct. 18, 1948, p. 109.

The progress of American industry toward safer, more healthful working conditions — leading to the Liberty Mutual program of Humanics — is one answer to those social critics who have accused business of seeking profits at the expense of human values. This progress has been an achievement of private insurance companies working with private business under the stimulus of the profit motive. It is exceedingly unlikely that comparable progress could have been achieved under programs of government business and government insurance.

Even if it were assumed that industrial and insurance leaders lacked any humanitarian motive — which would be an absurd assumption — it is obvious that the pressure to reduce costs, including the costs of workmen's compensation insurance, has worked at the same time to increase the welfare of employees. This "balance sheet stimulus" to progress is characteristic of private business; it is rarely felt in government business.[28]

Government is powerless to create anything in the sense in which business produces wealth and individuals produce ideas, inventions, and so forth. The sterility of government action is an old theme in the ideology: any reliance on government is an attempt to get something for nothing, and must necessarily fail. Thus Henry Ford: "Law never does anything constructive . . . As long as we look to legislation to cure poverty or to abolish special privilege, we are going to see poverty spread and special privilege grow." [29] A modern version of the same thought appears in an advertisement: "We run the risk in this country of substituting law for conscience, of feeling that passing a law makes something so. Laws are easy, work is hard. But only work ever got anybody anything worth having." [30] Another puts the same thought as follows: "America is at a crossroads: One is the way of easy promises by which we hope to arrive in the never-never land of abundance for all and hardship for none. The other way . . . is the road built by enterprise, and resourcefulness and hard work — and thrift." [31]

The sterility of government action is often explained on the grounds that government is essentially organized force; only voluntary action can be truly creative, and therefore government action, which is based on coercion cannot. Harper puts the thought as follows:

Government is, by definition, design and intent, an agency engaged in force. It is not necessary, for instance, to empower government to decree that the citizens shall eat when they are hungry, or sing and be thankful when they are happy, or to do any of the innumerable other things that free individuals

[28] S. Bruce Black, President, Liberty Mutual Insurance Company, "Humanics, a program for controlling human and financial loss in industry," Atlantic Public Interest advertisement, *Atlantic Monthly*, February 1952.

[29] Henry Ford, *My Life and Work* (New York, 1922), *passim*.

[30] Warner & Swasey advertisement, *Business Week*, April 9, 1949.

[31] Youngstown Sheet and Tube Co. advertisement, *Fortune*, November 1948.

do voluntarily. Government is engaged in issuing laws and decrees, and in their enforcement. Government conducts "war" on outsiders and "law enforcement" on insiders. Its purpose and operations are well characterized by the statement: "There ought to be a law . . ." Its operations involve force or the threat of force against certain persons, thus violating the liberty of those persons.

Based on all that has been said, one might easily conclude that government is an entirely negative force so far as liberty is concerned. He might conclude that anarchy — the complete absence of government — would be the ideal society, and that liberty would be complete under anarchy. That would be true if all persons were perfect. But they are not. With human frailties as they are, anarchy affords an opportunity for certain powerful and tyrannical individuals to enslave their fellow men, to the extent of their power to gain and keep control over others. So some degree of government function — or its equivalent performed some other way — is necessary if liberty is to be at a maximum; violators of liberty must be restrained so that the rights of liberty will be protected for those who respect them and play the game of society according to the rules of liberalism.

. . . To government should be delegated, of course, the powers necessary to preserve a maximum of liberty under limited, precise law. Up to that point, government is an instrument that increases the liberty of the people.

. . . Up to that point government can generate progress, but when it goes beyond that point in enforcing singleness of conduct it destroys liberty and progress in that society. The result of an expansion of governmental action beyond that defined as the objective of government in a liberal society is to make human conduct more and more similar to that of the social insects — involuntary servitude to the unknown.[32]

PUBLIC FINANCE IN THE CREED

The treatment of taxation, government expenditure, and the national debt mirrors the creed's general treatment of government. Since spending by government is unproductive, taxation is a diversion of resources from the hands of business and consumers, who can use them productively, into the hands of government, which cannot. The *U.S. Investor* expresses this view as follows:

. . . A million dollar subtraction from the purchasing power of business cannot possibly be offset by a million dollar increase in government expenditures. Briefly, a million dollars exacted from business in the form of taxes is a reduction of that sum in earning power, which might be capitalized at five-to-ten times that figure for the purposes of expansion and job creation. When the government spends the million dollars, there is only a single shot effect on the

---

[32] Harper, *Liberty, A Path to Its Recovery* (Irvington-on-Hudson, N.Y., 1949), pp. 49–50, 78–79. See also Dean Russell, *Wards of the Government*, FEE, 1950). Similar thoughts on the sterility of coercion and the identification of coercion with "planning" and government "intervention" are the main arguments of *Mainspring*.

economy which is quickly dissipated, whereas the same money left with business has a multiple effect and adds to permanent wealth.[33]

A similar sentiment, emphasizing taxation as a threat to liberty, is expressed by Bradford Smith, economist of the United States Steel Corporation:

. . . Taxation is the systematic taking, without specifically definable *quid pro quo,* of the individual's substance for the support of the government. Taxation, because it is necessary and because it is taking under constraint, is a principal danger to the maintenance of individual liberty in America.[34]

The threatening nature of taxation is frequently conveyed by descriptions of the sheer size of government expenditures or tax collections — usually those of the federal government only. A NAM pamphlet on taxes bears a huge dollar sign on its cover and the legend:

In the next fifteen minutes, while you are reading this pamphlet, your government will have spent more than a million dollars . . .
A MILLION DOLLARS OF YOUR MONEY
CAN YOU AFFORD IT? [35]

The First National Bank of Boston shows three maps of the United States, dated 1929, 1938, and 1947. In the first, the lower half of California is shaded; in the second, all the states from the Pacific eastward to the eastern boundaries of Montana, Wyoming, Colorado, and New Mexico; in the third, the Dakotas, Nebraska, Kansas, Oklahoma, and most of Texas have been added to the shaded area. The caption is "The Ever-Lengthening Shadow"; the text explains that the total incomes of the inhabitants of the shaded states equal the expenditures of the Federal government.[36]

In dealing with the specific evils of taxation, the ideologists claim that taxes are harmful in the following ways. High income taxes on

[33] *U.S. Investor,* May 21, 1949, p. 50.
[34] Bradford Smith, *Liberty and Taxes* a pamphlet distributed by the Foundation for Economic Education (Irvington-on-Hudson, N.Y., n.d.)
[35] NAM, *How Much Government Can You Afford?* 1948.
[36] First National Bank of Boston advertisement, *Business Week,* Mar. 26, 1948. This advertisement is interesting in several respects. It is an extract from the Bank's monthly newsletter, and as the text indicates, has previously been reprinted in *Reader's Digest.* The device of multiple use of a single piece of material is characteristic of the technique of dissemination of the creed; see Chapter 15, below, for further discussion. Another point of interest is the use of a representation device which cannot fail to create a false impression in the reader's mind, and which appears deliberately designed to do so. The "shadow" representing Federal expenditures begins on the West Coast, and thus can march rapidly over the sparsely populated, low-income mountain and plains states which cover so large an area of the map. Had the shading started in New Jersey, quite a different impression would have been produced. The use of clearly misleading material is much more frequent in advertisements than in other forms in which the ideology is presented.

individuals with large incomes restrict the supply of capital available for risky investment; they also make individuals less willing to take risks because success results only in handing over a substantial part of the gains to the tax collector. High corporate income taxes similarly cut into the supply of capital available in the shape of retained earnings, and thus have the same effect. The total result is a reduction in private investment, which in turn threatens the growth of the economy, leads to immediate inflation and ultimate depression.

The delegates to both the Republican and Democratic National Conventions in 1948 were presented with a petition for government economy, tax equality, and tax relief, signed by some 450 businessmen's organizations of the local chamber of commerce and trade association type. The tax relief portion of the petition read: "We urge that Federal taxes on individuals be further substantially reduced by overall Government economies and tax equality, to encourage incentive for more production, investment and employment." The signatory organizations ranged from the Akron Coal Exchange, Inc., Akron, Ohio, to the Wyoming Implement Dealers Association, Basin, Wyoming.[37] In a speech before the 1947 Congress of American Industry (the annual meeting of the NAM), the President of Sylvania Electric Products, Inc., speaking for the NAM Taxation Committee, described the NAM program as consisting of three closely related parts:

First, adequate capital formation to provide for greater production, better jobs, more pay, and higher standards of living for all the people.

Second, tax reduction itself, of a kind and in an amount that will provide tax relief where it is most needed, release income for capital formation, and re-invigorate the economic incentives to work, to save, to invest, and to venture.

And third, budget reduction of a size to make possible the necessary tax reduction within the framework of a balanced budget and a minimum of $2.5 billion annual debt retirement.[38]

It is not very surprising that businessmen express anxiety about federal fiscal operations in view of the size of federal expenditures and taxes in

[37] The petition was reproduced and distributed publicly; the authors have a copy in their files.
[38] NAM, *Call to Action on Taxes*, 1948, p. 3. The speaker goes on to estimate the "deficiency" in capital formation at $30 billion, and discusses the need for making it good as quickly as possible. The only two sources of the kind of "venture capital" which is most needed for growth are retained corporate earnings and savings from middle and upper incomes. These are hardest hit by present taxation, and therefore the urgency of the need for tax reduction and reform. NAM *Trends*, October 1948, p. 5, quotes the president of the American Bankers Association on the shortage of venture capital amounting to $75 billion, again dissociated with the impact of heavy taxation.

recent years.[39] But similar expressions, with the same gloomy portents can be found in ideological literature of the thirties and early forties, when the level of federal taxes was about one-eighth as high absolutely, and less than one-half as large in relation to national income.[40] W. J. Cameron in a 1938 talk on the Ford Hour analyzed the causes of the 1937–38 recession, and found them in the policies of the government, especially in taxes.

The time has gone by when the just complaint of Business can be confused with the common human distaste for paying taxes. . . . The complaint of Business is against unproductive and suppressive legislation imposed in the name of taxes or revenue, but in the language of its sponsors, imposed to restrict or punish. Even in the absence of the language, the punitive purpose would be plain. And its effect in operation is to choke the springs of revenue.[41]

Queeny, writing in 1943 about the experience of the thirties, attacks on a broader front:

Every year new and additional taxes were levied, each making the risking of capital in enterprise less attractive. Some of the taxes, such as the Undistributed Profits Tax, Capital Stock Tax, and pre-war Excess Profits Tax, were unorthodox and punitive and caused much apprehension in business circles as to the true motives of the sponsors. Some remembered Karl Marx's exhortation: 'If the Democrats propose proportional taxation then the workers must demand progressive taxation; if the Democrats themselves move for moderated progressive taxation the workers must insist on a tax whose rates are so steeply graduated as to bring ruin to capital.' Left Wingers who confidently predicted that private enterprise could never recover, even that it would pass away, were thinking mainly of the tax poison in its food.[42]

The menacing prospect of high tax loads has recently been summed up in a single measure: the "critical proportion" between taxes and national income. A figure of 25 per cent — total taxes 25 per cent of national income — has been given wide circulation in ideological literature as the critical proportion. A National Industrial Conference Board pamphlet entitled *Life with the Tax Gremlins* quotes former President Hoover:

The economists seem to agree that taxation beyond 25% of our national income will bring disaster. If you add up the actual and progressive annual

[39] Annual average Federal expenditures were $46.4 billion, 1946–52; net revenues, $41.1 billion. See *Statistical Abstract*, 1953, pp. 337, 340.

[40] *Statistical Abstract*, pp. 337, 340, and Seymour E. Harris, *The National Debt and the New Economics* (New York, 1947), table 23, p. 197.

[41] "What Stopped It?" Talk on the Ford Hour by W. J. Cameron, March 13, 1938, Ford Motor Company, Dearborn, Michigan. This discussion was aimed specifically at the undivided profits tax, but the language is general, and the tax is not mentioned by name.

[42] Queeny, *Spirit of Enterprise*, p. 54.

expenditures of the Federal Government and the state and local governments, and if you truly compute the national income, you will find this warning red light shines with an intensity considerably over 30%. This means far more than nearly one-third of the national income. It means a combustion of your savings and your possible standards of living.[43]

Tax-reform proposals advanced by business ideologists follow logically from their major criticisms of the present tax structure. In addition to a general demand for tax reduction, they center on lowering taxes on middle and high incomes, lowering or abolishing the corporation income tax, and if necessary, making up sufficient revenue to balance the budget and begin to reduce the national debt by a manufacturers' excise tax.[44] The degree of emphasis on various points in these proposals varies widely, as does the level of tax suggested. Thus, NAM spokesmen set great store on reducing the highest marginal tax rate on individual income to 50 per cent.[45] The managerial version, as expressed by the Committee for Economic Development, contains nothing specific on this point, although it

[43] *Life with the Tax Gremlins,* a supplement to the Spring 1950 number of *American Affairs,* p. 3. The same figure is quoted in the U.S. Chamber of Commerce pamphlet, *The Welfare State and the State of Human Welfare;* and Harper, *Liberty, a Path to Its Recovery.*

The figure of 25 per cent was proposed vigorously in an article by Colin Clark, "Public Finance and Changes in the Value of Money," *Economic Journal,* December 1945. The figure represents an estimate of a certain critical ratio of taxes to national income, and is presented with considerable diffidence. The critical ratio is defined as the ratio of taxes to national income which cannot be exceeded without setting into motion short-run inflationary forces. These forces are sufficiently powerful to cause a change in money national income great enough to bring the ratio of taxes to national income below the critical level. The argument assumes that a large enough share of government expenditures are fixed in money terms so that inflation can bring down the need for taxes in relation to money national income. The process of setting off the inflation is conceived as a bargaining process between rentiers on the one hand and entrepreneurs on the other, taking place within the government, in banks, etc. In no place is 25 per cent viewed as a critical limit of the value of taxes in relation to national income, above which *runaway* inflation begins. The whole argument posits a situation in which income transfers via taxation and interest payments on the national debt are large in relation to total income. Such a situation is not present in the United States. See the discussions by J. A. Pechman and Thomas Mayer and by D. T. Smith in the *Review of Economics and Statistics,* August 1952.

[44] This program is spelled out in many NAM publications in considerable detail: *Call to Action on Taxes;* a 1948 release, *Tax Reduction to Combat Inflation;* a 1950 pamphlet, *The Least of the Evils,* which, appearing in the context of the outbreak of the Korean War, recognizes the need for more taxes and proposes a uniform manufacturers' excise as the least of the evils; the NAM two-volume treatise, in outlining a program for America's future, treats future public finance along these lines, NAM, II: 981–984. A similar line appears in a speech by the president of du Pont before the Detroit Economic Club in 1954, "Can Tax Reform Promote Prosperity?," and, more sketchily, in a speech by a du Pont vice-president before the Kinston, North Carolina, Chamber of Commerce in October 1953 entitled "Blueprint for Disaster."

[45] See *Call to Action on Taxes.*

condemns the present rate structure as both unfair and uneconomic.[46] The general emphasis of the CED on the disincentive effects of the present tax structure, the need for lowering taxes on high and middle incomes and on corporation income, and the desirability of some Federal sales or excise tax is, however, very similar to that of the various NAM statements cited. On the other extreme, the spokesmen of the Foundation for Economic Education attack any progressive income tax as fundamentally immoral, and at variance with the principles of private property.[47]

We have already observed that the business creed's attack on the level and structure of taxes remains much the same despite large changes in the actual tax situation. This is characteristic of ideology. So is the tremendous selectivity of the creed's discussion of taxes and expenditures, and the ease with which the effects of specific taxes and the general tax structure are traced. A thorough study of the tax problem would have to compare the total national income under the particular tax structure being examined with that which might be expected under alternate tax structures. Such an analysis would make allowances for the fact that government as well as private expenditures may create additions to capital, or contribute to the satisfaction of consumer wants. The precise effect of income and corporation taxes on investment could be estimated only tentatively; the deterrent effects so obvious to business ideologists in recent years must be reconciled with one of the largest continuous surges of private investment in modern history. Further, the evaluation which underlies the whole of the creed's discussion of taxation — that capital growth should always be favored over present consumption — would be made explicit, and the possibility of other evaluations considered.[48]

[46] CED, *Taxes, National Security and Economic Growth,* a statement by the Research and Policy Committee, January 1954.

[47] Progressive taxation is identified with "the words of Karl Marx, 'From each according to his ability and to each according to his needs.'" Only proportional taxation is moral, and the old precedents of tithing are cited in its favor. Progressive taxation is "the simple looting through the law of the more productive by the more numerous but less productive. Its appeal is demagogic, and its result is communism . . . The endorsement of progressive taxation is, knowingly or unknowingly, the endorsement of communism, and sincere endorsement of progressive taxation, motivated often by generosity, is unwittingly one of the worst forces undermining individual liberty in America." Smith, *Liberty and Taxes,* pp. 3, 13.

[48] Some pioneer studies on the impact of taxes on business are currently being carried on at the Harvard Business School. See, especially, T. H. Sanders, *The Effects of Taxation on Executives* (Boston, 1951) and J. K. Butters, L. E. Thompson, and L. L. Bollinger, *The Effects of Taxation on Investments by Individuals* (Boston, 1953), both published by the Graduate School of Business Administration, Harvard University. These show none of the extreme effects which figure widely in the literature of the creed. An interesting technical point brought out by the second study is how widely effective tax rates actually paid differ from the theoretical rates which appear in the tax tables and the ideological examples. The effective rates, allowing for deductions, differences between capital gains and income tax rates, etc. show marginal rates below 50 per cent for even the highest incomes.

Moralizing on the evils of government deficits is even more frequent in the business ideology than decrying the impact of high taxes. Government deficits during wars may be tolerated in the classical version of the business creed,[49] but peacetime deficits are the quintessence of recklessness. While managerial writings approve peacetime deficit financing during periods of low employment, any "permanent" deficits are strongly opposed. Government budgets should be balanced over the cycle, if not annually.[50] In a period of very high taxes, when the NAM was pleading for every possible reduction in federal expenditures in order to provide tax relief for business, it nevertheless provided $2.5 billion in its planned minimum budget for debt reduction, so vital did it consider an immediate and continuing effort to reduce the national debt.[51]

The ideologists describe the national debt in terms of huge figures quite unconnected with any measure of relevance. The cartoon showing a startled farmer, about to burn the $8,000 mortgage on his farm in the presence of his wife and three children, being presented with another mortgage for $8,700 by a diabolical figure of Uncle Sam who tells him that it is "your share of the national debt"[52] is, in one form or another, one of the most widely repeated cliches in the whole repertoire of the creed.

The magnitude of the debt is regarded as a sign of approaching national bankruptcy, especially if the ominous upward trend continues. Often this threat is vague, resting on implicit analogies between private and public debt, and on the generally debauching effects of "spending." Often it is expressed in terms of historical analogies. The First National Bank of Boston warns of the example of Greece under Pericles:

Under this benevolent dictator the government embarked on a large-scale spending program to provide for the wants and entertainment of its people, a large proportion of whom were on the government payroll. But as the burdens accumulated and with bankruptcy imminent, Pericles led his people into a disastrous war, and that was the end of Greek leadership.[53]

[49] See Paton, *Shirtsleeve Economics,* pp. 321–337; NAM, II: 828.
[50] See Chapter 10 below for a fuller discussion of classical and managerial views on the relation of deficits to economic stability.
[51] *Call to Action on Taxes.* This was dated December 1947; it called for a $7 billion tax reduction for fiscal 1949.
In a 1949 statement, the first point of the program is: "There be a return to the historic policy of the retirement of debt as promptly as possible after the emergency giving rise to its issue has passed. Deficit financing is inconsistent with this policy and therefore deliberate resort to it in peacetime must be avoided." NAM, *A Program for the Management of the Federal Debt,* November 1949, p. 5.
[52] *Life with the Tax Gremlins,* p. 12. The cartoon is supplemented by a quotation from Senator Byrd of Virginia, the idol of the economizers, which conveys the same thought, and points out the contrast between the voluntarily assumed bank mortgage and the "other mortgage" which the farmer never "signed and blotted" (p. 13).
[53] *New England Letter,* Feb. 28, 1949.

In more specific terms, the threat of a large and growing federal debt is the threat of inflation; inflation in turn undermines the whole basis of the free enterprise system.[54] The threat of inflation, like the tax burden, is discussed in absolute terms, with little reference to changing economic circumstances or countervailing forces in other areas of the economy. A Chamber of Commerce report on the debt of December 1938, can be distinguished only by the actual dollar figures from NAM reports dated 1949 and 1952; although the alarming debt of the former year was some $37 billion, and that of the latter $260 billion.[55] The 1938 document shows the startling absolute size of the debt and its ominous rate of growth, compares it with the value of all U.S. farm lands, points to its origin in increased expenditures rather than decreased revenues, cites the warning lesson of European countries for the evil effects of large permanent debts, describes the debt and especially the sale of securities to banks as an inflationary engine, and recommends that all deficit-spending be stopped and debt-retirement be begun immediately. All this can be found in the later documents, with little change, except perhaps for a greater emphasis on the dangers of "monetizing" the debt through sales of government securities to the banks. This discussion has arisen in connection with recent controversies between the Treasury and the Federal Reserve Board over the desirability of the Treasury policy, abandoned in March 1951, of pegging the price of government securities. This practice was thought to have all the evils of promoting inflation, plus those of price-fixing and tampering with the free market.[56]

A dispassionate analysis of the impact of the federal debt would deal with many of the same problems discussed above. In particular, both the size of the debt and its management present real problems of monetary policy. But a dispassionate analysis would point to many variables other than debt and debt management which determine price levels; and it would give some importance to the role of Government debt both as a

[54] See Chapter 11 below for a fuller discussion of the problem of inflation.

[55] *Federal Debt and Expenditures, Chamber of Commerce* (Washington, 1938); and NAM, *A Program for Management of the Federal Debt* (New York, 1949) and NAM, *Public Debt and What to Do About It* (New York, 1952).

[56] See especially *Public Debt and What to Do About It*.

The wisdom of the pegging policy was a matter of much professional discussion among bankers, economists, and government servants. There was much to be said on both sides. An example of the projection of ideology into a quite technical discussion is provided by a pamphlet on this subject entitled *Treasury Debt Management and Federal Reserve Credit Policy*, distributed by Aubrey G. Lanton and Co., a government securities dealer, in 1950. Most of it is devoted to a reasoned and technically competent presentation of the anti-pegging view in a far from popular manner. The cover, however, bears the heading "Free Competitive Enterprise at Stake," and on p. 10 the summary warns, "Money and debt management can be conducted so as to promote free competitive enterprise, but if it is handled differently the machinations will consume vital organs without which free competitive enterprise cannot survive."

means of expanding monetary supply for our expanding economy, and as a lever without which monetary policy for stabilization could not easily be put into effect.[57]

NATURE OF THE DEMOCRATIC PROCESS

The continued "misbehavior" of government — especially in the twenty years of the Fair and New Deals — presents a difficult problem for the business creed. The bad results must somehow be squared with belief in the fundamental political system and affirmation of the values of individualism and democracy. The simplest conclusion, that the democratic process is itself corrupt and should be replaced by an aristocratic rule, is out of the question if the creed is to conform with the more general American values on which it is based.[58] The authors of the NAM volumes are evidently concerned with this problem, and they attempt to explain why the people continue to support dangerous government activity.[59] This explanation involves several factors. First is the reaction to the hardships of the early thirties. Second is the growth of a generation of young people who were inculcated with the desire for security and not taught the virtues of thrift, hard work, individualism, and self-help. Here it is implied, and elsewhere stated explicitly,[60] that the young have been the victims of propaganda by the government bureaucrats. Third is the fact that "vociferous groups of the 'intelligentsia' — many with rank pretense rather than training or authority to speak in this matter — have joined in the chorus of criticism of private enterprise." [61] Fourth is the past trend toward interventionism and totalitarianism in the rest of the world; fifth, the postwar increase in this trend, which makes it appear that interventionism is the wave of the future. The NAM study goes on to find,

[57] For the range of professional discussion of the problems of Federal debt, see *Our National Debt*, by the Commiteee on Debt Policy (Washington, 1949) and Harris, *The National Debt and the New Economics*. The first represents an extremely conservative approach which shares many of the values of the business ideology and its fundamental distrust of deficit financing and fear of inflation. The second emphasizes the importance of the income-creating effects of debt, and of the growth of debt as source of expansion of the money supply essential to the expansion of the economy.

[58] Compare chapters 2 and 12 below. There is, in private discussion, undoubtedly some expression of such sentiments. Moreover, the ideology does include certain anti-democratic statements, emphasizing, for instance, that the United States is not a "democracy" but a "republic." See, for example, Harper, *Liberty, A Path to Its Recovery*, ch. 7, "Democracy and Liberty." Also, Dean Russell, *The Bill of Rights* (Irvington-on-Hudson, N.Y., 1948). Also, during the depression of the thirties, there was some advocacy of depriving those on relief or on WPA of the franchise, but it hardly achieved responsible support.

[59] NAM, II: 1018–1023.

[60] See, for example, Forest A. Harness, *Federal Thought Control, A Study in Government Propaganda*, a pamphlet distributed by the National Industrial Conference Board, April 1948.

[61] NAM, II: 1023.

of course, that sound leadership and the natural qualities of the American people will reveal the virtues of free enterprise, and reverse the twenty-year stretch of bureaucratic domination.

At other times the popularity of alleged misgovernment is explained in terms of the pervasion of the democratic process through various kinds of vote buying and through the demagoguery of the political leaders of the New and Fair Deals. Thus the *Saturday Evening Post,* in a rueful editorial shortly after the surprising Democratic victory of 1948, said:

He [Truman] owes his election pretty much to the fact that some millions of people have come to accept the philosophy of the heroine of Gentleman Prefer Blondes: to wit, that love and affection are very nice, but a diamond ring lasts a lifetime. The sterling American farmer reasoned that Dewey might be wonderful, but it was Truman who was paying the support prices. Other groups were persuaded by promises that Uncle Sam would build them a house, pay their doctors' bills or guarantee hamburgers at thirty cents a pound.[62]

It goes on to speak of the Democratic platform and the President's promises: "Many of them sounded like irresponsible enticements by a man who realized that it was impossible to overestimate the number of crackpots on the voting lists. But Kansas-City-type politics do not altogether explain Mr. Truman's campaign . . ." Thus the editorialist managed to link together the themes of demagoguery and outright political corruption, old-style.

This type of explanation of the success of Fair Dealism also stresses the class appeal character of its policies. One of the strongest and most frequently repeated business criticisms of both F. D. Roosevelt and Truman was that they stirred up class warfare. Such tactics are said to be unfair; they deny the fundamental truth of the harmony of group interests in America which free enterprise produces, and on which free enterprise in turn rests.

DANGEROUS TENDENCIES AND INEVITABLE RESULTS

In discussing the relations of government and business in our society, the ideologists characteristically refer to dangerous first steps, inevitable tendencies, and logical conclusions. Here, of course, the logical conclusion of government intervention is socialism and slavery. Every measure of whatever character which carries government outside its proper sphere is seen as the next step down the road to socialism, a step which is always difficult or impossible to retrace. In general, our society stands on the edge of the fateful line: one further dose of intervention will carry us across, whence we can never return. This note is especially strident today,

[62] "Did We Buy Socialism with Truman?" *Saturday Evening Post* (editorial), Dec. 4, 1948.
See also NAM, II: 712, for a similar argument.

in the context of the great world ideological struggle between more or less decentralized, capitalist nations and the Soviet bloc of totalitarian nations with centrally planned economies. But it is an old theme, and was part of the business creed when Karl Marx was remembered more as an obscure scholar who had been grubbing in the books and papers of the British Museum than as the spiritual father of World Revolution.

Thus, Henry Lee Higginson spoke of government intervention in the eighties and nineties of the last century in these terms: "The Sherman Anti-Trust Law of 1890 is probably the most vicious and unreasonable law that was ever passed by any legislative body, and there is nothing in any state that I know of any worse than the Interstate Commerce Law and its various amendments, giving more power to a half a dozen lawyers than is possessed by the Czar of Russia . . ." [63]

Today the words are different; the same laws would hardly receive the same abuse, but the tune is the same. The financial editor of the *New York Times* complains: ". . . The American people are asked to believe not only that a little group of bureaucrats in Washington can run the economy better than it has been run for a century and three-quarters under the free-enterprise system, but that they can do so without interfering with democratic processes and freedom of the individual." [64] H. W. Prentis, Jr., then president of the NAM, put the problem as follows: "From past experience, a middle of the road course in respect to planned economy is out of the question. Competitive enterprise can be subject to regulations — as it should be — and survive, but it cannot be confined with government control and still function as competitive enterprise." [65] The Foundation for Economic Education distributes a pamphlet, *Planned Chaos* by Ludwig von Mises, whose theme is that interventionism equals socialism equals planning equals chaos; there can be no such thing as limited intervention by government.

First steps are dangerous because of the tendency to expand inherent in any governmental organization. Once started, a government agency always seeks new functions, new funds, new personnel; its efforts are successful, and it expands its size and scope. This expansionist tendency may be deduced from the nature of politicians, or it may appear as an independent attribute of government activity. In either event, it has become a favorite whipping boy among businessmen.[66]

[63] Perry, *Henry Lee Higginson*, p. 443.
[64] *New York Times*, March 7, 1950.
[65] Prentis, *Competitive Enterprise*.
[66] For example, three pamphlets recently issued by the Chamber of Commerce discuss various aspects of undesirable government intervention in business; a central theme of each of them is the inherent expansiveness of government activity. What starts as "creeping socialism" soon turns into galloping socialism. The pamphlets

Hostility between business and past Democratic administrations may partially explain the vehemence with which every proposed action of the federal government, whether it is concerned with aid to education or loans to Great Britain, is attacked as a step toward socialism; but the theme of inevitable decay is deeply rooted in the ideology. Perhaps, with a government more sympathetic to business the form of the idea will change, and the targets for some of the criticism shift, say, to unions, but the theme itself is likely to persist.

CONCLUSION

By their very nature, decisions on the ultimate purpose of government or the proper limits of government activity are based on value judgments. There are no absolute standards of "proper" versus "dangerous" government activities. In our own society the accepted evaluation of how a marginal unit of resources spent collectively, say, on education, should compare with the same unit spent individually on, say, entertainment, has shifted from time to time under the pressure of various forces. In no society has the calculus of economic rationality (as measured by what it would be profitable for the businessman to produce and sell in the market) been the sole criterion for the disposition of the society's resources; and there is no reason to suppose that it ever will be. But judicious attention to history does not provide the stuff of which ideologies are made.

---

are: *The Welfare State and the State of Human Welfare; The Drive for a CONTROLLED ECONOMY via PALE PINK PILLS* (Washington, 1949); *and Socialism in America* (Washington, 1950).

10

ECONOMIC FLUCTUATIONS

THE RESPONSIBILITY OF EACH INDIVIDUAL — whether business magnate or day laborer — for his own economic fate is one of the major tenets of the business creed. Virtue pays; hard work, thrift, initiative, imagination, and venturesomeness are rewarded not only in the next world but in this. Failure, like success, is deserved. This assumption of personal responsibility and the belief that the individual gets his just rewards or punishments are not, of course, confined to the business creed. They are attitudes widely diffused throughout American society, although less strongly held today than twenty years ago.

Events of this century have made people aware that the individual cannot completely master his own economic fate. A dynamic, interdependent, industrial economy is bound to produce discrepancies between virtues and rewards; and these discrepancies are bound to be disturbing to the individualist faith. This would be true even if the economy were on the whole stable. In fact, the American economy has been quite unstable, and its fluctuations between deep depression and inflation have revealed the economic impotence of the individual. In the great depression of the thirties, the unemployed assumed a remarkable degree of personal responsibility for their plight; they believed the fault lay with their lack of skill or industry or initiative. But the experience was disillusioning. It is hard to maintain the view that over ten million individuals become suddenly and simultaneously undeserving of employment. Since that time society has greatly widened the class of misfortunes for which it relieves the individual of responsibility.

The same events have perhaps made it clear that even the most powerful businessmen can be as helpless in the face of general economic tides as peasants confronting the weather. The plans of the most astute management can be ruined by depression or inflation. Economic fluctuations produce windfall profits and losses which are difficult to interpret as appropriate rewards for business skill and effort. There was a time when some businessmen could not only withstand financial crises but even overcome them. The Morgan contribution to stopping the efflux of gold in the nineties is a classic case, like the Rothschild episodes earlier.[1] But all that the sacrificial businessmen who responded to President Hoover's plea to spend money during the decline of 1929–32 could show for their patriotism was increased losses. Today businessmen are modest about their individual powers to produce economic stability, and they worry about the effects on their own businesses of fluctuations outside their control. Recognition of the importance of these uncontrollable forces is implicit in the tremendous business concern with forecasting general business conditions. Discussion of forecasts, much of it in terms which are more expressive than analytically useful, occupies a large part of the space of the typical newspaper financial page or business weekly.

The increased sensitivity of businessmen to the problem of economic fluctuations was evident in the mild recession of 1949. Even after a decade of unparalleled prosperity, the mild decline of 1949 aroused great apprehension. Throughout the postwar years, there had been growing expectation that the boom would end; indeed the boom went on in spite of the fact that people did not believe in it. Business publications in 1948 were full of warnings. Early in 1949, *Business Week* questioned businessmen: Their greatest worry? The coming recession.[2] A *New York Times* business commentator wrote in similar vein:

In spite of this increased ability to buy, people have been hesitant because of the apparent lack of confidence in the future, fear of depression, resistance to prices or in anticipation of lower prices, and perhaps because business men themselves are not doing enough to convert purchasing power into purchases . . .[3]

These apprehensions, conditioned by memories of the thirties, reflected a concern over more than business profits alone. Eric Johnston wrote:

All our efforts to create a stronger and better society would go by the boards if we had another depression in America. Naturally we expect ups and downs in a free economy such as ours. We can't stop the tide, but by a more purposeful direction of our economy for the common good we can prevent the tide from completely engulfing us as it did in the 1930's.[4]

Writers of both the classical and managerial wings of the creed agreed that the System could not survive another Great Depression.[5]

[1] Allen, *The Great Pierpont Morgan*, pp. 99–125.
[2] *Business Week*, Feb. 19, 1949.
[3] *New York Times*, May 22, 1949 (The Merchant's Point of View).
[4] Eric Johnston, *We're All In It* (New York, 1948).
[5] See NAM, II: 1030.

Business fluctuations present a difficult and crucial problem for the creed. The creed must reconcile to its basic individualist faith the impotence of individuals to deal with general instability. And it must contend with the ideological disaffection arising from the social consequences of business fluctuations. Economic instability jeopardizes public acceptance of such basic tenets of the creed as government noninterference, reliance on the free market, the virtues of hard work and thrift. Depression and boom lead the public to stress the values of security and social responsibility to a degree unwelcome to the business ideologist.

Both the individual businessman and the System as a whole are put on the defensive. In adjusting to fluctuations in demand beyond his control, the businessman takes actions which are bound to be unpopular — he cuts wages and lays off workers in depression, or he boosts prices in inflationary times. Even if he succeeds in convincing the victims that he had no more choice than they, his prestige suffers from this admission of helplessness. If he is at the mercy of outside forces, he is no longer the strong and skillful manager who gives employment and serves the customer. For the System as a whole, instability — unemployment and inflation — is certainly a major source of public disaffection. Anti-business sentiment and ideology would not get far without this issue.[6]

The central question for the business creed is whether or not cycles in economic activity are inherent in the System. Are fluctuations an endemic and inevitable consequence of capitalism? Or are they occasioned by outside forces impinging on an economic system which, left to itself, would be stable? Both views have advantages and disadvantages for the business creed. Both shift the burden of blame from the businessman's shoulders; in one case to "nature," in the other case to "outside forces," principally government. If instability is accepted as inevitable and natural, then the creed can argue it is the responsibility of individuals to adjust to this fact, and that no governmental action can eliminate the cycle without destroying the System. But then the creed must argue that the advantages of the System are worth this price. As the New York Chamber of Commerce put it: Depressions are the price we pay for freedom.[7] Another commentator, prepared to admit that communism can eliminate the cycle, points out that this is achieved only by maintaining a low standard of living and imposing slavery. Some writers, however, contend that cycles are inherent not only in capitalism but in any kind of economic organization.

---

[6] Income inequality is of course another major source of dissatisfaction. But it is noteworthy that anti-business ideology argues not only that inequality is unjust but also that it is responsible for booms and busts; this is a feature of both Marxism and what might be called "consumptionist Keynesianism."

[7] Quoted, S. K. Bailey, *Congress Makes a Law* (New York, 1950), p. 117.

The tremendous cyclical forces which underlie any economy and which express themselves in booms and depressions have never been successfully controlled — even under the conditions of "permanent depression" sometimes achieved by planned societies. No government has even been able to push down the peaks and hold up the valleys.[8]

If the other view is taken — that fluctuations can be avoided without destroying the System — then the door is opened for all kinds of governmental programs designed to avert instability and to relieve individuals of its consequences. It is not surprising, therefore, that the main outside force responsible for instability is, according to the creed, the government itself.

Some exponents of the business creed take the first answer to the question, and some take the second. A third viewpoint associated with the managerial wing of the ideology has found increasing acceptance since the war. The third school does not believe either that cycles are inherent and inevitable in the System, or that the economic system, left to itself, is automatically stable. This school believes that, although some government actions may unsettle the economy, others are necessary in order to stabilize it and can be adopted without destroying or damaging the System. These three viewpoints will be discussed in turn.

CYCLES AS INHERENT IN CAPITALISM

The view that cycles are an inherent part of the capitalist process is shared by economists as diverse as Marx and Schumpeter and by ideologies as far apart as Communism and the American Business Creed. Agreement does not extend to the significance of this fact. For Marx and the Communists, the cyclical process is part of the mechanism by which the proletariat is made progressively more miserable and capitalism collapses from its own contradictions. For Schumpeter and the business creed, cycles are a necessary and functional concomitant of the economic progress capitalism brings for the whole population.

Schumpeter's argument is that sustained prosperity spawns incompetence and inefficiency; during the ensuing decline, the cathartic phase of the cycle, inefficient producers are weeded out and the low-cost progressive firms survive. Just as the removal of an ulcer brings good health, so the elimination of the unfit is a necessary condition for a healthy and growing economy. In Schumpeter's phrase, the business cycle is part of the process of "creative destruction" — innovators of new techniques or new products destroy established business interests in the

[8] E. Holman, *The Public Responsibilities of Big Companies,* Address to the Economic Club of Detroit, Nov. 8, 1948, p. 9.

course of the very process by which they create a higher standard of living.

Another related theme is that the economy, having indulged in excesses in the boom, must make a retribution as inevitable as a hangover after a spree. Both ways of viewing depression imply that since painful adjustments are unavoidable and ultimately beneficial, government meddling and monetary or fiscal panaceas can do nothing but harm.

As long ago as 1857, Henry Lee Higginson graphically combined these two versions of depression:

> Looking at the thing from a philosophical point of view, this crisis is a very useful event for our country. People stop, add up their accounts, ascertain the truth concerning their money, see their awful pace, give up much of their wicked extravagance, discover the difference between necessaries and luxuries, go to work again, and they are wiser men. It stops the too great rush into trade, shows the danger of too extended credit, proves that one man cannot well do a dozen things at a time, and that we need railroad directors who will work and not play, etc., etc. It makes more room for young men, and more room for every man, and it turns the wheel which carries the rich and the educated down and brings the poor and the ignorant up to be educated and refined. It is a most effectual instrument for putting life and energy into our Republic. If we had no such troubles, the poor people would begin to think equality, etc., was a joke, and the rich people would agree with them. Of course, much suffering results from it, but it is healthy. There was a growing belief that all that was needed to be rich was to become a merchant. In the meantime, the country is very rich and powerful, and has enormous resources. All the real wealth is still in the land.[9]

More recently, the same attitude on depression was expressed by the National Industrial Conference Board.

> Thus one may note the birth of the idea that the Federal Government may be obliged to provide old age pensions for capital. That idea was bound to follow from the delusion that by the free application of federal subsidies to any seat of pain we may secure the great blessing of the painless economy. This of course is quackery. There is no such thing as a painless economy; and if you overcome the sensation of pain by anaesthetics, how shall the economy know when it is sick or why? The use of pain in a healthy body is to give notice of wrong living. The only way to cure it really is by right living . . . If it [the enterprise] could think of no way to get the profit back by improving its tools and methods, then simply it was lost — wiped out. But that is all that did happen. The great economic mechanism was not hurt at all. Indeed it was generally improved and worked much better when relieved of the weight of old and obsolete capital.

In discussing the repeated bankruptcies of railroads and the concomitant decline of rates, the N.I.C.B. concludes as follows:

[9] Perry, *Henry Lee Higginson*, pp. 114–115.

There was pain in it, of course, but it was pain that cured itself; and there came to be a hard saying of great wisdom — that the measure of the country's prosperity was the amount of bankruptcy it could stand. This meant only that the faster it sloughed off the dead and dying capital the faster it could go forward — provided always that the dynamic principles by which capital endlessly renewed itself were preserved.[10]

In summarizing the views of his business associates in the midst of the Great Depression, Eccles, a leading businessman and later a high government official, wrote:

"Do nothing," some business and financial leaders replied. They argued again that a depression was the scientific operation of economic laws that were God-given and not man-made. They could not be interfered with. Depressions were phenomena like the one described in the Biblical story of Joseph and the seven kine, fat and lean. The leaders said we were in the seven lean years that must inevitably follow the seven full years. And they further explained that we were in the lean years because we had been spendthrifts and wastrels in the roaring twenties. We had wasted what we earned instead of saving it.

He then rebuts this view by showing that the nation had not in fact been profligate in the twenties: damage of war had been repaired, the country had added $100 billion of new capital equipment and had advanced $10 billion to foreign countries, and the government had paid off $7 billion of internal national debt.[11]

The "sin and punishment" theory, it will be noted from the quotations above, admits that businessmen make mistakes. They become exuberant and over-optimistic during prosperity. They anticipate ever-growing markets and invest excessively, burden themselves with high-cost plants, hire inefficient workers, pay high prices for raw materials. Soon the markets become saturated. A price has to be paid for over-indulgence, in investment as in food, drink, or sex.

The *Saturday Evening Post* reflects the attitude that the economy must pay for past error when it writes:

One immediate lesson from what has been going on is that government officials and politicians who seek votes by yelling bloody murder every time economic changes occur deserve less popular attention than they have been getting. The average man who reasons that "what goes up must come down" has been a better predictor than the high-domed "economic advisors." [12]

The Guaranty Trust Company warned the nation in September 1949 that there was no easy way out of the recession, that "readjustment" to lower prices was required rather than "reflation" to higher prices:

[10] *American Affairs*, January 1950, p. 5.
[11] M. S. Eccles, *Beckoning Frontiers* (New York, 1951), p. 75.
[12] *Saturday Evening Post*, Feb. 26, 1949, p. 10.

Reflation is no substitute for sound readjustment. Price stability is of course highly desirable, provided it is a natural stability that reflects real economic equilibrium. But when that equilibrium is disturbed, price fluctuations are among the most important and least dangerous means by which it tends to restore itself.

The bank said, further, that business should strive for greater efficiency of operation and greater volume of output, at the cost of required price concessions; labor should abandon attempts to raise wages; and agriculture should also swim with the tide. The government should revamp its tax structure and cut burdensome taxes. "If these things were done, the orderly completion of the current adjustment could be anticipated with confidence." [13]

Impressed by the distortions brought on by war and controls, the McGraw-Hill Company approached the problem in a similar vein. Farm prices in 1946 were up 125 per cent and industrial prices only 32 per cent since 1941; the price of steel was up by 14 per cent; lumber, over 50 per cent; rents, 4 per cent; clothing, no change. Above all, uniform wage increases must be avoided.

Salvation both for the workers and for employers in the relatively profitless section, a peculiarly important group of industries, must be looked for primarily by increasing productivity, thereby decreasing the cost per unit. Part of this higher productivity can come only from individual efforts of the workers themselves. Another part can come from an elimination of bottlenecks in materials and parts which prevents the labor force from working most efficiently. Only by greater output per man-hour can workers and management solve their common problem.[14]

CYCLES NOT INHERENT IN CAPITALISM

The claim that a free capitalist economy is basically stable has an even longer tradition than the theory that cycles are an inevitable part of the capitalist process. From the classical economists on, the orthodox view has been that a competitive price system confers, among other blessings, continuous full employment. Through the price mechanism, resources are transferred according to the wishes of consumers, savers, and investors. General overproduction is impossible, for "supply creates its own demand." Saving cannot cause unemployment, because the market automatically channels it into investment. In a free labor market there can be no unemployment; for if wages are too high for the whole labor force to find employment, competition among workers will reduce wages to the proper level. It follows that if the economy is not stable, it must be because the price mechanism is not allowed to operate.

[13] Guaranty Trust Company advertisement, *Business Week*, Sept. 17, 1949.
[14] McGraw-Hill advertisement, *New York Herald Tribune*, Oct. 21, 1946.

A free market economy, responsive to discovery, invention, and shifts in technology and consumer demand, undergoes constant, ceaseless change. We produce in America some eight million different items, and provide thousands of different services. By and large, these commodities and services flow to the market in the right proportions, in response to consumer demand. Change is accomplished with a high degree of smoothness and dispatch, so that it is almost unnoticed by the public. The free market economy is self-coordinating and self-regulating, without master plan or central direction. The free price system acts as an effective guide, avoiding chaos and bringing about remarkable economic teamwork within a set of rules established by government.*

[Free competition] inevitably expresses itself in a higher and richer standard of living . . . The competition of job-makers for the services of workers pulled wages up, while the competition in the goods market helped to keep prices up . . . This rise in real income for all groups was the end product of our free, dynamic, progressive economy.[15]

* [Footnote in original] Economic depressions, closely related to war and the instability in the money and credit supply (both largely governmental problems) appear as a contradiction of these statements.

The creed recognizes three main factors which interfere with the operation of the free market: government, trade unions, and business monopoly. Government monetary and fiscal policies distort the mechanism by which the market automatically balances investment spending with saving; the consequence is either deflation or inflation. Government regulations and controls make prices and wages rigid and prevent the adjustments which the free market would accomplish by price changes. Labor organizations control wages and limit productivity, preventing the automatic adjustment of wages to full employment levels. Even the business monopolist who keeps his prices too high and too rigid is condemned. The force of this condemnation, however, is limited by the fact that the business creed defines monopoly so narrowly that virtually all business is competitive.

In one of the most elaborate analyses of the cycle in the literature of the business creed,[16] the NAM text places the main emphasis on government action. The authors admit that alternating waves of business optimism and pessimism contribute at least to the amplitude of fluctuations. But the causal factors they emphasize are outside forces — natural disasters, wars, and, especially, government policy.

In a long discussion of the 1929 collapse, the NAM authors hold that the government was responsible because of its misuse of credit, its encouragement of risky foreign loans, and its restriction of imports just when they should have been encouraged. This is a good example of the selectivity characteristic of ideological history. That the excess of foreign

[15] *The Welfare State and the State of Human Welfare*, pp. 10–11.
[16] NAM, 11, esp. ch. 16.

loans and their misrepresentation were the work primarily of private banks is not made clear. That the tariff policies were the result of strong business pressure is passed over. Not a word is said about other factors which have seemed important to nonideological students of the collapse — the failure of wages to rise with the large gains in productivity contributed to an insufficiency of consumption demand just when saturation was putting an end to the investment boom, particularly in the housing and automobile industries.

In the case of the 1937–38 decline, the NAM authors again emphasized the government's contribution:

. . . impairment of business confidence by tolerance of sit-down strikes; criticism of price level; proposals to reorganize the judiciary; arbitrary tightening of interest rates; taxation of undistributed profits; and sudden increase of wages when government was curtailing its pumping of other purchasing power into the system.

. . . It is further perhaps safe to say that all of them together would not have started a downswing, had it not been for the fact that the economy had been overstimulated and weakened through a long period of unwise governmental action which had resulted in a "consumption goods prosperity" as contrasted with a well-balanced prosperity based upon a backlog of investment as well as consumption.[17]

They do not mention the contribution of inventory speculation to the decline. One thing for which the authors do not berate the government is the change in the government budget from a cash deficit to a cash surplus; other observers have attributed to this some responsibility for the setback.

Similarly, business ideology has blamed government policy for the postwar inflation. Since this diagnosis is closely connected with the creed's discussion of monetary policy, it will be examined in the following chapter.

RECENT MANAGERIAL VIEWS

In recent years a third viewpoint has achieved expression in business circles, especially through the Committee for Economic Development.[18] According to this view, the system does not function perfectly; there may be problems of deficiency of demand and unemployment or excess of demand and inflation. Saving is not automatically converted into investment; nor is investment always limited to the available supply of saving.

[17] NAM, II: 861–862.
[18] Representative samples of this view are *Jobs and Markets* (CED, New York, 1946): and *Defense Against Recession* (CED Research and Policy Committee, New York, March 1954).

This analysis allows the government an important place not only in bringing about maladjustments but also in correcting them or compensating for them. In depression the government should add to purchasing power; in inflationary periods its objective should be to limit purchasing power. Although the exponents of this view do not recommend an ever-growing national debt, they see no virtue in an annually balanced budget. They are aware of the fact that a necessary condition for sustained and stable prosperity is adequate purchasing power, and that this condition is not fulfilled automatically but must be fostered by appropriate government policies. This approach differs from the older orthodoxy in reflecting the influence of Keynesian economics as well as of classical economics. As yet it is restricted to the CED and a few other managerial sources, such as *Fortune*, and receives comparatively little general repetition in the creed. This view is noteworthy as an example of the use and dissemination of quasi-academic and academic material by organized business groups.

NON-GOVERNMENTAL POLICY FOR COMBATTING FLUCTUATIONS

As the creed includes a number of diagnoses of the disease, so it contains a variety of recommended therapies. We shall first consider the policies recommended for private citizens, including businessmen themselves; and in the following section we shall examine the policies recommended for government.

The cry "harder work — more production" offers a universal antidote to any economic malady, be it depression or inflation. In recent years a common view has been that more production is the solution, and the only real solution, to the inflationary problem. This view ignores the fact that a rise in output, however desirable in itself, makes only a limited contribution to the reduction of inflationary pressure, because it adds to demand via the incomes of the people who produce it as well as to supply. An official of Willys-Overland Motor Company proposes as a solution to the problem of inflation: a rise of 10 per cent in productivity, which can be achieved by the elimination of waste and the restoration of pride in workmanship and the dignity of work.[19] Another firm advocates investment in machines to increase productivity as the cure for inflation:

We have high prices (inflation) today because there is more money than goods in people's hands.

Since nobody wants to surrender or lose his money, the only cure for high prices is more goods.

The only way to get more goods is better machines efficiently used to produce more.[20]

[19] *New York Times,* Nov. 19, 1948.
[20] Warner & Swasey advertisement, *Newsweek*, June 28, 1948.

The Advertising Council expresses a position congenial to the business creed when it assures us that economic virtue, and only economic virtue, will solve the problem of instability.

> But we ought to be able to do even better than we have in the past — if we all work together to increase our productivity and to spread its benefits. We can do this through increased wages, lower prices, shorter hours, more jobs and better collective bargaining, as well as more income to business. Only in this way can we hope to level off the ups and downs of prices and jobs, avoid depressions, lessen industrial disputes, and enjoy the good things which our economic system *can* give us! [21]

Senator Flanders, a business leader as well as a legislator, was, in 1949,

> . . . slowly and regretfully coming to the conclusion that it is difficult to end inflation by passing laws . . . Many of us are coming to believe that the exercise of mutual statesmanship by employer, employed, and consumer must be a large element in the control of inflation. It is the individual responsibility of all of us.[22]

At the beginning of this chapter we noted that businessmen are more modest about their ability to control the causes and consequences of general economic fluctuations than they used to be. But the fatalism of a National Dairy advertisement in 1948, "We don't like the high cost of living any more than you do . . ." [23] is not the only contemporary business estimate.

By contrast, in connection with "merit rating" adjustments of payroll taxes on employers for unemployment insurance, many businessmen believe that reducing the tax for employers with good employment records is an effective incentive to employers to stabilize employment. This position implicitly minimizes the significance of outside forces in determining the employment offered by a firm. Untenable as the position seems to most economists, business advocates have sold it to almost every state government.[24]

A distinguished businessman, Richard P. Deupree, President of the Procter and Gamble Company, which for many years has provided its employees with guaranteed minimum employment, insists that stability is

---

[21] *The Miracle of America*, p. 15.

[22] Quoted in *New York Times*, Oct. 20, 1949.

[23] National Dairy advertisement, *Harper's*, February 1948.

[24] The importance of the context of ideological discussion is illustrated by comparison of business positions on "merit rating" and on union proposals for a "guaranteed annual wage." In the latter context, the businessmen argue that they have little control over employment. It is further worth noting that business support of merit-rating is not a pure self-interest proposition, in which firms in stable industries take one position and those in unstable ones another. Rather it is endorsed on principle in the general ideology.

the responsibility of management; and he reproaches employers who have not stabilized their employment.

Steady year-round employment is so right from the standpoint of the employer, so right from the standpoint of the workers, and so right for the country as a whole, and, taken on an annual basis, so economical in the operation of a business that it is hard to see why we manufacturers have not made more progress in its application . . .

. . . .

There is no easy solution to this problem of stability. I believe it is management's problem and management's thinking, that, by considering all factors, will decide how a business can be changed to provide for steady year-round employment . . .[25]

Another leading industrialist takes a similar position:

If we can't avoid change, we may nevertheless manage our affairs in such a way that we eliminate many of the more painful effects of change. Favored companies in favored industries have been successes in this field. They have picked stability of employment as an objective and have made progress toward that goal. They haven't eliminated uncertainty, but they have made sure the bad effects of uncertainty are not destructive to the human spirit.[26]

A more balanced view is presented by the President of the Standard Oil Company of New Jersey. Admitting the difficulties of eliminating instability, he stresses the importance of minimizing insecurity without making the economy inflexible:

No government has ever been able to push down the peaks and hold up the valleys. I certainly am not under the impression that any big enterprise can succeed in this field. But I do believe that it should be a constant study of all of us to find ways of reducing the impact of these cycles on individuals.

We in America are more conscious than others of the value of enterprise and the taking of risks. Our wealth and high standards of living have come to us because a certain high percentage of men and women have been able, willing, and anxious to take chances. Our security as a nation lies partly in the fact that we have the strength which arises out of being an enterprising land — a place where great numbers of people invent new machines, develop new products, push back the frontiers of ignorance — because there are rewards available to those who take risks.

The American people know this. I think they will never retreat from their belief in opportunity and individual enterprise. At the same time, they are testing various ways of protecting the individual against the more damaging

[25] R. P. Deupree, "Management's Responsibility Towards Economic Stability," *Dun's Review*, August 1948, pp. 11–12.

[26] B. Ford, *Some Unfinished Business for Young Americans*, Address to the Department of Business Administration, Michigan State College, Dec. 8, 1949, p. 15.

effects of inevitable change. They are asking for constructive improvements which will defend the individual against forces which are too great for him to cope with.

So far as the management of my own company is concerned, we have formed the habit of thinking and speaking in terms of "career employment" or "lifetime employment." That is our goal. We have reached a point today where 90 per cent of our employees — wage-rated as well as salaried — have been continuously employed since the day they were hired. I am well aware that conditions in some industries are less favorable to steady employment than in others. But I am convinced that the will to achieve an answer to the modern problem of security is the most important factor.[27]

Taking a similarly modest but positive view, a steel executive praises the management of another company for reducing the impact of instability by branching out into new fields.[28]

GOVERNMENT POLICY

The business creed remains divided on the use of unbalanced government budgets to offset fluctuations in private spending. The classical position is opposed to compensatory fiscal policy and in favor of an annually balanced budget. The NAM, for example, does not believe that deficit spending is an effective method of recovering from depression. In arguing against it, it cites business reactions:

. . . Rightly or wrongly business men do not believe in the effectiveness of compensatory spending by government, and if the President announces that the outlook is so cloudy that such spending must be started, there is no question that business will start running for the storm cellar.[29]

But the NAM does believe that deficit spending causes inflation.

There is only one way to attack the problem and that is to call a halt to the present government policy of deficit financing and revert to the sound principle of living within our means. We cannot have our cake and eat it too. Government spending must be curtailed, money supply caused by credit inflation reduced, and incentives provided so that the more venture capital will be invested in productive facilities. The gap between money supply and the supply of goods must be closed.[30]

Senator Byrd, a leading exponent of the classical creed in the political arena, states the position as follows:

I shrink from the thought of the third course [deficit financing] . . . If we can't or won't run this government on a balanced budget now, I doubt that

---

[27] Holman, *Public Responsibilities*, pp. 9–10.
[28] B. P. Fairless, *Dedication to Success* (U.S. Steel Corporation, 1951), pp. 6–7.
[29] Hearings, House Committee on Expenditures, *Full Employment Act of 1945*, p. 554.
[30] NAM, *Trends*, October 1948, p. 2.

we shall ever return to sound financing. To you and me that means our credit would be destroyed and our system of government doomed.[31]

One of Franklin Roosevelt's few contributions to the business creed is a criticism he made of President Hoover in 1932 in words he was never allowed to forget:

The credit of the family depends chiefly on whether the family is living within its income. And that is equally true of the nation . . . But if, like a spendthrift, it throws discretion to the winds, and is willing to make no sacrifices at all in spending, if it extends its taxing to the limits of the people's power to pay and continues to pile up deficits, then it is on the road to bankruptcy . . .[32]

There has, however, always been some business support for the heresy that government spending could aid the economy. In 1931, Edward Filene wrote that government spending was a lesser evil than unemployment:

The greatest waste of all, however, is unemployment; for with graft and inefficiency rampant, some minimum of wealth at least is brought into existence whereas unemployment is total waste in that it produces no wealth whatever.[33]

Another retailer, General Wood of Sears Roebuck, had, according to a history of the firm, "a profound conviction that New Deal spending was helping the country, particularly the farmer, and was therefore helping his firm."

Another factor in mitigating the effects of the depression on the company was . . . government spending . . . not only did government spending in cities enable the residents of those cities to purchase farm produce, but a considerable share of the government outlays went directly to the farmers.[34]

The same views about government spending are reported by John Harriman of the *Boston Globe*, who, after numerous interviews in Wall Street, wrote:

. . . [Wall Street] does not want to see the government cut back on outlay for arms, or any forms of actual goods and services.

. . . .

Thus Wall Street thunder against Democratic spending has now become a whisper in the incoming Republican ear which says: "Economy in government is fine, but please don't make it too fast." [35]

[31] *New York Times*, May 5, 1949.
[32] Quoted in Eccles, *Beckoning Frontiers*, p. 97. These words frequently have been quoted by businessmen since.
[33] E. A. Filene, *Successful Living in This Machine Age* (New York, 1931), pp. 29–50.
[34] B. Emmet and J. C. Jeuck, *Catalogues and Counters: A History of Sears, Roebuck and Company* (Chicago, 1950), pp. 333–334.
[35] John Harriman, *Boston Globe*, Nov. 30, 1952.

These examples illustrate the difference between systematic ideology and pragmatic judgments which occur in specific contexts. The ideology stands in principle against the theory that government spending can bring and maintain prosperity, but businessmen cannot help feeling that increasing the demand for their products is favorable to business. But it is still the exception rather than the rule for a businessman to write as one did in regard to the 1949 recession:

. . . In other words, you advocate that the government should parallel and, therefore, magnify, the general decline in economic activity, or in plain language, make two unemployed grow where only one grew before. This is the economic philosophy of Hooverism which was highly respected twenty years ago . . .

In the old days the philosophy of governmental belt tightening was accepted because people did not clearly understand the workings of our economic system and regarded depressions as moral retribution for their sins. It was natural therefore to suppose that the period of retribution could be shortened by voluntary measures of penance . . .

Far from seeking to cut government expenditures, our obligation today is to increase the total amount of government expenditures in order to compensate for the temporary deficiency of private expenditures. In a word, we need to carry through a fuller investment program — of building schools, hospitals, roads, dams, etc. — to take up the slack created by the decline in private investment . . .[36]

The managerial wing of the creed, especially the C.E.D., accepts the validity of compensatory fiscal policy. These business spokesmen are content to balance the budget over a whole trade cycle rather than every year. They are not, however, prepared to support a persistent deficit as an offset to chronic deficiencies of private spending, which they consider unlikely to occur. They favor tax and other policies designed to encourage risk-taking, so that private investment will not prove to be persistently deficient. When demand nevertheless threatens to be inadequate, it is the responsibility of the government to fill the void. Of the two possible fiscal attacks on insufficiency of demand, the managerial creed, sharing the general business opposition to extension of government activity, prefers reductions in taxes to increases in expenditures.

Those who maintain that economic fluctuations are the outcome of government mismanagement and interference with the free market obviously will insist that proper restraint by the government will eliminate instability. In inflationary times, adherents of this position center their attack on excessive monetary expansion by the government; the NAM statement quoted above is typical.

[36] *New York Times*, May 23, 1949, Letter of M. Pennybacker, Connecticut businessman.

Frequently the creed emphasizes not so much the specific content of government policy as the uncertainties created by government actions. Business confidence is pictured as a fragile web, easily destroyed by government hostility and by doubts about what the government will do next. The explanation of the unsatisfactory recovery in the thirties often runs in these terms: investment and risk-taking were stagnant because the business community could have no confidence in the future under a New Deal regime. The NAM believes that business confidence was returning in 1932–33 before the new administration took office. But in the view of the NAM, the administration destroyed confidence, preventing full recovery and causing the decline of 1937–38.

The record also indicates that public confidence was not at such a low level as the proponents of pump priming would have had us believe. There was much talk of whether our system of individual enterprise was defunct, and probably many persons became convinced . . . Perhaps the clearest evidence of this was the trend of the stock market, for in those days it was unquestionably the best measure we had of the public's appraisal of the future, or at least the appraisal of that proportion of the public which economically was able to give expression of its opinion. And the records show that stock prices more than doubled.[37]

[37] NAM, II: 937–938.

11

THE MYSTERIES OF MONEY

MONEY IS NOT A SIMPLE SUBJECT, and experts on monetary matters frequently disagree. For that reason, we will endeavor to place the business creed's treatment of monetary problems in perspective by commencing this chapter with an ABC of money, stressing the problems on which ideological attention centers.

By "money" economists mean the medium of exchange of a society; any asset which is generally acceptable as a means of payment, from buyer to seller, employer to employee, debtor to creditor, taxpayer to government. Coin and paper currency immediately come to mind, but they are not the most important kind of money in the United States. Most of our transactions, if not in number then certainly in dollar value, we effect by transferring claims against banks. These claims we call "demand deposits" or "checking accounts," and we transfer ownership by writing checks. In late 1954, there were $30.5 billion of currency and coin in circulation, and $104 billion of demand deposits.

Other assets are close substitutes for these two kinds of money, although they are not generally used in making payments. Time deposits, of which there were $74 billion in late 1954, are not subject to check; but in other respects they are very similar to demand deposits as a way of holding funds. The same is true of various government securities. There is no clear-cut principle on which assets can be sharply divided between money and non-money. This is worth emphasizing because of the importance attached to the total supply or quantity of money in both professional and ideological discussion.

Since bank deposits are the most important kind of money, the first step in understanding our monetary system is to understand what determines the total amount of bank deposits in existence. The word "deposit" leads many people to think of banks as analogous to checkrooms: just as the number of hats in a checkroom depends on how many hats their owners have chosen to check there, so the number of dollars on deposit in banks depends on how many dollars the public has chosen to deposit there. There is some truth in the analogy, but on the whole it is exceedingly misleading. It neglects the crucial fact that banks can themselves create deposits, whereas checkrooms cannot create hats. Banks create deposits when they make loans and credit to the "deposit" accounts of the borrowers the amounts of the loans, or when they purchase securities from governments or the public. As borrowers spend the loans by writing checks, they transfer the ownership of the deposits to others. Transactions among depositors handled by checks cannot alter the total of bank deposits; they can alter only the distribution of ownership of deposits. Primarily as banks expand or contract the volume of their loans and investments will the volume of deposits rise or fall. The amount of credit extended by the banking system determines the total of deposits, rather than vice versa.

The ability of the banks to create deposits by extending credit is limited by their *reserves*. Reserves are, for the most part, defined by law as deposits to the account of the banks in the Federal Reserve Banks. The Federal Reserve Banks, twelve in number, are quasi-public banks which do not deal directly with the public but with "member" commercial banks. The twelve Reserve Banks are supervised and coordinated by the Board of Governors of the Federal Reserve System, an independent public agency responsible to Congress and appointed by the President. (An open market committee with representatives of the Board and the Reserve Banks plays an important part in determining policy.) Member banks are required to hold reserves equal to a stipulated percentage of their deposit liabilities. The required reserve ratio is set by the Board of Governors within limits established by Congress. Early in 1955, the required reserve ratio for demand deposits varied from 12 per cent for "country banks" to 18 per cent for Reserve city banks and 20 per cent for New York and Chicago banks. Reserve requirements for time deposits at 5 per cent were substantially less. For their $125 billion of demand deposits adjusted and time deposits in late 1954, banks had $19 billion of reserve balances with the Federal Reserve Banks, or 15 per cent. Generally banks will expand their earning assets, and create deposits, virtually to the ceiling permitted by reserve requirements. The volume of deposits is therefore determined by the volume of reserves, and the next question is what determines the supply of reserves.

Just as the total of commercial bank deposits is largely independent of the initiative of depositors, so the total of bank reserves — deposits to the account of banks in the Reserve Banks — is largely independent of the initiative of the banks. An individual bank may add to its reserves by gaining deposits at the expense of other banks — having a positive net clearing balance. But what it adds, other banks lose.

The major factors which in combination determine the volume of bank reserves are:

1. Federal Reserve Bank credit. Just as commercial banks can create deposits by lending and buying securities, so Federal Reserve Banks can increase their deposit liabilities in the same way. As these deposits pass into the accounts of member banks, the volume of reserves is increased. Like the commercial banks, the Federal Reserve Banks are limited by a reserve requirement. This requirement, set by Congress, is that the Reserve Banks hold gold certificates in amount not less than 25 per cent of their liabilities. However, the Reserve Banks are not primarily profit-seeking institutions and have no compulsion to expand their credit to the legally permitted limit. The volume of Reserve Bank credit is determined in accordance with the policy objectives of the reserve authorities.

2. Currency in circulation. Most currency in circulation consists of Federal Reserve Notes, a liability of the Federal Reserve Banks. If the public desires to increase its holdings of currency at the expense of bank deposits, banks have to obtain the currency to pay off their depositors by reducing their reserve balances with the Reserve Banks. If the public desires to hold its funds less in currency and more in checking accounts, banks obtain currency with which they can increase their reserve balances. This is the germ of truth in the checkroom analogy: the volume of reserves and of bank deposits is subject to the public's initiative in deciding how much currency it wishes to hold. Generally, however, the public's habits regarding relative use of currency and bank deposits are quite stable over short periods.

3. Other Deposits at Reserve Banks. The Reserve Banks have some depositors other than their member banks: non-member banks, foreign banks, and the United States Treasury. As the Treasury balance with the Reserve Banks goes up, as, for example, when Treasury receipts from the public exceed payments to the public, member bank reserves go down; and vice versa.

4. The monetary gold stock. The Treasury pays for the gold it buys by drawing on its deposit in a Reserve Bank. When the seller of the gold deposits his check in a commercial bank, the bank presents it to the Reserve Bank and obtains an increase in its reserve balance. The Treasury replenishes its own account by depositing with the Reserve Bank gold certificates in amount equal to the cost of the gold. The actual metal is stored largely in Fort Knox. Thus Treasury purchases of gold increase commercial bank reserves, and incidentally Federal Reserve Bank reserves, and Treasury sales reduce them.

The total supply of money in the United States is a superstructure built on gold. The size of the monetary gold stock limits the deposit and note liabilities of the Federal Reserve Banks, and hence the reserves of member banks. The amount of member bank reserves limits the total deposits in banks. In late 1954, a gold base of $22 billion supported a total supply of bank deposits and currency of $217 billion. But the list given above of other factors determining the volume of bank reserves makes it clear that the relationship of gold to total supplies of money is a loose one.

Is the United States on a "gold standard"? This is a question on which there is much popular discussion and confusion; and because the "gold standard" has symbolic connotations it is a question which receives considerable ideological attention. In the past, the gold standard had the following characteristics: (1) fixed prices of gold in terms of the currencies of various nations; (2) a commitment by the Treasury or central bank of each nation to buy gold with the national currency at the fixed price, in unlimited amounts; (3) a similar commitment to sell gold to holders of the national currency; (4) a commitment by the Treasury or central bank to sell gold at the fixed price, or to redeem currency with gold coin, in unlimited quantities, on the demand of anyone for any purpose; (5) a close relationship between the gold supply of a nation and its total money supply. Internationally these characteristics meant a fixed rate of exchange between any two currencies, determined by the established prices of an ounce of gold in terms of the two currencies. A deficit in one country's balance of payments with a second country would be met by a gold flow from the debtor nation to the creditor, though short-term borrowing often served as a substitute for gold movements.

Of these five characteristics, the United States monetary system now fulfills the first three. The Treasury will buy and sell gold in unlimited amounts at $35 an ounce. This has been the price since 1934. Previously the price had been fixed at $20.67 an ounce for a hundred years. But since 1933 gold coins have not circulated. The Treasury will not sell gold except for shipment abroad or for domestic industrial use. The Treasury will not redeem currency in gold just to enable residents of the United States to own gold rather than other assets. As for the fifth characteristic, we have already seen that the Federal Reserve System, which was founded in 1913, makes the relationship between gold stock and total money supply a loose one. This has long been true of every major country, as central banks have assumed an active rather than a passive role in monetary management.

For the purposes of the international gold standard, our present arrangements are sufficient. If other countries had similar arrangements, an international gold standard would exist. (Whether it would work well, in view of the loose connections between gold and money supplies in all countries and in view of other difficulties of adjustment to gold flows, is another question.) The fact is, however, that the United States is the only major country now (early 1955) prepared to exchange gold for its currency, and vice versa, in unlimited amounts.

The decision to withdraw gold from domestic circulation in 1933–34 was based on experience in the financial panic of 1932–33. The failure of public confidence in the banks and in the general financial stability of the country led to large withdrawals of gold for export or for hoarding. Both the reserves of the commercial banks and those of the Reserve Banks were depleted. Just at a time when many business and financial institutions, including banks themselves, needed credit to weather the crisis, credit had to be contracted because of this loss of reserves.

The Board of Governors has considerable discretionary power to influence the total supply of bank deposits. Its major instruments are two. First, within the limits established by Congress, the Board can alter the required ratios of bank reserves to deposits. In practice the Board is reluctant to use this power frequently, largely because of its uneven impact on individual banks. Second, the volume of Reserve Bank credit, which we have noted above as one of the determinants of the volume of bank reserves, may be altered, in two ways. One is to alter the total of Reserve Bank lending to member banks. By granting such loans more readily and at a lower rate of discount, the System encourages banks to expand their reserves by borrowing. By restricting these loans and charging a higher discount, the System deters banks from borrowing reserves. But for many years Federal Reserve discounts and loans have been rather unimportant. The second and more important method is purchase or sale of government securities on the open market. Open market operations are the major instruments by which the Federal Reserve can influence the quantity of bank reserves. The only legal limitation on the discretion of the Federal Reserve to vary the volume of outstanding Reserve Bank credit is the gold reserve requirement to which the Reserve Banks are subject.

RELATION BETWEEN MONEY SUPPLY AND NATIONAL DEBT

Federal Reserve open market operations affect not only the volume of bank reserves but also the prices and yields of marketable government securities. Traditionally central bank policy has been to curtail reserves and raise interest rates in periods of inflationary danger, and to expand reserves and lower interest rates in times of deflation. Since the Second World War, the Federal Reserve has faced a difficult dilemma, created by the large federal debt. The Federal Reserve could not attack inflation by the traditional method without letting government securities fall in price, making it necessary for the Treasury to offer higher yields whenever it borrowed to meet its maturing obligations. The Treasury, preoccupied with the perpetual problem of refunding maturing debt and concerned to keep interest charges on the debt low on behalf of taxpayers, was reluctant to see the Federal Reserve depart from the low interest rate structure which had been maintained by mutual agreement during the war. The

Federal Reserve, to the extent that it continued to support the government securities markets, was in the position of having to expand bank reserves whenever holders of government securities wished to sell them in order to make more profitable investments. Until July 1950, the Federal Reserve struggled gradually to escape from its wartime commitment and in a series of small steps, always with the delayed and reluctant acquiescence of the Treasury, raised the yields on short- and medium-term government obligations. Open conflict between the two agencies became a serious problem after the outbreak of war in Korea in 1950. It was resolved — at least for the time being — by a March 1951 "accord" between the two agencies, which freed the Federal Reserve from its last remaining commitment to the wartime interest rate structure, the 2½ per cent rate on long-term bonds. The assumption after this accord was that the policy of the Federal Reserve would not be oriented nearly as much as in the years 1941–1951 to keeping the price of government securities up; and much more to containing inflationary pressures. But an attempt by the Treasury to bring back a "free" market in 1953 encountered strong opposition and the policy was soon abandoned.

Monetary policy is designed either to increase the quantity of money and lower interest rates or to reduce the quantity of money and raise interest rates. But what effect do the money supply and the level of interest rates have on economic activity, as measured by employment, production, national income, and prices? On this question there are large differences of opinion among professional economists. At one extreme is the view which assigns strategic importance to the quantity of money. According to the "quantity theory," money national income is approximately proportional to the stock of money. This implies that expansion of the money supply at a time when physical output cannot be increased will raise proportionately the level of prices. At the other extreme is the view that economic activity is virtually unaffected by changes in money supplies and interest rates. In this view the forces influencing the spending decisions of business firms, households, and governments are not susceptible to monetary controls. Between these extremes are all shades of opinion concerning the importance of monetary factors. This diversity of opinion is symptomatic of the complexity of the question and of the lack of conclusive empirical evidence.

This review of the basic facts of our monetary system indicates the issues and problems which are likely to receive ideological attention. Briefly, these are: To what extent, and in what manner, should the government control the money supply and credit conditions? What measure of control should lie with Congress, the President, the Treasury, the Federal Reserve Board, and the Federal Reserve Banks, respectively? To what extent should we depend upon automatic forces rather than laws and management? Should domestic gold convertibility be restored? How far should monetary policy be governed by the objective of keeping prices of government securities up and hence yields down? How important are monetary factors and policies in causing or preventing inflation and depression? To what extent are unwise governmental monetary policies responsible for the instability of the United States economy? In addition, certain issues discussed elsewhere in this volume, for example, the classical vs. managerial approach, arise in an examination of credit, money, and finance.

THE BUSINESS CREED'S VIEW OF MONETARY ISSUES

We should expect the business creed to apply to monetary problems the major themes and attitudes which, we have found, pervade the creed's approaches to other subjects. But monetary ideology is a branch of the creed that raises special difficulties. In part, our problem arises from the failure of bankers and their representatives to speak up. An examination of about one hundred volumes of Congressional hearings since 1913 dealing with monetary issues reveals a surprising failure of bankers to testify and, when testifying, a failure to raise the ideological issues that they might be expected to raise. For this reason, we have paid some attention to views of bankers, and especially private bankers in earlier periods when they seemed to be more sure of themselves and expressed themselves more freely than they have in recent years.

Again, the views of bankers and other lenders may not coincide with those of other businessmen who are usually borrowers. Moreover, money is a complex subject, since some of the pervasive principles of the creed seem to come into conflict when applied to monetary problems. These difficulties explain to some extent the relative neglect of money in business ideology. Much of the ideology which does exist on the subject may be understood as an attempt to resolve the conflicts of principle.

The creed tends to blame government for economic ills, particularly for economic fluctuations. The monetary policies of the government are an inviting target. But an attack on them carries the tacit assumption, not always welcome, that it is government's duty to manage the monetary and banking system in the interests of economic stability. Moreover, the government's monetary policies are effected predominantly by restraining or stimulating private lenders and borrowers. To blame monetary policy for inflation, for example, implies that banks and other lending institutions and their customers were contributing to inflation and needed to be curbed by government action. This implication is not always a welcome one because it conflicts with a second major theme of the business creed: that the competitive market works adequately without government intervention.

It is no wonder, then, that the ideology criticizes the government as the source of inflation. "Experience affords ample demonstration of the fact that agencies of government for the creation of credit are less strict than private agencies and that losses by governmental agencies tend to be large . . . Exceptional circumstances must therefore exist if government is to be trusted with the extension of credit. . . ." Again, we are told that "government knows few limits in the amount of new money it can add to circulation." [1] Hence the demand for private ownership and administration subject to the minimum amount of government supervision, and hence the view that private banking should concentrate on "sound assets" and avoid currency or bank credit expanding indefinitely and secured by government securities.[2]

In the midst of the great depression the financial leaders were so fearful of inflation and so impressed with the forces of automatic recovery that they would not create money to deal with the decline. "Nature is doing her work . . . let us not underestimate our recuperative powers . . . We take resort particularly in cheap money devices in the hope and even in the belief that they will somehow or other wipe out mistakes . . . You do not want to overload your firebox with coal . . . You don't want, in other words, what is sometimes technically described as 'sloppy' money conditions . . . Even wise practitioners in administering cod-liver oil through the stomach will lay off at the end of the month." [3] This was the advice of A. C. Miller, member of the Federal Reserve Board, close associate of President Hoover and the spokesman for the financial interests. At this time commodity prices had fallen by one-third, income by one-half, and unemployment had reached twelve millions. But the fundamental assumption of the ideology that there was no substitute for hard work, for paying the penalty for past sins — this cropped out in the discussions of monetary policy.

Early in 1934, Mr. Burgess, then with the New York Reserve Bank, urged the Senate to be extremely careful lest an addition of reserves of a few billion dollars would ultimately bring a large inflation. The time will come "when confidence is more fully restored, when borrowers will want to borrow, and lenders will want to lend to the full amount of the available funds." [4] This fear of inflation and government intervention in monetary events is, as we shall see, especially evident in the discussions of the gold standard.

Banking — and credit in general — is a decentralized, private industry. It is difficult, especially for the members of the industry but also for

[1] NAM, I: 414, 421.
[2] NAM, I: 435.
[3] Hearings, Senate Banking and Currency Committee, *Restoring and Maintaining Average Purchasing Power of the Dollar*, May 1932, pp. 225, 237.
[4] Senate Hearings on *Gold Reserve Act of 1934*, part 2, January 1934, p. 178.

its customers, to accept the view that the competitive market is a satisfactory regulator elsewhere but not here. Neither a lending bank nor its borrowing customer is likely to agree that a bank loan can be inflationary. There is a long tradition, embodied in the original conception of the Federal Reserve System itself, that credit extended to meet the legitimate needs of trade cannot do harm. "But in most cases a large increase in the total quantity of money, not accompanied by an equivalent expansion of production, is likely to be a disturbing factor in our economy." [5] If a loan enables a firm to expand its production by building up its inventory of goods in process, does it not help to fight inflation? In the eyes of bankers and borrowers the purely business aspects of bank operations are likely to overshadow the fact that the banks are, in effect, mints which coin or retire money.[6]

Often this conflict is unresolved, and complaints that the government is too lax in applying monetary curbs are found side by side with complaints that the banking system is unduly regimented. But there are attempts to resolve the conflict by advocating monetary arrangements which would deprive the government of discretion but apply automatically to the banks the necessary checks and stimuli. The full gold standard is proposed as such an arrangement; it is supported partly because it appears to reconcile the principle of free competitive enterprise in banking and lending with the principle of government responsibility for sound money. But even here, there is a problem. The fixed price of gold is a government price-support plan fundamentally inconsistent with the free market principle that the market, not the government, should determine prices.[7]

---

[5] NAM, I: 415.

[6] Bankers' replies in 1952 to the Patman Subcommittee concerning their lending policies since July 1950 emphasize their concern that their loans be regarded as "productive" rather than "nonproductive" or "speculative."

[7] The difficulty presented by this inconsistency arises in connection with the question whether exchange rates between currencies should be fixed by government decision or determined in the free market. In the last few years, business spokesmen have tended to favor free markets in foreign exchange, particularly because a depreciation of foreign currencies was expected to reduce the burden of foreign aid on the United States. Says Hazlitt, the popular spokesman for business (*Newsweek*, Aug. 16, 1948): "A correction of the British (or French or Dutch or Norwegian) trade balance could be forced practically overnight, however, simply by allowing exchange rates to find their own market levels. This would discourage imports and encourage exports; it would make all currencies automatically convertible in any amount desired; and the 'dollar shortage,' in the sense in which the phrase is now used, would disappear. Any nation will have a trade deficit as long as it insists on overvaluing its currency." A similar view is expressed in the *New England Letter* of the First National Bank of Boston, Oct. 31, 1949. The point made is that uniform devaluation to new fixed exchange rates is a crude approach, and that the better solution is to allow exchanges to find their levels as determined by market conditions, not by bureaucrats.

CONTROL OF MONEY AND CREDIT

The central government had a long struggle to obtain control over the supply of money and bank credit, and bankers have been even slower to acquiesce to this control. At the turn of the century private bankers had the power and responsibility to determine monetary policy. In the latter part of the nineteenth century, Morgan and Company was strong enough to stop a dangerous outflow of gold. In 1907, it was private bankers who assumed the responsibility for stemming the panic.[8] In this century it became clear that only a strong central authority could effectively deal with crises. But it required a vigorous fight by President Wilson to make the Federal Reserve Board a public organization. And it required the fiasco of the late twenties to convince the country that control of speculation could not be left to private finance but was a central government responsibility.

Distrust of government was evident also in the attempts to restore confidence with the financial collapse after 1929. Indeed, the government was allowed to establish the RFC to bail out banks, insurance companies and railroads. President Roosevelt was told in confidence in 1933 by bankers that the government could safely put up tens of billions to bail out the banks. The bankers, in the course of the hearings on the RFC in 1931 and 1932, abandoned their ideology and were prepared to be bailed out by government. Secretary Mills made it clear that even the salvaging of the railroads could be supported in that depreciation of railroad bonds had impaired the solvency of the banks. If any bankers opposed this intervention, they were indeed silent.[9]

But once the issue of direct or indirect help to the banks was disposed of, the mistrust of government was still apparent. On the guarantee of bank deposits, proved to be a stabilizing influence of inestimable value, the bankers were silent or hostile. One of the few who testified said: "In discussing this matter with bankers, by correspondence and otherwise, I find a prejudice against any form of guarantee largely brought about, no doubt, by the failure of so many state guarantees, and, as I understand it, guaran-

[8] Higginson, a leading banker: "I know about the wickedness of some of our rich men, and deprecate to the last degree their accumulation of riches. Some of the great bankers I have seen and known intimately, and I can tell you from positive knowledge that, if the great bankers had not stood together in 1907 and done the best they could for the public, you would have lost your house, we might have failed, and the ruin of the land would have been excessive. Those men did not try to make money, and they did not produce bad results, but they risked their fortunes and their health in preserving the community from terrible disaster." Perry, *Henry Lee Higginson*, I, 439–441.

[9] See House Banking and Currency Committee Hearings on *RFC*, December 1931 and January 1932, and Senate Banking and Currency Hearings on S. 1 (*Creation of a RFC*), December 1931.

tees that were predicated somewhat upon the earnings of the banks." [10]

Nor were the bankers any more enthusiastic when the government approved a home loan relief bill, one of the early approaches to refinancing of home mortgages — again a program that over a period of more than twenty years has contributed greatly to home ownership and home building. The only banker witness had this to say:

> You cannot build a sound structure upon unsound foundations . . . building a Federal organization upon 48 different state systems, because, as has been pointed out in some of the testimony before Congress last year, there is the greatest diversity of character and of practice among the leading institutions of the different states . . .
> . . . I assert that the great bulk of the funds have not been employed for the purpose designed by you gentlemen when you passed this act [Federal Home Loan Bank Act]; that is to say, for the encouragement of home ownership, or of home building or for the relief of distressed home owners.[11]

In this branch of the ideology there is also to be found a strong preference for private management as against legislation. Writing to Ellery Sedgwick in 1925, Dwight Morrow, the former Morgan partner, commented on the freedom given to British bankers and the favorable results: "This results in investors being obliged to put their reliance upon the people who are managing the business rather than upon the statute . . . is it not well that people who have savings should be taught that no statute can really take care of them?" [12]

In 1927, Benjamin Strong, the great private banker and one of the leading figures in Federal Reserve administration, was also unwilling to depend on statutes: "Our examination of the past produces the most accurate knowledge of past action and reaction, but when it comes to a decision as to what we are going to do for the future, then just human judgment has got to govern. There is no mathematical formula for the administration of the Federal Reserve System or the regulation of prices." [13]

If Strong's views may be explained by an awareness of the complicated relationships of money and prices as well as distrust of government, Walter Stewart, another private banker who became an advisor of the Federal Reserve Board, supported gold because he stressed the limited capacities of men.

"The administration of the Federal Reserve System or of any central bank when it is on a gold standard has its actions tested, the wisdom of its

[10] House Banking and Currency Committee, *To Provide a Guaranty Fund for Depositors in Banks,* 1932, p. 58.
[11] Hearings, Senate Banking and Currency Committee on *Home Owners' Loan Act,* 1933, pp. 66–67.
[12] H. M. Nicholson, *Dwight Morrow* (1935), p. 143.
[13] Hearings, House Banking and Currency Committee on *Stabilization,* 1927, p. 302.

actions tested, by the judgment of many men, because the currency is convertible. The moment you reverse the convertible features or lodge the decision with some one as to the conditions under which the currency is to be convertible, you are greatly exceeding anything that any monetary system that I am familiar with has ever done, and you have consequently exposed it to that additional risk." [14]

In a similar vein, NAM warns us against management of the system. Authorities are in disagreement; those interested with authority "are not always entitled to be described as authorities." Nor are they always by training and experience qualified; and therefore management should be allowed to unfold only as we gain in experience and agreement.[15]

Once again, after the Second World War the issue of increased authority for the Federal Reserve has been under discussion. As before, the bankers oppose further grants of power to the Board. Here, as on other subjects, the ideology has undergone some change with the passage of time and the modification of institutions; but the central arguments of the application of the free market principle to banking remain.

Even after the passage of the Federal Reserve Act, the idea that the monetary and banking system should be managed by a central bank responsible to the people in the interests of general economic stabilization gained slow acceptance. The "needs of trade" philosophy has never lacked adherents. It cuts two ways. Not only is private commercial paper a suitable asset against which to create money, but government debt is not. In 1935, W. W. Aldrich, Chairman of the Chase National Bank, spoke out against permanently broadening the definition of eligible paper against which Federal Reserve Notes might be issued to include government securities. And he regretted tendencies which might change the banking system from one which "accommodates commerce and business to one which would plan to mitigate economic fluctuations." [16]

Soon afterward another banker expressed his opposition to the shift of monetary authority from the banks to Washington:

Since the Federal Government cannot spend without using the bankable funds of the nation, it is up to us to declare an embargo. We must decline to make further purchases. We must declare that we will not finance further spending by the government until a genuine, serious effort is made by the Federal Government to restore a balanced budget. The bankers of America should resume negotiations with the Federal Government only under a rigid economy, a balanced budget, and a sane tax program.[17]

[14] Hearings, Senate Banking and Currency Committee, *Gold Reserve Act of 1934*, pp. 296–297.
[15] NAM, I: 433–434.
[16] House Hearings, *Banking Act of 1935*, 1935, pp. 410–422.
[17] Quoted in Eccles, *Beckoning Frontiers*, p. 234.

The Employment Act of 1946 committed the resources and powers of the government, in the monetary field as elsewhere, more explicitly than ever before to the objective of economic stabilization. Many businessmen have accepted and applauded this commitment, and their views are expressed in the managerial branch of the ideology. Questioned by a Congressional Committee in 1949 on the proper objectives of monetary policy, three top businessmen (Clarence Francis, General Foods Corporation; John D. Biggers, Libbey-Owens-Ford Glass Company; and Meyer Kestnbaum, Hart, Schaffner, and Marx) all stressed economic stabilization. Many bankers shared the view of one who replied:

> The objectives . . . should apply principally to employment problems and to the maintenance at all times of sufficient credit facilities to assure as great a degree of stability in our economy as is possible.[18]

But other bankers still held to the view expressed by Aldrich in 1935 that stabilization was not the business of the monetary and banking system.

> It is not, however, the function of the banking system to shove up prices, or to depress them, or to lend forced stimulus to a theoretical level of employment as an objective.

> It was never the purpose of the Federal Reserve to attempt to regulate employment. Banks should be instruments of business, not masters of it. Banks exist for the accommodation of the public, not for the control of business or the control of employment.[19]

The continuing force of the opposition to centralized control over the banking and monetary system stands out clearly in the following statement by the President of the American Bankers' Association to the 1948 convention of that organization:

> I believe sincerely that the principal issue before the management of every bank is the future relationship between the banking business and the Federal Government. This has become a problem, partly from some of the things which have happened in banking in the past; partly from a worldwide trend toward more centralized government economic and financial controls; partly from the very nature of the banking business and very definitely from the financial and economic problems which face this country as a result of the war, the foreign situation and government inflationary policies of the last fifteen years.[20]

In fact the ideology often goes further, stressing the restricted scope of monetary policy. Whereas economists have tended in the last generation to raise questions concerning the potency of monetary policy, the ideology,

[18] Joint Committee on the Economic Report, *Monetary, Credit, and Fiscal Policies,* 1949, pp. 298–299.
[19] *Ibid.,* pp. 295, 325–326.
[20] *New York Times,* Dec. 19, 1948.

reflecting fears of central authority and hence for other reasons, also minimizes the importance of policy. "Hence the conclusion follows that monetary management is not likely to prove to be a panacea for the economic ills which have their manifestation in idle men, money and machines." [21]

But to return to the issue of powers to be given to the Board. Much the same views were held by bankers and other businessmen on the question of whether to grant the Board of Governors additional powers over reserve requirements. Bankers and businessmen were almost unanimously opposed to increasing the Board's powers.

Randolph Burgess warned that the Federal Reserve System:

. . . is threatened by the kind of thinking that created totalitarianism in Germany and Russia and Socialism in England, by the reasoning that efficiency calls for concentrating power in bureaus in Washington. This is a danger not for banking alone but for the whole country. It was the principle of Karl Marx that if a group of men could get control of the credit resources of the country they could control the whole country.[22]

An anonymous banker:

The determined drive to increase power over reserve requirements seems to be resulting in a circuitous, dead-water type of thinking as if the solution to all our problems was hidden in the mystery of reserve requirements. It is a crude and sweeping instrument that can be and has been used like a sledge hammer when knowledge and skill are required to deal with delicate situations. The instrument of reserve requirements was meant to be used in unusual situations such as an extraordinary inflow of gold or an excessive extension of Federal Reserve credit. If used arbitrarily or capriciously, the over-all power over reserve requirements could put banks out of commission or nationalize them.[23]

R. C. Leffingwell, of J. P. Morgan and Company, said:

[These powers] are too effective already as shown in 1920, 1929, 1937, and 1948. If the . . . Federal Reserve Board had exercised the powers over bank reserves which they again and again demanded of Congress, this country would have endured a deflation in the last twelve months which would have made 1932 seem like boom times.[24]

The connection between opposition to centralization and the creed's pervasive moral principle that governmental powers and clever schemes cannot really meet the nation's problems is made clear by the following:

[21] NAM, I: 434.
[22] W. Randolph Burgess, "The Marxian Sign in American Banking," *American Affairs*, October 1949, p. 201.
[23] *Monetary, Credit, and Fiscal Policies*, p. 536. Compare pp. 331–342.
[24] *Ibid.*, p. 330.

Otis E. Fuller, Security State Bank and Trust Company, Beaumont, Texas said:

None [additional powers] for Federal Reserve but a change in the attitude of people as needed — cut out "gimme" and go to work or we will go to hell.[25]

Bankers' views on the proper location of governmental monetary powers provide another example of the opposition to centralization. In the Treasury-Federal Reserve conflict in the years preceding the accord of 1951, bankers and businessmen were strongly on the side of the Federal Reserve; they were extremely anxious to preserve and strengthen its independence of the executive. But in other contexts, the Board of Governors of the Federal Reserve System has been pictured as the tyrant which should be restrained by strengthening the twelve regional Reserve Banks. Following are some bankers' replies to the Douglas Committee on a question concerning the division of authority within the Federal Reserve System:[26]

J. T. BROWN: *No further centralization of power.*

G. KEYTON: Decentralize power.

ANONYMOUS: More power to Federal Reserve Banks.

ANONYMOUS: More power to Federal Reserve Banks.

H. H. GARDNER: Board should not be an agent of Treasury; and Reserve Banks should be autonomous.

ANONYMOUS: Federal Reserve Board should be top authority.

J. R. GEIS: Too much centralization.

U. S. GRAY: More power for each Reserve Bank.

R. DUBOIS: Perhaps Board should have greater authority.

C. H. KLEINSTUCK: Wider representation on Board.

L. M. GIANNINI: Greater autonomy for Reserve Banks.

ANONYMOUS: More power to Open Market Committee and less to Board.[27]

D. WILLIAMS: Too much power in Board, which is subject to political pressures.[27]

The issue of centralization is also involved in the controversy over our "dual banking system." Banks can be chartered by the states as well as by the federal government. State banks need not be members of the Federal

[25] *Ibid.,* pp. 329–330.
[26] *Ibid.,* pp. 310–313.
[27] The Open Market Committee is composed of the seven members of the Board plus five representatives of the Reserve Banks.

Reserve System or subject to its reserve requirements. Economists and other students of our monetary system are virtually unanimous in the opinion that the existence of nonmember banks is an illogical weakness in the system; it discriminates against national banks and other members, and is a potential threat to Federal Reserve control over the money supply. But states' rights are successfully invoked against centralization of this kind, although coinage of money and regulation of its value are constitutionally federal functions. The "dual banking system" is such a powerful positive symbol in banking and business circles that hardly anyone dares to speak against it.[28]

GOLD AND "HARD" MONEY

The gold standard provides one possible escape from the dilemma between the chaos of unlimited freedom of the banks to create and destroy money and the centralization of monetary authority by the government. For it provides automatic restraints on the banks and on the government as well. In the opinion of its advocates these automatic restraints are more reliable than the discretionary decisions of governmental monetary authorities.

Above we have commented on the antagonism toward government control of money, on the need for minimum supervision and management by government, on the limited capacities of public officials to exercise discretion. Nowhere is the ideology more outspoken in its distrust of government than in its appeal for the old-fashioned gold standard.

The NAM authors are not sure that the monetary system can be wholly automatic, but they wish to reduce administrative discretion to a minimum.

In a governmental system such as ours, the area of administrative decisions should be limited as much as possible and reliance should be placed on automatic self-adjustments wherever feasible. Reliance on a fully automatic system of monetary and banking adjustment is obviously impossible; but our monetary and credit systems will serve our enterprise system better if the government authorities concerned make an effort to set up machinery for partly automatic control instead of constantly tinkering with a machine whose smooth functioning is essential to the economic health of the whole enterprise system.

One of the planks in the authors' platform for America is:

[28] Patman Subcommittee "Replies to Questions," 1168–1176 and 978–983, give the replies of bankers and state bank examiners, respectively, to the question of subjecting nonmember banks to the reserve requirements of member banks. Bankers were divided on the question, while state bank examiners were naturally opposed. The arguments used in opposition are full of references to the merits of decentralization, States' Rights, and the dual banking system. Even Federal Reserve officials, in supporting the proposal (pp. 720–723), felt that they had to give assurances that this would not be "a move to undermine the dual banking system."

Reestablish the right of private ownership of gold in any quantity private individuals desire, that is, reestablish a gold coin standard.[29]

Garet Garrett, the classical ideologist who edits *American Affairs,* contrasts the "century of sound money" preceding World War I with "the rule of planned money" which has followed:

> During one hundred years preceding World War I, government touched money hardly more than to establish standards of weight and measure, to lay down the laws of liability and to license bankers . . . In all that era of free exchange, free price, and sound money there were two things responsible governments did not do. The first thing was that they did not create money — or if they did, it was called *fiat* money and fiat money went bad so fast that no government having any regard for its credit could afford to do it again . . . The second thing was that governments in that century did not manipulate money and credit . . . Somebody must see to it that the quantity in circulation shall expand and contract as the need fluctuates. During that century of sound money it was the private banker who performed that office.[30]

Garrett explains that the bankers would expand credit indefinitely and dangerously were it not for their obligation to pay depositors "real money" on demand.

> The amount of credit money the banker can create is therefore definitely limited by the amount of real money he has in reserve. As he finds himself passing that limit he must not only stop lending but must call upon borrowers at the same time to pay off their loans. This is deflation. The pain function of money is then acting. . . .
> One of the uses of sound money is to produce that pain in the economic body; the ache tells it that by excess and wrong living it is doing its health a damage.[31]

Garrett argues that when the monetary function is in government rather than private hands, "the pain function will be suspended." For one thing, deflation is politically unpopular. The NAM authors agree:

> . . . central banks must "sit on the booms" if we are to escape the depression aftermath. They must administer our credit system with a view to the future as well as to the present; they must resist the ever-present political pressures for "easy money" credit expansion. That is one of the reasons why it is desirable that they should be private, rather than political, institutions.[32]

Another reason, according to Garrett, is that government learns how to finance itself by monetary creation and thus how to expand its activities

[29] NAM, I: 436; II: 986.

[30] Garet Garrett, "The Rule of Planned Money," *American Affairs,* April 1948, p. 79.

[31] *Ibid.,* p. 80.

[32] NAM, I: 422.

"free from the frustrations of sound money." "Every government, there-fore, was an enemy to the gold standard." And in 1933 the New Deal not only overthrew the gold standard. "One thing more was necessary, and that was to make *sound money illegal* . . . And so private property in gold was destroyed."

There is a long history of monetary experience. It tells us that government is at heart a counterfeiter and therefore cannot be trusted to control money.[33]

Inflation is the inevitable result, no less inevitable for the length of the lag that may intervene between cause and effect. Professor E. W. Kemmerer broadcast a speech for the National Economy League, December 20, 1934, "The Public Debt and Inflation." He warned then that inflation of prices would be the inevitable result of the monetary and fiscal policies of the Roosevelt administration. The failure of this prediction to materialize until after World War II did not prevent Kemmerer and his colleagues of the Economists' National Committee on Monetary Policy from repeating it again and again, frequently in the pages of *The Commercial and Financial Chronicle*. Garrett writes:

One source of confusion is the idea that the frightful cost of war was the primary cause of this inflation. War provided the volcanic spectacle. But the fire was already burning. It began in the thirties when governments overthrew the gold standard on the pretext that it frustrated the social aspirations of the people and took control of money. Long before the war governments had freed themselves from the limitations of sound money. They had found a way to socialize money, and one consequence was that the cost of the war was in-flated.[34]

The gold standard is clearly connected with the classical themes of free enterprise and limited government. Indeed, gold is one of the natural lim-its on government (although it seems unaccountably to have been omitted from the Constitution). According to Professor Walter Spahr, Executive Vice President of the Economists' National Committee on Monetary Policy, restoration of the gold-coin standard means "restoration to the people of their control over the public purse." [35] Professor Kemmerer wrote: " 'We have gold,' says an old proverb, 'because we cannot trust governments.' " [36] For the benefit of those who might think that representa-tive democracy gives the people power over the public purse, Garet Garrett points out:

[33] Garrett, "Planned Money," pp. 81, 79.
[34] *Ibid.*, p. 82.
[35] *It's Your Money,* pamphlet of Economists' National Committee on Monetary Policy, 1946, p. 36.
[36] E. W. Kemmerer, *High Spots in the Case for a Return to the International Gold Standard,* pamphlet of same committee, undated, p. 4.

Parliamentary control of government by control of the purse makes sense only so long as the quantity of money is limited; it ceases to have any meaning when government itself controls the supply of money and may fill its own purse.[37]

Both Garrett and Spahr see the gold coin issue as one facet of the issue between a free and a managed economy: planned economy and "planned money" are arrayed against free economy and "sound money."

Advocacy of a full gold standard, including return of gold coins to circulation, is generally found in the classical version of the creed. In this, as in other respects, the classical theme is ultimately indebted to classical economics. Ricardo and contemporaries discerned a "natural" distribution of the precious metals among nations, based largely on relative productive strength: attempts to disturb the natural distribution were bound to lead to disequilibrium. "When the currency consists entirely of precious metals, or of paper convertible at will into the precious metals, the natural process of commerce . . . adjusts, in every particular country, the proportion of circulating medium to its actual occasions, according to that supply of the precious metals which the mines furnish to the general market of the world. The proportion which is thus adjusted and maintained by the natural operation of commerce cannot be adjusted by any human wisdom or skill.[38] The hold of this doctrine is suggested by its virtual repetition by the author of the Bank Act of 1844 which dominated central banking theory until World War I.[39]

The quantity theory, asserting a simple proportionate relationship between prices and the money supply, also has a long tradition in economics. Those who adhere literally to this theory frequently consider any growth in the money supply to be *ipso facto* bad, even though the economy is also growing. They are inclined to approve the circulation of gold coin simply because it would reduce the reserves of the commercial banks and of the central bank and thus restrict the supply of money.

Monetary management by the government is opposed not only because the managers are bound to be humanly fallible but also because no government can be trusted to resist the temptation to debase the currency for its own advantage. B. E. Hutchinson, Chairman of the Finance Committee of the Chrysler Corporation, urged the NAM "to come out flatly in favor of a return to a gold standard in which paper money would be redeemable in gold, as the most effective anti-inflation measure that could be taken." [40] In an advertisement in the *New York Times,* June 14, 1948, Emmett C.

[37] Garrett, "Planned Money," p. 80.

[38] *The Paper Pound of 1797–1821: A Reprint of the Bullion Report,* Cannan ed., 1919, pp. 52–53.

[39] *British Banking Statutes and Reports, 1832–1928,* edited by T. E. Gregory (London, 1929), I: 28–29.

[40] *New York Times,* Dec. 4, 1948.

Barr insisted that "with sound monetary, banking and lending systems in operation, there would not be any inflation or deflation, or currency depreciation, or booms or depression. The great nation could then move forward to steady prosperity." Since the total supply of deposits and currency in 1947 was $108 billion and of gold only $21 billion, inflation, in his view, amounted to $87 billion. One banker has expressed a widely held diagnosis of our recent economic history:

> If we had returned to the gold standard after confidence was restored in the early stages of the New Deal Administration, there would not have been the extravagance, waste, inefficiency, incompetency, and reckless abandon then or now, as we have and are experiencing. There should be a firm basis for our money to rest upon . . . Steps should be prepared and taken toward going back on the gold standard. And unless we do so, the road we are in will lead to ruin.[41]

Throughout the advocacy of the gold standard runs the feeling that only metallic money is of real, honest value. Other kinds of money are, in contrast, just pieces of paper. The attitude that gold is sound, honest, "hard" money, while paper irredeemable in gold is not, is consonant with certain very general attitudes in the business creed. Money is suspect when it can be created at will, without the hard work of mining it. To command goods and services by paper money not directly tied to gold seems to be an attempt to get something for nothing. We have noted repeatedly the business creed's disdain for easy panaceas, its insistence that moral virtue is the only true solution. You can't get something for nothing, and you will be penalized if you try. For nations as for individuals, the ideology stresses hard work, thrift, sound judgment as the indispensable requirements of economic success, and the dangers of seeking the fruits of success without meeting the requirements. Tinkering with money is too easy to be effective, and too easy not to be dangerous. "Hard money" is a symbol which summarizes the application of these moral principles to monetary affairs. It is a defense against those who would seek prosperity or economic reform through governmental monetary management, including the many varieties of monetary cranks — the Greenbackers, the Bryans, the Major Douglases — who become especially vocal in depressions.

Professor Spahr ruefully notes:

> There is endless hope, apparently, that man can find a way to make a cheap thing like paper as valuable as gold, without direct redemption into gold, and its functioning even superior to that of the gold-coin standard. History and science provide no support for such hope.

Referring to the French of 1790, he continues:

[41] *Monetary, Credit, and Fiscal Policies,* p. 363.

They learned in the hard way . . . that after all paper is paper and gold is gold.[42]

It is possible to agree with the preference for an automatic monetary system over a managed system without favoring the gold standard. Indeed, without other institutional changes in our system of banking and central banking, a return to a full gold standard would still leave a good deal of discretion to the Federal Reserve. One school of economists advocates that the money supply be determined neither by gold nor by discretionary decisions of government agencies. Their system would not involve gold, because they consider it a waste of productive resources to mine monetary tokens which can be otherwise provided at virtually no cost. They would deprive the central bank of discretion by a Congressional directive defining specific and objective rules for its behavior (for example, whenever a certain price index falls by a point, the Federal Reserve must buy a certain quantity of government securities). They would divorce money from bank credit by requiring 100 per cent reserves against demand deposits.[43] It is noteworthy that these proposals receive no support in business ideology. The gold standard has symbolic overtones which an alternative automatic system lacks. And bankers are understandably opposed to the 100 per cent reserve proposal, which would limit their sources of loanable funds to the savings they are able to attract from the public.

The gold standard and "hard money" are prominent symbols in the business creed of recent years, partly because the great economic evil for which the government was blamed was inflation. But the views of financiers and other businessmen are not always the same, nor are they always on the side of gold and monetary orthodoxy. As debtors, businessmen have often been on the side of monetary expansion. Henry Ford, who had his share of trouble with the financial interests, can be taken as an example. He emphasized the unproductiveness, selfishness, and irresponsible power of bankers and the dangers of tying the economy to gold.

Money is not worth a particular amount. As money it is not worth anything, for it will do nothing of itself. The only use of money is to buy tools to work with or the product of tools. Therefore money is worth what it will help you to produce or buy and no more. If a man thinks that his money will

[42] Spahr, *American Affairs,* April 1948, p. 87; compare Herbert L. Satterlee, the official biographer of *J. Pierpont Morgan,* 1939, pp. 277–279. Satterlee, reflecting Morgan's views, held that "When that unhappy day [failure to redeem gold in 1895] should arrive, our government, despite the vast natural resources of the country and its material wealth, would be in the position of an individual who could not meet his notes . . . and he would be thrown into bankruptcy."

[43] Examples of this school are provided in the following: H. Simons, "Rule v. Authority in Monetary Policy," *Journal of Political Economy,* February 1936; M. Friedman, "A Monetary and Fiscal Framework for Stability," *American Economic Review,* June 1948; L. Mints, *Monetary Policy for a Competitive Society* (New York, 1950).

earn 5 per cent or 6 per cent, he ought to place it where he can get that return, but money placed in a business is not a charge on business.[44]

The danger of having bankers in business is that they think solely in terms of making money, not goods:

> They regard a reduction in prices as throwing away of profit instead of a building of business. It requires less skill to make a fortune in money than in production . . . Yet the banker through his control of credit practically controls the average business man.
> . . . the country's production has become so changed in its methods that gold is not the best medium with which it may be measured, and . . . the gold standard as a control of credit gives, as it is now . . . administered, class advantages. The ultimate check on credit is the amount of gold in the country, regardless of the amount of wealth in the country.[45]

But views of this sort are uncharacteristic and not widely enough represented to form a significant strand in the ideology.

DEBT MANAGEMENT AND MONETARY POLICY

The sympathies of businessmen were with the Federal Reserve in its battle with the Treasury over supporting the prices of government bonds.[46] In 1953–55, however, when the Treasury was under the control of respected businessmen and when the Treasury assumed the leadership in a return to a "free" money market, business now joined the Treasury in favor of a free market and higher rates. The creed contends that money markets, like other markets, are governed by certain natural laws; government should be subject to these laws, not attempt to tamper with them. Throughout the debate the ideology held that Truman and his Treasury deliberately invited inflation, putting narrow governmental interests ahead of economic stability, by shackling the Federal Reserve. This argument was particularly telling in the context of the controversy over direct controls, to which the creed was opposed. It was claimed that these controls would be ineffectual so long as the monetary engine of inflation was permitted to run, and unnecessary if it were stopped.

Economic self-interest does not obviously or directly dictate advocacy of a restrictive monetary policy, either by bankers or by businessmen. Although bankers as lenders might be expected to favor higher interest rates, it must also be remembered if the Federal Reserve ceased to support the bond market there was a smaller reserve base for the extension of credit than if support were continued. Opposition to a low interest rate policy on the part of other businessmen, especially debtors or potential borrowers, was even less in their immediate self-interest.

---

[44] Ford, *My Life and Work,* pp. 39–40.
[45] *Ibid.,* pp. 176–177, 178.
[46] For a managerial view, see CED, *Flexible Monetary Policy,* 1953.

The prevailing view that in peacetime government should be subject to the market, not the master of the market, is exemplified by the following reply of a banker to the Douglas Committee:

Though every national facility must be utilized to implement a war effort even at the cost of financial orthodoxy, in a post-war period the Federal Reserve should revert to its primary status as the regulator of credit conditions . . . The resources of the Federal Reserve System should not be used to exempt government from the disciplines, which, for the good of all, are applied to the citizens, whether in an individual or corporate capacity.[47]

Many bankers, although agreeing that prices of government securities should not be pegged, stressed the need for Federal Reserve action to maintain "orderly markets."

Instead of manipulating reserve requirements, the Federal Reserve should permit or cause interest rates and government bond prices to vary, but should maintain orderly markets. . . . Its action should be prompt but mild in either direction. The guiding principle is to maintain an orderly market and a favorable atmosphere, but not a frozen market. It is not the function of the Federal Reserve to fix prices and yields of the government securities. The general welfare is more important than the price of par.

A minority believed in stable prices of government securities.

. . . the government should at all times maintain its bonds at par and should never let them go below par in the open market at any time.[48]

A businessman of the managerial wing was less concerned than bankers over orderly markets.

As a primary consideration, the Federal Reserve Board should give *no* attention to interest rates on the government debt or to the price of government securities.[49]

Nowhere are there wider divergences between the classical and managerial strands of the creed than in regard to monetary and fiscal policy. For the managerial wing, gold-coin is not a live issue. Governmental management of the currency is accepted as inevitable and desirable: It is taken for granted that monetary adjustments cannot be wholly automatic and that monetary policy must be subject to the discretion of the central bank. The managerialists are concerned that the Federal Reserve have sufficient powers and be free to act independently of the Treasury. They regard the federal debt not as a calamity but as a tool that can, if managed wisely, contribute to economic stability.[50]

[47] *Ibid.,* p. 305.
[48] *Ibid.,* p. 304.
[49] Clarence Francis, General Foods Corporation, *ibid.,* p. 308.
[50] See, for example, CED *Flexible Monetary Policy.*

MONEY AND ECONOMIC FLUCTUATIONS

The claim that unsound monetary policies on the part of the government produce instability has an obvious plausibility even, or perhaps especially, for those businessmen who do not fully understand the mechanics of the monetary system. Little attention is paid in the creed to the analytical problem which bulks so large in professional economics — namely, just what is the significance of monetary factors in determining the level of economic activity. The ideologists frequently assume that a naïve quantity theory is self-evidently true, and the doubts which assail economists on this subject seldom trouble them. Often this is because the link between the supply of money and the rate of spending of money is not analyzed or because no distinction whatever is made between the two concepts. The dictum so often found on the financial pages — if there's more money and the same amount of goods, prices must rise — is not such an obvious truth as it seems. If *spending* rises while output remains constant, prices will certainly increase. But there is no hard and fast relationship between spending and the amount of money in existence. We have experienced increases in the stock of money which did not stimulate spending, and we have had increases in spending while the stock of money was not rising.

An excessively simple view of the relation of money and prices is exhibited even by a United States Chamber of Commerce pamphlet, *The Economics of the Money Supply* (1948). The author traces the expansion of money in the forties and shows correctly how this was connected with the rise of government debt. To this expansion he attributes the increase in prices, and he is surprised that the price level has not risen as much as the supply of money. The more modern approach to the analysis of inflation emphasizes the balance between consumption, investment, and government expenditures and available supplies of goods and services. Had this approach made a greater impression on the writers of the business creed, they would have viewed monetary expansion as one link in a chain of causes of inflation rather than a sufficient explanation in itself. Why does the Chamber of Commerce pamphlet devote a separate section to government debt and inflation and no section to private investment and debt? By this we do not mean to imply that private investment and debt are unrelated to monetary expansion. Far from it. But the recognition that monetary policy is related to inflation via its effects on spending decisions makes the whole story of postwar inflation more complex and less suitable for the deployment of ideological symbols.

EARLIER MANAGERIAL STRAINS IN MONEY AND FINANCE

Although in general we have concentrated on the current ideology and have not sought additional evidence in history, at times we have broken this rule. The reluctance of financiers and bankers generally to present their ideology in the last generation tempts us to examine briefly the period of high finance when the bankers had great power, self assurance and even were prepared to take on executive leadership of the highest order — for example, for Grover Cleveland and Theodore Roosevelt. When, in 1902, President Roosevelt opened up the Northern Security Case, Morgan was outraged. "If we have done anything wrong," persisted Morgan to the President, "send your man to my man and they can fix it up." After Morgan's departure, President Roosevelt said to Attorney General Knox, "That is a most illuminating illustration of the Wall Street point of view. Mr. Morgan could not help regarding me as a big rival operator, who either intended to ruin all his interests or else could be induced to come to an agreement to ruin none." [51]

In the area of money and finance one can find managerial strains as early as the latter part of the nineteenth and early part of the twentieth Century.[52] The great private bankers of the latter part of the nineteenth and the early part of the twentieth Century exercised great power. They controlled a vast industrial empire, though perhaps not to the extent suggested by the politically minded Pujo Committee. It is well to recall that, in the absence of a central bank, the Morgan interests stepped in and paid off the Army in 1877 when the Public Treasury was empty; replenished the country's gold reserves in the 1890's by selling gold to the government for bonds and guaranteeing that the gold would not then be exported; saved the credit of New York City by setting up a syndicate to pay the City's bills in the panic of 1907; and organized the banks of the city and imposed upon them gold levies to strengthen the weak banks in the midst of a great panic. It could be said with some justice by Mr. Lamont, the Morgan banker, that, if the Morgan interests were so determined to monopolize finance and industry, they would not have played the significant part they did in helping to create a rival power, namely, the Federal Reserve.

Throughout much of this Morgan literature runs a refrain to the effect that the large financial firm had a responsibility beyond earning profits; that they had to serve the public as well as improve its financial statements. When the public was served, the small profits or even losses incurred were emphasized. In the absence of central banking, time and again large responsibilities were put upon the financial leaders, and they apparently at times assumed the role of servant of the people. What is more, the empha-

[51] L. Allen, *Pierpont Morgan*, pp. 220–221.

[52] See, among other books, Allen, *The Great Pierpont Morgan;* Satterlee, *J. Pierpont Morgan;* T. Lamont, *Henry P. Davison;* Nicolson, *Dwight Morrow;* O. H. Kahn, *Reflections of a Financier;* O. H. Kahn, *Of Many Things; They Told Barron,* 1930; N. W. Stephenson, *N. W. Aldrich;* and H. O'Connor, *Mellon's Millions.*

sis frequently was that power rested not on money or credit but on character. Money was available only to those who could be trusted.[53] Under constant hammering of the Pujo Committee, Morgan could explain the purchase of the Ryan stock of the Equitable Insurance Company at a price yielding a fraction of one per cent as follows: ". . . the only reason I did it, on which I am willing to stand up before the community, is that I thought it was the thing to do." And numerous contemporaries support the Morgan emphasis on service.

Mr. Morgan's purchase from Thomas F. Ryan of the stock of the Equitable Life Insurance Company was another subject from which the Committee's Counsel [Untermeyer, counsel for the Pujo Committee] brought all his guns to bear. From his reiterated statements, it seemed difficult for him to realize what was the fact, namely, that Mr. Morgan had locked up several millions of dollars of good money, not for the sake of profit but so as to be certain that, in his hands, the assets of that great life insurance company would be conserved for the benefit of the company's policy holders.[54]

The apologists for the great Pierpont Morgan could time and again insist that Morgan had taken action to save the credit of banks, to protect impecunious depositors, to preserve the credit of the government — and often at a loss and to serve the country.

Well, said the latter [J. P. Morgan], some way *must* be found to help these poor people. We mustn't let them lose all they have in the world . . . That means the firm can't lose more than $6,000,000, doesn't it? [55]

In a similar vein O. Kahn, the famous banker, wrote: "The undisturbed possession of the material rewards now given to success, because success presupposes service, can be perpetuated only if its beneficiaries exercise moderation, self-restraint and consideration for others in the use of their opportunities, and if their ability is exerted, not merely for their own advantage, but also for the public good and the weal of their fellow men. Democracy rightly insists that a part of every man's ability belongs to the community." [56]

Again, E. H. Harriman, the Railroad financier, is the hero of a successful attempt to contain the overflowing Colorado River. ". . . virtue being its own reward, because Congress has not seen fit to pay us back our outlay, though the President sent it a message asking that we be reimbursed." [57]

[53] Allen, *Pierpont Morgan*, pp. 273–274.
[54] T. W. Lamont, *Henry P. Davison*, 1933, p. 140; Compare Allen, *The Great Pierpont Morgan*, pp. 272–274.
[55] Lamont, *Davison*, p. 126.
[56] O. H. Kahn, *Reflections of a Financier* (London, 1921), pp. 238–239, 257.
[57] O. H. Kahn, *Of Many Things* (New York, 1926), pp. 138–139.

The buccaneer was, however, still around. Mr. Mellon may be considered the prototype of this type of financier. He did not hesitate to allow his rival bank in Pittsburgh to shut its doors, apparently in part because he knew the depositors would shift their business to his bank. Unlike Morgan who, once his position was established, would help competitors, Mellon would crush them. Also he would not hesitate to use his power in the Treasury to save vast sums for Andrew Mellon, the taxpayer.[58] Perhaps the ruthless position of the great Mellon may be explained in part by a realization of helplessness and hence a submission to Darwinian principle. (It will be recalled that the ideology is explained in part by the strains to which businessmen are subjected, for example, their helplessness before cyclical forces.) Judge Mellon (Andrew's father) was disillusioned by the panic of 1873. He decided to close his banking house. Apparently there was no way for a provident man to escape the hazard of ruin in a business which depended so much on credit and confidence. It gave him, he confessed, "more vexation and mortification than all the other adverse circumstances of my business life put together." [59]

[58] H. O'Connor, *Mellon's Millions* (1933), pp. 343, 354–357.
[59] *Ibid.*, p. 31.

12

THE VALUES OF A GOOD SOCIETY

SO FAR THE VALUES inherent in the business ideology have not been examined as such, although they are implicit in many of the policy recommendations and flatly evaluative propositions examined in previous chapters. In this chapter we shall explicitly examine the ideology's set of values. Of course, it is not possible to contrast these values with any objective account as it often was in the case of ideological descriptions of social and economic phenomena. There is no objective counterpart to statements like "Freedom is good." But it is possible to do three things: to point out the main values in the creed and how they are linked together; to see whether any of these values conflict seriously and, if so, how they are reconciled; to see whether they are applied consistently or selectively. For these purposes we must pay attention to those evaluative propositions and symbols which are so broad that they have not fallen into any of the divisions so far used in this book, and we must look at the material already examined from a different standpoint. In this way we may achieve one kind of synthesis of the myriad statements that together form the business ideology.

INDIVIDUALISM: MORAL RESPONSIBILITY AND FREEDOM

A note of individualism sounds through the business creed like the pitch in a Byzantine choir. We have heard it repeatedly — in the emphases on "self-reliance," on the importance of private business decisions, and on the dangers of collective dependence on the welfare state. It is the keynote of the classical creed, around which the themes of freedom and liberty are woven.

Individualism has two main aspects, an injunction of responsibility and an affirmation of freedom. First, it involves individual moral responsibility in the sense that each individual must direct his actions according to moral norms and be prepared to accept the consequences of his actions. It is the antithesis of passively accepting the decisions of others or of evading responsibility for the consequences of one's actions. Second, it asserts the desirability of autonomous choices by individuals in their own interest.

Loosely expressed, it involves the pursuit of individual values without regard to the attitudes of others or the needs of a collectivity.

The business creed is individualistic in both these senses. Like Oliver Cromwell it wants men who make some conscience of that they do. In sharp contrast to ideologies like Marxism in which the moral qualities of individuals are secondary to historical conditions, the business creed makes the moral individual decisive. "Whatever our scheme of national government, whether socialistic or capitalistic, the system will be no better and no worse than the cross-section of the characters of the men who administer it," we are told.[1] A good society is one in which men of solid integrity act with a full sense of personal responsibility.

The emphasis on these values is so great that extreme conclusions occasionally follow from their application. One writer for the Foundation for Economic Education has even questioned the legitimacy of majority decisions. With Tolstoy he rues the day when men "recognized the decisions of men united in councils as more important and more sacred than reason and conscience . . . On That Day Began Lies." He abhors an "almost blind faith in the efficacy and rightness of majority decisions" and finds that responsibility to make compromises in Congress "leaves shattered and destroyed any basis of moral action." [2]

But few of the business ideologists are so radical, although they maintain the same moral tone and frequently resort to religious values and symbols. They worry over the so-called immoral climate of the United States,[3] and the alleged disintegration of morality which has afflicted the Twentieth-Century World.[4] They assess the "welfare state" by the moral standards of individual responsibility and find it grievously wanting.[5] The ideologists call for honesty, sobriety, industry, and prudence on the part of every man. The elder Morgan made moral character the basis of credit but the business creed typically goes farther and puts it at the base of a good society.

[1] James Mooney, *The New Capitalism* (New York, 1934), p. 196.

[2] Leonard Read, *On That Day Began Lies*, #3 of the series, *In Brief*, July 1, 1949, p. 23. The Tolstoy quotation is from *The Law of Love and the Law of Violence*. The other quotations are from pages 15 and 11 of the pamphlet, respectively. At pp. 7–8, Mr. Read produces a remarkable colloquy at the "Pearly Gates" between "Mr. Joe Doakes" and "Mr. St. Peter." Joe is denied admission because he once went along with the majority of the Updale Do-Good Association to deprive widows and orphans in the interests of a golf course. Joe complains that this nefarious act was the act of a committee but "Mr. St. Peter" reminds him that "up here" only the acts of individuals are recognized.

[3] Hiland C. Batcheller, Chairman of Allegheny Ludlum Steel Corporation, in address to National Association of Purchasing Agents, *New York Times*, May 27, 1952.

[4] Philip D. Reed in *Creating an Industrial Civilization*, p. 163.

[5] F. A. Harper, *Faith and Freedom* (Irvington-on-Hudson, N.Y., December 1951), pp. 3–8.

VALUES OF GOOD SOCIETY 253

The permissive aspect of individualism is found mainly in the torrent of imprecation against the dangers of the welfare state. The moral individual not only has responsibilities; he has rights of individual autonomy, above all against the state. The freedom of business enterprise tends to be fused with other freedoms and the simple, unqualified symbols of freedom and liberty are set before us in all the available media. The Advertising Council shows subway riders an attractive picture of Independence Hall and reminds them of "175 years of American independence" with the injunction, "Now Freedom needs you!" The NAM distributes a film entitled *The Price of Freedom* to "re-create the desire to preserve individual freedom and revive ability to recognize attempts to encroach on that freedom." [6] Even that familiar feature of the American landscape — the business club's welcoming sign at the edge of town — may add "Liberty — let's keep it." The good society in the business creed is vaguely but emphatically a free society.

While the autonomy of private enterprise naturally occupies a prominent place among the specific freedoms the creed extols, it is by no means the only one. The usual civil liberties are included as in the following exhortation by Harvey S. Firestone, Jr.:

On Independence Day this year, let us consider the spiritual freedom, the personal liberties, and the material possessions which we enjoy. Let us compare our American way of life and its system of competitive free enterprise with that of people who live under other forms of government.

Let us turn our thoughts to the founding fathers who risked their all to win for us the right to work, to worship, to speak and to live as we choose. And let us ask Divine Providence to instill in our hearts that dauntless spirit of 1776 so that we, too, will have the strength and the wisdom to preserve and to protect the priceless blessing of freedom for ourselves and for the generations to come. [7]

Freedom is also prominent in the theme of consumer sovereignty. This is a theme of free individual choice: the consumer should be free to spend his income as he chooses with no dictation from either business or government, "for without a free exchange of goods, you cannot have a free people." [8]

The individualism of the business creed thus consists of a balance of rights and responsibilities. The ideal model is that of a society in which individuals can be entrusted with wide freedoms which they will use with a sober sense of moral responsibility. Moral obligations typically involve

[6] *Trends,* September 1949, p. 8.
[7] Harvey S. Firestone, Jr., "The Spirit of 1776," *New York Times,* July 4, 1948. Mr. Firestone was Chairman of the Firestone Tire and Rubber Company.
[8] "Let Us Count Our Blessings," *Saturday Evening Post,* Feb. 19, 1949 (Brand Names Foundation). See Chapter 7 above for discussion of this theme.

obligations to consider the welfare of others as well as of oneself. But the creed stresses the individual's responsibility for his own welfare and warns against the dangers implicit in more collective responsibilities. It does not draw a clear or consistent line between the two, because there are obvious limitations to the explicit expression of selfish individualism. Characteristically, a frankly positive valuation of individual self-interest does not appear by itself, in isolated symbols. Egotism[9] requires a supporting body of doctrine and thus appears more diffusely in the ideology.

INDIVIDUALISM IN THE CLASSICAL CREED

The entire classical strand of the business creed can be viewed as an expression of individualistic values, and in particular as an argument for the social virtues arising from the pursuit of individual self-interest. The model shows that maximum satisfaction and distributive justice result from individual egotism. Certain moral qualities of the individual are essential to the operation of the model: integrity in transactions; willingness to live up to one's commitments and to accept the consequences of one's actions. But a whole range of possible moral responsibilities to others are excluded. The transactions of the market place are not guided by morally calculated, just prices, but by impersonally given conditions and the self-interested actions of individuals. If a transaction is carried out honestly, the individual need not ask whether he is morally justified in getting the best possible terms from the other party; the acceptability of terms to the other is a matter solely for his own judgment. The individualism of the model thus eliminates a host of possible moral problems. As the NAM volumes remark, there should be, strictly speaking, no talk of just wages, prices, or returns on investment.[10] The argument for the model is that it is precisely this sort of egotism which assures the benefits of the system.

The classical model also implies a remarkable unwillingness to impose substantive evaluations on tastes and behavior. The model assumes a great variety of people engaged in a great variety of production and consumption activities. The doctrines of consumer sovereignty and the rational direction of production with an eye to profitability imply rejection of substantive standards as to desirable products and tastes. No business is better than any other business because it produces a more worthy commodity, and pushpin is as good as poetry in consumption.[11] To stress the right of the

[9] We use the term "egotism" here and in the following discussion simply to denote the individual pursuit of self-interest. Incidentally, Bentham once called political economy the "dogmatics of egoism," a label which might fairly be applied to the classical strand of the business creed. See Elie Halevy, *The Growth of Philosophical Radicalism* (London, 1949), p. 15.

[10] NAM, I: 489–490.

[11] We are not suggesting that this implication of the classical model is always rigorously drawn and applied. See the further discussion of the relative valuation of business activities in Chapters 16 and 17 below.

individual to make his own free choice in consumption and the responsibility of the producer to "serve" that choice is to refuse in principle to set down norms as to which production and consumption activities are worthwhile and which are not. The system itself sets up no norms, and the individual is both free to and obligated to make his own choices.

MATERIALISM AND PRODUCTIVITY

The absence of norms in the classical creed is intimately linked to its frank praise of materialistic advantages among the "achievements of American capitalism." Material advantages are an essential part of a good society. The "Miracle of America," is, in large part, a miracle of bathtubs and two-car garages. Even the opportunities in America are apt to be material. "America is a place where any boy can dream of being President and any family can afford a fine carpet by Lees." [12] The demands of product advertising obviously stimulate this kind of proclamation, which regularly confronts us in the daily press. The Burlington Mills held forth on the things we might live without:

A refrigerator. You can live without it.
A yellow convertible car. You can live without it.
A television set. A Chippendale chair. . . . You can live without any or all of these.
But Who in America Wants to?
In America these things represent LIFE rather than mere subsistence. In America the things we don't *need* for mere existence are more important than the bare necessities, so abundant in this land.
Take ribbon — gaily colored ribbon . . .[13]

The business creed becomes ambiguous over the ultimate significances it assigns to material abundance; it certainly does not advocate a sybaritic enjoyment of wealth. Much of its apparent materialism arises from a tendency to value material riches without special regard to their ultimate uses. It does this above all in stressing the active pursuit of material wealth through *productivity*. Business ideologists are not ashamed to stand with John Bright against Matthew Arnold and measure the greatness of a society in terms of its size and industrial equipment. For Henry Hazlitt, productivity is a more important requirement in an economic system than distributive justice. If it comes to a choice between a productive social system and a less productive system with greater virtues in other respects, Hazlitt thinks we would choose the more productive one:

What is "justice" in an economic system? Is it the equalization of rewards regardless of the contribution that anyone makes or fails to make to the social

[12] Advertisement, *Christian Science Monitor,* Sept. 19, 1952.
[13] *New York Times,* Business Section, Dec. 12, 1948.

product? To many of us a system under which the talented and skilled and industrious received no more than the incompetent and shiftless and lazy, and which equalized rewards irrespective of effort would not only be unjust but, what is worse, unproductive (!) Most of us, if we thought that it were the only alternative, would prefer an enormously productive if not equally "just" system to one which provided a perfectly "just" distribution of scarcity and poverty.[14]

The ideologists do not always face up directly to the obvious question, "Productivity for what?" But often their boasts of material achievements and their eulogies on the virtues of productivity make the question inescapable. The NAM volumes are devoted to the material concerns of society, as the authors note in their preface,[15] but they hasten to add that this does not imply an indifference to or lack of recognition of spiritual values. Clarence Randall also faces up to the importance of the problem with characteristic forthrightness:

> Production, as I see it, is merely a tool to be used by society for its own advancement. To produce more and more with less and less effort is merely treading water unless we thereby release time and energy for the cultivation of the mind and spirit, and the achievement of those ends for which Providence has placed us on this earth. Better production does not in itself accomplish these ends. It merely gives us more time for trying.[16]

Characteristically, the creed does not get beyond this sort of generality and indeed there are good reasons why it cannot. With the ultimate goals of human action left so largely in the private domains of individual decision it would be illogical to prescribe those spiritual values which should be pursued. Moreover, the force of emphasis on productivity would be seriously weakened if productivity itself too clearly were placed in a merely instrumental status. An appearance of shallow materialism is the price paid for the high valuation of economic activity.

Materialism complements individualism. As consumption goods, material riches gratify individual needs. More important, the material emphases on thrift, saving, and capital accumulation are a necessary condition of personal autonomy. Both material advantages and productivity are based on moral qualities; according to Batcheller, "One may not believe that widespread immorality will send a people down the road to Hades, but it will certainly send them down the road to poverty." [17]

---

[14] Henry Hazlitt, "The Ethics of Capitalism," *Newsweek,* Sept. 20, 1948. (Reprinted and distributed by the Foundation for Economic Education.) Walter Gifford makes a similar point, see below, p. 262.

[15] NAM, I: xiii.

[16] Randall, *A Creed for Free Enterprise,* p. 16. See also Meyer Kestnbaum, President Hart, Schaffner & Marx, *Creating an Industrial Civilization,* p. 172.

[17] Batcheller, address to NAPA.

PRACTICAL REALISM

Productivity is one of a group of values in the ideology which bear on the conduct of individuals and the nature of desirable institutions. Another is practical realism. Every individual has a serious moral responsibility to face the material facts of life and to provide for physical needs. These things have positive value; they are not just necessary evils to be accomplished as quickly as possible to leave time for higher pursuits. For while the ideologists pay homage to spiritual values in general, they give little praise to other-worldliness, romantic idealism, or noble impracticality. On the contrary, romantic fantasies are dangerous. Time and again the ideologists solemnly warn us that we disregard the basic laws of human nature at our peril; we must, like it or not, heed the law of supply and demand, "the law that cannot be repealed." In adopting governmental measures to control the economy, we are seeking some easy, illusory escape from the hard demands of existence. We should not put our faith in such magic as currency experiments but face up to the fact that production and distribution are the things that matter.[18]

Practical realism appears in the ideology not only as an attribute which, in fact, gives the businessman superior moral worth; it is frequently also a moral injunction addressed to businessmen. In the aftermath of the 1948 Presidential elections, *Business Week* proclaimed that it was a responsibility of management "to adjust their business thinking to the kind of community they actually work in, rather than to the kind they would like to . . . The realistic businessman will learn from this election the kind of world that — like it or not — he has to live and work in."[19] The editors of this business journal eulogize an economist who they think attends to facts rather than to speculation. Wesley Mitchell is "an economist business men should know." Unlike Keynes he did not simply toss off "ideas and theories which politicians recognized as valuable weapons." His *Business Cycles* "will no doubt stand up to anything Keynes did," but after he produced this theoretical work he went after facts rather than headlines. "If men of practical affairs, particularly in the realm of politics, could be animated by the spirit of Wesley Mitchell, this would be a relatively happy state of affairs. Then we might find out what actually makes this economy of ours work as it does, find out before it is smashed by the clash of detached theories propelled by politicoes."[20]

Practical realism complements individualism. It stresses the importance of those problems which no adult can avoid, and it demands that each

[18] Mooney, *New Capitalism*, p. 180.
[19] "A Fact that Businessmen Must Face," *Business Week*, Nov. 6, 1948, p. 124.
[20] *Business Week*, Aug. 27, 1949, p. 88.

individual meet them with competence. Built into the classical model it
becomes a justification of individualism. In Chapter 8 above we stressed
the prominence of incentive arguments in expositions of the classical creed,
and hence, in particular, the prominence of the "profit motive." But for
all its prominence in the creed, the "profit motive" hardly stands as an
ultimate value in itself. It must be accepted and utilized because it is
fundamental in human nature; the virtue of a free enterprise system is that
it permits an honest recognition of this individualism in human nature.[21]
In this sense the creed is individualistic, not so much because individualism
is an ultimate value in itself, but rather because it is a fact of human nature which it would be impractical and unrealistic to ignore.

ACTIVISM BASED ON REALISM

Close attention to the practical side of life demands a kind of relentless
activity repugnant to moral philosophers. Our own Christian tradition is
full of denunciations of the neglect of higher values which results from
attention to business. St. Augustine thought that "Business is itself an evil
because it deflects man's attention from true rest, which is God"; and St.
Thomas Aquinas argued that priests should abstain from trade not only
because it was acquisitive but because it demanded so much in the way of
immediate worldly attention.

The bustling activity of the American businessman both at work and
in the community has been the subject of awe, amusement, and ridicule.
But the ideology is not evasive or apologetic. Some time ago, Roy Durstine asked, "Are we so ready to laugh at the Rotary Clubs because they
are really funny or because some one tells us they are?" From here he
proceeded to a defense of the speedy pace of American business and American life generally.[22] A letter to *The Rotarian* gives an alphabetical array of
virtues: "A is for Action all wise men should seek, . . . E is for Endeavor
better things to do, . . . V is for Vigor used rightly every day, Z is for
Zeal to apply in all our ways." [23] The spectacle of a people engaged in
"relentless efforts" is not simply painful evidence of the difficulties of life
but something to be proud of.[24] The business community boasts about the
great number of highly productive jobs in America, and hence about the
magnitude of human effort itself. There are many specific panegyrics of
effort for its own sake. The Statler Hotels' management prepared a brochure which shows the history of the organization in cartoons. It concludes, "And this story of Statler is but one example of freedom in action.
There are countless others — in fact, America is the sum total of all the

[21] Compare Grape, p. 265, below.
[22] Durstine, *This Advertising Business,* p. 67.
[23] *The Rotarian,* June 1949, p. 55.
[24] This point has already been noted in our discussion of "achievements," see
Chapter 2 above.

ideas, the plans, the work, the *relentless efforts* of people to broaden and expand the gains . . . the opportunities . . . the security . . . and the way of life which is the exclusive property of free men. THIS IS THE AMERICAN ADVENTURE." [25] The authors close with a *tutti* bringing in most of the business creed's value-symbols, but "relentless efforts" wins the unique distinction of underlining.

THE CONTINUING GOAL OF PROGRESS

The emphasis on sheer activity and effort in the creed has its natural complements in high valuations of rationality, adventure, and progress. The activism of the business creed is not the activism of random, impetuous enthusiasm but of systematic effort based on a sober assessment of the facts. This implies more than passive adjustment; if the conditions of action must be faced squarely, this does not mean that they must be fatalistically accepted. The increase of knowledge and rational control are fundamental values in the creed. They imply a constant dissatisfaction with the existing state of affairs and a willingness to take calculated risks in trying something new. A good society is progressive.

What is meant by progressive? Once again the business creed becomes ambiguous. The ideologists see America and its free enterprise system as a permanent revolution, but the meaning or direction of this revolution are not defined beyond the material level. Progress is measured very largely in terms of the nation's material growth, and otherwise its content remains vague.[26] But however vague it may be, to regard progress as a permanent value assures a place for continuing effort. We are told not to be satisfied with the greatness of America. "This is a picture of the richest and most self-contained country in the world — but an *unfinished* picture, a picture in process; for the glory of America is not finality but fertility." [27] The International Business Machines magazine, *Think,* once quoted Senator Paul H. Douglas giving a picture of toiling generations in the path of progress. "No generation of Americans really finishes the business in hand . . . we move on from generation to generation on a wide and broad horizon, straining to do the tasks we set ourselves, and strengthening our fibre because we do so." [28]

THE NEED FOR OPTIMISM AND THE SPIRIT OF ADVENTURE

Progress thus means continuing human effort arising from dissatisfaction with the contemporary state of society. The businessman or the citizen who finds a new and effective way of doing things is a hero. This

[25] Statler Hotels, "An American Adventure," 1948. (Dots in text; they do not indicate omissions.)
[26] Compare Chapter 2 above.
[27] Cameron, Ford Hour, October 12, 1941.
[28] *Think,* April 1949, p. 25.

implies an intense but qualified devotion to rationality. A good society involves continually growing scientific knowledge and an educated citizenry. The managerialists, in particular, stress the virtues of education and the need for improving our schools.[29] But the ideologists' praise of rationality and the power of knowledge remains qualified by their devotion to individualism and practicality. The problems of our society cannot be solved by a centralized planning agency, the complexities of the society are too great for this — such have been the objections against governmental measures like the Full Employment Act of 1945.[30] The application of reason must be left to those who are actually confronted with all the bewildering facts and who possess that spirit of adventure and bolstering optimism necessary to shoulder the inevitable risks. The Statler Hotels call their business history "an American adventure," and *Business Week* reminds its readers of the "flexibility, daring, and imagination that are needed for a powerful, productive economy." [31] The theme is ubiquitous in simple positive form or combined with denunciations of the desire for *"security."* The kind of pessimistic caution which favors a secure place in preference to a challenging but insecure one is "not what made this country great." [32] One has a moral responsibility to show faith in the future; this has been put with characteristic solemnity by W. J. Cameron:

. . . no credentials should be more rigorously examined than those of the prophets of calamity. If they speak not according to experience and the facts, they *may be* firebrands of defeatism, certainly they are *not* beacons of warning. We may set it down as almost a rule that in *this* country we are thinking wrongly unless we are thinking hopefully.[33]

COMPETITION AND UNIVERSALISM

The classical model is universalistic in its very fundamentals. It represents a system in which individuals gain or lose according to an impersonal gauge of their performance. What individuals get in the system is not dependent either (a) on the opinions which others may hold of them, or (b) on the sense of responsible concern they may have for others or others for them. The model is one which is peculiarly atomistic and as such suited to a creed which is in other respects universalistic; that

---

[29] See, for example, Alfred P. Sloan, Jr., "Big Business Must Help Our Colleges," *Colliers,* June 2, 1951, pp. 13–15, 68–69. Frank W. Abrams, "The Stake of Business in Public School Education," address, Cleveland, Ohio, Jan. 12, 1951, dist. by National Citizens Commission for the Public Schools, 2 West 45 St., New York 19, N.Y.
[30] Hearings before a subcommittee of the Committee on Banking and Currency, U.S. Senate, July–Sept. 1945, S. 380.
[31] *Business Week* (editorial), Nov. 6, 1948, p. 142.
[32] Don G. Mitchell, President, Sylvania Electric Products, Inc., *Creating an Industrial Civilization,* p. 158.
[33] Ford Hour, October 5, 1941 (italics in original).

is, devoted to the principle that individual merit should be judged impersonally. By the fact that everyone acts egotistically, the system allegedly puts every individual up against the same impersonal conditions and in this sense treats them fairly.

The competition symbol probably gives the most tangible and direct expression to universalism as a value. It is, of course, usually applied to competition among business firms but, not infrequently, it is implied that everyone ought to be subjected to "competition." Thus Mr. Mooney disparagingly remarks that the government has no competitors in the tax-collecting business,[34] and his confreres denounce "monopolistic" labor unions. The symbol competition seems to have a very general connotation, signifying fair and approved conditions for measuring merit.

DEMOCRACY AND UNIVERSALISM

It is because of its stress on fair competition and equal opportunity that the business creed may be called egalitarian or democratic. We have avoided these latter terms, preferring the more neutral term, universalism, in order to avoid the ambiguities which are frequently found in popular language. The creed is certainly not "egalitarian" in some senses of the word. It defends differences in income, opposes limitations on profits, and claims for businessmen the rights and responsibilities of community leadership. But it does insist on the fundamentals of equal opportunity, and resists inequalities based on ascribed status. The American businessman who proudly announces in his preface, "I have no family tree — I don't want one" [35] provides an illustration of this point. Although some business firms have in fact become the bases of established families with aristocratic pretensions, no elitist doctrine has won representation in the ideology; indeed some of the abuse of England in the business ideology has been aimed directly or indirectly at its "aristocracy, upper-classism, caste and title." [36] There is a warm regard for "family life" but this centers on the nuclear family[37] and has little to do with status.

The classical model is one in which society is composed of individuals without fundamental differences in worth. Businessmen remain faithful to the model in the ideology. We have not, for example, found any explicit demand for property qualifications in voting, although there are veiled attacks on universal suffrage.[38] Certain gratifications which commonly go

---

[34] Mooney, *The Economics of Free Enterprise*.

[35] J. Edward Jones, *My Country 'Tis of Thee* (New York, 1941), p. 4.

[36] *Ibid.*, p. 16.

[37] Sociologists distinguish between the unit consisting of parents and immature children and the larger units suggested by such terms as the "Vanderbilt family" or the "Rockefeller family." The former is the "nuclear family," the latter, an "extended family." See George P. Murdock, *Social Structure* (New York, 1949), ch. 1.

[38] Leonard Read, "On that Day Began Lies," pp. 16–17.

with authority and responsibility tend to be muted and restrained. Even within the contexts of his own enterprise, the businessman claims he should not expect gratitude from his employees for giving them jobs. The business enterprise is not to be one in which workers gaze upward in disciplined respect toward their executive betters, but a cooperative venture in which the executive serves the general needs of an industrial community. This feature does not tally with the charge that business shows "fascist" tendencies. In contrast to the typical fascist emphases on discipline and respect for the leadership of an elite, the business creed calls for leaders who are "simple men with the common touch," [39] men who can elicit voluntary cooperation in a humble spirit of "service."

There is still another sense in which the business creed is strongly universalistic. The achievements of American capitalism vaunted in the creed are nearly all concerned with the common welfare; they imply an ideal of a democratic distribution of rewards and opportunities. The yardstick of achievement is in this sense universalistic although restricted by the nationalism of the creed; the welfare of all humanity gets far less attention than the welfare of all Americans, but within our national borders the common welfare is a prime measure of achievement. Walter S. Gifford, former head of American Telephone and Telegraph, once extolled the American devotion to the underlying "democratic" values as follows:

The democratic conception came first in politics, then in education and third in prosperity. A universal participation in government as a practical matter was an American conception. A universal participation in education was likewise first tried in the United States, and a democratic and widespread prosperity is peculiarly an American ambition and American accomplishment. The force and strength of this ideal cannot be overestimated. A prosperity of the few at the expense of the many is subject always to the danger of attack by the many whether they be inside or outside national boundaries. And what is more serious than this, a prosperity for the few does not invite the energy, resourcefulness and ambitions of the multitude to its support and enlargement.[40]

Mr. Gifford's concern about maintaining the "ambitions of the multitude" raises an important question: how can this devotion to the common welfare be reconciled with the egotistic pursuit of self-interest? The creed achieves some reconciliation between these two norms by interpreting and qualifying them.

[39] David J. Mahoney, Inc. advertisement, *New York Times,* Sept. 15, 1952, p. 33.
[40] Walter S. Gifford, "Planned Progress for Cultural Development," *A Philosophy of Production,* edited by J. G. Frederick (New York, 1930), p. 60.

"SERVICE" AND SOCIAL RESPONSIBILITY

Managerial ideology is so prominent at the present time that it may be questioned whether or not we have done justice to the creed in stressing its individualism as a dominant characteristic. The managerial strand of the creed certainly does not proclaim unfettered individual freedom; above all, it stresses the mutual interdependence of the people related to a business firm and the importance of managers having a sedulous regard for their welfare. The doctrine that the evil days of rugged individualism have now passed and that a new era of business responsibility has emerged wins increasing praise.[41]

But it is entirely too simple to see the managerial ideology as a "socially responsible" replacement for an older individualistic creed. A theme of responsibility for service to the community and the common welfare appears throughout the whole business creed. indeed, it would be extraordinary if the long record of philanthropy and communal devotion of American business were not reflected in the creed, and in fact the managerialists have certainly had no monopoly on claims to "service." Such claims have appeared side by side with a vigorous emphasis on individualism. The Radicals of early nineteenth-century England were ready to draw the harsh but logical conclusion that they had to restrain altruism if they were to promote individual responsibility; the Poor Law of 1834 was a monument to their unflinching consistency. But most popular ideology displays less concern with logical rigor, and the American business creed has accommodated both self-reliance and service with apparent ease. It has done so by stressing that service is voluntary and is not due to the recipients as a matter of right. The managerial creed essentially preserves this pattern of thinking. It responds to the problems of the large public corporation not by calling for a legal redefinition of the social responsibility of managers but by exhorting them to assume new responsibilities voluntarily.[42] It maintains a vigorous opposition to governmental assumption or dictation of responsibilities and the model of a transformed American capitalism remains decentralized and quasi-individualistic.

INEVITABLE INCONSISTENCIES IN VALUE SYSTEMS

Our review has shown that the many values of the business creed hang together in a meaningful way. But against this suggestion of coherence must be set some inconsistencies and contradictions.

[41] Staley, *Creating an Industrial Civilization*, p. 16, and the special issue of the *Saturday Review of Literature*, Jan. 24, 1953.

[42] For an instructive contrast, compare George Goyder, *The Future of Private Enterprise; A Study in Responsibility* (Oxford, 1951).

In the nature of their function, value-symbols and moral injunctions must suffer from logical inconsistencies if they are to be part of working ideologies. If they were qualified to the point where they could be applied literally, they would lose their evocative force. An old dilemma of ethical theories is that they must either impose a dogmatic rigidity on human efforts to deal with the complexities of the world, or lose their force in a misty indefiniteness; this problem is particularly prominent in any doctrine which like the business ideology clings to the values of "realism."

This is because any decision to act is complicated by the various consequences that action may have, and by the difficulty of knowing what significance to attach to these consequences. Any given situation imposes some elements of strain and deprivation on the human actors in it and confronts them with various possible courses of action. Action which is possible in the service of a proximate goal is always subject to critical evaluation in terms of other, especially more remote, goals, and in terms of generalized values; what seems to be desirable in terms of its immediate effects may not seem desirable when alternatives or remote consequences are envisaged. One obvious problem of choice lies between *resigned acceptance* and *efforts at alteration* of the elements in the situation. Our society is not, in a broad sense, a fatalistic one, although it approves of some forms of patient acceptance — business ideologists praise the acceptance of competitive pressures and the sometimes harsh consequences of the free enterprise "game." Our society contains complex patterns which impose responsibilities — on the one hand to "do something" in the face of strains and frustrations, and on the other hand to bear up patiently. A radically consistent position in one direction or the other would disrupt the present social fabric.

Furthermore, this problem of activism versus passivity involves choices between proximate, instrumental goals and more ultimate goals. The balancing of activities between the things "one does to live" and the things "one lives for" involves intrinsic uncertainties. An active impetuousity in grasping the immediate problems of existence is always open to the criticism that it leaves insufficient place for idealistic aspiration and the quiet virtues of leisure and contemplation.

Finally, since human action always takes place in a social context of some sort there are always problems of individual independence versus interdependence or social responsibility. Strictly speaking, the radical individualist who makes up his own mind on all questions, independent of what others think or expect, does not exist. People are so profoundly sensitive to the expectations of others that all action is inevitably guided by these expectations. On the other hand, some measure of individual independence is also a functional necessity. One need only recall the familiar psychiatric problems of excessive "dependency relations."

In short, unqualified prescriptions for human behavior must either be vague in their applicability or be manifestly unsound. This very problem has led the great ethical traditions into dependence on mystical pronouncements or exemplary parables. As a result, moral pronouncements tend to have a simple, direct character and as such are molded by the behavior which they are designed to influence. Depending on which pole of the various dilemmas above is seized in a particular case, they will have a varying character, and since either pole may from time to time need to be emphasized, they may show fundamental inconsistencies as a total corpus of doctrine.

SELECTIVE APPLICATION AS A BASIS FOR COHERENCE

It is obvious that the coherence of business creed values depends largely on the fact that they are applied in an area which is tacitly circumscribed. The creed is not equally concerned with all of the institutions and aspects of our society. Like other ideologies, it has special foci of interest. The great French historian of utilitarianism, Halevy, has pointed out that the clarity of emphasis on individualism, which the utilitarian forefathers of the business creed achieved, was due in good part to their neglect of kinship as a social phenomenon.[43] James Mill and Francis Place were good family men who must have perceived that they acted on other principles than utilitarian egotism in their families but to recognize this in their social theory would have been fatal to its simple coherence. Similarly the business creed's devotion to the dominant value-configuration we have presented is dependent on a special concern with business enterprise; when other aspects of social life are recalled, conflicting value emphases appear.

The link between the dominant values of the business creed and business enterprise is often explicitly made and becomes an ultimate justification of business enterprise. Theodore S. Grape's recent summary of the values we have been discussing won the valued back cover spot on the NAM magazine, *U.S.A.:*

I like business because it is competitive, because it rewards deed rather than words. I like business because it compels earnestness and does not permit me to neglect today's task while thinking about tomorrow. I like business because it undertakes to please, not reform; because it is honestly selfish, thereby avoiding hypocrisy and sentimentality. I like business because it promptly penalizes mistakes, shiftlessness, and inefficiency, while rewarding well those

---

[43] Halevy, *The Growth of Philosophical Radicalism*, pp. 503–504. Since it was outside the main focus of interest, kinship could be taken for granted and Marshall could hence argue that "economic man" had never been really treated as "perfectly selfish." Preface to 1st ed. of *Principles of Economics*. Marshall says explicitly, "(economic man's) normal motives have always been tacitly assumed to include the family affections."

who give it the best they have in them. Lastly, I like business because each day is a fresh adventure.[44]

On the same theme, Calkins asserted:

Business is today *the* profession. It offers something of the glory that in the past was given to the crusader, the soldier, the courtier, the explorer, and sometimes to the martyr . . . (Business is the field of) high adventure . . . with opportunities greater and rewards larger than in learned professions.[45]

When the creed takes notice of other sectors of our society, it often presents a contrasting set of values. This is most striking when the family or the home is under discussion. Like many other ideologies the business creed gives very little substantive attention to our kinship system; the home, when it is mentioned at all, is generally treated as an ultimate value which may be threatened by unsound developments and which must be protected against any such threats. While the businessman may in fact have to leave his parental home in search of opportunity, protect his business rationality against the claims of relatives, or struggle bitterly to balance the claims of office and family on his time and energies, little or no call for "progressive" evolution of our kinship system appears in the ideology. The tone is eminently conservative, stressing traditional duties and reflecting the spirit of a title from across our Northern border, "Let's Preserve Family Life." [46]

It is not only in domestic institutions that the creed shows a conservatism to balance its demands for restless adventure and progress. As in any ideology which emphasizes moral values, there is a tendency to sentimentalize the past. The self-reliance of the pioneer, the moral fibre of a more agricultural America,[47] and the simple unity of old-fashioned small towns win rhapsodies. There is a real mistrust of the large urban agglomerations which are in fact so intimately conected with business, and even a sentimental concern that the merely quaint be preserved. Ford's Dearborn Museum has its ideological counterparts, and we hear an enthusiastic American advertising man worrying lest the quaintness of Europe be spoiled by Americanization.[48]

It is not surprising that there are areas of the social structure in which the business ideology lauds change while deploring it in others. There are many contrasts between actual behavior in business offices and that in such contexts as churches and homes to parallel the ideological contrasts. But also in the domain of governmental activities, where alertness to demands for change is certainly expected, the business creed shows stub-

[44] Theodore S. Grape, *U.S.A.*, September 1952.
[45] Calkins, *Business the Civilizer*, pp. 51, 232.
[46] The Royal Bank of Canada Monthly Letter, December 1951.
[47] NAM, vol. I, ch. I.
[48] Calkins, *Business the Civilizer*, "Europe on the American Plan," pp. 100–113.

born conservatism. When focusing on the welfare state, the growth of labor's political influence, or the sheer expansion of government, the ideology sees patterns of change which it greets pessimistically, indeed in jeremiads. A gloomy tone predicting imminent catastrophe in our economy and society has pushed the businessman into a conservative position which he sometimes finds embarrassing.[49]

The creed's tempering of restless activity and innovation with conservatism represents one major departure from radical and dogmatic consistency. Another appears over the dilemma of individual autonomy versus collective responsibility. Although a loose sort of resolution of this dilemma is contained in the creed, it is a precarious one. Again selective application has favored coherence; the immense numbers of ideological assertions about the proper behavior of government have clearly emphasized voluntarism and individual autonomy. But the concern of the managerial writers with the structure of the firm and its relations to stockholders, consumers, and the community have blurred the picture. Similarly, the nationalism of the creed has not favored a dogmatic individualism. Vis-à-vis other nations, nationalism can represent the analogue of self-interest in more private spheres, but within the United States it calls for something more than self-interest.

Other examples of inconsistencies and counter-tendencies in the creed might readily be added. Perfect consistency in the application of values is no more characteristic of working ideologies than it is of social systems themselves.[50] Efforts at working out a systematic ethic are not very common or popular in the modern world and it should not surprise us to find the business ideology little equipped with imposing, rationalized bodies of thought in this quarter.

RELIGION IN THE CREED

A favored means of justifying values and working out their relative priority in our society is that of linking them to our religious heritage. The ultimate grounding of value systems must be sought either in some kind of secular metaphysics or in appeal to religion. At the present time, American business ideology is not strongly tied to any secular philosophy; there is no philosophy which has the general acceptance which Social Darwinism seems to have had at the end of the nineteenth century. This has left the field open for religious doctrines but there can hardly be said to be a clear systematic orthodoxy which ties religious ideas to the rest of the business ideology. The NAM treatise on the individual enterprise system

---

[49] For example, Cameron, Ford Hour, Oct. 23, 1938.

[50] On the general question of the value-integration of social systems, see F. R. Kluckhohn, "Dominant and Substitute Profiles of Cultural Orientation: Their Significance for the Analysis of Social Stratification," *Social Forces*, XXVIII: 370–393 (1950); and Parsons, *The Social System*, pp. 177 ff.

does not make economics a handmaiden of theology, and a great part of the moral exhortation depends on no expressed religious principles.

Nevertheless, the place of religion in the business ideology is a conspicuous and honored one. Klein begins his creed for loyal supporters of our capitalist system with a solemn, "In the name of God, Amen." [51] Conrad Hilton would have America on its knees, fearing "nothing or no one . . . except God!" [52] Solemn and respectful symbols or broad exhortations to religious piety like these examples are sprinkled through the creed. They recall the common use of prayer and religious sentiments in American political life and have a similarly vague relation to specific ideological doctrine.

More focused efforts to supply religious authority or guidance in social conduct are often found. The *Wall Street Journal* once suggested in a Christmas message that the coming of Christ was the beginning of liberty and quoted St. Paul's "words he would have us remember afterwards in each of the years of his Lord: Stand fast therefore in the liberty wherewith Christ hath made us free and be not entangled again with the yoke of bondage." [53] An unwillingness to mix religion with business practice has often been alleged of business but the ideology does not admit or approve of it. The NAM *Trends* proudly reports instances in which successful businessmen claim guidance from God in their business lives. Thus, R. B. Le Tourneau (a manufacturer of earth-moving equipment) is reported holding weekly Gospel meetings in all his plants, and proclaiming, "God runs my business." J. C. Penney is "a man who applies Christian principles in business as an essential part of free enterprise." [54] One company has a vice-president in charge of Christian relations, and there is apparently sufficient general activity of this sort for a newspaper editorial to suggest that business is "getting religious." [55] But, although we hear of much deliberation on the "Christian Role of Management," [56] there can hardly be said to be clear systematic orthodoxy which emerges to take an important place in the business creed.

[51] Klein, *How to Stay Rich*, p. 169.

[52] From an address, *The Battle for Peace* distributed with a color reprint, *America on its Knees* by the author (Beverly Hills, Calif., 1952); also appeared in national magazines, summer 1952.

[53] *Wall Street Journal*, Dec. 23, 1949, reprinted in *Faith and Freedom*, December 1951, p. 2.

[54] NAM, *Trends*, September 1948, pp. 1–4, 12–14.

[55] *Boston Herald*, May 6, 1949, p. 46. Stimulated by "Business and Religion." *Harvard Business Review*, May 1949.

[56] Title of a program at Wilson College (Chambersburg, Pa.) reported in *Trends*, September 1949, pp. 5–7. Stuart Chase reports a YMCA conference on the problems of management in summer 1949. (*Social Responsibility of Management*, New York, 1950, p. 7.) These are certainly only random examples from a spate of similar activity.

Thus, the place of religion in the business creed is an honored, but ill-defined one. The creed bows to the importance of religion, admits seeking religious guidance, but continues to be a predominantly secular ideology. The Deity is reverenced and His laws respected, but the explanations of business cycles or the workings of the price system are seldom deduced from theological premises. What coherence the creed shows in its values derives not so much from deliberate systematization under religious guidance but from the more spontaneous influences which we have briefly outlined. In Part II we shall explore this coherence more deeply, seeking its roots in the cultural heritage, the institutional framework of our society, and the strains of the business executive's role.

PART II

AN ANALYSIS OF BUSINESS IDEOLOGY

Our survey of the American business creed is now completed. We have set it forth as coherently as we could, organizing our exposition in part after the pattern of the creed's own emphases, in part in accordance with the logic of a systematic survey of our society. Thus far, we have kept our analysis deliberately meager. However, we have done more than simply state the content of the creed; we have compared the special views of the creed with the complexities of concrete social reality; we have stressed possible alternative views of society and pointed out the incompleteness of the business creed and its frequent inconsistencies. If our exposition deserves to be called "critical" it is not because we have sought to demonstrate where the creed is "right" or "wrong," but rather because we have striven to make clear that the creed is not an exhaustive and inexorably compelling account of contemporary America (or of modern industrial societies generally). We have repeatedly pointed to situations which are simply obscure, and on which a detached judgment could do no more than admit ignorance and uncertainty; the business creed has often been strongly dogmatic in its analyses of these situations, and we have set this dogmatism in relief. Where the creed has shown patent misconceptions we have not hesitated to point them out, but it has been our aim to avoid polemics.

Our purpose in Part I, aside from an intrinsic interest in what the business creed says, has been to raise a series of problems about the roots of this ideology. Such analysis as we have put into the foregoing discussion has served primarily to point up the implicit questions as to why the business creed takes the shape it does. We now turn to the task of examining these questions squarely.

Analysis of the roots of ideology — why particular ideas appear, receive emphasis, and win emotional support while others are muted, neglected, or suppressed — may proceed in a number of directions. There are three modes of analysis which appear to be important. In the first place, any ideology stands in a particular cultural heritage. The ideas which are proclaimed and accepted in American society must be expected to bear the marks of American cultural traditions. Every society's culture has some coherence, stemming from the common historical background of its elements and from the demands of mutual compatibility among them. Not all of the elements of a culture must fit into one neat configuration, but a moderate compatibility of any ideology with the broad cultural heritage is to be expected. The American business creed is conspicuously related to broader sets of ideas which are partly American and partly the communal property of the Western world, and we can develop a considerable insight into the business creed by tracing out these relations.

In the second place, any ideology is manifestly dependent on certain institutional frameworks for its continued viability. The current examples of totalitarian states have made us uncomfortably aware that the diversity of ideologies with which we are familiar in the United States is dependent on a particular set of institutions. It is also clear, on the other hand, that popular government, as we know it, is dependent on the existence of flourishing ideologies. The free discussion on which popular government rests must necessarily be largely ideological in character, and the agencies of government, official and unofficial, provide a basic framework for the dissemination of ideologies. An examination of the role of political and economic institutions in stimulating the production and dissemination of business ideology and shaping its content is a second approach to understanding its roots.

The third direction of analysis takes us to a different and deeper level. In explaining social behavior, it is never sufficient to point out the nature of cultural prescriptions, and the habitual patterns of organizing behavior crystallized in institutions. The questions always remain: why are individuals motivated to conform to the prescription? to grasp the opportunities which institutional situations offer? to exploit a particular one among available alternatives? The cultural heritage, as we shall show, presents broad ideas from among which the business ideology selects and emphasizes some; other creeds emphasize other elements of the heritage; we must explain the selection. While institutions constrain ideology to some extent and shape its characteristic modes of expression, the content of what is expressed and the emotion with which it is invested cannot be *explained in institutional terms. To do this a motivational analysis is required. We must study the motivations of the businessmen who are the producers and consumers of the ideology.*

In Part II, we explore all three of these modes of analysis — cultural, institutional, and motivational — but we put our chief emphasis on the last, as central to our explanation. This part comprises six chapters. Chapters 13 and 14 examine, respectively, the cultural heritage and the institutional framework of our society in relation to the business creed. Our examination of these subjects is not exhaustive; it proposes, however, to bring out their salient points and indicate what we think needs to be explained in motivational terms. This explanation, developed in Chapters 15, 16, and 17, constitutes the major part of our analysis.

In the final, Chapter 18, we take up a question which we have avoided up to now, that of the temporal stability of the business creed. Our material is drawn chiefly from the period 1948–49; only occasionally, in search of a comparison or a statement on a problem poorly covered in our current materials, have we ventured back to examine the creed over a longer time span. We have not attempted to treat our topic historically, and the analysis which follows is couched in terms which show no particularly restricted temporal reference. The concrete political and economic situation of the period plays no great role in our analysis of the business creed as it was expressed in the years 1948–49. We have sought to explain the ideology in terms of certain persistent forces, not confined in their relevance to a narrow period of time. If our analysis is correct, we should expect to find that the business creed, viewed broadly, is fairly stable over time, since the motivational forces which we view as its chief determinants change only slowly. In Chapter 18 we attempt, in a modest way, to consider the extent to which the creed has been stable, by examining its treatment of a particular problem over a long period. Such problems as the changes in the creed which the New Deal has brought, the effects of the recent revolution in professional economic thought, or the change in the relative prominence of classical and managerial doctrine in the creed get at least some treatment in this way. This discussion is necessarily summary; it would require another volume for anything like a full historical treatment of these issues. This we cannot undertake; but placing this chapter at the end of our study gives some impression of the changes which have come about and some idea of the pressures which may lead to further change. And, thereby, we are able to delve further into our problem than a survey of the confusing present usually allows.

13

THE IDEOLOGY AND THE
CULTURAL HERITAGE

WHETHER AN IDEOLOGY is devoted to conservative rationalization of the existing society or stoutly demands a revolution, it is always grounded in the culture of the society in which it appears. The American business creed is obviously dependent on the American cultural heritage in the most intimate ways. The very obviousness of these relations frees us from pointing them out in detail, but there are dangers in assuming too much on these matters. One of the many consequences of heightened sensitivity to cultural differences in modern social science has been the realization that we take for granted, as inescapably "natural," ways of interpreting human experience which are in fact cast in our own peculiar cultural molds.

In this chapter, we shall distinguish three elements of the business creed — its general character, its descriptive ideas, and its set of values. We shall show in broad outline how these derive from our general Western heritage and from traditions peculiar to America.

THE BROAD CHARACTER OF THE CREED

The stamp of Western tradition is clearly set upon the general character of the business ideology. It is overwhelmingly secular in character; its values are temporal — almost embarrassingly so. Despite its use of religious symbols, the creed does not proclaim the workings of God's ways to men nor exhort them to bow in humility before the mysteries of supernatural forces. It does not consist as, for example, the classical Chinese heritage so largely did, of traditional precepts and exemplary tales. It is not a body of sacred writings or traditional texts for esthetic savoring. Rather, it is a structure of logical argument and empirical description which attempts to explain and direct the workings of society according to humanly understandable principles.

Writers like Alfred North Whitehead, Max Weber, and Marcel Granet made clear to us that this kind of intellectual approach to the world is dependent on the special characteristics of our Western tradition. The development of a sense of the "order of nature" out of the Greek achievement, the "disenchantment" of the world in favor of the awesome dignity of a remote Judaic-Christian deity, and the Roman Law's encouragement of broad application of general principles to human affairs, were some of the major elements shaping this heritage. The tenets of the business creed which make complex societies humanly understandable as coherent "systems" subject to general laws fit into this pattern; they would be completely alien to other cultures.

This Western heritage is, of course, more than permissive. It not only makes ideological systems of this kind possible; it demands that acceptable explanations of, and guides to, human action have some degree of logical coherence and that they deal directly with the empirical world. Mr. Baer's famous assertion that the anthracite miners owed him their obedience in the station to which God had called him was altogether too simple a justification of his authority in this broad cultural heritage. The business creed must treat the structure of the firm, the province of the government, the causes of business cycles, or the growth of American society in terms of rationally coherent empirical argument if it is to be considered plausible in the modern world.

The business creed has good precedent in the Western heritage for treating the world as rationally knowable and manipulable for human betterment. But the detailed emphases of American business ideology find little agreement or acceptance elsewhere. The prospcts of rationally guided betterment which much of the Western world cherishes, involve a far kindlier attitude toward the state and correspondingly less emphasis on individualism. The "free enterprise system" is not a beloved symbol throughout the Western world, and indeed some of the nationalism of the creed must arise from recognition of this fact. It is common intellectual property in the Western world, at least since the nineteenth century, to regard economic activity as an "inner system" about which the "outer system" of other social action revolves. But the outer system may, elsewhere in the West, be given the brilliance of Saturnian rings about a darkened center. *Rerum Novarum* tells us that work is not shameful but it hardly makes work and material activity the bright expressions of human worth.

THE VALUES OF THE CREED

Two important values which the creed shares with the broad American heritage are those of individualism and the importance of work. In this heritage, continuous, narrow application to work and private affairs is not just a concession to the unpleasant demands of practical life; it is a positive value in itself. Charles E. Wilson, telling a Senate committee that he believed in keeping his mind on his own work and not worrying about its rewards or significances, stands solidly in an American tradition.[1] So does David Sarnoff, arguing recently that a businessman who did a good job at work did not have to apologize for not "improving" himself after work.[2] This confidence that work in an occupation may in itself be a legitimate and rewarding focus of a man's best energies and not merely a means to "higher" things is deepset in American values. It provides a natural background for an ideology extolling the importance of work and productivity. And the absence of a leisured aristocracy devoted to self-cultivation has given the bourgeois values of work and productivity a relative freedom from competition.

American mistrust of social systems which do not rest on morally responsible individuals is not confined to the business ideologists. When Professor Sheldon Glueck of the Harvard Law School put together a set of critical essays on the welfare state, he was able to find educators, lawyers, scientists, politicians, journalists, and soldiers who denounced "the threatening tendencies of our times." The impressive and varied list of his contributors included Dwight D. Eisenhower, Bernard Baruch, Vannevar Bush, John Foster Dulles, Roscoe Pound, and Herbert Hoover.[3] The business creed, in demanding freedom for individual initiative, sober self-reliance, and brakes on governmental paternalism, is merely accenting, in special contexts, broad values which gain general assent in American society.

The creed gives individualism a moral emphasis, and in this it also follows an American pattern. As Margaret Mead has repeatedly emphasized, American society is particularly disposed to view issues in moral terms and to stress the importance of moral character in the functioning of society.

These aspects of the American heritage are variations on common Western value themes. If the American business creed differs from other ideologies in the modern world, it is not because others have been unaffected by the same basic values. The modern West is worldly and materialistic and its ideologies demand that we all be Marthas. Even the aristocratic D'Annunzio would have only producers in his constitution of

[1] *New York Times*, Jan. 24, 1953, p. 8. The words are remarkable: "Now, actually, it sounds a little funny, maybe, but I have been a great believer in our American system. I have figured that if I worked in my job, the system would take care of me. I sort of neglected my own affairs, really, in a certain way — but they did pretty well because I worked at the things I was supposed to be working on."

[2] *Creating an Industrial Civilization*, pp. 54–55. Mr. Sarnoff also remarked (p. 61): "We encourage our executives to go out and play a game of golf once in a while. We think a lot of business is done on the golf links."

[3] *The Welfare State and the National Welfare*, edited by Sheldon Glueck (Cambridge, Mass., 1952); a symposium on some of the threatening tendencies of our times.

Fiume. Nevertheless, in its emphasis on individualism and practical effort, the American heritage stands clearly differentiated from the Western tradition of which it is a part. These emphases have roots in the confluence of the Puritan movement in religion and the Enlightenment in the sphere of political thought. The absence here of any long established competing traditions — Catholic, monarchical, aristocratic, conservative — gave these developments a clearer field in America than in Europe.

The special achievement of the Puritan tradition was to give a religious sanction to individualism and occupational effort as values. At the core of the Calvinistic, Puritan tradition[4] as it worked itself out in social life were the linked values of *austerity, individualism,* and devotion to *occupations as callings*. The dramatic pathos of predestination and the reaction against a sacramental church implied a sharp isolation of the individual in his chances of salvation. From this a complex edifice of individualism was built up. The nothingness of the individual before the awful majesty of God made suspect direct concern with worldly gratifications; an austerity which demanded selfless disregard of prestige, self-esteem, and the delights of the flesh was thus a natural expression of religious interests. This austere selflessness could be achieved in a strictly limited number of ways. The path of mystical other-worldliness was suspect because it invited too much attention to merely human, psychological states. Devotion to an occupation, not primarily as a means to earthly reward, but for itself as a "calling" fitted admirably the pattern set by the religious postulates. This view of occupations as callings gave to the work of the world a special dignity as a path to salvation.

The importance of this tradition in giving a distinctive cast to American values has certainly been very great. Seeking to define "the most characteristic qualities of the American temper," Parrington has put Puritanism on a very exclusive list of two (the other was "optimism").[5] Taking a wider perspective, Troeltsch has argued for a more important place of Puritanism in the Anglo-American tradition than elsewhere in the Western world.[6] Within this tradition the American businessman need make no apologies for a narrow, specialized existence filled with the cares of producing and distributing material goods. The "dignity of work," the worth of material gains, and the propriety of a strong individualism are solidly grounded in the heritage.

We venture here to recall this religious heritage of contemporary American values because it seems to have had great importance in legit-

[4] The tradition is broader than New England Puritanism, being also represented in Scotch-Irish and Huguenot influences.

[5] Parrington, *Main Currents in American Thought* (New York, 1930), vol. III, p. 326.

[6] See Troeltsch's admirable *Deutscher Geist und West-Europa* (Tübingen, 1925) for contrasts to Germany and the Lutheran heritage.

imizing and defending values which are highly vulnerable to critical opposition. The sorts of difficulty we encountered in the business ideology over "productivity" indicate the nature of the problem. Occupational activity inevitably bears an instrumental character: whatever the intrinsic satisfactions which it may offer, there is always some relatively tangible end product to which the activity is directed. Thus the natural tendency is to see in work a means to living rather than an ultimate value in itself. Even in our American heritage there is a strong tendency to dissent from the view that work is valuable for its own sake and in the European heritage the tendency has certainly been stronger.[7] Moreover, insofar as occupations tend to be concerned with providing the material needs of life, they may be contrasted with those spheres in which more ultimate values are sought, and thus fall into the domain of the "material" as invidiously contrasted with the "spiritual."

The Puritan heritage, by combating these tendencies, has opened the path for ideologies which, like the business creed, extoll the importance of work. In a broad way, the Enlightenment reinforced those values of individualism stressed in the Puritan heritage; above all it was a critical attack on existing hereditary aristocracies and the governmental authority associated with them — particularly monarchical prerogatives. Individualism and universalism became the new ideals. The United States as a political entity was, to a peculiar degree among the Western nations, founded on explicit ideology with the values of the Enlightenment as guiding principles. Born in a mood of hostility toward strong government and status-distinctions, the nation was able to gain a remarkable unanimity of ideology about these fundamentals. Whereas elsewhere in the Western world the ideology of the Enlightenment had to contend with ideologies which approved class distinctions and less synthetic governments, in the United States it has had a relatively clear sweep of the field. One consequence of this is the great openness and explicitness in ideology, stressed by foreign observers from Alexis De Tocqueville to Gunnar Myrdal.

Hostility to a strong centralized government and a corresponding positive emphasis on individual initiative form a general ideological climate in which the specific doctrines of the business creed can readily flourish. This heritage has been applied directly to the freedom of business enterprise and the minimization of governmental economic activity — par-

[7] We would suggest that there are subtle but important differences between the lauding of effort in the American business creed and the aggressive assertions of the dignity of work in much European ideology. Hitler's "Ehret die Arbeit und achtet den Arbeiter" associates in a sentence the defense of work and the defense of "workers" exemplifying the common tendency to treat work as a symbol belonging to the critics of society. The business creed may applaud work in American society without "class" implications; it is attacking no legitimately established elite less devoted to work than the manual "worker."

ticularly since the post-Civil War era. The concrete forms in which individualism was conceived by the political theorists have been peculiarly suited to this process. Beginning with Locke, the ideological reaction against monarchical prerogative had seized upon property rights as the basis of political freedom. To attack one form of established right, the current of political ideology directly fostered the growth of another kind of established right. As Keynes has remarked, "The purpose of promoting the Individual was to depose the Monarch and the Church; the effect — through the new ethical significance attached to contract — was to buttress Property and Prescription." [8] The later drift toward radical democracy leached the elements of prescription out of this structure but private property remained. While this emphasis on private property later provided a target for socialist criticism, it first enabled those with business property to set themselves up as the defenders of political liberty. If the American business ideologist now sees a free enterprise economy as essential to political liberty in a free society, he is well within the American tradition.

The egalitarianism of the Enlightenment has also greatly smoothed the course of the business creed. In a society in which a less aggressive assault on status pretensions has occurred, the confident assertion of the primacy of business or the forthright proclamation of its merits would be more difficult. There is no country in the Western world in which the businessman has had the assured self-confidence in his own merits and the importance of his work which he has had in the United States. If the Reformation made work respectable, the Enlightenment, by assaulting the status of unspecialized, leisured aristocrats, has made it possible for "busy" people to believe with unabashed confidence that they are the crucial elements in our society.

We could elaborate further on the close relationship between our cultural heritage and the values of the business creed. For instance, the spirit of rational criticism of existing institutions and the optimism about the future found in the business creed are expressions of leveling tendencies of the Enlightenment. But, if we have given the reader some idea of how this relationship works, we have succeeded in our purpose. Roughly speaking, the effect of the cultural heritage is to define the range of values which the ideology may legitimately express. Businessmen have extolled certain values more loudly and more openly in America than in other Western countries. The role of the businessman is much the same in all Western countries, so the businessmen tend to hold the same views independent of national boundaries. That certain values are strongly expressed only in America is due as much to a congenial cultural heritage as to any peculiarities of American business itself. The most outstanding

[8] J. M. Keynes, *Laissez-Faire and Communism* (London, 1926), p. 7.

example is individualism. There are intrinsic difficulties in defending extreme individualism. Human existence is critically dependent on the observance of mutual obligations and the acceptance of collective responsibilities in some form. Cultural traditions, illogically or otherwise, nearly always stress the importance of these obligations and responsibilities. By giving individualism religious sanction, the Puritan tradition has helped to protect it against attack. Business ideology is thus enabled to take a stronger individualistic stand in America than in cultures where the traditions of Puritanism and the Enlightenment have been weaker.

The cultural heritage not only permits certain values to be expressed in the business creed; it inhibits the expression of others. A society strongly attached to universalistic values inhibits the expression of "anti-democratic" or "elitist" values. The form of the business creed thus depends, not only on what it includes, but also on what it rejects.

IDEAS AND THE HERITAGE: THE CLASSICAL CREED AND AMERICAN ECONOMIC INDIVIDUALISM

The business creed gives a high place to the role of ideas in history and at the same time is sharply critical of intellectual experts. It depicts societies as capable of choosing which sort of "system" they will adopt and makes economic progress dependent on correct understanding of how the various systems work. At the same time it shows a great confidence that straightforward practical men can understand the system.

This is rooted in psychological needs, but it draws on material from our broad Western heritage. The conception that a society may be planned in advance and its guiding principles set down in a written constitution would be completely bizarre in more traditionalistic cultures. In the West, however, the human intellect and rationality have always had a fairly august position and the Enlightenment glorified them. Thus, in a nation founded on a written constitution and nourished on the idea that societies can be vastly improved by the persistent use of reason, the business creed can plausibly emphasize the importance of understanding the System correctly. Moreover, both the faith in the reason of the practical man and the correlative distrust of professional qualifications are natural developments from the universalism of the Enlightenment.

But it is the substance of the business creed which provides the most striking evidence of the influence of American traditions. For various reasons, the ideas of the political economists of the nineteenth century have gained more enduring acceptance in America than in Europe. It is these ideas — of Adam Smith, Ricardo, Malthus, the Mills and their popularizers — which form the preponderant classical strand in the business creed, and give it its most distinctive character in the modern world.[9] The ideas of the managerialists sound fresh and distinctive in America only because they are set against the background of the classical theme in the business creed. Outside the United States the theme that the workers must be integrated into the business firm and that business must assume broad responsibilities to customer, community, and nation has become a flat banality.[10] It is in its vigorous cries against "government interference" and "socialism" and in its persisting faith in the workability of a vaguely defined "free" economy that the business creed is genuinely distinctive. The Western world has not swung over to totalitarian collectivism but outside America it no longer nourishes a Spencerian distrust of the state and a goal of maximal freedom for private enterprise. Even in England a figure like Sir Ernest Benn appears to be regarded as a gifted but tedious eccentric rather than as a spokesman of the plausible Right.[11] Some British and Western European businessmen may be extreme individualists but they do not form national associations to broadcast their opinions.

Why have the ideas of the classical economists become so firmly

[9] Explicit reference to the classical economists is remarkably rare. In the great mass of material we have examined in this study, we recall only a few instances in which Adam Smith, Ricardo, Malthus, or J. S. Mill is quoted as an authority. The attitudes which lead Communists to stud their writings with quotations from Marx, Engels, Lenin, or Stalin are evidently absent from the background of the business creed. It would be out of keeping with the individualistic and rationalistic values of the creed to admit such recourse to "wisdom" or authority. The creed is presented as something which is fundamentally clear and simple (hence not to be groped after as we do with the traditional wisdom of the Bible). It should be something on which each man is able to make up his own mind and not accept as the dictum of authority. There is probably also a disadvantage in leaning on classical authorities; they may readily be represented as "out-of-date" or at least needing reexamination to verify that their doctrines still hold.

Classical economics had of course many characteristics which ill fit it for the optimistic doctrine of the business creed. The somber conclusions from the Malthusian population doctrine and Ricardo's laws of distribution do not readily make popular ideology. It is perhaps suggestive that the Foundation for Economic Education has revived Bastiat, an optimistic popularizer, rather than the classic figures themselves. The continued study of the classics is left to the academics and it is almost exclusively to such purposes that we get new editions of them. An abbreviated edition of the *Wealth of Nations* has indeed appeared which is explicitly designed to broadcast Smith's lessons for our times, but the new edition of Ricardo now appears in the solemn majesty of ten handsome volumes for the scholar. The Constitution and the Declaration of Independence may be "sacred" texts for the business creed; the *Wealth of Nations* and Ricardo's *Principles* are not.

[10] Such doctrines were prominent in Fascist ideologies but also in what has been called "welfare capitalism." See R. A. Brady, *Business as a System of Power* (New York, 1943), p. 44, *et passim*. They are an obvious reaction to strains discussed in Chapter 15 below and have appeared in both pro-business and anti-business ideologies.

[11] See the review of his *The State the Enemy* in the *Economist*, Jan. 24, 1953, and contrast the treatment of Clarence Randall in the *Saturday Review of Literature* on precisely the same date.

established not only in the minds of businessmen but also, to a considerable extent, among the American people at large? To answer this question thoroughly would require an elaborate historical analysis. But, broadly speaking, one can say that the predominant ideology in a society tends to reflect its social structure. Since America has not had, and has been antagonistic toward, a rigid class structure, its people have found little appeal in organic conceptions of society. Where people feel free to improve their position in society whenever the opportunity presents itself, an ideology which stresses the social functions of various status groups would be out of place.[12] The acceptance of structural divisions into classes, either in the aggressive forms of the socialist heritage or in the mild conservatism of *Quadragesimo Anno,* which assumes "various ranks of society," is inhibited by our universalistic values.

The classical model of the utilitarians, on the other hand, has given concrete and intellectually sophisticated expression to inchoate tendencies in American society. The Reformation and the Enlightenment had previously disposed American thought to some form of economic individualism. The classical model, which treats the nation as a collection of individuals with no fundamental difference *inter se,* provides an expression of the central values of our cultural heritage in a systematic form.

A glance at the nature of academic economics in America reveals the very strong place of the classical heritage. Of course, there have been historicists and institutionalists who have attacked the views and methods of classical economics. But these critics have not succeeded in dislodging abstract analysis on the classical model from its solid place of acceptance at the core of economics as an academic discipline. Whereas in a country like Germany the method of economics remained profoundly at issue for a long time and the classical analysis won a footing only very late,[13] in

[12] In particular, it discourages a conception of "business" as representing a distinctive segment of the total structure. Much business ideology has been devoted to sharp attack on those who would divide the nation by "class" arguments or legislation. (The outraged cries against Mr. Roosevelt's assault on "economic royalists" were typical of the theme which has been regularly voiced for at least half a century; see Chapter 18 below.) That businessmen could deny with great evidence of moral outrage that they represented a distinctive "interest" or group in American society has surely been based on individualistic ideas of "freedom of entry." The notion that anyone with thrift and ambition could be a businessman has certainly not been a monopoly of businessmen. We know that large numbers in the American population still think of themselves as potential businessmen (see Centers' study cited in Chapter 18 below) and are thus not likely to favor views which give sharp and persisting distinction to businessmen as against other social classes.

[13] Myrdal has asserted that theoretical economics won a firm place in German universities only after the popularization of Cassel's text in the first decade of the present century. Gunnar Myrdal, *The Political Element in the Development of Economic Theory* (London, 1953), p. 13. The pedestrian but extensive survey by T. Suranyi-Unger, *Twentieth Century Economics* (New York, 1937), is very instructive on national differences.

the United States it has long dealt with critics from a place of established eminence.[14] If the American businessman has often been at odds with the academic economist, he has pitted himself against a foe who took much the same stance and used much the same weapons. Classical views have likewise pervaded other spheres of American life. Our legislation has been hostile to conditions which would disturb freedom of competition and contract. The unique American venture in anti-trust legislation does not represent a pure deduction from the doctrine of free enterprise, but, insofar as it has had a solid rationale, it has had to depend on such doctrines. The "liberals," like Thurman Arnold, who have vigorously prosecuted business firms under this legislation, have done so under the aegis of a free enterprise ideology. Similarly, in the sphere of judicial decisions we need only recall the famous series of Supreme Court decisions outlawing wage and hours legislation as breaches of freedom of contract.

How closely does the classical theme in the business creed conform to classical economic doctrines? First and foremost, the creed's fundamental tenet — that it rests on certain general laws of human nature and society — represents loyal adherence to the classical tradition. Resistance to classical economics in the continental, especially the German, tradition tended to take the form of denying the subjection of the human will to universal laws, with a corresponding stress on the unique characteristics of each society and individual.[15] Thanks in good part to the acceptance of classical economics, this battle has been avoided in the United States. When Mooney writes that the "functioning of economic units and groups are universal in their general characteristics and classically similar throughout history" and that they are "never altered by changes in the complexions of governmental or political structures," [16] he is restating postulates which form the core of classical economics as an abstract discipline. While the American "free enterprise" system is said to be unique in history, it is also conceived as "natural" and, like all other systems, subject to the inexorable workings of general natural laws. In his conceptions of these laws the contemporary business ideologist sticks tightly to the model of his utilitarian predecessors.

The business creed states that society is at one and the same time highly

---

[14] We do not overlook the great influence of the German universities through men like Ely, Clark, and Patten in the closing decades of the nineteenth century, and we remember that the American Economic Association and the *Journal of Political Economy* were founded in opposition to the classicists. But all activity issued more in a stress on empirical investigation rather than a seriously altered set of theoretical views on the nature of society, and indeed many of the youthful critics of classicism were ultimately transformed into its mature exponents. The Keynesian revolution is a palace revolution from the broad perspective here adopted.

[15] Max Weber, *The Methodology of the Social Sciences,* trans. by Shils & Finch (Glencoe, Ill., 1949).

[16] Mooney, *The New Capitalism,* p. 181.

complex and delicate, and subject to laws that are evident and simple. These views were shared by the classical economists. Ricardo and his disciples sought simple general laws governing the economy but at the same time feared the imposition of any general norms upon it. The conception of economic law which emerged from this tradition was one which put no tools in the hands of legislators; it counseled only "systematic abstention," putting faith "not on the power of knowledge but on the *vis medicatrix naturae*." [17] As ideology, the doctrine is a curious one, but nicely adapted to the sentiments of men subject to the peculiar problems of the business executive's role.

In substance as well as in formal conception, the fundamental laws of human nature found in the business creed are largely those with which the utilitarian tradition endowed it. The special twist given individualism by the utilitarians was to make of it not merely a matter of freedom from social constraints, but a principle of motivation. The egotism of this tradition, the famous doctrine of the primacy of individual self-interest, of course goes back to the fountainheads of modern secular ideology in Locke and Hobbes. Adam Smith and the utilitarians turned it into a systematic philosophy with particular application to the economic affairs of society. Doctrines of individual self-interest originally conceived in the defense of political liberties could be readily used to rationalize the self-interest which is institutionally part of the businessman's role. The "profit motive" could be abstracted from its institutional context and labeled the pursuit of individual self-interest — the fundamental condition of human happiness. If the contemporary business ideologist shows an almost obtuse stubbornness in making a concept as intrinsically vulnerable as the "profit motive" a prominent feature of his defense of free enterprise, he is not without long established precedent.

Other connections between the contemporary ideology and the classical heritage might be pointed out. The ideology's views on the unproductiveness of government, the efficacy of a "neutral," "unmanaged" currency, and many other subjects are cases in point. We have discussed enough examples to make clear the intellectual lineage of modern business ideology. Why classical ideas persist in the business creed is another question, which will be discussed later.

THE SPECIAL EMPHASES OF THE BUSINESS CREED

If it is important that the American business creed derives much of its character from the American cultural heritage, it is equally important to recognize that it is not wholly determined thereby. The variety of ideologies which flourish in twentieth-century America attest to the selectivity of the business creed among the materials which the heritage

[17] Halevy, *Growth of Philosophical Radicalism*, pp. 371–372.

supplied. Some of these ideologies differ from, or are even frankly hostile to, the business creed; yet they too are closely linked to the American heritage — although businessmen may hotly deny it. The vague doctrines of the two major political parties are good examples. The doctrines of the Republican party are not identical with those of the business creed, while the New and Fair Deal doctrines of the Democrats are in open conflict with them. There are also, within the general American tradition, ideologies linked to organizations such as churches or to status groupings such as the labor movement, and ideologies that are not based on any clearly defined organization or group such as the "liberal" ideology of many intellectuals.

The distinction between the business creed and other current American ideologies is one of substance, not merely of source. It is true that we have taken the source as our guiding criterion of what constitutes business ideology; but the body of ideology so delineated has proved remarkably uniform and has a discernible structure. It is an ideology which differs substantially from others on the American scene, as the policy recommendations it contains make quite obvious. Indeed, the last twenty years of ideological struggle in the United States have, to a striking degree, been fought out along the lines laid down by business and anti-business forces. It might be possible to interpret this struggle solely in terms of clashes of concrete interests between the various forces. But it is more easily explained in terms of opposition between broader ideological tendencies.

Despite conflicts, the business creed and other American ideologies share the same broad American inheritance and hold certain values and ideas in common. America has largely escaped the type of ideological dispute which has tortured some other Western nations. There has been no irreconcilable opposition of clerical Royalists and anti-clerical republicans as in France or bourgeois monarchists and revolutionary socialists as in Germany. The broad values which we have encountered in the business ideology and in the American cultural heritage have not been the values of one partisan class group but values to which all must at least make a show of obeisance. The symbols of democracy — political and religious freedom, equality of opportunity, and progress — have been accepted by all the major American ideologies. It is rather in the matter of emphasis that ideologies differ, and here their differences are great and conspicuous. The contrasts between the business ideology and the ideology of labor unions on such symbols as security, adventure, self-reliance, and productivity provide an obvious example. The business creed certainly does not assert that security is a bad thing, any more than labor unions deny the virtues of self-reliance.

Or, again, individualism and equal opportunity win general support throughout American society; but it is only the business ideology which lays special stress on the competitive struggle that these values imply. Religious and "intellectual liberal" ideologies tend to stress cooperation and collective responsibility. American society is unquestionably "moralistic" in many respects, but Americans have also fostered the doctrine that better conditions make better men and given less stress to moral character than does the business creed.[18] Practicality and straightforward simplicity are highly regarded throughout American society; but the business ideology puts exceptional stress on them and does battle with "experts" and "planners" who would deny them.

We see the business ideology then as solidly based in the American heritage but representing a special set of emphases within that heritage. Whether or not it can claim (as it is so frequently pleased to do) that it represents the dominant American heritage is a difficult question of judgment which we need not try to resolve here. There is certainly much to be said for the view that this has been a "business civilization," that our culture is the culture of capitalism, and that the Benthamite model of society which has dominated much of our thought has been elevated to its honored position by the very fact of business dominance. On the other hand, it may be argued, as Denis Brogan has done recently,[19] that the Coolidge view that the "business of the United States is Business" was a deviation from the main path of American history and the New Deal was a return to normalcy. These are difficult questions of historical judgment which we believe we can legitimately dodge. What we wish to stress is that businessmen are motivated to make special uses of the common heritage and that this poses problems which cannot be answered by historical or cultural analysis alone.

There remains one point which we must make by way of caution. In stressing that the business creed takes the American heritage and uses it selectively, we have used examples which may have suggested an oversimplified interpretation. We might dismiss the different respect for "security" shown by labor leaders and businessmen as an obvious result of the different interests of the parties involved. Some of the emphases of the creed can be explained as simply as this, but others cannot. For example, the stress on "competition" can hardly be a simple reflection of "interests" since competition is in fact a source of trouble and dangers to businessmen. We clearly need something more than a common-sense theory of interests to take care of examples of this sort, and much of the remainder of our work will be concerned with building and applying such a theory.

[18] If Riesman's thesis of the shifting balance between the "inner-directed" and the "other-directed" in our society is sound, the business creed would appear to represent one of two major value tendencies in contemporary American society.

[19] Denis Brogan, *Roosevelt and the New Deal* (London, 1952).

14

THE INSTITUTIONAL FRAMEWORK

AMERICAN PLURALISM

AMERICAN INSTITUTIONS both stimulate the production and wide dissemination of ideology by business leaders and influence its contents.[1]

The great number and diversity of our formally organized associations have been commented on by every observer of the American scene since De Tocqueville. The pluralism of American society has two aspects. First, different social functions usually involve different social structures — thus one set of institutions provides for formal schooling; another, largely separate, set of institutions for religious activity. Second, within each major functional area of organized social activity, there exist many separate organized groups, operating with a significant degree of independence and displaying a variety of goal values, modes of action, and "memberships." Not only are Church and State separate, but there exist many churches rather than one Church.[2]

Both aspects of pluralism contribute to the diffusion of social power. Because of functional separation, those who hold political power — political leaders and high government officials — are not identical with those who hold economic power — corporate executives, wealthy families, trade union leaders — who in turn are not identical with those who hold what might be called cultural power — religious and educational administrators,

---

[1] Both these topics are necessarily treated sketchily, since they are not central to the main theme of the study. Because of this summary treatment, there will be no attempt to document in detail each proposition offered, especially since the material is essentially familiar. The chapter draws on many expositions of the American scene; two which were used heavily were: V. O. Key, *Parties, Pressure Groups and Politics* (New York, 1952, 3rd ed.); and R. M. Williams, Jr., *American Society.*

[2] Currently there are at least 230 "religious bodies" in the United States operating through some 200,000 local congregations and claiming about 80,000,000 members, or roughly half the population. A dozen denominations with more than one million members, ranging from the 30,000,000 in the closely organized Roman Catholic Church to the little more than 1,000,000 in the loosely bound Congregational Churches, accounted for more than nine-tenths of the church members. *World Almanac,* 1953, p. 705.

leaders of the learned professions and of science, owners and managers of the mass media. Within the major functional areas there is a similar dispersion of power: federalism and the tripartite separation of powers in government; the large number of decentralized production units in the economic area,[3] as well as the separately organized power of labor unions;[4] religious pluralism.

The character and number of "voluntary organizations" — associations other than business enterprises and organs of government — are illustrated by a volume entitled *National Associations of the United States,* published by the U.S. Department of Commerce (1949). This lists the functions, headquarters locations, and officers of some 4,000 such associations. A sample of the list ranges from the U.S. Chamber of Commerce and the American Tariff League through the American Library Association, the Cooperative League of America, the National Council of Negro Women, and the American Legion to the American Kennel Club, the American Federation of the Physically Handicapped, and the National Association of (State) Insurance Commissioners. Classified functionally, the 4,000 include:

> 1,500 trade associations
>   300 other national associations of businessmen (such as the NAM)
>   500 professional associations
>   200 labor unions
>   100 women's associations
>   60 veterans' and patriotic societies
>   55 farmers' associations
>   50 Negro associations
>   50 associations of public officials
>   25 fraternal associations
>   100 recreational associations
> 1,000 other types

The groups organized primarily around economic interests number more than half the total, and most of these are business groups. As will appear below, these have a special significance in the production and dissemination of ideology.

[3] There were some 4 million business firms, 5.4 million farms, 600 thousand consumer cooperatives, and 250 thousand self-employed professionals operating in the U.S. economy in 1951. *Statistical Abstract,* 1952, pp. 441, 575, 907 for the first three figures; and C. Wright Mills, *White Collar* (New York, 1951), pp. 64–65, for the last.

[4] Themselves organized in a multitude of units. There were in 1948 about 60,000 union locals, organized into about 200 national unions. About half of these, in turn, were united in the A. F. of L.; 40 more in the C.I.O.; and 21 more loosely tied in the Railway Labor Executives Association. The remaining 30-odd national unions were independent of larger units. See *Directory of Labor Unions in the United States,* U.S. Dept. of Labor, 1948.

These associations facilitate and stimulate the production of ideology, primarily through interaction with one another; this is especially true of those organized around economic interests and the machinery of government. Their profusion also has certain minor consequences. One is the lack of any one generally accepted set of answers to social (or other) questions, which would inhibit ideological discussion, and, indeed, do much to make it unnecessary. Another is the tremendous stream of print and other public communication which the voluntary associations generate, both to unite their memberships and to "explain" themselves to the other groups and the public at large. Thus the national associations listed by the Department of Commerce typically spent between 10 and 20 per cent of their budgets on printing, and nearly every one produced some kind of newspaper, journal, or bulletin.[5] This stream of publication provides both the occasion for the generation of ideology and an important means of disseminating it.

POPULAR GOVERNMENT AND SOCIAL ACTION

There can be little social action in America without involving some level of government either positively or permissively. If this is most obvious in the economic sphere,[6] it is no less true of others, such as the regulation of marriage, the care of the sick, education, the maintenance of the old and disabled; but the major significance of government activity for the business ideology lies in the economic field. While the present extent and character of government activity, especially on the federal level, have been shaped by the New Deal, the Second World War, and the present international power struggle, the general importance of government action in the economic sphere extends back to the earliest history of the nation.[7]

At all levels in the United States, government is popular government:

[5] At a guess, based on the typical budget figures shown in the Commerce study, this might amount to some $40–80 millions per year for the associations listed therein.

[6] Even the sketchiest list of the major areas of economic activity in which the federal government intervenes significantly is very long. Thus, for example, F. H. Cook, *Principles of Business and the Federal Law* (New York, 1951) a recent elementary textbook contains fourteen chapters, each devoted to the discussion of one major federal statute regulating business directly. These include no discussion of taxation, monetary policy, tariffs, other controls on foreign trade, Federal lending activities, government procurement, to name but a few Federal activities of major impact on business.

[7] See, for example, E. L. Kirkland, *A History of American Economic Life* (New York, 1951), esp. chs. IV, VI, VII, X, XI, XIV, XVII; any other standard text on American economic history would make the same point. For detailed studies of the large role of state governments in economic activity in the period between the Revolutionary and Civil Wars, see L. Hartz, *Economic Policy and Democratic Thought; Pennsylvania, 1776–1860* (Cambridge, Mass., 1948) and Oscar and Mary Handlin, *Commonwealth, A Study of the Role of Government in the American Economy: Massachusetts, 1774–1861* (New York, 1947).

most executive officers and all legislators are elected at short and regular intervals. All government action is therefore undertaken with some attention to public opinion. Here, organized groups with particular interests, continuity, consistency of purpose and long memories are in a better position than the general public to influence the legislator. Every group which commands the resources to express itself, and every group which influences, may influence, or appears to influence voters gets a hearing.

In particular, the groups organized around economic interests necessarily make it part of their function, if not the major part, to represent their interests before the legislature, and, to a lesser extent, before other parts of the government. Even groups originally organized for technical rather than political purposes, for example, many trade and professional associations, become converted into agencies which try to influence legislation and government action because of the impact of government action on their interests.

Further, the constitutional separation of powers and the loose structure of the two major political parties gives a special importance to organized "pressure groups." Sometimes they are even referred to as a fourth branch of government.[8] The hearing procedure of the Congressional committees in which legislation is produced provides the formal machinery through which groups can express their views; these formal channels are not, of course, the only available or necessarily the most important ones. American political parties are loose coalitions of the representatives of various interests and viewpoints, rather than clearly differentiated parties of principle subject to central discipline. This further increases the importance of pressure group activity in the functioning of the government, since there need not be agreement between members of a party in Congress and members of the same party in the executive branch on any

---

[8] See E. P. Herring, *Group Representation before Congress* (Baltimore, 1929). Several recent studies have traced the pressures on the Congress involved in the enactment of specific pieces of legislation: S. K. Bailey, *Congress Makes a Law,* and Bertram Gross, *The Legislative Struggle* (New York, 1953), both on the Full Employment Action of 1946; Fred. W. Riggs, *Popular Pressures on Congress* (New York, 1950) on the repeal in 1943 of the Chinese Exclusion Act; and Earl Latham, *The Group Basis of Politics* (Ithaca, N. Y., 1952) on the proposed basing point legislation of 1950–51.

The discussion of the present chapter is in terms of the federal government; so are all the works cited above. The situation in the states and in local government is essentially similar. Yet there are sometimes cases at these levels in which some particular pressure group so far outweighs all others in strength that it can operate by direct negotiation with government, rather than by argument and persuasion addressed as much to the public as to the legislature. Crude oil producers in Texas and copper mining interests in Montana are or have been in this position. In such situations, the stimulus to ideology production simply disappears.

This realistic differential in business power is one reason that the ideology expresses preference for state and local over Federal government, but not the most important one. See below, Chapters 17, 18, where this point is further discussed.

particular piece of legislation. In fact, some disagreement is the rule; it is one of the functions of Congress to oppose the executive.[9]

Illustrations of the mechanics of the hearing process and of the variety and nature of groups which put opinions before Congress (and before the public, by reports of the hearings in the press, and by circulation of statements, etc.) are easily provided. Thus the hearings on the extension of price control [10] in June 1945 drew the testimony and statements of 156 witnesses, filling a volume of some 1,250 pages. Of the 156 witnesses, 58 were representatives of trade associations and business groups such as the National Association of Manufacturers, local Chambers of Commerce, etc.; 28 were businessmen speaking for their own businesses; 25 were members of Congress; 12 were representatives of national and local farm organizations; 12 were representatives of consumer organizations and women's clubs; 11 were representatives of unions; 10 executive officers from the Office of Price Administration or other departments dealing with stabilization problems; 2 represented professional associations. Again, the hearings later that year on the Full Employment Act of 1945[11] produced 1,163 pages of testimony, in which 59 witnesses were represented. Of these 26 were representatives of non-profit voluntary organizations, ranging from business groups like the National Association of Manufacturers, the U.S. Chamber of Commerce, and the Committee for Constitutional Government, to the Roman Catholic Diocese of San Antonio, the American Legion, the National Education Association, and the Young Women's Christian Association; fourteen congressmen and government officials; five union representatives; four corporation officials; four representatives of farm organizations; and six private citizens expressing personal views.

The organized group which makes its views known to Congress will find, as the above examples show, other organized groups offering conflicting views. They must impress Congress with the great weight of votes which lie behind their arguments, since in the last analysis, it is the "pres-

[9] On the influence of the machinery of government as a stimulus to the production of ideology, the contrast between the separation of powers and the parliamentary system is most instructive. In the latter the executive controls the majority of the legislature; both parties in the legislature are under strong discipline, and all but a few members owe their election to the party. It is the government departments which draft legislation in detail as well as in general; and interest groups exert their influence much more through direct negotiation with ministers and members than through public propaganda in committee hearings and outside. See W. I. Jennings, *Parliament* (Cambridge, 1936) and *Cabinet Government* (Cambridge, 1951, 2nd ed.).

[10] Hearings on H. J. Res. 101, Seventy-ninth Congress, 1st Session, House of Representatives, Committee on Banking and Currency, 1945 Stabilization Extension Act, June 1945.

[11] House of Representatives, Committee on Expenditures in the Executive Departments, Seventy-ninth Congress, 1st session. Hearings on HR 2202. November 1945.

sure" of votes to which Congressmen do respond. The widespread dissemination of ideology is designed to create such "grass roots pressure." The techniques of creating "grass roots pressure" are described in the General Interim Report of the 1950 House Select Committee on Lobbying as follows:[12]

If a descriptive label is needed, this new emphasis on pressure tactics might best be called "lobbying at the grass roots." What it amounts to is this: Rather than attempt to influence legislation directly, the pressure group seeks to create an appearance of broad public support for its aims, support which can be mobilized when the legislative situation demands it. The general premise underlying this effort is that if people are made to feel deeply enough about an issue they will translate their feelings into action which will affect that issue's resolution by the Congress. This expression of public opinion may be genuine in the sense that the views expressed are expressed spontaneously and with conviction. Or, on the other hand, such expression may be artificial and contrived. In either case, the process is one which has been deliberately and specifically instigated by one group or another having a particular stake in legislative issues.[13]

Under the law on the registration of lobbyists which the House Committee was inquiring into, 5 labor organizations, 4 farm organizations and 153 corporations reported their expenditures "to influence legislation" in the period January 1, 1947–May 31, 1950. Their reported expenditures totaled some $33.4 million, with the major part of the total reported by the corporations.[14] The most important type of expenditure was the donation of nearly $27 million by corporations to organizations producing and disseminating ideological material, such as the Foundation for Economic Education, the Committee for Constitutional Government, the National Association of Manufacturers, the United States Chamber of Commerce. Of the remainder, expenditures on advertising and printing were many times larger than expenditures on travel and Washington

[12] House of Representatives, Select Committee on Lobbying Activities. Eighty-first Congress, 2nd Session, 1950, H. Res. 298. See esp. pp. 23–51. See also Edgar Lane, "Some Lessons from Past Congressional Investigations of Lobbying," *Public Opinion Quarterly,* Spring 1950, which discusses Congressional investigations of 1913, 1929, and 1935. The 1913 investigation dealt chiefly with NAM activity in urging high tariffs; the later ones were broader.

[13] *General Interim Report,* p. 29.

[14] The figures were: corporations, $32.1 million; American Federation of Farm Bureaus, National Grange, National Council of Farm Cooperatives, and National Farmers Union, $0.9 million; A. F. of L., C.I.O., the Railway Brotherhoods, United Mine Workers, and the American Federation of Machinists, $0.55 million. The union and farm organization figures did not include the cost of publishing their respective newspapers; if these had been included, the respective totals for farm organizations and labor organizations might have reached some $2 million and $11 million. See H. Doc. 3137, *Expenditures of Corporations to Influence Legislation,* and H. Doc. 3238, *Expenditures of Farm and Labor Organizations to Influence Legislation,* both reports of the Select Committee on Lobbying, 81 Cong., 2nd Session.

offices or, in other words, the costs of dealing directly with legislators.[15]

Business executives, who desire to produce and circulate ideological material in order to influence legislation or for more general reasons, create a demand for the kind of services supplied by organizations such as the Foundation for Economic Education and the Committee for Constitutional Government.[16] Or, alternatively, existing organizations created for other purposes start to produce and disseminate ideology; examples of this are provided by many trade and professional associations.[17]

Apart from these specialized organizations, individual business firms themselves produce (or have produced by advertising agencies and public relations counsel) and disseminate ideology in the form of advertisements, house organs, pamphlets, and so forth. There are various advantages to both methods, and the balance of advantage for a particular firm may lie with either method, or, frequently, with some combination of both. The specialized organizations may be more efficient for a firm wishing to spend only a small amount on the production and distribution of ideology. An organization may provide an air of expertness and disinterestedness, of activity on behalf of the public good which a business firm speaking for itself may be unable to achieve. Finally, these organizations provide a significant degree of anonymity for the firms which support them.[18] On

[15] On the basis of the totals suggested in the preceding footnote which include the publication costs of union and farm organization newspapers, the ratio of expenditures for the general dissemination of ideas, excluding the donations to organizations engaged in this activity, to expenditures on maintaining direct contact with Congress (and other branches of the Government) is at least ten to one.

[16] Businesses are not the only creators of such groups; the Lobbying Committee reports reveal that the Bureau of Public Affairs of Washington, D.C., a research and propaganda organization, receives most of its support from the Brotherhood of Railroad Trainmen. See *General Interim Report*, p. 13. The contributions of the Brotherhood amounted to some $200,000 in the three-and-one-half-year period covered by the reports; see H. Doc. 3238, p. 30. But business is the major source of financial support for such groups, as the Committee reports clearly show.

[17] The American Medical Association provides a good example. See below, and also O. Garceau, *The Political Life of the American Medical Association* (Cambridge, 1941), pp. 96–103, 122–124. (This book is largely devoted to the internal politics of the AMA, not to its activities in national politics.)

The National Association of Manufacturers shows this pattern too. It was founded in 1895 chiefly to promote American foreign trade, although among its original principles were "to disseminate information among the public with respect to the principles of individual liberty and ownership of property; and to support legislation in furtherance of these principles; oppose contrary legislation." Quoted from the original statement of principles reproduced in the NAM pamphlet, *The Public Be Served* (n.d.). See also the address of Wallace F. Bennett, then president of the NAM before the American branch of the Newcomen Society in 1949, "The Very Human History of the NAM."

[18] Anonymity is important to some contributors, for it enables them to sponsor more extreme views than they are willing to admit publicly. In large corporations with wide stock ownership, the protection from stockholder criticism may be very important. In fact, the desire for anonymity in the expression of extreme views may offer a large part of the explanation for the success of promoters like E. A. Rumely,

the other hand, to the extent that businesses and businessmen rely on such specialized organizations for ideology production, they relinquish all but rather general control over what is said, and what media of distribution are used. This, and the existence of the natural channels for ideological expression provided by advertising in the mass media account for the fact that specialized organizations are only one of the sources of the stream of business ideology.[19]

Ideology which is produced to influence legislation may be confined to particular pieces of legislation or generalized. The American Medical Association spent some $1.5 million, raised by levies on its membership, in its successful 1949 campaign to defeat "socialized medicine" in the form of President Truman's proposed national health program.[20] On the other side, the Committee for Constitutional Government distributed 82,000,000 pieces of "literature" — pamphlets, books, reprints of speeches and articles, paid for the broadcast of more than 10,000 radio transcriptions, and took more than one set of full-page ads in 536 newspapers. This effort covered everything from arguing the advantages of the Taft-Hartley Act to pointing out the general failings of the New Deal; the latter exemplified by the distribution of 750,000 copies of John T. Flynn's *The Road Ahead*.[21]

THE MASS MEDIA AND ADVERTISING

American society is permeated by the media of mass communication — newspapers, the radio, television, and general circulation magazines. The media are all in the hands of commercial institutions, supported

---

Joseph Kamp, and Merwin K. Hart in getting financing for their organizations from large corporations. *General Interim Report,* esp. pp. 6–23.

[19] Some influence on decisions as to the allocation of business expenditures on ideology between the support of organizations for the purpose and advertising, pamphlet distribution, etc. directly by individual firms is probably exerted by the tax laws. Certain propaganda organizations such as the Foundation for Economic Education have received tax-exempt status, so that contributions to them are deductible as contributions for educational, charitable, or religious purposes. The law forbids deductions for any contributions to groups "seeking to influence legislation." On the other hand, advertisements proclaiming the benefits of free enterprise and the dangers of government can be treated, along with other advertising expenditures, as business expenses and deducted from gross income. It might be that any business which spent an unusually large sum in this kind of advertising would meet with an unfavorable ruling from the Bureau of Internal Revenue as to its legitimacy as a business expense; this apparently has not happened, but its possibility might stimulate some contributions. Dues to such organizations as the NAM and the Chamber of Commerce are business expenses. In any event, no clear uniform stimulus in one direction or the other is provided by the tax laws, but the decisions of individual firms may reflect the impact of taxation. *General Interim Report,* pp. 13–20.

[20] *General Interim Report,* p. 8.

[21] Lobbying Committee, H. Reps. 3239, p. 24, and 3024, p. 15, Eighty-first Congress, 2nd Session.

entirely or largely by advertising, and through advertising linked intimately
to the business world. In 1951, total advertising expenditures were some
$6.6 billions; the mass media accounted for about 60 per cent of the total;
billboards, direct-mail advertising, and other forms for the rest.[22] Nearly
one-half the subject matter of the mass media is advertising — less for
radio and television, more for magazines, just about half for newspapers.[23]
Complete analysis of the reach of the media is difficult, but various partial
figures are available. In 1952, the 1,773 English language daily newspapers
in the United States had a daily circulation of 54,000,000;[24] In 1942, it
was estimated that 95 per cent of urban families read daily newspapers.[25]
At the same time, it was estimated that 30,000,000 families listened to
radios for an average of five hours per day; this is 85 per cent of the
number of all families in the United States at the time.[26] The present proportion of families listening to radio is probably not smaller, and television
has come into the picture. In January 1951, it was estimated that 35 per
cent of the families in United States owned television receivers; the present
figure is probably nearly 50 per cent.[27] Circulation of 700 magazines
carrying advertising was some 140,000,000 copies per issue in 1942.[28]

The mass media have created an audience and a technique for reaching
it. The intimate connection of the media with advertising has created a
channel from business to this audience. The advertising industry exists to
utilize this channel; it has a reservoir of personnel skilled in the techniques
of mass communication and mass appeal.[29] Thus business finds a familiar means at hand through which it can disseminate the business creed:
the "selling of ideas" could naturally use the same techniques and means
as those already made familiar by the selling of goods. Advertisements
in newspapers and general circulation magazines, on billboards and post-
ers, "talks" on the radio such as those of W. J. Cameron and Henry
Taylor are the media through which the business creed achieves its
widest audience. "Literature" distributed by organizations specializing in
the production and distribution of business ideology usually reaches a
relatively small audience; the speeches and books of business leaders an

[22] *Editor and Publisher*, Jan. 12, 1952.

[23] See Committee on the Freedom of the Press, *A Free and Responsible Press*
(Chicago 1947), p. 64. Also A. M. Lee, *The Daily Newspaper in America* (New
York, 1937), pp. 324–325.

[24] *Editor and Publisher, International Yearbook 1952*, p. 17.

[25] P. F. Lazarsfeld, "The Daily Newspaper and Its Competitors," *Annals of the
American Academy of Political and Social Science*, January 1942. Lazarsfeld estimated that the average time spent reading the newspaper was fifteen to forty-five
minutes per day.

[26] Lazarsfeld, "Daily Newspaper," p. 33.

[27] *Printers Ink*, Jan. 18, 1952, p. 246.

[28] Lazarsfeld, "Daily Newspaper," p. 33.

[29] In 1948 there were some 3,300 advertising agencies in the United States with
some 38,000 employees, *Census of Business*, VI: 109 (1948).

even smaller one. It is the mass media which are the most important carriers of the business creed in terms of size of audience.[30]

The use of advertising to disseminate business ideology grew very rapidly during World War II, although it did exist beforehand.[31] The very high rate of excess profits taxation made the marginal expenditure of a dollar on advertising nearly costless to the firm. At the same time, many firms had no products to sell in the civilian market. With various motives — stimulating patriotic sentiment, purchasing postwar good will, keeping their names before the public, going through the accustomed motions, responding to the pressures created by advertising departments and advertising agencies — firms advertised themselves as institutions, their contributions to war production, the benefits to be expected when industry once more could turn to peaceful pursuits and the American Way of Life.[32] In addition to this burst of ideological advertising by

[30] The smaller audiences of the specialized organizations are undoubtedly selected with a view to their role in influencing the opinions of others.

[31] Examples of advertisements which were almost entirely ideological were found frequently by 1937 in such journals as *Fortune, Business Week,* and the *Saturday Evening Post.* Thus, in *Fortune,* January 1937, p. 37, appears an advertisement of the Association of American Railroads with a high ideological content: progress, service, high payrolls, no subsidies, high tax payments. The *Saturday Evening Post,* Feb. 13, 1937, pp. 29–30 carries a General Motors advertisement, "Who Serves Progress Serves America," occupying a double page spread in color, and making it clear that it is Industry which is serving progress. The prominence of ideological themes in advertisements more clearly devoted to advancing the advertisers' sales is noticeable much earlier. In the *Saturday Evening Post,* March 5, 1927, N. W. Ayer and Sons (p. 109) and the Pennsylvania Railroad (p. 79) point to the "service" which advertising and railroads, respectively, give to the general community. As long ago as 1918, an advertisement for Goodyear Tires appearing in the *Saturday Evening Post* (Feb. 9, 1918, pp. 50–51) sounded the service theme; at this time, it was unusual. An examination of four earlier issues of the *Post* — April 13 and Sept. 31, 1907, Oct. 18 and Nov. 8, 1913 shows no single example of this or other ideological themes in the advertising: it was all strictly business, addressed to persuading consumers of the virtues of particular products.

[32] A look at any issue of a general circulation magazine during the war period provides a plethora of illustrations. Thus *Time* shows the postwar wonder theme displayed in advertisements by Radio Corporation of America (Jan. 3, 1944, p. 38), Dow Chemical Company (p. 9), and Continental Can Company (inside cover). The frequently repeated statement of war service, sometimes coupled with emphasis on the fact that private industry performed the service, is exemplified by the Standard Oil of New Jersey advertisement (Jan. 3, 1944, pp. 74–75), and the Irving Trust Company story of how "Bank Credit Cushions a Paratroop Landing" (p. 77). The American Way is extolled by Nash-Kelvinator (inside front cover), General Motors (Mar. 20, p. 41), Bryant Chucking Grinder Company (Feb. 14, p. 97), and Rustless Iron and Steel Company (Mar. 6, p. 93). Warner & Swasey (*Business Week,* Jan. 22, 1944, inside front cover) contributes an example of the stimulation of patriotic sentiment without any specific business ideological content.

The double-page color spread of Pan American World Airways (*Time,* Jan. 10, 1944, pp. 52–53), one of a series entitled "Forum of the Future," offers an example of ideological advertising on material far removed from the business creed — a statement by Archbishop Stritch of Chicago on the importance of religion and family life as the foundations of society in the postwar world. This is an extreme case of the nonbusiness motivation of much wartime advertising.

individual firms, a systematic campaign of advertising to promote the war effort was developed by the War Advertising Council, an association of advertising agency executives. This body arranged for the donation of space by advertisers and the preparation of advertisements by member agencies urging readers to purchase war bonds, to buy fewer consumer goods, to salvage waste and scrap, etc.[33]

The Council extended its activities into peacetime, and it now functions as the Advertising Council. Most of its efforts are devoted to the Red Cross, National Heart Week, the need for more expenditures on, and more widespread citizen concern with, public schools, and similar topics which are not specifically business ideology. But it sponsors one continuing advertising campaign devoted to the business creed: the "Miracle of America" series. The advertisements of this series portray American productivity and America's high standard of living, identify them as the achievements of freedom and cooperation, and emphasize that by "pulling together," continued progress can be ensured.[34]

Nowadays, then, there are many more advertisements devoted wholly to ideology than was the case fifteen years ago. In addition, ordinary advertisements devote more space to the merits of the advertiser and the merits of the system, and relatively less space to expounding the virtues of particular products. Continued high corporate taxes may provide a partial explanation of the persistence of this type of advertising; so may the increased pressure of counter-ideology as compared with the prewar situation. But an important explanatory factor is simply the desire of business to continue to utilize this technique, which was "discovered," so to speak, during the war.

Advertising is not the only vehicle of business ideology. In newspapers and magazines, much of the editorial material also repeats the business creed. This is true of editorials proper, of feature-writing and syndicated columns, and of most of the material in the financial sections of the daily press other than straight news. This is largely due to the fact that the mass media are in the hands of big business, run by businessmen subject to the same ideology-producing forces as other businessmen, and thus, naturally, exponents of the same ideology. The point that the press is a big business

[33] See T. S. Repplier, "Advertising Dons Long Pants," *Public Opinion Quarterly,* Fall 1945, for an account of the genesis and activities of the Council. He estimates that it used $1 billion worth of advertising during the war.

An example of a Council advertisement appears in *Time,* Jan. 3, 1944, p. 94.

[34] An Advertising Council offering on the theme of "Pulling Together" appears on p. 116 of the *Saturday Evening Post,* Nov. 6, 1948; it is typical of the series. We have quoted this and other releases above.

The postwar history of the Council is discussed by J. A. R. Pimlott, "Public Service Advertising," in *Public Opinion Quarterly,* Summer 1948. For the year ending February 1947, Council advertising amounted to $100 million, a considerably lower volume than that maintained during the war.

is put clearly and succinctly by the Commission on the Freedom of the Press:

> The agencies of mass communication are big business, and their owners are big businessmen. The American consumers just prior to the war (World War II) paid the 40,000 mass communications establishments nearly 2.5 billion dollars for their services, representing one dollar out of every twenty-seven spent that year for all goods and services. The press is a large employer of labor. With its total wage and salary bill in the same year nearly a billion dollars, it provided 4 per cent of the country's total salary and wage expenditures. The newspapers alone have more than 150,000 employees. The press is connected with other big business through the advertising of these businesses, upon which it depends for the major part of its revenue. The owners of the press, like the owners of other big businesses, are bank directors, bank borrowers, and heavy taxpayers in the upper brackets.[35]

Since most of the non-advertising content of radio and television is entertainment, business ideology other than advertising is not so important in these media. It is, of course, not entirely absent: witness some radio commentators, and the Ford Hour talks of W. J. Cameron.

That the agencies of communication are themselves private enterprises in the United States excites little comment; it is generally accepted as a natural state of affairs. But, of course, it would be considered highly unnatural in some other countries. Neither the British radio, controlled by a government corporation, nor the French press, with newspapers linked to and subsidized by various political parties, presents a similar picture.

COUNTER-IDEOLOGIES

Obviously enough, competing ideologies influence the formulation and propagation of the business creed. The major competitor of the business creed in recent years has been what may be termed the New-Deal-trade-union ideology. This is a rather less well-integrated system of beliefs than the business creed; indeed the New Deal and trade-union parts of it might for some purposes be separated and treated as two ideologies, resembling each other, but distinct. Their major themes are the necessity of strong government regulation and supplementation of business activity in a variety of ways, and the desirability of an egalitarian, consumption-oriented, high-wage, low-profit society.

New-Deal-trade-union ideology is disseminated in many ways, although

---

[35] *Free and Responsible Press,* p. 59. The quotation is from a section entitled "The bias of owners." This, and the following section entitled "Advertising and sales talk" are pertinent to the present section of this chapter, though needless to say they are addressed to an entirely different context of problems.

The quotation cited is followed by quotations making the same point from three important figures in American journalism: William Allen White, Virginius Dabney, and Erwin D. Canham.

it gets little representation in the mass media. Its most important channel is directly through trade union activity to union members, of whom there are currently some 16,000,000.[36] A more revealing measure of trade union strength is given by the following estimates: (1) in 1945, 31 per cent of the United States population twenty-one years or older was associated with labor unions by membership or by belonging to the families of members; (2) 33 per cent of the male wage and salary workers in cities (2,500 population or more) were union members.[37] These people receive trade-union ideology partly by word of mouth and partly through the union press. There are some 650 weekly and 250 monthly labor papers, although there are no dailies. Their readership is variously estimated at 20 to 30 millions, but this figure includes duplications, readers of more than one paper.[38]

In addition to reaching their own members, the unions, especially the two national federations — A. F. of L. and C. I. O. — reach the general public. They do this in part through speeches and statements by their leaders, in part through the activities of their political affiliates — Labor's League for Political Action (A. F. of L.) and the C. I. O. Political Action Committee. These operate in the same way as other political pressure groups, whose activities were sketched above. Both currently sponsor radio news commentators.

During the period when the Democratic Party held national office (1932–1952) the speeches and public statements of the President and of many Cabinet officers were an important medium for the propagation of New Deal ideology, and the federal government bureaucracy was an important organ for formulating it. At present, certain Senators and Congressmen play a continuing part in disseminating the ideology of the New Deal, but their role is relatively minor.

Certain small political groups, active mostly among professionals, small businessmen, and ethnic minorities in large cities play some part in formulating and spreading New Deal ideology: the Americans for Democratic Action, and the Liberal Party in New York are examples of two currently important groups of this type. Also, a few journals of small circulation such as the *Reporter,* the *Nation,* and the *New Republic,* read to a large extent by the same social groups, play a similar role.

The existence of a counter-ideology which gets the hearing of a very large public and is sponsored by organized groups with considerable politi-

---

[36] *Handbook of Labor Statistics,* 1952.

[37] See C. W. Mills and T. E. Anderson, in *The House of Labor,* edited by J. B. S. Hardman and M. F. Neufeld (New York, 1951), ch. 3, "People in Unions." The first of these estimates was based on a National Opinion Research Center Survey of a national sample of 2,500 people twenty-one years of age and over.

[38] See M. H. Hedges, "Why a Labor Press," and H. C. Fleisher, "The Union Press," in Hardman and Neufeld, *House of Labor.*

cal and economic power both stimulates the propagation of business ideology and shapes it to meet the arguments of trade unionists and New Dealers. The first kind of response is exemplified by the recent growth of "employee education programs" in business.[39] These programs, which appear under various names, are efforts to teach the business creed directly to their employees by firms, through the use of pamphlets, lectures, films, company meetings, and so on. The programs have grown to the point where certain firms specialize in providing them: *Fortune* found nearly 100 such firms in New York City alone.[40] Examples of the second response have already appeared above; in Chapter 6 we showed that the assertions of employer "rights" in the business creed have been made in direct opposition to employee "rights" which unions claim.

The New Deal and the present strength of organized labor are both recent phenomena. The second, in fact, has come about largely as a result of the first. In the period before the 1930's, no equally important, equally widespread counter-ideology with adherents of great political strength existed.[41] But, throughout this period, and into the present, socialism in all its variants, Marxian and non-Marxian, democratic and revolutionary, has served as an important counter-ideology to the business creed. This is remarkable in view of the small direct influence of socialist thought and

[39] Much information on these programs is contained in an unpublished student paper prepared for a course given by one of the authors at Harvard: Otto Lerbinger, "An Approach for the Evaluation of Economic Education," January 1952.

[40] *Fortune*, July 1951, pp. 84–86.

See also C. W. McKee and H. G. Moulton, *A Survey of Economic Education* (Washington: 1951). This survey gives no basis for an estimate of the global magnitude of employee education programs; but it does provide certain fragmentary figures. It lists among "educational agencies" other than schools the following, with estimates of their annual budgets:

Advertising Council, Economic Systems Program	No budget figure
American Viewpoint Inc.	$50 thousand
(1945–50, distributed 6 million pamphlets)	
American Heritage Foundation	No budget figure
Public Relations Society of America, Inc.	$60 thousand
Committee for Constitutional Government	$532 thousand
Federal Council of Churches	No budget figure
National Protestant Council on Higher Education	No budget figure
American Economic Foundation	No budget figure
Foundation for Economic Education	$350 thousand
Americans for Competitive Enterprise, Inc.	$50 thousand
Joint Council for Economic Education	No budget figure

The authors surveyed by mailed questionnaire 2,500 business firms; 280 answered and said that they engaged in some kind of economic education program for their employees. The authors report (p. 47) numerous firms as spending $100,000 to $500,000 per year on such programs.

[41] This was true for at least the preceding sixty years. In the eighties and nineties, agrarian populism was the most significant competitor of the business creed, and many of the creed's dogmas on money and foreign trade still bear the marks of that struggle. See Solon Buck, *The Granger Movement* (Cambridge, Mass., 1913), and John Hicks, *The Populist Revolt* (Minneapolis, Minn., 1933).

socialist politics in the United States, at least until after World War II, when Marxist communism became, because of Russian foreign policy, a real force in American life. But long before it presented the world in terms of a life and death struggle between "socialism" and "free enterprise" (a view which receives equally strong and frequent expression in Pravda and in the publications of the National Association of Manufacturers) the business creed directed many of its arguments against the evils of socialism.[42] Today, of course, the symbol of communism appears constantly in the business creed, as do those of socialism and the welfare state.

The persistent use of socialist ideology as a negative symbol in the business creed, irrespective of its actual influence as a counter-ideology in the United States, is due to its intrinsic properties. First, it is a "foreign ideology"; this is especially true of Marxian variants. Second, it is in some sense a polar ideology to the business creed: its ultimate values — hedonism, materialism, efficiency, activity — are much the same but the part it assigns to the businessman and to business institutions is diametrically opposed. It is therefore useful as a dialectical punching bag, while it can be made into a strong negative symbol because it is foreign. Any ideology which simply ignored the values enthroned in the business creed and emphasized, say, passivity, equanimity, the repression of desire, and alienation from the material world could hardly fulfill the same function no matter how alien it was.

Both Marxist and New-Deal-trade-union ideologies are strongly associated with "intellectuals." Professional academicians, civil servants with professional training, and other professionals have been among the leading spokesmen for these ideologies in the United States. This in itself has had an important influence on the business creed, quite apart from the specific content of the ideologies. The learned professions have a socially recognized authority in ideological realms which businessmen lack. This type of intellectual authority is frequently challenged in the business creed, where it is claimed that the businessman's practical wisdom is superior to the academician's unworldly theorizing.[43]

INSTITUTIONS AND THE CONTENT OF THE CREED

The institutional arrangements which stimulate the production of ideology, and provide for its propagation also shape its content in varying ways. The deeper themes of the creed reflect the fundamental strains in the business role in our society; but the particular selection of topics, the language in which these topics are treated, and the relative importance of extended argument or use of symbols show the impact of the institutional factors we have just examined.

[42] Compare NAM pamphlet cited in Chapter 19 below.
[43] This point is discussed at some length below, in Chapters 16 and 17.

For example, a substantial part of the ideological discussion of labor markets and unions takes the form of an assertion of managerial "rights" as opposed to "rights" asserted by trade-union ideology. The ideological defense of profits, with its elaborate discussion of the "proper" size of profits is shaped both by the attack on profits in the New-Deal-trade-union ideology, and by taxation and other government regulation of profits. The "right" level of profit taxation must be determined by ideological discussion in our kind of government. The same can be said of any major decision of government policy; the particular arguments about undesirable government intervention which fill the literature of the creed take their specific form from the activity of government in imposing price-control, or supporting agricultural prices, or building power dams.

The language and symbolism in which the creed is expressed, especially in its more popular versions, bears the heavy impress of the techniques of advertising. The symbolism used to portray the relations between big and small business, the identification of corporate ownership with "plain people," the manipulation of profits to sales ratios and the use of the questionnaire, all show the application of the techniques of selling commodities to the propaganda of the creed.[44]

PREVALENCE OF THE BUSINESS CREED

In simple terms of the volume and variety of statement, it is clear that the business creed enjoys a far wider dissemination than its chief rival — the New-Deal-trade-union ideology. This advantage arises from the intimate association of business with advertising and the interdependence of advertising and the mass media. Every general medium of mass communication carries a heavy freight of business ideology; the representatives of opposing creeds are limited to more specialized channels, except to the extent that public statements made by political and union leaders are in the news. To what extent the business ideology is believed by the public compared to other creeds is another question, and one we cannot go into here.

[44] Much of this has been discussed above, especially in Chapters 3 and 4.

An amusing and revealing satirization of these techniques appears in William H. Whyte, *Is Anybody Listening?* (New York, 1952), esp. pp. 30–33 and the ill. on p. 31.

The illustration shows a street scene outside a small-town corner drugstore, with the druggist and "a plain guy, name of Joe Smith." The rest of the text is filled with the rambling reflections of Joe and Doc Hibbard on the state of the socio-economic world. The picture bears the title "Bull Session," and the text ends with the slogan, "Everything is everybody's job." Whyte observes that when the "ad" appeared in *Fortune*, one company asked for 1,000 reprints because it was "such a magnificent expression of real Americanism." This shows not so much that the company executives lacked a sense of humor, as that the subject matter of the ideology is serious business, not to be trifled with.

15

STRAINS AND IDEOLOGY

BOTH OUR CULTURAL HERITAGE and our institutions have influenced the business ideology; but they alone do not explain its specific
form and content. Something more is needed — a reason why the business
ideology differs from others within the same cultural heritage and institutional framework.

THE SELF-INTEREST THEORY

The most common explanation put forward is that businessmen say
what they do out of self-interest. As their interests differ from those of
other groups within the society, so their ideology differs. Accordingly, the
businessman stresses self-reliance, the necessity of free enterprise, and the
dangers of the welfare state because it is in his interest to do so. This theory
is strong in the Marxist tradition, but many who are not Marxists subscribe to it.[1]

The difficulty with this theory lies in the meaning of the word "interests"; either the term is clearly defined, in which case the theory becomes
patently inadequate, or the term is stretched to cover every contingency,
so that the theory loses all meaning. Why do businessmen so fiercely
oppose deficit financing on the part of the government? Such opposition
cannot be the result of a rational calculation of their tangible interests. In
the short run many businesses (for example, construction firms) stand to
gain from this policy. It is possible that in the long run, business interests
may be injured by deficit financing, but it is certainly not inevitable. In
any particular instance it is exceedingly difficult if not impossible to assess
the remote consequences of deficit financing. And so there is no rational
basis for the simplicity and certainty of business opposition. If we stick to
a theory of rational self-interest we can only dismiss examples such as this

---

[1] The authors have repeatedly encountered it in connection with this project.
To many persons, often of acute and sophisticated intellect, the business ideology was
so obviously a reflection of businessmen's interests that they could conceive no
problem in accounting for its content.

as evidence of ignorance or error.[2] But this is obviously unsatisfactory.

A broadening of the concept of "interests" to take into account non-rational action is of course possible. The problem is to do it in some reasonably clear and systematic way. We take it as axiomatic that what businessmen say is somehow related to their motivations and hence that, in a very diffuse sense, they are speaking in their own "interest." To use the term "interest" in such a broad way, however, is to deprive it of all special character and an "interest theory" becomes little more than the bald proposition that ideologies are motivated.

The clearest way to give the theory a definite character is to equate interests with objective, private economic advantage.[3] Formulated in this way, the interest theory, as our deficit financing example shows, simply cannot account for a considerable part of the business ideology.[4]

---

[2] It is very important to keep a clear distinction between the point of view of the actor and the point of view of the observer. The businessman may think he is acting in his own interests (or in certain cases, against his own interests) without it being possible for an observer to decide whether he is or not. We are here concerned with the point of view of the observer and the types of theoretical apparatus he may bring to his observations. Compare the classic discussions of Pareto, *The Mind and Society* (New York, 1935), vol. 1; and Talcott Parsons, *The Structure of Social Action* (New York, 1937).

[3] Some people include power considerations also on the ground that they are objectively verifiable. Compare the efforts of W. E. Hutt, *Economists and the Public* (London, 1936), to utilize Briffault's conception of "power-thought."

[4] Critiques of "interest" theories have seldom approached the subject with clarity and generality. The prevalence of these theories is a complicated subject in intellectual history. It has much to do with the peculiarities of the utilitarian framework of thought, in which the "interests" of individuals were set over against the common interests. (To a modern sociologist, imbued with the conception that action follows institutionalized patterns, opposition of individual and common interests has only a very limited relevance or is thoroughly unsound). The Marxian theory has stimulated some of the better critiques; see H. De Man, *Psychology of Socialism* (New York, 1927), ch. I; and Richard Behrendt, *Politischer Aktivismus* (Leipsig, 1932), pp. 65–95. Mannheim's famous analysis of ideology is thin on the motivational side. While Mannheim was very critical of the Marxian theory of ideology he essentially took over its motivational analysis (or lack thereof). "Vulgar" Marxism has shown a persisting tendency to interpret ideology as rational action in terms of "interests," but the more sophisticated tradition is at once more subtle and more vague. The famous view that ideas are determined by class position does not in itself supply an analysis of the psychological mechanisms whereby ideas are acquired and believed. By its assumption that "class position" could be defined in terms of "objective conditions," the Marxist theory can be regarded in some sense as an "interest" theory of ideology but it is not, strictly speaking, a theory which assumes rational orientation in terms of perceived interests. The *Wissenssoziologie* which has flourished in Germany in the twentieth century has been strongly influenced by the Marxist tradition (and in part sprung from common roots) and it has largely shared this weakness of motivational analysis. The basic viewpoint of this tradition, namely that the motivation of ideological belief must be sought in reference to social status, is now certainly axiomatic but it needs to be integrated with the advances in sociology and psychology which permit a more substantive and explicit analysis of motivation. An admirable account of the theoretical developments here very briefly and inadequately discussed may be found in the papers of Merton, *Social Theory*, chs. VIII, IX. See also Sutton, *The Radical Marxist*, ch. 2.

STRAINS AND IDEOLOGY: THE THEORY OUTLINED

Before applying our own theory to the business ideology, it may be well to formulate it in general terms — to indicate the part played by ideologies in individual and social life. The general framework of our theory can be stated in terms of the following propositions:

(1) By far the greater part of human action is performed unreflectively. We do not stop to think how we should walk, wash our hands, or greet our friends. In contrast to older, more rationalistic theories of human action, modern thought tends to stress the unreflective, automatic course of most human action. There may very well be explicit ideas which are on occasion brought to bear in interpreting and justifying action, but they are not persistently resorted to in the normal course of action. Far from being the reflection of consistent and regularly applied systems of ideas, ordinary human action appears inevitably to proceed with the "carelessness and inattention" which Hume advocated as the only remedy for man's estate.

The most dramatic evidence that inattention is essential to normal human action appears in psychopathology. It is precisely a self-conscious attention to matters ordinarily ignored that characterizes many of the bizarre phenomena known as obsessions and compulsions. For example, Janet has reported the case of a young girl who was always aware of the number of fingers with which she touched an object, and bound herself to certain rules which made touching a very complicated venture.[5] Still other cases display long deliberation and indecision over matters which are ordinarily passed over without the effort of conscious choice.

If the psychoneurotic reminds us that we execute most daily actions without reflection, more normal but exceptional persons remind us of our inattention to problems of the society in which we live. Men like André Gide who question the propriety of accepting advantages of birth trouble themselves about a problem which could trouble many people but rarely does. Our society is one with very marked egalitarian values and much ideology in support thereof. Still it does not demand any radical denials of the ties of kinship, even though these ties inevitably lead to differential advantages which are difficult to justify. Most parents who give financial support to their children's education are not seriously and persistently troubled by moral issues, nor are the children forced to explicit decision about the propriety of having their tuition paid. The familiar figure of the radical born in comfortable surroundings who is troubled by his "unfair"

---

[5] P. Janet and F. Raymond, *Les Obsessions et la Psychasthènie* (Paris, 1903–8), vol. II, p. 324. (Another patient of Janet's insisted on jumping rather than walking, allegedly because he was conscious of an asymmetry of sensations in the more normal form of locomotion.)

advantage is a reminder, by exception, that most of the infinite gradations of kin-determined advantage do not call forth explicit justification.

(2) The roots of this normal unreflectiveness lie in the very nature of societies and the way in which they mold the personalities of their members. No society simply presents its members with a random set of choices of possible behavior; it indicates the approved ways, and rewards or punishes as these are adopted or rejected. The molding of human behavior is so definite, even in societies like our own, that many alternative ways of doing things remain unconceived or stoutly rejected as "unnatural." (That the study of cultural anthropology has been so illuminating is an index of the feebleness of imaginations cramped by our special cultural traditions.) Explicit discussion on social action springs from the contemplation of alternatives. In the nature of human socialization, the great mass of possible questions for discussion are, as it were, resolved in advance, and the solutions are internalized to become working parts of personality.

(3) Fortunately or unfortunately, societies and personalities are never completely free from difficulties and disturbances. Any society must cope with a variety of functional problems. It must provide means for dealing with the natural environment, for allocating goods and services among its members, for maintaining order, etc.[6] Complete success in handling these problems is never attained. Weather conditions, health matters, external military threats, economic conditions, and many other sources give rise (either chronically or occasionally) to problems which are only imperfectly manageable. The classic antinomies of freedom and security, of efficiency and humane flexibility also remind us that meeting one problem effectively may weaken a society's capacity to meet others. Individuals living in societies experience these imperfections as *strains;* they must at times face situations where the expectations they have learned to view as legitimate are thwarted, or where they must wrestle with conflicting demands. In addition to the difficulties of the immediate, contemporary situation, we know that human personalities are apt to carry a heavy freight of unresolved problems arising in earlier experiences. Like societies, personalities are *systems* but systems with persisting imperfections which add to the burden of strains experienced at any given time.

(4) Strains then are "normal" in any society. Situations regularly arise in which the individual must work out solutions in the face of difficult or conflicting demands. It is at these points that he must think explicitly about the courses of action he may take, and hence looks for guiding principles which can help his decisions. If the fundamental pattern of human action is unreflective conformity with the cultural tradition, there is nevertheless

⁶ See D. F. Aberle, *et al.,* "The Functional Prerequisites of a Society," *Ethics,* January 1950, pp. 100–111.

a general need for bodies of explicit ideas which may be used when strain arises.

While we tend to exaggerate the importance of conscious thought in action (simply because it is there that our attention focuses), we must not go to the opposite extreme. No society could function effectively without some means of guiding conscious decisions, and in a society like ours they assume exceptional importance. One of the critical functions of modern governments is precisely in this area; much of any national society runs by itself but, in those matters where conscious manipulation is required, the government acts as an agency diagnosing the problems and investigating alternative solutions to them. In some cases, explicit ideas have a clear empirical reference and help directly in the solution of well-defined empirical problems; in other cases they have no such reference but they still play an important part in the functioning of societies. Older rationalistic views which damned empirically unfounded ideas as prejudice or error, have now given way to a better understanding of their functional significance, particularly in the study of myths and religious systems.[7]

(5) The strains to which the members of a particular society are subject do not simply vary at random; they are patterned. Human behavior in social systems is patterned in a body of institutions and role, and strains are patterned accordingly. The difficulties which, say, adult women experience in fulfilling their roles in our society vary greatly, depending on individual experience. Yet, there are certain built-in strains arising from a conflict between our universalistic ethics and educational system on the one hand, and our kinship system on the other. The "career-marriage" problem represents a patterned strain in the role of the adult female. Any role in a social system is likely to involve patterned strains of greater or lesser severity.

(6) The reactions to a given strain are not entirely random. There is some patterned linkage between strains and reactions. It is true that reactions to strain in human personalities may be of the most varied sorts, and may lead to manifestations very distant from the seats of trouble. Strains can lead in various ways to a bewildering array of psychosomatic and neurotic symptoms, as well as to less spectacular character disorders, crotchets, idiosyncrasies, etc. Emotional energy generated in one context can become displaced and symbolically linked to other activities, functions, or contexts. Because of this mobility, the linkage of strains and reactions is bound to be loose.

(7) Ideology is a patterned reaction to the patterned strains of a social

---

[7] C. Malinowski, *Myth in Primitive Psychology* (New York, 1926); Kluckhohn, "Myth and Ritual," *Harvard Theological Review* 35: 45–79 (1942); and, classically, Durkheim, *Elementary Forms of the Religious Life* (Glencoe, Ill., 1947).

role. We have seen above that explicit thought about action is typically a response to conflict. Where a role involves patterns of conflicting demands, the occupants of that role may respond by elaborating a system of ideas and symbols, which in part may serve as a guide to action, but chiefly has broader and more direct functions as a response to strain.[8]

The fundamental relation we consider, then, is one between strains and ideology. But the links between them are by no means simple: a one-to-one correspondence between particular strains and specific ideological content is not to be expected. First, the elaboration of ideology is not the individual's only response to strain; many non-ideological responses — from nail-chewing to alcoholism — are possible. Second, the general mode of relation between strain and ideology is that of symbolization: the ideology is a symbolic outlet for the emotional energy which the strain creates. As we have remarked, symbol systems in general are multiply-determined, more than one symbol can refer to a given strain, and a particular symbol may be used in response to more than one strain. While the relations between strains and the content of ideology are not simple, neither are they merely chaotic. The objects on which reactions ultimately settle may be only symbolically related to their origins, but presumably not just anything is appropriate as a symbol. A hostility to "capitalists" is engendered by certain strains in our society, and the choice of capitalist as a symbol is not just a random choice. It is conditioned on the one side by something in the nature of the underlying strains and on the other by the susceptibility of business executives to symbolic treatment.

(8) The business role is filled by many individuals of varying personalities. Individual businessmen will vary widely in their quantitative reactions to the strain-producing situations in their role. What might overwhelm some, will appear as exciting stimuli to others. But the patterned strains of the role, arising from basic conflicts in it which all businessmen feel to some degree, can be expected to show strong qualitative uniformities; and correspondingly the ideological reactions can be expected to be qualitatively similar.

---

[8] We here repeat a cautionary remark which appeared in the first chapter. We focus on the significance of ideas in the emotional adjustment of personalities because we wish to understand why certain ideas are expressed, repeatedly and vehemently. The fact that holding a particular belief may serve to ease emotional strains for the person who holds it, in itself carries no implications for the validity or invalidity of the belief. The popular reaction to stress on the psychological function of belief — that it implies casting doubt on its validity — nonetheless contains some truth. Where a particular belief is so clearly dictated by objective circumstances that any other would be spectacularly wrong, there is little interest in psychological analyses. But this is a far cry from regarding all motivational analysis as radical debunking of discussion of complex social issues. The views of individuals on the income tax may be profitably analyzed in terms of strains in their personalities without the implication that all discussion of the level of the income tax is sound and fury which might better be dispensed with.

In addition to the patterning of behavior imposed by particular role definitions in a society there is the further patterning of personalities due to a common cultural tradition. American businessmen come to their roles with personality structures susceptible to certain general types of strain and prepared for coping with role demands in particular ways. It seems very plausible that Americans, Frenchmen, or Germans when they become businessmen will react in ways which are not simply a consequence of national differences in business organization as such, but in part at least because they are Americans, Frenchmen, or Germans. There is here obviously another reason to expect patterning of strains and reactions and hence common tendencies to ideological reaction.

Role-patterned strains are not, of course, the only problems in the personalities of individual businessmen. Many other problems may lie deeper, below the level of conscious worries and conflicts. In this respect, as in others, the personalities of individual businessmen may be presumed to vary widely. Characterizations of the personalities of business executives[9] are at best modal descriptions of populations with large variances in several dimensions. The way in which individuals choose occupations in our society no doubt reduces the variability of personality within an occupation. But it is still too great to permit generalizations about the *total* personalities of individuals of a given occupation. For this reason, the total personalities of businessmen would provide an unsure footing for an analysis of ideological dispositions. This does not mean that our analysis is blind to strains arising from sources other than the business executive role itself. Strains arising in one role-context may be heightened in their seriousness by strains generated in other role-contexts, past or contemporary. This is, of course, a matter of everyday experience, the petty annoyances of life being more or less tolerable, depending on the general equilibrium of the personality, which in turn depends on the strains from the various role-contexts each person fills or has filled. The strains of one role-context thus may become symbolic points of discharge for affect generated in another context. The strain-producing features of the business executive's role may, we suggest, act both (1) as primary sources of strain, and (2) as secondary symbolic foci for strains generated in other contexts. For our purposes, it does not greatly matter what the relative importance of (1) and (2) may be. It might very well happen that, for large numbers of business executives, the "intrinsic" strains of the role — that is, type (1) — are weak; still, insofar as other strains become focused on the business role, the consequences in ideology should be similar.[10]

[9] As, for example, W. H. Henry, "The Business Executive: The Psychodynamics of a Social Role," *Amer. Jour. of Soc.*, 54: 286–291 (1949).

[10] This is far from a full discussion of the question as to why basic personality strains should be channeled through occupational role strains, rather than being discharged directly into ideology.

CONSTRAINTS ON IDEOLOGY

Ideological propositions are subject to constraints imposed by their audience; in particular, they must be *plausible* and *legitimate* in terms of the going standards of the audience. There are all sorts of reactions to strain which do not get beyond the private domains of fantasy; they may be gratifying, but they depart too much from acceptable standards of plausibility and legitimacy to be openly propagated. Later we shall see that there are many symbols which do not appear in the business ideology but which may serve as reactions in more private contexts, and commonly do. The "government," for example, may be publicly abused by businessmen without bringing the kind of discredit upon them which public castigation of "the Jews" would arouse.

In certain situations constraints of this sort may produce serious divergences between "public" and "private" beliefs. In a totalitarian state, the available forms of public ideology may be so narrowly circumscribed that there is little latitude for variation in response to the strains of particular roles. If this were the state of affairs in the United States today our analysis of the business ideology would be to little purpose; if what is said is dictated by external conditions, then further motivational analysis becomes irrelevant. As it is, we do not believe that the business ideology is narrowly determined by external conditions. A number of legitimate ideologies exist side by side in America, although some of them — labor ideology, for example — conflict with the business creed. Some sort of motivational analysis is clearly necessary. But a question persists as to the discrepancies which may exist between this ideology and the beliefs which are expressed privately or implied in actions. At the end of this chapter we discuss this question in detail.

NATIONALISM AND ANTI-CAPITALISM: THEIR ROOTS IN OUR SOCIETY

Before analyzing the business ideology in terms of our theory we shall apply it to two widely used groups of ideological symbols. By examining nationalist and anti-capitalist symbols in terms of strains that are generally felt throughout our society, we shall illustrate the methodology and technique which will later be applied to the business ideology. These symbols are analyzed in terms of certain pronounced strains in American society; but they are shared in varying degrees in all Western countries. Nationalist and anti-capitalist symbols have been shared by groups of very different political colors. They have appealed to radical left-wing parties and to extreme right-wing groups. The Soviet Union has become nationalistic, while Hitler denounced the selfishness and greed of the capitalist society.[11]

---

[11] F. Borkenau, *Socialism; National or International* (London, 1942) gives a perceptive discussion of the relations of nationalism and socialism.

Even in the United States, Wall Street, Big Business, and "economic royalists" have been abused.[12] Both sets of symbols have common roots which can be characterized as the lack of psychological security afforded by our society compared with earlier societies or others which exist today.

Our society is peculiar in the broad perspective of cultural anthropology in that it gives only a very limited place to ascribed status, that is status which is fixed independently of individual performance and is generally determined by sex, by race, or, within the same ethnic group, by kinship. Instead, high or low status is nearly always determined by the individual's achievement, especially in his occupation.[13]

In particular, the relations between kinship patterns and occupational patterns have been largely severed. In many societies a son will automatically succeed his father at work, whatever his own abilities may be. With us, the new generation must make its own way; obtaining a particular job is (ideally) dependent on one's abilities and not upon one's social status. Of course, there are exceptions — family businesses are an example. But normally the behavior of an employer who gives a job to a friend or relative rather than to a better qualified person is negatively viewed as nepotism or favoritism.

Our society certainly has some ascribed patterns; kinship ties are of this sort. The new-born child is ascribed a position in a particular family and will remain a member of it for the rest of his life. But this particular type of ascribed status is less important than it is in other societies. Our effective kinship units are isolated nuclear families consisting only of parents and immature children.[14] The young adult can choose whom to marry and where to live, free from intimate control by, or responsibilities to, his own family or that of his spouse. In this way his ties with a particular location are weakened.

It is the same story with other ascribed patterns. Sex and skin color are still the basis of ascribed statuses. But the fight for equal rights and non-discrimination are gradually whittling down the importance of ascription in favor of achievement. In general, our society has peculiarly uni-

[12] It is noteworthy that the businessman has seldom been made an attractive figure in American literature. (See Walter Taylor, *The Economic Novel in America* (Chapel Hill, N.C., 1942). Recently, John Chamberlain, *Fortune* (November 1948) and Allan Nevins (in a speech at Stanford University Institute of American History, Summer 1951) have deplored the negative use of the businessman in literature. See also *Capitalism and the Historians,* edited by Friedrich A. Hayek (London, 1954).

[13] The distinction used here has been popularized by Ralph Linton in *Study of Man* (New York, 1936); see also the systematic treatment of the ascription-achievement variable in Parsons and Shils, "Values, Motives, and Systems of Action," *Toward a General Theory of Action,* Part 2.

[14] See *The Family: Structure, Function, and Destiny,* edited by Ruth Nanda Anshen (New York, 1949); in particular the papers of Talcott Parsons and Ruth Benedict.

versalistic norms; these norms constitute a basic feature of our government, business organization, and countless voluntary associations. To cite one example: our retail markets will sell to anyone who chooses to buy, whereas in traditional India, merchants, artisans, and customers were tied together by hereditary bonds.

This emphasis on achievement patterns avoids some of the frustrations which are felt in traditionalistic societies but it leads inevitably to other strains. Primarily, the individual does not have a stable secure place in society in which he is largely protected from the vicissitudes of fortune whatever his performance may be. The lot of the small urban family today is often contrasted bleakly with the family's security in more stable rural societies. Lack of psychological security has led the most mobile Americans to cling fervidly to their sense of having a "home town" or roots in a particular community.[15]

The occupational structure about which so much of modern life is organized thus limits our sources of security in assured solidary ties. In addition, it contains intrinsic sources of strain which may aggravate the need for such ties. Personal preferences have to be rigidly controlled in favor of "fairness" in recruitment, promotion, and in countless other ways. The professor cannot legitimately favor the dull student he happens to like over his abler but unattractive classmate, nor can the businessman advance only those employees who win his personal affection. Such institutionalized patterns of *affective neutrality* are widely familiar to the sociologist and have a fundamental place in the functioning of our society.[16]

In a highly differentiated economy equal dignity for all types of work is a romantic ideal beyond the bounds of possibility. Our emphasis on achievement patterns has thus led to fierce competition for high status through success in the more prestigious occupations. Occupational success is a profoundly important if vaguely defined goal for every American male. The sky is the limit for young men from all kinds of family and educational backgrounds. But the top jobs can be attained only by a few. Most people must accept modest positions in the hierarchy, and must accept them without the comfortable assurance that they have been ascriptively assigned these positions. The process of adjustment must involve strain. The strains

[15] Compare Margaret Mead, *And Keep Your Powder Dry* (New York, 1942). Incidentally, the strains which are imposed on business executives by the moving which climbing the ladder of advancement may entail, are evidently troublesome. A *Fortune* study has reported the following striking case: "One executive who recently changed to a non-transferring company . . . has no trouble recalling the exact moment of his decision. One night at dinner his little boy asked him a question. 'Daddy,' he said, 'where do you really live?' " Whyte, *Is Anybody Listening?*, p. 197.

[16] On their importance in the physician-patient relationship: Parsons, *Sociological Theory*, ch. VIII, and *Social System*, ch. 10.

imposed on those at the bottom of the ladder are obvious; in terms of the dominant values they are failures.[17] But at any level there must be strains in adjusting to the status actually attained.

Nationalism as a widespread ideological reaction has its affective basis in these strains. National membership is normally an ascribed status. It is not, like being a doctor or a $20,000-a-year executive, a status that one "works" to attain. However well or badly one does in occupational competition, one is still a citizen. Moreover, an emphasis on nationalities does not encounter the disqualifying opposition which universalistic norms bring against many appeals to ascriptive statuses. It is certainly likely that anti-Negro prejudice in the United States is stimulated by the strains of a competitive status system; by emphasizing the ascriptive status of being white, the bigot puts a solid floor under his status. But reactions of this sort do not lend themselves well to ideological justification; they run counter to the great traditions of egalitarianism and as such are derogated as "prejudice." Similar, if lesser, difficulties arise in attempts to use other ascriptive statuses as a cushion against the strains of competition. "Being of good family" may be made into a useful cushion in some special contexts but it has obvious limitations. Other possible solidarities, such as local communities, are greatly weakened either by the facts of mobility or the force of universalistic norms and their supporting ideology. The nation, in contrast, is likely to be both a life-long ascriptive solidarity and a legitimate tie to emphasize.

Anti-capitalist tendencies in modern ideology may be related to the same fundamental patterned strains. A system which operates so largely under the norm of universalism can easily seem cold and indifferent. People who feel insecure for other reasons find it difficult to accept impersonality in their relationships with others; they desire assurances of responsible concern. Business enterprise becomes a convenient target for hostile reaction in this pattern. By definition it has no communal responsibilities, as do, for example, the medical profession or the government. Among all the major institutions of modern society, business enterprise is most vulnerable to the charge that it operates with no responsibility for the security of any of the citizenry. A business is conducted for profit; it supplies bubble gum rather than inspirational tracts to juveniles if the former sells better. It provides for those who can pay rather than those in need. Attacks on Wall Street or Big Business have no doubt gained much of their political force because they alleged that private concerns with limited

---

[17] See Merton, *Social Theory*, "Social Structure and Anomie," where the strains of generalizing status criteria are well analyzed.

On the adjustment of the lower-class in our society, see the survey of Genevieve Knupfer, "Portrait of the Underdog," *Public Opinion Quarterly*, Spring 1947.

responsibility control many things that should be in the hands of those with full responsibilities to the whole community.[18]

The special vulnerability of the role of the individual "capitalist" or businessman should also be noted. Because business is institutionally oriented to private profit, he can be made to appear irresponsible, selfish, and greedy. In addition, one regular form of attack on the functioning of our society is the allegation that the stratification system is not "fair" or does not really work as it is supposed to; that success is dependent not on effort and ability so much as on ascriptive advantage, favoritism, and luck. There are obvious motivations among those dissatisfied with their own place in the system to show that others have not gained their status by fair or proper means or that their statuses do not merit the rewards that go with them. The inevitably large numbers of people who attain no very honored status must have some means of rationalizing their position. Individuals of lower class and occupational status are less likely than their higher status countrymen to accept American orthodoxy on the relations of success to ability and effort.[19] Even among those who attain fairly high status, such as the professionals, we know there is a large amount of dissatisfaction which may lead to attacks on the system.[20] Business executive roles are a convenient point of attack for the dissatisfied.

In defense of his high status, the businessman claims first that he has earned it by performance of difficult and responsible tasks; but here he is hampered by the inherent elusiveness of the content of the executive role.[21] Second, he must claim that he has reached his position in a fair and free competitive race through his own initiative and ability; here also he must overcome some resistance. The new entrant into business does not have to have tangible professional qualifications. The charge of nepotism and favoritism is therefore easily made; and it is supported by observation of the realistic importance of family ties, "contacts" and personal ingratiation. Furthermore, the line between grasping opportunities in a legitimate manner and being over-aggressive and "pushing" is very thin. Initiative and

[18] A recent study by the Survey Research Center of the University of Michigan (conducted under a grant from General Motors Corporation), revealed that the most commonly expressed complaints against big business among a national sample of respondents had to do with excessive power. See Burton R. Fisher and Stephen B. Withey, *Big Business as the People See It* (Ann Arbor, Mich., 1951), pp. 19–22, and part IV, pp. 111 ff. "Too much power," particularly in the area of inter-business practices, was most commonly suggested as a "bad" feature of big business, and there was very widespread sentiment for reduction of the power of business relative to state and national governments.

[19] See R. Centers, "Motivational Aspects," p. 200; R. Centers and H. Cantril, "Income Satisfaction and Income Aspiration," *Journal of Abnormal and Social Psychology*, 41: 64–69 (1946); J. Useem, P. Tangent, and R. Useem, "Social Stratification in a Prairie Community," *American Sociological Review*, June 1942.

[20] Centers, "Motivational Aspects."

[21] See Chapter 5.

aggressiveness are qualities which are generally admired and approved as means to occupational success. But it is easy for the disappointed to believe that the successful have achieved their positions in an improper manner. Business, perhaps more than any other occupation, involves aggressive grasping of opportunities in relation to other persons, and thus is intrinsically adapted to being a symbol of over aggressiveness. Jews have been another such symbol, and their close association with business has certainly contributed to the plausibility of this symbolic use. Like the Jew, the businessman may be accused of gaining material rewards through cunning and unscrupulous behavior rather than through hard work and intelligence.

Doubts about the legitimate limits of self-assertiveness are thus a pervasive source of anti-business sentiment in the Western world. But we may expect this source to be the more important, the more strongly a society is oriented to status references — more important, therefore, in much of Europe, especially Germany than in America. Status-reference means that what can be done is prescribed by the social context and that the scope for individual initiative is restricted. American life in contrast, say, to German life has been marked by an informality and an avoidance of relationships frozen in terms of status-references. This should mean more latitude for self-assertion, fewer delicate conflicts over its propriety, and hence lesser need for projective symbols to be attacked in relation to these conflicts. A society which gives rewards of prestige and esteem for the close observance of status proprieties and yet gives material rewards of income to a role with elements of aggressive self-assertion must inevitably be subject to strains. No part of the Western world has escaped this kind of conflict in some degree but if "capitalism" is still respectable in the United States, the fluidity of "informal" social relations has greatly contributed.

Not only the "capitalist" but the business organization is the target of hostile reactions to the strains generated in a competitive status system. Fisher and Withey found that 24 per cent of their respondents condemned the power of big business over its competitors, while less than 10 per cent condemned its power in matters where their own interests might be adversely affected.[22] The anxieties of those respondents who were worried about the power of big businesses over their competitors can scarcely be explained in terms of a rational farsighted view of their own interests. The ultimate consequences of business concentration are very difficult even for experts to assess. Instead competition among businesses must have a symbolic importance for many people who are not engaged in business. Very

[22] Fisher and Withey, *Big Business,* table, p. 22. The sample was composed of U.S. adults living in households (appendix B) and thus businessmen made up only a small fraction of the sample.

probably they have come to think that size gives an unfair advantage from their own personal experience of competition,[23] and they project this presumption into the field of business rivalry.

This analysis of the sources of nationalist and anti-capitalist sentiment in Western societies has traced their appeal to fundamental and pervasive strains inherent in the structure of these societies. The analysis has illustrated the underlying theory and method, which we shall apply specifically to the businessman and his ideology in subsequent chapters. In addition, our examples have made some substantive contribution to that task. Nationalism is a prominent feature of the American business creed, as of other ideologies, and the strains that motivate the businessman to his nationalist views are only a variant of the general insecurities to which, we have found, nationalism is a general ideological reaction. Anti-capitalism, of course, is not shared by business ideology, although the appeal it has to small businessmen makes the preservation of a united ideological front among businessmen a difficult and important task. But the anxieties and resentments that lead to anti-capitalist sentiments among non-businessmen are shared by businessmen. As we shall see, the reactions of businessmen to these strains play an important part in the generation of business ideology.

THE STRUCTURE OF IDEOLOGIES

Three elements in the general structure of ideologies, which we noted in Chapter 1, can now be explained in terms of our theory; they are selectivity, oversimplification and the use of symbols.

Selectivity. Ideologies resemble all systems of ideas in that they must abstract from reality. But ideologies are selective in particular systematic ways, for they must be built up around the affective needs engendered by the kinds of strains we have analyzed. Concepts which are not connected with these needs can not become part of ideology. The picture of society given by any ideology must, therefore, be very imperfect and incomplete. This point is often lost from sight. The tendency to equate ideology to "basic underlying assumptions" or some other inexplicit aspect of societies is common[24] and implies that discrepancies between ideology and social structure could conceivably be eliminated.

Others recognize the discrepancy between ideology and actual social structure, but consider it to be an intrinsic source of strain, leading to ideological rationalization or attempts to adjust the social structure to the

[23] It may also be a corollary of this presumption that the profits of big business are thought to be too large, whereas small local businesses escape this charge. See Fisher and Withey, *Big Business,* pp. 80 ff. and polls in Cantril, *Public Opinion,* pp. 685–686.

[24] See, for example, the collection of papers edited by F. C. S. Northrop, *Ideological Differences and World Order.*

ideological model.[25] This view is more credible — particularly in America where the quasi-rational criticism of social practices in terms of the dominant ideology is customary. If Negroes are not in fact treated as the American Creed directs they should be, the situation must either be rationalized or altered under ideological pressure. Some observers of the business creed view it as an effort to defend or bring about change in actual practices which depart from the supposed dictates of ideological orthodoxy — and with some justification. Discrepancies may indeed be seized on for ideological discussion, but they need not be. They are of quite general occurrence, and hence the mere existence of discrepancy is not a sufficient explanation of the motivation "to make something of it." [26] Just as the substance of his complaints about an irrational, insincere world provide no sufficient explanation of the radical's motivation, neither do the discrepancies between a classical model of free enterprise and contemporary realities sufficiently explain the motivations behind business ideology.

Oversimplification. Ideologies tend to envisage intricate systems which are, paradoxically, supposed to be easily understood by the simple untutored mind. Marx accused Lassalle of misunderstanding the true doctrine of labor power while simple workers understood it.[27] Similarly, an American industrialist in the 1930's promised that "A remarkable improvement and a healthier equilibrium in our national economy could be hastened by a widespread understanding of economic laws, and public acceptance of these laws in the spirit of the American tradition . . . These economic laws are simple and self-evident. Almost all men know them and apply them in their personal lives, but many are ready to disregard them completely the moment a collective or national problem is discussed." He promised to present these laws in a way "to bridge the seeming yet actually non-existent gap between the simple economics of housewifery, housekeeping and village life and the large-scale economics of America." [28] Ideologies are driven to oversimplification because they must be linked to the direct experience of the ordinary individual in order to win affective support. The complex operations of a social system cannot easily be grasped. To be dealt with, they must be translated into familiar terms, at whatever cost in accuracy. Thurman Arnold has pointed out that the government is thought of as a Big Man;[29] this follows a pattern universal in human experience, of anthropomorphizing the unfamiliar. Complex

[25] Myrdal, *American Dilemma,* is a classic instance.

[26] Examples have been given above on the conflict between kin-determined advantage and the ideology of equality of opportunity. They might easily be multiplied. The admissibility of "discrimination" among women on grounds of physical beauty is not widely challenged in our society but it certainly does not accord well with our general ideological principles.

[27] *Critique of the Gotha Programme* (New York, 1938), p. 15.

[28] Mooney, *The New Capitalism,* pp. vii–viii.

[29] Arnold, *Folklore of Capitalism.*

social processes, viewed in detail, would appear ". . . impersonal forces and factors, eternally remote." [30] And the government is particularly susceptible to this kind of symbolic treatment. The symbols of national unity must center around it in any working political structure. People must in some degree identify themselves with government actions, and equate them with the actions of the whole society. Hence the alarm, for example, at the image of a nation fast going bankrupt, and of every man, woman, and child in debt for several thousand dollars. Here the government functions symbolically as a summary indicator of the state of society, for which all individuals have responsibility.[31]

Use of symbols. Despite the inherent difficulties of constructing a logically coherent ideology relating to a total society, ideologies commonly discuss societies in terms of abstract systems of ideas. Business ideology is greatly concerned with the "system" of "free enterprise" or the "American system" and with various contrasting alternatives such as "statism," "socialism," etc.[32]

Placing global systems in opposition would logically call for the construction of systematic abstract models; in fact these either do not exist or are not set forth in the ideology. The history of human thought is full of reference to systems which are posited as conceptual possibilities without being explicitly worked out. Even as doggedly persistent a thinker as Marx left the depiction of "socialism" in the vaguest form. On the other side, orthodoxy has often, implicitly or explicitly, rested on conceptions that somewhere, at some time, somebody had worked out the model of a laissez-faire economy; but, as Keynes once remarked,[33] such an impressive achievement is not in fact to be found.

"Systems" as grand alternatives are discussed not merely because they promote logical and precise thought but because they serve a special purpose as symbols. By the use of such symbols we can dissociate ourselves, our institutions, or our society from actions or features we dislike. All the

[30] Sigmund Freud, *The Future of An Illusion* (London, 1949, Robson-Scott trans.), p. 28. The passage continues: "But if the elements have passions that rage like those in our own souls, if death itself is not something spontaneous, but the violent act of an evil will, if everywhere in nature we have about us beings who resemble those of our own environment, then indeed we can breathe freely, we can feel at home in the face of the supernatural, and we can deal psychically with our frantic anxiety. We are perhaps still defenceless, but no longer helplessly paralysed; we can at least react; perhaps indeed we are not even defenceless, we can have recourse to the same methods against these violent supermen of the beyond that we make use of in our own community; we can try to exorcise them, to appease them, to bribe them, and so rob them of part of their power by thus influencing them . . ."

[31] See S. S. Alexander, "Opposition to Deficit Spending for the Prevention of Unemployment," *Income, Employment and Public Policy,* by Alvin H. Hansen *et al.* (New York, 1948).

[32] Chapter 2 above.

[33] Keynes, *Laissez-faire and Communism,* p. 17.

admirable features are incorporated into the system, while the unpleasant ones are "not part of the American system" or are "not part of our true selves." Psychological research has shown that an individual constantly formulates or adopts formulations of what he himself, his society, and various institutions "really are." These conceptions are typically vague and loose, and they change presumably in response to changing demands for adjustment. When these formulations become marked and rigid, they are signs of pathological traits in the individual or of malintegration in the social system.[34] The normal functioning of personalities and social systems would thus seem to preclude constant reference to clearly defined, consistent systems. Conversely, if such constant reference occurs it is the result of strains within the social system.

A large social system like the United States is much too complex to be fitted neatly into any one conceptual scheme, and any global characterization of it which has the coherence to serve as a symbolic guide for attitudes and action must be patently oversimplified. Yet such simplified systems serve important functions in ideology: they provide the symbolic means for focusing the inchoate aggressive impulses produced by the strains which generate ideology. The very complexity of the social system lends itself to ideological use. Determinations of whether the United States is "still a free society," or "dangerously far on the road to socialism," contentions over the mean level of "self-reliance" in the population and its trend over time — all are important as targets for the discharge of emotion and as symbols in the "struggle" between adherents of the business creed and those of threatening hostile "systems," unprofitable as they might be as subjects of realistic discussion.

There is something strikingly similar in the evident desires of Marxists to be engaged in "the heat of a struggle" and of many contemporary American businessmen to take a "fighting stand" against something or other. An indispensable requisite for a "fighting stand" is some definition of what one is fighting for. Narrow issues may suffice for many needs but the symbolic use of a total "system" has advantages. The opponents of the "system" may, of course, be left in vague fantasy or defined in terms which can gain some measure of plausibility. The business ideology includes "intellectuals," "underpaid and underworked professors," "demagogues," "planners" among its symbolic opponents.[35]

Here a delicate balance must be maintained. On the one hand, a

---

[34] Schilder has studied psychopathological phenomena extensively from this point of view. See Paul F. Schilder, *The Image and Appearance of the Human Body* (New York, 1950), and *Goals and Efforts of Man* (New York, 1942), esp. ch. XXIII, "Ideologies," pp. 224–239.

[35] They are sometimes used very specifically as opponents in imagined arguments. This is the literary technique of James Mooney in *Economics of Free Enterprise* (Toledo, Ohio, 1939).

vividly conceived opponent has advantages as a target for aggression. On the other hand, this use of projectively defined scapegoats is vulnerable to rational criticism.[36] Because of this vulnerability, opponents may remain very shadowy and inexplicit. But this does not mean that they are not important in motivating a view of the world as a struggle between global systems, in which one must take an emphatic stand.

PUBLIC EXPRESSION AND PRIVATE BELIEF

Our theory relates ideology to deep-set motivations; yet we recognize that ideological expression is constrained by the boundaries of legitimacy and the demands of effective influence. The relevance of the theory depends on some assurance that ideologies like the business creed express the "real beliefs" of their adherents. We must consequently turn again to the question of the conformity of public expression to private belief, with specific attention to the case of businessmen. There are two obvious approaches: first, to compare the business ideology with such evidence as there is of more private statements or evidences of belief; and, second, to examine theoretically the relations we might expect between them. We shall start with a brief word on the second.[37]

It is often assumed that "real" belief is that which finds expression in action and hence that overt actions are the ultimate criterion for judging

[36] It was one of the notable characteristics of the "anti-rationalism" of the Nazi movement that it enforced a blatantly unrealistic use of Jews, Freemasons, and Communists as scapegoats. The impulses to the use of concrete scapegoats are presumably endemic and constantly restrained by rational criticism. On the scapegoat theory of prejudice, compare Gordon W. Allport & Bernard M. Kramer, "Some Roots of Prejudice," *Journal of Psychology*, 22: 9–39 (1946), Gardner Lindzey, "An Experimental Examination of the Scapegoat Theory of Prejudice," *Journal of Abnormal & Social Psychology*, 2: 296–309 (1950), ibid., "An Experimental Test of the Validity of the Rosenzweig Picture Frustration Study," Journal of Personality 19: 315–330 (1950) and literature there cited.

[37] No systematic discussion of the problems of "public" and "private" belief seems to be at hand in the technical literature. Social psychologists whom we have consulted on the question have agreed that the older discussions did not get much beyond recognizing the distinction and that neglect of the question produces a distinct "hole" in the recent literature. The extensive review by Quinn McNemar, "Opinion-Attitude Methodology," *Psychological Review* 43: 289–374 (July, 1946), reveals no significant work on the subject. Scattered articles may be mentioned which bear on the relations of action and assertion: Herbert Hyman, "Do They Tell the Truth?," *Public Opinion Quarterly*, 8: 557–559 (1944); D. F. Blankertz, "Motivation and Rationalization in Retail Buying," *ibid.*, 13: 658–668 (Winter, 1949–50); R. K. Merton, "Discrimination and the American Creed," in *Discrimination and the National Welfare*, edited by R. M. MacIver (New York, 1949), pp. 99–126.

Any profound study of this question would, of course, have to take into account the psychoanalytic literature on rationalization and give it a social psychological extension — a venture of forbidding difficulty. Beginnings in this direction are being made (See, for example, G. Bateson and J. Ruesch, *Communication, The Social Matrix of Psychiatry* (New York, 1951), but seem not to have attained clear results as yet.

the sincerity of expressed beliefs. But a moment's reflection reveals that the connection between action and belief is obscure; people often do things which directly contradict beliefs they hold strongly. True, we tend to reproach people who do not practice what they preach; but it does not follow that actual behavior would be a reliable basis for inferences regarding beliefs. What businessmen actually do in the conduct of their own affairs may be a more treacherous guide to what they really believe about their society than is their ideology. We therefore do not regard the actual practice of American business as the ultimate criterion for the beliefs of businessmen.

A more attractive criterion is provided by views businessmen express in private when they are less constrained than in public. For instance, Professor Cochran has pointed out that even in the gaudier days of American capitalism, businessmen would boast of their power over the public only in private conversations or correspondence.[38] Public ideology certainly does not tell the whole story of business beliefs. It would, however, be reckless to assume either that the public and private views of an individual are radically inconsistent or that the private views necessarily represent "true" belief. In private a businessman may "let off steam" in ways which are prohibited in public; but this certainly does not mean that all his deeply-felt opinions are denied public expression. Even on the same subject, he may have ambivalent attitudes, some of which are publicly legitimate whereas others are not. Also, many of the views that he keeps *in petto* or expresses cautiously in private confidence are likely to be of a concrete, personalized nature. As such, they are not directly relevant to ideological beliefs; the effects of censorship on those generalized private beliefs which can be directly compared with public ideology are probably slight.

We have not collected any large body of interview material which might indicate the private views of businessmen on the subjects of business ideology.[39] The only data for a comparison lie in public opinion polls. A fair number of polls of business executives or of general polls with breakdowns showing businessmen's views have now accumulated.[40] The polling situation is a "private" one in the sense that anonymity of the individual is preserved; it lacks, of course, the intimacy of rapport which presumably

[38] Compare T. C. Cochran in *Change and the Entrepreneur* (Cambridge, Mass., 1949).

[39] The only extensive study of this sort known to us is currently underway at the Center for International Studies, Massachusetts Institute of Technology, Cambridge, Mass., under the direction of Raymond Bauer and Ithiel De Sola Pool. It concerns the private views and public expressions of American businessmen on foreign trade.

[40] The following discussion is based on all the polls in which businessmen's opinions are shown separately, reported in Cantril, *Public Opinion;* and issues of *Public Opinion Quarterly* 1946–1952.

would be present in discussions among businessmen, but it is at least freed from many of the constraints on identified statements for a public audience. This material reveals a close correspondence between polls and ideology.

Poll evidence is in general agreement with the broad emphases of the ideology on "competition," "opportunity," "freedom," etc. It is, of course, the beginning of wisdom in the interpretation of poll results to recognize the great influence of the precise phrasing of questions on the results attained. Consequently, polls are not easy to summarize, so we must discuss specific examples.

1. On May 14, 1947, the Gallup poll asked the following question of a national sample: "Which one of these statements do you most agree with? (1) 'The most important job for the government is to make it certain that there are good opportunities for each person to get ahead on his own.' (2) 'The most important job for the government is to guarantee every person a decent job and standard of living.' " [41]

In the national sample, 50 per cent chose the first statement, 43 per cent the second, and 7 per cent were undecided. A breakdown by occupational categories shows that 67 per cent of professionals and businessmen, as compared with only 37 per cent of manual workers, favored the "opportunity" choice. The impression which their ideology conveys that businessmen are especially concerned to foster openness of opportunity is thus bolstered by their expressed reactions in another type of situation.

2. When questioned about the actual state of competition in their own industries, businessmen have tended to be in favor of the *status quo*. Many complain that competition is too severe, while relatively few find it too weak.

A *Fortune* poll of a national cross-section of executives in July 1950 asked the following question: "Regardless of the number of companies in it, do you think the competition in your industry is too intensive, not intensive enough, or about right?" [42] The results, tabulated in percentages by size of industry, were as follows:

	TOO INTENSIVE	NOT INTENSIVE ENOUGH	ABOUT RIGHT	NO OPINION
Large	34	2	58	6
Medium	36	3	55	6
Small	37	3	54	6

Another result from a poll of October 1943, indicates similar sentiments. The *Fortune* executive poll then asked: "In your own business

---

[41] *Public Opinion Quarterly*, Summer 1947, p. 284.
[42] *Public Opinion Quarterly*, Winter 1950–51, p. 802.

field, do you think after the war it would be a good thing if there were about the same number of competitors as now, more competitors, or fewer competitors?" The replies showed 74.5 per cent favoring the same number of competitors, 11.6 per cent favoring more competitors, and 13.9 per cent favoring fewer.

When the question is put in more generalized form, we find relatively more enthusiasm for competition (an approach to the public ideological position).

A *Fortune* poll of executives in October 1943, asked the following question: "Do you think that, as compared with 1939, business in the United States after the war needs about the same amount of competition within business, more competition, or less competition?" 76.2 per cent chose more, 4.5 per cent less.[43]

Another result, very difficult to interpret because of its presumed "contamination" by attitudes toward the New Deal and one of its prominent figures, is the following, again from the *Fortune* poll of executives (December 1940): "Today, the Department of Justice is following almost exactly the opposite policy from NRA on price-fixing, and Assistant Attorney General Thurman Arnold has launched the greatest campaign in history to enforce the anti-trust laws and prevent price-fixing agreements. He says, 'The first concern of every democracy is the maintainance of a free market.' Do you agree with Mr. Arnold?" The replies (in percentages) were as follows:[44]

YES	IN MOST CASES	IN A FEW CASES	NO
27.7	31.0	18.3	23.0
58.7		41.3	

From this, one can claim that there are distinct differences in the way businessmen feel about competition as a real factor impinging on their own business operations, and about "competition" as a symbol for a general state of the economy. In general, businessmen do not renounce their broad espousal of competition when asked to discuss their own industries; nevertheless, statistically speaking, they are less enthusiastic about competition in their immediate affairs, than they are about competition in general. This is not a difference in private and public utterance, but rather a difference in specificity of application of the ideas in hand. The public and private ideologies agree on competition in general; it is when businessmen are called upon to speak of their own affairs that we get significant differences. These are to be expected, and we discuss

[43] Cantril, *Public Opinion*, p. 133.
[44] Cantril, *Public Opinion*, p. 481.

them in Chapter 17. Obviously, competition means difficulties and dangers for the businessman, and he has strong motivations to reduce competition; it does not follow that his public praise of competition is insincere.

On more specific topics, business opinion as expressed in polls supports related themes of business ideology. The general themes of economy in government, sound governmental finance, and criticism of actual governmental policy gain solid support. The outcries of business against New Deal measures were not merely public "window-dressing." When questioned privately (in the *Fortune* poll) on a long list of them, the prevailing sentiment was that they had "always been bad" or were "good ideas badly handled." [45]

The percentages finding various measures "always bad" were as follows: silver subsidies, 90.2; Guffey Coal Act, 75.3; taxation policies, 67.7; pump priming, 61.7; NRA, 57.4; WPA, 39.3. In general, as percentages decline in the "always bad" column, they rise in that headed "good ideas badly handled." Exceptions where the measures found widespread approval were the Hull reciprocal trade treaties, and the Housing and Home Loan acts.[46]

A 1943 poll [47] indicated that the most widely approved measure for the alleviation of a depression was economy by government departments; 73 per cent chose this measure.

The proportions in favor of other measures were:

Lower corporation taxes: 51.9 per cent
A cooperative credit and employment effort on the part of business: 53.6 per cent
A huge public works program: 27.1 per cent
Liberalization of bank credit: 15.2 per cent
Devaluation of the dollar: 1.3 per cent.

We know of no simple and direct expression of feeling on the desirability of balancing the budget, but it is clear that the sentiments expressed in the business ideology are those of the population at large; a variety of polls indicate that the people as a whole are "budget balancers," [48] and it seems safe to infer that the polled sentiments of businessmen would show the same pattern.

Expressions on labor matters found in polls are consistent with the ideology. Businessmen prove to be more critical of labor than of other

[45] *Fortune*, December 1940, p. 168.
[46] FDIC, which won heavy approval in another poll, *Fortune*, October 1939, pp. 53 ff., was not included.
[47] *Fortune* executive poll, reported in Cantril, *Public Opinion*, p. 65.
[48] Compare Gallup polls of June 19, and July 13, 1949, reported in *Public Opinion Quarterly*, 13: 541 (Fall 1949), also that of Nov. 17, 1950, reported in *Public Opinion Quarterly*, 15: 169 (Spring 1951).

segments of the population, but we have discovered no expressions of opinion which are radically different from the expressed ideology; businessmen do not expose a mailed fist under the anonymity of the poll.

An old poll (October, 1935) showed 58 per cent of business proprietors believing that "in general labor is fairly treated in this country today." [49] Sixty-seven per cent of the "prosperous" group in this poll found labor treated fairly, whereas only 32.3 per cent of the "poor" were so convinced.

Many polls have shown that mistrust or criticism of labor unions is widespread among the general population. Thus, a Gallup poll in October 1941 found 61 per cent believing "many labor leaders are Communists." On the same date, 74 per cent expressed a belief that "many labor leaders are racketeers." [50] A *Fortune* poll in 1946 showed very modest popularity for the most approved labor leaders and widespread disapproval of some, such as John L. Lewis.[51] In a milieu of this sort we should hardly expect that businessmen would have to censor their public utterances severely.

[49] *Fortune* poll, reported in Cantril, p. 393. This result may be compared with later ones showing similar differentials, for example, the *Fortune* poll of February, 1948 on labor relations, reported in the *Public Opinion Quarterly,* Summer 1948, p. 356.

[50] Cantril, *Public Opinion,* p. 397.

[51] *Fortune* poll, reported in Cantril, p. 397.

16

STRAINS IN THE BUSINESS ROLE

THE ROLE OF THE BUSINESS EXECUTIVE

APPLIED TO THE BUSINESS CREED, our theory of ideology links
the special emphases of the creed to patterned strains in the businessman's
role. We shall now examine the businessman's role as a first step toward
establishing this relationship. Since the term businessman applies to thousands of men in occupations ranging from the President of General Motors to the proprietor of the local ice cream stall, we must at the outset
decide upon one of two courses. We can distinguish between the roles of
various businessmen on the grounds that they impose very different strains
upon their incumbents[1] or we can look for the common elements in the
roles of different types of businessmen that give rise to the same patterned
strains. We have chosen the second alternative on the ground that fine
distinctions are not relevant to our purpose; and we shall speak indis-
criminately of *business executives.*

Executive roles are not a monopoly of business firms. They are an
essential ingredient of government, universities, hospitals, and a host of
other formal organizations. All executive roles have certain elements in
common. They may be defined as roles involving authority to direct the
work of subordinate personnel, responsibility for the performance of this
work, the making of decisions on behalf of the organization, and coordination of the various parts of the organization. In contrast to labor roles,
specialized routine technical performance plays only a small part in the
role of an executive. In contrast to an author, a research scientist, or a
salesman, the executive has responsibilities not only for his own performance but for that of others.[2] Business executives are distinguished
from others principally because they work in organizations whose purpose
is to make profitable transactions in the market. Working in this type of

---

[1] One type of classification might be that used by R. A. Gordon in *Business
Leadership in the Large Corporation,* ch. I, where he distinguishes entrepreneurs,
salaried managers, and owners.

[2] Chester I. Barnard, *Functions of the Executive* (Cambridge, Mass., 1938) and
Herbert Simon, *Administrative Behavior* (New York, 1947).

organization subjects them to the characteristic strains of all executives.

This conception of the business executive covers all levels of management in large corporations down to the foremen, and all kinds of business organizations from large corporations to individual proprietorships. Although the role of the manager of a specialized division of a large corporation obviously differs from that of the owner-manager of a small independent business, the two have important elements in common. It may be difficult to think of the owner-manager of a very small business as an executive; but, where there are any employees whatsoever, the element of responsibility is certainly present. Even where there are no employees the separation of the business from the owner-operator's personal affairs imposes a quasi-executive framework on his role.

BUSINESS ACHIEVEMENT, RESPONSIBILITY AND RESULTING STRAINS

The business executive must make at least a moderate success of his career if he is to win the respect of his fellows and satisfy his own ambitions. He is, therefore, subject to the basic strains that beset every adult American as the price we pay for a society with careers open to talent. For the business executive these are given special forms by features peculiar to his role. In America we have probably pushed the importance of occupational achievement farther than any of our neighbors in the Western world. Our successful businessman, like our successful doctor or scientist, is constantly preoccupied with his specialized work to the neglect of his physique, his literary and artistic accomplishment, and his civic duties. Unlike a Continental businessman, an American business executive loses little prestige by neglecting general cultivation.[3] The occupational specialization we emphasize and reward would win little respect in civilizations which, like classical antiquity, demanded more rounded accomplishments of their citizens.

In our society achievement in an occupation is such an important goal of adult life that its attainment may cause strains and tensions. One obvious example of such strain, with which we are not directly concerned here, lies in the difficulty of choosing an occupation. Initially the individual has immense freedom of choice; but once he has chosen he is confined within a narrow specialism. His talents and efforts must be focused on competing successfully within his occupation, and his other interests and abilities are left to atrophy. The difficulties of making the initial choice are therefore very great.

Another basic source of strain lies in the fact that each person must constantly measure his achievement against those of his competitors. Here the businessman's role gives rise to pronounced anxieties. What are the

---

[3] See Robert H. Lowie, *The German People, a Social Portrait to 1914* (New York, 1945). Also, E. A. Sugimoto, *A Daughter of the Narikin* (New York, 1932).

criteria of business achievement? In the business ideology they are said to be clear and tangible. Theodore Grape likes business because "it rewards deeds rather than words . . . because it promptly penalizes mistakes, shiftlessness and inefficiency, while rewarding well those who give the best they have in them." [4] Such prompt justice, one would suppose, would be very welcome. Although it would give rise to some strains in that shortcomings would be revealed immediately, businessmen could rest assured that their success or failure would be a direct reflection of their abilities.

Actually, there are no such simple and direct criteria of individual performance in the role of business executive as the business ideology would have us believe. On the contrary, one experienced observer puts a sharp emphasis on the intangibility of business achievement in large firms:

These strains (on management) are not compensated by immediate tangible accomplishment. The joy of attaining a definite goal has been submerged in the vastness of space and time. Management must learn to get its satisfactions vicariously, trusting that its contribution will sometime fructify to the benefit of the community as well as to the enterprise. It has no single limited objective that it can perceive, measure and take pride in achieving. Its goals are multiple and are judged by criteria other than dollars and cents. [5]

This quotation concerns the goals of top-level executives; for executives at lower levels, the criteria of achievement are likely to be even more obscure and ill-defined.

Nevertheless, in contrast to such organizations as governments and universities, the prime criteria of business achievement are relatively definite and tangible. These standards include profitability, percentage control of the market, size of firm, and rate of growth.

The generalized character of these standards means that the particular products and methods of various business activities lose their intrinsic significance. By these criteria, pills are as good as poetry, and a hat factory may be more successful than a bookstore. A firm making sewer pipes, cheap dresses, or artificial flowers may be more successful than one producing elegant china.

The admiration of the American businessman for sheer size is a result of these generalized achievement standards. Where the particular content of business activity is minimized as a goal in itself so that the intrinsic prestige of a fine product is subordinated as a source of satisfaction, more or less quantified standards of general accomplishment must emerge. These standards have a relatively conspicuous and tangible character; one may dispute whether a tomato farmer or a tachometer manufacturer

---

[4] See page 265 above.
[5] Knauth, *Managerial Enterprise*, p. 181.

is making greater contributions to human needs and displaying greater industry and skill, but it is relatively easy to see which has the bigger or more profitable business.

Coupled with this generalization of achievement standards is a high valuation of novel rather than traditional methods of business. The heroes of American business are not those who have behaved most graciously and scrupulously in terms of traditional standards but those who have shown initiative and struck out on new paths which have paid off. Of course, there are limits which one cannot overstep; Frank Costello made money but his social status is not enviable. Nevertheless, within wide limits, the emphasis is on results, however unorthodox or inelegant the means. The business that is only holding its own in a traditional pattern is thought to be stagnant or otherwise undistinguished. The firm that ruins its competitors by "stealing" their market with a new product is a success. So is the one which makes a fortune through the use of clever singing commercials or by advertisements featuring eye patches. There is constant pressure to do something new.

Because of the generalized character of the standards of business success, any businessman can feel that success is within his reach no matter what his line of business. The goal of success is peculiarly open and fluid as befits a society with egalitarian ideals.[6] There are inevitably some intrinsic rewards which go with the status of a university professor, a doctor, or an industrialist, but in a society which minimizes status deference, the judgments of worthiness to regard tend to be individualized in terms of what the particular person can do or has done, and this requires general standards divorced from particular occupational contexts. The focus on a generalized standard of success makes achievement in the most varied types of activity worth while and protects many types of business activity from intrinsic derogation. The president of Dydee Diaper Service can sit in conference with business school professors and steelmen.[7] Tendencies in our society to narrow the standards of "success" are a threat to the general position of businessmen and are an important stimulus

---

[6] See Margaret Mead's perceptive discussion in *And Keep Your Powder Dry.*

[7] Compare Allen, *Individual Initiative in Business.*

We are not denying that important differences in the intrinsic prestige of particular types of business do exist. Quite aside from the generalized criteria of size, profitability, etc. there have been familiar status-distinctions between investment bankers and night-club operators. (We have heard a sales manager who had shifted from whiskey to housing proclaim with satisfaction that he was now in a "clean business.") But relative to other societies, even to western Europe, we have apparently had an exceptional blurring of such distinctions in the United States. (Compare a stimulating discussion of the occupational specialization of Jews as a reflection of these distinctions in F. R. Bienenfeld, *The Germans and the Jews,* London, 1939.) It is this blurring that we are concerned to stress at this point; the relevance of distinctions between different types of business is discussed in Chapter 17.

to ideology. As long as "success" is measured in generalized terms of occupational achievement, and income is a dominant criterion of status, the businessman is in an advantageous position; the goals which are institutionalized in his role are precisely of the sort which conduce to good positions in a stratification system emphasizing achievement and "democracy."

GENERALIZED STANDARDS AS A SOURCE OF STRAIN

The subordination of other concerns to the generalized criteria of business success must be a source of anxiety to many businessmen. An intrinsic interest in the processes of manufacture or the quality of products is certainly compatible with much "good business." But such interests must always be controlled and subjected to the economic criteria of profitability; a business executive cannot give himself over unreservedly to technical delights or to enjoyment of the esthetic qualities of his merchandise. He must produce and sell those things which "pay," and there are surely strains over this constraint on his activities. As we have repeatedly stressed, a capable businessman is likely to be interested in much more than sheer questions of profitability. Walter Rathenau once remarked that he had never known a successful businessman who was only interested in making money and he doubted that a mere money-maker could be a good businessman. The more important the "technological" or substantive aspects of business are in motivating a man to undertake a business career, the more the conditions of high motivation may in themselves be a source of strain.

The incidence of strains of this sort no doubt varies widely throughout the business community. They may be strongest where artisanal or professional skills compete with more strictly business interests. The druggist who takes an interest and pride in his pharmaceutical competence does not like to judge his achievements merely by the profitability and size of his business. To have to meet competition and struggle with purely business problems all the time is irksome and felt to be an unworthy deflection from the more dignified activities of responsible professional service.[8] A similar clash of motivations appears in artisanal groups.[9]

The close relation of engineering and executive roles in industry is a source of serious strains. The engineer is in a position where the interest and prestige of technical accomplishment are likely to be uninsulated from the competing interest and prestige in executive roles. Given the fact

---

[8] This point has been developed in a paper written by a student of one of the authors, Charles E. Sletten: "The Retail Druggist," unpublished paper in possession of the authors.

[9] See Louis Kriesberg, "The Retail Furrier: Concepts of Security and Success," *American Journal of Sociology*, 57: 478–485 (March 1952).

that appreciable numbers of executives are recruited from the ranks of engineers and other professional specialists there is good reason to believe this competition is felt by many corporate executives.[10]

The lot of the industrial worker has often been sadly contrasted with that of the traditional artisan making a product which had a manifest use and finished character; working in a detailed specialization, which has been set up not because of its intrinsic interest but because of its sheer technical efficiency, is freqently decried as meaningless. The same charge could be made against the work of the business executive. If he cannot give full rein to his interest in the quality of shoes, typewriters, or milk shakes, what is he working for? The institutional goals of profitability or building a great business can easily seem a shallow and unworthy pursuit of "filthy lucre" or power. Yet, he must control or even subordinate his interest in more concrete and meaningful goals in the service of these dubious ones.[11] Profit, far from being a "motive" inherent in nature, is a goal which cannot be maintained without strain. The conspicuous and tangible achievements which are taken as the goals of business enterprise are very readily attacked if only because they impinge so closely on the status concerns of non-businessmen in our society. Personal money income plays a highly important role in our society as a *symbol* of achievement. A man with a large income is likely to gain respect — not because of the income itself but because of the presumption that it is an index of his importance or competence. The possibility that symbols of this sort may be exploited is obvious, and society has difficulty keeping money income in line with other status symbols. The man who "goes after money" directly is particularly vulnerable to being thought a seeker of short-cuts and even a "cheater" who debases the currency of symbolic ranking.

[10] The situation of the engineer has particular interest because it is a relatively prestigious profession but one in which a "practical" emphasis deprives it of some possible advantages over executive roles. Independent artisans who come to concentrate their interest on their own technical work seem in general to have no doubt about their status relative to those in the same trade who have subordinated their own technical interests to "business." In Kriesberg's interesting study of Chicago furriers (cited in note 9), the commercial furriers were the "successes" and the artisans knew they were not. But such a definition of the situation has much to do with the intrinsic content of the roles in question. In a university, the balance is apt to be tipped the other way, the prestige of technical academic accomplishment being so powerful that those who "go into administration" are widely thought to have stepped down from pursuit of the highest goals. In manufacturing, the competing sides are apt to be more balanced and the clearly superior status of the executive not easily accepted.

[11] The businessman's role brings out with peculiar force the general problems of giving meaning to complex, rationalized activities of the modern world. Compare Troeltsch's classic discussion of the comparative problems of the medieval and modern worlds in *The Social Teachings of the Christian Churches*. The tasks of business ideology are not easy ones.

Businessmen share these general concerns of American society which make businessmen susceptible to misgivings about the merit of their own efforts.

UNCERTAINTY, LIMITED CONTROL AND RESPONSIBILITY

Business executives feel great responsibility for what happens in their businesses; yet, actually, the outcome of an executive's decision is likely to be very uncertain. This combination of responsibility and uncertainty is bound to produce strain. The businessman judges his performance by the state of the balance sheet. But the balance sheet does not reflect his performance alone; it is affected by a host of unforeseeable and uncontrollable factors, such as general business conditions. To make the business executive completely responsible for the state of the balance sheet is to give him undue credit for successes and undue blame for failures. Insofar as the business executive does influence the concrete.outcome of his business's ventures, it is through the making of those decisions which constitute the primary content of executive performance. Genuine decisions, in contrast to routine, habitual action, necessarily refer to uncertain situations. To say that the function of the business executive is to make decisions is, therefore, to give him responsibility for outcomes over which he has only limited control.

Decisions of this kind weigh on the business executive for at least two fundamental reasons. In the first place, the over-all coordination and direction of the organization are his responsibilities. But the very need for executives as a standard feature of modern organizations arises from the fact that no organization ever quite attains to the smooth, routinized functioning in which only specialized technicians are needed. There are always elements of uncertainty and conflicting demands which must be resolved in some authoritarian way; hence the need for the executive to be a "specialist in generality" endowed with high status and authority in the organization. The following example illustrates vividly the kind of organizational uncertainty and conflict to which the top business executive must give an authoritative solution:

Not long ago a major tire manufacturing company was faced with the problem that a new car had appeared without sufficient space under the fenders for a tire which would wear well. Much internal dissension developed in the company as to what should be done. The sales force urged supplying a tire which would fit and threatened that they "wouldn't be responsible for keeping the account" if tires weren't made. The production force urged against the tire and "wouldn't be responsible for its wearing." Resolution of the issue had to be made at the top executive level; the chief executive "assumed responsibility," deciding in favor of the sales force, and now "shudders every time he sees one of those cars." [12]

[12] Personal communication from participant.

In the second place, the businessman cannot predict exactly the future of the environment in which his business operates. At best he can only make predictions which have some probability of error. To make a man fully responsible for the specific outcome of his decisions is to ask the impossible, and subjects him to serious strain. The strain on the executive is partially eased to the extent that he is expected to be right only part of the time. However, behind such tolerance lies the presumption that someone could conceivably have been consistently right. Indeed, many business decisions lend themselves peculiarly well to Monday morning quarterbacking; if you buy raw materials for inventory and then their price goes down, you have no doubt that you should kick yourself.

There is abundant evidence that the making of difficult decisions proves a source of strain among business executives. The capacity to make decisions is recognized by businessmen to be one of the prime qualifications for a capable executive. It won second place, outranked only by "ability to handle people," in a *Fortune* Executive Poll.[13] Interviews reveal that businessmen try to appear decisive and confident, and to suppress signs of anxiety, since these are evidence of "weakness." [14] It is surely no accident that businessmen attach importance to the traits of confidence and decisiveness. In roles which have less to do with influencing concrete courses of action and more concern with sheer understanding, a confident appearance is much less notably approved; professors are more likely to be applauded for their diffidence and modesty. (A comparison of the photographs which appear in the book review and financial sections of newspapers is instructive and amusing. The businessmen on the financial pages are likely to wear sober, level gazes and orderly, conventional attire. Authors, in contrast, are apt to be lost in introspection, and to be smoking or informally attired.)

The executive's need to appear confident and decisive means that he cannot always candidly admit, either to others or to himself, his areas of

[13] Question asked in Executive Poll, *Fortune*, October 1946: "Most people who achieve success have a combination of many outstanding qualities. Which *one* of the following qualities do you rate as having contributed most to your success? Which next?"

Replies	Most (per cent)	Next Most (per cent)
Ability to handle people	30.0	22.6
Ability to make decisions	24.5	26.1
Technical or special knowledge	18.9	10.4
Great capacity for work	16.2	13.3
Ability to see things through	10.2	13.4
Other	1.0	1.6

(Percentages add to more than 100 because some gave more than one answer.) Cantril, *Public Opinion*, p. 831.

[14] Learned, Ulrich, and Booz, *Executive Action,* ch. 5, esp. pp. 77–80.

ignorance or inexpertness. Often this suppression of his uncertainty hinders him when he has to obtain information; he cannot explore the facts and solicit advice too avidly for fear of betraying anxiety or incapacity.[15] Research has revealed widespread fear of failure among businessmen for which the repression of misgivings about personal capacity in the interest of maintaining a front of confident decisiveness must be partly responsible.[16]

REACTIONS TO UNCERTAINTY

Between the businessman's action and the final outcome of this action a host of uncontrollable or unforeseen factors may intervene. The discrepancy between efforts and outcomes imposes a strain on the businessman; similar discrepancies between human efforts and concrete outcome have plagued mankind in every society. Never do we reap exactly as we sow; the flourishing of the wicked and the blighting of the good have long been a problem for religious questioning. Malinowski and others have observed that magical and religious practices in primitive societies flourish in situations where there is a marked discrepancy between efforts and results, due to weather and other natural forces. For, by such practices, primitive peoples attempt to control those external forces which frustrate their efforts. Clear expectations as to the consequences of action seem to be an essential condition of unperturbed human action; unexpected or uncertain outcomes occasion strain. We need not expect to find rabbits' feet or crystal balls in the inner offices of business firms, but we should expect to find some functional equivalent.

The most obvious reaction to this kind of strain is to attempt to control the situation so that uncertainties are minimized. Since competition

[15] Compare the interesting remarks of Learned, Ulrich, and Booz, *ibid.*, on the significance of raising questions about "how things are going." The line between "keeping informed" and betraying neurotic anxiety is a delicate one of which executives seem to be conscious. For a sensitive probing of the relations of normal and neurotic decision-making see H. S. Sullivan, *Conceptions of Modern Psychiatry* (Washington, 1945).

[16] Henry, "The Business Executive: The Psychodynamics of a Social Role." This is a very perceptive paper on the personality characteristics of successful and unsuccessful executives.

The enormous importance of a "fear of failure" among executives is commonly stressed. Chester Barnard has remarked that it is much more important than the hope of gain in the over-all balance of motivations. The roots of this "fear of failure" are complex but one important root certainly lies in the suppression of doubts which go with a role demanding decisive action. In a role which, paradoxically perhaps, has some notable features in common with the business executive's — that of the activistic political radical — something amounting to a "certainty of failure" has been observed. Richard Behrendt, *Politischer Activismus* (Leipzig, 1932), notes some interesting examples from the French Revolution (Robespierre, Marat, etc.). See also Elton Mayo, *Some Notes on the Psychology of Pierre Janet* (Cambridge, Mass., 1948), ch. I; and Sutton, *The Radical Marxist*.

among business firms is one obvious and important source of uncertainty, there is strong motivation to reduce it or eliminate it. Monopolies, cartels, "fair trade" legislation, and market agreements are well-known devices for restraining competition. Less obvious, but performing much the same function, are innumerable conventions and tacit agreements, both among firms and among departments of the same organization. The usual explanation for these phenomena is, of course, desire for profit and for power; but we believe that the desire for security is at least equally important.

Another possible reaction is that of avoiding decisions and escaping responsibility. But, although the businessman may wish to take this course, he finds it difficult to do so. In the business ideology the responsibility of the businessman is contrasted with alleged buck-passing in government offices. The point is exaggerated, but contains an important truth. Within a bureaucracy, areas of responsibility and authority are clearly defined. Frequently the lower-level bureaucrat can act in accordance with a routine defined by an explicit set of rules. He can play safe by sticking to the rules. If the bureaucratic organization is later charged with inefficiency, he may escape blame by pleading that he did what was expected of him in terms of the definition of his office.[17] To some extent, the same reaction open to civil servants and officers in the armed services is open to junior business executives. But it is not open to top-level business executives nor to those at lower levels from whom initiative rather than narrowly circumscribed performances are required. For these businessmen, there can be no escape from responsibility by inaction or by sticking to well defined rules. For the responsible executive, inaction is a decision.[18] In the tire manufacturing case cited above, for example, inaction would have been, in effect, a decision for the engineers.

The enormous power ascribed to executive action by the definition of the businessman's responsibility seems to imply that in any situation there must be something he can do. Hence the executive's reaction in the event of strain is not to evade action but to "do something." There are abundant impressions that activism, even to the extent of "wheel spinning" overactivity, is a common pattern of reaction to the strains of the role. Walter Bagehot remarked "Even in commerce, which is now the main occupation of mankind, and one in which there is a ready test of success and failure wanting in many higher pursuits . . . (a) disposition to excessive action is very apparent to careful observers." [19] Chester Barnard's admonition to the executive not to do anything in many situations suggests that he

---

[17] Merton, "Bureaucratic Structure and Personality," *Social Theory and Social Structure,* pp. 151–161.

[18] See Barnard, *Functions of the Executive,* p. 193.

[19] Walter Bagehot, *Works,* IV: 566–567, quoted in Barnard, *Organization and Management,* p. 67.

thinks executives are disposed to overactivity. Again, businessmen who have difficulty in handling their jobs show a harried, overworked appearance.[20]

Excessive activity in the office or plant is often carried over into leisure hours and into the deeper layers of the businessman's personality; recent research shows that the constant, driving activity of the executive often makes him unable to relax and sometimes leads to psychosomatic disorders.[21] The prevalence of ulcers among top business executives may well be connected with such personality disorders.

BUSINESS HIERARCHIES

No thorough investigation has been made of the way responsibilities impinge upon various types and ranks of business executives. But we can assume that our general analysis applies without significant qualification to the salaried managers of large corporations and to the owner managers of small firms. It is generally believed that the latter feels his responsibilities more keenly than the former; but if anything, the reverse may well be the truth. However many other executives may, theoretically, share the praise or blame in large corporations, in practice responsibility tends to be pushed onto the top figure in the hierarchy.[22]

Our analysis will be valid for the lower levels of the hierarchy to the extent that business organizations have not settled into stable, routinized patterns of divided, circumscribed responsibilities and of regular promotion.[23] Insofar as they have, the particular strains we have been discussing are mitigated. However, there are good reasons to believe that few businesses are, or could readily become, rigidly bureaucratic at the executive level. Ideally, business firms are well integrated organizations with flexible, dynamic qualities; this ideal imposes heavy demands for initiative and cooperation from executives at all levels.[24] A company which rest-

[20] See Learned, Ulrich, and Booz, *Executive Action.*

[21] Franz Alexander *et al., Studies in Psychosomatic Medicine* (New York, 1948). In an extremely interesting study of executives at the Benjamin Franklin Clinic of the Pennsylvania General Hospital, Philadelphia, a diffuse "inability to relax" and an impression of high incidence of psychosomatic disorders associated with high activism has been reported. (Unpublished work, personal communication.)

[22] We refer to the symbolic use of leading figures as heroes or scapegoats. It was through this mechanism that President Hoover was blamed for the depression and President Roosevelt lauded for getting us out of it (or, alternatively, blamed for prolonging it).

[23] The subject does not seem to have been well studied as yet. Over a decade ago, M. E. Dimock and H. K. Hyde, *Bureaucracy and Trusteeship in Large Corporations* (T.N.E.C. Monograph #11, U.S. Government Printing Office, 1940), p. 132, lamented that the bureaucracy problem had "not received the attention it deserves . . . This apathy has been reflected in the relative lack of detailed studies." The subsequent years do not seem to have fundamentally altered this situation, but the subject is a difficult one.

[24] Barnard has given special emphasis to this point in *Organization and Management,* p. 10.

lessly seeks new products and methods and rapidly adjusts to competition and other external pressures cannot be rigidly organized. Its component parts must be adjustable — ready to respond to ever changing demands of the central coordinating authority. This implies that the standards of performance of executives, at low levels as well as near the top, may be ill-defined; they can only be clearly defined at the price of steady routine and rigidity. Moreover, the demands that component divisions of a firm respond quickly and willingly to demands from higher coordinating authority run counter to the familiar tendencies of all organizations to develop their own internal organization which tends to resist pressures from outside. The total business firm itself shows these tendencies to develop "its own ways of doing things" and resists "dictation" from outside, but it must overcome the same tendencies as they appear within the firm.[25]

The demands made upon junior executives for initiative, flexibility, and cooperation are a major source of strain. The junior executive must control any proprietary feelings he may develop about his special department and functions. He must show initiative and attempt to work out problems for himself; yet he must immediately abandon his cherished ways of doing things should they be out of line with the latest company policy. Loyalty to the total organization is always demanded of an executive, but demands of this kind seem to be especially emphasized in American business organizations.

In the absence of bureaucratic routine, there are no clear standards by which a junior executive's performance can be judged. His prospects depend to an unusual degree upon the opinions of a very few superiors, or perhaps of one man.[26] He is judged by practical results but, like his superiors, he may be judged by results over which he has very little control.[27]

Thus, the junior executive is subjected to the same kind of strains associated with responsibility as is the top executive. If the responsibility itself is not so great, other factors add to the strain. Not only does the junior executive have to get results which are not entirely within his own control; he has to convince a single superior or a very few superiors that he is getting results as well as, or better than, others might do in his

[25] The pattern here referred to is, we stress, perfectly general in formal organizations. It has been much studied by industrial sociologists among work groups — particularly as it affects level of output. Although it has not, to the writers' knowledge been as exhaustively studied in other types of organizations, it is obviously present in governmental departments and military organizations.

[26] This is one of the fundamental reasons for the extremely careful observation of superiors which has often been noted. See Learned, Ulrich, and Booz, *Executive Action*. J. P. Marquand's *Point of No Return* contains a beautiful account of the phenomenon.

[27] A group of young executives interviewed by the authors had considerable to say about the pains of being praised for what they thought was indifferent work and being dressed down for what they thought had been the best they could do.

position. In the absence of objective standards he is very dependent on the idiosyncratic likes and dislikes of his superiors. Personal ingratiation rather than objective performance may be, or may be thought to be, the road to promotion. Moreover, the executive cannot easily move from one firm to another, because his talents, experience, and reputation are not readily transferable.[28] This means that success for the junior executive is most realistically defined in terms of promotion within one particular firm. His promotion therefore depends not only on the judgment of a few superiors but on the arbitrary chance that suitable vacancies will occur at the right moments. A recent president of the New York Central Railroad has stated: "There are no great men; somebody quits, somebody dies, or you happen to be the right age . . . so much of it is luck . . ." [29]

The junior business executive is hardly assured that his merits will be justly rewarded. There is a definite gamble in his commitment to a particular firm which must produce very ambivalent feelings toward it. Unlike the man in the labor role, however, he is not in a position to express his doubts openly. The demands for flexible, coordinated functioning require a high level of loyalty from business executives. Their doubts and hostilities regarding satisfactory recognition and prospects cannot readily get the kind of frank statement which the demands of labor get through union spokesmen. The presumption is that they are suppressed and tend to find indirect expression in a compulsive loyalty to the firm (or business firms in general) and a complementary hostility to real or symbolic opponents of the firm. The potentialities of this mechanism for ideology are evident, particularly in assaults on governmental interference and the iniquities of labor unions.

THE SOCIAL RELATIONS OF BUSINESS AND ATTENDANT STRAINS

By comparison with much social action, business enterprise involves highly rational focusing of action on clearly defined empirical goals. The sharp eye of Adam Smith long ago noticed that efficiency in carrying out business transactions demanded an exclusion of amenities and concerns which surround other kinds of action. He emphasized that we do not have to behave in the market place in the same way as we do with friends or relatives and that the brusqueness and forthrightness of market behavior are essential to expedition and efficiency.[30]

There are two institutional features which distinguish personal relations

---

[28] There are of course some industries (such as the automobile industry) in which there is apparently a considerable circulation of executives between firms. But there are strong tendencies favoring internal recruitment. See "The Nine Hundred," *Fortune*, November 1952, pp. 132 ff; Randall, *Creed for Free Enterprise*, pp. 131–132; P. W. Litchfield, *Autumn Leaves* (Cleveland, 1945), p. 109.

[29] William White, *Time*, July 7, 1952, p. 75.

[30] Smith, *Wealth of Nations*, p. 14.

in business from interpersonal relations in general: *affective neutrality* and *self-orientation*.

AFFECTIVE NEUTRALITY

In any social relationship, individuals tend to like or dislike each other rather than remain indifferent. The extent to which they can express their feelings depends upon the institutional context of the relationship. Within the family loving others is not merely permitted; it is a responsibility. At work one usually has to restrain one's likes and dislikes, to behave impartially. This *affective neutrality* pervades the business world.[31] The businessman who allows his salesman to deal with customers only as he likes or dislikes them is apt to be regarded as a poor businessman.

SELF-ORIENTATION

In any social setting the individual feels some responsibility for other individuals or for the system as a whole, and the limits of this responsibility are defined by a set of institutionalized rules.[32] In the case of the business enterprise, these limits are narrow; the enterprise may be legitimately self-oriented and the interests of others or the community at large rarely have to be considered. What is desirable for the individual enterprise has a claim to legitimacy by this very fact. Of course, these patterns are not peculiar to the business enterprise alone; they apply to all parties to economic transactions. The shopper is expected to buy to please himself, not to help the merchant or the national economy.

Affective neutrality and self-orientation are usually found together in the same circumstances, and the strains they raise are closely interconnected. The kind of strain they produce on business executives is often seen in connection with personnel problems of various sorts. When the authors asked a group of junior executives which were the decisions which gave them the most anxiety and difficulty, the answer was those involving personnel matters; these were the "real bastards." These decisions always involved a conflict between the norms of efficient business conduct and feelings of personal attachment or responsibility for others. For example, there is X who is a "swell fellow" and who needs a promotion, but whose work does not merit one, and may indeed not merit a job.[33] A correspondent in *Dun's Review* reflected the same tensions when he wrote: ". . . to wonder if it is not time to get rid of a person who cannot do a

[31] The development of this concept as a tool of sociological analysis is due to Talcott Parsons. For a systematic, technical exposition, see Parsons and Shils, *Toward a General Theory of Action*, pp. 75–80. Application of the concept may be found in the references cited in ch. 15, note 16.

[32] See on these and related matters, Parsons and Shils, *Toward a General Theory of Action*, pp. 75–80.

[33] Discussion with Sloan Fellows at Massachusetts Institute of Technology, Cambridge, Mass., by two of the authors.

thing correctly . . . to reflect that the person in fault has a wife and seven children . . . No other executive in the world would put up with him for another moment . . . but that . . . in all probability . . . any successor would be just as bad . . . and probably worse . . ." [34] In the *Fortune* poll cited above, ability to handle people was listed first among the qualifications necessary for a good executive. The responses may have been sober reflections that the practical results of handling people well are very important, or that this particular ability is very scarce; it is probable, however, that the sense of tension involved in handling people is an equally important reason for the respondents to answer as they did.

The conflict which the businessman feels on this score is not simply one between expediency and humanity. He feels it is his *duty* to judge people fairly according to their competence. When businessmen have to make hardhearted decisions, these are not without the reinforcements of moral norms. The norm of affective discipline in dealing with employees is closely tied to norms of universalism, whereby there is a moral responsibility to judge employees "fairly" according to their competence and performance. We have heard businessmen say, with the finality of a categorical imperative: "You *have* to judge men on what they can do." Sometimes the discipline of affective concerns in the interest of universalism is carried to such a point that the businessman complains that he is unable to admit to motives other than "good business."

We kid ourselves a lot . . . we talk about doing all this because it pays off in the annual report. We'd be scared to admit to ourselves anything else. But I think I know why we're doing it — it's because these people here have a right to express themselves. Putting the emphasis on efficiency as the reason is like Stakhonovism, and that's not really what we are doing anyway. I think we'd do better to face up to the fact.[35]

Affective neutrality and limited responsibility are part of the role of the businessman, but conditions that produce strains over these norms are inevitably present. The contractual character of employer-employee relationships limits the mutual responsibilities of both sides, but this does not mean that personal acquaintance and "friendliness" are avoided. To the contrary, the shirtsleeve democracy with the friendly, informal boss

[34] *Dun's Review*, July 1951, p. 8. The dots, except at beginning are included in the writer's text.

[35] Whyte, *Is Anybody Listening?*, p. 39. See also, the comment of William A. Orton in *Fortune*, October 1948, p. 118. "Many a corporation director is more interested in his concern as a working community than as a money-making machine; but he is usually shy to admit it — partly because he thinks the stockholders or the bankers would kick, partly because he is genuinely afraid of being 'unbusinesslike.' "

is an outstanding characteristic of American business.[36] The businessman strikes up a great many friendships at work. At the same time, anyone with authority over others tends to feel moral responsibility for their well-being. It is not always easy for the businessman to keep these feelings of responsibility within the very narrow limits of contractual obligation. Feeling that his employees are dependent on him for their livelihood, he tends to develop a paternalistic sense of responsibility toward them.[37] While the norms of good business may back him up if he has to discharge an employee, his sense of moral responsibility rarely permits him to do so without strain. Certainly many businessmen have suffered over discharging men whom they scarcely know.

The worn slogans, "Business is business," and "Sentiment has no place in business," surely derive much of their currency from the strains we are depicting. Within the contexts of his own organization, the "sentiments" which these adages warn against are evidently those which arise from personal likes and dislikes or feelings of responsibility, and control of them must be a constant source of strain.

Affectively neutral relationships have a distinctive character within the business organization, but in somewhat different forms they are characteristic of all economic relationships in our society. It is unbusinesslike to patronize a particular merchant simply because of ties of kinship or friendship. By contrast, in many other societies economic transactions would never bring together those who are otherwise unrelated strangers.[38]

Relationships built on the norms of universalism, affective discipline, and limited responsibility hold obvious advantages for economic development. They provide the means whereby men with nothing in common other than economic interests can work together; they give some assurance of reliable action and fair treatment. But relationships founded on such narrow grounds can easily be disturbed. In consequence, various patterns have developed which provide confidence that the market relationship is not merely a hostile opposition of naked self-interest. Salesmen assume a cheery enthusiasm and friendliness; the clerks in women's stores

[36] Perhaps the "informal organization" which has now become a classic study of American industrial sociologists, following Roethlisberger and Dickson, is a specially important and conspicuous phenomenon in our particular variant of industrial organization.

[37] It seems to be very common in American business to talk of the "boys" in the shop, or out in the plant. Such references to grown men as "boys" seem to occur in our society where there is a diffuse sense of dependence and subordination like that of children in families. (Compare references to "soldier boys.") In business organizations, they certainly suggest something of this sort and consequently more than contractual responsibility.

[38] See, for example, Raymond Firth, *Primitive Polynesian Economy* (London, 1939).

behave with saccharine familiarity; business in general claims that it "serves" the customer.

Assumed friendliness has an even more obvious significance in the problems of initiating business relationships. A network of personal acquaintances is of greater importance in our mobile and fluid society than in more traditional, ascribed orders. American society is notoriously concerned about possibilities of "contacts." "Contacts" tend to be clothed in the guise of "friendship" even though they rest on very tenuous bonds of common schooling, home towns, or casual encounter. Outgoing "friendliness" in this sense has obvious functional importance in a dynamic progressive economy.

It also gives rise to considerable strain. There is an abundance of cynical comment about "contacts," "buttering up," and the shallowness of "business friendships" which reflect this strain. Similar suspicions extend to advertising, and public exhortations in general.[39] Where narrow self-oriented relationships are clothed in the forms of more intimate relationships, suspicions about sincerity can hardly be avoided. If a salesman is friendly and attractive, it may be necessary to be on one's guard lest he exploit the confidence he inspires. And under strain he may be viewed with exaggerated and cynical suspicion.

Strains in this area arise on both sides of a relationship. Those who are importuned must assure themselves they are not being taken in; those who importune must also avoid disillusionment and disgust over their actions. The demands of aggressive friendliness are not easy to meet. Ambivalence about the legitimacy of aggressive tactics, widespread in our society, is one of the roots of anti-business sentiment. The salesman or executive trying to put across a "deal" or a "proposition" by winning the

---

[39] Compare Merton, *Mass Persuasion, passim*. This is a valuable study of the problems of convincing the public of "sincerity." Merton speaks of the kind of relationships we have been describing as "pseudo-Gemeinschaft" relationships. The possibilities of exploiting friendly acquaintances are legion and one important example will have to suffice for illustration. One of the characteristic problems of establishing business relationships is getting access to executives. Because of the very nature of the executive's function he must be careful in the allocation of his time; not all executives are really busy but they all are potentially busy (either through preoccupation with the always available detail or through avoiding delegation of decisions). If an executive is to control situations, he must be able to control the use of his own time — hence among other things the protection of executives by encapsulated inner offices and a secretarial carapace. To be a "friend" of an executive gives a nice leverage point for getting at his time; since friendship is a symmetrical relationship and permits one to presume on the other's time, access which might be impossible on more formal grounds thus becomes possible through the claim of friendship. (This situation is nicely depicted in an advertisement of *Nation's Business* in the *New York Times*, March 24, 1929, where a salesman is being turned away even though he "knew" Mr. ————; the implication is that this approach is a familiar one but that it may fail while the pages of *Nation's Business* may slide past the politely firm secretary.)

confidence and assent of others must convince himself that what he is doing is not dishonest, insincere, or presumptuous. The "shallowness" which European observers see in back-slapping American gregariousness can be detected by the Americans engaging in that very activity. Maintaining confident action in the face of such awareness may produce a great deal of tension.

THE BOUNDS OF LEGITIMACY

The self-orientation of business means that the businessman as such feels only limited moral responsibilities toward other persons and groups. But there are always boundaries on legitimate means of pursuing business success. The emphasis on achievement implies a constant pressure on these boundaries of legitimacy; and in particular instances it is very difficult for the businessman to determine just where his responsibilities lie. The man who builds up a great business by exploiting every opportunity is applauded; but he is not applauded if he uses "illegitimate" coercion or fraud. Nor is concern with the boundary only a matter of keeping within the law, or avoiding the condemnation of others; each businessman internalizes in some measure the rules of "honest business." Any departures or pressures to depart from these rules are thus felt internally as a source of strain.[40]

There are good reasons why the businessman finds it difficult to define clearly the boundaries of legitimacy. Basic moral training takes place in the family; much of it concerns relations to friends and relatives and may provide little that can be applied to the more tenuous and less particularistic interpersonal relations of business. The standards which grow up within the business community need not be integrated with those taught and practiced elsewhere. The adage "business is business" seems to reflect the fact that practices are legitimate in the business world which fall short of some ideal moral standard. Further, the great sensitivity of businessmen to criticism by "outsiders" who don't understand their problems again points to internal standards which fit only poorly with other standards of the community, and which are in themselves not too clear. Were there a firmer sense of what is proper business, the businessman's sensitivity to outside criticism and his dependence on the supporting judgment of his associates would be much less.[41]

The pressure on the businessman to pursue an aggressive business

[40] There is a tendency to think of the "bad old days" as completely lawless; in fact there has always been some body of practices which were considered illegitimate. The boundaries are indefinite and changing; but at any time they are perceptible to most businessmen.

[41] Comparison to the medical profession is instructive: the fear of "socialized" medicine is probably reinforced by a sense that things are done by doctors which they would not like to have to justify to laymen.

policy, with heavy penalties for crossing boundaries none too well marked, results in strain. He has difficulty in keeping a balanced moral judgment of his practices. One direction of reaction is emphasis on the hardheaded pursuit of self-interest. He may even become cynical, declaring in his disillusionment that all business is dirty business.[42] To the extent that reaction in this direction is conducive to ideology, it favors ideology of a classical sort rather than requiring the acceptance of moral responsibility. At the opposite extreme, the businessman may try to invest the whole business world with moral dignity and responsibility. This reaction is the mainspring of the managerial element of the creed.

But the assumption of feelings of heavy responsibility to others as an alternative to cynical acceptance of self-interest is not without its problems. To whom must the businessman feel responsible? The responsibilities assumed by business firms to customers and competitors, community and nation remain relatively narrow. For example, American businessmen are more ready than their European counterparts to see their competitors driven to the wall.[43] This readiness has undoubtedly contributed much to the strength of the American economy; it has also made it difficult to define responsibilities which limit the self-orientation of an American business. Similarly, there is potential conflict between good business and devotion to the nation.[44] Very frequently the businessman must be forced by the pressures of "good business" to courses of action which are something less than generously patriotic. Given the strong pressures in the modern world to show general community responsibility, and the importance of the government as a symbol of broad national loyalties, this conflict is bound to produce much strain, arising in a context which is particularly suitable to ideological reaction.

THE BUSINESS EXECUTIVE IN THE SOCIAL STRUCTURE

Those who are business executives also fill other roles. The relation of the executive role to these other roles, and the place of the executive

[42] The disguised autobiography, *High Pressure*, by J. R. Sprague, is a most interesting case study of a reaction at this pole. "Peter Kent" remains an honest businessman but he has a passionate hatred of moralizing about business, in particular the effort to reconcile it with Christian principles.

[43] See J. Sawyer and D. Landes, *Modern France*, edited by E. M. Earle (Princeton, 1951).

[44] These difficulties are no special feature of national emergencies, but are grounded in the relations of business and government as fundamentally represented in our legal system. The fundamental point lies in the essentially negative character of the obligations imposed on business by the legal system. The legal rules and principles are enforced by the government but this enforcement is segregated from such demands for generous loyalty to the nation as may be exacted or expected in other contexts. Legal rules constitute boundaries to what may be done rather than diffuse ideals of what ought to be done. Thus, in relation to the law, it is permissible to be technical, seek out loopholes, and try to "get away with" things.

in the system of social stratification have important consequences for the forms of ideological reaction. Our previous discussions of the strains of the role and of its vulnerability to ideological attack might suggest that the role of business executive brings limited satisfactions and modest regard. This is not so. The available evidence indicates that American society is one in which businessmen can and do look on themselves with self-satis-faction. Numerous studies of the relative prestige of occupations produced recently by American sociologists accord businessmen a position which, if below the top, is at least very respectable. Various governmental posi-tions have regularly outranked any business executive role — United States Supreme Court Justice being monotonously first in all studies, and ambassadors, state governors, United States Senators, cabinet members taking closely following positions. Perhaps surprisingly, professional roles — above all that of the physician — have outranked important business roles (such as directors of large corporations). But various types of business executive roles have at least attained medium status and often pressed toward the highest levels of prestige.[45] Moreover, there is reason to believe that occupational status alone gives an undervaluation of the class status accorded to businessmen and their families. While occupational status is probably the prime determinant of class status, the business executive's occupational prestige is reinforced by his participation in many highly valued extra-occupational activities to which business is the natural entree. These activities boost the individual businessman to high status in local communities. In smaller American communities, business-men typically are looked up to as leaders and constitute a sort of local aristocracy. The nature of business activities and the possession of rela-tively high personal incomes join to give businessmen a sense of respon-sibility and prominence in local affairs. These, in turn, give in small compass the kinds of increments to prestige which bring high place on the national scene to those in governmental executive roles. Integration of occupational status with a prominent place in local communities is probably more important for businessmen than for most types of profes-sional men, and accounts for differences in local prestige and the abstract valuation of the occupations as such.[46] We find here one of the roots of a certain local emphasis in the business ideology.

The relatively high rewards in income and prestige which accompany

[45] The most thoroughgoing study of these matters is that of North and Hatt cited above, Ch. 5, note 55. Older studies were largely conducted with students at various places in the country. See the extensive review of the literature in A. F. Davies, "Prestige of Occupations," *Brit. J. Sociology*, June 1952.

[46] Some good remarks are found in C. Arnold Anderson, "Sociological Elements in Economic Restrictionism," *Amer. Soc. Rev.*, 9: 345–358 (1944).

"(The small businessman's status) is . . . local in focus. More than any other vocational group, the small business man tends to be identified with his community; he is the spokesman for the values of community life." (p. 350)

the business executive's role lead us to expect an ideological reaction of an essentially conservative sort. The contrast with those ideological reactions which are congenial to the strains of the labor role is instructive.[47] The labor role is not one of high prestige; despite leveling tendencies in the income distribution and the pressures of egalitarian ideals the worker remains in a poorly regarded status. Given this fact, the rewards for successful performance in his role are inevitably modest and little is to be gained by glorification of coping with its strains and difficulties. The business executive, on the other hand, is in a much more favorable position to react to strain by introjection, accepting the sources of strain as indicators of the difficulty and worthwhileness of achievement. The difference is not simply one of vested interests in a property sense, but rather of the differential value of positions in the stratification hierarchy.

The presumption of a conservative ideological reaction assumes that businessmen are adjusted to their roles, that basically they accept its goals and practices as legitimate and worth while. There are some businessmen who "hate business" and are disposed to strongly "anti-business" ideological reactions; no role ever integrates fully all who may become its incumbents. And indeed, some aspects of the structure of the business world lead in the direction of anti-business reactions.[48] But the dominant pattern is certainly toward satisfaction and acceptance of the role. Despite the ulcers and worry, business executives show the highest levels of satisfaction with their jobs of any occupational group in our society. They also, not surprisingly, show the highest percentages satisfied with their incomes *at all income levels* (except for high income farmers).[49] In view of this evidence, we may turn to relate strains and ideology with confidence that reactions which "defend" the business system are likely to gain broad sympathy among businessmen.

[47] For a detailed analysis of the strains of the labor role, see Sutton, *Radical Marxist,* ch. 7.

[48] Two important possibilities arise over: (1) the conflicts between artisan or professional motivations and business standards, and (2) the inevitable cases of limited success or outright failure. The strains among groups on the professional fringe (such as druggists and morticians) have been noted, as well as similar strains among artisanal groups such as furriers. Kriesberg's study cited these strains. "Unsuccessful" furriers tend to emphasize their artisanal skill and denigrate their "successful" competitors as dishonest or unscrupulous.

[49] Richard Centers and Hadley Cantril, "Income Satisfaction and Income Aspiration," *J. Ab. and Soc. Psy.,* 41: 64–69 (1946). Compare the notably higher levels of dissatisfaction among professionals revealed by this study.

17

THE CREED ANALYZED:
STRAINS AND IDEOLOGY

WE SHALL NOW EXAMINE THE CONTENT of the business ideology in the light of our theory, considering first the general "tone" of the creed as set by its pervasive themes and showing how it relates to the strains experienced by businessmen. The broad strands of ideology represented in the classical and managerial creeds will then be analyzed in relation to special ideological themes, discussed in roughly the same order as they were presented in Part I. Limitations of space prevent our examining *every* proposition in the business creed; but, by showing the systematic relationships between the principal themes in the ideology and strains in the businessman's role, we hope to convince the reader of the usefulness of our theory.

THE TONE OF THE CREED: PRACTICALITY, AUSTERITY, OPTIMISTIC AFFIRMATION

Throughout the business creed runs a characteristic tone, compounded of emphases on: sober, practical realism; responsible, moral austerity; and optimistic affirmation.[1]

The qualities of practicality and realism are assigned to the image of businessmen themselves — they above all other elements in the community possess these qualities. The whole ideology is shaped by a certain distrust of abstract theory and systematic argument, of theorists and intellectuals. The creed prefers common sense to abstract argument, "shirt-sleeve economics" [2] to academic theories, the ordinary meanings of words to professional niceties of definition,[3] the testimony of purchasing agents

---

[1] Chapter 12 has expounded the values of the business creed as they appear in explicit symbols and themes. By the tone of the creed we mean to characterize more diffuse emotional dispositions manifested in the creed.

[2] The title of a book by W. A. Paton (New York, 1952), a professor of accounting.

[3] The NAM text appeals ostentatiously to common-sense usage against professional refinements in accepting the accounting definition of profits rather than any economic definition, and in refusing to worry about the different kinds and degrees of competition which concern economists. NAM, I: 440; NAM, II: ch. 12.

about prices to the analyses of economists,[4] and the sales experience of a Paul Hoffman to years of governmental service or university study. Even those more esoteric pieces of ideology which essay systematic analysis exhibit marked distrust of abstract theory, as the NAM text illustrates. The long theoretical tradition in support of the business position, from which the classical creed draws much of its argument, is paid little explicit honor in the ideology. Adam Smith is not revered, even though the coincidence by which 1776 is the publication date of *The Wealth of Nations* would enhance his usefulness as an ideological symbol. Unlike Marxism, the business creed does not insist on its "scientific" character, although it would resist characterization as "unscientific." It disclaims the need for any intellectual authority; the wisdom and experience of businessmen or the common sense of any American are a more reliable guide to understanding the economy.[5]

There are, no doubt, sound dialectical reasons for the business creed to refuse to be drawn into full-blown logical and abstract arguments. At best, the blacks and whites which contribute to the effectiveness of ideological pictures would be blurred by qualifications, exceptions, and matters of degree; at worst, the inconsistencies and contradictions characteristic of any ideology would be exposed. However, the anti-theoretical stand of the creed is so pervasive and so pronounced that it can hardly be explained by dialectical expediency alone. It is an attitude which the creed proclaims with pride, rather than a weakness which it attempts to conceal.

In spite of this distaste for abstract, systematic analysis and argument, the creed extols rationality and insists that businessmen are peculiarly rational. This claim is best appreciated if "rational" is understood as the antonym of "sentimental." Against the wishful thinking and unrealistic hopes with which the public is constantly being deluded, businessmen insistently call attention to the simple hard facts of life which limit the possibilities of action. (Certainly it would be nice to raise wages, but businessmen must point out that enterprises cannot pay out more than they take in.)

[4] NAM, ch. 10. Compare our discussion in Chapter 12 above.

[5] "The arm-chair economists are at it again — the boys of the 'hot stove' league who always have the answer . . . Let's do a little analyzing, just as average Americans, using just average common sense." Standard Steel Spring advertisement in the *New York Times*, April 5, 1949.

"To a certain extent, economics consists of ability to present plausible phrases as an alternative to the progress of practical production." E. Howard Bennett, editorial, *Textile Reporter*, Aug. 14, 1952, p. 41.

"To me, as I imagine to every executive of a competitive American business, the economic principles that I have attempted to elucidate are in fact nothing less than workaday laws we are forced to observe as surely as we observe the law of gravity." President Dunlop of Sun Oil Co., *Hearings on Profits* (Flanders), p. 269.

Closely related to this emphasis on cold, rational practicality, is the note of austerity that pervades the business creed, especially the classical version. It is not, of course, austerity, in the sense that an ascetic indifference to worldly pleasures is commended as a personal ethic either to businessmen or to other individuals. It is, rather, that the realities of economic and social life, as the creed describes them, are such that a resolute attitude of austerity is the only hope of avoiding disappointment. Moreover, an austere attitude is morally right both for individuals and for nations in the sense that excessive eagerness for the material good things of life, unaccompanied by the will to earn them, is morally wrong. In these respects, the business creed recalls both the "dismal science" of nineteenth-century economics and the Protestant ethic which Max Weber found so important for the growth of capitalism.

Various propositions of the ideology contribute to its general tone of austerity:

The only road to greater economic welfare, either for the individual or for the nation, is hard work and thrift. There are no shortcuts to Canaan. The real wages of the worker are determined by his productivity; and that depends on his own effort plus the tools provided by the thrift of savers. Whether the national problem is unemployment or inflation, the basic — and only — solution is production and still more production. Security is an illusory goal — ultimately it too rests on individual productivity and thrift; it cannot be provided by *ad hoc* governmental institutions.

Certain fundamental laws govern economic affairs. Attempts to circumvent them are bound to fail and be punished. Monetary and fiscal panaceas are untrustworthy; departures from the principles of a sound currency are bound to be disastrous. What goes up is bound to come down. You can't get something for nothing. If Keynesian economics says that national self-indulgence in spending will lead to prosperity, and frugality and thrift to depression, then Keynesian economics is immoral and must be wrong.

Many economic and social reforms with worthy objectives sound good on paper or in theory, but in practice they will founder on the rock of the immutability of human nature.

The ethic which the creed commends to individuals is individual self-reliance. The world owes no one a living. Everyone gets what he deserves in terms of his own efforts and abilities. Things aren't the way they used to be — people have degenerated morally. Workers don't work as hard as they used to. People don't stand on their own feet any more. Everybody is too interested in security nowadays.

These emphases on practical realism and austerity give much business ideology a somber character. When unrelieved they issue in gloomy scoldings or harsh fundamentalism. But there is another emphasis in the creed which supplies a brighter note: confident optimism about future progress, proud boastings about America and its achievements under free enterprise, refusal to see insoluble problems in labor-management relations, in business ethics, or anywhere else. (This provides a sharp contrast to an ideology like Marxism with its critical stance toward Western society and its fatalistic insistence that only the ripening of history can bring a change.)

This quality of the business ideology — which we may call "optimistic affirmation" — is unevenly represented in the classical and managerial strands but has its place in both. Indeed it has a ubiquity which calls for the recognition we are here trying to give it.

. Accepting this characterization of the business creed's general tone, let us consider how it is related to the strains of business. It appears that the businessman responds to the strains of his role in American society by vigorous acceptance, rather than by evasion, withdrawal, or rebellion. Because strain is involved, this acceptance must be more than quietly unreflective; it must have the compulsive character which ideology shapes and reinforces. The businessman's creed defines his activities as morally proper and as serving worthy goals. In a loose sense, the dominant psychological reaction which the ideology expresses is "introjective" rather than "projective." Sources of strain are not defined as arbitrary or pernicious impositions, either of human agents or of inescapable conditions. Instead, they are accepted aggressively; transformed, they shape the definitions of merit and achievement. Room is left for scapegoats and dangerous historical tendencies, but complaint and warning about these evils are balanced by a positive definition of the business role in the existing society.

The *practical realism* of the business creed is a theme with various roots. In the first place, the business role is a self-interested role[6] and this orientation is bound to be a source of anxieties and doubts regarding its worthiness. The pathways to rationalizing the pursuit of self-interest are few. If the businessman is to escape cynicism or a sense of merely yielding to expediency he must have an ideology that gives some positive valuation to his self-interested action. Since self-interest (in itself) is a poor subject for lyrical idealism or warm romanticism, the tone of a suitable ideology must be somewhat restrained and sober. The business creed achieves an effective tone by making practical rationality a virtue and an obligation.[7]

[6] In the sense discussed in Chapters 5 and 16.

[7] All the various possibilities which come to mind for an ideology supportive of independent business seem to have common elements. They legitimize business activity at some basic level, then extol it as an instrument to nobler ends. Thus in medieval Christianity (See Troeltsch, *Social Teaching of the Christian Churches*, vol. 1) the doctrine of relative natural law gave most forms of business activity a legitimate place in an imperfect but not thoroughly evil world. Under an ideology of this sort the businessman could feel a modest merit in what he was doing. Other possibilities (as in nationalist ideologies) emphasize the contribution of business activity to the good of the whole community and thereby lend it at least the

It does this not only by direct exhortation and injunction but also by the conception of human nature which it advances. In the classical creed, self-interest is not a peculiarity of business, but the universal and immutable motivation of every man. The choice of ideals of human motivation is not, on this view, a choice between nobler ideals of altruism and the ignoble pursuit of self-interest, but a choice between idealistic error and sober realism. Intellectuals, "do-gooders," and reformers are, accordingly, apt to be naïve about human nature and many of the reforms they propose are doomed as impractical by the self-interest of individuals. The creed's view of human nature is of course, not just an "hypothesis." Asserted as reality, it carries a moral obligation of acceptance, and those who deny it abjure the moral responsibility of practical realism. Moreover, the businessman's armament against critics of his self-interest is strengthened by a view of human nature which impugns the integrity of those intellectuals and bureaucrats who proclaim the general welfare as their only real concern.[8] This realistic view of human nature is strengthened by those strains in business life connected with the manipulative use of personal relationships and the resulting suspicions of insincerity. A generalized attitude that "you can't get something for nothing" is a natural consequence.

Other roots of the business creed's emphasis on practical realism may be found in the problems of justifying the relative importance of the businessman's productive functions.

There are some doubts, within the business organization and in the society at large, concerning the substantive content of the role of the business executive, especially when his role is compared with the well-defined jobs of professionals, specialists, and experts. Although the businessman may be confident of the importance of his function, the fact that others do not always share this confidence cannot fail to concern him and may even shake his own faith. The content of the business executive role in skill, effort, and accomplishment is certainly less easy to identify in concrete terms than the content of a specialized professional role. (This does not mean, of course, that it is any less real; the contrary may be the case.) Moreover, the business executive must rely on the advice and performance of specialized subordinates. He is inferior to them in their fields of competence, yet it is he who ultimately makes the decisions and gives the orders. To justify his superior position in business hierarchies and, frequently, his higher income and status in society, the businessman needs

---

dignity of a necessary function. But satisfactory logical closures of arguments along this line are made difficult by the "irresponsibility" implied by the self-interest of the business role, which may in fact have to be overlain with a mass of conflicting obligations to bring a satisfactory sense of legitimacy. Further analysis of these problems appears later in this chapter.

[8] Note the criticism of bureaucrats reported in Chapter 11 and analyzed later in this chapter.

some reason to feel superior to professionals and experts, a reason which identifies the businessman's peculiar functional virtue. Emphasis on practicality answers this need.

As an executive, the businessman is a "specialist in generality" who must always see the "whole picture." Specialists and experts are, on the other hand, narrow. They are apt to take positions and advocate decisions which have good justification within their own fields of competence but fail to take into account other considerations which are often decisive. The executive has good reason to identify his comprehensive view of the many elements in a situation with practicality, and the narrowness of specialists' views with impracticality. With the help of the ideology, it is easy to carry this identification from the single enterprise to larger arenas.

The business creed's *austere emphasis on moral responsibilities* derives in part from the strains already noted and more particularly from some others. We have stressed that the business role demands decisiveness and confidence in the face of uncertainties that obscure the outcomes of business decisions. The businessman cannot escape the necessity for decisions or responsibility for results which are beyond his powers to control fully. He is conscious, therefore, of a strong compulsion to base his decisions on a sober assessment of the facts, undiluted by wishful thinking and sentiment. He is conscious, also, of the inevitability with which the concrete outcomes of his decisions will expose error and penalize him for it. He may rely on many for information and counsel; but his alone is the decision, his alone the responsibility. He is, in consequence, receptive to an ideology which extols as virtues the necessities of his role — sober realism, responsibility, self-reliance. These necessities lead him to view the process of business decision as peculiarly rational, that is, uninfluenced by extraneous considerations and attitudes.

The note of austerity appeals to the businessman because of the strains due to the exacting responsibility placed on him. If he is to meet the institutionalized demands of his role, the businessman must be prepared to be judged by results, come what may. As we have argued, there is a genuine sense in which the businessman thereby accepts "unfair" judgments. He could, by purely objective standards, quite legitimately beg off responsibility for much that happens (both for results better and worse than reasonable men could expect). However, since he characteristically does not, the businessman opens himself to a compulsive emphasis on self-reliance and responsibility. It follows from his own need for such emphasis that others too should be self-reliant and judged rigorously by their objective achievements. Those who are not called to account in the same way are morally inferior to him: politicians, bureaucrats, intellectuals, academicians, reformers, union leaders. If he finds the discipline of the balance sheet an exacting one, he likes to believe that a similar discipline should and ultimately does govern affairs outside the business enterprise. Eventually everyone must be brought to account; those who think otherwise are impractical and immoral.

This generalization of moral demands is reinforced by another fact of the businessman's responsibility. The businesman's responsibility for results which are in considerable degree dependent on the skills and efforts of others makes him susceptible to the feeling that his associates and subordinates are not doing their part, that they are letting him down. This feeling will not serve as an excuse to relieve him of any responsibility for failure, because part of the skill of the executive is supposed to lie precisely in the selection of subordinates, in the organization of "teamwork," and in inspiring the greatest skill and effort in personnel throughout the hierarchy. Hence these feelings can find acceptable outlet only in the more general context of ideology, in generalized exhortation and in unfavorable comparisons of the moral qualities of people in subordinate roles with those of previous generations. Thus businessmen are quick to believe ideological assertions that labor productivity isn't what it used to be, that workers nowadays are more interested in security than in craftsmanship, and so on.[9]

The business role also defines the relationships of the businessman to other individuals in a way which is conducive to emphasis on austere acceptance of responsibility and indeed to belief in practical realism as well. The businessman is supposed to be neutral in these relationships, in two senses. First, in his pursuit of the profit of his enterprise, he must resist the intrusion into his decisions of likes or dislikes of the individuals and groups affected by his decisions. This requirement of *affective neutrality* conflicts with the general expectation in our society that inter-personal dealings will be influenced by the affective feelings of the parties. Second, the definition of the business role specifies certain moral responsibilities which the businessman is expected to assume. But it does not impose on him obligations to all the individuals and groups directly and indirectly affected by his actions. Indeed the role sets certain norms which tell the businessman it is wrong to assume diffuse moral responsibilities. (For example, the norm of universalism says that individuals should be treated in business dealings and in occupational competition according to their performances, not according to their needs and virtues.) This requirement of the role conflicts with a vague but strong feeling in our society that individuals should be guided by "social conscience" as well as by private conscience. The businessman must resist the intrusion into his decisions of feelings of diffuse moral responsibility beyond the specific obligations of his role.

[9] There is a general tendency of ideologies with moral stresses to find "golden ages" of human virtue in the past, and the business ideology falls in line with this tendency. It is easier to argue the possibility of moral improvement in the future if better standards are alleged to have been attained in the past.

The strains of conducting the personal relationships of business life on this neutral basis are alleviated by the ideology insofar as it makes virtues of these requirements. Thus businessmen can take pride in being hard-headed, practical, and unsentimental.

A tone of *optimistic affirmation* in the business creed obviously fits with our general suggestion that the creed reflects a basic acceptance of the business role and an effort to transmute its strains into criteria of merit. Some of the previously outlined reactions to particular strains have natural and essential complements in notes of optimism. Thus the responsibility of the business role and its demands for decisive action produce a need for optimism, even a sense of moral obligation to be optimistic. Action in the face of uncertainty normally requires an optimistic bias. The business creed makes activism and optimism virtues in themselves, thereby setting up diffuse moral norms which suit the specific needs of business-men. Optimism about one's own enterprise usually requires an optimistic view of local and national society, both present and future. The proud and hopeful vision of a progressive Middletown in a progressive America conforms to this need.

The business creed's acceptance of self-interest as a practical and re-alistic view of human nature needs a brighter touch to relieve its sobriety. The ideology, selecting the rosier conclusions from the tradition of eco-nomic thought, readily finds cause for optimism in the aggregative results of self-interest.

It is important to remember that sometimes the businessman is able to do things that are easy and pleasant. There is in fact a real basis for his claims that he serves the interests of others, that he can minimize the need for hardboiled decisions, or that he can make his firm operate like a big family. Conscientious pursuit of these responsibilities and ideals requires the kind of ideological support which stresses that such things can be done. It is natural to find a vigorous business community urging itself on with an optimistic, affirmative ideology such as American businessmen possess in some major strands of their creed.

THE CLASSICAL AND MANAGERIAL VIEWS ON MAJOR TOPICS

Profit and Ethics. Possibly the most fundamental source of strain in the business role is an inconsistency in the ethical norms by which Ameri-can society expects business behavior to be governed. On the one hand, self-interested actions by businessmen are tolerated in law and approved in social mores. On the other hand, self-interest is considered to be an unworthy goal of action which conflicts with ethical norms to which society attaches great importance. This inconsistency creates ambivalence in social attitudes toward business; and since businessmen share the values which support both sides of the dilemma, it also produces strains within businessmen themselves. One of the major concerns of business ideology is, there-fore, the place which self-interest does and should have in business action. The classical and managerial answers to this basic question stand at oppo-site poles; they may be viewed as alternative resolutions of the fundamen-tal inconsistency in ethical norms.

Some social norms support the profit orientation of business. In the vast majority of our day-to-day dealings with business firms, we accept without moral indignation their orientation to profit. Furthermore, we em-phasize occupational achievement as the proper goal of personal action; and we define occupational achievement in business in terms of profit or some related measure. In comparison with other societies, America gen-erally places such a high premium on the goal of success, as measured by money income and wealth, that the social norms which constrain the means used to pursue the goal are relatively weak.[10] At the same time, our culture provides businessmen with certain norms which are defenses against the intrusion of other orientations in business action. These defenses are for the most part derived from the value which we as a society place on uni-versalistic treatment of individuals — treatment, that is, according to what they can do rather than who they are — in relationships outside the family and the home.

But the ethical norms which call for modifying the profit orientation of business decisions are also very powerful. As explained previously, these are of two main kinds. First, it is expected that an individual will form affective dispositions — likes and dislikes of various intensities — toward his associates and acquaintances, even in occupational life, and that his actions toward other individuals will be influenced by these. Second, it is expected that, in taking actions which affect others, an individual will as-sume some moral responsibility for their welfare, quite apart from his feel-ings toward them. Besides these two norms, other prevalent social attitudes diminish the acceptability of a self-interested orientation of business action. Unvarnished self-interest is not an admissible explanation of action; to be socially approved, the actions of an individual must be interpretable as contributing something to society. It is true that American society awards social status on the basis of highly generalized criteria of occupational achievement, such as wealth and income. But we are far from being com-pletely indifferent to the specific content of the achievement or to the methods by which success is attained.

Many businessmen doubtless find it possible to make an unreflective adjustment under these conflicting demands most of the time. But strains regularly arise from such conflicts and they produce overemphasis either on self-interest or on responsibilities to others. In the former case, disillu-

---

[10] For a development of this point, see Merton, *Social Theory and Social Struc-ture*, ch. 4.

sionment and cynicism, with acceptance of a complete divorce between the worlds of business and morality, is one extreme reaction. At the opposite pole, we may find Utopian denial of conflict or compulsive acceptance of social duties. Not all of these reactions can be suitably fitted out with ideology, but in the classical and managerial creeds the businessman has a possibility in each direction.

The classical creed affirms the moral propriety of profit orientation in the business role. To the businessman, torn by a conflict of values, it explains that devotion to private profit is not inconsistent with serving the social welfare but is, rather, a prerequisite of economic efficiency. At the same time, it assures the businessman that he really has no choice in the matter anyway, since he is merely the agent of inexorable market forces. The classical creed also strengthens the businessman's defenses against the intrusions of orientations other than profit in his decisions. It defines the business organization in terms of property rights and contractual relationships. This definition directs the moral responsibility of the business manager to the owners of the business and confines his responsibility to others to the fulfillment of contractual obligations. Similarly, the classical description of the firm — which describes employees, customers, and suppliers as outsiders — strengthens the businessman's resistance to the influence of affective dispositions toward these individuals on his decisions.

Likewise, the classical creed fortifies the businessman in his adherence to the universalistic ethic of our society. On the one hand, it extols the virtues of practicality and hardheadedness in businessmen, telling him that if he gives a man a job just because he needs it or favors a particular salesman with an order simply because of his congeniality, he is not being a good businessman. On the other hand, it commends to all, businessmen or non-businessmen, the virtue and the necessity of self-reliance: each must make his own way, stand on his own feet, and fare as he deserves. This doctrine relieves the businessman of responsibility for the effects of his actions on other individuals. Further, it tells him that if he does not insist that others be independent, he really does disservice to them and, more important, to society at large. The importance of this function of the ideology may be understood by reflecting that the affective discipline required by universalism is difficult to maintain in many roles in our society, outside, as well as within business. Generally it requires the reinforcement of a set of beliefs which give moral justification to actions which would otherwise appear unfriendly or even unjust. (Thus, university professors in grading students face problems quite similar to those which confront businessmen in selecting, firing, and promoting personnel. Professors, who must flunk attractive students who have worked hard and need to pass in order to get into law school, need their ideology about the social function of a university to persuade them of the importance of applying universalistic criteria to the evaluation of students.)

The managerial strand of business ideology takes the opposite tack. It relieves the businessman of the onus of selfishness by denying that private profit is or ought to be the principal orientation of the business enterprise. Excessive profits are unfair and sinful. To the businessman, discomfited by moral claims which he thinks it unbusinesslike to consider in making decisions, the managerial creed says: "These are, in truth, moral responsibilities which it is your duty to assume. You, the manager of a business, are responsible to your stockholders, your employees, your customers, and the general public. You must balance their competing claims on the fruits of the enterprise, and determine fair wages, fair prices, fair dividends, and prudent reserves." To the businessman who finds affective neutrality uncongenial, the managerial creed says: "Your business is not just a network of property rights, contractual relationships, and lines of authority. It is a family of human beings cooperating in a common purpose; it is proper for you to like them and to worry about their personal problems."

The managerial creed also modifies the definition of personal achievement in a business career; as long as achievement is measured in terms of profit, the drive for occupational success conflicts with the enthusiastic embrace of moral responsibilities which the managerial creed recommends. There are two important aspects of this redefinition of business achievement. One is the insistence that a business management is to be judged not only or even principally by its stewardship to its stockholders but also by its success in promoting satisfying human relationships among its employees, its progressiveness in scientific and technological research and in providing new products for consumers, and its contributions to the local community. The second is the view of business management as a profession. This too weakens the identification of occupational achievement in business with financial success. Professions are accorded by outsiders social status which, while not uninfluenced by pecuniary criteria, depends in large measure on the specific content of professional work, both in skill and in service to society. Status within a profession is influenced less by money income than by the appraisal of fellow-professionals. A profession is also equipped with a strong set of ethical norms which limit the approved means to professional achievement. Thus definition of business management as a profession provides ideological reinforcement for the social attitudes which oppose identification of success in business with maximum profit.

These, then, are the two polar ideological resolutions of the psychological strains due to the conflicting moral requirements of the business role. At first glance, the picture which the managerial ideology paints of the business role certainly seems to be the more appealing. Would not any businessman prefer to see himself, and have others see him, as presiding with wisdom, justice, and affection over a family of loyal individuals in a common enterprise dedicated to service, rather than as a hardboiled profiteer? The managerial creed has the additional advantage of relative simplicity. Both versions of the ideology claim that business serves the general interest, but the classical version requires an involved abstract argument in order to reach this conclusion. Moreover, the managerial creed faces up to the facts of business size and concentration and of separation of business ownership and control, which the logical exigencies of its argument compel the classical creed to dodge in one way or another. (A principal reason for the emergence of the managerial strand of business ideology is precisely the discrepancy between the classical model of small and weak business proprietorships and the real world of great corporate enterprises.) Yet, despite these patent disadvantages, the classical creed persists. Indeed, the managerial strand must be considered a variant of the more basic classical theme of the ideology rather than a parallel alternative. Why?

Part of the answer lies in the logical incompleteness of a purely managerial view, which is discussed further below. But ideologies are constrained by logic only to a limited degree, and the principal explanation of the continued prevalence of the classical creed is to be found in the ideological motivations of businessmen. The managerial definition of business responsibility leaves the businessman at sea without a compass. The moral responsibilities toward others which the managerial view would have him assume are numerous, conflicting, and incommensurable. By what standards shall he weigh competing moral obligations in making his decisions? It is not accidental that the codes of managerial behavior which appear in ideology are extremely vague, studded with such operationally meaningless concepts as "fair wages," "as low prices as consistent with management's other obligations," and the like. To accept this revision of the definition of the business role is to undertake a burden with more potential for anxiety for many businessmen than to cling to the alternative ethical norms which support orientation to profit. Those norms defend the businessman from all kinds of troubles which he would have to worry about if he permitted them to be broken down. If he must concern himself with X's six children, Y's attractive personality, and Z's need for his patronage, he is lost. If he must balance the merits of claims to higher wages, lower prices, and higher dividends, he is a judge rather than a businessman. The businessman has strong motivational disposition to any ideological explanation which fortifies his defenses against moral responsibilities and affective ties and at the same time exonerates him of social irresponsibility and indifference. This is the accomplishment of the classical doctrine — no wonder it persists.

The utility of both the classical and managerial creeds to the businessman accords with the combination of emphases which we found in the tone of the creed. The classical creed gives form and structure to the elements of practicality and austerity. In its moralistic quality, the managerial creed represents the same elements; but it does more evident service in giving form to the brighter, optimistic side of the creed.

The Extent and Legitimacy of Business Power. Closely connected with the issue of moral responsibility is the question of the amount of discretion and power at the disposal of the individual businessman. This is a sensitive area for the ideology, and we have noted the symptoms of a strong ideological motivation to minimize the size and power of the business enterprise.[11] The businessman is beset by moral claims conflicting with each other and with the profit orientation of the business; he can ease his difficulties if he can tell himself and the claimants that he has no choice, that he simply does what he has to do and what any other man in his place would do. The classical creed enables him to say this by telling him he is simply the agent and victim of impersonal market forces. His power and discretion, according to the classical creed, are severely limited by the competition of actual or potential rivals for the "votes" of consumers.

The managerial creed is relatively silent on the question of power, and its silence is as eloquent testimony to the sensitivity of businessmen to the issue as the disavowals of power characteristic of the classical creed. Implicitly, by its acceptance of moral responsibilities on corporate management, the managerial creed recognizes a substantial area of discretion in the decisions of the executives of large corporations. The economic determinism of the classical argument is not available to the managerial creed. There have been isolated efforts to replace it with a sociological determinism, according to which the corporation executive is powerless, not so much because of economic factors, as because of organizational and social pressures;[12] but on the whole the managerial ideology ignores the power implications of management's moral responsibilities.

In the managerial description of the business role, positive description and moral exhortation are never clearly distinguished. Although American capitalism is said to have undergone, or almost completed, a great moral transformation, the strong element of moral exhortation in the managerial creed suggests that there are still some businessmen who are insufficiently transformed. If the mid-century executive extolled by *Fortune* has great power for good, the unreconstructed businessman presumably has great power for evil. The managerial creed is logically weak in providing no mechanism by which managers who fail to live up to their broad social responsibilities will lose power.

[11] See Chapter 3.
[12] C. Barnard, in *Change and the Entrepreneur* (Cambridge, Mass., 1949), pp. 9–10.

This is a sensitive issue because our culture demands that power, where it is admitted to exist, be legitimate power. There are a number of ways in which power can be made legitimate. One way is to interpret power as the exercise of a recognized individual right, such as the rights of private property. This is the method used in the classical creed in those contexts, principally labor relations, where it admits the existence of such power. But this method is not open to the managerial ideology, in which the business enterprise is conceived in broader terms than as the agency of the legal property owners. Another way of making power legitimate is to show that the person who holds this power was selected, directly or indirectly, by those to whom he is responsible. In the classical picture of the firm, hired managers have legitimate power because they are selected, if not in fact then at least in law, by the shareholders. But in the managerial version the acknowledged constituency of the business executive is much larger, and it cannot be contended that this constituency chooses the management. A third way lies in the systematized self-prepetuation of a professional elite in which recruitment and advancement are regulated by definite, objective, and universalistic rules. This is the source of power of the university faculty or the church clergy. Here is another reason why managerialists desire to view management as a profession. If management is a profession, its power has a flavor of legitimacy; but as yet the ideology can claim no system of recruitment and promotion for business executives comparable to those of the traditional professions.

Although the managerial creed makes some attempt to argue that public opinion constitutes in some vaguely defined way a check on managerial power, ultimately it has to fall back on the classical arguments of competition and consumer sovereignty.[13] The test of the faithfulness of corporate management to its public responsibilities is its continued success in attracting customers. An inefficient or irresponsible management would be displaced by competition.

The Businessman and the Consumer. Any conservative ideology is likely to picture existing social relationships as harmonious. "Service" is the main symbol in the business ideology used to describe the relationship of businessman to consumers.[14] This symbol is obviously related to anxieties about the shallowness of profit as a goal. The buyer-seller relationship in our society is singularly devoid of moral or affective content, and the maintenance of this neutrality is a source of strains for the business seller. He prefers to see himself as the servant of consumers than as a cold bargainer seeking the most advantageous terms for himself. He would

---

[13] An alternative argument for the managerialists might be found in the theory of countervailing power of J. K. Galbraith, *American Capitalism* (New York, 1952). But this has certain disadvantages as ideology, depending as it does on the countervailing power of government.

[14] See Chapter 7.

rather embrace his customers in the family of his enterprise than view them as an anonymous shifting mass.

The businessman must restrain his feelings not only toward his customers, but toward his products. Sales are the criterion by which he must judge these products, not beauty or technical perfection. Subservience to consumer tastes is not always a welcome discipline; many a manufacturer must have occasion to regret that consumers are so unappreciative of workmanship, ingenuity, and design. This is all the more reason for the ideology to affirm the symbol of service to consumers. Service is an excuse for and denial of any compromise of technical and aesthetic standards to the demands of the balance sheet. From the same source comes some of the emotional steam in the creed's defense of non-price competition; anyone can compete by cutting prices, but it takes skill to compete by offering variety and quality of product.

The service symbol fits into both the managerial and classical versions, depending upon its interpretation. Service may be an inevitable by-product or prerequisite of profit, or it may be an obligation which conflicts with profit. The individual businessman may serve the consumer in the sense that the competitive mechanism in which he is a cog operates to the ultimate benefit of consumers, or in the sense that he takes consumers' interests directly into account in his actions and decisions. Thus service may support the businessman's orientation to private profit; it describes that orientation in more attractive terms and carries the implication that he serves best who profits most. Or service may be one of the principal moral obligations which the businessman assumes in order to give dignity to his station.

The power attributed to the consumer in the doctrine of "consumer sovereignty" is a principal manifestation in the ideology of the sensitivity of businessmen about the amount and legitimacy of their power. One way of shedding awkward responsibility is to believe that the consumer is the real boss, that the businessman merely carries out his (or perhaps more frequently in the ideology, her) orders. Even managerial ideology ultimately relies on consumers' ratifying the stewardship of management. It is not by chance that consumer sovereignty is generally described in terms suggesting the processes of political democracy. In the "balloting" of individuals in the market place, business management seeks the same legitimacy which political elections give public officials.

The repeated affirmation of consumer sovereignty also springs from the businessman's attempts to influence the sovereign consumer. The more the businessman — through advertising and the many other forms of aggressive American salesmanship — attempts to mold the tastes of consumers, the more he proclaims that the consumer is sovereign and his tastes are autonomous. Advertising, branding, and salesmanship are

extremely sensitive subjects for the businessman. Attacks on these practices evoke violent ideological reaction; all the "first step" arguments,
which bring the whole System to the defense of any part, are brought into
play. A partial explanation may be found in the ambivalence in businessmen's attitudes toward aggressive friendliness in selling and in the vagueness of the ethical standards which govern business behavior in this area.
Doubts on the propriety of the initiative which sellers take toward consumers lead to a compulsive affirmation of both consumer sovereignty
and the propriety of sellers' initiative. Defensive solidarity and exaggerated sensitivity to external criticism are reactions typical of groups
uncertain of their moral standards. This symptom is abundantly present
in the ideology relating to advertising and salesmanship. Outside critics
are condemned for their ignorance of the field and told now as they were
told twenty-five years ago[15] that business can deal with malpractice without external assistance.

The Legitimation of High Status. In an essay, "Social Psychology of
World Religions," Max Weber remarks:

The fortunate [man] is seldom satisfied with the fact of being fortunate.
Beyond this, he needs to know that he has a *right* to his good fortune. He
wants to be convinced that he "deserves" it, and above all, that he deserves it
in comparison with others. He wishes to be allowed the belief that the less
fortunate also merely experience their due. Good fortune thus wants to be
"legitimate" fortune.
Strata in solid possession of social honor and power usually tend to fashion
their status-legend in such a way as to claim a special and intrinsic quality of
their own, usually a quality of blood.[16]

The business ideology fulfills a major psychological need in legitimiz-
ing the high status of businessmen in American society. This legitimation
must be accomplished under the constraints of the values of the American
cultural tradition which businessmen share with the rest of the population.
That tradition rules out legitimation in terms of any intrinsic "quality of
blood" or ascribed status from birth. At the very least, the universalistic
values of American culture rule such legitimation out of explicit expression.
(There is evidence that in private opinion Americans of high status do
not entirely exclude genetic differences in quality as explanations of differences in status — the poor are just poor stock, trash, a different species
of man.[17]) No doubt many businessmen sometimes feel in sympathy with

[15] Compare the replies to Bernard de Voto, *Fortune*, April 1951, and the reply
of Carpenter in *Dollars and Sense* to Stuart Chase and F. J. Schlink, *Your Money's
Worth* (New York, 1927). See Chapter 7.
[16] Max Weber, "Social Psychology of World Religions," *Essays in Sociology* (New
York, 1946), pp. 271, 276.
[17] See, for example, the Tops' opinion of the Bottoms in the South Dakota town
studied by Useem, Tangent, and Useem, "Social Stratification in a Prairie Com-

Mr. Baer's well remembered assertion of the divine rights of business management. But the very fact that his remark is still notorious indicates that today no businessman could broadcast such views. Publicly expressed opinions are more consistent with our main cultural values than are privately held beliefs. But social censorship operates on private beliefs also, and few people will privately legitimize their status in terms which are radically unsuitable for public expression.

Legitimation in terms of the values of American culture means legitimation in terms of universalism and achievement. The businessman must justify his status by claiming, to himself and to others, that he has earned it by his own efforts in a race which was open to all. The need for this justification is made more acute because the businessman is aware that in fact the race is not completely fair.[18] Individuals may defeat others in the race for high executive rank by nepotism, favoritism, and bureaucratic "politics" rather than by sheer ability. The criteria for initial selection and subsequent advancement of executive personnel in corporations are necessarily far from objective. Success is won by some businessmen who ignore the ethical, or even legal, restraints by which other businessmen feel themselves bound. These discrepancies within the business world increase the need for an ideological explanation of status differences. On the one hand, the successful businessman needs to have his success legitimized vis-à-vis competing businessmen as well as in relation to other social groups. On the other hand, the less successful businessman needs to feel that he is in his proper niche in the business hierarchy.

Furthermore, status must be achieved in a socially approved line and by socially approved means. The self-interested elements in the business role may make the need for assurance on these points more acute for businessmen than for the occupants of other roles.

Clearly there are many parts of the ideology which help to meet these needs. In a sense the whole ideology serves as a legitimation of the high status of business. A few of the most directly relevant features of the ideology are as follows:

(1) *Business is a skilled profession and businessmen work hard at it.* It is not the managers who have the forty-hour week, and it *is* the man-

---

munity." Similar sentiments are revealed in anti-Negro prejudice and in the feelings which underlie the size and geographical distribution of our immigration quotas; however prejudices of this kind are probably to be explained less as legitimations of high status than as efforts to achieve self-esteem on the part of, say, Anglo-Saxons of low status. In the South Dakota study, the Tops and the Bottoms were of similar ethnic origins.

[18] "The need for an ethical interpretation of the 'meaning' of the distribution of fortunes among men increased with the growing rationality of conceptions of the world . . . Individually 'undeserved' woe was all too frequent; not 'good' but 'bad' men succeeded — even when 'good' and 'bad' were measured by the yardstick of the master stratum . . ." Weber, *Essays in Sociology,* p. 275.

agers who get ulcers from overwork. It is not an easy job to manage a business; it requires skills which few possess. These ideological themes relieve the businessman's doubts about the emptiness of his job and his inferiority in skill compared with the technicians on his staff.

(2) *Competition for business leadership is an equal race.* In this way the status of businessmen is legitimized in terms of the universalistic values of American society as well as in terms of its achievement values. Ideological biographies point with pride to the humble origins of successful business leaders. There is always room at the top. And everyone has a chance to get there by his own efforts — either by climbing the hierarchical ladder in an established business or by starting a new firm of his own. To the extent that the successful businessman subscribes to these tenets, he need not feel apologetic toward the less fortunate. The doctrine of self-reliance tells him that the less successful could be in his shoes if they had the stuff. To the less successful businessman, the ideology says that in the last analysis his relative failure is due to his own shortcomings — others have conquered worse handicaps.

(3) *Business owners and managers are entitled to high incomes.* The main symbol of the businessman's high status is his income and wealth relative to other occupational groups; and the main ideological defense of his status centers on his claim to the profits and salaries he receives. The business creed is much more concerned with this than with other dimensions of the status of the businessman: his rank and authority in the hierarchies of business organization, his social prestige, his leadership in community affairs, etc.

Status in America is to a remarkable degree measured in the generalized medium of money income and wealth, which enables comparisons to be made between individuals whose occupational differences would otherwise make their achievements incommensurable. The use of this pecuniary measure is especially pronounced in gauging business success. Businessmen are especially vulnerable to any narrowing of the social definition of achievement and to any weakening of the pecuniary criteria of status. They are vulnerable because, in the absence of large monetary rewards, the content of their jobs — what they do, the products they make, the methods they use — would leave them only with their executive responsibilities as a claim for high status in the eyes of society. The status of a businessman, in comparison with that of a professional man, is relatively more dependent on consumption activities than on occupational activities. Economic leveling is thus a greater threat to the status of businessmen than it is to the status of other relatively high-income groups. The business creed's defense of income inequality is not simply the reflection of the economic greed of a fortunate class. It is a defense of high status by an occupation which might lose status if it should lose its income advantages.

Actually, the creed does not justify the rewards of businessmen only; it defends high incomes of all kinds, whoever may receive them. The creed of the nineteenth-century English businessman condemned the high rents of landlords; and opposition to the "unearned" incomes of passive absentee property-owners and of *rentiers* has in the past found some support among business elements in this country. It is certainly not obvious that high interest incomes are to the economic advantage of businessmen, or that a sweeping defense of "unearned" incomes eases the dialectical tasks of the ideology. But the generalized defense of high incomes in the business creed serves the function of maintaining the integrity of the pecuniary criterion of achievement and status.[19] Throughout the economy, according to the creed, rewards are a reliable measure of contributions and achievements. If businessmen, among others, do well by this standard, then they deserve high status.

The creed emphasizes that monetary rewards are proportionate to the importance and difficulty of the services for which they are paid, and that high rewards are necessary as incentives to insure that the more important and difficult services are performed. But there is a significant divergence between the ideology and the classical economics from which much of the incentive line of argument is derived. This divergence arises over economic rent. Economists recognize that a high income may have to be paid to all who offer a given service in order to obtain the service in sufficient quantity, but that many individuals would be willing to offer the service for less. These "intra-marginal" individuals receive economic rents, surpluses above the incomes necessary as incentives for them. Also, economists recognize what may be described as the vicarious incentive function of high incomes. Thus the existence of high profits in a particular line of business may be quite unnecessary as incentive for the individuals who are actually engaged in that business and receive the profits. But it may serve as an incentive for other individuals to enter business careers along quite different lines. These economic arguments constitute a formidable defense of income inequalities on incentive grounds. But they receive relatively little exposition in the business creed. Why?

The answer seems to be that they divorce to an intolerable degree the connection between *individual* services and *individual* rewards. The individual businessman does not want to be told that his income is high because there must be high incomes somewhere in order to encourage entrepreneurship in the next generation. He wants to be told that his income is high because he has earned it and because his specific services are very important.

---

[19] This defense of high incomes derives also from other roots. The businessman's position as an executive with broad authority over others disposes him to a belief in the unequal competences and deserts of individuals.

Competition. The great ideological symbol, "competition," is intimately linked to the concerns about status which we have just been analyzing. Competition is the logical cornerstone of classical ideology. Through competition the pursuit of private profit is reconciled with the general welfare, and the concentration and abuse of private economic power is avoided. Managerial ideology places less emphasis on competition, since it proclaims that private economic power is administered for the general welfare and has little need of external discipline; nevertheless it too keeps competition as an ultimate check against any possible abuse of power for private ends.

But competition plays much more than a logical role in the ideology. It is an emotional symbol, set off by its antithesis, monopoly, and there is much evidence that it has a wide appeal outside business. The reason seems apparent — it symbolizes the basic patterns of universalism and achievement in our society.

In all kinds of contexts — athletic, scholastic, political, occupational, as well as business — we have a strong moral commitment to open the race equally to all, to impose the same rules on all contestants, to expect each to do his best within the rules to win, to award prizes to the winners, to applaud the efforts of the losers and expect them to be "good sports." Nothing is more important than "fair play" — an equal chance for all contestants and adherence by all to a set of impartial rules. Competition implies all of these things, and business competition draws much of its symbolic appeal from the wider reference of the word. All of us have disappointing experiences with competition; we lose, or think the race was unfair, or suspect the rules were broken, or believe the race was fixed. But such experiences only intensify our emotional attachment to the symbol. In particular, the keen rivalry for personal achievement in business careers provides plentiful opportunity for resentments and anxieties which contribute to the adherence of businessmen to competition and fair play.

Since competition is so integral a part of the classical creed, the motivation for adherence to this symbol is in large part the motivation, described above, for adherence to the classical resolution of the moral conflicts of the business role. That is, competition enables the businessman to shed moral responsibilities. If wages, prices, and profits are competitively set, he need not worry about whether they are fair and just, too high or too low. He has a ready answer not only to himself but to outsiders who question his decisions on moral grounds and seek to regulate them in the interests of their conception of justice.

A symptom of the importance of this motivation for ideological belief in competition is the creed's failure to exploit the cogent arguments of Schumpeter.[20] His analysis provides a ready-made defense of large-scale

---

[20] Schumpeter, *Capitalism, Socialism, and Democracy.*

enterprise and of imperfectly competitive markets. It is a defense which would fit in well with the managerial creed's recognition of the realities of large-scale corporate enterprise. Schumpeter argues essentially that progress is the result of innovation, inspired by the hope of building or maintaining monopoly positions; the economy can well afford to concentrate power in monopolies at any one time because their power will in time be checked by innovators who aspire to become monopolists themselves. Even though the creed's generic concept of competition could easily be stretched to cover this process, and even though innovation and progress are themselves important positive symbols, the argument is scarcely used. Businessmen cannot admit even the temporary existence or limited desirability of monopoly. The Schumpeter argument gives too much power and responsibility to the self-interested manager. The businessman prefers to believe in a kind of competition which relieves him of these burdens — or, failing that, in a kind of manager who is not self-interested.

Given an initial disposition to believe in competition, the emotional attachment to the symbol of competition is enhanced by certain strains in the business role associated with competition itself. The competition of rival firms increases the uncertainties involved in the decisions for which the businessman is accountable. Competition threatens profits, and destroys the comfortable security of stable relationships with customers and suppliers. Competition is an important element in producing the strains to which the exaggerated activism of businessmen is a common reaction. Competition keeps the businessman under continuous pressure — while he rests, his rivals may steal his market, pirate his labor, invent a new gadget, or launch a new selling campaign. For these reasons, businessmen are under strong temptation to shelter themselves from competition, in a host of ways (mentioned in Chapter 8). Their complaints about "unfair competition," and the legislative remedies they seek to deal with it, indicate the strains of doing business in a competitive market. But the greater the burdens of competitive discipline and the stronger the temptations to avoid them, the louder it is necessary to pledge, in the ideology, allegiance to competition.

Competition is at the same time a description of the working of the economy and a set of moral norms for the individual businessman. These norms are strongly internalized in the average businessman by the positive values attached to business competition, not only in business ideology but in the attitude of American society at large where "antitrust" has long been a popular rallying cry. For the individual businessman, the norms supporting competitive practices often serve a useful function by confirming the propriety of self-interested actions. They enable him, for example, to destroy a business rival without worrying about the rival's wife and children. But in other circumstances the competitive norms can produce a sense of guilt, for they conflict with a self-interest which prompts him not to destroy his rivals but to collude with them. For this reason, the distinction between business practices which are consistent with competitive behavior and those which are not becomes an important subject of ideology.

Not surprisingly, the ideology's conception of competitive behavior is extremely catholic. It contrasts with the economist's narrow definition of pure competition, assumed in the classical argument on which business ideology lays so much stress. But economists' notions of competition are dismissed as impractical, with a unison and an impatience of external moral criticism which again are symptomatic of a solidarity protecting internal moral standards of which the group is none too sure.

The existence of the Sherman Anti-trust Act serves the ideology well in this connection. The Sherman Act reduces the question of adherence to competitive norms to one of conformity with the Act. Failure to be prosecuted under this extremely vague law can be interpreted as a kind of certificate of conformity with the competitive code. Because of the ambiguities of the law, no one can be sure whether or not he is violating it without actual litigation, and not always then. So long as the antitrust division of the Department of Justice leaves him alone, the businessman can extrapolate his general character as a law-abiding citizen from the context of specific laws to conformity with the canons of competition. The ideology does not fail to exploit the Sherman Act in this way — if there is monopoly anywhere it must be because the government is not enforcing the law.

HOSTILITY TOWARD THE GOVERNMENT

In its attacks on government, the business ideology provides many points of discharge for emotions generated in the strains of business life. An exhaustive discussion of all the detectable links between strains and this great focus of ideology would be prohibitively long but we seek to analyze some of the more prominent and important ones.

The pervasive hostility of the business creed toward government appears to have a simple explanation: rational, calculated, self-interested opposition to the New and Fair Deals. It would be foolish to deny that the political color of the national administration since 1933 has exacerbated business hostility to government; but there are several reasons why the explanation is too simple. First, complaints about government antedate 1933. Second, a rational calculation of the self-interest of businessmen would not lead to a wholesale condemnation of government, even of government under the aegis of Roosevelt and Truman. It would call for selective and discriminating judgments of diverse measures. If the labor policies of these administrations can realistically be taken as opposed to business interests, the proliferation of federal agencies anxious to lend money to business exemplifies a policy which can only be interpreted as friendly. Actually the hostility of the creed to the Democratic administrations centers to a remarkable degree on one area: fiscal policy — the size of the budget, deficit financing, and the magnitude of the national debt. This is an area where, as we have argued before, no simple explanation in terms of business interest will do justice to the intensity of the creed's opposition. Third, the opposition to government is more than disaffection from the policies of a particular party or administration. The creed contains a generalized distrust and scorn of politicians and bureaucrats, whatever their party and whatever the policies they advocate and execute.

The strains of the business role generate anxiety, resentment, and aggression. Let us consider why the government and its politicians and bureaucrats are appropriate symbolic targets for these feelings.

(1) The government is a convenient personification of the obscure forces which cause the outcomes of business decisions to differ from expectations.

One popular explanation of uncertain outcomes deals in terms of good and bad luck. Luck is often used in explanation of business successes and failures, but mainly in specific personal situations, to display the modesty of the successful or to bolster the self-esteem of the unsuccessful. As a generalized explanation suitable for ideology, it runs counter to the demand that status in our society be earned by personal achievement. For businessmen to assign to the whims of fortune the determination of successes and failures would be to forfeit their claims for the high status associated with business success.[21]

The dimly understood external forces which cause the outcomes of human actions to differ from expectations are often personified. Personification makes these forces more understandable in terms of everyday human experience, and, apparently, subject to control by the common techniques of social intercourse. In other societies and other situations the disturbing forces of uncertainty may be embodied in supernatural entities, but our cultural tradition is too strongly rationalistic, especially in the spheres of business and technology, to admit a supernatural ex-

---

[21] It is of incidental interest to note that the unsuitability of luck as an explanation of differential fortunes could not be easily explained by an "interest" theory of ideology. For luck definitely has conservative implications which could serve the interest of businessmen in the maintenance of the existing social structure. To the extent that the less fortunate are persuaded, as many of them believe anyway, that their poor fortune is a matter of chance rather than an inevitable result of the social structure, they are not inclined to wish to alter existing institutions. (See Merton, *Social Theory and Social Structure*, pp. 138–139, and the references there cited.)

planation of economic events. Individuals may privately believe in such explanations, but they can hardly express them in public.[22]

If personification is needed and supernatural persons will not do, the government is the best available candidate. The government stands in such a representative and symbolic position in the society that it lends itself readily to anthropomorphizing. At the same time, it involves no departure from our rationalistic and naturalistic ways of thinking about economic events to attribute great influence over them to the government. That the government does impinge on business decisions and operations in many ways is a fact of common observation and experience for every businessman. These interventions are often unpleasant — taxes, regulations, filling out forms — and they are often new and disturbing to business routine. What is not a fact of common observation and experience but a highly complicated question of social science is the net effect of all of the government's interventions on the course of economic events. But the experience of the businessman is enough to dispose him to believe that the government's actions have unfavorable effects and to personify the "government" as the main source of the troubling discrepancies between results and expectations in business operations.

The government also contains another essential ingredient of the needed explanation: it is subject to human control. The psychological need is not merely for an explanation to gratify curiosity but for an explanation which indicates how the disturbing uncontrolled forces may be controlled. Personification accomplishes this by suggesting that the social techniques which influence the actions of other human beings may be of use here too. If the forces are supernatural beings, the means of control are prayer, ritual, magic, or some functional equivalent, designed to persuade, cajole, bribe, or coerce. Man's quest for understanding as an instrument of control is accentuated in the businessman by those features of his role which lead to activism. He is not likely to find congenial an explanation of his sufferings which consigns him to passive acquiescence. The sun-spot theory of business fluctuations is a naturalistic explanation, not without evidence in its favor. It would at least remove from businessmen's shoulders the blame for economic instability, and the implied inevitability would shield them from unwelcome interventions in their affairs. But neither it nor any other fatalistic theory of economic fluctuations finds much favor in business ideology. If, on the other hand, the

[22] It is true that religion may be involved in the explanation, but in an ethical rather than a metaphysical capacity. Thus the ultimate explanation of a business recession may be found in the moral failings of certain individuals, and these failings may in turn be attributed to their departure from traditional religion. But the explanation of the recession will not be that God willed it. Even those in our society who believe that in an ultimate sense God wills everything that happens, business recessions included, would need a subsidiary explanation along naturalistic lines.

government is responsible, the means of control are naturalistic means, readily understood by businessmen. They consist in accomplishing a change in government policy and personnel by various political techniques. That the color of the government may be as far beyond business control as the spots of the sun is beside the point. It is important that the means of control, while being understandable and feasible enough to offer some hope, should not be too readily available to the individual businessman; otherwise he could blame only himself for miscarriages of his decisions. The government serves very well; it is a force whose control the business-man understands but a force which he alone cannot in fact control. Even when he occasionally blames himself for taking too small a part in politics, he is by implication castigating the government.

(2) The government is a suitable focus for the strains associated with the maintenance of confidence and optimism in the business role.

The alleged effects of government on business confidence illustrate more directly than any other part of the ideology the connection between the strains of decision in the face of uncertainties and the ideology's hos-tility to government. The businessman has realistic cause not to be con-fident in the outcome of his decisions. He must be decisive nonetheless; and he must not betray lack of confidence to his associates and sub-ordinates or even, if he can help it, to himself. One reaction to this strain is a compulsive optimism; a realistic sensitivity to all the possible ways in which things could go amiss would be unbearable. Optimism easily becomes not merely a personal attitude but a social imperative. On the local scene, the invidious distinction between the "booster" and the "knocker" is a familiar one. It is sinful not to believe that Plainville is destined to double its population and industry in the next ten years. The skeptic, even if he is not opposed to Plainville's expansion or to policies designed to foster it, is an outcast just because of his pessimism. The social disapproval evoked by his lack of confidence betrays the fear that pessimism might be contagious and disruptive. On a national scale business ideology displays a similar compulsion to optimism.[23]

One of the ways in which the government exerts its unfavorable in-fluence on economic events, according to the creed, is to destroy business confidence.[24] This the government does by creating uncertainties con-cerning future government policies, or simply by adopting an unfriendly attitude toward business. The economic system, sometimes depicted as stable, tough, and impersonal, is in this context pictured as so fragile

---

[23] The "New Era" of the twenties applied the "booster" psychology of the home town to the national economy. During the thirties one of the major sins alleged of the New Deal was that it was pessimistic concerning the economic future of America and thus undermined the nation's confidence. The ideology has been more concerned to denounce the "mature economy" thesis as morally reprehensible than to prove that it has no factual basis.

[24] See Chapters 2 and 9.

a web of mutual confidence that an unkind word from the White House can cause collapse. It is understandable that the businessman struggling to maintain confidence in his own decisions in the face of inescapable uncertainties will be receptive to cries against the government for destroying confidence and creating uncertainties.

Fluctuations in the level of general business activity are, of course, one of the principal sources of discrepancies between expectations and outcomes in business. Waves of depression or inflation engulf the individual businessman. The general business tide is a focus for the anxieties we have been discussing. It is a focus which, because of its generality, requires an ideological explanation appropriate for wide and common consumption, rather than the diverse private *ad hoc* explanations which might suffice for fluctuations in the fortunes of individual businesses. The government's actions, for the reasons we have advanced, provide the major ideological explanation of business instability. The mechanisms by which the government produces depressions and inflations may vary, but the fact that the government is responsible is an invariable article of business faith.

We have said that the disposition to personify government as a scapegoat is strengthened by the fact that businessmen do have direct unfavorable experience of government interventions. It is important to emphasize, however, that, once the government becomes the personification of the forces of disturbance, much more is attributed to it than can logically be deduced from the businessman's direct experience. That taxes are onerous to the businessman does not prove they are breaking the nation, though his experience disposes him to believe so. That the businessman is disturbed because he does not know what some government agency is going to do next month does not logically entitle him to conclude that the government is causing general economic stagnation; but it is not surprising that he is disposed to make the larger claim, or at least believe it when he hears it made by others. The mechanisms by which government is supposed to cause undesirable economic fluctuations are complex, and remote from the direct experience of any single businessman. These mechanisms are monetary and fiscal processes which the individual businessman can feel, if at all, only indirectly and which he cannot distinguish from nongovernmental influences to which his operations would normally be subject. If thousands of businessmen are convinced that the federal debt is the source of great economic difficulties, it cannot be because they have any direct experience of the evils of the debt. If the President of the Sun Oil Company believes he has observed the quantity theory of money operating in the everyday conduct of his business, it only shows the sway of ideology in molding his interpretation of his immediate experience.

(3) Business ideology denigrates government and its personnel be-

cause of their supposed freedom from the kinds of responsibility and accountability which are imposed by the businessman's role.

The discipline of accountability to which the profit orientation of the firm subjects the businessman is an exacting one from which he at times longs to be freed. But, in a familiar kind of psychological reaction, business managers exalt their burden into a virtue and feel superior to those who are not subject to the same discipline. As government personnel appear strikingly exempt from the accountability imposed by business, businessmen can scorn the "irresponsibility" of politicians and the "impracticality" of bureaucrats. Politicians are vulnerable to the charge that they make extravagant promises in the pursuit of elective office, unrestrained by any mechanism for calling them to account. Their policies in office are, it appears to the businessman, unchecked by financial balance sheets; the financial costs of their projects are balanced largely by vague, unmeasurable nonfinancial benefits. Nepotism, favoritism, corruption, and "just politics" have, the businessman believes, full rein in the selection of government personnel and even in the determination of government policies and administrative decisions. No balance sheet discipline enforces the universalistic norms to which businessmen must adhere. Bureaucrats have, in contrast to businessmen, the option of playing safe and sticking by the rules in the face of difficult decisions. Theirs is a responsibility for adherence to bureaucratic rules rather than for results. They can be accused of an unworthy longing for a security which the businessman, sometimes to his regret, cannot achieve. Yet, in many cases, these inferior breeds of men sit in moral judgment on businessmen whose problems they cannot understand.

To a remarkable degree the creed's opposition to government centers on government deficits and debt. But abundant, if unsystematic, observation suggests that the private attitudes of businessmen focus on this issue even more than the published ideology. This concern over federal debt is, in large part, a logical misunderstanding. The businessman naturally applies to government the same fiscal strictures which apply to an individual enterprise, but the analogy is mistaken. It is natural for the businessman to make the national government the symbol of the national economy, and to construe the government's budget as the report of the economic condition of the nation; this identification is also mistaken. There are economic disadvantages, even perils, in deficit financing and the existence of a large national debt; but they are quite different from the dangers which the business creed commonly prophesies. Economists worry about such things as: the effect on incentives and on income inequality of the internal transfer of income from taxpayers to bond holders; and the limitations which the existence of a large debt places on freedom of fiscal and monetary action to stabilize the economy, par-

ticularly in times of threatening inflation. Businessmen are more likely
to be concerned over a vaguely defined future catastrophe — national
bankruptcy, national insolvency, collapse of the government's credit. They
point with alarm to an equally vague burden of debt which weighs down
every man, woman, and child, apparently without discrimination between
taxpayers and bondholders. It does little good to point out the mistakes
of analogy and identification which are at the root of these fears, or to
explain the mechanics of internally held debt and of our central banking
and monetary system. The business creed's anti-intellectual strand comes
into play and rejects all such arguments as unreliable, impractical, and
sophistical. The subject is held to be so simple and obvious that no
experts are needed to understand it; Mr. Micawber, in his celebrated
defense of the balanced budget, had the last word.

The appeal to ordinary practical average common sense against expert
logical argument on this issue suggests strongly that the views of the
business creed on the national debt are not simply an understandable
intellectual mistake. Furthermore, as we have argued, it is difficult to
explain the concentration of attention on the debt in terms of the rational
economic interests of businessmen. We suggest that the immense concern
of business ideology with the debt is rooted in the strains of the businessman associated with responsibility and accountability. These strains, we
have been arguing, find ideological reflection in the personification in
government of the obscure forces which cause business plans to go awry
and in the condemnation of the irresponsibility and impracticality of
government personnel. The government debt and deficit financing provide
the most dramatic symbol of the departure of government from the principles of accountability which constrain the businessman; and the strains
of adhering to these principles motivate scornful indignation against an
institution which ignores them.

Another feature of the ideology's treatment of government may be
viewed in this general context. The tendency to reduce government to its
"essence" as coercive police power is common in the ideology. Bureaucrats, in contrast to businessmen, can force people to do their bidding
and as such are relieved from the major constraints of securing the
cooperation of the people they ostensibly "serve."

(4) The scorn in which the business creed holds politicians is reinforced by the ambivalence of business feeling toward that aggressive
exploitation of personal relationships which is common to both business
and politics.

The business role generates anxieties about the sincerity of personal
friendships in business and about the propriety of aggressive cultivation
of the favors of others as an avenue to business success. These anxieties
are reflected, outside the ideology, in the business variants of anti-

Semitism, which invest the Jews with the disapproved extremes of behavior. Some of the businessman's feeling against the politician, which can find ideological outlet, has the same motivation. The politician is made to symbolize a pattern of insincere and selfish camaraderie for which the business role itself provides strong temptation. After all, politicians and business salesmen have many points of similarity. Both are experts on "how to win friends and influence people." Both slap backs, make contacts, do and seek favors. In a society which places great stock on sincerity in affective relationships, both are vulnerable to the charge of seeking friendships only to exploit them for their own gain. The intensity of business feeling against the politician and the emphatic distinction drawn between politicians and businessmen may well be a projection onto the politician of some of the things the businessman dislikes about himself and his colleagues.

(5) The common epithet "impractical" as applied to government derives appeal not only from the freedom of government from businesslike responsibilities, but from the role of government as a regulator of business practices and as an external judge of business morality.

Government controls over business practices rival government financial policies as a target for the business creed. There are obvious elements of simple economic interest here: for example, profits are higher without price controls. But a different motivation for hostility is revealed in the indignation that "they" in Washington should assume that they know better than "we" do how to run our business. This kind of indignation is typically evoked by the details of government controls of business. For example, in order to enforce price controls the government may prescribe just how livestock must be slaughtered, how and where commodities must be marketed, what records a business firm must keep, what qualities of a product must be produced, and similar details. Now an organization like a business firm develops, both within itself and in its external dealings, particular routines of teamwork — "the way we do things around here." The personnel of the organization build up expectations based on these patterns, and much of their feeling of competence consists in familiarity with the routines. Naturally they resist all efforts to destroy patterns on which their feelings of security and competence rest. They distrust and resent the agents of such efforts, and they regard outsiders as incompetent because they are unfamiliar with the special procedures. Any new top executive who attempts a reorganization must encounter this resistance. Any efficiency consultant who endeavors to rationalize an organization must be resented. In these cases the expression of resistance and resentment may be inhibited. But there is nothing to inhibit it when the government is the agency of disturbance to established routines or organization.

The vagueness of business ethics provides, as we have argued in two specific cases above, motivation for hostility to outsiders who make moral judgments of business behavior. Government, both in legislation and in administration, judges the propriety of business practices of many kinds. In regulations concerning labor relations, pricing practices, advertising claims, product qualities, tax deductions, health and safety provisions, and many other matters, government agencies decide, in effect, what is legitimate business and what is not. The agencies, it is claimed, just don't understand the problems and make facile moral judgments unsupported by knowledge.

This source of hostility to government is closely allied with the general anti-intellectualism of the business creed. Bureaucrats are specialists and experts; and, especially in the New Deal era, the vulnerability of government to the hostilities directed generally against intellectuals was increased by the prominence of academic personnel in the federal service.[25]

(6) The government is a suitable target for suppressed resentments of business life.

Business offers many occasions for mutual resentments among businessmen. These are inevitable in a competitive race for success, in which the ethical norms controlling the choice of means to success are only vaguely defined and subject to wide differences of interpretation. Within an enterprise, an aspiring executive may feel he is being outstripped by others in the race up the hierarchy not because of their superior business ability but because of nepotism, favoritism, "apple-polishing," and the like. As between enterprises, a businessman may feel that his competitor has injured him by resorting to unfair practices which his own ethical standards deter him from duplicating. In many instances one party to a contract or oral understanding may feel that the other has violated the spirit or even the letter of the agreement. The obverse of these resentments is the guilt which the businessman may feel about certain actions which lead to his gain at the expense of others.

The overt expression of these resentments among businessmen is in large degree suppressed by the social convention of being a "good loser," reinforced by the reflection that "business is business." A junior executive whose rival gets the coveted promotion may complain in confidence to his wife; in public he is supposed to rejoice in the good fortune of a friend. A businessman whose competitor steals his market may growl to his colleagues about the rival's ethics; he does not buy newspaper space to denounce his competitor. One article of the code of business ethics is, indeed, that a businessman does not publicly impugn other enterprises. Of course serious friction may break into the open in litigation; but there are many instances of friction where law is not involved.

[25] See Merton, *Social Theory and Social Structure,* ch. 6, "Role of the Intellectual in Public Bureaucracy."

These suppressed resentments, and their corresponding feelings of guilt, can be unloaded onto a suitable scapegoat external to business. A suitable scapegoat, in this context, is one which can be plausibly alleged to violate the ethical norms by which business is guided. The emotional steam against the scapegoat derives from the feelings of resentment and guilt surrounding real or imagined departures from these very norms within business itself. Trade unions often serve as a symbol of violation of business ethics. Intense feeling can be aroused by the accusation that a union is violating a contract, in letter or spirit, or a verbal agreement. There are few industrial disputes in which such an accusation is not made. The government is a particularly suitable symbol, for two reasons. First, government is notorious as the locus of particularistic criteria in selection and advancement of personnel. But indignation about "politics" in government surely is motivated by the prevalence of "politics" in non-governmental organizations. An executive who has doubts about the purity of his own business hierarchy in this respect will have a large capacity for moral indignation against nepotism, favoritism, and patronage in government. Second, in purchasing from business or in competing with business, government is a target for accusations of unfairness. Government purchasing, contracting, and lending operations are areas where there is wide scope for irrelevant particularistic criteria. The businessman who resents the fact that he lost an order to another business because he was competing with the purchaser's brother-in-law, and the businessman who feels guilty because he buys from his brother-in-law rather than from a cheaper source, will find the corruption of government a convenient outlet for their feelings. In its contractual dealings with business, the asymmetrical legal position of government makes it a vulnerable target. Government is accused both of violating its own end of the bargain and of holding business too strictly to the letter of its end. In this connection it is worth recalling that one of the greatest moral outrages of the Roosevelt administration was the abrogation of the gold clause in government obligations. Since the indignation aroused by this action was surely disproportionate to the injury suffered by business interests, we may conclude that the incident was seized upon as symbolic of governmental disrespect for business ethics. As a final example, publicly owned utilities are repeatedly accused of competing unfairly with private utility companies. Businessmen other than utility executives are responsive to this charge, it may be hazarded, less because of the manifest claim that such competition is a "first step" toward socialism than because of resentments and guilts surrounding their own relationships with competing businesses.

(7) The political localism of the business creed, while partly a matter of dialectics, corresponds to the fact that businessmen have higher status locally than nationally.

The business creed exhibits a decided preference for local and state governments over the national government. The creed favors decentralization of political power, states' rights, and local autonomy; it deplores the centralization of power in the federal government. What are the reasons for this attitude?

One reason is simply dialectical. Anyone hostile to government in general will find in the federalistic American political tradition a ready argument to oppose the expansion of government activity. He need only claim that the function in question is properly the province of some other level of government. Since the federal government is the most rapidly expanding government, anyone opposing more government will naturally seek to exploit the traditions of localism and states' sovereignty.

A second reason lies in real differences in businessmen's powers to control governments. The influence of businessmen over government has long been — certainly since 1933 and probably before — inverse to the size of the government. It is not accidental that these differences are correlated with differences in the social prestige of businessmen. Businessmen have relatively more prestige as individuals within a local community than in the nation at large; and the local ranking of individual businessmen relative to individuals in other occupations is higher than the ranking of business as an occupation in the abstract.

A third reason may be found in the appeal of the symbol of independent, local, "grass-roots," initiative in political affairs to businessmen convinced of the virtues of decentralized, individual initiative in economic matters. Local governments, it can be argued, offer greater possibilities than the central government for directly enlisting the energies, skills, ideas, and loyalties of the public. They offer scope, as central administration cannot, for diversity, flexibility, innovation, experiment, and even competition. Confronted with the colossus in Washington, the businessman finds it easy to see in local government the same virtues of neighborliness, independence, and simplicity which the ideology attributes to the model small local enterprise.

The political localism of the business creed provides another counter-example against the simple interest theory of ideology. Although the creed expounds localism as a fundamental principle of government, a calm assessment of business interests would lead to a much more pragmatic approach to the problem. It is not in the interest of New England businessmen but of their Southern competitors to be for states' rights in labor legislation. In other cases, there is not even any geographical divergence of business interest, so great are the disadvantages to businessmen of multiple administration and conflicts of jurisdiction.

(8) Guilt over self-interested dealings with the government, to which, as the major symbol of the nation, the businessman acknowledges a

responsible loyalty, probably is one source of a compulsive affirmation of nationalism.

The national government symbolizes the nation as no other institution does, and the business creed is a major ideological carrier of American nationalism. Very commonly nationalistic creeds identify closely the nation and the government; but the business creed's hostility to government seems to run counter to its nationalism. The creed's hostility to government must therefore be expressed so that it does not connote disloyalty to the nation. This is accomplished by distinguishing between our national system of government in the abstract, to which the business creed is loyally devoted, and the incumbent administration, which itself may threaten the true national principles of our system of government. Only in emergencies — wars and the deep depression of 1933 — is the existing government accorded nationalistic loyalty.

This distinction in the ideology serves an important function for the individual businessman. We have paid considerable attention to the moral responsibilities which intrude upon the businessman and make it difficult for him to hew to the line of private profit without strain. The nation is a group to which the businessman unhesitatingly acknowledges responsibility and loyalty. In business dealings with the government he must feel some misgivings about treating the nation's representative on a "strictly business" basis. The ideological distinction between the actual government and the national system of government enables the businessman to maintain a sense of national loyalty while doing the best he can for his enterprise. Any residue of guilt for dealing with the nation's prime representative on the basis of calculated self-interest serves to exaggerate the affirmation of nationalism. To the primary sources of this affirmation of nationalism we now turn our attention.

ATTITUDES TOWARD SOCIAL CHANGE

American society has a strong institutional commitment to rationalism, outstanding in comparison with other nations in the Western cultural tradition and even more striking in a broader comparative perspective. One of the consequences of this commitment is a constant questioning of the utility of existing technological and social institutions. Existing institutions are subjected to rational criticism and to comparison with possible alternatives. The rationalist strand in our culture is intolerant of sentiment, tradition, and custom as justifications of any institution which, viewed as a means of attaining its manifest end, has outlived its usefulness. In the fields of science and technology, the process of rational criticism and consequent innovation has been spectacularly developed. Change is itself institutionalized, and high value attaches to keeping up to date technologically, whether in the realm of consumer gadgetry or that of industrial engineering. But the process of rational criticism does not confine itself to science and technology. Political institutions, economic arrangements, educational procedures, religious organizations, moral conventions are also subject to its searching glare. Moreover, the process of technological change itself disrupts existing relationships among individuals. For both reasons, rationalism is a source of instability in our society; and instability in social relationships and expectations is in turn a source of psychological insecurity.

The businessman is perhaps the major agent of the rationalism of our culture. He presides over the process of technological change. He is conspicuous for guiding his actions by rational norms. In making his decisions — whether they concern technological innovation, reorganization of the enterprise, a new promotional campaign, or novel price policies — he is expected to emancipate himself both from reverence for convention and tradition and from particularistic concerns for the individuals involved. Part of his role, in summary, is to apply the process of rational criticism and innovation to the fields of his jurisdiction. When he is attacked for this function by those whose sense of security is undermined by technological innovation and business rationality, he replies with a defense of progress and rationalism in the main stream of the ideas of the Enlightenment. The ideology contains a full quota of paeans to progress, with the businessman pictured as a pioneer, an Edison or a Ford. It is also loud in praise of the individualism and freedom which obliterate old social divisions and permit men to follow the rational pursuit of their own desires. The pictures of society in both classical and managerial creeds relegate coercive restraint to mistrusted governments and happily assume that the rest of capitalist society can operate through the enlightened cooperation of reasonable men.

Given these facts, it is perhaps surprising that the creed is nationalistic and presses its austere, practical emphases to the point of being anti-intellectual. Instead, business might be expected to loom as "the great civilizer," opposing superstition, treating men everywhere on the same basis, breaking down irrational group loyalties and antagonisms. In his essay, "On the Sociology of Imperialism," Schumpeter contended that business is essentially an internationalist and pacific social class, in contrast to the class of "professional warriors" which is a feudal relic doomed in the rationalistic milieu of capitalism. He endeavored to refute the Marxian connection of capitalism with nationalism and imperialism by deducing anti-nationalism from the universalistic and rationalistic norms which guide business behavior.[26]

What Schumpeter failed to notice is that universalistic and rationalistic

<hr>

[26] J. A. Schumpeter, *Imperialism and the Social Classes,* edited by P. Sweezy (New York, 1952).

norms are never easy to adhere to without strain. The businessman is no exception. The process of rational change which the businessman is forced to guide is not a comfortable process for him. It accentuates his uncertainties about the results of his decisions. In its effects on established routines and relationships, it disrupts his own sense of security as well as that of others. He cannot react, as others often can, by opposing rational change in the fields of business and technology; indeed his anxieties about the process only compel him to affirm more vigorously the virtues of progress and to condemn more scornfully the obscurantism of those who would impede it. But if his role compels him to be rational in this area, he can seek the security of tradition elsewhere.

Thus it is that the business creed, progressive in matters of science, technology, and business practice, is conservative with regard to other institutions. The creed opposes the application of the process of rational criticism and innovation outside of science, technology, and business. It opposes them in a manner characteristic of a group whose security — and status and authority as well — are dependent on traditionalized patterns of social relationships. It opposes them, that is, with the very kind of appeal to traditional and particularistic values and symbols which businessmen dismiss as obstacles to innovation in their own sphere. The businessman reacts by defending values which are themselves vulnerable to rational attack and attacking the symbols of rationalism.[27]

Nationalism plays a prominent part in this fundamentalist reaction. Nationalism has a general appeal in a society where universalism and rationalism destroy other group solidarities which might provide psychological security to individuals. It is not surprising that nationalism should be part of businessmen's own reactions to the insecurities which they feel as a result of the disruptive effects of rational criticism. In this nationalistic reaction the grand theme of progress is not discarded; instead it is dressed in the American flag. Technological progress is an American national tradition, and the technological achievement of America is unique.

As an antidote to insecurity, nationalism provides the feeling of superiority. If social critics and their disturbing ideas can be tagged as alien, they are also automatically tagged as inferior. For, no matter how good the ideas may sound "in theory," the fact remains that it is the United States which has the most motor cars and wins the wars. The need for such feelings of superiority is probably related not only to businessmen's insecurities in the face of rational criticism and innovation,

[27] See Parsons, "Certain Primary Sources and Patterns of Aggression in the Social Structure of the Western World," *Essays in Sociological Theory*, pp. 251–274, esp. pp. 266–270, and "Some Sociological Aspects of the Fascist Movements," *Social Forces* (November 1942). Parsons calls this kind of reaction a "fundamentalist reaction."

but to inadmissible doubts about their own adequacy in the face of responsibilities of their role.

A second and related element in the fundamentalist reaction involved in business ideology is anti-intellectualism. The practical emphasis, which we found throughout the ideology and traced to certain strains in the businessman's role, gains reinforcement from the strains of adjusting to a rapidly changing society. As more matters come within the grasp of rational technology, the province of the practical man is relentlessly invaded. At a somewhat deeper level, the questionings of traditional patterns by rational criticism arouse defences and lead to bitter counterattacks. Intellectuals are attacked as undermining traditional institutions and as alien and disloyal, at least in spirit.

A third element in the reaction of business ideology to social criticism and social change is the affirmation of the traditional religious values of the society. The nationalism of the business creed is a religious nationalism; the fundamental principles on which our nation and our economic system have been built are religious principles. The intellectuals whom the creed castigates are likely to be described as atheistic as well as un-American. Some business ideologists even find it difficult to resist identifying opposition to their economics with opposition to God. Just as the moral reformation which managerial ideology discerns in American business leadership is an application of both Christian and Jeffersonian ethics, so the moral decay which the creed often detects in other elements of the population is attributed to a departure from these ethical traditions. The roots of this reaction seem clear: it is very difficult for any individual to stand in the stream of a process of social change and to view it with a dispassionate and scientific neutrality. He is under strong compulsion to dramatize the process in moral terms; in doing so, he tends to think of the process as revolutionary rather than continuous and to picture it as a struggle between moral right and moral wrong. Given the traditional associations between morality and religion and between socialism and secularism in our culture, religion is bound to be invoked to support the morally right side of the struggle.

THE CREED AND THE SOLIDARITY OF THE BUSINESS COMMUNITY

American social structure tends to leave a large gap between the family and the nation, a gap in which there are no social groupings to which an individual automatically belongs. This vacuum is filled, for various Americans, in various ways. Trade unions, ethnic solidarities, home town loyalties, college and school allegiances, social clubs — all may have, in part at least, the function of alleviating the insecurities of a cold competitive world.

Businessmen are subject to the same insecurities. We have frequently emphasized the strains involved in the maintenance of affective discipline in the business role. Like others, businessmen need the comforting security which may be derived from a group solidarity. Individual businessmen may, of course, find this in non-occupational groups. But it would be surprising if some occupational solidarity were not sought in addition. One of the important functions of the ideology is to promote this solidarity.

There are, of course, many aspects of business life which set one businessman against another. Within a given firm, they compete for advancement; or one must obey the order of another; or one must correct another's mistakes. In inter-business dealings, they may be rivals in the same market; or they may have to haggle over the terms of a contract. The race for achievement in business gives plenty of scope for mutual resentments; but their uninhibited display would be disruptive of business and hard on the individuals involved.

Loyalty to a group which embraces all the contestants in the race effectively inhibits disruptive feelings. The suppressed resentments are thus channeled on to external scapegoats, where they serve to promote rather than to disrupt the solidarity of the group. Loyalty to the enterprise itself may be the important solvent for frictions within the organization. An individual will find his position within the firm easier to accept if he convinces himself it is right to give his all for the organization. But the frictions of inter-firm dealings require a wider solidarity, and this is the function of the ideology. It provides both positive and negative symbols to evoke sentiments of solidarity. On the one hand, it demands loyal support for the American Business System, Free Enterprise, Competitive Business, and the like. On the other hand, it castigates government, unions, socialists, and intellectuals.

The function of the ideology in unifying the business community explains the relative silence of the ideology on issues on which the interest of businessmen diverge. The achievement of the ideology in preserving this solidarity is impressive, for, after all, there are countless issues of government policy on which the interests of businessmen diverge. Indeed the defection of small business from large, or Southern and Western business from Eastern, is always a possibility. Anti-business movements usually attempt to capitalize on the natural divergences within the business camp. No doubt Roosevelt was, temporarily at least, quite successful in his efforts to enlist small businessmen in his fight against "economic royalists." Many businessmen, as well as other people, distrust Eastern capitalists and Wall Street. Nevertheless it is possible to speak of a "business community" which exhibits a remarkable solidarity; it is difficult to see what would hold it together in the absence of the ideology.

18

STABILITY AND CHANGE
IN THE CREED

OUR ANALYSIS HAS BEEN BASED on the presumption that the basic features of the business creed could be understood in terms of enduring institutional patterns of American society; the ideology of the forties is not, in our view, simply a reaction to the specific historical circumstances of postwar and post-New-Deal America. This static analysis we believe to be fundamentally justified, but it ignores the problem of change. For the varied purposes of checking the assumptions of our analysis, discriminating between stable and fugitive elements in the contemporary business creed, and offering some guesses about future developments, we devote this final chapter to change. But this book makes no pretense of being a history of business ideology. We have undertaken no thoroughgoing comparison of the business creed of the immediate past with that of earlier decades, or of the last century. Our conclusions must therefore be regarded as tentative.[1]

[1] Our task is complicated by the fact that this particular field has been neglected. Possibly the closest approach to a general survey is Chapman, *Development of American Business and Banking Thought*, although it is really much more a history of the Federal Reserve System than a catholic survey of business thought. A recent book by James Warren Prothro, *The Dollar Decade* (Baton Rouge, 1954) surveys business ideas in the 1920's. There are, of course, histories of American economic thought which cover the period from the nineties to the recent past with some thoroughness. We may mention Joseph Dorfman, *The Economic Mind in American Civilization* (3 vols., New York, 1946, 1949), Vol. 3, or J. Normano, *The Spirit of American Economics* (New York, 1943). Unfortunately, these studies restrict themselves very largely to academic economics. Among general intellectual histories, Parrington, *Main Currents in American Thought*, and R. H. Gabriel, *Course of American Democratic Thought* (New York, 1940), have been found of some use. Among more specialized studies we have used R. G. McCloskey, *American Conservatism in the Age of Enterprise* (Cambridge, Mass., 1951; excellent analysis of Carnegie); Walter Fuller Taylor, *The Economic Novel in America;* Donald McConnell, *Economic Virtues in the U.S.* (New York, 1930). But for the most part we have had to depend on primary sources, as indicated variously in the text and footnotes following.

THE STABILITY OF THE CREED

A basic stability, indeed almost a stubborn intellectual conservatism, in many elements of business ideology is evident from the most cursory examination of past business pronouncements. The classical picture of a society in which business firms compete freely with one another under the inflexible rule of simple economic laws has been drawn with the same broad strokes, decade after decade. The evils of monopoly, governmental interference, and socialism have been constantly drubbed with the familiar weapons of classical doctrine. Not only do the articles of faith, but the very form and detail in which they are argued, remain the same. The sober, scolding emphasis on the immutable laws of economics which we find in contemporary discussion (and have noted in the writings of James Mooney and others from the thirties) appears earlier in forms only slightly altered by our forefathers' greater weakness for pompous rhetoric. In 1910, we hear John Kirby, Jr., President of the National Association of Manufacturers, telling the Manufacturers Association of Erie, Pennsylvania, that the purpose of a labor union "should not be to antagonize the natural law of economics, which, in the nature of things is as irrevocable as the law of gravitation." [2] Earlier we hear Mr. Searles, Secretary of the American Sugar Refining Company, assuring the Lexow committee that the same law protected the nation from monopoly:

There is a law, let me tell you, sir, higher than the State of New York. That is the law of supply and demand. No trust has ever been yet organized, no corporation has ever been created, and there has never been any combination of capital of any sort big enough to violate that law. As I told you, hundreds of millions of dollars are in New York waiting to be put into industrial pursuits; but if all the hundreds of millions were put into one industry, the violation of the law of supply and demand would bring about the destruction of all the wealth. The consumer is amply protected by the operation of this law, just as the combination of capital is held in check by it.[3]

Even in the days *Fortune* now terms the Age of the Tycoon, when great monopolies were in the making and businessmen privately boasted of their power with an impudence which would not be ventured today — even then the public ideological picture showed lots of little businesses competing under natural law. Not all businessmen were as stubborn in their denial of power as was the elder Morgan in his famous appearance before the Pujo Committee (1913); there was often concrete admission of the power of influencing the prices of commodities, but this did not

[2] John Kirby, Jr., *Facts vs. Platitudes and Sophistry* (No. 18 in a series of pamphlets published and distributed by the NAM, New York, 1910).
[3] Quoted by Henry Clews, *The Wall Street Point of View* (New York, 1900), p. 40.

disturb a broad confidence that competition under the ineluctable law of supply and demand basically prevailed. Witnesses before investigating committees stubbornly pointed to such things as the competition for capital and depicted trusts as under basically the same competitive tests as firms within an industry.[4] The symbol of competition has had the stable value of honest currency, and efforts to depict existing conditions as conforming to the symbol have been untiring.

Antipathy to control, interference, and ownership by government is an ancient theme in the business ideology. Long before the New Deal, the dangers of government intervention were pointed out in terms strikingly similar to those used today;[5] government ownership of the railroads would cause "no end of trouble" by suppressing the stimuli of competition and the spirit of business enterprise; government meddling was to blame for business depressions.[6]

In its steadfast adherence to the classical tradition, the ideology serves dead economists; it has not sought new masters. The subject of economics has undergone profound changes in our times, but the business ideology has not followed its lead. It has rejected the Keynesian revolution and has refused to follow economists' modifications of assumptions.[7] Whereas the economist now talks cautiously of "models," the ideologist confidently asserts that there are "laws every housewife knows," and the "laws" are stubbornly classical.

This long devotion to the classical view of our economy has been matched by a persisting loyalty to certain symbols. The vigorous nationalism of the contemporary creed, with its emphasis on the peculiarities of American society, the extraordinary achievements of America, and the un-American qualities of socialism and other "isms," is hardly less pro-

[4] *Ibid.,* p. 37; testimony of F. B. Thurber before the Lexow committee.

[5] See statements of Morgan, Higginson, etc. in Chapter 8. Also, C. A. Destler, "The Opposition of American Businessmen to Social Control During the 'Gilded Age,'" *Miss. Valley Historical Review,* xxxix:641–672 (March 1953).

[6] Clews, *Wall Street Point,* pp. 25, 115. Here Cleveland's government is made responsible for the depression of the nineties. "When Mr. Cleveland took possession of the White House, March 4, 1893, the country was prosperous. When he went out of office, March 4, 1897, the country was almost on the verge of bankruptcy and the worst prolonged depression in business that the nation has ever experienced prevailed during the greater part of the time. Had it not been for the agitation regarding free-trade theories, together with certain other Utopian schemes of reform, the good times which the country enjoyed during the last years of General Harrison's administration would in all probability have continued indefinitely." (See also p. 125, where free trade theories are made responsible for the loss of hundreds of millions in panics.)

[7] Except of course for the C.E.D. wing and the *ad hoc* acceptance of newer economics on some policy questions. The very infrequent appearance of marginal analysis in the ideology might even be taken as evidence that the ideology has not absorbed the great transformation to neoclassical economics in the late nineteenth century.

nounced than it was a half century ago. The popularity of Social Darwinism tinged many of the pronouncements of the Gilded Age with an
international, global quality. But, if a figure like Andrew Carnegie spoke
in catholic terms of "the race," there were swarms of orators and
pamphleteers holding to the proudly nationalistic themes which America
has always heard. Readers and listeners were given statistics on the greatness of America, assured by an NAM president that "Americanism" was
"the true solution of the labor problem," [8] or that "the next step in
education" should be toward "real Americanism." [9]

Values too have been unchanging. The emphases on individual self-
reliance, the virtues of thrift and saving, practicality, and austere moral
responsibility run through pronouncements of earlier business leaders as
they do through those of the last twenty years. The businessman of the
late nineteenth century may have echoed McGuffey's Eclectic Readers more
loudly and naïvely than does his twentieth-century descendant, but the
fundamental values are identical. Carnegie epitomized the central values:
"A man's first duty is to make a competence and be independent." [10]

The managerial strand of the business ideology we might expect to be
quite new and without precedents, as it seems to evolve from the
emergence of the large, stable public corporation and, as such, to be a
phenomenon of the middle twentieth century. In its core propositions
about the responsibilities and motivations of business management, this
may well be the case; even here, however, it is evident that the theme
antedates the New Deal. It is easy to collect quotations from the 1920's
and even earlier which sound very much like those of 1952. Managerial
protestations of social responsibility are evidently more than responses
to the political and trade union pressures of the last twenty years. Thus,
Owen D. Young, Chairman of the Board of the General Electric Company,
in 1928:

We think of managers no longer as the partisan attorneys of either group
against the other. Rather we have come to consider them trustees of the whole
undertaking, whose responsibility is to see to it on the one side that the invested capital is safe and its return is adequate and continuous; and on the
other side that competent and conscientious men are found to do the work and
that their job is safe and their earnings are adequate and continuous.[11]

[8] James W. Van Cleave, Americanism: The True Solution to the Labor Problem
(NAM pamphlet, 1908).
[9] Dr. F. W. Gunsaulus, "The Next Step in Education" (NAM pamphlet No. 4,
1908).
[10] Quoted in McConnell, *Economic Virtues*, p. 64. This volume contains a considerable survey of the values expressed by American businessmen, from the period
following the Civil War to 1930.
[11] *Bulletin of the International Management Institute*, vol. 2, no. 2, February
1928, quoted in McConnell, p. 123. See quotations, *Economic Virtues*, pp. 121 ff.

It may be that, formerly, such pronouncements were restricted to a handful of successful, conspicuous leaders like Henry Ford, Edward A. Filene, and John D. Rockefeller, Jr. But, if we think of the managerial strand as including broader assertions of community responsibility than those peculiarly appropriate to managers of large, public corporations, then the older literature burgeons with "managerial" statements. For instance, the service ideology flourished in earlier decades.[12]

On more concrete matters we should expect considerable change in the ideology. There have certainly been great changes in American society regarding such matters as the legitimacy of labor union activities, the nature and range of governmental activities, experience of depressions, and the form of business activity itself. But no ideology is a simple reflection of the changing social system, and there are many instances where the business creed has shown a surprising stability in the face of profound changes in its subject matter. We shall illustrate this in one major area, that of labor union activity and collective bargaining.

Businessmen have been very reluctant to accept collective bargaining and have been slow to concede the legitimacy of labor unions' power. One might conclude from this that labor unions have only recently been accepted in the ideology. But this is emphatically untrue. When the Industrial Relations Commission of 1913–1914 sounded business on the legitimacy of unions, it gained almost unanimous assent from more than two hundred witnesses; a few were very reluctant to concede organizational rights of labor, but almost no one denied them categorically.[13] This was, of course, a situation in which there were presumably very strong pressures on the businessmen testifying to express "democratic" sentiments, but the testimony was not exceptional. Reading the literature of the NAM at about this period, we find the most vigorous attacks on the leadership and practices of labor unions, coupled with solemn declarations of respect for organization and bargaining rights. John Kirby, Jr., in accepting the Presidency of NAM in 1909, told the organization that they had selected him "not on account of my ability, not on account of my national reputation; nothing of that kind, but simply because you know where I stand on the labor question." With this mandate, he went forth to do battle against Samuel Gompers and the American Federation of Labor, which he was pleased to call "this beast with seven heads and ten horns . . . stalking up and down the earth, demanding that no man should work, buy, or sell, save that had the name or mark of the beast upon his right

---

[12] See references cited in Chapter 6. "Service" was a conspicuous symbol in the 1920's but we are unclear as to its earlier history. A sample check of issues of the *Saturday Evening Post* in 1907 and 1913 showed no use of the service symbol in advertising.

[13] Chapman, *American Business*, p. 23.

hand or on his forehead." The force of his rhetoric could hardly be matched on the side of business today; he saw mortal dangers to our civilization in a movement which has latterly become synonymous with conservative unionism:

> The foundations of Rome became morally rotten, and its superstructure came down with a crash. So will our superstructure tumble if we permit the spirit of socialism and anarchy to penetrate its foundations, and the germs of Gomperism to eat away its industrial footings.[14]

> No organization of men, not excepting the Ku Klux Klan, the Mafia, or the Black Hand Society, has ever produced such a record of barbarism as this so called organized labor society, which through misdirected sympathy, apathy, and indifference, has been permitted to grow up to cripple our industries and to trample in the dust the national and constitutional rights of our citizens.[15]

Still, Kirby was always careful to condemn men and abuses, not the principles of labor organizations as such. In a speech on "The Disadvantages of Labor Unionism," he wished it distinctly understood:

> . . . that anything I may say condemnatory of trade unions is in no manner intended to reflect discredit upon the labor organizations which are founded upon an enlightened public conscience and which base their operations on legitimate principles . . . I am not opposed to wage unions as such, and never have been . . . I freely accord to wage earners the same right to unite in lawful organization for the advancement of their mutual interests as is accorded to all classes of citizens.[16]

He repeatedly asserted that the NAM had always taken this stand, as the words of previous NAM officials testified. James W. Van Cleave had said:

> Mark You! I have no fault to find with labor organizations. Workers have just as good a right to organize as have employers. They have not only the right, but it is a laudable undertaking to bring the workers together into societies, and these societies into larger aggregations for mutual benefit, and for combating autocracy and oppression when found in combinations of capitalists or employers. We have no more right to quarrel with workers for forming unions and for consolidating these unions into federations, than we have for opposing the formation of the great leagues of capital, like the railroads into the great trunk lines of today. We demand, however, that the right of free competition, whether among manufacturers, railroads or laborers, must not be assailed.[17]

[14] John Kirby, Jr., "Where Do You Stand?" (NAM, 1909), pp. 5, 10.

[15] John Kirby, Jr., "The Goal of the Labor Trust," address to the Springfield Employers' Association, Jan. 11, 1910, p. 23.

[16] John Kirby, Jr., "The Disadvantages of Labor Unionism," address to the Young Men's Hebrew Association of New York, Nov. 7, 1909, p. 4.

[17] Van Cleave, *Americanism*, p. 5.

The attack was on "abuses" and not on the organization of labor unions as such.

Much of the agitation at this early period was directed at specific contemporary issues. There was great alarm about the legal status of boycotts and injunctions, and about proposals for amendment of the Sherman Act to exempt labor unions.[18] But, while the specific issues have changed, there is remarkable similarity between the arguments which were advanced at the beginning of the century and those which flourish at mid-century. Today's labor unions allegedly threaten freedom either by establishing monopoly or by restricting the freedom of contract of the individual worker and subjecting him to the dictates of labor "bosses." The epithet "labor trust" was liberally interspersed through business speeches in the early part of the century.[19] On more specific questions of union practice — the legitimacy of the closed shop, the boycott, or aggressive picketing — it was claimed then as now that individual rights should be protected from organized coercion.[20] What businessmen may now be willing to accept in practice from labor unions certainly differs from what an older generation would accept, but there has been no corresponding shift in ideology.

A thorough historical study would, no doubt, reveal other instances of ideological stability in the face of social change. The Honorable Chauncey M. Depew, inviting the New York Chamber of Commerce to fill Delmonico's with "hallelujahs to the truth" because "the people of this country, educated, intelligent, redeemed, prosperous, stand here upon the grave of the fetich (sic) and the superstition of free silver" [21] sounds quaint today. It would be strange to find a group of businessmen solemnly toasting the Gold Standard, and giving a great round of cheers when the speaker identifies it with "honest money." [22] Yet the symbol of "honest money" still wins regard if not applause; the contemporary issues change, but they are discussed in terms of perennial symbols.

Our venture into the history of the business ideology has been sketchy and impressionistic and must be treated with caution. But the evidence of ideological stability supports our general hypothesis of the relation

[18] See the series of NAM pamphlets (1909–1910): No. 11, *Class Legislation*, by Hon. Charles E. Littlefield; No. 12, *Injunctions*, by a Member of the New Jersey Bar; No. 13, *The Doom of the Boycott*, by James W. Van Cleave; No. 14, *Class Legislation for Industry*, by James A. Emery; No. 15, *The Boycott*, by Walter Drew.

[19] In the title of Kirby's 1910 address to Springfield Employers' Association. See also "Where Do We Stand?", p. 17; "Disadvantages of Labor Unionism," p. 36.

[20] See, for example, the pamphlets above and No. 16, *Closed Shop Unionism*, by Walter Drew (1919).

[21] Chauncey M. Depew, *Speeches on the Occasion*, Chamber of Commerce of New York, 132nd Annual Banquet, 1900, p. 29.

[22] Governor Roosevelt at the 131st Annual Banquet, 1899, p. 32. A toast to the Gold Standard was a regular feature of these gastronomic prodigies.

between ideology and patterned strains in social roles. Institutional patterns do not change overnight; were the business ideology to change radically with superficial changes in current political issues, our theory would be untenable. To be sure, the role of the business executive has undergone some changes in the last half-century. But we have stressed broad, persistent features of the business role. Correspondingly, if ideology is shaped by the strains of the role, we should expect to find stability in its basic symbols and doctrines.

The inertia of cultural heritages is a familiar fact of social science but needs explanation. Our theory explains ideological continuity by the continuity of the institutional patterns which give rise to the ideology. The functions of ideology are such that it must reflect the continuity of the institutions it serves. Ideology cannot have the relative freedom of pure intellectual investigation. Ideologies seem to display a common intellectual conservatism, whether they are "radical" in their content or conservative. Marxism is certainly a notable example. While the oscillations of the Communist Party on specific issues are violent and spectacular, the basic theoretical structure of Marxism and the form of arguments have scarcely altered since Marx and Engels laid them down. No amount of cogent logical criticism or new empirical evidence has shaken the loyalty of Communists to primitive orthodox Marxism. *Das Kapital* is never viewed as obsolete or in need of revision.

This example suggests reasons for the intellectual conservatism of ideologies. To be a Marxist means to have faith in the truth of the broad Marxist principles; fundamental alteration in these principles can be made only with a sacrifice in distinctiveness of faith. The diffidence toward theories and conceptual schemes which is characteristic of science can hardly be maintained toward a working ideology. The framework of an ideology is not looked on as a convenient set of abstractions but more naïvely as a necessary description of the real world. The broad concepts of ideology come to have the status of symbols and are not readily manipulated with intellectual detachment.

Ideologies affect the attitudes and actions of large numbers of people; this also imposes a rigidifying influence on them. If symbols are to have an impact, they must be familiar and they must have an uncluttered simplicity. The path of intellectual development is likely to lead through complexities and ambiguities which make poor material for ideology. The anti-intellectualism of the business creed may have a special rigidifying effect; the creed demands that valid concepts be those which are intuitively intelligible to housewives and practical men. But something of the same kind characterizes ideologies generally; they tend always to be out-of-date in their general concepts, which get "reinterpreted" to fit new situations.[23] The reason lies, not in the stupidity of those who subscribe to them, but in their emotional needs as generated by the society in which they live.

THE CHANGING PLACE OF THE CREED IN AMERICAN SOCIETY

Time has brought changes less in the substance of the business creed than in its tone and in the kind of adherence which it gains. The business ideology now reflects less confidence that it is the accepted orthodox creed of the whole society.

Karl Marx pointed out in the *German Ideology* that all ideologies are couched in terms which demand the assent of everyone, even if their adherents in fact constitute a small minority. But before the Great Depression, the businessman might correctly claim that his creed was the creed of nearly all sections of society, that it was *the* orthodox American ideology. The creed carries the stamp of an orthodoxy, as we have seen. The emphasis on the integrated, harmonious System of free enterprise, for example, stands in contrast to the "contradictions" which hostile critics see in the society.[24] The classical strand's picture of the "naturalness" of the System in its correspondence with fundamental traits of human nature is the mark of an orthodoxy. So is the emphasis throughout the creed on the unifying features of the social order and its denial or suppression of divisive ones. With these qualifications and in an atmosphere where the President could proclaim that "the business of the United States is business," the creed could show a comfortable sense of general acceptability.

Two decades later the creed does not show so much confidence. Rather, it is marked by concern over the supposed lack of appreciation and understanding of business among the public at large. And, though still retaining its fundamental shape as an orthodox creed, accepting and reinforcing the going social system, the creed is now filled with violent attacks on certain institutions as they have developed since the Great Depression — notably the government, and, to a lesser extent, organized labor. Further, the signs of insecurity are strong in its supporters: the tone of their defense is often violent, as are the attacks on the forces which threaten the system.

Compare Elmo Calkins' *Business the Civilizer* (1929) with Ernest Klein's *How to Stay Rich* (1950). The former deals with critics of business to be sure, but with an almost condescending buoyancy of spirit — the errors of the unwise need to be pointed out but the "system" is not

---

[23] McCloskey, *American Conservatism in the Age of Enterprise,* describes this process in the history of American political ideology.

[24] That ideological critics in a society devoted to rationality should pillory the society they attack as anarchic, meaningless, and full of contradictions is precisely what we would expect. Not only the Marxists, but a host of critics, from Saint Simon to Veblen, have followed this line.

fundamentally threatened. Klein thinks the situation far more desperate; he wants us to take a stand, here and now and "in the name of God, amen," for democratic American capitalism and against the deadly threats to it. There are, of course, reasons which we have already indicated, why ideologies are full of references to "first steps" and fundamental decisions, but there is an insistency in the contemporary business creed which suggests a more chronic fear that the ideological tide may be turning against it. It is not only Mr. Klein who deplores lack of clarity about the nature of our system and the necessity of profit. The following appears in a solemn pre-election editorial by the NAM: "These concepts of statism are now accepted throughout most of the world and only a forthright and vigorous affirmation of the principles of American freedom can arrest, and perhaps reverse, the trend toward them in our own country." [25] H. E. Humphreys, Jr., President of the United States Rubber Company, is one among a great many who think there is "widespread misunderstanding of our business system" and a "failure of government to recognize the true role of profit in the path of prosperity." [26]

Social systems commonly develop the sorts of malintegration which are evidenced in groups feeling that they are misunderstood and improperly appreciated by the rest of the society.[27] Those who live in academic communities in the United States need only reflect on the conversation of professors to note that such feelings are not restricted to the business community. Businessmen have shown evidence of feeling misunderstood, not merely since the New Deal, but more or less chronically. Even in the heyday of business dominance around the turn of the century, businessmen were frequently moved to protest against the misunderstandings which they had to face.

It has been the habit of too many people — well meaning people too — to decry Wall Street as hurtful to the morals of the country and injurious to our best business interests — all of which is mistaken.[28]

But recently the protests have been stronger and more frequent, and the note of anxiety which they reflect is louder.

THE STRENGTH OF COMPETING IDEOLOGIES

The claim of business ideology to be an American orthodoxy has never gone unchallenged. First, there has always been plenty of room for argument as to what constitutes the "American System." An ideology can be

---

[25] *U.S.A.,* October 1952, p. 4.

[26] United States Rubber Company advertisement, *New York Times,* Oct. 27, 1952, p. 17.

[27] See Alfred Schuetz, "The Stranger," *American Journal of Sociology,* May 1944, for a penetrating discussion of this problem.

[28] Clews, *Wall Street Point,* p. 22.

a conservative affirmation of existing institutions without giving so central a place to "free enterprise." Second, innovation as such has a positive value in American society; it is perfectly legitimate to subject many features of our society to critical scrutiny. Ideological competition in American society must be fought out in both these fields. The business creed seeks to defend American institutions from "misguided liberals," "intellectuals," and "foreign ideologists," but it also proclaims the service of business to progress and resists being put in a purely conservative position. It is equipped to answer opponents but hardly to monopolize either the field of conservative affirmation or the field of liberal criticism. If there has been a diminution in the general acceptance of the business creed, we should seek its roots not so much in the emergence of basically new and "alien" ideologies as in a growing strength of competitors for the common symbols of the American heritage.

There certainly are indigenous tendencies to ideological differences in modern Western society. Different roles tend to produce distinctive strains and correspondingly varied ideological reactions. Broad tendencies to division are inherent in the process of social change and in the stratification system, and, as we have emphasized above, the institutions of business become a point of attack in many reactions. Anti-business ideologies have evidently gained more force in the recent past, and this apparent gain must either be due to increased pressures behind these ideologies or to improved opportunities for their legitimate expression.

The opportunities for expression of other ideologies have indeed improved. The businessman's views that the growth of strong labor unions and "big" government represents a threat to business are sound intuitions, although perhaps for reasons which the businessman cannot usually make clear and explicit. These developments, whatever their substantive effects on business operations, have great significance in facilitating the expression of counterideologies.

GOVERNMENT AS AN IDEOLOGICAL COMPETITOR

The extension of governmental activities in the United States has altered the structure of American society in a way which is not easily handled in the business creed. In 1910 the modern kings of commerce could be represented as natural successors of the medieval kings,[29] and Americans were told that "in the course of evolution and a higher civilization we might be able to get along comfortably without Congress, but without Wall Street, never." [30] "Big" government seems now an ineradicable feature of American society, and its growth is inseparable from the expression of ideology uncongenial to the business creed. The nature of

[29] Depew, *Speeches*, p. 29.
[30] Clews, *Wall Street Point*, p. 4.

modern governments is grounded in the values of universalism and collective responsibility. Legislators and government officials play the role of disinterested "servants" of the people; as such they can legitimately claim to speak for the "people." Given the universalism demanded in our society, with its implications of radical democracy, political figures must represent not only those in high statuses but the whole range of statuses in our society. They must represent the "general interest" and not "selfish, private interests." The endemic tendencies to anti-business sentiment in the society can gain expression through figures who are in a legitimized position as representatives of the general interest. The claim of business to represent the "common interest" may thus be opposed by political figures to whom business is one special "interest" among many.

The peculiar heritage of the American government made it easy for the government to be viewed as merely a service agency with certain limited regulatory functions — the view which was dominant in America in the fifty years before the Great Depression. Here, as nowhere else in the Western world, government was dominated by business. Most of the present governments in the modern Western world still reflect their origins in what Max Weber called patrimonial governments — in which the state was conceived basically as the personal domain of the ruler. In such governments, the role of the state as an essential symbolic focus of the nation — as, for example, the British monarchy — still depends on that heritage. The absence of such a tradition in America made it easy to take a purely instrumental view of the state. In this context, it was not difficult for businessmen to see themselves as the kings of commerce, the *real* locus of American power, and for others to share the view summed up in Coolidge's dictum, "The business of the United States is business." As the prestige of businessmen in America has depended on the absence of a hereditary aristocracy of landowners and governmental servants, so the power of business, independent of government and often *de facto* over government, has depended on the corresponding absence of patrimonial tradition.

The Great Depression, the Second World War, and the continuing national emergency have brought to an end the older pattern of limited national government and have reduced business power. These developments, pushed by practical necessities, have had great ideological consequences. A government which controls and directs economic activity must have ideological rationalizations of its actions. As a "servant" of the people, government must have a "welfare" ideology and present it as a national orthodoxy. The growth of government also means that ideology will have an array of spokesmen among the relatively high status figures in our society. The growth of government inevitably bolsters the authority of technical and professional experts, and the growth of the influence of this corps of "experts" has been a notable feature of recent American life. In crying out against braintrusters, Keynesian economists, bureaucrats, and intellectuals, businessmen have not been attacking a pure phantasm. Our analysis of the strains in the business role which lead to positive emphases on practicality is one very important side of ideological determination in these matters, but only one; the competing authority of professionals in a new national constitution cannot be ignored.

The working ideology of a government must claim to be general orthodoxy. If it is not proclaimed in Washington that America is a "free enterprise society," then those who claim that it is must regard themselves not as loyal supporters of an unchallenged truth but rather as the pleaders of a special cause. The twenty years of Democratic administrations, 1933–1953, were not years in which the White House voiced the business creed. The defensive, injured tone of business pronouncements has suggested an unwelcome estrangement. One course of reaction has been a running fire of accusation that the government was not acting as a proper American government should. There have also been many oblique and displaced reactions. The enormous amount of attention given to the symbols of freedom, and the virulence of attack on the Communist "slave" states as well as on the domestic Communist threat, have certainly been linked to the irritations from a government acting on the "wrong" symbolic principles.

The return of a Republican administration has doubtless eased businessmen's feelings of estrangement from the government. It is still very early to assess this new era, but our general argument points to broad changes that are not likely to be reversed in it. The voice of government may harmonize better with the creed in future than it has in the recent past, but it will not carry precisely the same tune.

ORGANIZED LABOR AS AN IDEOLOGICAL COMPETITOR

The other major institutional change facilitating the expression of ideologies competing with the business creed has been the growth of labor unions, in membership and in strength. The business creed's acceptance in principle of organization of labor was, as we have seen, at one time combined with vigorous efforts to deny legitimacy to the particular forms of the labor movement existing at the time. There was an aggressiveness and abusiveness in business' statement of its case which would not be heard today. Probably no responsible national figure from business would now venture to describe the leaders of organized labor as "men of muscle rather than men of intelligence" (as did David M. Parry, President of the National Association of Manufacturers, in 1903).[31] The weapons of rhetorical abuse are now brandished more openly by labor leaders. (In the steel strike of 1952, Philip Murray publicly referred to the leaders of the steel

[31] Quoted in John K. Galbraith, *American Capitalism* (Boston, 1952), p. 157.

industry as "those big baboons," while apparently no steel executive publicly questioned Mr. Murray's intelligence or humanity.) In recent years,
business spokesmen have come to accept the legitimacy and respectability
not only of abstract, ideal labor unions but of those organizations actually
existing and opposing them, often militantly, on the issues of the day.

The coming of age of the labor movement has had profound consequences in pushing the business creed away from its central position of
orthodoxy toward an uncomfortable position of minority conservatism.
There was a time when the notion of a "labor point of view" on such
broad questions as fiscal policy, price controls, or nationalization could
have been scoffed at by business. Now, following certain pressures in its
own internal dynamics, the labor movement is heard not only on the
classical problems of wages, hours, and working conditions, but on a host
of subjects throughout the fabric of the national society. There is a well-
developed labor ideology — not in the Marxian or social democratic traditions of European labor movements but indigenously American — which
could serve as the subject of another book. In a universalistic society the
labor movement is in an especially strong position to claim representation
of the "people" and to pose as the champion of alteration of our society
for the greater benefit of the "people." It engages in heavy battle with the
spokesmen of business for the great symbols of the heritage, for "progress,"
"freedom," and "human dignity."

CHANGING VALUES AND THE ACCEPTABILITY OF THE BUSINESS CREED

These institutional changes are the conspicuous and tangible results of
deeply rooted and pervasive changes in American society; changes that
involve important shifts in values. These shifts represent the working out
of a set of values well grounded in our heritage — activism, universalism,
and social responsibility.

The first is that people are now less willing to accept and rationalize
large differences in income and status. A new egalitarianism has been
growing in American life. In the early nineteenth century, Fisher Ames
could speak smugly of the "wise, the rich, and the good" as though the
three terms were synonymous.[32] At the beginning of the twentieth century,
businessmen could openly blame the poor for their poverty — D. O. Mills,
founder of the Mills Hotels, called the urban poor "the most wasteful and
extravagant people in the world today." [33] But by the middle of the twentieth century, one can no longer say in public that the fate of the poor is
their just reward and no one's responsibility but their own. Even the

---

[32] Fisher Ames, letter (1802) quoted in *Dict. Amer. Biography*, 1:246.

[33] D. O. Mills, *Cosmopolitan,* 1902, p. 292, quoted in McConnell, *Economic Virtues*, p. 118.

Christian tradition of the laudable omnipresence of the poor has been repudiated by such august bodies as the Federal Council of Churches of Christ in America.

The second change can best be summed up as growing collective responsibility on a national scale. It may well have been easier to accept differences of status and income in narrower, local contexts than it is to accept them on the broad stage of a national society. Improved transportation and communication, the forces of nationalism, and the cohesive effects of two world wars have enlarged the domain of application of the values of universalism and social responsibility. Differences in status and economic well-being may now be given *de facto* tacit recognition but they cannot become public policy. It cannot be a government's policy that only a certain fraction of the people should receive professional medical attention, have certain forms of insurance, or enjoy a certain type of housing. Nor can the condition of those who fall below certain universally applicable minimum standards be fatalistically accepted. Our tradition is one that calls for actively "doing something" about evil conditions.

As we have earlier remarked, the business executive is likely to acquire a more solid and prestigious status in the concrete contexts of a local community than he does more abstractly in the nation at large. William B. Given, Jr., Chairman of the Board of the American Brake Shoe Company, remarked in a Bernays Foundation Lecture in 1950:

> Old school business managers felt that everyone who worked for them was in their debt. Some even felt that the pay check was, at least in part, charity. We, who are older, experienced this. Now we know that the opposite is true — that every company has a long term debt to those who contribute to its success. Managers who are not realistic about this do not belong to today's management.[34]

In the older forms of our society, when local and kinship ties were more embracing than they are at present, the status distinctions in a local setting had an apparent inevitability and hence a legitimacy which the more fluid distinctions of a large-scale, mobile society do not possess. If Mr. Given finds the modern manager compelled to feel less paternalistic, the increase in scope of business operations and the wider perspectives of employees must bear a large part of the responsibility.

These changes have clear implications in the emergence of "service" conceptions throughout the society. Governments in the modern world represent themselves ideologically as "servants" of the people, but increased demands for social responsibility have been imposed not only on government but on other agencies in our society. Business and the professions as well are subject to increasing demands that they "serve" the

---

[34] *Social Responsibilities of Management*, p. 72.

general populace. The recent history of struggle over the responsibilities of the medical profession in the United States is important evidence of the generality of these demands. It is now certainly ideological orthodoxy in the United States that professional medical attention conforming to "adequate" standards should be availbale to all citizens. Medical attention has thus become regarded, at least ideologically, not as a privilege of those who are able to afford it but as a "right" of everyone. Pressures on the medical profession to abandon "private practice" in favor of some scheme of "socialization" have paralleled those on business and have produced a political sympathy between business and medicine especially prominent on the contemporary scene.

A third shift in values is in a sense the opposite of the first two. The individualistic values which we found so conspicuously extolled by the business creed — the values of industriousness, personal integrity, thrift, and self-reliance — have declined in relative importance. David Riesman has recently put in vivid and provocative form a thesis that there has been a fundamental change in the character structure (and hence the ruling values) of Americans.[35] He contends that American society has changed so that it now produces personalities that are "other-directed" rather than "inner-directed" as our ancestors tended to be; conduct is said to be now more commonly directed by the shifting expectations of others than by fixed, internalized moral principles which the individual applies regardless of "what people think." One of the most impressive kinds of evidence in support of Mr. Riesman's thesis has to do with child-rearing practices, presumably the matrix of character formation. Anthropologists have pointed out to us the remarkable degree to which we have traditionally taken a moralistic stand in rearing our children.[36] This moralistic pattern, symbolized in the homilies of the McGuffey readers, has now been invaded by a more rationalistic pattern, symbolized by the psychiatric articles in parents' magazines. To a remarkable degree, children are now raised according to what are currently conceived to be sound psychological principles rather than according to traditional moral norms. The implications are that these standards will be shifting ones and that parents and children alike come to give more attention to contemporary "authorities" than to unchanging moral laws.

This rationalizing of the process of child-rearing is but one example of the greatly increased force of norms of rationality. Whether or not contemporary Americans are in any absolute sense more "rational" than their fathers, they place an increasing emphasis on science and rationality as

[35] Riesman *et al. The Lonely Crowd,* chs. I, II.

[36] See Margaret Mead's writings. She also sees a shift from the "Puritan" character which is now "increasingly rare" to a more flexible character structure: "Social Change and Cultural Surrogates," in Kluckhohn and Murray, *Personality in Nature, Culture, and Society* (New York, 1948), p. 521.

the sources of proper norms for conduct. The values which demand that we avoid fatalistic acceptance of frustrations but attempt to "do something" about our problems are implemented by rationalistic efforts. Moral self-sacrifice, stolid patience, and resigned pessimism are perhaps sometimes given their due, but the main weight of the value-system is toward active betterment of conditions rather than "noble" acceptance.

The decline of "inner-direction" in American character weakens the general force of an ideology as individualistic and moralistic as the business creed. It is, of course, conceivable that individualistic values persist along with strong feelings of universalistic national solidarity. But their strength is likely to be less than in an era of local self-help and particularism. If America is slipping down the fatal path to "socialism," the trend is hardly one which can be explained purely as a result of fuzzy-minded thinking or pernicious influences from abroad. It seems an inevitable consequence of integration as a nation. A loss in general assent to the business creed, especially in its classical form, seems equally inescapable.

Similarly, the replacement of traditional moral principles by up-to-date scientific findings as norms of conduct weakens the potential support of the business creed. The creed has, it is true, some tendency to subordinate moral precepts to the rational pursuit of tangible goals. The worker is often urged to be industrious and thrifty, not for the sake of these values alone, but because this is the way to success and prosperity. Still, by contrast with an ideology like Marxism, the business creed is fundamentally less in tune with rationalistic trends. Where there is a strong tendency to seek solutions to problems in terms of rational effort — "planning" and the like — the appeal of an ideology which gives such prominence to individualistic moral values is likely to be lessened. The persistence of doctrines as gloomy and resigned as the Ricardian economics has no doubt been dependent on an older set of values; the future of such doctrines is unpromising in a society more firmly wed to values of hopeful activism and rationality.

These shifts in value emphases have been accompanied by a decline in the relative importance of business as a focus of career aspirations. Business could claim to speak for the whole nation with more conviction were there a more widespread tendency for individuals to link their own career aspirations directly to the problems of business firms. The hope of having one's own business, still strong in the American population, strikingly enough, is most common among manual workers.[37] Those who occupy occupational roles higher up in the status scale may have their aspirations fixed on some managerial role, but they tend to think more in terms

[37] See R. Centers, "Motivational Aspects," *Journal of Social Psychology*, and the various studies summarized in Kurt Mayer, "Business Enterprise: Traditional Symbol of Opportunity," *British Journal of Sociology*, IV: 160–180 (1953).

of a salaried role in an established organization than in terms of new ventures in private enterprise. This sort of situation probably did not exist in anything like the same degree in the past. Our economy has developed to the point where large numbers of people think of their careers in terms of collective interdependence and rewards within a given organization. The large, established firm has come to stay. A society in which large numbers inevitably think of their occupational careers as set within a technical and professional mold, and in which their rewards are in terms of promotion or increased salaries within an organization, is not one in which the businessman's problems easily gain the sympathy of all. It is perhaps ironic that in the ranks of labor — the group with most crystallized opposition to business — there most commonly exist career aspirations of a sort that might conduce to deep sympathies with the business creed.

To summarize, two influences have arisen in American society to challenge the business creed. In the first place, government and labor organizations have been greatly strengthened as agencies for ideological expression, and in the second place, some broad changes in the social structure and in dominant values have strengthened other ideological tendencies at the expense of the business creed. The first consequence we draw from these developments is a decline in the appeal of business ideology; the second has to do with a possible response of the business creed. The managerial strand in the ideology emphasizes social responsibilities. If American business is to preserve a strong sense of legitimacy in the ideological climate of the present, it must respond to the increased demands for general responsibility; and the growth of the managerial strand may doubtless be seen as a response to a growing challenge. Its logical incompleteness has been stressed above, and this incompleteness seems not merely a consequence of immaturity. As long as managerial ideology clings to the autonomy of individual business enterprises, it is not easy to see how it can be filled out to encompass the workings of our total society in its logical embrace. The picture of society wholly controlled by beneficent managerial decisions would be so much like "socialism" that it could hardly serve as a symbol in the business creed.

THE FUTURE OF THE BUSINESS IDEOLOGY

Thus, the business ideology is basically a stable body of doctrine, shifting its emphases and making concrete *ad hoc* changes, but not undergoing any fundamental revolutions. The biggest changes have been less in content of the creed than in the confidence it shows in its own general acceptance. It is now more definitely a "business" creed standing in opposition to other ideological positions firmly established in American society.

Would it be fair to conclude that the business creed is stubbornly reactionary and that businessmen are becoming more intransigeantly op-

THE AMERICAN BUSINESS CREED

posed to other groups in American society? The recent American past shows a remarkable history of business opposition to changes which have been deliberately engineered by legislation or less consciously brought about by social forces. Even such familiar and basically accepted institutions in our society as the Federal Reserve system, the personal income tax, federal taxation of corporate income, or the exemption of labor unions from anti-trust prosecution were hotly opposed by businessmen at their inception.[38] The outraged opposition of much of the business community to New Deal and Fair Deal measures and policies remains a vivid memory.

However, the rigidity of the business creed should not be exaggerated. American business now gives at least *de facto* acceptance to a multitude of laws and practices which it earlier opposed as dangerous to the commonwealth or morally repugnant. As against an occasional voice denouncing the progressive income tax as a "Marxian idea" which has destroyed the true America,[39] there is now a much greater volume of argument over the magnitude of the tax, its principle being tacitly accepted. As early as 1939, the *Fortune* Forum of Executive Opinion found considerable support for some modification of New Deal legislation but relatively little for its outright repeal.[40] In more recent years there has been continuous criticism of dangerous tendencies and excesses, but little evidence of a fully "reactionary" program of return to pre-New Deal practices. There has thus been, in effect, substantial change in what is accepted as the normal working of the society. Measures once opposed with the greatest alarm and evidence of unalterable opposition have come to be accepted.

The impression of extreme business conservatism which may appear from following the course of political events is thus likely to be misleading. There is a curious pattern of behavior here, which Thurman Arnold exhibited with telling sarcasm in *Folklore of Capitalism*. At any given time the focus of ideological discussion is likely to bear heavily on certain concrete issues of the day. These are discussed in terms of broad principles, so that the passage of a particular bill is claimed as a deadly threat to "free enterprise" or the "American System." It would be a misreading of these events to assume that the apparent ideological excitement on these occasions represented either unalterable opposition on the one hand, or simply

---

[38] See, for example, *Proceedings of the 40th Annual Meeting of the National Board of Trade* (1910) for opposition to any central banking system (pp. 106–107) and to the corporation tax of 1909 (p. 174). The NAM pamphlets cited above were full of alarm over the proposed exclusion of labor unions from the reach of the Sherman Act, which became law in the Clayton Act. The exclusion was opposed on principle as "class legislation."

[39] Garrett, *Ex-America.*

[40] *Fortune*, October 1939, pp. 52 ff. There was of course wide variation in the reactions to different measures, with only 3.1 per cent wanting to eliminate the Federal Deposit Insurance Corporation, while 44.4 per cent would do away with the WPA.

"window dressing" for calculated effect on the other. It seems far more likely that the issues in question have become a strong focus of sentiment not because of their intrinsic, foreseeable import but because they have assumed a broader symbolic significance. The intense concern over contemporary issues represents a channeling of reactions to strain onto specific objects. States of strain which might otherwise result in the discomforts of diffuse anxieties can, through this process, gain the more gratifying discharge which a definite object for attack provides. This view of the symbolic importance of concrete contemporary issues gives a good basis for understanding the capacity of the business community to move on from what has seemed to be unalterable opposition to at least *de facto* acceptance of new policies and practices.[41] The issue did not in fact have the crucial significance which was alleged for it, and hence its unfavorable resolution could in fact be accepted.

In recent decades the great issues of American public life have been ones in which there has been a large scope for disagreement as to long-run effects or tendencies. It is certainly true that the government debt can get too large, government intervention and control become too intrusive and confining, or mismanagement of the currency lead to disastrous upsetting of "confidence." It is also true that precedents in governmental assistance to particularly handicapped groups or governmental support for particular prerogatives of unions may, once established, be used as leverage for less worthy demands. The practical question has always been quantitative judgment as to what variations in practice and policy can be attempted without setting up serious structural disturbances throughout society. This uncertainty gives an opportunity for the insecurities provoked by strains to be focused on the "dangerous tendencies" involved in particular decisions. Exaggerated statements of the dangers and implications of particular decisions, concessions, or legislation have regularly emerged. Yet new practices, instead of bringing about predicted dire consequences, have become a part of the familiar framework of institutions. Although the business community grants *de facto* recognition to social innovations violently opposed a short time previously, the business creed does not grant what we may term *de jure* recognition until much later, if at all.

Partly for this reason, partly because of the basic conservatism of ideology, there are constant tendencies for some wings of business opinion to lose their flexibility and to shift into a polarized, fundamentalist reaction. We have at various times in this study been very hard put to decide whether or not to give serious attention to documents which at first seemed grossly irresponsible or fantastic, as considerable business ideology adopts

---

[41] See R. Lane, "Law and Opinions in the Business Community," *P.O.Q.*, 17: 239–257 (Summer 1953), which discusses this problem from a somewhat different point of view.

extremely rigid moralistic positions and paints lurid pictures of the degradation of modern American society.[42] A more frequent position, exemplified in such writers as John T. Flynn and Ernest Klein, advocates an uncompromising stand for a vaguely defined "free enterprise" against further concessions in the vaguely defined direction of socialism. Support for some extremely fundamentalist or even "fascist" groups has certainly been found among business groups.[43] Business ideology also has "crackpot" fringes, puzzling to assess. We were, for example, initially disposed to dismiss *Mainspring* as something no responsible businessman would assent to; on closer inspection we discovered that it had been published and distributed through the assistance of General Motors.

Analyzing the importance of these tendencies in the creed is difficult, but it is not proper to dismiss them as inconsequential aberrations. Thoroughly "sensible" and "hardheaded" businessmen may subscribe to ideology which is far from common sense and practicality. Businessmen who know the working difficulties of their own roles may still nourish romantic hopes and fancies; our whole analysis of the strains of the role points to pressures which may find appropriate outlets in thoroughly "romantic" ideology. In our moralistic society we are very familiar with ideals which are not in fact operative, which are perhaps demonstrably Utopian, but which win the assent of sober people. The Sermon on the Mount is a hallowed part of our heritage, but hardly a practiced code of working ethics. Since even businessmen can lose the clarity and common sense with which they tackle their own problems when they venture into the generalized domain of government and national problems, it is not surprising that a sensible businessman can yield to a very romantic fundamentalism when he writes or reads about the state of our society.

The shift in the business creed from a neutral orthodoxy to a clearly conservative ideology increases the danger that businessmen are likely to move ideologically in the direction of their more extreme right-wing fringes. The more they do so, the more their opponents are pushed to the poles of other ideologies. Especially adverse conditions, whether due to business depressions or international tensions, may periodically increase the dangers of polarization. But we see no necessary secular trend of this sort. The business creed is at best ill-adapted to rationalize a process of increasing governmental influence in the economy, and this process is certainly not one which is likely to be arrested. But the creed is not completely unsuited for new conditions or incapable of adapting to them.

---

[42] See, for example, the writings of Mr. Leonard Reed and other publications of the Foundation for Economic Education.

[43] See H. R. 3137, a report of the House Select Committee on Lobbying Activities (Eighty-first Congress, 2nd Session). It is worth noting that some corporations gave contributions to groups covering a wide range of the spectrum of business ideology, while others were more "consistent" in their donations.

There is, after all, a persisting need in the development of American society for ideology like the business creed. The broad doctrines of the classical creed are not simply obsolete. If the model of a freely competitive system in which everything works out to the maximum satisfaction of all has had intellectual flaws and a highly qualified empirical relevance, it still expresses considerations which cannot be ignored in the conscious shaping of any society like ours. The notions of supply and demand, of competition and efficient allocation of resources, remain pertinent and need to be voiced in ideology. The issues as to efficiency of a centralized socialist economy as against a decentralized capitalist one are far more complicated than the business creed would have them, but they remain issues. Strong cases can certainly be made out for the kind of decentralization we now have in the American economy, and there is need that these cases be heard.[43]

We have suggested above that the managerial strand can hardly be filled out with its own concepts to take the place of the older classical strand. This does not mean that transformation of the classical strand cannot come about. The strains of the businessman's role do not necessarily enslave him forever to the nineteenth-century economists. The very nationalism of business thinking gives a strong leverage for a transformation to newer outlooks on the total economy. Business hostility to government is likely to persist in some form. But, always provided that the levels of strains which produce shrill-voiced rigidity can be avoided, there should be ample scope for a more effective and constructive representation of the conservative position on the national scene.

[43] See R. A. Dahl and C. E. Lindblom, *Politics, Economics, and Welfare* (New York, 1953).

APPENDIX

A NOTE ON SOURCES

The source materials on which this study was based included five types:
(1) pamphlets, leaflets, journals, and other material distributed by business
firms or by business organizations such as the National Association of Manufacturers; (2) statements of businessmen and business spokesmen in Congressional hearings; (3) advertisements by business firms or associations of business
firms in periodicals of general circulation; (4) articles and editorials in business
periodicals and in the financial sections of newspapers; (5) speeches, books,
pamphlets, and other forms of public utterance by individual businessmen.

(1) Organizations from which literature was solicited and received in
some volume included: Advertising Council; American Tariff League; Association of American Railroads; Brand Names Foundation; Chamber of Commerce
of the United States; Foundation for Economic Education; National Association of Manufacturers; Machine Tool Builders Association; National Association of Real Estate Boards; National Industrial Conference Board.

(2) Congressional hearings examined in detail included:

1935, Banking Act of 1935; House Banking and Currency Committee 74:1
1935, Banking Act of 1935; Senate Banking and Currency 74:1
1939, Social Security Amendments; House Ways and Means 76:1
1944, Emergency Price Control Extension, House Banking and Currency 78:2
1944, Emergency Price Control Extension, Senate Banking and Currency 78:2
1945, Stabilization Act Extension, House Banking and Currency 79:1
1945, Full Employment Act of 1945, House Committee on Expenditures in
    Executive Departments 79:1
1946, Extension of Emergency Price Control Act, House Banking and Cur-
    rency 79:2
1948, Corporate Profits, Joint Committee on the Economic Report 80:2

(3) Periodicals clipped systematically, 1 July 1948–30 June 1949
   (A) Magazines of general circulation: *Atlantic Monthly*; *Colliers*;
       Fortune; *Harper's*; *Life*; *Newsweek*; *Saturday Evening Post*;
       Time; *Women's Home Companion*.
   (B) Newspapers: *New York Times*; *Boston Herald*.
   (C) Business Magazines: *Business Week*; *Dun's Review*; *Rotarian*;
       United States Investor.

In Part I of the study (Chapters 2–13) in which the substance of the
business creed is set forth, 703 references to source materials for ideology
appear. These are distributed as follows among various types of material:

1. Publications of business associations, including books, pamphlets, and journals: 186

those most widely used were: National Association of Manufacturers, Economic Principles Commission, *The American Individual Enterprise System* (91); other NAM material, for example: *Competitive Enterprise versus Planned Economy* by H. W. Prentis, *Who Profits from Profits?* (38); U.S. Chamber of Commerce publications, for example: *Measuring Monopoly, Socialism in America, The Drive for a Controlled Economy via Pale Pink Pills* (21); Foundation for Economic Education publications, for example: *Outlook for Freedom*, Leonard E. Read, *31¢* by F. A. Harper, *In Search of Peace* by F. A. Harper (18); other Business Associations (18).

2. Books by business authors: 156

the five most frequently quoted are: Edgar M. Queeny, *The Spirit of Enterprise* (30); S. Wells Utley, *The American System* (16); Henry G. Weaver, *Mainspring* (13); Ernest L. Klein, *How to Stay Rich* (8); G. Carpenter, *Dollars and Sense* (10).

3. Advertisements 117

4. Speeches by individual businessmen, pamphlets, etc., by businessmen, not distributed through organizations listed above, business house organs, annual reports, newsletters, etc. 83

5. Testimony by businessmen before Congressional Committees:

for example: Robertson Committee. *Economic Power of Labor Organizations, Hearings* before the Senate Committee on Banking and Currency. Eighty-first Congress, 2nd session.

Celler Committee. *Study of Monopoly Powers, Hearings* before the Subcommittee of the House Committee of the Judiciary. Eighty-first Congress, 2nd session.

Flanders Committee, *Profits, Hearings* before the Subcommittee of the Joint Committee on the Economic Report. Eightieth Congress, 2nd session. 65

6. Editorial matter in business publications,

for example: *Fortune*; *Newsweek*; *Business Week*. 60

7. Miscellaneous sources:

Includes film scripts, radio scripts by business commentators, editorial material in publications of general circulation, statements of the creed from other than business sources.

INDEX

Activism, as a value, 258–259
Adams, Phelps, 43, 44, 47, 177
Advertising: informative function of, 147–148, 150–151; honesty in, 144–147
Advertising Council: activities of, 296–297; advertisements, 1, 21, 46, 140, 253; literature, 19, 22, 218
Advertising Federation of America advertisements, 140
Alcoa advertisements, 60, 173
Aldrich, W. W., 235, 236
Allen, Frederick Lewis, 187
Allis-Chalmers advertisements, 37,48
American Association of Advertising Agencies, 145, 146
American Electric Light & Power Companies advertisement, 194
American Steel Spring Co. advertisement, 173
American Telephone & Telegraph Co. advertisement, 61, 89
Appley, Lawrence A., 134, 135
Arnold, Thurman, 402
Association of American Railroads advertisements, 82, 156–157
Atchison, Topeka & Santa Fe Railroad advertisement, 38
Avondale advertisement, 62

Bagehot, Walter, 92, 335
Banker's Trust advertisement, 173
Banking System, 224–230; distrust of Federal control over, 233–239
Barnard, Chester, 107, 160, 335–336
Barr, Emmett C., 242–243
Barron's advertisement, 42–43
Batcheller, Hiland G., 86, 92, 256
Bell Telephone System: advertisements, 24, 60, 87; *Annual Report,* 140, 156
Bennett, Wallace F., 136
Better Business Bureaus, 147
Better Homes & Gardens advertisements, 157
Biggers, John D., 236
Black, S. Bruce, 194–195
Boston Consolidated Gas Co., 159–160
Boston Globe, T. G. M.'s column, 74

Boston Herald, 127
Boulware, L. R., 91, 97, 128, 137
Brand Names Foundation: organization and activities of, 148n.; advertisements, 148–149, 253.
Brogan, Denis, 286
Brown, E. C., and Millis, H. A., 117, 120
Brown, J. S., 136
Brown, J. T., 238
Bullis, Harry A., 134
Burgess, Randolph, 237
Burlington Mills advertisements, 172–173, 255
Business creed: materials used in study of, 10; channels through which disseminated, 294–298; pervasive themes in, 347–354. *See also* Ideology
Business enterprise: distinguishing features of, 53–56; as a family or team, 62–64; monarchical structure of, 98; importance of discipline in, 112–113; lack of unifying emotional symbols in, 111–112; and social mobility, 110–111; size of, 58–61; and values in the creed, 265; in the classical creed, 57; in the managerial creed, 57–58
Business executives: definition of, 326–327; uncertainty and decision-making in role of, 90–92, 332–334; doubts about substantive content in role of, 351–352; power of, 97–99, 359; responsibility for results in role of, 93–97, 208–209, 352–353; criteria of achievement of, 327–330; responsibility to public of, 343–344; income of, 103–104, 330–331, 365; social relations in role of, 338–343, 353–354; status of, 345–346, 362–364; junior executives, 336–338
Business Week editorials and reports, 63, 70, 90, 92, 115, 116, 125, 126, 209, 257
Byrd, Sen. Harry F., 220–221

Cadillac advertisement, 154
Calkins, Ernest Elmo, 141, 145, 151, 266, 392–393
Camels advertisement, 154

SCHOCKEN PAPERBACKS

At your bookstore. For complete catalog write to

SCHOCKEN BOOKS   67 PARK AVENUE   NEW YORK 16, N. Y.